This book describes the spread of new agricultural practice in the half millennium after 1350, and reconstructs a neglected part of Europe's agricultural past: the introduction of fodder crops, and the continuous reorganization of traditional botanical inputs within a new system of farming.

New agricultural systems, based on convertible husbandry, clovers, turnips and other roots, were introduced to some areas of Europe from the 1750s, and gave new impetus to productivity. This so-called 'agricultural revolution' involved a learning process in which recourse to ancient and medieval botany helped farmers and scholars to overcome a situation of stalemate in early modern technology.

The book breaks entirely new ground by showing the distant historical origins of a major transformation in land potential and farm productivity. A vast range of evidence is cited from Italy, France, England and elsewhere to produce in effect an economic, social and cultural history of Europe in which the focus is on the long-distance consequences of the 'agricultural revolution'.

Past and Present Publications

The wild and the sown

Past and Present Publications

General Editor: JOANNA INNES, *Somerville College, Oxford*

Past and Present Publications comprise books similar in character to the articles in the journal *Past and Present*. Whether the volumes in the series are collections of essays – some previously published, others new studies – or monographs, they encompass a wide variety of scholarly and original works primarily concerned with social, economic and cultural changes, and their causes and consequences. They will appeal to both specialists and non-specialists and will endeavour to communicate the results of historical and allied research in the most readable and lively form.

For a list of titles in Past and Present Publications, see end of book.

The wild and the sown

Botany and agriculture in Western Europe:
1350–1850

MAURO AMBROSOLI

University of Turin

TRANSLATED BY MARY McCANN SALVATORELLI

CAMBRIDGE
UNIVERSITY PRESS

Published by the Press Syndicate of the University of Cambridge
The Pitt Building, Trumpington Street, Cambridge CB2 1RP
40 West 20th Street, New York, NY 10011-4211, USA
10 Stamford Road, Oakleigh, Melbourne 3166, Australia

Originally published in Italian as *Scienziati, contadini e proprietari:
botanica e agricoltura nell'Europa occidentale 1350–1850*
by Giulio Einaudi editore, Turin 1992
and © Giulio Einaudi editore s.p.a.

First published in English by Cambridge University Press 1997
as *The wild and the sown: Botany and agriculture in Western Europe,
1350–1850*

English translation © Cambridge University Press 1997

Printed in Great Britain at the University Press, Cambridge

A catalogue record for this book is available from the British Library

Library of Congress cataloguing in publication data

Ambrosoli, Mauro.
[Scienziati, contadini e proprietari. English]
The wild and the sown: Botany and agriculture in Western Europe,
1350–1850 / Mauro Ambrosoli; translated by Mary McCann
Salvatorelli.
    p.   cm. – (Past and Present Publications)
ISBN 0 521 46509 5
1. Botany, Economic – Europe – History. 2. Botany, Economic – Italy –
History. 3. Agriculture – Europe – History. 4. Agriculture – Italy –
History. I. Title. II. Series.
SB87.E8A5313 1996
338.1'733'094 – dc20   96–300   CIP

ISBN 0 521 46509 5 hardback

To my parents

Contents

Illustrations

PLATES
(*Between pages 264 and 265*)

1. The oldest illustrations of forage-crop plants, Poligalon (polygala, *onobrychis*); in Dioscorides, sixth century, facsimile, Graz 1965–70, fo. 265r, Turin, Biblioteca Nazionale.

2. The oldest illustrations of forage crop plants, Trifullon (*trifolium bituminosum*); in Dioscorides, sixth century, facsimile, Graz 1965–70, fo. 265r, Turin, Biblioteca Nazionale.

3. Melica (*Surghum vulgare*) replaced *medica* (*Medicago* sp.) on poor soils. *Tacuinum sanitatis*, Rome, Biblioteca Casanatense.

4–5. Clover (*T. pratense*, bottom left) appears together with other meadow plants in paintings. Gentile da Fabriano, *Saint Dominic and Saint Mary Magdalen*, panels from the polyptic of Valle Romita, Milan, Pinacoteca di Brera. By permission, Ministero per i Beni Culturali e Ambientali, Milan.

6. A new sensitivity to nature: clovers from the illustrated manuscript of Serapion, British Library, Egerton ms 2020, fo. 7r.

7–9. Lucerne and clovers were recognized and represented with their distinguishing features. Red clover (*T. pratense*), white clover (*T. repens*) and lucerne (*Medicago* s.), from the Roccabonella, later Rinio Herbal. Venice, Biblioteca Marciana, Lat. ms VI, LX, 2548, fos. 152v, 153v, 396v.

10–11. Sixteenth-century botany identified many varieties; Polygala (*Onobrychis sativa*) and lucerne (*medica* s.). P. A. Michiel, *Erbario o Istoria generale delle piante*, I, Red book, Venice, Biblioteca Marciana, Ital. ms II, XXVI, 4860, fos. 216r, 345r.

12. Reader's markings of famous texts. A copy of Corniolo della Cornia's *Divina Villa*, made, with corrections, by ser Giorgio, son of Jacopo Di Bonaparte; mid-fifteenth century, Florence, Biblioteca Nazionale, cod. Magl. XIV 3, fo. 1r.

FIGURES

Tables

Foreword

JOAN THIRSK

It is only rarely that a book on a familiar subject manages to open up wholly new vistas in every direction. This is one such treasure. We English readers and writers treat the introduction of clover onto the farming scene as a piece of relatively straightforward history. We know that the process was slow, because farmers were cautious. We have discovered that some of the more adventurous were experimenting in the 1630s, and a few more summoned up the courage to try clover in the 1660s and 1670s. But it was well after 1700 before any considerable number of farmers grew it in the country as a whole. It was then absorbed into a thoroughly satisfactory four-course rotation, of turnips, barley, seeds (i.e. mostly clover), wheat, and farmers from the Continent of Europe visited England to admire the system. Only after 1800 did it become a routine, and the wheel had turned to complete a revolution in arable farming.

This England-centred account is eventful enough, but, in fact, it uncovers only a few layers of the full story. We have never penetrated to the deeper layers of men's efforts to identify and separate different legumes, test their merits, and exploit their virtues. Nor do we have any inkling of the devious route by which success was finally achieved. Clover was not the only choice for a nitrogen-fixing legume, which would restore fertility to the soil after more exhausting cereal crops; we might have chosen lucerne, as farmers on the European Continent preferred, or sainfoin. At the beginning, the issue was open and undecided.

This book from an Italian historian peels away the deeper layers of the story, and carries us to the heart of the matter. It reveals the most fruitful cooperation across Europe among botanists, herbalists, landowners, diplomats who travelled with their eyes and ears open, and observant, practical farmers. It pays full tribute to the vital contribution of small peasants, who, by virtue of their very situation, observed small things closely, and attended to detail. For them, riches were counted not in the extent of their land but in the quantity and quality of the family labour given to cultivating it. All these many different people contributed to the solution of a vital farming problem, managing to carry agricultural production forward to new heights, without abusing the land; the new regime kept it in good heart for future generations. Through the alliance of these many different people, the several legumes were finally correctly identified and named, the best growing procedures were established in the different countries of Europe, and sufficient pure seed was supplied to sustain the system. It comes as a shock to realize that the clover revolution in England and northern Europe depended heavily, throughout the nineteenth century, on the supply of seeds gathered by small peasants in southern Europe. It anticipated by two centuries the present situation when the Third World is deprived of its own germoplasm in order to sustain the productivity of the Western economy.

This is a timely book in many different senses. It reveals the truly European dimension of agricultural progress in one farming sector. But the lesson has much broader significance. It shows how new ways forward are always sought in the dark, without certainty of success, amid conflicting information and among conflicting viewpoints. Many different people, with different interests, and different training, make unexpected contributions. No one can foretell the outcome. The historian comes along at the end, traces the sequence of events, and identifies the major milestones. But even historians, with assumptions inculcated in one period, do not always see all the issues involved in a world ruled by other assumptions. As this book vividly shows, a new interpretation of our past is always possible, offering a challenge to the present.

This story of the legumes in farming, of lucerne, sainfoin, and clover, builds up a rich tapestry of events and people linking Italy with France, Spain, Germany and England. The partnership of humanist scholars, curious travellers, scientists, small farmers and large, was essential for their ultimate success. But it illuminates an experience from the past, which it is is also of great moment for us to understand in the present. While it enriches our historical understanding with a multitude of original insights, it should prompt many sober reflections on the practical lessons to be remembered when we Europeans take decisions about our future.

JOAN THIRSK

Preface

In the late 1960s, when research on this volume was begun, one could still approach the question of 'agricultural revolution' with reasonable optimism, as a necessary precondition for the transformation of traditional economies into so-called modern industrial society. Since the 1750s new agricultural systems had increased productivity, first in certain parts of Europe and thence in other areas of the world. Today, however, there is no escaping from the fact that these two hundred years of capitalist agriculture have created large, agriculturally uniform regions competing for economic priority, yet have failed miserably to free mankind from the shackles of starvation. Many valuable agricultural practices and cultivars have been abandoned. As a result, mankind still depends on the plants developed at the time of the first agricultural revolution, which took place between 7500 and 3500 BC, in Central Asia, South-East Asia and Mesamerica.

The so-called 'nouvelle agriculture' or 'agricultural revolution', founded on convertible husbandry, clovers, turnips and other roots, highlights the value of botanical input, originating outside, but rapidly absorbed into, the framework of capitalist farming. However, a process of innovation is always linked to a process of learning, involving continual choice between two or more solutions. Historians of innovation have often forgotten these choices, describing historical events as if there had been only one possible solution, whereas, in practice, the present position of industrial (or post-industrial) society has been reached largely thanks to errors, delays and/or rearrangements which in no way followed a linear progression.

Despite my apparent reluctance to hand over the final script, I warmly welcome the opportunity offered to me by the Cambridge University Press, to make this work available to English-speaking readers, since I believe that changes in the public's attitudes may eventually make a significant contribution to the defence of our common agricultural assets. Unquestionably, the present edition would never have been brought to press without the continuous support and encouragement of Dr Joan Thirsk, to whom I am deeply grateful. We have been discussing its contents over the years, since we met in Oxford in 1977. The many hours she has devoted to the revision of the translated text go beyond anything one could hope for from the most generous of editors. While never failing to respect the thinking of the original, her suggestions have greatly helped to present the book in a form more familiar to the English reader. Obviously, I alone am responsible for the views and judgements expressed in it.

Of the many colleagues and friends who have given me their support during these years I particularly wish to mention the late Professor Franco Venturi, who followed most attentively, with the interest and curiosity for which he was distinguished, each new step of my research. Marino Berengo and Carlo Poni have read earlier versions of the text; Diego Moreno has always been very ready to back up my interest in the history of agriculture. Giovanni Levi, Edoardo Grendi, Gianni Toniolo and Patrick O'Brien have all devoted a great deal of their time to me. Many specialists have shared their knowledge with me, as did the late Frank Emery, who presented me with his unpublished paper on matters closely related to my studies. Much of the work has been the subject of lectures and seminars with my students at the University of Turin and other distinguished institutions, such as the Institute of Historical Research, London 1977, Ca' Foscari, University of Venice 1988, the Berenson Foundation, I Tatti, Florence 1989. The University of Oxford and Magdalen College, Oxford, honoured me with an invitation to give the Waynflete lectures in 1987 and granted me a Fellowship which provided an opportunity to revise all the material that I had been collecting over so many years and to insert many missing links. Conversation with J. Stoye, C. Grayson, M. Gilsenan, D. Norbrook, A. Boltho, J. Enos and L. Brockliss was always interesting. Unfortunately, Angus MacIntyre, then acting President of Magdalen College, who had the rare gift of turning an academic event into an occasion for lively communication between scholars of different extractions, is no longer with us. His recent, untimely death is a sad loss to all who benefited from his friendship.

I also wish to thank Monsieur Gilles Postel-Vinay, of the Institut National des Recherches Agronomiques, Paris, and Dr Anna J. Schwartz, of the National Bureau of Economics, Washington DC, for valuable indications of sources; as well as those many librarians and archivists who have patiently met my countless requests. Documents from the Samuel Hartlib Papers, University of Sheffield, are quoted here with the permission of their owner, Lord Delamere. The Ministero degli Affari Esteri, Rome, the British Academy, London, the Consiglio Nazionale delle Ricerche, Rome, Magdalen College, Oxford and the Italian Fondi Universitari per la Ricerca, Rome, have all met some of the expenses incurred in the years 1973, 1977, 1980, 1986–87, 1981–90. The Dipartimento di Storia of the University of Turin has also generously granted permission to use some of their local Fondi Universitari per la Ricerca, to cover part of the translation expenses. Gian Felice Mura of the same Dipartimento has helped me a great deal with the preparation of this manuscript.

My translator, Mrs Mary McCann Salvatorelli, has edited a number of papers for international meetings and articles on agriculture published in English and American reviews. She approached the daunting task of translating this volume with the insight that stems from her Oxfordshire farming background and many years of delving into the intricacies of Italian thought patterns. Thanks to her powers of persuasion the reader has been spared much of the obsolete, archaic language to which I have decided leanings, natural and acquired.

This new edition, too, owes a great deal to the intelligent support, tempered with affection and a large measure of English humour, which my wife Vanessa has always given to me. I am also grateful to Stefano for the many interests he likes to share with his parents and the many more he wishes to develop in the coming years.

Abbreviations

Avignon
    AADD   Archives Départmentales du Rhône
    MC   Musée Calvet
Bologne
    AA   Biblioteca Archiginnasio
    BU   Biblioteca Universitaria
Brescia
    AS   Archivio di Stato
    BQ   Biblioteca Queriniana
Cambridge
    UL   University Library
Carpentras
    AACC   Archives Comunales
    BI   Bibliothèque Inguibertine
Die
    AACC   Archives Comunales
Florence
    BL   Biblioteca Laurenziana
    BM   Biblioteca Marucelliana
    BN   Biblioteca Nazionale
    BR   Biblioteca Riccardiana
London
    BL   British Library
    GL   Guildhall Library
    PRO   Public Record Office
Milan
    AS   Archivio di Stato
    BA   Biblioteca Ambrosiana
    BN   Biblioteca Nazionale Braidense

Modena
    BE   Biblioteca Estense
Montpellier
    EM   Ecole de Medecine
Oxford
    BO   Bodleian Library
    DPS   Department of Plant Sciences
Paris
    AANN Archives Nationales (now known as CARAN)
    BM   Bibliothèque Mazarine
    BN   Bibliothèque Nationale
Sheffield
    UL   University Library
Turin
    AS   Archivio di Stato
    BC   Biblioteca Comunale
    BN   Biblioteca Nazionale
    BR   Biblioteca Reale
Valence
    AADD Archives Départmentales de la Drôme
Venice
    BN   Biblioteca Nazionale Marciana
    MC   Museo Correr
Winchester
    CL   College Library

Libraries which are quoted in full in the text do not appear in this list.

NOTE ON BOTANICAL NOMENCLATURE, CHRONOLOGY, METRIC SYSTEM

We have adopted the Linnean system for naming botanical species. Wherever another nomenclature has been used, the fact has been indicated, unless it is clear from the context that it derives from the nomenclature of Dioscorides, from Italian, French or English, or from botanists earlier than Linnaeus.

English local plant names follow C. E. Hubbard, *Grasses*, Harmonsworth 1968 and W. Keble Martin, *The Concise British Flora in Colour*, London 1969.

The measures used in agriculture are those in use in the place in question in the past, unless the source of the conversion is specifically indicated.

The prices are always given in local currency (£ s d), without repeating the obvious references to the *livre* of Tours for France, the pound sterling for England, or the *lira* of Venice or other Italian States, for Italy.

The spelling of old English, French and Italian documents has been kept, while abbreviations have been replaced by the full form. English dates are given according to the Old Style Calendar when necessary, with the New Year beginning on 15 March, not 1 January.

Metric conversions of ancient measures used in the text:

Volume:
1 pint = 0.57 l; 2 pints = 1 quart = 1.14 l; 4 quarts = 4.55 l; 2 gallons = 1 peck = 9.09 l; 4 pecks = 1 bushel = 36.37 l.
1 *quarta* = 12.16 l; 1 *somata* = 146 l; 1 *carra di fieno*, Brescia = 11 mc, Turin = 5.022 mc.
1 *éminée* = 23 l.

Weight:
1 pound = 0.45 kg; 1 quarter = 12.60 kg; 1 hundredweight = 50.80 kg.
1 load of hay = 18 cwt = 914 kg; 1 load of hay = 12 cwt = 610 kg.
1 *carra di fieno*, Turin = 553.26 kg.

Land:
1 acre = 0.40 ha; 1 *arpent* = 0.34 ha; 1 *arpent commun* = 0.42 ha.
1 *piò* = 0.32. ha.
1 *éminée* = 0.05–0.08 ha.
1 *tese* = 0.00 ha.
1 *pertica* (perch) = 2.85 m.
1 *pertica* = 0.065 ha.

Introduction

The subject of this book is the elaboration and subsequent spread of new farming methods in Europe between pre-capitalist and modern times. The sources have led us to focus on three key areas – Northern and Central Italy; the region round Paris, plus Provence; and Southern England. The main aim of the work, which has involved interdisciplinary and comparative research, is to bring out the continuous, albeit forgotten links between the past and the present, between the Mediterranean environment and northern societies, capitalist agriculture and the peasant economy, cultured readers and scientists on the one hand and the common run of people on the other. It should be kept in mind that the spread of the agricultural system which, for the sake of convenience, we call the 'new agriculture', founded on a continuous crop rotation, on the integration of agriculture with stock-keeping, through the growing of forage and other intercalary crops, was necessarily preceded by a period of learning, supported and spurred on by the reorganization of ancient and medieval botany. By tracing the spread of forage crops (particularly clover, vetch, lupins, sainfoin, Spanish sainfoin and lucerne), we get an instructive picture of the continual re-elaboration of botanical knowledge, at the root of all agricultural activity, set against an economic background dominated increasingly by capitalist farming. Starting from the medieval crisis in agriculture and keeping in mind the many individual solutions that were applied to the new problems, and the fact that they could be solved only by comparing the present of the fifteenth and sixteenth centuries with a past that dated back to Classical times, the work examines the reorganization of modern agriculture with reference to the continual tension between scientists and ordinary people, between landowners and peasants, tenant-farmers, sharecroppers and small landowners, within a framework of farming founded on an unstable equilibrium. The continual exchange between the natural and cultivated environments eventually set up a process of domestication and

1

commercialization of plant species, and created a new routine characterized by a thoughtless and dangerous reduction in the number of varieties.
The natural history of lucerne before the fifteenth century goes to the
heart of the matter surveyed in this book.

The most ancient evidence concerning lucerne is contained in
archaeological findings from the first agricultural revolution, dating from
7500 BC, which occurred on the plateau of Iran and in Central Asia,
where plants such as wheat (*triticum dicoccum*), barley and wild
oats, and animals such as the gazelle, the onager and the pig were
domesticated for human consumption. Findings on the site of Ali Kosh,
datable between 7500 and 5600 BC, show that the lucerne genus grew
there together with other species, such as *astragalus* and fenugreek.
Ninety-four per cent of the carbonized seeds found were small clover
and/or lucerne seeds, though these amounted to no more than a third of
the total weight of the carbonized plants. *Medicago, trigonella* and
astragalus were native to Khuzistan.

There is no botanical difference between cultivated species and weeds.
It is man who makes a selection, by cultivation and the choices arising
from it, and who labels plants as suitable for food or ornament or merely
as weeds. In the case in point, with the spread of wheat and barley, wild
leguminous plants and other grasses (*lolium*, for example) were allotted
the status of weeds and removed to make room for cultivated cereals. The
leguminous plants withdrew either to the mountainsides or along the
edges of the cultivated land. They ceased to have a place in human diet
around 6000 BC and from then on became food for sheep and goats. In
Iran and the Near East *astragalus* and *trigonella* are two of the plants
most commonly gathered, even today, as fodder for domesticated goats.
Medicago was associated since the very beginning of human cultivation
with *trigonella* and *Onobrychis crista galli*, Lam., which, together with
vicia narbonensis, are found on the site of Beidhan (Southern Jordan),
dating from the pre-ceramic Neolithic Age. Amongst their weeds, on the
same site, were found *Aegilops* sp., *lolium* sp., and *avena ludoviciana*,
plants on the rather thinly marked borderline between cultivated
crops and weeds. The Middle-Eastern origin of *Medicago* should be
remembered and emphasized, as it has not been found on any archaeological excavation sites in Southern Europe, Greece, Macedonia or
Bulgaria.[1] Lucerne came down from the Iranian plateau much later, in

---

[1] See Flannery, in P. S. Ucko and G. W. Dimbleby (eds.), *The Domestication and
Exploitation of Plants and Animals*, London 1969.

700 BC, being listed as *aspastu* or *aspasti* among the plants that grew in the garden of the Assyrian king Merodachbaladam, in Babylonia. The name itself reveals its Persian origin, and it remained the same in the inventory of King Merodachbaladam, who boasted that he had acclimatized, in the region between the Tigris and the Euphrates, plants such as lucerne, horticultural plants such as garlic, leeks, cress and lettuce, as well as spices such as cardamom, coriander and hyssop.[2] It seems, however, that these species were only cultivated in the king's garden, not yet in the field. But, here again, it seems that lucerne did not grow alone. When it was transplanted, fenugreek, a semi-parasite and weed, was taken with it. Thus, from the time when it was first cultivated and began to spread from one region to another, lucerne has always had fenugreek as a fellow-traveller, growing side by side with it in a variable relationship of dominance or subjection, closely linked with agricultural work. *Aspastu* means literally 'forage for horses', and with this name (or equivalent variations) lucerne spread on the one hand through Syria and on the other through China, while it was also native to regions like Afghanistan and Pamir. Lucerne is a debt that Chinese agriculture owes to the ancient Sassanid Empire, together with Persian horses.

When General Can'k'ien's mission brought pure-bred Persian horses back to the Emperor Wu (140–87 BC), they also brought seeds of the plant that served them as forage, lucerne, or *mu su* in the Chinese translation from the Persian (126 BC). Again in this case, the Imperial gardens were the centre of domestication and diffusion of lucerne. The Chinese also discovered lucerne in Kashmir during the same period. Later it was cultivated in the gardens of another Emperor Wu (265–90 AD) and the horses used in the postal service were fed on it. The book of agronomy *Ts'i min you su*, of the fifth century AD, gave rules for its cultivation. Lucerne continued to spread through China, used both for cattle and horses, and even for the human population in times of famine. In China, connected from the start with the celestial horses and the care that the Emperors took over their rearing, it was mostly cultivated intensively, which delayed crossbreeding of the species. Only towards the end of the sixteenth century (AD) were plants identified which might be wild species of *Medicago sativa*, i.e. lucerne (for example, *medicago denticulata*, *lupulina* and *minima*). There was never

---

[2] See V. Hehn, *Kulturpflanzen und Haustiere in ihrem Übergang aus Asien nach Griechenland und Italien . . .* , Berlin 1894, 6th edn, O. Schrader and A. Engler eds., pp. 390–401; see also B. Meissner, *Babylonien und Assyrien*, Heidelberg 1920, p. 210.

any confusion with fenugreek, the seeds of which were always associated with imports and foreigners.[3]

It is essential to remember that lucerne spread eastwards and westwards from the Iranian plateau at practically the same time. It reached China and crossed the Mediterranean in the fifth century BC, at the time of the Persian Wars. Mentioned by Aristophanes in the *Knights* (v. 606), it was only in the fourth century that lucerne (*poa medike*) appeared in the western world, rather hidden away in the scientific treatise of Theophrastus. Theophrastus, pupil and follower of Aristotle in Stagira, opened his school in Athens in 317–307 BC. He was known chiefly for his writings on botany, *De causis plantarum* and the *Historiae plantarum*, for which he collected a huge amount of data on the effect of cultivation on genetic change in wild species. Theophrastus based his research on the external characteristics of plants, the roots, leaves, flowers, seeds and fruit, taste and smell. He went on to examine the propagation of plants, the difference between wild and cultivated trees, the problem of genetic mutation, and so on. Unfortunately, he did not produce a systematic herbal. He mentioned lucerne because of the way its characters change if sheep graze and leave their droppings on it for long periods. Elsewhere in the work lucerne is included among the plants that improve in taste and quality after cutting. The same passage speaks of it being mown as forage for animals, saying that mowing produces a better crop and prevents bloat in sheep.[4]

However it is only in the Latin writers on agriculture, the *Rerum Rusticarum Scriptores*, that we come to the more substantial, lasting work on lucerne and forage crops bequeathed to us by the ancient world. Varro, Columella, Palladius, even Virgil and the Elder Pliny, all speak of the cultivation of meadowland or lucerne. The plant was introduced into Italy in the first century BC; thus Cato the Elder, the first of the Latin writers on agriculture (second century BC), makes no mention of it

---

[3] See E. Bretschneider, *Botanicon Sinicum*, Shangai 1893, III: *Botanical investigations into the Materia Medica of the ancient Chinese*, pp. 16–18, 402–3, and the irreplaceable work by B. Laufer, *Sino–Iranica. Field Museum of Natural History*, publ. 201, X series, vol. XV, Chicago 1919, pp. 208–19, 446–7. Concerning Chinese agriculture see also J. Needham, *Science and Civilization in China*, vol. VI (with the collaboration of Lu gwei-djen and Huang hsing-tsung), *Biology and biological Technology*, I: *Botany*, Cambridge 1986, pp. iii, 163–4, 341, 500; II (by F. Bray): *Agriculture*, Cambridge 1984, pp. 4, 293.

[4] See Theophrastus, *De causis plantarum*, transl. by B. Einarson and G. K. Link, Loeb Classical Library, London–Harvard 1976, Introduction, *passim*; II, 15.6; idem, *Historiae plantarum*, VIII, 8.7.

although he speaks at length of meadows; while Varro (second to first century BC) and the others do speak of it.[5] Perhaps Columella contributed unwittingly to its etymological uncertainty by writing that lucerne was a fodder crop appropriate for sick cattle ('aegrotandibus pecudibus'). For his part, Pliny the Elder (first century AD) explained the name with reference to the Persian origin of the plant, adding that it had passed through Greece at the time of the Persian Wars, around 400 BC. The rules for the cultivation of lucerne were never very different from those outlined by Columella (first century BC). The land, he explained, was to be ploughed for the first time in October, ploughed again at the beginning of February, and finally, in March, divided up into areas ('in morem horti') of three metres by fifteen, for manuring. The lucerne was only to be sown at the end of April (at the rate of about half a litre of seed per plot). Tilled in this way the land looked much more like a garden with flower beds than a field. The farmer could use the paths between one plot and another both for irrigation and for weeding and hoeing. The cultivation of lucerne as described by Columella became highly labour-intensive but repaid its cost by high productivity – one *jugerum* (slightly smaller than a statute acre) provided forage for three horses for a year. The *Rerum Rusticarum Scriptores* also associated lucerne with a number of other forage crops – spring oats and barley, vetch, clover and fenugreek. But only lucerne enjoyed a privileged position, being the only grass cultivated with an almost horticultural technique. According to Palladius (fourth or fifth century AD) the calendar for the cultivation of lucerne was as follows: in February, ploughing and tilling of the field to be sown; in April, sowing and tillage; the lucerne to be mown from May on, as needed; in September, rotation of sesame and lucerne; in November, the lucerne given to the sheep as dry fodder. Although the *Rerum Rusticarum Scriptores* had dealt with the plant at length, they had not given a description of it. It was Dioscorides, a Greek doctor serving in the Roman army in Asia Minor in the first century BC, who left us a scientific description of it in his treatise *Materia Medica libri V*, one of

---

[5] Of the vast bibliography on the *Rerum Rusticarum Scriptores* we indicate only the following passages by M. P. Cato, *De agricultura*, VIII, XXVII, LIII, LIV (on meadows); M. T. Varro, *De re rustica*, II 1.17, 2.19; L. I. M. Columella, *Res rustica*, II 7.1, 10.24, 10.26, 12.6; VI 38.4; VII 3.19, 4.2; XI 2.75; T. R. A. Palladius, *Opus agriculturae, Febrarius*, VI; *Aprilis*, I; *Septembris*, VII; *November*, XIII; P. Vergilius Maro, *Georgicon libri IV*, I 215; C. Plinius Saecundus, *Naturalis historiae libri XXXVII*, XVIII 26.

the most famous works of ancient times.[6] Lucerne, he wrote, looked like clover but grew higher and straighter and produced pods with a curious spiral shape (*siliquae corniculatae*). Unfortunately, he did not state the colour of the flower (perhaps because he rightly considered that it was not important) and this was to make it more difficult to identify the plant during the Renaissance. While the *Materia Medica* described a total of four hundred plants, it did not give a list of the species that are weeds of lucerne, since Dioscorides was more interested in the medicinal properties of the species than in their agricultural uses. However, he did speak of plants such as fenugreek, *onobrychis* (today classified as *hedysarum* sp.) and *polygala* (today *onobrychis* sp.). The Classical world, to a lesser extent the medieval world – though Dante (*Inferno*, IV, 140) mentions him among the great figures of Greece – and above all the Renaissance, were to find in Dioscorides a master to be first imitated, then surpassed. Unfortunately, the complete text of the *Materia Medica* in the Greek original was buried deep, for centuries, in a very few libraries, such as the Vatican Library, and it was only after Aldo Manuzio's edition, published in Venice in 1499, that the study of this master of ancient thought could be taken up again.

The importance and commercial value of lucerne in the ancient world was such that it was included in Diocletian's edict *De pretiis rerum venalium*, which regulated the sale of its seed at 150 *denarii* per *modium*, together with that of hay (30d), hemp (80d) and vetch (80d).[7]

In practice, the late Classical and medieval worlds knew the botany of Dioscorides through the herbal of Apuleius Barbarus (fifth century AD), the only herbal that has come down to us from Classical times. It has often been reproduced incorrectly and incompletely in medieval manuscripts (even when the pictorial standard is high), as in the well-known Bodley MS 130, from the Abbey of Bury St Edmunds. No entries on lucerne appear in the manuscript tradition.[8] The *Etymologiae* of Isidore of Seville (570–636 AD), directly inspired by Pliny the Elder's *Natural History*, mentions lucerne, but the author's knowledge seems to derive entirely from books, though his interest may indicate an attempt

---

[6] For the numerous textual problems concerning *Materia Medica* see the edition of Pedacios Dioscorides, *De Materia Medica libri V*, II 5 (M. Wellman ed., Berlin 1906–14).

[7] See S. Laufer (ed.), *Diokletians Preisedikt*, Berlin 1971, p. 100.

[8] See C. Singer, 'The herbal in antiquity and its transmission to later ages', *Journal of Hellenic Studies*, 47, 1927, pp. 1–52; R. W. T. Gunther, *The Herbal of Apuleius Barbarus* (Ms Bodley 130), Oxford 1925.

to put a stop to the semantic wavering between *medica* and *melica*, which was to contribute to its disappearance in the West during the Middle Ages.[9] Dioscorides' text, re-elaborated in Latin in the eighth century under Longobard influence, provides us with two points of the greatest interest, because of the variations in the original text and the place where it was composed, certainly in the Benevento area despite the Longobard influence (*b* and *v* are constantly inverted in the titles of the text, as is the rule in the dialects of Southern Italy). Moreover, in the chapter on lucerne (chap. X) it states 'Of *medica*, that is *sulla*' ('De medica id est sulla').[10] That is, *medicago* was substituted by the more resistant, semi-wild species, *sulla*, which is *hedysarum*, or Spanish sainfoin, typical of the dry Mediterranean area (Calabria, Sicily, Spain). The scribe and interpreter of Dioscorides' text was adding and perhaps explaining the most difficult plants to his Germanic patrons; but he was explaining in terms of the flora of his own region. For the species clearly described by Dioscorides he substituted another, which does not look like clover (Spanish sainfoin looks more like vetch) and which was later to be confused with *onobrychis*, 'which donkeys eat too' ('quae herba et asini comedunt', as the text runs). This is the Latin version of Dioscorides most frequently copied in manuscript form and finally printed in 1481. The most illustrious owner of the Latin MS 337, now housed in Munich, was Marcello Virgilio, a Florentine doctor and Humanist. He realized that the Longobard Dioscorides was a corrupt edition which showed little respect for the original, and so he did not have the text of the manuscript printed, preferring the older Latin version, which was a more faithful rendering of the Greek original.[11] Soon after this came another Latin book produced outside Italy, Palladius' *Opus agriculturae*, copied in the oratory of Troyes in the Ile-de-France, in fine Merovingian script of

---

[9] See Isidorus, *Etymologiae sive originum libri XX*, XVII 4.8 (W. N. Lindsay ed., Oxford 1911).

[10] See K. Hofman and T. N. Auracher, 'Der Longobardische Dioskorides der Marcellus Virgilius', *Romunische Forschungen*, 1, 1883, pp. 49 ff., especially pp. 49–51, 157; continued by H. Stadler, 'Dioskorides Longobardus (Cod. Lat. Monac. 337)', X, 1899, pp. 181 ff., 369 ff., especially p. 228, the chapter on lucerne; XI, 1899, pp. 1 ff.; XIII, 1902, pp. 161 ff.; XIV, 1903, pp. 601 ff. Ms. Lat. 337 was acquired by the Hof- und Staatsbibliothek of Munich thanks to a series of gifts, from Marcello Virgilio to Salnuccio Sangiminianese, from him to Cardinal Capuano hence to a Widmestadt and to a Johan Rebauer, chemist, in Munich, who died without an heir on 25 November 1557. This is the text which was printed in the Latin *editio princeps*: Dioscorides, *Opera*, Venetiis 1478.

[11] See Marcellus Vergilius, *P. Dioscoridou De Materia Medica libri V . . . Commentarius doctissimi M. V. . . .* , Cologne 1529.

the ninth or tenth century. Where the word *medica* occurs for the first time, it has a marginal note: 'sorghum, like melick grass' ('surgus ut meliga herba').[12] Clearly, sorghum (*Surghum vulgare*), another African and Indian plant that was spreading over the Mediterranean area after the Islamic conquest, was taking the place of lucerne.[13] The scribe of Troyes was following a pattern not unlike that of his colleague of Benevento; both of them were substituting a plant more familiar to them for an unknown one. But whereas in the first case, Spanish sainfoin was simply a distant, wild variety of lucerne, in the second it was the transformation of *d* into *l* (*medica* into *melica*) that led to the false identification of a now-forgotten species with a more recent one frequently found in the fields of medieval Europe.

In the Byzantine world, however, the Classical tradition continued unbroken in the *Geoponics*, a collection of earlier writers compiled by Cassianus Bassus, by order of Constantine, Emperor of Byzantium (probably Constantine Porphyrogenitus). Although the date of this composition is extremely uncertain – somewhere between the seventh and eighth century AD – lucerne often appears in it both as a cure for sick animals and as a means of increasing the yield of milking cows; it is mentioned together with cytisus (*Medicago arborea*), fenugreek, oats and clover.[14] Unknown to Western agronomy until the translations brought out by sixteenth-century publishers, the *Geoponics* were never to become a fundamental text for Western technique, serving mostly as a source drawn on by many authors.

It is also interesting to compare the European documents so far examined, with experience gained in the Eastern Mediterranean. Syrian writers, of whom we will mention only Bar Serapion here (Ibn Serabin in Arabic), had access to the Greek texts of Dioscorides, Galen, Paulus Aegineta or the Syrian translation of Dioscorides, the above-mentioned

---

[12] See Montpellier, EM, ms 305.

[13] On the diffusion of sorghum see A. M. Watson, *Agricultural innovation in the early Islamic world. The diffusion of crops and farming techniques, 700–1100*, Cambridge 1983, pp. 9–14 and the bibliography. Sorghum (in Italian also known as *meliga*) (*Sorghum bicolor*) should not be confused with millet (*Milium effusum*) and panic (*Panicum miliaceum*), another grain of Indian origin, widespread in the Mediterranean region during the first millennium BC and known to ancient authors. See Chap. 1, note 13.

[14] See H. Beckh (ed.), *Geoponica sive Cassiani Bassi Scolastici de re rustica eclogae*, Leipzig 1895: *medike*, III 1.8, 2.4; XVI 9.4; XVII 8.1, 14.6; XVIII 2.6; *trifullos*, II 4.1; X 77.6; XII 17.1; A. Toynbee, *Constantine Porphyrogenites and His World*, Oxford 1973.

Geoponics and the Arabic translation of the book on agriculture by Junius (i.e. Iunius Moderatus Columella). In these texts the same name was given to several kinds of forage crop, melilotus being both melilotus proper and fenugreek. *Handaquq* stood both for lucerne (*medike*) and for clover (the *trifullon* of the *Geoponics*), at least as long as they were used as green forage; but in Egypt and Syria the same word *handaquq* was also used for *trigonella* and *melilotus* in the wild state. In the southern oases *medicago* was called *abede*, while it became *cadab* in the Fezzan area and the small oases. Lucerne was called *barsim* in Cairo, as in central and southern Syria. This great variety in the nomenclature, which bears witness to the continual presence of lucerne, fenugreek and melilot, and the substitution of one for the other, shows that the name *handaquq* indicated a type of forage rather than a botanical species.[15]

In the thirteenth century, which marked a return to original writings on agronomy, there was again considerable debate and division in European agronomic thinking, between the Spanish and Italian peninsulas in the Mediterranean, and between Northern and Mediterranean agriculture. Hence, while St Hildegard of Bingen recorded the agricultural properties of clover, no mention whatever was made of clover, lucerne or sainfoin in the *Opus ruralium commodorum* of the Bolognese Pier de' Crescenzi, the collection on agronomy which is the equivalent of Dante's and Thomas Aquinas' systematic re-ordering of medieval thought. However, the absence of lucerne in the Italian botany of this time is compensated for by the presence of melilots and fenugreek, which are to some extent weeds and parasites of lucerne and which take its place when tillage is discontinued.[16] Thus even Rufinus, a Florentine botanist, author of a herbal, probably compiled before 1287, which groups and describes specimens on the lines of Dioscorides, Macer, the *Circa Instans*, the masters of Salerno, Isaac and a few others, knew neither lucerne, onobrychis, melilot nor fenugreek. Yet Rufinus unexpectedly turned his attention to 'cockshead'(*caput galli*), which from the description of the flower might be identified with Spanish sainfoin or sainfoin proper[17] (described as *Onobrychis caput galli*, Lam. by French botanists). In contrast, Arab-Andalusian agronomy in the Spanish peninsula moved

[15] See I. Low, *Aramaische Pflanzennamen*, Leipzig 1881, pp. 5, 11, 18, 19, 94–5, 421–2; on Bar Sarapion see G. Sarton, *Introduction to the History of Science*, Washington 1949, vol. II, p. 229.
[16] See below, Chap. 2 for the bibliography on Pier de' Crescenzi.
[17] See L. Thorndike, *The Herbal of Rufinus, edited from the unique manuscript*, Chicago 1946, n. 26.

away from the two- and three-year rotation prevalent in Europe from the tenth to thirteenth centuries. Crops were grown intensively for several years, then the fertility of the soil was built up again by planting lucerne and clover. From such authors as Ibn-Al-Awwàm, Ibn Bassal and Abù-l-Khayr we can reconstruct the fundamental details of an agricultural system in which continuous crop rotation was possible thanks to the practice of a tilled fallow, which took the place of manuring by breaking up the soil very finely. Lucerne (*fisfisah*), Alexandrian clover (*kurt*), grey peas (*nadjil*) were planted on the fallow land and well irrigated, then mown once or twice a year. These legumes were presented not only as a botanical species, wild or cultivated, but as crops fully integrated into the agricultural cycle, substituting tillage and manuring, as pointed out above. Leguminous plants were being chosen on the lines of Classical agronomy, according to what was best for the cereals, giving preference to short-rooted species, such as vetch, lentils and lupins. Broad beans were given preference as green manure, since they could be harvested before being ploughed into the soil. Andalusian agronomists, better botanists than other Europeans, integrated their knowledge of the properties of plants into the agricultural system, by studying the Classics.[18]

Outside the Classical tradition, Anglo-Norman agriculture produced its own treatises in the thirteenth century. They were widely read among the administrators of the great estates, both of the nobility and of the Church. However, they focused on corn-growing, sheep, and the collection of rent and feudal dues. We shall search in vain in the pages of Walter of Henley, in the rules laid down by Robert Grosseteste, Bishop of Lincoln, for any reference to grasses, to forage or botany in general. The abundance of the natural grassland of England, where meadows and woods covered so much of the country, restricted interest in forage crops, even though clover is a species native to the British Isles.[19]

The natural history of lucerne is like that of other forage crops, clover, trefoils, fenugreek, sainfoin, melilots and Spanish sainfoin. When it is founded on historical documents, it always reveals a continuous chain binding these species, and a connection between them and cultivation. It

---

[18] See L. Bolens, *Les méthodes culturales au moyen-age d'après les traités d'agronomie andalous: traditions et techniques*, Geneva 1974.

[19] See D. Oschinski, *Walter of Henley*, Oxford 1979, *passim*. For an analysis of historical evidence regarding the ecology of medieval pastures and lands otherwise used for grazing, such as woodlands and commons, see now O. Rackham, *The History of the Countryside*, London 1986, pp. 62 ff., 119 ff., 282 ff., 305 ff., 328 ff.

shows, moreover, how species used in the history of agriculture from time immemorial appear and disappear from the scene as a result of historical vicissitudes that are by no means restricted to the mere struggle for survival and the predominance of one species over another. Very ancient plants are transformed into innovations when they become part of a plan to introduce them into a system that previously ignored them. These innovations, in their turn, throw light on the effort to learn which was made by individual farmers, laymen and scientists, and on their relations with the economic institutions of their times. Rather than thinking of agricultural development as the result of uninterrupted progress, we need to see it as the product of continual tension between two systems of agriculture, the first favouring the transformation of work into capital and economizing in labour, the second tending as far as possible to maximize the produce of the land. To reconstruct this effort and to learn how it was put into practice, we have started, in this book, with the plants at the root of the revolution in forage crops, and endeavoured to trace the continual change in the natural environment brought about by all agriculturalists in the course of production.

1. *Translations and classification of the natural environment from the fourteenth to the sixteenth century*

Social and economic growth came to a standstill during the fourteenth century, as a result of a well-known series of disasters. Harsh winters caused a dramatic fall in wheat yields; from 1348–50, after the renewal of trade with Eastern countries, the plague, brought to Europe by infected vermin from the holds of ships, found ideal breeding-grounds in unhygienic, crowded ports and other urban areas. The population was practically halved, whole villages were deserted and labour shortages changed the face of the land. Arable farming gave way to animal husbandry and fields once fertile lay neglected for decades beneath a tangle of weeds and brushwood. Yet grain was still needed for human consumption, and landlords and owner-occupiers were faced with the alternatives of tilling larger areas of land for extremely low yields or cultivating smaller fields more intensively. While the social groups involved varied considerably, interest in Classical culture emerged as a common denominator of their response. Indeed, it can be said that the confrontation of the Classical and medieval systems of botany and agriculture gave rise to the process of change which is the subject of this study.

1. THE AGRONOMY OF PALLADIUS' *OPUS AGRICULTURAE* IN MEDIEVAL LATIN

Comparison of the old and new systems had to take into account how the relationship between them was mediated by written texts and tradition. The *Opus agriculturae* of Taurus Rutilius Aemilianus Palladius, the last of the Latin writers on agricultural economy, was used constantly by writers in Latin all through the Middle Ages, from the Carolingian Renaissance to the invention of the printing press. Hence he plays a double role as mediator between us and the past and between the medieval reader and well-defined Roman-Mediterranean economic practice. What we want to bring out especially is the spread of Classical knowledge, the careful reading of copyists, translators into the vernacular and annotators, which has enabled us to understand how the static model provided by the Classical writers moved on to a transitional phase that lasted from the mid-fourteenth to the early sixteenth century.

Rather than simply reading and annotating the texts of ancient writers, these industrious students of Palladius might have produced new texts. Being mainly landowners and bailiffs, none of them actually took this step; however, their manuscript notes, and suggestions concerning problems of translation, show that, although they were untrained in the critical interpretation developed later by Humanist philologists, their reading was not passive. Their interpolations reflect the economic perspective of the *Opus*, in which plant and animal production was part of a precise plan for the exploitation of the natural environment, as a means of preserving the prevailing social structure.[1] Of Palladius himself we know nothing, except that he was writing in the fourth or fifth century AD and that he was the owner of two estates, one in the Lazio region, the other in Sardinia. The structure of his work was much nearer the medieval tradition than Columella's accurate calculations of the cost of farm labour. Book I deals with the general principles of agriculture; books II–XIII give a calendar of agriculture work, under the headings of produce, cultivation, weather conditions and weather forecasting; book XIV is a *Carmen de insitione arborum*, on grafting and the cultivation of trees, often not included in manuscript copies. Palladius had the advantage of basing his treatise on Columella and on the work of Gargilus Martialis, now lost. It afforded the medieval reader a synthesis of organized instruction in the form of a calendar of rustic tasks which was to become so common in medieval iconography. At the same time, Palladius' estate seemed nearer to the medieval *curtis*, being concerned with problems of subsistence and self-sufficiency in produce and labour,

---

[1] See P. Zumthor, *Parler du moyen âge*, Paris 1980; the present writer dissents from the opinion of R. H. Rodgers, 'The Moore Palladius', *Trans. Cambridge Bibliographical Society*, 5, 1971, p. 204: 'Book production for its own sake seems to have been the raison d'être of at least some of the Manuscripts'. As a general introduction see now *L'ambiente vegetale nell'alto medioevo, 30 marzo–5 aprile 1989*, Settimane di studio del centro italiano di studi sull'alto medioevo, Spoleto 1990, 2 vols. (especially the contributions by G. C. Alessio, *Glossografia altomedievale alle Georgiche*, pp. 55–102, and J. L. Gaulin, *Tradition et pratiques de la literature agronomique pendant le Haut Moyen Age*, pp. 103–35).

and not advising costly tillage by slave labour for commercial production as did Columella, the outstanding agricultural expert in Rome in the first century. Moreover it was a short work, which made it easier to circulate in manuscript, in luxury copies or simpler versions, according to the status of their purchasers.[2]

For a long time, nobles and churchmen seem to have been the chief beneficiaries of Palladius' text. They included the monks of the Oratory of Troyes (ninth century), the De la Meres, the Norman aristocracy, but also a certain William Reed, Bishop of Chichester, one Wying, vicar of Westwell in Kent, Petrarch, the Florentine monks of Santa Maria Novella and the Alli and Strozzi families of Florence. And then later on, in the fifteenth and sixteenth centuries, Humphrey, Duke of Gloucester, Sir John Pilkingtom (*sic*), a Valerio Dionisi of Turin, the Puits friars, Sir John Prise, the Venetian Humanist Ermolao Barbaro and the versatile Florentine writer Bernardo Davanzati.[3] Even the bindings of the agricultural manuscripts recall the old medieval habit of putting works together according to their subject or the needs of the reader. This opens up the larger context to which Palladius belonged and the inter-disciplinary links through which we can achieve an understanding of the text in a literary as well as a social sense. Let us take a look at the *Tacuinum Sanitatis* and the *Marescalcia*, by Lorenzo Ruso, which were copied and completed in 1499 by Arnold Irhout of Brussels, working in the city of Naples. They contain various writings on astronomy, medical astronomy (*sic*), a *Tacuinum Sanitatis*, the cosmography of Albert the Great and Lucius Apuleius. Another copy is bound together with Macer's *De Viribus (virtutibus) herbarum* and a copy of Theophilus' *De diversis artibus*; while six manuscripts, now separated and housed in Rome,

---

[2] See R. T. A. Palladi, *Opus agriculturae. De veterinariae medicinae, de insitione*, edited by R. H. Rodgers, Leipzig 1975, and idem, *An Introduction to Palladius*, Univ. of London, Institute of Classical Studies, Bull. Supp. 35, 1975; R. Martin, *Recherches sur les agronomes latines*, Paris 1971; Palladius, *Traité d'agriculture (Liv. I, II)*, edited by R. Martin, Paris 1976; J. C. Webster, *The Labours of the Months in Antique and Medieval Art to the End of the XIIth century*, Princeton 1938.

[3] See in the following order: Montpellier, EM, ms 305; Paris, BN, ms Lat. 7131; Rodgers, 'The Moore Palladius'; Florence, BN, Conventi Soppressi, ms D.l.835; Florence, BN, Fondo Naz., MS II.II.91; Oxford, Merton College, mss CCCXI/6, CCCXII/3. See also London, BL, Add ms 38.818; Carpentras, Bibl. Inguibertine, ms 314; Paris, BN, ms Lat. 6830 F; Florence, BN, Fondo Naz., ms II.II.92. The Parisian manuscript, BN, Lat. 6842, once belonged to Francesco Barbaro: cf. A. Diller, 'The Library of Francesco and Ermolao Barbaro', *Italia medievale e umanistica*, 6, 1963, pp. 253–62, nn. 1230, 1292.

London, Paris and Cambridge, came before the text of Vitruvius' treatise on *Architecture*.[4]

There are many copies with page references in the margin and manuscript notes in different hands, from which we can make well-founded hypotheses on the relationship between the text and the reader. Petrarch is the outstanding figure among those who used Palladius' work. The manuscript that includes the *Opus agriculturae* was copied by or for him and also contained the writings of Apuleius Platonicus, two of Cicero's orations, *Pro Marcello* and *Pro Ligorio*, and the military writings of Frontinus and Vegetius. The text of the *Opus agriculturae* is embellished with miniatures of agricultural tools and there are two short pages of notes on agronomy in the poet's own hand on the end-papers.[5] These notes concern both field cultivation of vines, laurels, olives, willows and grassland, and horticultural plants such as rosemary and hyssop, among others. Petrarch was not greatly interested in lucerne-growing, though he showed a practical interest in agriculture both in Arquà and in Vaucluse. He left evidence of this in the same way that many lesser students of agriculture were to leave something of themselves on the end-papers of their manuals on agronomy. Petrarch also owned the works of Pliny the Elder, the *De Proprietatibus rerum* by Bartholomew Glenville, and Pier de' Crescenzi's work. His interest in Palladius was mainly theoretical. However, though he may not have been involved in farming, he cultivated his own gardens in Rome, Arquà and Vaucluse and in his correspondence with Cardinal Colonna, in the *Senilia*, in the *De montibus, silvis, fontibus, lacubus* and in the *De remedis utriusque fortunae*, he made further explicit reference to the interest he felt in the natural environment.

It is very important to stress the cultural link that was established between books and their readers. Great writers and small landowners alike have left us testimony of their reading, their learning and their experience in the margins of the most prestigious works of their time. There are markings of all descriptions. Some would read the text, pen in hand, and add the name of the month as a heading at the top of the page,

---

[4] See in the following order: Venice, BN, ms lat. Cl.VII, 57; Paris, BN, ms Lat. 10.264; Cambridge, UL, ms Ee.6.39; K. W. Grandsen, 'The Interpolated Text of the Vitruvian Epitome', *The Journal of the Warburg and Courtauld Institute*, 20, 3–4, 1957.

[5] See P. de Nolhac, 'Pétrarque jardinier' (1892), *Pétrarque et l'Umanisme*, Paris 1907, n. 2, pp. 259ff., 264–8. This manuscript volume is in Rome, Biblioteca Vaticana, ms Vat. Lat. 2193. See also F. Marconi, 'Il Petrarca nella storia dell'agricoltura', *Atti della R. Accademia dei Georgofili*, 16, 1893, abstract.

or would add their own comment on the text, at the beginning of a new paragraph – on the birth of bees, for example.[6] Elsewhere there is an incredibly curious detail on the reproduction of plants from cuttings (*surculus*). Sometimes the markings and notes in the margin run right through the text, indicating the reader's special interest in, and care for, this or that produce. Signs of interest in Mediterranean botany are always very vivid, though somewhat erratic. Explanations in Latin or in the vernacular are given whenever plant names occur, especially if the plants are not native to the place where the text is being read, or if an attempt is being made to cultivate them. Then, in one case, a careful sixteenth-century English reader makes a complete little glossary of Latin–English botanical terms, so as to achieve a better understanding of the original text, bound together with Macer's work on medicinal herbs. All these approaches led on to the vernacular translation of Palladius' text in the years between 1350–1450.

Readers did not simply want to peruse the ancient text, but to interpret it and learn from it.[7] For the first time we find real evidence of the relationship between North and South, between Mediterranean and Northern agriculture, which grew into a comparison between the various agronomic cultures of Europe and Classical agronomy.

A number of adaptations of Palladius' text were also made and the *Opus agriculturae* became available throughout Europe. The conflict between North and South can be seen clearly from the oldest adaptations and rearrangements, such as the one made in the thirteenth century by Gottfried von Franken (see 3.1 below), which dealt mainly with grafting, the cultivation of fruit trees, and wine used for medicinal purposes. An anonymous French writer culled from Palladius warnings about wheat, pigeons, ants, moles and rats (terrible competitors with man for the consumption of food), as well as nuts, dates, olives, apples, pears, cherries and peaches. As a supplement to these extracts he added a short treatise on bees, a cookery book in Latin and a second in French, and for good measure the *Geoponics* on wine translated by Burgundio Pisano. In Florence in some cases only a few chapters from each month were chosen for the version in the vernacular, while agricultural tasks and

---

[6] See Paris, BN, ms Lat. 15.112, XIV century.

[7] See Montpellier, EM, ms 481; Paris, BN, ms Lat. 15.112; Paris, BN and Montpellier, EM, ms 305; Paris, BN, ms Lat. 6830 F; London, BL, Add. Ms 22.015. See also Montpellier, EM, ms 305, as the oldest example of this new way of perceiving the natural environment and London, BL, Add. Ms 44.922; a more recent example is Cambridge, UL, ms Ee.6.39 (1–2).

botanical features were simplified to suit what must have been the commonest farming tasks, comprising cultivation of the vineyard, of flax, asparagus, hedges, quince and other apple trees, filberts, lettuce, cumin, besides the keeping of swine and boars. Finally in Naples, the calendar-form of the text was changed completely, merely giving summaries of the chapters on the house, farm buildings and various ways of storing products; these were followed by others on how to build a plough and a few points about domestic economy and stock-breeding. It is worth noting that absolutely no reference was made to botany. This is an indication that the Classical texts not only created longlasting relations between ancient and modern, but simultaneous relations between the economies of Northern Europe and Italy and the Mediterranean world as well.[8]

Lastly, while reading the *Georgics* in Latin does not seem to have led directly to problems in the identification of plants and tools, the flat, prosaic style of Palladius spurred the average reader to assess the everyday life of his time by the yardstick of the ancient text.

It is important to notice that while translations of Palladius' text came out in Italy, Catalonia and Castile towards the middle of the fourteenth century and a hundred years later in England, a contemporary translation of Pier de' Crescenzi's *Agricultura* delayed the publication of Palladius in French until the early sixteenth century (see Chap. 2, 3.).

2. PALLADIUS IN THE FLORENTINE VERNACULAR

Let us look first at the translation into the Florentine vernacular and the relation between the original and the adaptation in a Mediterranean setting. Reference to the Classical tradition of agronomy would seem less

---

[8] The manuscripts by Gottfried von Franken are quoted below, in notes 18 and 19; in the following order see Paris, BN, ms 7131, f. 100: please note that the *Catalogue des mss. Latins* is somehow incorrect in the description of nn. 5 and 6. The following is a more careful reading of ms 7131: f. 90v, 'Incipit tractatus de aedificatione, nutricione, conservatione et transportacione apum' (Anonym); f. 91r, 'Tractatus primus de planctationibus arborum. Et in primo de planctacionibus pomorum et pirorum'; f. 94r, 'Explicit Tractatus ecc.'; this is the tract by Gottfried von Franken, as we read also in the top right-hand corner of f. 91r, missing in the Catalogue of the BN. Furthermore see Florence, BN, ms Palatino 562, and the already quoted Paris, BN, ms Lat. 10.264. On pests in the history of agriculture see now K. H. Dannenfeldt, 'The Control of Vertebrate Pests in Renaissance Agriculture', *Agricultural History*, 56, 1982, pp. 542–59 and K. Thomas, *Man and the Natural World. Changing Attitudes in England 1500–1800*, London 1983, pp. 143–65.

out of the ordinary here, where corn, wine and oil were as typical of the Florentine countryside as they had been of Roman agriculture.

The translation of the *Opus agriculturae* into the Florentine is generally attributed to the notary Andrea Lancia and can be dated 1350. It was one of the favourite texts used by the Accademia della Crusca for compiling its great dictionary and for the explanations of agricultural and botanical terms. The plan to publish the complete text, as was done for Pier de' Crescenzi, never got further than a series of handwritten notes, probably by Salviati; and it was only in the early nineteenth century that the text of a Venetian copy was printed.

Florence was a city of merchants but she had not lost touch with the land. In the next chapter we shall see more clearly how complex her economic relations with the country often were. By no means negligible names of the Florentine aristocracy appear at the foot of manuscript translations of Palladius. Tommaso degli Alli, son of Giacomo, left his copy to Giovanni degli Alli in his will and from him, at the end of the seventeenth century, the manuscript passed to the library of Tommaso Strozzi. Bernardo Davanzati, a highly versatile writer, who made an early attempt to formulate the quantitative theory of money, and who was the author of a well-known treatise on the agriculture of Tuscany, owned another copy which ended up among the papers of the Accademia della Crusca and in the hands of Salviati. Zenobio Bartolini, who defines himself as a distinguished Florentine, ordered a copy from Bartolomeo Filarco of Pistoia. A copy is also to be found among the papers of the monastery of Santa Maria Novella, with the part on the month of November missing; the good monks who commissioned Paolo Uccello to carry out the naturalistic decoration of their cloister obviously did not have a merely artistic interest in Nature. As we shall see later, the artistic representation of Nature drawn from life went hand in hand with the new interest in writings on agriculture. A final touch – the inventory of the belongings of a certain Giuliano Pierozo, probably a craftsman, made on his death in 1419, included just one book, a translation of Palladius.[9]

---

[9] The following manuscripts are those mentioned in the text (letters A, B . . . N in brackets indicate Mss in the text): Florence, BL, cod. Ital., Plut.43, mss 12 (A), 13 (B), 28 (C); Florence, BR, mss Ricc. 1646 (D), 2238 (E); Florence, BN, Fondo Naz., ms II.II.91 (F), 92 (G); Florence, BN, Conventi Soppressi, ms D.I.835 (H); Florence, BN, ms Palatini 562 (I); Venice, BN, ms Ital. Cl.I cod.C (L); Paris, BN, ms Ital. 930 (M); London, BL, ms Harley 3296 (N). See also L. Salviati, *Avvertimenti della lingua sopra il Decamerone*, Firenze 1584–6; Accademia della Crusca, *Gli atti del primo vocabolario,*

The codices are divided into the following parts – two dating from the fourteenth century and seven from the fifteenth, one from the sixteenth and one from the eighteenth century. Hence it is a mainly fifteenth-century production, which fits in well with the rest of the information we have on Northern Europe. The chapters on lucerne will serve to clarify the difficulties that arise in comparing classical late medieval agronomy and thought and this specialized product of Classical agriculture proper.

Where the Latin text always speaks of *herba medica* under the months of February, chapter VI (tilling the field where lucerne is to be sown), April, chapter I (cultivation of lucerne), September, chapter VII (rotation of sesame and lucerne), November, chapter XIII (lucerne as forage for sheep and goats), we find in the Florentine translation a whole range of variants. Codex B (fourteenth century) lists *erba saggina medicinale*, *saggina*, *melleca*, *medica-melega-saggina*, *erba medica*, *saggina*. All this muddle occurs in a single text, when it is quite clear from the original that it is referring to the same species all the time. The copy owned by Bernardo Davanzati is less confused. Most of the other manuscripts (A, B, C, G, H, M) follow the Davanzati codex, but here too there is considerable wavering and uncertainty. There are few variations in the remaining codices, where we find some phonetic substitution of *melica* for *medica* and a great many synonyms. It is probably not by chance that when Bartolomeo of Pistoia copied the D manuscript for Zenobio Bartolini of Florence, he added, in the margin, that the Latin *jugerum* was the equivalent of 'sixteen of our Florentine *stajora*'[10] (the land needed to sow a bushel of corn) and translated the Latin *ciatus* as 'a tankard of seed'. The same goes for the M codex, now in Paris, which represents the month of April as the 'First chapter on the sowing of lucerne'. All the copyists and rearrangers of the text obviously knew that lucerne was a kind of grass, but they were in doubt about exactly what sort of grass it was.

What at first sight looks like a mere phonetic change – where *m* changes to *l* – becomes, in fact, a semantic change. Lucerne, a forage

Firenze 1974; B. Davanzati, *Coltivazione toscana delle vite e di alcuni arbori*, Firenze 1600; idem, 'Lezione sopra le monete ecc.', in P. Custodi, *Scrittori classici italiani di economia politica, Parte antica*, vol. II, Milano 1804. L. Perini, 'Un patrizio fiorentino e il suo mondo: Bernardo Davanzati', *Studi storici*, 1976, pp. 161–70. On Bartolini see R. Goldthwaite, *La costruzione di Firenze rinascimentale*, Bologna 1984, pp. 129–30, 132–3, 165, 238–40. See also Chap. 2, note 39. In general see also: L. Martines, *The Social World of the Florentine Humanists, 1390–1460*, London 1963.
[10] See c. 98*r*.

crop (*Medicago sativa*), becomes sorghum (*Surghum vulgare*), a secondary cereal called *meliga* or *saggina* in Tuscany. Lucerne was thus cut out of the classical texts during the time when it disappeared from the fields and meadows of medieval Europe, replaced by a plant that was extremely common in the medieval world. The *Tacuina sanitatis* gave ample illustrations of it, Pier de' Crescenzi spoke of it, Pollaiolo placed it in the background of his famous engraving, the *Battaglia di ignudi* (Battle of naked men). But sorghum, a spring corn, was not grown like lucerne, though its sowing-time might be more or less the same. Besides, it is clear from the original that, once sown, lucerne could last for ten years, as it still does in the best lucerne fields, whereas sorghum is an annual, like all cereals. Forage crops such as clover, lucerne and sainfoin restore the nitrogen that corn-growing has drained from the soil, the irrigation they require makes it essential to check more carefully the moisture in the soil, the harvesting of the seed becomes a fundamental stage in the conservation of the species. In these texts a forage-crop worthy of promotion under an improved agricultural system is replaced by a minor cereal which nowadays provides food for the poorest African countries, in semi-arid lands where wheat or maize cannot be grown. It rightly belongs on the borderline between cultivated fields and marginal wasteland, between the farm and the wilds. A medieval source went so far as to speak of melega as suitable for *Porcis et rusticis* (hogs and peasants).[11]

2.1. Uncertainties concerning ancient botany: melica *for* medica

In any case the choice involved in translating and epitomizing Palladius' text always made for simplification, as the Florentine, English or French

---

[11] See P. Aebischer, 'Les noms de Sorgho dans les dialectes modernes et le latin médiéval d'Italie', *Zeits. für rom. Phil.*, 65, 1949, pp. 434–41; the printed edition of *Tacuinum sanitatis* has been edited by A. Pazzini, E. Pirani and M. Salmi, Parma 1970–1; on the same problem see also L. Cogliati Arano, *Tacuinum sanitatis*, Milan 1979; in one of the illustrations of the *Tacuinum sanitatis* kept in the Biblioteca Casanatense, Rome, a wild boar is rooting in a sorghum field; P. J. Jones, 'Italy', in *Cambridge Economic History of Europe*, vol. I, Cambridge 1966, p. 371. In Italy we have only a few statements in favour of sorghum and millet: a notable exception was Agostino Gallo (see Chap. 3. 8 ff.), whose comment should spark off new discussion together with some pages by L. Messedaglia, *Per la storia dell'agricultura e dell'alimentazione*, Piacenza 1931, pp. 143 ff., J. D. Snowden, *The Cultivated Races of Sorghums*, London 1936 and now Watson, *Agricultural Innovation*, pp. 9–14; see now M. S. Mazzi and S. Ravelli, *Gli uomini e le cose nelle campagne fiorentine del Quattrocento*, Firenze 1983.

reader adapted the data to the conditions with which he was familiar. Even in the context of Mediterranean agriculture, not only was *medica* or lucerne turned into *meliga* or sorghum, but the text was simplified, keeping in mind the chief forms of tillage used in the region and the way they were carried out. So the L manuscript, which follows Andrea Lancia's translation so faithfully that it could be included among the other codices, only gives a few chapters for every month; the text, too, is generally abridged. Only the headings of the other chapters are kept. Thus, though the codex mentions 'medicha' for the months of April and September (the February section is incomplete), it makes no reference to the fundamental relationship between seed and field, merely repeating that the yield from a *jugerum* is sufficient to feed three horses for a year. Moreover, it does not explain how the lucerne field should be prepared and reduces Book III, Chapter VIII – on the care of vines in the month of February and the sowing of barley (*hordeus galacticus* in the Latin text) – to a summary of work on the vineyard, omitting the sowing of barley. It continues for the month of February with details mainly on growing trees, vines and olives, as well as quinces, pears, blackberries and filberts. Manuscript I gives a foretaste of the individual effort that would become apparent from the reading of the handwritten notes to Pier de' Crescenzi's work on agriculture, made by dozens of landowners and other readers, from central Italy to England. The manuscript and printed text both provide a link between the reader-landowner and his agricultural-economic setting.

2.2. The Humanists' explanation

It has already been mentioned that Palladius' fame does not rest only on translation into the vernacular or on the fourteenth century. Twenty-three of the seventy-five codices of the *Opus agriculturae* were produced in the fifteenth and early sixteenth centuries and during the Christmas season of 1478 (21 to 24 December) Arnold Irhout of Brussels was still abridging the Latin text in Naples. The invention of printing had already produced its first fruits and the complete text of the *Rerum Rusticarum Scriptores* (by Cato, Varro, Columella and Palladius) was to be one of the volumes most frequently reproduced and annotated, from 1472 on, in Venice, Paris and Strasbourg. Columella's text had already been available to readers of Latin in the early fifteenth century, since Poggio Bracciolini had found a copy in the Benedictine Abbey of Fulda; many copies of codices of the *Res Rustica* were to be made throughout the century. In the same way, those who knew Greek could satisfy their curiosity concerning lucerne by reading the complete text of Dioscorides, which Aldo Manuzio had published in Venice in 1518, unless they had already done so by consulting Cristoforo Landino's translation of Pliny's *Naturalis historia*.

But how many readers had direct access to works of this kind? Incunabula were expensive, reserved to the scholar. The same was true for manuscripts. Of the three oldest Florentine manuscript translations of Palladius, the one that remained longest in private hands was Bernardo Davanzati's copy, which passed to his son Giovanni and then to the Accademia della Crusca; the other two have been chained to the stalls of the Laurenziana Library in Florence since it was first opened. By this time there were many Latin texts (by Varro, Columella and Pliny, besides Palladius) that spoke of *Herba medica*. Landino himself, who put the question of the nomenclature of grasses correctly, wisely translated it as medick. In any case, Humanist philologists could not but give some explanation of the term, and Filippo Berualdo points out that the letter *d* changes to *l* in Vulgar Latin, as Varro says, hence *medica* and *melica*, at least in the Latin of the Golden Age, would be equivalents. But, we should add, *melica* or *milica* is also a late form of Vulgar Latin and has always been used to indicate the *milium* of Classical Latin, which is millet (*Panicum miliaceum*), and which in the medieval world is sometimes confused with sorghum. Hence it seems that Beroaldo, while understanding Columella's original text properly and clarifying that lucerne (*medica*) was a meadow grass, afterwards slipped into the usual transformation of lucerne into sorghum.[12] But how could a forage-crop, capable of surviving for ten years, become an annual, thus clearly

---

[12] See in the following order: C. Pliny, *Historia naturale di latino in volgare tradotta per Christophoro Landino et nuovamente corretta per Antonio Brucioli*, Venice 1543; on translators from Latin into Italian see L. Olschki, *Geschichte der neusprachlichen wissenschaftlichen Literatur*, Heidelberg 1919, and C. Dionisotti, *Geografia e storia della letteratura italiana*, Turin 1967, pp. 151–5. Paris, BN, ms Lat. 10.264, fos. 172–83; on Palladius cf. J. Svennung, *Untersuchungen zu Palladius*, Uppsala 1935, and R. H. Rodgers, *Palladius R. T. Ae.*, in *Catalogus translationum et commentariorum*, edited by F. E. Kranz and P. O. Kristeller, Washington 1980, vol. III; on Columella see A. V. Josephson, *Die Columella Handschriften*, Uppsala Un. Arsskrift, 1955; S. Hedberg, 'Contamination and interpolation. A study of the 15th C. Columella mss.', *Studia latina Upsaliensia*, 5, 1968; also Cod. Lat. 212, Modena, BE, T. Varro, *De agricultura* [*sic*], another fifteenth-century Ms maintains in the index (c. 62*r*) and in the text (c. 81*v*) the ambivalence between *melica* and *medica*. Millet-meliga-sorghum were confused in the well-known *Tacuinum sanitatis* today housed in Vienna; this inaccuracy is also found in Watson, *Agricultural Innovation*, p. 13.

contradicting the text? It was not the philologists, for all their merits, but the agronomists and botanists of the following century, who were to find the definitive solution to the problem of identifying lucerne.

2.3. Palladius in Troyes

It was not only in Florence that the phonetics of the Florentine vernacular changed *d* into *l* and twisted the meaning of Palladius' text. In the oldest manuscript of the *Opus agriculturae* (ninth to tenth century), now in Montpellier – where it was transferred from the Oratory of Troyes,[13] and hence from the Paris area – a contemporary hand made annotations, in Carolingian, on the grasses and plants and the tools mentioned in the course of the text. The manuscript invariably gives *medica*, as always when the text is in Latin, and where it appears for the first time the annotator adds *surgus ut meliga herba* in the margin. Therefore the phonetic change from *d* to *l* and the consequent demotion of lucerne to sorghum occur in a very much wider and older area, albeit of Romance tradition. The French monks of the oratory of Troyes, and Andrea Lancia and the Florentines who copied and made use of his work in the mid-fourteenth century, changed the unknown to the known in the same way.

2.4. Palladius in sixteenth-century Italy

The renown of Palladius' slim manual of agricultural and domestic economy was not confined to the manuscript tradition, and had spread so widely that sixteenth-century publishers and booksellers felt bound to take advantage of it by printing a translation for readers quite untrained to use the philological editions of the Classical authors. On 14 June 1526 the bookseller Simone di Nicolò published a translation in Siena 'so that those who do not know Latin may reap benefit and great delight'. The translation is more accurate than that in the Florentine vernacular, at least as far as lucerne is concerned. The semantic corruption of *medica* into *meliga* is avoided and the original phonetic value is respected. Pietro Marino da Foligno dedicated this translation to Vittorio Colonna, mentioning both his military prowess and his wonderful knowledge of agricultural matters. He was translating Palladius for those who did not know Latin but wanted to learn the science of cultivating the land, which

---

[13] Montpellier, EM, ms 305.

requires 'practice and theory'. Pietro Marino da Foligno also knew
something about agriculture. He spoke of his 'rustic solitude' and also
mentioned that he made the translation from Latin into his own idiom,
the Umbrian dialect. Thus Palladius' influence extended beyond the
town but lucerne was still presented in mythical garb. The printed
version met with rapid, albeit shortlived success. It was reprinted in
Venice in 1528, first by Zoppino and then by Bernardino da Lessona,
who later issued it, together with Pier de' Crescenzi's *Agricultura*, in
1538.

It is rather surprising to find Francesco Sansovino, a really important
polymath, architect, writer and printer of Venice, insisting, as late as
1560, in the April section of his new translation of Palladius (published
once more together with Pier de' Crescenzi) that *melica* has to be sown
in fields divided into large sections by irrigation channels. He was clearly
quite unconcerned with cost–benefit ratios.

In the mid-sixteenth century no well-informed and careful reader
should have continued to mistake lucerne for sorghum on the strength of
a misreading of the Latin text. By then botanists and agronomists had
defined many more species than those known to the ancient and medieval
worlds, and agronomists were well aware of their existence. Sansovino
may have been working on a copy of Andrea Lancia's translation and
merely set out to make it more readable. This version of Sansovino's may
have been responsible for another, very bad mistake almost a hundred
years later. For in 1640 Vincenzo Tanara of Bologna, a well-known
agronomist, military man and traveller with great practical experience,
no longer feeling any need to consult the ancient texts, suggested that
perhaps *melica* (*sic*) was also called *medica* 'because it came from
Media', turning the question upside down once more.[14] And then, as

[14] See in the following order *Palladio dignissimo et antiquo scriptore della agricultura
traducto vulgare* [. . .], Siena 1526, a very rare edition missing in F. Argelati,
Biblioteca dei volgarizzatori, Milan 1767, vol. III, p. 173, in Florence, BN, and New
York, Columbia UL; P. Marino, *Palladio* [. . .], Nicolò d'Aristotele detto Zoppino,
Venice 1528, in 4°; P. Marino, *Palladio* [. . .], Bernardino Viano da Lessona
vercellese, Venice 1538, in 8°; on Vittorio Colonna see *Dizionario biografico degli
italiani*, *sub nomine*; T. R. A. Palladio, *La villa tradotto nuovamente da Francesco
Sansovino*, Venice 1560. On Francesco Sansovino see P. F. Grendler, 'F. Sansovino
and Italian popular history 1560–1600', *Studies in the Renaissance*, 16, 1969,
pp. 179–80, and A. Cicogna, *Delle iscrizioni veneziane*, Venice 1834, vol. IV,
pp. 31–91; V. Tanara, *L'economia del cittadino in villa*, Bologna 1640, Libro VI
(p. 408, ed. Venice 1680).

the new American products began to spread in the seventeenth century, millet and sorghum were even taken for maize.[15]

3. DUKE HUMPHREY OF OXFORD AND THE ENGLISH TRANSLATION OF PALLADIUS

The Middle English translation of Palladius is later but none the less significant. Humphrey, Duke of Gloucester, brother and uncle of kings, as he liked to call himself, was deeply involved in English and foreign politics and in the wars in France and Flanders against Philip of Burgundy. He was accused of conspiring against the Crown and figured in other scandals, including a trial for witchcraft. In 1439 and 1443 he donated to the University of Oxford a certain number of manuscript volumes as a token of his interest in Humanism. Among the volumes donated in 1443 was a copy of the *Opus agriculturae* in Latin, while an English translation of it was among the work produced under his patronage. It has been said that Duke Humphrey's court was the gateway to Italian Humanism. His role as patron of the arts and scholarship certainly encouraged the spread of more than one Classical work, and more generally speaking the exchange of Humanist culture between England and the Continent. The acquisition, donation and translation of Palladius, a text so widely used among Norman nobles in the Middle Ages, was not of exceptional importance in the framework of Duke Humphrey's interests. Among the works sent to him from Italy by the Italian Humanist Decembrio were a treatise on botany by Pseudo-Apuleius, the works of Vitruvius, Ptolemy, Columella, Cato and Varro; and Humphrey himself made a careful study of Pliny's *Naturalis Historia* and Florius' *Epitome*. One might ask why Humphrey chose to have Palladius' text translated rather than Columella's, since Decembrio had sent him that too. We can only guess that the *Res rustica* would have presented too many difficulties of the kind we shall be looking into later, and that its size discouraged translation as it had discouraged its circulation in previous centuries. The question is not merely rhetorical, as Heinrich Osterreicher translated Columella's text between 1472 and 1482, avoiding the complicated problems involved by leaving the

---

[15] See Messedaglia, *Per la storia dell'agricoltura*, pp. 73 ff.

juridical terminology in Latin.[16] But in England Palladius' *Opus agriculturae* was the recognized text of noble agriculture. It reflected the interest and curiosity that the upper classes felt for exotic plants and crops, exotic and Mediterranean being one and the same to them. The prose treatise was rendered in clumsy verse, for Chaucer had established English as a literary medium and fired lesser men to imitate him. The attempt served to illustrate the difficulties inherent in the change of form as well as conveying an idea of Mediterranean conditions. It became a work of didactic poetry, one of the many calendars of months, strung between Chaucer and Spenser's beautiful *Shepherd's Calendar*, part of a literary tradition which in its turn bridged the gap between the scientific genre of the *Secreta secretorum* or the above-mentioned *De proprietatibus rerum* and the Virgilian tradition of the *Georgics* and the *Eclogues*; the world of the shepherd moved on to that of the knight, in which animal and plant life adorned the aristocracy in classical garb.

The difficulties that the medieval Italian and French reader encountered in identifying plants, agricultural tasks and tools come up again all the more understandably in the English translation. Just as John Trevisa, editor of two rightly famous texts, that of Pliny (in Robert Cricklade's version, be it noted) and Bartholomew of Glenville's *De proprietatibus rerum*, had faced the problems of botanical and agricultural terminology,[17] so the anonymous translator of Palladius shows

---

[16] See in the following order: H. Anstey, *Munimenta academica*. Pt. II. *Libri cancellarii et procuratorum*, London 1868, pp. 758–22; K. H. Vickers, *Humphrey Duke of Gloucester. A Biography*, London 1907, pp. 394–5; W. L. Newman, 'The correspondence of Humphrey and Pier Candido Decembrio', *English Historical Review*, 20, 1905, pp. 484–93; R. Weiss, *Humanism in England during the 15th Century*, Oxford 1941, pp. 59, 62–3; Bodleian library, *D. Humphrey and the English Humanism in the Fifteenth Century. Catalogue of an Exhibition*, Oxford 1970; A. Sammut, *Umfredo duca di Gloucester e gli umanisti italiani*, Padova 1980, and idem, 'Tra Pavia, Milano e Oxford: Trasmissioni di codici', in *Vestigia. Studi in onore di G. Billanovich*, Rome 1984, vol. II, pp. 613–22; see also D. Hay, 'England and the Humanists in the 15th century', in *Itinerarium Italicum. The Profile of the Italian Renaissance in the Mirror of its European Transformations. Dedicated to P. O. Kristeller, Studies in Medieval and Reformation Thought*, 14, 1975; J. T. Rosenthal, 'Aristocratic Culture Patronage', *Bull. J. Rylands Lib.*, 64, 1982; R. Tuve, *Seasons and Months. Studies in a Tradition of Middle English Poetry*, Paris 1933, and as an example see I. Gollancz and M. M. Weale (eds.), *The Quatrefoil of Love*, London 1935, EETS, n. 195, and E. Curtius, *Europäische Literatur und lateinisches Mittelalter*, Bern 1961, p. 194; K. Loefflerer, 'L. J. Moderatus Columella De re rustica übersezt durch Heinrich Oesterreicher Abt von Schussenried', *Bibliothek des Literarischen Vereins in Stuttgart*, Tübingen 1914, 2 vols.

[17] Cf. K. Rück, 'Das Exzerpt der Naturalis Historia des Plinius von Robert von Cricklade', *S. B. der k. bayer. Akad. der Wissenschaften philos.-philol.-hist. Klassen*, 1902 [1903],

us what the natural environment and the economy of the Mediterranean looked like to an Englishman of average-to-advanced cultural level in the mid-fifteenth century. Since he attempted a rendering of the whole work, this translator was forced to be more accurate in dealing with specialized terminology, or else to paraphrase when he could not find the exact equivalent.

The English version of Palladius is almost certainly the first text in which a translator whose mother-tongue was English (probably Thomas Norton, Humphrey's chaplain) was confronted with continuous cropping.[18] As in the case of the Florentine translation, it is especially important to check the outcome of this confrontation, looking carefully at the nomenclature. *Trifolium*, for example, became trefoil, certainly an English word, though less common than clover. It seems to come directly from the Latin or from the French *treffle*. In more recent times, trefoil is used for *Medicago lupolina*, but in earlier times it could be used simply to indicate any three-leafed plant. In any case, the translator did not choose the commonest name, *clover*, or its variants *clafre, cloure, cleuvre, claver*, of which we have traces in England from the eleventh century on and which are linked directly with German dialects. Actually, a version made at the same time as that in the vernacular ran *Trifolium quando* s*impliciter ponitur anglice dicitur cleure*, which shows a better understanding of the relationship between the wild and the cultivated plant in a Latin–English context.[19] Hence, while grass is a correct

pp. 195–285; E. W. Gudger, 'Pliny's Historia Naturalis the most popular natural history ever published', *Isis*, 6, 1924, pp. 269–81; A. C. Klebs, 'Incunabula editions', *Isis*, 24, 1935–6, pp. 120–1; L. Thorndike, 'Epitomes of Pliny', *Isis*, 1936–7, 26, p. 39; M. Le Bonnec, *Bibliographie de Pline*, Paris 1946; J. Trevisa, *On the Property of Things. J. T. Translation of Bartholomaeus Anglicus De proprietatibus rerum*, Oxford 1975, vols. I–II.

[18] On English manuscripts see Oxford, BO, ms 29620, 31, 502, photographic reproduction of the copy prepared for Duke Humphrey, ms 31369, papers concerning the discovery, date and possible authorship; a forgotten partial copy in the possession of the Hunterian Museum, Glasgow, has to be added, see *Catalogue of the Manuscripts in the Library of the Hunterian Museum in the University of Glasgow*, Glasgow 1908, pp. 108–9. The two printed editions are: B. Lodge, *Palladium on Husbondrie. From the unique ms of about 1420 A.D. in Colchester Castle*, London 1873, EETS, nn. 52, 72; M. Liddell (ed.), *The Middle-English translation of Palladius de re rustica* [*sic*], Pt I, Text, Berlin 1896. See also C. Struever, 'Die mittelenglische Übersetzung des Palladius. Ihr Verhaltnis zur Quelle und ihre Sprache'. Inaugural-dissertation [. . .] an der G. A. Universität zu Göttingen, Halle 1887; recently D. R. Howlett, 'Studies in the Works of John Wethamsteade', PhD Thesis, Oxford 1975, suggested that the text had been translated by Thomas Norton.

[19] See *Alphita* c. 1400, Anecd. Oxon 1887, in *Oxford English Dictionary*, 'clover'.

rendering of the Latin *gramen* or the generic *herba*, the new term *foenum graecum* is more ambivalent and the translator wavers between Greekish hay, the literal translation, and the phonetically based form fenugreek.

But the greatest complications appeared when the translator came to the March text, Chapter VI, *De agris medicae parandis*, where the word *medica* disappeared from the translation altogether and the text was ruthlessly carved up and inserted in Chapter V, *De serendo cannabo*. The sowing of hemp was a much more familiar subject than the cultivation of lucerne, which was not to appear in England for another hundred and fifty years (cf. Chap. 6, 1–3). In the other passages, *medicine* (Book III, v. 25) or *medick* are suggested as the translation of *medica*, based on the Latin *medicus*, *medeor* (to treat or medicate etc.), without recognizing the reference to place in *Media*, *medicus*, which clarified the Middle-Eastern origin of the grass. Indeed the term *medick*, which appears to be modelled phonetically on Latin, referring to and insisting on the supposed medical properties of the grass, was to meet with some favour until the time when seed was imported from France, and preference was given to the French *luzerne*. In the second half of the sixteenth century, the famous botanist William Turner wrote that he had never yet found it growing wild in England, and suggested the translation *horned clover* (from the shape of the pods) or *medic fodder*.[20] It is not surprising that the English translation of Palladius produced a wealth of phonetic associations, since Italian Humanists and translators had proceeded in exactly the same way, just as many Greek words had also been trans-ferred into Latin. So, at least, said Cristoforo Landino, insisting that there was great uncertainty particularly with regard to grasses and that many people used the same name for different grasses (see above 2.2 and note 14). This was all the more understandable in the transition from ancient to modern or from the Mediterranean area to Northern Europe. Once more it is a question of a different relationship with the objects described. The difficulties it created for the English translator were such that in the end he chose to keep the Latin word wherever he felt uncertain. Numerous alternatives were given between the lines throughout, so that the reader was left to decide what interpretation to give to the Latin text. One might think the anonymous translator had little knowledge of agronomy (but why then should Duke Humphrey have commissioned him to carry out such a hard task?), and yet he translated the text on

---

[20] W. Turner, *The names of herbes in Latin, Greke . . .* , London 1545 (see below, pp. 263–7).

ploughing cornfields confidently, and did not hesitate over *fallowland* (*ager novalis* in Latin, *falowis* in the English translation), a constant feature in English agriculture in his day.

3.1. The Tractatus Godefridi supra Paladium *and the English reader*

That the English translation of Palladius' text was not made by chance, and that interest in the agriculture and produce of the Mediterranean was constant, is confirmed by the story of a lesser text, which is, however, of great importance for the understanding of the background to the spread of Palladius' work. The *Tractatus de planctacionibus arborum* or the *Tractatus Godefridi supra Paladium*, also known as *Geoffrey upon Palady*, is a short text often met with from the thirteenth century on, which became famous between the fifteenth and early sixteenth centuries. For a long time it was uncertain who its author was. In some catalogues it is attributed to the well-known rhetorical writer Geoffrey Vinsauf, author of the *Poetria Nova*, which was said to have eclipsed the fame of Horace's epistle on the same subject. In other catalogues he is simply called Galfridus, and in yet others he is anonymous. It was Pits who hypothesized that the author of the *Poetria Nova* might have been called Vinsauf precisely because he had written this short treatise on how to store wine; actually there is little mention of wine in the *De planctacionibus arborum*. In the 1868 printed catalogue of the manuscripts of the British Museum they have tried to put the matter right by reading 'Bononiensis', where the text speaks of 'Bononienses' (Bolognesi) in connection with storing wine. According to Fattorini and Tiraboschi, Geoffrey Vinsauf taught in Bologna and so used the title *Bononiensis* in honour of that city. However, in Bologna he was known more simply as Galfridus Anglicus. W. Stubbs, with greater insight, suggested (1864) that the little treatise on grafting was attributed to Geoffrey Vinsauf precisely because of his name, well fitted to persuade his contemporaries of the excellency of the advice given in the text. If we add to this the fact that the *Poetria Nova* and the *De planctacionibus arborum* are never found together in the same codex, a less familiar Geoffrey would seem to hover behind Vinsauf. Anyone who had read one of the oldest and most complete versions (the Add. MS 18752 and the Arundel MS 251 in the British Library, for example), as the compilers of mid-sixteenth-century catalogues were aware, would have noticed that this author had travelled widely and spoke of Calabria, Greece, Bologna, Bamberg and Wurzburg at first hand. Actually, Geoffrey had visited

Paris, Bologna and Rome, where he had awaited the homecoming of Richard I after the latter was imprisoned by the Emperor. Besides, we come across certain phrases in the *De planctacionibus arborum* such as 'vulgari nomine amarellen . . . vocantur vulgariter wisselen . . . arbor vulgariter dicitur Erle' (fos. 3*r*, 5*v*, 8*r*), in which 'Erle (Eller), amerellen, wisselen' for alder, egriot, and sour cherries, clearly come from Middle-Low German rather than Middle English. At this point a new figure emerges – Gottfried von Franken, frequently found in the catalogues of German libraries because of his epitome of Palladius' book. The oldest manuscripts in English libraries are German, like the Arundel MS 251, or were copied from the many texts produced in Germany. The couplets placed before the Add. MS 18752 of the British Library – a German original or a copy made in England, bound together with various books of secrets, in Latin and English, of the fourteenth, fifteenth and sixteenth centuries – are the same as those that appear before other German specimens. Gottfried von Franken's Latin version was to be translated into many languages before being printed anonymously. There are three German versions, one Swabian and two Bavarian, followed by one in Bohemian German and another in Czech, besides the one in English that we shall examine shortly, which has been passed over in the literature on Gottfried. Let us now leave the good Gottfried to drink bad wine in Bamberg (as he himself complains) and turn to the codices of *Galfridus supra Paladium* in England.[21]

---

[21] The studies useful for the identification of the author are as follows: E. Faral, *Les arts poétiques du xe et du xiiie siècle*, Paris 1924, pp. 14–17; D. Kelly, 'Theory of composition in Medieval narrative poetry and Geoffrey of Vinsauf's Poetria Nova', *Medieval Studies*, 31, 1969; W. Stubbs (ed.), *Itinerarium peregrinorum et gesta regis Riccardi* (*Chronicle and memorials of the reign of Richard I*), Coll. rolls, London 1864, vol. I, p. lviii; M. Sarti, *De claris Archigymnasii Bononiensis professoribus a saeculo xi usque ad sec. xiv*, Bologna 1769, vol. I, part I, pp. 505–7; M. H. Laurent, 'Fabio Virgili et les bibliothèques de Bologne au début du xvie siècle d'après le ms Barb. Lat. 3185', *Studi e testi*, 105, Città del Vaticano 1943; Svennung, *Untersuchungen zu Palladius*, pp. 627–8; quotations are taken from London, BL, ms Arundel 251; other collections in the British Library, such as Cotton, Harleian, Sloane, Add. Mss, have more recent copies; the oldest English manuscript is kept in Cambridge, Gonville and Caius College, ms 200; other copies are in the Bodleian Library, Oxford; amongst German manuscripts we quote only Vienna, Kaiserliche Biblioteck, ms 2357; München Bayerischen Biblioteck Staats, *Catalogus Codicum Latinorum*, vol. II, part iv, München 1881, mss 2487, 2634; *Catalogus Codicum Latinorum*, vol. I, part i, München 1892, ms 615; *Verzeichnis der Hss in Preussischen Staate, Göttingen*, Berlin 1893, vol. II, ms BL.226b; on the text and its author see J. Haupt, 'Über das md. Arnzeibuch des Maisters Bartholomaeus', *Sitzungsberichte der Kaiserlichen Akademie der Wissenschaften, Wien*, 71, 1872, pp. 451–565; G. Eis, *Gottfrieds Pelzbuch*

It is not easy to define the text of the *Tractatus Godefridi*. Grafting and the growing of fruit-trees, storing wine and cultivating the vineyard make up the greater part of it. The English codices (in English or Latin but copied in England) are generally a shortened version of the original text (for example the Arundel MS 251), more or less following the Cotton Julius D MS VIII (a variation on the Arundel MS 251, with omissions and additions) or the MS 200 of Gonville and Caius College, shortened to nineteen chapters. Nor was Palladius the only source of our Gottfried; Galen and his sources were also added, as we learn from the couplets placed before various specimens. He also included his own experience, recalling at first hand the Duchy of Brabant, Calabria, Greece, the people of Bologna, a 'certain monk', a 'Magister Richardus' not otherwise specified. We are dealing here with a minor traveller but nonetheless well informed and curious about other people's experiences. In any case it would seem that the *Tractatus Godefridi* served to condense the experience and knowledge contained in the *Opus agriculturae* to suit the needs of circles less interested in scholarly work and more closely involved in the practical problems of grafting and of storing wine. Godfridus' style is very near to that of Palladius. He followed the Latin author carefully, month by month, especially in the case of March, and annotated the practice of grafting and various experiments on fruit-trees. Quotations from the ancients (Palladius and Galen) and more recent experience (Master Richard) guaranteed to readers that the instructions and advice were reliable, that they formed part of the pure medieval tradition of gardening and horticulture, in which the quality of the fruit was maintained by grafting onto wild plants as Pier de' Crescenzi taught. Such cultivation was a kind of amateur gardening, its aim being to produce rare, unusual fruit, without stones, with strange colours, sometimes even grown on trees of another species. It did not form part of an organized system of fruit-growing like that adopted by Pier de' Crescenzi on his own land. Nor was there any serious attempt to develop a system for turning wild trees into orchard

(München 1944), Wiesbaden 1966; R. Ankenbrand, 'Das Pelzbuch des Gottfried von Franken', Inaugural Diss., Heidelberg 1970, mentions a Latin manuscript kept in Italy: Florence, BL, ms Laur. Ashb.1011, but omits other copies of Gottfried's text in Italy, Brescia, BQ, ms B.V.14, ff. 76–95 and in Rome, BV, see L. Schuba, *Die medizinischer Handschriften der Codices Palatini in der Vatikanischer Bibliothek*, Wiesbaden, 1981, p. 532, nos 1240, 1242, 1255, 1155. See also S. Sudhof, 'Das deutsche Pelzbuch des Mittelalters und seine Einflüsse auf die europäische Gartenliteratur der Neuzeit', *Zeitschrift für agrar Geschichte*, 2, 1954, pp. 105–14.

specimens. These experiments were made only by the aristocrat or at most the town-dweller, in Northern Europe, where they loved Nature as she was described in medieval romances, full of miraculous woods and plants, flowers and fruit that were also poetic and social symbols.

3.1.1. *Godfridus and Nicholas Bollard*

To judge from the manuscripts that have come down to us, the fame of Gottfried's text was at its height in England in the fifteenth century.[22] The English translation and adaptation certainly increased its circulation. It was probably made by a Nicholas Bollard, clerk of Oxford. He no doubt based it, very literally, on an abridged Latin version common in England, for example the MS 200 in Gonville and Caius College. To it were added a few pages entitled *Of gendrynge . . . graffyng . . . of alterations of trees . . .* , signed by Bollard himself. They merely repeat advice like that in the translation, on grafting and fruit-bearing, with some quotations from the apocryphal work *The secrets*, by Aristotle and Ptolemy, and a marked insistence on the relationship between astrology and plant growth. No detailed analysis can be given here, but the following points need to be borne in mind. Godfridus' Latin text is still hesitant about botanical terms and keeps the non-Latin names in Middle-Low German (Erle, Amerellen) for greater clarity. These disappear from Bollard's English translation, which seems to be more accurate and more confident than the translation of the *Opus agriculturae* with regard to terminology. Yet the two texts and the two translations have some obvious points in common. The brevity of Godridus' work and its focus on the cultivation of trees and the storing of fruit may explain why it was given preference, in the same way as the concise Palladius text gradually ousted the Columella and made it virtually unobtainable. Nicholas

---

[22] For an example see: London, BL, ms Sloane 122, *Geoffrey upon Palady* (in English), fos. 72–83v, *Bollard*, fos. 84–8; London, BL, ms Sloane 686, *Geoffrey*, fos. 16–40v, *Bollard*, fos. 41–47v; on Nicholas Bollard see *Dictionary of National Biography* (hereafter quoted as *DNB*), *sub nomine*; A. M. T. Cecil, *A history of gardening in England*, London 1910, p. 62; B. Henrey, *British Botanical and Horticultural Literature before 1800*, London 1975, vol. I, pp. 55–7; the text was printed as R. Arnold, *The Names of the Baylifs Custos Mairs and Sherefs of the Citie of London*, Antwerp 1503, London 1521 and 1811; *The crafte of graffynge and plantynge of trees*, n.p., n.d. [Caxton 1520]. A partial edition was published in J. Halliwell, *Early English Miscellanies in Prose and Verse, selected from an unedited Manuscript of the 15th century*, London 1855. The whole text has been transcribed from Oxford, Balliol College, ms 354, by D. C. Browning, 'Commentary on ms Balliol 354', B. Litt. Thesis, Balliol College, Oxford 1935, unpublished.

Ballard's English translation was circulating in manuscript form at the same time as the printed edition. It is so rare that it may have been prepared specifically for publication, though only part of it came out in *Arnold's Chronicle* and the *Craft of graffynge*, which Caxton was to print in 1520. It can be reasonably supposed that it was the translation of Palladius made for Humphrey at or in the immediate vicinity of Oxford that prompted Nicholas Bollard, also from Oxford, to translate Godfridus' text, obviously for a different kind of reader. The number of extant copies of Godfridus' Latin text goes to show how many people wished to own and use a work of this kind in the fifteenth and sixteenth centuries. The influence of the difficult, shortened text of Palladius is to be found in lower circles, having more material aims, rather than in the small group of readers able to appreciate Duke Humphrey's Humanism.

The text is rarely found alone; generally it is copied on paper, in unskilled, often quite illegible lettering, bound together with miscellaneous texts, fragments and short poems, extracts from the Statutes of the Realm, in what came to be known as *commonplace books*. A certain Richard Hill, a citizen and wholesale mercer of London in the early sixteenth century, owned a particularly well-crammed one. His transcription of *Geoffrey upon Palady*, as it was called by then, is very long, almost complete. It is preceded by a short, incomplete treatise on the veterinary art. Hill was an educated, middle-class man. He also copied out extracts of poems in English and Latin, from the *Gesta Romanorum* and the *Boke of Curtaisie*, and added information about his children. He is the model husbandman who enlarged his concept of domestic economy to include plants and animals, ahead of his time by almost a hundred years. Actually, he copied part of his book from a kind of almanac, known as *Arnold's Chronicle*, in which a long extract from Geoffrey and Bollard's text was printed; and part from a much more complete, manuscript copy, also adding further notes on grafting. Hill was not the only man in London to possess the Geoffrey–Bollard text and to take an active interest in trees and grafting. Robert Robynson has left another *commonplace book* in which his Geoffrey–Bollard is bound together with notes on the moon, on how to calculate the date when Easter fell, on the zodiac, on the value of coins, the rose-garden, as well as the usual notes on his own life. He was born in the county of Lincoln in 1454, moved to London as an apprentice in 1470, married in 1482 and on 19 September, at the age of 78, he wrote his notes on the 'vyne', the hours and saffron. Was he just one more *pater familias* following Cato's example and devoting his old age to the care of trees and grafting? He too read Geoffrey–Bollard, prompted by a wish for greater control over nature, on something rather like Pier de' Crescenzi's plan. He too pointed out the possible connection between the growth of plants and the influence of the stars. So we are confronted with a complex situation – on the one hand Palladius and the translation commissioned by Humphrey; on the other Godfridus–Geoffrey–Bollard and *Arnold's Chronicle*, the commonplace books and the almanacs.[23]

3.1.2. *Godfridus and Palladius made accessible lower down the social scale*

Godfridus' success was not to end with Caxton in 1520. The passing of the years, the new spate of books on agriculture, gardening and botany put on the English market, the economic situation, deeply changed after the dissolution of the monasteries and sale of Church property, quickly made an old text obsolete, even though it had been revised in the early sixteenth century, as was the Geoffrey–Bollard version. But the title of the treatise, with its mixture of Latin and the vernacular, wisdom of the ancients, practical advice and links with the stars, was too fascinating to be discarded straight away. And for English printers of the sixteenth century it was too easy a matter to get hold of a book or a text and republish it. The ancients, the Classical texts, science, astrology, magic, all the themes dear to Duke Humphrey, were being corrupted. Godfridus was turned into the author of an almanac brought out in London, undated, by Robert Wyer – *Here begynneth the Boke of Knowledge unknown apperteyninge to Astronomye with certayne necessarye Rules, and certayne spheres contaynyng herein Compyled by Godfridus super Palladium de agricultura. Anglicatum.* All the information on the cultivation of fruit-trees and so on was suppressed, while the astrological part, the influence of the stars and planets on man's life, were left and expanded. Godfridus and Palladius were reduced to a mere title, for people who bought printed almanacs, probably quite unlike those who had so eagerly perused the little treatise on trees fifty years earlier. Yet as they had previously copied the text on trees, they now copied the almanac. One edition followed another. The one printed in London in 1585 had additions exclusively on astrology; another, undated one,

---

[23] See in the following order Oxford, Balliol College, ms 354; Browning, *Commentary*; R. A. B. Mynors, *Catalogue of mss. of Balliol College, Oxford*, Oxford 1963, pp. 352–3; W. P. Hills, 'Richard Hill of Hillend', *Notes and Queries*, 177, 1939; London, BL, Harley ms 1785, fos. 21*v*, 31*v*, 54*r–v*, 56*r*.

added weather forecasting and details about the seasons for farmers, with an engraving of Ptolemy on the frontispiece. The same title appeared again in 1619; and then thirty years later in 1649, came a mistake. In *Godfridus super Palladium de Agricultura, Anglicarum* the original *t* in *Anglicatum* has become an *r*, while a comma was left to complicate the interpretation of the obvious printer's error. Times had changed. Cheap literature was hawked in the streets and Godfridus held his peace until the early eighteenth century. Then, when the publisher H. Rhodes of London took up the last edition, he noticed what seemed to him a mere printer's error and corrected it to *Godfridus super Palladium de Agricultura Anglicorum*, as if Palladius had written a book on English agriculture. A certain John Small read this almanac in 1764 and had no fault to find with it.[24]

But John Small was not the only one to have lost all touch with the ancient text. Between 1714 and 1719 the medical student Samuel Cook of Wantage annotated in beautiful handwriting a parchment specimen of the *Opus agriculturae*, written in the fourteenth century. We might expect the comments of a scholarly gentleman, like Jethro Tull, who transposed the agriculture of the ancients in modern key; actually, what we find is such wisdom as 'money makes the mare to goe as saith the Proverbe' (fo. 11*r*), 'nothing can I more commend than pure and perfect love' (fos. 8*r*, 13*v*), 'an Honest Imployment is an Excellent Patrimony' (fo. 14*r*), 'Mrs Sownly the most celebrated Beauty in London Died of the small pox Aug 13:1716' (fo. 33*v*), to quote only a few examples. Benjamin Bikeman, another owner of the same codex, used the *Opus* to keep account of the money he borrowed in January 1796.[25]

So the text of the *Opus agriculturae*, which had constituted a link with, and a substitute for, the text of Columella, was reduced to a few hints and practical details exclusively on grafting and the cultivation of fruit trees and finally to a mysterious title for readers of almanacs. Once prized by members of the Norman aristocracy, then by their gardeners, it finally fell into the hands of readers of chapbooks. But obviously this was only one of the paths followed by ancient writings on agronomy from the fifteenth to the eighteenth century. The other was the tradition that took

[24] Godfridus, *The knowledge of things [. . .]*, London 1707; Oxford, BO, Douce G.335, bears a signature on the frontispiece: 'John Small His Book 1746'. On almanacks and their readers see now M. Spufford, *The Great Reclothing of Rural England: Petty Chapmen and Their Wares in the Seventeenth Century*, London 1984.

[25] See Oxford, BO, ms Rawlinson G.61, fos. 11*r*, 8*r*, 13*v*, 14*r*, 33*v*.

into account the editions and criticism of Merula, Beroaldo, Vettori and the other Humanists and comparison with Cato, Varro, Columello, Pliny and the *Georgics*, the Classical writings on agriculture. That tradition kept alive the metonymic connection of these texts with the agriculture of the Mediterranean, the unfailing interest of English agriculturalists in the techniques and production of that area, where the botanical species were more numerous and the connection between wild and cultivated species could be exploited. They also saw the need to go beyond their own material conditions to exploit the teachings of ancient techniques. These would lead to Jethro Tull, Dickson, John Symonds and finally the critical editions of Gesner and the translations of the mid-nineteenth century. The stream of abridgements of the original text was destined to dry up because it represented the last stages of a medieval style of learning which consisted in synopses and generalizations for a social-economic model which offered few alternatives. What was still to prove fruitful was the individual's struggle with the original texts, when every reader-owner began to organize his personal answers to various economic problems.

3.2. Sir John Prise – antiquity as a source of innovation

It was John Prise who brought out the practical value of the study of Palladius. He was writing scarcely a hundred years after the English translation, yet in that time a whole series of abridgements had tended to associate Palladius' name exclusively with grafting. Along the lines of his approach, a contact at once scholarly and practical was established with the agricultural techniques of the Continent.

Prise was one of the commissioners appointed by Thomas Cromwell to administer the monastic lands taken over by the Crown in 1538–9 and to oversee their subsequent sale. He bought some of them himself. He combined his administrative post with a scholarly interest in the history of the British Isles and crossed swords with Polydore Vergil over his history of England. The sale of Church property also enabled him to acquire a good many manuscripts. These included a copy of Pliny's *Naturalis historia* in Robert Cricklade's version, and a Latin copy of the *Opus agriculturae*. Between 1539 and the year of his death, 1555, Prise made notes on his text of Palladius. They were probably written around 1540 when he was having Treago Castle built in the county of Hereford: an impressive symbol of his new status as a landowner.

He seems to have had no philological or other set scheme for his notes and underlinings. They reflect the interests of a man reading an ancient text, pen in hand, expecting to reap immediate benefit from it, and clearly endeavouring to cut down a still very useful work to his own measure. The notes and underlinings are restricted mainly to the first three books, the introduction, January and February, and to Vitruvius' *De architectura*, which is bound together with the Palladius. On the end-papers he entered an alphabetical index. Only the letters N, O, P, Q and R, with a couple of references to the text, are extant. Nonetheless they reflect a deeper interest in the work than would appear from its present state. Prise's interests fall roughly into four categories, the construction of the house, cultivation in general, botany and the cultivation of trees. He often makes comments in Latin or translates certain words into English. Thus in Book I, *De aedificio*, he translates *tufus* as *soft stone*, *argilla* as *clay* and also gives the names of trees used for timber (*cerrus*, *fagus*, *farnus*) and copies in the margin the sub-title of the chapter on *aestivae mansiones* (summer-houses) to be built in wood. He underlines and annotates in the margin the chapter on *lime*. He also looks carefully at the problems of building a granary and storing grain (I 19). He proceeds in the same way in the section on cultivation. He studies the quality of the soils as revealed by their colour (V 5), the level of moisture and the need for manuring, the time for sowing and care of the vegetable garden and field. He is also interested in fruit and vegetables. He translates *lactuca* as *natural cress*, *eruca* as *rocket*, *allium* as *garlick*, *pomus* as *cormior* and goes on to underline the month of February, where Palladius speaks of the pear tree and apple tree and of grafting quinces. Then he jumps to the month of November, once more to study the apple tree. All this provides us with an example of an individual reader, illustrating the many problems connected with the transfer of Mediterranean crops to a northern environment. They include problems in translating the text, factors which reduce the range of Mediterranean plants to those that can be grown in the English climate, and problems of introducing the author's message into a very different social-economic situation.

On all this Prise is most illuminating. The picture that emerges from his underlining is of young men bowing to the will of their elders in farming matters; of the hopeless battle against creditors of those who till land, burdened with debts and tithes; of the small, well-tended property more fruitful than the large, neglected one; the dangers of letting out land on the boundaries of one's property or of choosing friends as bailiffs, since they will not be ready to answer for any faults (actually, the ancient text outlined warm relations between master and servant). By now the lessons that Prise is culling from the work are clear. Husbandry enriches the land, not the size of an estate, which must in any case be freely and absolutely held, right up to its boundaries; there must be no links of friendship between the owner and his bailiff. As Prise builds his home at the centre of his new property, he seems to be searching for a new model to take the place of the great ecclesiastical and feudal estates, to be based on the absolute authority of the owner, on careful supervision, preserving the limited size of the property which ensures control over those serving him. By excluding everything that had nothing to offer him, Prise has managed to extricate, from Palladius' thousand-year-old text, the economic model that was to prevail after the dissolution of the monasteries. For lack of a more modern text, which had still not been produced either in England or on the Continent, the *Opus agriculturae* provided the details necessary to plan the economic reorganization of the one-time Church lands. Two factors are at work here; a leaning towards Roman private law, as applied to the *ager privatus* or estate; and the Mediterranean agronomic tradition, which provides a series of agricultural rules based on a wider botanical heritage and knowledge of the qualities of the soil. In his largely unfinished commonplace book, Prise also mentions, almost as if it were something to be avoided, masters' over-indulgent treatment of their servants. His is a hierarchical society; he is seeking to achieve the greatest productivity possible on his estate by exerting authority over the younger generation and all his dependants. Introduced into this kind of social-economic context, interest in Mediterranean agronomy, with its wide choice regarding production, takes on a quite different meaning.[26]

4. SUMMARY

The analysis made in this chapter shows the initial stages of a continuing interrelationship between ancient and modern, North and South. During the Middle Ages, and above all in the fourteenth and fifteenth centuries, Palladius' text served to bridge the gap between Classical agricultural technology and landowners more effectively than Pier de' Crescenzi,

---

[26] See London, BL, Add. ms 44.922; T. Kendrick, *British Antiquity*, London 1950, pp. 88–94; F. J. Levy, *Tudor Historical Work*, The Huntington Library, San Marino Cal. 1967, pp. 67, 127, 132; N. R. Ker, 'Sir John Prise', *The Library*, series V, 10, 1955, pp. 15–21; Oxford, Balliol College, ms 353.

whose writings were new from every point of view, although they made use of Classical sources to some extent. On studying the abridgements and marginal notes to Palladius we discover that the medieval entrepreneur was not interested in the whole world of Classical agriculture. What is most striking is that, despite medieval additions, the botanical species were extremely few. Comparison with the Latin text forced translators, in Oxford as in Florence, to proceed in much the same way. They tried to make some sense of the text wherever the ordinary man (neither Andrea Lancia nor Thomas Norton was a scientist) could not understand its real meaning. In France and Italy the transformation of lucerne into grain, such as sorghum, came about by way of the phonetics of the Romance languages, but also because sorghum actually grew in the fields in Mediterranean countries; whereas in England the transliteration *Herba medica-medic-medicine* was something abstract and totally foreign to the English scene. The climatic conditions of the country were such that her plant life, wild and cultivated alike, included neither lucerne nor sorghum.

The translation of Palladius' work in England was not an isolated phenomenon. Together with that of the equally successful Gottfried von Franken, it spread very widely both in Latin and in English in many different circles, among nobles and merchants, in the upper and middle classes. Sir John Prise, fierce opponent of Polydore Vergil because he based his history of the British Isles exclusively on the Latin chronicles, did not scruple to ransack Palladius for a model for capitalist exploitation of the land, which he could not get from any contemporary English text.

John Prise was probably alone in reading Palladius with such clear economic intent. In common with his contemporaries, he made little distinction, in his study of the classics, between past and present, the ancient and the contemporary world. They on the other hand were reading Palladius and Gottfried von Franken to learn the rules for growing fruit-trees. Apple and pear trees and above all the vine were fascinating to landowners, whether or not they had overcome the problems of subsistence farming by successful corn-growing and stock-keeping, and so felt free to spend their energies on extending their control over plant life. They were enthralled by the magical world of links with the moon, the reproduction of trees by grafting, the production of fruit, and methods for storing and keeping food, which were also status symbols. In this way they started a process of learning which was not restricted to the production of rare, prestigious foods. For in their work on grafting they were facing the problem of growing and developing cultivated species with the help of those that were still wild. The patient, delicate work of adapting Mediterranean species to the northern climate brought with it progress in botanical knowledge which was to be more completely developed, scientifically and economically, over the next hundred and fifty years.

It was in the Classical texts that readers found the technology necessary to make full use of that continual interplay between the natural, wild environment and cultivated plants which was so important in the Middle Ages. In the following chapters we shall be dealing further with the capacity of one social group to transform the experience of former generations to their own advantage, by exploiting both the information to be culled directly from Nature in the wild and the knowledge of Mediterranean types of agriculture. The result was to be what, for the sake of convenience, we continue to call the Agricultural Revolution.

2. From medieval agronomy to Renaissance agriculture – the success of Pier de' Crescenzi between 1474 and 1561

On 23 June 1320 Pier de' Crescenzi dictated his last will and testament in the monastery of the Dominicans in Bologna. He divided his property, consisting of house, vineyard, and tree-lined ploughing fields at Villa Olmo, near Rubizzano, in the country round Bologna, to his sons. Later changes in the boundaries of the farms, in an area now largely marshland, have made it impossible to identify his property today. His work as a farmer and agronomist is known to us only from the *Liber cultus ruris*, which he wrote when he retired from public office at the age of seventy, after being appointed to various judicial offices, held in a number of central and northern Italian cities. Father Almerico Giliani of Piacenza, a discriminating collector of rare books, Prior of San Domenico in Bologna and for a short time General of the Dominican Order, encouraged Piero to complete his work, which he did around 1305. The *Liber* was dedicated to Father Almerico, as a token of the close connection its author had established with the Dominicans. Finally it was presented to King Charles II of Sicily.[1]

---

[1] De' Crescenzi's work is known under various titles: in Latin as *Liber cultus ruris, Duodecim libri ruralium commodorum, Opus ruralium commodorum*; in Italian as *Crescentio, l'Agricultura di Crescenzio, Utilità villerecce*; in French as *Livre des prouffitz champêstres*. Of these many titles *Liber cultus ruris* is highly preferable since it keeps the original concept of general cultivation of the countryside (*rus*), as de' Crescenzi himself made clear in the introduction. The essential bibliography is indicated by P. Toubert in the *Dizionario biografico degli italiani*, Rome, 1984, vol. XV *sub nomine*; it is particularly useful to quote here: F. Re, *Sulle opere agrarie di Pietro Crescenzi*, Milan 1807; idem, *Elogio di Piero de' Crescenzi*, Bologna 1812; L. Savastano, 'Il Contributo allo studio critico degli scrittori agrari italici. Pietro dei Crescenzi', *Annali della Stazione sperimentale di agrumicultura e frutticultura*, Acireale 1922; A. Röding, *Studier till Petrus de Crescentiis och hans antika källor*, Göteborg 1927; Societa' agraria di Bologna, *Pier de' Crescenzi (1233–1321). Studi e documenti*, Bologna 1933. More recent work includes S. Polica, 'Lettori cinquecenteschi di Pietro de' Crescenzi', *La Cultura*, 24, 1986, pp. 231–55, and J. L. Gaulin,

Various problems are connected with the composition of the *Liber*. Although Palladius is the Latin author most frequently mentioned in it, it does not have the structure of a calendar, but is arranged according to subject. Book I deals with the structure of the house and the choice of a favourable site; book II with matters commonly concerning the cultivation of the fields; book III with the work in the fields and the produce harvested from them; book IV with vines and wines; book V with trees and their fruit ; book VI with vegetable gardens; book VII is on woods and meadows; book VIII on gardens; book IX on animals; book X on hunting and wild animals; book XI is a general summary of the whole work and book XII a calendar of tasks on the land. Savastano, even now the greatest authority on Pier de' Crescenzi's work from the agronomic point of view, was of the opinion that the agricultural thinking of the *Liber* was completely Palladian, that is, inspired by and drawn from the *Opus agriculturae*. Nevertheless, the question of Palladius' influence on the text is still open to debate. The very long, fundamental chapter on manure, book II, chap. XIII, is an instance of this. Palladius speaks of manure at length but without going into detail about how it should be constituted; whereas Crescenzi links all his own experience with his written sources; Palladius, Varro and Columella, and the experiments of the alchemists appear beside the procedures of the farmers round Milan, in Tuscany and in his own district, with regard to the nourishing of plants and the transformation and improvement of agricultural land.

The most important issue concerning Pier de' Crescenzi's text is whether or not this author had read Columella's *Res rustica*. Columella's book disappeared during the Middle Ages, hidden among the pages of three codices, one in the Abbey of Fulda (Hesse), one now in St Petersburg, but formerly in the monastery of Saint-Germain in Paris, and a third now lost but known to the Humanist philologists. It was only after Poggio Bracciolini discovered the Fulda codex that Columella's work spread once more throughout Western Europe.[2] Most of the *Rerum Rusticarum Scriptores* (Cato, Varro, Columella and Palladius), collected in a single codex, dates back to the fifteenth century and so does the copy which belonged to the library of San Domenico in Bologna (founded

'Sur le vin au Moyen Age. Pietro de'Crescenzi lecteur et utilisateur des Géoponiques traduites par Burgundio de Pise', *Mélanges de l'Ecole française de Rome*, 96, 1984, pp. 95–127.
[2] V. Josephson, 'Die Columella Handscriften', Uppsala Un. Arssk., 1955.

between 1218 and 1223) and hence to be dated much later than Pier de' Crescenzi and Father Almerico's time.[3] Filippo Re and Luigi Savastano have already shown that all the quotations of Columella in the *Liber cultus ruris* are borrowings from Palladius' *Opus agriculturae*. More recently an attempt has been made to show that certain chapters of Pier de' Crescenzi's IXth book are more or less literal translations of Columella. But it is above all in the form that the two works are most alike. They are both divided into twelve books and the subject matter of books I, IV and V correspond to a certain extent in their general advice on the house and its site, the cultivation and produce of the fields, the vine and other fruit trees.

The *Res rustica* and *Liber cultus ruris* undoubtedly have something in common but it is certainly not due to imitation; just as Pier de' Crescenzi does not try to outdo Palladius, who, to judge from the number of codices of his work produced in the fourteenth and fifteenth centuries, was still much esteemed. Palladius and Pier de' Crescenzi are often indexed together in old library catalogues and some publishers were bringing out both even in the late sixteenth century. It was in the fifteenth century that they were most widely circulated, but it is clear that these were Palladius' last days of splendour. Only eighteen manuscripts of the *Opus agriculturae* were produced in the fourteenth and fifteenth centuries, while the *Liber cultus ruris* was already very widespread in Italy, France and England (twenty-four codices were produced in Latin in the fourteenth century as against fifty-six in the fifteenth). Thanks to the extremely successful printed editions, it was on the way to becoming the standard text of European agriculture until the mid-sixteenth century.[4]

1. TEXT AND READERSHIP

The reaction of readers to the *Liber cultus ruris*, which we can attempt to reconstruct from an examination of handwritten notes and marks of ownership in the margins of the printed editions, is a necessary phase in understanding how Renaissance man perceived the natural agricultural

---

[3] Cf. M. H. Laurent, *Fabio Virgili*.
[4] The complete description of the extant manuscripts (123 in Latin, Italian, French, German) is given in the Società agraria di Bologna, *Pier de' Crescenzi*, pp. 260–306; ms V E 26 of the National Library in Prague has to be added to the above list, see V. Smelyaus and K. Neradova', *Crescenti Bohemi. Partem primam, Libros I–VI. Partem alteram libros VII–XII Continentem*, Pragae 1966–8.

environment. After being widely circulated in manuscript, the text of the Bolognese writer was very soon issued by fifteenth-century printers. In 1471 it came out in Augsburg, in 1474 in Louvain, in 1486 in Strasbourg, in Latin, in 1479 in Florence, and then in Vicenza in 1490 in Italian.[5] These dates show that the hundred and more manuscripts on the European market were insufficient to satisfy the demand for a text of this kind. In the same years Italian and French presses produced critical editions of the *Rerum Rusticarum Scriptores*; which were to dominate the market for such works until the mid-sixteenth century, at least in continental Europe. But while it would never be clear how far the works of the Latin agronomists were read for purely practical purposes and not as specimens of Latin too, Pier de' Crescenzi's treatise is not open to doubts of this kind.

The editions that have been taken into consideration here go up to 1564, and hence exclude the one brought out by the Accademia della Crusca in 1605 and all the later ones that reproduce essentially the same text. Two reasons have led to this exclusion. While Pier de' Crescenzi's text could be used throughout the West roughly until 1550, from that date on various agricultural experts in each country were capable of producing original treatises which showed how far they had moved away from the *Liber*. From 1550 onwards, Pier de' Crescenzi's work once more became the concern of Italian publishers only. The last edition printed outside Italy is the one published in Latin in Basle in 1548, on which Sansovino's new Italian translation of 1561 was modelled. The years 1550–1600 will be examined, to bring out the difference between the attitudes of those who used the last editions of de' Crescenzi's text and what the local agronomists in Northern Italy, France, the Rhineland and England were producing. The period 1471–1564 must be dealt with as a whole, taking into account the reactions of European readers over long years of change and transition. This is in part because the new capitalist agriculture was founded on a new economic relationship with nature, and so was reorganized in the course of the sixteenth century.

The analysis given here is based on the reading of the notes and under-linings of the text in the specimens now housed in the most important European libraries. In Italy this means the libraries of Bologna, Florence, Milan, Modena, Turin and Venice; in France Avignon, Carpentras and Paris; in England Cambridge, London and Oxford. There are 172 printed

---

[5] Cf. the complete list of the extant printed editions, in A. Sorbelli, *Bibliografia delle edizioni*, in Società agraria di Bologna, *Pier de' Crescenzi*, pp. 307–69.

specimens in all, published between 1471 and 1569. By carefully examining the marks of ownership, signatures, *ex libris*, and all the notes that various owners and readers have left in the margin of their copies, we can get a fairly clear idea of the relationship between local conditions and the use made of the text.

As a rule, we should expect the libraries mentioned to have collected mostly works bequeathed by people living in the surrounding district, and this is confirmed by indications such as 'Moreau Medicus Parisiensis', or 'Carolus Pavarus Cremonensis' or the Venetian 'Messer Meollo Pitton'.[6] Sometimes the relationship with the text appears from corrections made in the index, in wrong headings or chapters or in the numbering of pages, as well as corrections of the text itself. In other cases the interest of the reader-owners seems to have flagged after the first few pages, or they were perhaps forced to interrupt their study, while in some cases the marginal notes are in handwriting so tiny that it is illegible. The only example of a young man's handwriting occurs in the case of Edward VI of England.

It has generally been difficult to add anything to the information on ownership, or the notes, which was not already in the text. The nationality of the anonymous hands can generally be ascertained from the nomenclature of the herbs or other terminology in the reader's mother tongue.[7]

There is always some doubt as to whether or not the authors of the notes were the owners of the books, and the time when the anonymous notes were made may not correspond to the date of publication of the editions examined. In general we can tell from the context when the latter do coincide; the almost complete absence of notes in editions later than 1550 is certainly significant. There is also the problem of two or more hands annotating the printed text successively; we shall take this into account in the following analysis.

Precisely for the reasons given above it is worth focusing attention on Italian–French–English territory, moving up from Tuscany, the Po Valley, Provence, to a vast area around Paris, and then southern England. The sample of readers from this territory have one thing in common. They all have connections with the Mediterranean world, which acquired a privileged position from the very fact that Crescenzi, his model the

---

[6] See for example: Paris, BN, S.4404; Milan, BA, SNS.37; Venice, BN, 52.D.230. A key to the shelf marks is given below in table 1.

[7] For an example see: Paris, BN, S.15034; Oxford, BO, Douce C. Subt. 45.

Rerum Rusticarum Scriptores and the scientific culture which integrated them, were all products of Mediterranean civilization. The links seem to run from Italy (Venice and Florence) to England, or from Provence to Paris, Provence to England, and Paris to England; thus a North–South relationship prevailed, while the East–West relationships seem slighter, at least in this phase, in which the individual was facing the question of the economic organization of his natural environment.

First, we must consider the yield of our sample, the number of specimens extant as compared with those containing handwritten notes and/or marks of ownership. The information would be complete if we knew the name of the owner and his economic status for every copy with handwritten notes. This could be partly, but never completely, achieved, despite months of work, since old library catalogues very rarely give the date when the volume in question entered the library and/or the name of the donor. Similarly, only after an extended and frequently unfruitful search in notaries' archives, for tax returns or estimates, could we hope to reconstruct something about the economic substance of their owners. In the case of Pier de' Crescenzi himself, no one has managed to identify his country properties in the Bolognese area. Yet his work is none the less significant for the history of agriculture. In the many examples quoted by this writer we can find farms which represent all the possible types of cultivation in use at that time in his given agricultural area.[8] Pier de' Crescenzi presents in his text plans of work from which the reader is free to choose the part most necessary and interesting to him.

Either we find names of owners or else notes and markings. By putting the two types of information together we can attempt to make something more than a mere hypothesis concerning the social class to which readers of the *Liber* belonged. For example, we do not need to know the name, surname and profession of the owner to realise that whoever underlined exclusively the pharmaceutical part of book VI was a reader of a different standing (a chemist, maybe, or a burgher who had an ambition to own land but had none) from the one who also underlined book II on manuring, hemp and corn, or who revealed his attachment to the aristocratic way of life by only underlining the part on falcons, hawks and goshawks. The sample presents problems of internal dating,

---

8 A. Serpieri, *Corso di economia e politica agraria*, Firenze 1943, vol. II, Chap. 1, put forward the theory that one way of measuring the efficiency of farms was to consider them as ideal models of all the crops that could be grown in the area. He was following the theory of J. H. von Thünen, *Der isolierte Staat*, Berlin 1826.

involving a redefinition of the rather long period under examination (1471–1605), a determination of regional boundaries, and the continual confrontation of reader and text. How long did de' Crescenzi's *Liber* hold the monopoly of the market, not just because there were no real alternatives, but because the text enjoyed the complete and immediate approval of its readership? This needs to be studied in depth.

1.1. A European sample

Altogether, the sample of 172 specimens (see Appendix, table 1) shows how easily such a large number of copies of the *Liber* can be found today. For the sake of convenience we confined our search to the major libraries, those which provided links with other themes in this research. The bias of the Italian specimens has emphasized the Mediterranean qualities of Pier de' Crescenzi, confirmed by the higher ratio of copies with readers' underlinings and markings in comparison with the number of clean copies (sixty-six as against twenty-three). It would seem possible to link these two characteristics because examination of the copies shows that the inscription of the owner's name was often the first step towards a more careful reading of the text, though this was sometimes not completed.[9] For French and English readers, the proportion of annotated and unannotated copies was around 50 per cent. The effort required of the reader was, however, lightened by the French translation, by Gorgole de Corne's short epitome, and by a greater familiarity with the Mediterranean region. For the English it was more complicated, forming part of a process of learning about and confrontation with the Mediterranean world.

Since even the printed catalogues of the great libraries give only vague indications, the sampling has had to be made randomly. New, more closely annotated copies may emerge here and there in the future to confirm or modify what follows. By and large, however, the pattern of reading and perception of the natural environment indicated here will probably not be essentially modified. The reason for this claim is as follows: since 172 copies of the *Liber* can be quite easily found, and 69 per cent of them show signs of attachment to, or involvement in, the text, and signify a use of the book that went beyond mere possession,

---

[9] See for example: Turin, BN, O.VII.45.VE 1561; Milan, BA, 1560.VI 1490; Venice, BN, 203.D.151.VE 1519; Modena, BE, 2.3.20.VE 1538; Paris, BN, M.S.15.LO 1474; Cambridge, UL, L.3.4.BA 1548.

how many copies lost or unknown to us showed a similar degree of interest? On the basis of the data on book production in the fifteenth and sixteenth centuries elaborated by Henry Martin and Rudolph Hirsch,[10] it can be supposed that around 12,500 printed copies of the *Liber cultus ruris* were put on the market between 1471 and 1564. Books were still rare commodities during this period, and Hirsch rightly deals with book sales as a whole; only those that would sell well were published. The publication of Pier de' Crescenzi's *Liber* must have required a fair amount of capital, at least until the cheap and very inaccurate editions began to come out in Venice in 1534. On the other hand, though the price of paper was still high, the cost of the illustrations was certainly lower, since German and French editions very often reproduced previously used engravings. Fresh plates were made for the Basle edition of 1548 and for the one published in Venice in 1561 by Sansovino who, shrewd businessman as he was, made use of the same drawings of herbs that had appeared in other works on agriculture that he brought out in those years. So, at a rough guess, including the rare editions of 1471 onwards, often incomplete even in the most important libraries, and the more complete ones of 1480, 1490 and 1495, we can calculate an average of 300 volumes for every re-print; while for the 1511–64 period 800 copies may be considered plausible, since that was the number of Dodoens' *Frumentorum historia* printed by Plantin for more or less the same readership, albeit only for sale outside Italy. Probably the number of copies of the *Liber cultus ruris* printed was never so high as for school books or books of devotion. This would seem to be confirmed by the fact that, to judge by our sample, the only institutions that had a copy of it were abbeys and monasteries in Italy, Paris and Avignon, or the Jesuits' in England. They seem to have been copies read for practical rather than for literary purposes. Finally, the very rare indications of price tell us nothing about the connection between the year of publication and the price. The 172 copies of the sample examined represent only 1.3 per cent of the hypothetical 12,500 copies which it may be supposed were in circulation between 1471 and 1564; thus it would be unwarranted to assume, on the basis of the ratio found in the sample, that as many as 8,625 copies in all may have contained notes, underlinings, indications

---

[10] Cf. L. Febvre and H. Martin, *L'apparition du livre*, Paris 1958, pp. 326–31; R. Hirsch, *Printing, selling and reading 1450–1550*, Wiesbaden 1967, pp. 125–53; A. Quartucci (ed.), *Libri, editori e pubblico nell'Europa moderna*, Bari 1977, is a useful collection of essays.

of ownership or other evidence of careful reading or attachment to the text in the vast area encompassing Italy, France, England and the German-speaking countries. We have aimed at making an essentially qualitative analysis of the sample, and it is only the recurring pattern of reading in it which acquaints us with the readers' degree of adherence to the text, and suggests that they may have been spurred to apply its lessons on their own land.

2. ITALIAN READERS

The Italian sample is made up of ninety copies which cover the whole 1471–1564 period. A description of them is given in table 1 of the Appendix.[11] Over the very long time-span changes occurred in both the way books were produced commercially, and the material conditions in which the study of a text like Pier de' Crescenzi's would prove useful. In 1501 Aldo Manuzio decided to print a thousand copies even of the *Georgics*, at a reasonable price, rather than the 150–300 copies he had brought out in previous years.[12] One is immediately struck by the large gap between 1563 and 1605, that is between the editions of Sansovino and that of the Accademia della Crusca. The ratio of the copies with and without annotations was inverted, falling to one in three in 1563, and this seems to constitute a prelude to the long silence after which Pier de' Crescenzi's text disappeared from the market. For it was in the 1560s that, in response to local needs, the new sixteenth-century agronomy began to produce texts with more marked regional features. But the gap between 1471 and 1563 is long too, covering generations during which the Italian economy grew to maturity, a large part of the peninsula lost its political liberty for ever and the first symptoms of economic decline appeared. Actually there are two cycles, 1471–1519 and 1539–63. In the first we find a continual increase in the number of copies extant. The 1478 Florentine edition, in Italian (together with Italian manuscripts of the same period) discouraged the sale of the Latin editions from

---

[11] The following printed editions (arranged in chronological order) can be found in Italy: Augsburg 1471: 1; Florence 1478: 6; Louvain 1480: 1; Strasbourg 1486: 3; Vicenza 1490: 7; Speyer 1490: 1; Venice 1495: 4; Venice 1504: 1; Venice 1511: 9; Venice 1519: 3; Venice 1534: 2; Venice 1536: 6; Venice 1538: 1; Basel 1538: 2; Venice 1542: 3; Venice 1543: 2; Basel 1548: 5; Venice 1554: 2; Venice 1561: 4; Venice 1564: 4. Total: 67 copies; Latin texts: 13 copies; Italian texts: 54 copies.

[12] See in general M. Lowry, *The world of Aldus Manutius. Business and scholarship in Renaissance Venice*, Oxford 1979, and in particular R. Romano, *Tra due crisi: l'Italia del Rinascimento*, Turin 1971, p. 81.

Strasbourg, Augsburg and Speyer; the 1495 edition, with its fine woodcuts, made the text more practical and accessible. But it was the 1511 edition which first had the characteristics of a less expensive edition and monopolized the market for almost twenty years. The one issued in 1519 was essentially a reprint of the 1511 edition and, given its success, was probably made to satisfy the last ripples of demand.

The 1519 edition marks the end of the first editions, those of 1511 and 1519 still having all the characteristics of incunabula, though they are in octavo, not in folio. It was another fifteen years before Bernardino da Lessona (Vercelli) republished de' Crescenzi in less impressive editions as *Opera di agricultura*, together with a translation of Palladius' *Opus agriculturae*, so as to bring out the link with the Latin writer, but also with a view to greater profit. For at this time there were few alternatives to de' Crescenzi's text. There were the scholarly, philological editions of the Latin agronomists, which were costly and more difficult for the wider public to use. The manuscripts produced in by no means negligible numbers in the years 1471–1519 should also be taken into account.

Then silence fell. When de' Crescenzi reappeared it was in a series of more popular editions, with the print and paper less and less refined. They were probably intended for a different kind of purchaser; there were no more coats-of-arms of noble households carefully drawn on the frontispieces of these incunabula. Suddenly, the Latin text also appeared, printed in Basle in 1538, while the five 1545 copies, also from Basle, seem to mark an inversion of the trend, in a way confirmed by Francesco Sansovino's 1561 edition. The printing of the two editions requires careful scrutiny. Henricus Petrus, following the example of the German editions of Petrus Drach of Speyer (c.1490), added figures of plants and animals, besides the illustrations of agricultural work which had embellished previous editions (Paris 1486 and Venice 1496). It was these very plant illustrations, drawn from life, not reproduced from the now out-dated models of the medieval herbals of the French and German traditions, which made people trust de' Crescenzi's text more.[13] The original text gave no botanical description of plants, herbs or vegetables. It was the new dimension in man's relationship with Nature, now firmly directed along the path of empirical research, in the first half of the

---

[13] Amongst the oldest printed herbals we quote: *Herbarius*, Peter Schöffer, Mainz 1484; *Gart der Gesundheit*, Peter Schöffer, Mainz 1485; *Arbolayre ou Le grand herbier*, Pierre Metlinger, Besançon 1486–8.

fifteenth century, which prompted the publisher to make this choice, thus enabling the average reader to identify the specimens of medieval botany at once, directly and personally. Moreover H. Petrus in some ways restored the status of the Latin text, which had been corrupted in many versions. Sansovino did the same in Venice. He printed a new translation in Italian, added drawings of plants and herbs perhaps more finely executed than those of Basle, added a page of agricultural tools very like those that were later to appear in Agostino Gallo, and an index and explanatory table of technical terms. But since Sansovino was a businessman and an expert publisher, he reprinted Palladius in the same years and brought out a compilation of his own in which he did not scruple to reproduce many chapters from Pier de' Crescenzi's book VI, obviously making use of the same engravings mentioned above.[14]

2.1. Milan

But how was de' Crescenzi read, from Milan to Florence? In Milan his work came into the hands of readers who carefully underlined the passages where it recalled the Lombard landscape. In other cases the reading was linked to the everyday interests of the reader-landowner. The books circulated and had many readers. A copy of the 1490 Vicenza edition, for example, was bought in 1495 by Giovanni Garofalo and his friends and passed into the hands of the Dean of Brembo, Giulio Borroni, in 1659.[15] But it was only the first hand, very likely that of Giovanni Garofalo, that left marks of reading where the text speaks of the medicinal properties of rue, mustard, yew, *testiculus canis, vulpis,* thyme, bindweed and nettles.

An anonymous sixteenth-century commentator made lengthier annotations. He was reading the text with an eye to timber (book I), the laurel, blackberry, peach, juniper, briar, melons and scabious, to which he often added handwritten notes on their medicinal properties, in good Lombard dialect. At the end he added a page of notes on wood for barrels and vats and how to stop wine going mouldy. He recorded that in Milan, at the Mulino delle Armi (now the street of the same name) you could get the best whetstones for sharpening knives; that by sowing

---

14 See A. Gallo, *Le vinti giornate dell'agricoltura et dei piaceri della villa,* Venice 1567, see below, chap. 3.7; *La villa di Palladio traducta nuovamente da Francesco Sansovino,* Venice 1560, and *V libri d'agricoltura di Francesco Sansovino,* Venice 1560. See also chap. 1.

15 Milan, BA, inc. 1560.

flower seeds at new moon in March and August you could get marvellous results. He was focusing on the natural environment as it existed within city walls.

The anonymous owner of the 1511 Venice edition[16] went deeper into the text. He read, pen in hand, the whole of book II, *Of the nature of trees*, underlining only those parts of chapters VIII, X, XII and XIII that mention grafting in the trunk of the willow, and how cultivation and soil change the characters of a plant; how sterility is connected with age and varies from tree to tree; how trees are to be planted, at what distance from one another, at what depth; how to modify chalky or sandy soil; and then the whole chapter dealing with manure and trees, manuring and irrigation. Further on (chaps. XXII and XXVIII), he looks at grafting and the hedgerow, which should be made of blackthorn bushes. Then it is book V on trees that attracts his attention, where it mentions improvements to sandy soil again. He was also interested in the seeds and grafting of the almond, filbert, cherry, chestnut, quince, cornel cherry, fig, laurel, apple, pomegranate, mulberry (it is not by chance that this Lombard reader underlined the whole chapter here), medlar, hazel, olive, pear, plum and peach, as well as the pine, rowan and jujube. He carefully marked in the margin the whole of the seventh chapter of book VIII (*Of what gives delight in trees*) where it describes how the good householder must be careful to 'have plenty of good trees, of several generations, on his land'. His interest in trees is the more evident since he only marks one point about vegetables in the whole book, though he does take note of the qualities that bulls must have at the time of purchase, of doves and dovecotes, and does not miss the least detail on the improvement of sandy soil (book IX, chap. IV and book XI, chap. XXIX). Agricultural land well lined with trees (*la piantata*), and the problems of overly sandy soil were just what he was up against.[17] Orchards and tree planting were so widespread and important that constant estimates were made of them on the property of Count Barbiano di Belgioioso in the first half of the sixteenth century. The cultivation of trees was linked with the widespread irrigation of crops, which produced an economic pattern of

[16] Milan, BA, 5Q.O.VII 6.
[17] Of particular interest, D. Sella, *Crisis and continuity. The economy of Spanish Lombardy in the seventeenth century*, Cambridge, MA. 1979, and A. De Maddalena, 'Vespri e mattutino di una società preindustriale', *Rivista storica italiana*, 93, 1981, pp. 599–611; see also E. Sereni, *Storia del paesaggio agrario italiano*, Bari 1961, pp. 130–6 (forthcoming in English translated by Professor B. H. Litchfield).

intensive agriculture, while the diversification of tree species provided the botanical support necessary for this capitalist agricultural development.

The barefoot Carmelite Friars of the Friary of Saints Cosimo and Damiano in Milan practised a simpler, humbler kind of farming. They took note of the influence of the moon on newly planted trees and marked a few things about grafting (book II, chaps. XXII, XXIII); they also had some trouble about keeping wine (book IV, chap. XI), registered that ash wood was good for barrels and 'to make pikes for soldiers', since times were what they were; and finally they ignored all the vegetables with the exception of garlic, betony, pumpkin, watermelon, cabbage, onions and parsley. They did pay some attention to hens and hatching chickens (book IX, chap. XV); their markings go up to 1542, at least, since they record the locust plague of that year.[18]

The notes contained in the 1536 Venice copy are short but not random.[19] The anonymous reader focused on the farmstead with courtyard; the granary for good storage of hemp, corn and rice; chick-peas for the workers and dodder for the treatment of dysentery contracted from drinking the stagnant waters of the *Bassa*, the low-lying area of the rice-fields. This reader clearly had in mind a model of capitalist agriculture based on large-scale cultivation. Another city-dweller gave two recipes for making mortar, Cremona-style, then underlined 'beans, chestnuts, lime, fig, nut, plum and damson', and among the vegetables in book VI 'beetroot, watermelon, cabbage, onions, saffron, lettuce and sage'. Obviously cabbage, saffron, lettuce and sage were already typical of Lombard cookery even in those days.

But de' Crescenzi was of use to the householder not merely to provide advice, inspiration and ratification of economic procedures which he already followed in their essentials. The book served for jottings in the margin on everything concerning the natural environment, almost like a commonplace book for those not in the habit of keeping a written account of their daily business. So the passing of the seasons acquired a private dimension, and space was taken to note down certain exceptional events,

---

[18] Milan, BN, A B XI 21, Venice 1511: the Po Valley was deeply affected by the 1542 plague of locusts, which destroyed many crops from Friuli to Piedmont and occasionally swarmed beyond the Alps and the Appennines. Locusts were killed in great quantities, however large numbers of eggs survived and hatched the following year, see A. Corradi, *Annali delle epidemie occorse in Italie dalle prime memorie fino al 1850*, Reprint, Sala Bolognese 1973, vol. I, pp. 481–2 and vol. V, p. 313.

[19] Milan, BA, SPM IV 151.

such as the coming of locusts, the death of a great number of people during the plague of 1576, or a moral comment on the ups and downs of fortune, in verse, on the predominance of moral values, virtue, kindness, on love that takes precedence over social status, on silver and gold (social status being more important than wealth) or simply on 'our daily bread'.[20] The *Liber cultus ruris* hovers between the natural environment, the organization of work and the duties of the householder; and the marginal notes made in it have something of the same ambivalence. The text was meant to be an open work, assisting the reader in the use of his natural environment, through good husbandry, whether based on large- or small-scale cultivation.

2.2. Venice

In the course of the sixteenth century, Venetian society grew ever more interested in its hinterland. From the 1520s, the rising price of corn made investment in draining swampy land constantly more profitable. The Peace of Cateau-Cambrésis (1559) confirmed the influence of Venice in the Po Valley. Managing landed property in the country, traditional activities connected with trade and the work of the craftsman, old and new, all contributed to the accumulation of capital.[21] As was mentioned earlier, it was just this expanding market that forced Venetian publishing to transform itself into an industry and achieve national and international pre-eminence. The history of Italian publishing in the sixteenth century is largely the history of Venetian publishing, and the many Venetian editions of Pier de' Crescenzi were throughout accompanied by careful reading. Venice and Brescia were also the centres where the new works of Italian agronomy were published for the first time, after 1560. Agostino Gallo, another great name in the field, recalls how in his day (around 1550) the noble Gianfrancesco Gambara of Brescia studied and annotated the whole text of the *Liber cultus ruris* 'which was so full of

[20] Milan, BB, AB XI 21, AK XIII 18, 25.15 K 24.
[21] A. Ventura, 'Considerazioni sull'agricoltura veneta e sull'accumulazione originaria del capitale nei secoli xvi e xvii', *Studi storici*, 9, 1968, pp. 674–722; I. Cervelli, *Machiavelli e la crisi dello stato veneziano*, Napoli 1974, chaps. vi, viii; G. Borelli, *Un patriziato della Terraferma veneta tra xvii e xviii secolo*, Milan 1974, and M. Berengo, 'Patriziato e nobiltà: il caso veronese', *Rivista storica italiana*, 87, 1975, pp. 493–517. On printing and publishing in Venice see Martin and Febvre, *L'apparition du livre*, and Lowry, *The world of Aldus Manutius*.

mistakes that no one could make any sense of it'.[22] The private interests mentioned above, which turned both land and books into merchandise, were subtly intertwined. Most of the copies of de' Crescenzi still in Venice were published earlier than 1561, and the marginal notes and underlinings bring out especially the tone of the aristocratic agricultural circles where life had been organized to combine pleasure and profit. They emphasize the most striking features of this system of values, in which animals, ornamental plants and flowers conferred prestige. 'Pavones suo decore nobiliores ceteris avibus sunt' (Peacocks are nobler in their own right than other birds) writes an unknown reader of the 1486 Strasbourg, Latin edition,[23] inevitably bringing to mind Mantegna and the image of the peacock, which became almost a symbol of the court of the Gonzagas in Mantua, not so far away. Or else, in another copy, instructions on how to feed and breed red hawks are underlined. And perhaps the dichotomy of those who had only a small flower- or kitchen-garden in town (not a few Venetian patricians set up their own gardens of simples within the city walls)[24] and those for whom agricultural management proper was of equal importance with traditional merchant trading is clearer in Venice than elsewhere. The same hand that cared for red hawks also underlined his copy of de' Crescenzi at length all through book I, on advice to the farmer ('vilicus non ambulator . . . ' he commented in the margin); the classification of plants; the transformation and alteration of the genetic features of a plant; manuring; improvement of the soil; cultivation of hilly and mountainous ground; how and when to plough; how to recognize soil fertility; the care of trees and grafting. He went on to book II on wheat, flax and millet; book III on how to treat sick vines; book IV on trees (the lemon, fig and the laurel bush); he paid attention to the question of cultivating wild plants and, ahead of his time for the Venetian mainland, doubtless because of the extent of marshy ground there, he realized the importance of

---

[22] See in general F. C. Lane, *Venice: a Maritime Republic*, Baltimore 1973, pp. 240 ff., 296 ff., 308 ff.; D. Sella, *Commerci e industria a Venice nel xvi secolo*, Venice–Roma 1961. On Gambara cf. A. Gallo, *Le vinti giornate dell'agricoltura* . . . (1567), Brescia 1775, p. 445 (giornata decimanona): see below, chap. 3.7. Amongst other achievements Gianfrancesco Gambara set up a printing press in his Pralboino castle: cf. O. Rossi, *Elogi de Bresciani illustri*, Brescia 1620, p. 261.

[23] Venice, M.C. INC. E 251.

[24] Venice, BN, INC. 565, Strasbourg 1486; G. Marsili, *Dei patrizi veneti dotti nella cognizione delle piante e dei loro orti botanici più rinomati*, Padova 1840.

water-meadows;[25] and, finally, hawks and crossbows for hunting. Here we have a plan for farm administration that does not leave out any sector – field, meadow or wood. But it is also a model for the *villa*, a foretaste of the advice of Agostino Gallo (1564, 1566, 1569) and Camillo Tarello (1567)[26] on water-meadows. Among the many products, he carefully chose corn, millet and flax, wheat being both a cash crop and for consumption in the owner's family, millet for the bailiff, and linen to be woven in the home. It is a model of the relationship between town and country too. The reference to a resident bailiff seems to suggest that the owner lived in town. Obviously it is only in a few cases that the single copy reveals such an organic plan.

In Venice, however, where the land–water opposition might have produced an attitude to Nature based on a geographical division of labour, we do not get that cleavage of town and country so typical of Italian cities, with gardens and kitchen-gardens outside the city walls. Venice controlled large-scale cultivation on the mainland, while day-to-day consumption was provided for by the small gardens and kitchen-gardens within her boundaries. The food most commonly produced was corn and beans, but medicinal herbs were included too, as well as corn-cockle, rye-grass, lentils, lupins and wine. Almost all the trees mentioned in book V were valued by this anonymous writer, as they could be used to make rose-water, syrups and the like; he also marked borage, basil, betony, camomile and maidenhair, translating the better-known species into the Venetian dialect.[27] Surprisingly, for the late sixteenth century, there is also a whole calendar of times for sowing and of work to be done in the garden, the vegetables including onions, cabbages and chicory, artichokes, peas ('bisi' in the local dialect), asparagus, fennel and thistles, besides parsley, sage and rosemary for flavouring.[28] It is difficult to get an idea of the quantity of these plants produced, since no account was taken of them in public records on food supplies. The annotations are mostly scattered here and there and become significant only when we connect them up and relate them to their economic and agricultural background. Seen in this way, though filtered

---

[25] See D. Beltrami, *Saggio di storia dell'agricoltura nella repubblica di Venice durante l'età moderna*, Venice–Roma 1955, pp. 30 ff.; Ventura, 'Considerazioni sull' agricoltura', and on early rice cultivation in swamps see M. Lecce, *La coltura del riso in territorio veronese: xvi–xviii secoli*, Verona 1958.

[26] See below, chap. 3, 7–10.

[27] Venice, BN, 162 D.224, Venice 1534.

[28] Modena, BE, X.10.34, Venice 1519.

through de' Crescenzi's formal, traditional style, they reveal considerable organizational capacity, modelled by the ends that each individual reader had set himself. Questions of reclaiming marshy land come up in references to hedgerows and ditches, wells and the quality of drinking water, in the healthiness of the site of a house or the improvement of the soil (dry, acid or salty); while little notes on peas, laurel or pomegranates alternate with ideas for large-scale projects for the land or the study of cultivation and nomenclature of the best-known plants in the district.

2.3. Bologna

Bologna boasts a large number of well-annotated and underlined copies. Landowners were prompted to purchase, read and annotate the text by the renown of their fellow citizen and the constant interest in agriculture in a city deeply attached to the land. Their reading seems to depend on the general conditions obtaining in the area and the fact that de' Crescenzi's text was nearer to the type of agriculture practised in the region. Some of the structural problems that had to be faced were to be finally solved only with the deep mechanical ploughing introduced in the nineteenth century.[29] Manuring drew most attention, since it could counterbalance the dominant characteristics of the soils, according to the products and how the land was to be used (as field, meadow or vegetable garden). This was often followed by careful reading of the chapters on pigeons, dovecotes and how pigeon-droppings could be used in the garden. Next came the connection between manuring and flax-growing.[30] Nor was this study restricted to the Italian editions of the text. Two of the three copies produced in Basle were closely annotated in Latin. Bartolomeo Richelmi changed the title of the chapter on rice to 'Peas' (actually de' Crescenzi's Latin text never included the chapter on rice, which was an addition made to the Italian translation);[31] he made

---

[29] Sereni, *Storia del paesaggio*, pp. 132 ff.; C. Poni, *Gli aratri e l'economia agraria del Bolognese*, Bologna 1963, especially pp. 169–80; idem, *Fossi e cavedagne benedicon le campagne*, Bologna 1982.

[30] Bologna, BU, KK IV 15, Florence 1478; Bologna, BU, A IV T I 9, Basel 1548; Bologna, BA, 16.D II.8, Vicenza 1490; Bologna, BA, 17 W IX 30, Venice 1526; Bologna, BA, Ercolani G 8.36, Venice 1536.

[31] On the introduction of rice cultivation into Italian agriculture see E. Motta, 'Per la storia della coltura del riso in Lombardia', *Archivio storico lombardo*, ser. IV, 32, 1905, pp. 392–400; L. Messedaglia, 'Per la storia delle nostre piante alimentari. Il riso', *Rivista di storia delle scienze mediche e naturali*, 29, 1938, pp. 2–15, 50–64; Lecce, *La coltura del riso*.

marginal notes to mark the paragraphs in book IV on trees in general, on the ageing and care of trees, and on hoeing the soil at the foot of the tree. Then he went on to book VI on gardens, noting 'soil, water, manure-heap, site of the garden, quantity of seed, sowing procedures, the mixing of seed, deficiencies in and remedies for garden soil and how to get rid of mice and moles'; the herbs to be gathered for medicine; lettuce, in book VI; and, in book VIII, small greenhouse plants and average-sized ones ('inter arbores plantandae vites', planting vines between trees). Then we come once more to the countryside with the *piantata*, where trees such as the poplar, willow, elm and mulberry were planted along ditches to enclose fields and bind the soil firmly (chap. V). The same chapter also discusses the advantage of owners exchanging inconvenient patches of land and planting hedgerows along boundaries – one more piece of evidence of the strengthening of private property, so necessary to the good organization of production based on private ownership of the land. In the interpretation of Rolandino Passeggeri, professor of Law at Bologna University, and a contemporary of Pier de' Crescenzi, Roman Law concerning land became a weapon wielded by the urban middle class against the feudal aristocracy.[32] Then comes more about grafting vines, about wines and grapes of different taste and colour, the delights of gardening, of roses, cherries and peaches. The marginal notes on seeds and kitchen-gardens conclude with lettuce seed, leeks, watermelons and cucumbers, suggesting that a good farm must have a well-defined plan for renewing all its plants.[33] As he omitted books II and III, Bartolomeo Richelmi must have had only a garden and kitchen-garden. Nonetheless he did not simplify the criteria of his scheme for the constant renewal of the Mediterranean farm – choosing suitable land, manuring to correct its dominant qualities, gathering and selecting seed. The anonymous reader of the 1548 Basle edition was more involved in the cultivation of a real estate. He ably interpreted and corrected the printed text and even suggested different versions in some cases.[34] His is a critical reading of outstanding interest, with many references to the text, suggesting that the

---

[32] See A. Palmieri, *Rolandino Passaggeri*, Bologna 1933, p. 90; on the growth of *franc alleu* within the feudal estates of the Bolognese countryside in the thirteenth century see idem, 'Le condizioni agricole bolognesi', in Società agraria di Bologna, *Pier de' Crescenzi*, p. 44. Relevant comments on juridical land institutions in the Bolognese area and De' Crescenzi agronomy are made by P. Jones, 'Per la storia agraria italiana nel Medio Evo: lineamenti e problemi', *Rivista storica italiana*, 76, 1964, pp. 310 ff.

[33] Bologna, BA, 13 CC.VIII.7, Basle 1538.

[34] Bologna, BU, A IV T I 9, Basle 1548.

reader had studied it carefully. It is densely underlined throughout. As in the case of the Lombard and Venetian copies, book I is not overlooked. Water, farmhouse and courtyard, wells, building materials, the duties of the farmer and householder are all considered. Of the larger trees, our reader was only interested in cypresses and fig-trees, but he did not neglect the chapters on the differences between trees or their trans-mutation, on seed, the choice of trees and grafting. He went very carefully through the chapters on manure, ploughing, fields in the hills or mountains, but paid little attention to fallow ground. Had he perhaps cut it out, in favour of a rotation of corn and hemp with the addition of large quantities of manure?[35] In book III, on products, he made a very clear choice – the threshing floor, corn, beans, hemp, flax, rye and vetch. The chapters he studied in book IV on the vine were few but well chosen. This kind of close-knit commentary on the Bolognese countryside seems almost to herald Innocenzo Malvasia (1609) or Vincenzo Tanara (1640). It is the work of an entrepreneur, carefully clarifying his mind on a few well-chosen subjects concerning cultivation and passing over all the part on husbandry and the pharmacopoeia (i.e. the list of drugs and directions for their use) as well as stock-breeding, meadows and woods. Rather than finding chronological differences between the 1478 copies and those of the sixteenth century, we find clear-cut differences according to the point of view from which the text was read, whether by town-dwelling house-holders whose interest in the land was restricted to the orchard and kitchen-garden, by monks confined within their monastery walls, in town, or by landowners. So Friar Alessandro Garganelli, of the above-mentioned San Domenico friary, after marking the 1511 Italian edition somewhat randomly, took especial note of the fact that lettuce seed dampens the sexual urge. The de' Crescenzi editions later than that published in Basle in 1548 were very little read, or at least very little annotated; the Sansovino text is found more often, but with nothing to suggest the impact that the illustrations had on his readers, in contrast with his other works of the same time. Among the many well-known and lesser-known names of readers – Alessandro Garganelli (1511), Giovanni della Fonte (dated 1552), Bartolomeo Richelmi, Count Marsili, Baldassare Ruggeri[36] – is a most illustrious one, Ulisse

---

[35] On crop rotations in the Bolognese area see R. Finzi, *Monsignore a suo fattore. La 'Istruzione di agricoltura' di L. Malvasia (1609)*, Bologna 1979, pp. 114–42.

[36] Bologna, BU, a.IV T VII, Venice 1511; Bologna, BU, A IV Q V 31, Venice 1511; it is bound with L. Ruso, *Mascalcia*, Venice 1548; Bologna, BA, 13 cc VIII 7, Basle 1538; Bologna, BU, A IV T 21, Basle 1548; Bologna, BA, 17 W VIII 9, Venice 1561.

Aldrovandi,[37] who made a marginal note, in his almost illegible hand-writing, of several kinds of grapes grown for wine (book IV, chap. III): these were *schiava, albana, tribiana, cerasuola, malvasia* and others; he then underlined the passages concerning a few larger trees. It is not much, but is sufficient to show that the great naturalist had already gone beyond the botanical knowledge of Pier de' Crescenzi.

2.4. Florence

Pier de' Crescenzi's work on agriculture left its mark in Florence before the printed editions became common. Two outstanding figures of fifteenth-century Florence have left at least two references to the *Liber cultus ruris*. In his short, incomplete treatise on the *villa* Leon Battista Alberti reminds us that agriculture is the highway to riches. He follows the *Proemio* to the *Liber cultus ruris* closely, where Pier de' Crescenzi himself is close to Cicero's *De officiis*, I 151.[38] It was the Alberti family who first showed how shrewd investment in land and houses guaranteed greater security against the ups and downs of trade, as in 1315 and 1319, and this combination of land and money had enabled the 'Alberta' family to keep up their position, notwithstanding their political mis-fortunes, as Leon Battista himself pointed out. Indeed, in the fifteenth century countless farms were set up, enlarged and merged to form the so-called 'bel paesaggio', the beautiful Italian landscape, with farmland arranged in terraces and contour ploughing, which became almost a permanent feature of Tuscan agriculture. From the evaluation made for tax purposes in 1427 it was already clear that the wealth of Tuscany was now firmly in the hands of the Florentines. The hundred richest families of Florence owned more property than the 37,000 rural households, and the 3,000 richest families had at their disposal a larger slice of the state than the 57,000 families who made up the Republic. Within this pattern it was real estate, land and houses, that constituted the bulk of Tuscan wealth. Exemption from the payment of taxes on fixed capital, which

---

[37] The Garganelli family was deemed to have 9 and 729 *tornature* in 1502: see B. Farolfi, *Strutture agrarie e crisi cittadina nel primo '500 bolognese*, Bologna 1977, p. 69 (also Aldrovandis were measured, pp. 53–4). On Count Marsili, see G. Fantuzzi, *Memorie della vita del generale Marsigli* (*sic*), Bologna 1770, and R. Gherardi, *Potere e costituzione a Vienna fra Sei e Settecento*, Bologna 1980. Bologna, BU, A IV T IX 27, Venice 1561.

[38] This fortunate and programmatic definition was to be remembered by the compilers of the *Dizionario* of the Accademia della Crusca (Florence 1605).

was necessary for the continuance of the system, guaranteed agricultural property from the risks incurred when financial assets were invested in merchandise. However, real estate produced little income in comparison with financial assets and the public debt. Hence, the reason for the conversion of Florentine family fortunes into landed estates is to be sought in the security conferred by the ownership of land. The Florentines' control of the land went beyond the boundaries of the Republic, into the Pisa area, for example, thanks to the local custom of sharecropping. By this arrangement, the owner contributed to the running of the farm by advancing capital for seed, oxen and tools, even paying a wage in kind in years of famine; the outlay returned to town in the form of farm produce.[39] Giovanni di Pagolo Morelli advised his sons to keep a firm hand over his labourers and tenants (*mezzadri*), the produce, and the property, in terms not unlike Pier de' Crescenzi's chapter on the duties of the householder.[40] The text of the Italian translation, printed by Nicolao of Breslau, first appeared in Florence in 1478 with the title *Liber Petri De Crescentis de agricultura*.

There are twenty-five copies still in the libraries of Florence, only ten of which have no contemporary references at all; the notes and references are most plentiful up to 1511; nine out of fifteen copies are annotated. The two types of reader, one interested in farm management and the other only in the agricultural produce, are, of course, to be found in Florence too. So a contemporary hand annotated one of the very rare copies of the first edition (Augsburg, 1471), carefully underlining and marking the chapter on water and wells, then the connection between water, manuring and grafting by which wild plants soon become cultivated; from there he passed on to discussing how the rose-garden could be used to make sweets and syrups, how to give water and oil the

---

[39] Of the vast bibliography on the subject we will mention here only: L. B. Alberti, *Opere volgari*, edited by C. Grayson, Bari 1960, vol. I, pp. 357–63; A. Sapori, 'La famiglia e le compagnie degli Alberti del Giudice', in idem, *Studi di storia economica*, Florence 1955, vol. II, pp. 975–1012; E. Conti, *La formazione della struttura agraria moderna nel contado fiorentino*, Roma 1955, 3 vols.; Sereni, *Storia del paesaggio*, pp. 157–74; P. J. Jones, 'Florentine families and florentine diaries in the XIV century', *Papers of the British School at Rome*, 24, 1956; R. Goldthwaite, *Private wealth in Renaissance Florence. A study of four families*, Princeton 1968; D. Herlihy, 'Family and property in Renaissance Florence' (1977) in idem, *Cities and society in medieval Italy*, London 1980, pp. 3–24; D. Herlihy and C. Klapisch-Zuber, *Les Toscans et leur families. Une étude du Catasto florentin du 1427*, Paris 1978; *Contadini e proprietari della Toscana moderna*, Atti del Convegno di studi in onore di Giorgio Giorgetti, Florence 1979, *passim*.

[40] V. Branca (ed.), *Giovanni di Pagolo Morelli: Ricordi*, Florence 1956, pp. 234–6.

taste and colour of roses (book V, chap. XLVIII), and noted borage (mixed with honey, as a remedy against heart trouble), gentian, papyrus (the paper reed) and penny royal.[41] Another early reader had a rare interest in the names of great masters to be found in the text – Varro, Scrofa, Cato, Palladius, Columella, Ysac, Avicenna, Galen, Isidore and Dioscorides – almost as if the prestige of the name were a guarantee of the excellency of the cure for lice or worms or a recipe for barley cakes.[42] He also paid due attention to the text, going through book I, on air, water and farm; book II, on the generation of plants, the parts of plants and their growth; the choice of fertile or arid land, the position of the fields; book III, on the threshing-floor, granaries, chick-peas, corn, broad beans and other beans, rye-grass, lentils, lupins, flax, barley, millet, panic, spelt and rye; book IV on the vine. Here, in chapter XII, *On pruning the vine*, he adds 'note, gentle graft, three things are to be taken into account in pruning'. These chapters are essential for the management of a typically mixed farm, of no small size, since he can afford to diversify corn production to include the lesser grains, probably intended as food for his servants and workers. The chick-peas, broad beans and other beans, and barleymeal, point to both production and consumption that was typical of Tuscany. The cereals marked in another copy of the 1478 Florence edition are once more corn, broad beans and other beans, spelt, corn-cockle, rye-grass and lentils.[43] Wine was also of interest to town-dwellers like the pharmacist Giovanni Valentini, who paid special attention to the harvest-to-bottling phase, almost suggesting that he purchased grapes and made his own wine; or to those who tried to make wine out of sour or over-ripe grapes or even out of vinegar. And then we have Angelo Morosini, who underlined in ink much of the text of book IV, on the various types of vine, time of harvesting, grapes to be pressed, vinegar, care and storage of wine, bottling, wine-tasting, what to do when wine goes sour, and the beneficial and harmful effects of wine.[44]

While the complete model of Tuscan agriculture was made up of fields, vineyards, orchard and kitchen-garden,[45] it also existed in

---

[41] Florence, BN, LF inc.7.

[42] Florence, BR, Ed.R 64.620, Florence 1478.

[43] Florence, BM, R A.251.

[44] See in the following order: Florence, BN, D.7.5.29, Speyer 1490; Florence, BN, 13 B 4.3.2, Venice 1511 (book IV, chaps. xxi, xxiii, xxiv, xxx, xxxix, xlii); Florence, BM, R.O.16, Venice 1511; Florence, BN, 20, B.1.2.23, Basel 1538 (book LV, chaps. iv, xxi, xxiii, xxiv, xxvi, xxxii, xxxiii, xxxiv, xxxv, xxxvi, xxxvii, xxxviii, xxxix, xlvi).

[45] For an example although in a different area, see M. Berengo, *Nobiltà e mercanti nella Lucca del Cinquecento*, Turin 1965, pp. 305–16, and in general G. Pinto,'Ordinamento

simplified versions, such as Giovanni Valentini's vineyards and stables; or just house, field and orchard; or again vineyard, orchard, kitchen-garden, stable and hunting grounds.[46] In practice, the context is more urban than rural, revealing how far Florentine society dominated the countryside. To put it shortly, agriculture and the country were defined as such in towns where cultivation was no longer the dominant feature of the socio-economic system. The first iconographic representation of agriculture as *ars mechanica*, side by side with the other crafts, was Florentine, (now housed in the Museo dell'Opera del Duomo, in Florence). But agriculture, or rather the cultivation of the countryside, came into town either in the form of country produce, or in the garden and kitchen-garden. The handwritten comments to de' Crescenzi's notes and text reveal the economic basis of the lovely fifteenth- and sixteenth-century Tuscan landscape portrayed in so many paintings. There is a correspondence between the trees and plants that were depicted with ever greater care at the foot of, or as a back-drop to, figures of saints and Madonnas, until they themselves took pride of place in Botticelli's *Primavera*, and in the emphasis given to plant life in the underlinings of books V and VI of Pier de' Crescenzi.[47] Almond trees, hazels, junipers, cherries, the cornel cherry, the fig, apple, pomegranate, millet, walnut, olive, pear, plum, palm, oak and bay-oak, jujube, reeds, rose-trees and millet are among these plants, all very common; even the palm grown in sunny spots and never missing in Christian iconography of Palm Sunday or in the background of the Flight into Egypt. The evidence is not only iconographical but is to be found in unpublished sixteenth-century Tuscan treatises too.[48] The kitchen-gardens produced aniseed, dill, hyssop, curled dock, mallow, mint, horehound, poppy, parsnip, purslane, rue, mustard and thyme, but also beetroot leaves, pumpkin, watermelon, cabbages, onions, artichokes, coriander, endives, fennel, sweet marjoram, turnips, asparagus and shallots. The lily, symbol of the city, was naturally

culturale e proprietà fondiaria cittadina', in *Contadini e proprietà nella Toscana moderna*, pp. 223–77, on the relationship between soil quality, crop choice and consumption. On the achievements of mixed farming in Tuscany compared with the existing bibliography and the 1427 cadastre see C. Klapish-Zuber and D. Herlihy, *Les Toscans et leurs familes*, Paris 1978.

[46] See in the following order: Florence, BM, R.A.251, Florence 1478; Florence, BR, Ed.R.681; Florence, BN, 13 B 4.3.2, Venice 1511, with monogram TGN.

[47] On these problems see *Storia d'Italia Einaudi. Annali*, 5, *Il paesaggio*, Turin 1982.

[48] See A. Del Riccio, *Trattato*, Florence, BN, ms Pal. Targioni 56.2.

given prominence in Florence.[49] Even the kind of hunting practised tended to be bird-catching, with nets and lime, which could be practised by ordinary people without special training, rather than the elaborate system of control of birds of prey and wild animals required for falconry, which was reserved to the nobles. Whoever made a note of Ariosto's name beside the chapter on the sparrow-hawk probably had a literary rather than a direct, personal knowledge of the matter.[50]

So it seems that in Florence a frankly utilitarian reading predominated and in more relaxed moments tended to emphasize the delights of the villa, trees and vines, while the more theoretical part seems to have been passed over. In the first place the *Liber cultus ruris* was an 'open' book and so left the reader ample margin for his own preferences. But even in Florence the chapter on decay did not pass unnoticed. It was fundamental because it gave general rules for the reproduction of every plant or tree, according to the grower's needs. One anonymous reader, perhaps belonging to the same family whose coat-of-arms was reproduced on the flyleaf, commented, at the point where the text claims that from a cartload of straw you can get four cartloads of manure, 'you can't get anything much from a cartload of straw'. While further on, where the text says that manuring with manure from large animals enriches the earth for six years, he adds cryptically 'manure lasts until it is used up'.[51] Obviously his experience did not tally with Pier de' Crescenzi's remarks. The *Liber cultus ruris* was not studied as an authority to be followed religiously. In an era of independent thought such as the late fifteenth and the first half of the sixteenth century, when technology and knowledge of the workings of nature were growing, it acquired the role of a compromise between the more restricted natural environment of the single reader and the boundless environment beyond the city walls. It encompassed work and economic planning which enabled the owner to create a link between himself and Nature, only broken by the division of labour between owner and farmer.

---

[49] Florence, BR, Ed.R.681, Venice 1495.

[50] Florence, BR, ED.R.681, Venice 1495; Florence, BN, 13.B.4.3.2, Venice 1511. See K. Linder (ed.), *Das Jagdbuch des Petrus Crescentius*, Berlin 1957; G. Innamorati, *Arte della caccia. Testi di falconeria, uccellagione e altre cacce*, Milan 1965, 2 vols.; *La chasse au Moyen Age*, Actes du Colloque de Nice, Nice 1980; H. Zug Tucci, 'La caccia, da bene comune a privilegio', in *Storia d'Italia Einaudi. Annali, 6, Economia naturale ed economia monetaria*, Turin 1983, pp. 399–447.

[51] Florence, BN, D.7.5.13, Vicenza 1490.

2.4.1. *Corniolo della Cornia and books on agriculture in Florence*

The work of Florentine agronomists has always been foremost in the field, beginning with the fourteenth-century translations of the work of Pier de' Crescenzi and Palladius, and even in our own day it affords a quantity of data which should be compared with the personal interpretation presented here. Oddly enough, the central position of Tuscan agriculture in the economy of the region has produced more unpublished manuscripts (della Cornia, Tanaglia, Tedaldi, del Riccio, Vettori and Fiorenzuola, besides the unfinished writings of Alberti and some memoirs, also unfinished, from the monastery of Vallombrosa) than printed volumes (Vettori and Davanzati).

To these unpublished works must be added a manuscript copy of the *Divina villa* of Corniolo della Cornia of Perugia, composed at about the same time and too near geographically to escape the notice of some Florentine readers. It is so clear that the *Liber cultus ruris* was the model for it that we cannot avoid mentioning it here nor fail to include this long manuscript in any study of Pier de' Crescenzi's contemporaries. Indeed, the parallel is so striking that an old librarian, perhaps Magliabechi himself, whose library contained the manuscript, felt bound to entitle it *Liber de agricultura composta su Crescenzio*. The copy was made just after the *Divina villa* was written (however, for the date suggested by recent scholars, between the last decades of the fourteenth century and the early fifteenth century, there is too little evidence so far) and it affords interesting hints on its composition and on the recently published sixteenth-century text, though the manuscript only contains three texts – Macer's *De viribus herbarum, La Divina villa*, and various extracts from medical works and prescriptions for the plague. In the large paper volume we find collections of notes made by a certain *ser* Giorgio son of Jacopo di Bonaparte di Santa . . . , who copied Corniolo della Cornia's work as part of his studies on agriculture, botany and medicine, a practice we have seen in so many readers and annotators of Pier de' Crescenzi. In these notes, Corniolo is reflected in his reader-annotator, master Giorgio, and each clarifies the role of the other in dealing with the two texts. On the one hand, Corniolo della Cornia completes and brings up to date the *Liber cultus ruris*, proving to be one of Pier de' Crescenzi's most scholarly readers; on the other, *ser* Giorgio copies and translates the text of the *Divina villa* to such an extent that the chapters mostly on pharmaceutics in book VI are replaced by extracts of a real medical text. These commonplace books are really open works, within which the scribe operates as reader, student and author all at the same time.[52]

In this case, *ser* Giorgio had access to a much older text than the well-known codices of the *Divina villa*, probably from the Latin original. The Latin preamble is followed by the Italian translation; then come the chapters up to chapter VII, directly in Italian; from that point Latin and Italian alternate once more; after which, from chapter XIV to the end of book III, the text is all in Latin, while the Italian translation starts again only with the pruning of the vine, going as far as the early chapters of the book on kitchen-gardens. A few paragraphs further on *ser* Giorgio inserted some Italian chapters on hygiene and healthy food which are missing in the sixteenth-century manuscript; he noted some remedies for lice, mice and vipers; and he outlined the principal parts of the human body. The transcription of the *Divina villa* stops at the chapter on precautions against predators,[53] and the following 150 rather difficult folios deal, in Latin, with the treatment of fractures and wounds, other prescriptions and treatment, in Italian and Latin, ending with notes by or after Teobaldo Lozieto di Anzigno, of the diocese of Bologna, on country ailments and the treatment of the plague. It would indeed seem that *ser* Giorgio took to heart the advice given by Pier de' Crescenzi at the beginning of book VI, to go more deeply into the pharmaceutical properties of wild herbs and cultivated plants, useful to everyone but above all to those living in the country, where there were no medicines.

---

[52] See Florence, BN, ms Magl. XIV 3: *Libro di agricoltura composto su Crescenzio. xv secolo* (on the flyleaf, in pencil, was written: *Anonimo. Trattato d'agricoltura e medicina*), manuscript book all in the same hand, paper, 349 fos., fifteenth century: fos. 1–27v, *Incipit Liber Macri de viribus herbarum*; fos. 29–50, index of the second and third parts of the book, fos. 51–349v, *Divini ruris gloriam*. The texts are interleaved with a number of blank pages, unnumbered, with hardly legible script of the mid-sixteenth century. In the margin of fo. 1 of the *Divina villa* a more recent hand, probably of the early sixteenth century, wrote 'Scriptum per manum ser Gregorij domini Jacobj de Bonaparte de Sancta . . . '. Neither the title, *Divina villa*, nor the authorship, Corniolo della Cornia, seems to appear anywhere in the long manuscript. Towards the end of the manuscript there is mention of doctor Teobaldo Lozieto d'Anzigno from the diocese of Bologna (fo. 349v). Although unfinished, this manuscript precedes those mentioned by L. Bonelli Conenna, *La Divina villa di Corniolo della Cornia. Lezioni di agricoltura tra xiv e xv secolo*, Siena 1982, pp. xxxiii–xxxvii. This manuscript confirms the supposition that there was a Latin version of the *Divina villa*: see M. G. Marchetti Lungarotti, 'Note di Museografia agricola', *Rivista di Storia dell'Agricoltura*, 3, 1976, p. 99, an opinion not shared by Bonelli Conenna, *La Divina villa*, p. xxxv.

[53] The manuscript by *ser* Giorgio presents a number of discrepancies with the published text of the *Divina villa* (for example 'salvatico' for 'salutifero', I, II; the whole of chap. xvii is different in the Latin version).

The *Divina villa*, written during the demographic recovery after the plague, was certainly breaking new ground by insisting that caring for the sick was one of the good husbandman's duties.[54] Just as Corniolo brought the text of the *Liber cultus ruris* up to date, using principally Columella's text, so this anonymous scribe added to the parts on medicine, surgery and pharmacy and, for good measure, began his handwritten book by copying Macer's book on herbs.

The greatest novelty of the *Divina villa*, which also gives some indication of its date, is its wide use of the Latin agricultural writers and even more of Columella, sometimes quoted directly, sometimes just conveying his ideas. This places the *Villa* after the date when the codex of the *Res rustica* was found (1418) and rapidly spread throughout Italy. The insistence on the accurate calculation of the benefits reaped from work and on doing work at the right time is of particular interest.[55] So are the updating and completion of the text from Columella and Pliny (who often used Columella without quoting him) on the cultivation of produce, which we shall look at later.

Corniolo's book, the contemporary copy made by *ser* Giorgio, and the readings of Crescenzi discussed above are all part of the renewed interest in Classical agronomy, so well represented by the books owned (and probably read) by a large number of Florentines between 1413 and 1608, and which obviously go back to the translation of Palladius.[56] In the fifteenth century, copies of Cato, Columella, Varro, besides multiple copies of Pliny the Elder and Virgil (the *Georgics*) were already appearing, not merely in the great libraries. The choice of Giuliano di Perozo, who was recorded, in 1419, as possessing only one book, fell on the Italian translation of Palladius. In the following century, the greater number of books on agriculture after 1550 modified, but did not fundamentally change, the way agriculture was taking over the natural world, which was brought out clearly by readers and annotators of the *Liber cultus ruris*. Landowners not only from Florence – Pierfrancesco di Folco Portinari (1531), Inghiramo di Gerolamo Inghirami of Prato (1579), Jacopo Marescotti (1592), for example, who were collectors of

54 See Bonelli Conenna, *La Divina villa*, p. 27.
55 See *ibid.*, pp. 9–11, 29. On the Columella manuscripts see Josephson, *Die Columella Handschriften* .
56 See L. Perini,'Libri e lettori nella Toscana del Cinquecento', *Ricerche storiche*, 11, 2–3, 1981, pp. 575–92; C. Bec, *Les livres des Florentins (1413–1608)*, Florence 1984; S. Polica, 'Lettori cinquecenteschi di Pietro de Crescenzi', *La Cultura*, 24, 1986, pp. 231–55.

great personal libraries – but humbler people, economically speaking, such as Stefano Lippi D'Arezzo (1543), Ippolito Buondelmonti (1563), and Bernardo Baroncelli (1579), all owned at least one copy of Pier de' Crescenzi. To him they often added the Latin agronomists, at least Palladius, or often, in his place, Luigi Alamanni (1570, 1571, 1579) or Giovanni Tatti (1573); *L'orto*, by Carlo Stefano (1573); *La coltivazione degli ulivi*, by Vettori (1576, 1599); *L'agricoltura*, by the Spaniard Herrera, in Italian translation (1601). The interest of Florentine readers in technical treatises appears from all these works, not only on law, commerce and medicine but also in the specific field of agriculture and natural history. Xenophon's *Oeconomicus*, Dioscorides, Mattioli, Cesalpino, Tommasi, the *Geoponics* and Georg Bauer's *De re metallica* were all easy to find.[57] In other Italian and European circles too, but particularly in Florence, it is obvious that Pier de' Crescenzi prepared the way for the reading and writing of new works on agriculture.

3. TEXT AND READERSHIP IN FRANCE

So widespread was Pier de' Crescenzi's text in France that, thanks to a fourteenth-century translation, it was looked on almost as a French text. We do not know who made the 1373 French translation of the *Liber cultus ruris*, which became *Le livre des ruraulx prouffits du labour des champs* and, like the Latin original, was dedicated to a king. For Charles V of Valois, more a man of letters than of war, had the thankless task of reigning over France after the defeat of Poitiers (1356), during the worst of the Hundred Years' War. The translation of the *Liber cultus ruris*, made at his behest, can be considered part of his attempt to reorganize the French state, before and after he came to the throne (1364). By careful attention to finance, the army, and agriculture which was in a state of upheaval after the peasants' revolts, he hoped to bring about his

---

[57] See Perini, 'Libri e lettori', and Bec, *Les livres des Florentins*, especially pp. 29, 59, 71, 123, 127 ff.; I suggest that '*l'Agricoltura* dello Spagnolo' should be identified with the Italian translation of the '*Agricoltura*' by Gabriel Alonso Herrera, Venice 1557 and later editions (*ibid.*, pp. 71, 290) and that '*Agricoltura* di messer Giovanni Zati' should be corrected to 'Giovanni Tatti', published under this pseudonym by Francesco Sansovino in Venice 1560 and later reprints (*ibid.*, p. 312).

country's recovery and halt the English king's advance.[58] The work of the middle-class Pier de' Crescenzi, who in his dedication to King Charles of Sicily had made a formal act of homage to a distant sovereign, moved in this way beyond the framework of middle-class agriculture and entered into that of the aristocracy. In the same years Peter of Aragon had Palladius' *Opus agriculturae* translated into Castilian, while, at a rather similar time of civil strife, Duke Humphrey of Gloucester had the same text translated into Middle English. The figure of a sovereign who commissions a work on agriculture, or who has one dedicated to him, was to recur again in the sixteenth century, with Agostino Gallo's homage to Charles Emmanuel I of Savoy; then, in 1601, Olivier de Serres dedicated his impressive treatise to Henri IV.

The patronage conferred by the monarchy on Pier de' Crescenzi's treatise certainly helped it to spread widely in both Latin and French. At least seven Latin manuscripts were copied in France. They were specimens embellished with miniatures or with the initials of the Bibliothèque Royale, of Michel Reynault, lord of Champrouber, and of Louis Raquier, Bishop of Troyes. Even more precious were the manuscripts in French that once belonged to Antoine, the bastard of Burgundy, the Du Fou family and others. Against this background of feudal agriculture, a change of meaning was made in book I, where mention is made of the bailiff's duties (in Latin *villicus*), while the French speaks merely of 'celui qui a charge de la ville' and in the course of the paragraph even turns him into the mayor. This is highly ambiguous, since 'ville' can mean village, community, or else property in the fourteenth- to fifteenth-century sense of the word. Ambiguities of this sort reappear with regard to the householder, who no longer visits his farm, as suggested in the Italian translation, or the *fundus* of the Latin text; instead, 'le Seigneur ancien de l'hotel vient a la ville . . . ' Similarly, the burgher's sincere wish not to have a farm 'infra quei campi che mutano spesso signoria' (in fields whose ownership often changes) but to have authority over the estate, becomes 'Se il y a assez champs qui ne remuent pas souvent seigneurs' (if there are enough fields that do not change owners frequently). Cato's advice that the householder should go

[58] See Societa' agraria di Bologna, *Studi e documenti*, pp. 277–83, 298, 300–4; see also P. Boyer, 'Le "Ruralium commodorum opus" de Pierre de Crescent. Etude d'Histoire économique', Pos. Thèse Ecole des Chartes, 1943, pp. 29–35. See also R. Bousshat, *Le moyen age. Histoire de la literature française*, Paris 1967, pp. 209–11. The Bibliothèque de Dijon, Cod. 453, owns another version of the de' Crescenzi text produced by a certain Domenican friar, Brother Nicolas, in 1413.

to the market to sell and not to buy is cut out, while there is an addition, freely translated from the Latin, to the effect that certain things double in value if they are kept for long enough.[59]

Novelties appear all through the French text. To begin with it is not just a translation but an adaptation of the original subject-matter to the French situation. This is true especially of book V, on the vine and wine, where the French terminology obviously does not adhere to the Latin, since it is based on a form of cultivation with well-defined characteristics; and, what is more, the procedures, of chapters VII and IX, for example, are different, simpler than in the original. Another by no means negligible novelty in the French text is the idea of sowing turnip seed in the ley, before introducing corn into the rotation (book VII, chap. II). It still has to be established whether this was a practice common in the French translator's home district, or whether it is an addition to the original text based on another passage in which Pier de' Crescenzi mentions green manuring by ploughing in roots and turnips, as was usual in Tuscany and Lombardy (book II, chap. XIII, towards the end).[60]

Another novelty missing in the Italian translation, which gives some warning of how the *Liber cultis ruris* was to be read in the French version, is a minor text based on de' Crescenzi himself. A certain Gorgole de Corne extrapolated the rules for planting and growing every kind of tree, according to the title. What we actually have is an epitome on domestic economy (storing of products, production of various wines with many different flavours, how to keep the house free of insects, and so on). This text was to be amplified in the early sixteenth century by one Nicole du Mesnil, who claimed he had gathered his knowledge of grafting and various ways of planting trees from Palladius, Galen and Aristotle and that he followed the method of Pier de' Crescenzi.[61] In this context, Antoine Verard's first printed edition, published in Paris in 1485, fell on extremely fertile ground, with readers prepared to make full use of the text, as the large number of editions brought out and reprinted

---

[59] This and the following quotations are from the copy in the possession of the Biblioteca Nazionale of Turin, Philippe Le Noir, Paris 1529, fo. VIIv.

[60] See F. Fleurot (ed.), *Ce livre est nommé Rustican . . .* , Dijon 1864, pp. 18–19, 22–3. Titles such as *Rustican* or *Bon Mesnager* were often used to indicate various printed editions of the *Prouffitz champêstres.*

[61] Following the *Divina villa* by Corniolo della Corna one could possibly identify Corniolo with Gorgole de Corne. Although it is useless to compare the four small sheets of Gorgole de Corne and the 326 pages of the *Divina villa*, one might even suggest that Nicole du Mesnil and Friar Nicolas, author of the second translation of de' Crescenzi, were the same person.

between 1486 and 1540 testifies. Evidence of the great demand for, and rapid buying up of, the first edition is to be found in a manuscript copy of Jean Bonhomme's edition.[62] We cannot make such a detailed analysis of the French sample as of the Italian one. Nonetheless, it does reveal interesting characteristics, based on the contrasts between North and South, the different kinds of owner (laymen or religious institutions), the agricultural background of the original text and that of its readers.

3.1. French readers

Our French sample of texts definitely focuses on the area round Paris. However, by good fortune, the boundaries of the Bibliothèque Nationale in Paris go beyond the geographical area and hence we have some testimony from Liège and Tours. Southern France is represented by an area round Avignon and Carpentras, yet at least one copy takes us as far as Lyons and extends into the Languedoc area. Other French copies have crossed the Alps and the English Channel.

A manuscript note at the foot of a 1474 Louvain copy can be dated 1502, which comes to us from the monastery of Saint Laurent in Liège and the underlinings and notes in the margin would seem contemporary; but this reader did not go beyond the first part. He read, carefully, the chapters in book I on air, healthy climate, winds, water, where to build a new house, on wells and fountains and building materials; and then went on to book II, on the growth of plants, where the importance of moisture for the growth of leaves and fruit is pointed out. The reader also paid attention to the changes that take place inside trees and made marginal notes on the chapter on manure where it deals with the manuring of grafted trees and the cultivation of wild trees. Finally, in the slightest of references, he recalled Palladius on the time for ploughing; from other copies we get an idea of the changes taking place. The copy that once belonged to the Parisian monastery of the Guardian Angels of the Blessed Virgin yields even more scanty information.[63] Among those that give nothing more than an indication of who owned them are three belonging to the Celestine Order in Avignon, which owned the most important friary in the city.[64] The second and third copies have footnotes

---

[62] See Paris, BN, ms Franc. 19084; see the comments of E. Chiovenda, *Archivio di storia della scienza*, 3, 1922, pp. 311–18 on a copy of the first edition.
[63] Paris, BN, RES.361; Paris, BN., RES.285, Paris 1486.
[64] See in the following order: Avignon, MC, 4°.1024; Avignon, MC, MR.FOL.200, book I, chap. lxxxviii, xc, xci, xcii, xcv, xcvi; Avignon, MC, 8°.1.476.

with the dates when they were introduced into the catalogue, 1591 and 1620 respectively, but perhaps they were volumes acquired or at least read previously. What did the Catholics, loyal subjects of the Pope, underline? Chapter XIII of book II, on how to plant trees and convert (*sic*) wild or hybrid trees into good trustworthy ones (*franches*); grafting (Paris 1529); they noted the properties of various herbs – mugwort, centaury, rocket, fennel and everlasting-flower. In another copy (Paris 1536) they noted how to tell whether must (new wine) contained water and how to separate one from the other; they also noted dove-keeping and bee-keeping. In chapter CXVIII a second signature, of a certain Claude Rogier, appeared, which shows that the same volume was definitely read by more than one person. Though we can only be sure of the identity of the person making the annotations in a very few cases, there is never any doubt that many copies passed from hand to hand. Perhaps the greatest surprise awaits us in the third copy, the one from Venice, unfortunately with no signs to indicate if it was ever taken to Avignon in an Italian monk's bag, but which has a contemporary cardboard binding, with Antonino Venuto's extremely rare little book on growing trees attached.[65] The reading or ownership of Pier de' Crescenzi's text prompted people to widen their knowledge of the subject. Antonino Venuto dealt mainly with fruit trees, and on the sixteenth-century book-market his work must still have been of some value to a reader interested in the subject. If we also take into account that Provence already served as a botanical garden, providing trees and vegetables for the rest of the country, the choice of those who annotated Pier de' Crescenzi's advice on growing fruit-trees gives a clue to the way the *Prouffitz champestres* was read in France.[66]

By a curious coincidence two other annotated examples have come down to us for 1502. A certain Chastilhon purchased his copy, published in Paris in 1486, on 14 January 1502, for 15 *sous*, so it says after the colophon. Many people saw that copy. After the prologue there is a note in ink to the effect that the volume belonged to the College of the Jesuits in Lyons, in 1694, and the stamp of the public library of the same city was placed on it later.[67] But the dense underlinings and the rare

---

[65] See A. Venuto, *De agricoltura opusculum*, Naples 1516, Venice 1538; see the comments of L. Savastano, 'Contributo allo studio critico degli scrittori agrari italici, III, . . . A. Venuto', *Annali Stazione Sperimentale di Agrumicultura e Frutticultura di Acireale*, 6, 1919–21 on this extremely rare agricultural tract.
[66] See E. Le Roy Ladurie, *Paysan de Languedoc*, Paris 1966, chap. ii, *passim.*
[67] Paris, RES.S.365.

manuscript notes are all in the older hand, presumably that of Chastilhon, whom from the context we can take to be a landowner of the region round Lyons, since he underlined all the chapters on bailiffs and landowners very closely; indeed, he read the whole of book I with care. In book II he read the two opening chapters on the nature of plants and the principles of propagation attentively, then his interest flagged a little; however from chapter X to the end there is an unbroken series of references and often illegible marginal notes. So Chastilhon must have been directly interested in the cultivation of the land, manuring, soil improvement and sowing, but also in grafting and the domestication of wild plants. In book III come references and notes on products and places of production, including the threshing-floor and granaries, wheat, beans, lentils, barley, chick-peas, peas, rye and vetch. Actually he paid most attention to oats, beans, chick-peas and vetch, less to the other products. The book on the vine and wine interested him too. There are a few marks in the first chapters and then his pen runs on busily through the chapters on the time of harvest, mulled wine and must, on keeping wine, on making various kinds of wine, on how to make barrels, wine jars and on storage.[68] Then he puts in a recipe for mulled wine on a separate slip of paper; apparently he liked to add carrots and ginger to it. He was less interested in the larger trees and there are very few markings concerning the elm, or the laurel, pomegranate, medlar, rose-tree or rosemary bush. The long list of herbs that Pier de' Crescenzi describes in book VI on the kitchen-garden seems not to have confused him; he carefully picked out garlic, sorrel, the beet, borage, pumpkin, watermelons and cucumbers, cardoons (here he made a correction, 'Note that *chardons* are artichokes'), turnips and rapes at those points where the text tells how to grow them. Chastilhon's use of the text was not exclusively utilitarian; he shared Crescenzi's taste for the delights of the villa, the garden, flowers, rare-coloured fruits. He included in his underlinings the chapters on gardens that tell, mainly on the basis of Classical experience, how to create the enchanted gardens of the medieval romances. He was also interested in the diseases of horses and oxen, went over the chapters of book XI where the reader is reminded of the contents of the whole work; and lastly, carefully marked the tasks to be carried out month by month.

Who was this Chastilhon? His name was common in the region around Lyons, and a great many Chastilhons are known to us, especially if we take into account the various possible spellings (Châtillon, Casteilon,

---

[68] *Ibid.*, chaps. Ii, v, viii, ix, x, xxi, xxxii–xxxiv, xxxvii, xxxviii, xl, xlvi.

etc.). Very probably they were a family of middle-class origin, who settled in Châlons, were granted the title of nobles in 1555, and were to produce a Nicole, court engineer, in the second half of the century. In any case, his interests as a reader tell us a good deal about him. He had not yet acquired the nobles' taste for hawking, since he omitted the part on hunting completely. To the hawk and the falcon he preferred the book on gardens, and the cultivation of what would have been looked on in his day as exotic fruit. His property was not large, for he took no note of large trees, with the exception of the useful, common chestnut (probably he owned no woodland). He kept his kitchen-garden to a minimum, just a few products for the table, for cooking or agricultural use, as the chapter on manure suggested to him. He passed over the cultivation of the meadow, with that most innovative part on sowing turnips as forage. Indeed, a text like the *Prouffitz champestres*, whether in Latin, Italian or French, is interesting not merely for its intrinsic value, but for the readings of it made by many more or less anonymous owners who culled its novelties and brought traditional procedures to a halt. However Chastilhon leaves us some traces of an interest in turnips, perhaps connected with oats and vetch. It is clear that he concentrated mainly on field cultivation. He may have had some livestock and a little wine (as a rent in kind), but the villa and social structure he was examining formed part of his own interests. In any case, Chastilhon was rather an exception to the general rule in the region, at least as far as the agricultural use of his farm is concerned.[69] He had no meadow or vineyard, perhaps because the soil was unsuitable for them (like those to the south of Lyons, for example), but was interested in the garden and shared with his fellow-citizens the enthusiasm for breeding cattle. If a series of estimates for 1413 are to be trusted, Chastilhon paid between a fifth and a tenth of the value of a good-sized ploughing ox for his copy of the *Prouffitz champestres*.

Another copy, published in Louvain in 1480, still being read and annotated in 1502, suggests a reading in part philosophical, in part pertaining to domestic economy, regarding the relationship between substance and nucleus dealt with in book II, chapter IV. On the subject of storing wine, the rule about keeping wine-jars clean is noted and

---

[69] See M. T. Locrin, *Les campagnes de la région lyonnaise*, Lyons 1974, pp. 28, 50, 282–8; on the Chasteilons see *Dictionnaire de biographie française*, Paris 1959, vol. VIII, *sub nomine*; on French interest in turnips in the sixteenth century see *Rapinae seu raporum enconium, auctore Claudio Bigotherio poeta rapicio*, Lugduni n.d., quoted by A. J. Bourde, *Agronomie et agronomes en France au xviiie siècle*, Paris 1967, vol. I, p. 44.

finally the qualities of boars and sows are marked. Another more recent hand, we might guess late sixteenth century, added a slip of paper between books IV and V, on which he wrote a poem beginning 'Omne brutum est sensibile', full of syllogisms and assonances, which ended 'Omnis philosophus est risibilis'. The text of the *Prouffitz champestres* exudes a system of values that leads its readers to give precedence to the body and material matters, rather than philosophical abstraction.[70]

While for the Italian sample of texts there was a clear division between those who read the *Liber cultus ruris* with an eye to large-scale cultivation and those who were interested mainly in the medical side of the work, very few Frenchmen consulted Pier de' Crescenzi with any attention to (his) pharmacopoeia. Perhaps this was because illustrated books like the *Platearins* were common in France. A certain Silvanecter owned a 1474 Louvain copy, which he probably got from previous owners (there is another illegible signature at the end of book IV). It contains just a few notes on the vine and on trees, after which the whole chapter on the properties of herbs is underlined (book VI, chap. I), besides the section on gardens and their cultivation (book VI, chap. II) and the parts on garlic, fennel and mustard.[71] To judge from the bindings, the *Prouffitz champestres* must often have been bound together with manuscripts concerning medicine. Another sixteenth-century, dated copy (the 1486 Strasbourg edition in Latin) was bound by a certain Magister Petrus Valctrenisse of Antwerp together with medical manuscripts of the sort written for Peter Engel of Brabant – *Liber de consolatione medicinarum* (1418), *Practica Cyrurgiae, Quaedam recepte medecinae* and others.[72] In other cases it was bound together with such famous texts as Aristotle's *Animals*, Theophrastus' *Plants* and commentaries on them.[73] Even the copy that ended up in Turin has some mainly medical-botanical notes, on the cultivation of trees, the transformation of wild into cultivated trees (book II, chap. XIII) and then on the almond, fig, laurel, chaste-tree and rosemary (book V, chaps. I, II, VI, VII, XXIV and XXXV). Then come a series of underlinings and marginal notes (often cut out by later binding) on mugwort, birthwort,

---

[70] Paris, BN, RES.S.359; IV, xxxi; IX, lxxvii. On the philosophical quarrel between high and low, spirit and body, see M. Bakhtin, *L'oeuvre de François Rabelais et la culture populaire au Moyen Age et sous la Renaissance*, Paris 1970; on Aristotelian thinking and syllogism see R. Lenoble, *Les origines de la pensée scientifique moderne*, Paris 1957.

[71] Paris, BN, M.S. 15.

[72] See Paris, BN, RES.S.362.   [73] See Paris, BM, 3990, Basel 1548.

betony, cress, calamint, maidenhair, cowbane, samphire, larkspur, dittany, heather, dock, mandrake, onion, nettles, parsley and purslane. Other brief notes concern horse and ox diseases (book IX, chaps. XIX, XXI, XXV, LV, LXVI).[74]

In France too it is the sixteenth-century copies from before the forties that have most notes and underlinings. This was the period before the publication of the treatises by the printer Charles Estienne, later collected under the title *Praedium rusticum*, when, for lack of a more recent and geographically defined work, the reader was forced to make a greater effort and struggle with the ancient text.[75] One anonymous reader of a copy published in Strasbourg in the sixteenth century was careful to trace the inner connections of the work and made marginal notes of the pages that interested him most. So in book XI he marked the reference in book XI which also deals with the house and its management. He did the same in book II, underlining the theoretical parts, the general principles, the parts on plants, manure, the connection between manure and water, the choice of plants and the position of the fields. In book III, on work in the fields, he marked only the threshing-floor, the granary, oats, wheat, spelt and rye. He read the whole of book IV, on the vine, with care, noting the choice and layout of the vineyard, the grafting and pruning of the vine, the chapters on the grape-harvest and wine-making. He went through book VI very quickly, almost as if the cultivation of gardens, kitchen-gardens and fruit trees did not concern him very closely. Whereas nothing escaped him in book IX, on animals, or book XI, he underlined in ink all the chapters (II–IX) dealing with the breeding and care of horses, then of mules and donkeys, goats, dogs, hares, fish, peacocks, pheasants, geese, hens, pigeons and bees.[76] He compared book XI with other pages in the text and, lastly, checked the calendar in book XII with a text of Palladius, which he obviously owned. All this involved long, hard application and reveals a considerable capacity to deal with the great themes of cultivation, the fields, care of the vineyard and animals. No reference appears to any kind of noble agriculture, the choice focusing shrewdly on whatever is useful, not forgetting fishpond, dovecote or beehive.

[74] See Turin, BN, RIS.25.17, Paris 1529.
[75] Ch. Estienne, *De re hortensi*, Paris 1535; idem, *Seminarium*, Paris 1536; idem, *Vinetum*, Paris 1537; idem, *Sylva*, Paris 1538; idem, *Pratum*, Paris 1543; idem, *Praedium rusticum*, Paris 1544. See below, chap. 4.
[76] On bee-keeping in France see Musée national des arts et traditions populaires, *L'abeille. L'homme, le miel et la cire*, Paris 1981.

So not only were Pier de' Crescenzi and the *Opus agriculturae* often published together, but we now have evidence that they were also read together and compared with each other. For lack of more specific texts, the early sixteenth-century reader used what the publishers of his day provided for him, but he did not absorb the published texts passively. He was capable of correcting them where they were obviously ungrammatical; and above all he made a choice, which was an economic choice because it was made with a view to solving some particular problem, which lies hidden in the reader's notes.

It was the concept of the good householder, by then merely an empty formula, that in 1809 prompted an English nobleman, James Stephens, to purchase a copy of the 1516 Paris edition of the *Prouffitz champestres* for the sum of one pound fifteen shillings. The volume had belonged to a Frenchman of the sixteenth century, who left us his thoughts on nuns and abbots in the footnotes.[77] Probably it was this older hand that lightly marked, in the index of book I, the chapters on water, the site of the villa, the courtyard and the cistern; in book II the general chapter on ploughing, the field, fallow and grafting; in book III the chapter on beans; in books IV and V the introductions; in book IX the parts on mares, the birth of the colt, the care of the horse, signs of good character in the horse, certain horse diseases (chaps. XVIII and XIX) and little else in the rest of the book. He underlined the text of book V, where it speaks of the medlar (the chances of growing it from seed, with much time and patience), the apple-tree (he noted the spacing of trees), the pear-tree (grafting procedures). His aim was to emphasize with discrimination a few simple, practical rules of cultivation.

We come now to another group of landowners who left scarce indication of their reading, but took pride in displaying their ownership of the *Prouffitz champestres* – Schynchee, a Parisian doctor, Moreau and a Camille Maret.[78] Two readers even struggled with Italian in order to read Pier de' Crescenzi. The one who left us underlinings and short marginal notes in a 1511 Venice copy is unfortunately anonymous. He had quite clear ideas about what to keep in mind. He picked out chapter XXII of book II, on how to make ditches, how to plant seeds in the month of January and the influence of the moon on the growth of plants, according to Albert the Great. He went on to chapter XIII on grafting,

---

[77] See Paris, BN, RES.M.S.19.
[78] See Paris, BN, S.288, Paris 1536; Paris, BN, S.4404, Basel 1538; Paris, BN, RES.S.366, Paris 1540.

some general rules and how to cut the shoots and the tree on which they were to be grafted, with references to chapters XXV and XXVI, on the position of land and how to recognize good quality soil. He took note of how to defend the fig tree from ants (book V, chap. X). He dwelt longer on the book on the kitchen-garden, noting the properties of herbs, the chapters on dill, mushrooms, rape-seed (another example of the French interest in turnips and rape-seed, mentioned earlier). In the chapter on roots he revealed his linguistic origins by adding a marginal note in the usual mixture of Latin and French – 'Napo non anis refort'. He marked book VII, chapter II, which describes how, by the use of irrigation, grass and corn can be rotated without having to leave the land fallow. He concluded his reading with two very short notes, one on the horse and the other on the quality of the air.[79] Claude Le Comte of Paris used both Italian and Latin on the frontispiece of his copy, published in Venice in 1534.[80] It had belonged, or was to belong to the library of Saint-Éloy. No doubt it was Le Comte who underlined book X alone, on birds of prey (chap. I), how to tame them (chap. IV), how to use them (chap. V), and the differences between falcons (chap. IX) and different kinds of owl (chap. XVI). He was an example of a middle-class Parisian, aspiring to an aristocratic life-style typified by hawking. For all his delight in grafting and agriculture and the symbolic value of the *Liber cultus ruris*, Le Comte was a man of the middle classes who had not assimilated Cato's model of the good householder still present in Pier de' Crescenzi. By focusing on the chapter on falconry he once more revealed that desire for social standing already apparent when he called himself 'honnuorato'.[81]

3.2. French gardens and kitchen gardens

It has already been pointed out that our French readers have left us less obvious marks of the continual contrasts found among Italian readers – between high and low, town and country, consumers and producers. An outstanding clarification of the text is contained in the pamphlet printed at the end of the fifteenth century, entitled *La manière d'enter et planter extraite de P. Crescenzi*. It consists of four octavo pages printed for the

[79] See Paris, BM, 14856, Venice 1511.
[80] See Paris, BN, S.15034; see also E. Picot, *Les français italianisants au xvie siècle*, Paris 1906–7, 2 vols.
[81] See in general G. Huppert, *Les Bourgeois Gentilhommes. An Essay on the Definition of Elites in Renaissance France*, Chicago and London 1977, pp. 34 ff.

first time in 1486[82] with the first edition of the *Prouffitz champestres*. The short rules extracted from de' Crescenzi had an enormous success for such a slight text.[83] The author was a gardener, and his name, Gorgole de Corne, only appeared in 1533, when his pamphlet was published for the first time as an appendix to Pier de' Crescenzi's text. It came out later in a slightly larger edition, under the name of a certain Nicole du Mesnil and was reprinted for the last time in 1550. Besides the rules on gardening, on storing food produce, making wine of various flavours and how to get rid of insects, Nicole du Mesnil amplified the part on grafting and planting trees, but cut down the long list of trees in the original text to three kinds of pear-tree, the apple, chestnut, cherry and almond (the most southerly species in this text), the oak, peach, plum and vine. These were followed by other rules on growing cereals, flowers, and, to conclude, for the benefit of admirers of the *Roman de la Rose*, he gave advice on how to keep roses fresh throughout the year.[84] The short rules at once impressed his readers, who made their own additions[85] in the margin on how to grow stoneless medlars sweet as honey, while one anonymous owner seems to have been especially moved by the formulae for favouring the growth of trees planted at new moon, or immediately after.[86] He also underlined how certain trees can be defended from ants; how pith can be used as slips in planting trees and how all kinds of fruit can be protected from the frost; at this point he added a long note in the margin on storing fruit, now cut out by careless binding, except for the words ' . . . they will be so fresh at Christmas . . . '.

Another anonymous figure, underlining a 1560 edition, marked the chapter on wild trees, among other things. Finally there is a contemporary copy, which passed through the hands of a certain Gerard to L. Machon and ended up in Paris, among the books of the Pères Gardiens de Saint-Honoré, bound together with other short treatises on the same subject.[87] The underlinings, in pencil, are of some interest. They

---

[82] See Paris, BN, RES.S.834.

[83] This small booklet was often printed under different titles (for an example: *La manière de enter et planter en jardins choses bien estranges*: see Paris, BN, RES.S.713).

[84] On the essays on gardening see J. Meuvret, *Agronomie et jardinage au xvie et xviie* (1953), reprinted in idem, *Etudes d'histoire économique*, Paris 1971, pp. 153–61; also see Bourde, *Agronomie*, vol. I, pp. 59–67. On the symbolism of the rose see now J. Goody, *The Culture of Flowers*, Cambridge 1993, pp. 120–65.

[85] As Elaine de Sav . . . did (the missing part of the name was cut out by a more recent binding), Paris, BN, RES.S.834.

[86] See Paris, BN, RES.Z.2755.

[87] See Paris, BN, S.1075, Paris 1560.

focus on how to make trenches for planting trees in dry or wet soil, the time for planting them according to local conditions, and how to plant them so that they do not keep the sun from others. Then this reader, obviously disagreeing with the text, crossed out a paragraph on the moon and the time for planting trees. Nor did he believe that cherries could grow without stones or that vines should be pruned in spring in cold regions and in autumn in hot climates, or that there was a connection between the phases of the moon and the growth of the vine.[88] But where some readers corrected and crossed out, others copied faithfully. Thirty-nine lines of an edition of Gorgole de Corne were copied in the end-papers of an older volume.[89] So some believed in, while others denied, the positive influence of the new moon on the growth of plants. In general the influence of the stars on the life and growth of plants was not questioned in the sixteenth century; yet there were disagreements on the matter within the group of readers applying the practical rules of Gorgole de Corne and Nicole du Mesnil.

This same pamphlet, in a carefully made manuscript copy, with some variations, was brought to Turin at the time of Emmanuel Philibert.[90] The eighty-nine chapters include the usual rules but add a greater variety of Mediterranean trees such as the orange, lemon, medlar, date and a long list of commonly used herbs, vegetables and roots taken from the complete text of the *Prouffitz champestres* or one of the many editions of the *Platearius*. Here, too, the lack of a printed book on agriculture prompted the compilation of a written manual, probably with the additions and corrections dictated by the author's own interests. The printed text never completely excluded the manuscript, which was produced according to need. A number of codices of de' Crescenzi's *Liber*, in Latin, Italian, French and German, were copied from printed editions. This provides further confirmation that the number of readers of the sample under examination here was certainly greater than the number of volumes actually printed.

---

[88] In general see P. Saintyves, *L'astrologie populaire étudiée spécialment dans les doctrines relatives à l'influence de la lune*, Paris 1937.

[89] See Carpentras, BI, E 1763, Paris 1515. The paragraphs in question have the following *incipit*: 'Quiconque veult edifier jardins; L'on peut planter sans larme toutes arbres; Le premier jour du croissant fait bon edifier; Pour enter bien; Qui veult enter vigne; Se un arbre detende trop; Qui veult xavoir pesches deux moys plus tot; Enter nesples, ceriscier et pesches . . . '

[90] See Turin, Biblioteca Reale, ms Varia 271: *Le livre de agriculture composè* [sic] *super de planter et hanter* [sic] *arbres et de semer noyaux et semences* is the title given by an anonymous gentleman to his agricultural book.

The cultivation of trees would seem to provide the most significant key to the understanding of the *Prouffitz champestres*. Unlike the printed herbals, the guidelines provided by Pier de' Crescenzi can be traced back to a plan of cultivation in which the feature that distinguishes North from South is the inclusion of plants that require a milder climate. Even in the early sixteenth century Provence was acquiring specialization as a nursery for trees and plants and providing seed for Northern France. In the 1620s Claude Lemasyeux or one of his friends, as the colophon tells us, underlined book II, on the things necessary for all plants (chap. I), the reproduction and growth of plants (chap. XII), manuring and the nourishment of plants (chap. XIII), how to make the field fertile at sowing-time (chap. XVII), the general method of sowing (chap. XXVI) and the quality of the soil (chap.XXVI). All he marked in book VI, on the vine, is how to make vinegar (chaps. XLIII–XLVI) and in book V , on trees, he underlined the oak, the bay oak, the turkey oak, the walnut and the box-tree. He also added 'time for planting' in the margin, where book II specified that spring was the best time for planting trees.[91] The trees noted in another edition, of 1521, are more numerous. It was a Provençal, or at least a southern reader who annotated this copy, which later entered the library of Francis Douce (1757–1834), the well-known English bibliophile and collector. The reader's region of origin is apparent from the point in the printed text which speaks of *fraxinagol* (*Celtis australis*, L.) and he writes in the margin 'falabreguier', one of the names commonly used for celtis in the *Midi* and the south-west of France. The tree was much appreciated for its berries and for its straight, ungnarled trunk.[92] The same reader went through the whole of book V on fruit-trees, excluding only rowan, jujube and juniper. For non-fruit-bearing trees he was more selective, marking the chaste-tree, the cypress, maple, whitethorn, ash, celtis, the rose-garden (closely annotated in the margin), willow and elder. From here he passed to book VI, underlining or noting in the margin the names and properties of eighty-one herbs and vegetables, from the very common ones such as garlic, pumpkin, cress, chicory, endive, fennel and fenugreek, to such rare ones as large dodder, ginger and savory, to name only a few. He had already underlined something on must, vinegar, oats and corn-cockle in the other books.

---

[91] See London, BL, 1501/157, Paris 1529: in 1753 the book belonged to the Sainte Geneviève convent in Paris.

[92] See H. Coste and C. H. Flahault, *Flore descriptive de la France*, Paris 1937, vol. III, p. 250.

Lastly, on the flyleaves, he stuck two woodcuts, one showing a harrow drawn by a horse or mule, with a peasant sowing, the other a more complex scene in which an owner inspects his estate and observes one peasant ploughing and another pruning the full-grown vine.[93]

Generally speaking, the French readers made a botanical selection and, unlike Italian readers, took into account the separation of town and country. The little booklet of Gorgole de Corne and Nicole du Mesnil was added to by other readers; only the commonest trees in the country-side of northern France appear in this sample. Only one Provençal writer, like the one examined above, branched out into citrus fruit and pepper. For French readers were still attached to the reproduction of an old scheme of tree-growing, which is precisely what the *Capitulare de Villis* was to describe – apple- and pear-trees of various kinds, black-thorn, rowan, chestnuts, peaches, quinces, hazels, almonds, mulberries, laurels, pines, fig-trees, walnuts and cherries.The products of gardens and kitchen-gardens were also essentially the same, with a few variations – the lily, rose, fenugreek, sage, rue, fennel and mint, to mention just a few.[94]

We get the impression that Chastilhon, Claude Le Comte, and other readers who remained anonymous, were middle-class gentlemen. The *Prouffitz champestres* provides a good illustration of the long process of buying up land and manors at the expense of impoverished nobles and peasants. The years of its publication coincide with the beginning of the irreversible advance of the urban middle classes, which began at the end of the fifteenth and continued into the sixteenth and seventeenth centuries. There is no lack of examples, nor are they restricted to the Paris area. The Franche-Comté and Languedoc have provided the subject-matter of famous works of French history on this question. The names and professions we have traced correspond to the world depicted by Gilles de Gouberville, which moves constantly between the sphere of law and that of agriculture. It was a world in which Gilles supervised the reaping and other agricultural work and gave up hawking with a party of nobles rather than neglect his rural responsibilities. None of our readers, with the single exception of Claude Le Comte, took any interest in

[93] See Oxford, BO, Douce C. Subt.45, Paris 1521: see below, chap. 3, 6–11 *passim* concerning Gallo and Brescian agriculture.

[94] See A. Boretius, 'Capitularia regum francorum', in *Monumenta Germaniae Historica. Legum sectio*, II, vol. 1, Hanover 1883, pp. 89–90; W. Metz, 'Das Problem des Capitulare de Villis', *Zeitschrift für Agrargeschichte und Agrarsoziologie*, 2, 1954, pp. 96–104.

woodlands or hunting. They might take no direct part in agriculture, except to cultivate some exotic fruit trees. The *bail à ferme* was still the most common form of land management. Fernand Gauthiot, a rich burgher who became a noble in the second half of the sixteenth century, passed his time on his property, alternately in Gray and Besançon, and owned a well-stocked library, in part inherited from his father. Among the many works of literature, on law and medicine, we find Antoine Mizauld (?), the *Maison Rustique* and two editions of Pier de' Crescenzi (*Le Bon Mesnager* and the *Prouffitz champestres*), besides a small pamphlet on hunting the wolf, which must have been most useful in the woods of the Franche-Comté. Woods and meadows became an important part of the lord's manor, to the detriment of the peasants' land, and these middle-class owners tended to give new shape to the landscape by putting up farm buildings and courtyards.[95] By and large, from the time when it existed only in manuscript to when it appeared in print, the French version of the *Liber cultus ruris* changed its readership from the hereditary aristocracy to an aggressive middle class of entrepreneurs.

4. TEXT AND ENGLISH READERSHIP

The success of Pier de' Crescenzi in England is set in a different context. It was the complex relationship between Classical antiquity and the Mediterranean world, between North and South, which inspired English readers of the *Liber cultus ruris* to make an intellectual effort to comprehend a new natural environment. Between 1471 and 1564 England was transformed from a feudal into a national monarchy. During this time the ruling family received political and social support through the Reformation against the movements of revolt that continued throughout the first half of the sixteenth century. The dissolution of the monasteries (1536–9) provided the opportunity to create a class of landowners and officials whose support for the new order was based on personal advantage and who guaranteed social order at home and

---

[95] See in the following order: L. Febvre, *Philippe II et la Franche-Comté* (1912), Paris 1970, pp. 107–241; Le Roy Ladurie, *Paysans de Languedoc*, pp. 263–313; M. Devèze, *La vie de la forêt française au xvie siècle*, Paris 1961; J. Jacquart, *La crise rurale en Ile-de-France, 1550–1670*, Paris 1974, chap. ix, *passim*; S. Dontenwill, *Une seigneurie sous l'ancien régime. L'Etoile en Brionnais (1575–1778)*, Roanne 1973; M. Venard, *Bourgeois et paysans au xviie siècle*, Paris 1957. Gilles sire de Gouberville is mentioned by Huppert, *Les Bourgeois Gentilshommes*, p. 112; Fernand Gauthiot's library was mentioned by Febvre, *Philippe II*, pp. 219–221.

political independence from Catholic powers abroad. This social and political change was reinforced by the desire for economic self-sufficiency. The rise in prices prompted the nobles to take over the management of their own estates and this renewed interest in the direct administration of upper-class property, the shift from cereal-growing to sheep-breeding, to supply the European wool industry, the very creation of new estates within the boundaries of old ecclesiastical properties, gave rise to more intensive farming. The sixteenth century became a period of economic transformation; it was the workshop in which the social-economic changes of the following decades were forged.

Of the sixteen codices of the *Liber cultus ruris* in Latin still to be found in English libraries, at least three were produced in England in the course of the fifteenth century. One in Italian and two in French were copied in Bruges for King Edward IV, with designs and illustrations to make the book fit for a king, perhaps in imitation of the French copies made for Charles V of Valois (see above, 3.). The oldest cathedrals, such as Winchester and Hereford, had copies, as well as institutions like Merton College, Oxford, Winchester College and St John's College, Cambridge.[96] Since both the manuscripts and printed copies were mainly in Latin, the *Liber cultus ruris* seems to have been addressed to a different kind of reader from those who had read Palladius in previous centuries. It was not by chance that the only French copies were made for a king. French was the language of the Anglo-Norman aristocracy but the imitation of the French model was not a success and the *Liber cultus ruris* never became an essential text for the fifteenth-century English gentleman. The printed editions began to compete vigorously with manuscripts, and the translation of Palladius' *Opus agriculturae*, commissioned by Humphrey, Duke of Gloucester, and the English translation of the *Tractatus Godefridi* (see Chap. 1, 3–3.1) already showed that the new writing on agriculture was linked up with the Latin-English tradition, leaving French, as well as Italian, to bridge the gap between Classical and Modern when there were no other direct sources. Very probably the *Liber cultus ruris* was still seen as a recent text in the mid-fifteenth century, while, by having Palladius' *Opus agriculturae* translated, the Duke would earn further title to be numbered among the Humanists.[97]

---

[96] See the de' Crescenzi manuscripts in England recorded in Società agraria di Bologna, *Pier de' Crescenzi*, pp. 304–5, 285–90 and also Winchester College Library, ms 11.

[97] See chap. 1, 3.

But was Pier de' Crescenzi ever translated into English? Filippo Re maintained that it was, though he was unable to quote a definite source for his hypothesis. However, more recent scholars hold that it was not, claiming that Filippo Re was mistaken, despite his deep knowledge of ancient books on agriculture. But Filippo Re was only partly wrong, for a little study on fishing was going around London in the early seventeenth century. It was composed in Latin by Ian Dubravius, bishop of Olmutz in Moravia, who in his turn had copied much of Pier de' Crescenzi's book X, at the end of the sixteenth century.[98] Agricultural studies had grown, the *Liber* had a good number of competitors, the fiercest of them by now translated into English, and Pier de' Crescenzi's fame was in part overshadowed by publication of the Latin Classics. Yet in this strange, roundabout way Dubravius' Latin text transmitted a part of that applied science so much sought after in the early seventeenth century, when man was eager to experiment on, and gain control of, the natural world.

4.1. English readers

In the period under examination, the number of copies of the *Liber cultus ruris* to be found in England were undoubtedly fewer than those in Italy, France or Germany. No publishers in England were ready to bring it out unaided, though there was no lack of voluminous works like Bartholomew of Glenville's *De proprietatibus rerum*, or even Pliny's *Natural history*, on which publishers could make larger profits, given the wider market for encyclopaedic works in English. The Latin Classics were all brought in from the Continent and Pier de' Crescenzi's book, too, continued to belong to the category of goods imported for a fairly homogeneous group of readers, who went on using these works over a slightly longer period. In this, more restricted, English sample there is evidence that the work was read well after the year 1600. Thomas Knyvett, who discovered Guy Fawkes and his gunpowder in Westminster on the evening of 4 November 1605, wrote his signature in a copy of the book in 1610; Henry, Prince of Wales, son of James I,

---

[98] See F. Re, *Sulle opere agrarie*, p. 14; see also idem, *Dizionario ragionato di libri di agricoltura veterinaria e altri rami di economia campestre*, Venice 1802, and the manuscript version of this bibliography kept in Bologna, Biblioteca Universitaria. See also Ianus Dubravius, *De piscinis et piscium qui in eis aluntur naturis libri quinque . . .* , Zürich 1559, and the English translation as idem, *A new booke of good Husbandry . . .* , London 1599.

left a copy dating from before 1612, the year of his death; Thomas Wriothesley, Earl of Southampton, owned a copy in 1635, when he returned home after ten years spent in Holland and France; and, lastly, Thomas Belasyse, Lord Fauçonberg (1627–1700), determined supporter of Cromwell, though a Royalist after the Restoration, and ambassador to Italy signed his copy in 1677.[99] These are merely marks of ownership, unaccompanied by indications that the text was actually read. They designate a small group of people whose lives spanned the Stuart monarchy, the Civil War and the Restoration and who never moved away from the noble form of agriculture which was to be in such troubled waters in the mid-seventeenth century.

English readers showed an overall interest in the first six books of Pier de' Crescenzi, in the following order: on cultivation in general (book II), trees (book V), arable land and produce of the field (book II), the herb garden and the produce of the vegetable garden (book VI), the house and the good householder (book I), the vine and the care of wine (book IV). They read with a certain amount of care the book on hunting (book X), the one on animals (book IX), that on gardens (book VII), and the summary of the whole work (book XI). Not all readers dealt with the text in this way, but it is clear that the effort to learn was directed to some extent towards the fundamental parts of the work. Moreover, the cultural background was different here and the link between text and environment less direct. The owners who signed their names in their copies all seem to have belonged to the upper class, for example Guerardus Digby – Sir Everard Digby, one of the leaders of the unsuccessful Gunpowder Plot (1605),[100] liked to sign himself thus – as well as those mentioned above. Catholics and Protestants alike owned copies, even the English Jesuits had theirs.[101] We get most information from the oldest, anonymous copies; it is merely confirmed by the others.

A very early hand annotated a 1474 Louvain copy, carefully scrutinizing the index and numbering the chapters and pages of the whole volume.[102] Manuscript notes are added here and there. 'Wonderful experiments on the planting of trees' is the note to book II, chapter VIII, where the text speaks of the cultivation of wild trees. The reader goes on

---

[99] See *DNB*, *sub nomine*.

[100] See *ibid.*, vol. V, *sub nomine*.

[101] See in the following order: Cambridge, UL, INC.3F.2.2.3167, Louvain 1474; Cambridge, UL, INC.3F.2.2.3197, Louvain 1481; London, BL, C14 B.12, Louvain 1480.

[102] See Oxford, BO, Douce.

to chapter IX, on the same subject, noting where the author quotes Varro on grafting, trying to learn the use of the slip (*surculus*) and the wedge. Of the produce of the field, only wheat and beans interest him; indeed, he is only concerned with their pharmaceutical properties. He is attracted once more to grafting, on the vine (book IV, chap. XI), then he notes the qualities of cherries, according to Dioscorides and finally, after so much Latin, lapses into his mother tongue and *lactuca* and *plantagine* become *letyse* and *plantagenes* respectively (book VI, chaps. LXVI and XCI). Another very old copy, from Louvain (1480), which was to end up among the books of Leonard Plukenet (a botanist to the Queen at Hampton Court after the Restoration)[103] was probably annotated in the early sixteenth century. The anonymous reader carefully added the titles of the missing chapters in the index and made some short notes to some passages. He marked in ink the whole of book I, chapter II, on the reproduction of plants; then, again in the same book, in chapter VIII, where it speaks of grafting sprigs of blackthorn or cherry on to the willow, and how to get fruit without stones, he comments on the positive results of these practices. Though modern fruit-growers do not think such grafts are possible, we cannot but pass on this story, which purports to have been based on practical experience.[104] This reader also went through chapter IX, but seems to have made notes only of the parts he found most striking – the chapters on trees that do not bear fruit (book V), the kitchen-garden and herbs (book VI), the chapters on woods (book VII) and the rules of book XI. His was almost exclusively an interest in trees, fruit-bearing or not, cultivated or wild. Unfortunately, he gave no indication of which trees interested him most.

A contemporary copy, which at some time came into the hands of the Jesuits in England, provides more information. Everything seems to suggest that the underlinings and manuscript notes date from before 1580.[105] After a rather hesitant beginning on winds and waters, the

103 See London, BL, B.492010, and *DNB, sub nomine.*

104 We have already mentioned that Luigi Savastano (*Contributo*, p. 113) thought this way somehow possible, without considering it as a true graft. The shoot of the cherry or the plum-tree fastened into moist earth to strike root while attached to a parent plant, the willow in this case: it produced roots without becoming attached to the foot of the willow, and so eventually it bore fruit. This method is called 'layering' in English gardening practice, see *OED, sub nomine* (see also O. Rackham, *The History of the Countryside*, p. 181). Many of these hints on grafting are also mentioned by Giovanni Maria Bonardo, active around 1584: see S. Malavasi, *Giovanni Maria Bonardo agronomo polesano del Cinquecento*, Venice 1988, pp. 51–5.

105 See London, BL, C.14 B 12, Louvain 1480. Campion went on his mission to England in 1580.

markings go straight to book II, where the chapter on manuring is underlined. Once more in book II, chapter XI, on sowing, gives an interesting
indication of how the relationship between the moon and the growth of
plants was understood. Pier de' Crescenzi said that the moon could do in
a month what the sun does in a year. Our anonymous reader seized this
chance to give a clear explanation of this mysterious relationship and
added 'The moon goes through spring, summer, autumn and winter in a
month'. The chapter on manure was not read in vain, since it provided an
opportunity to note the harmful effects of using slurry from the pigsty as
manure (book II, chap. XXII). Only wheat, barley, beans and peas were
marked in book III, the main interest seeming to lie in the pharmaceutical
properties of these foods, very common indeed in the early sixteenth
century. It is no novelty that the book on the vine and the vineyard should
attract attention beyond the English Channel. We have emphasized this
elsewhere. Here the storing of grapes, fresh or dry, was underlined, and
how to make vinegar, the beneficial effects of vinegar and also of wine.
The main points of chapter I, book V, on trees, were marked in the
margin; then the cherry-tree, the fig, laurel, apple, rose, rosemary,
bramble and savin are underlined and annotated. The same procedure
was followed in book VI, where the reader studied everything that could
harm the vegetable garden and what could be done to defend it from ants,
mice and moles. Of the 130 plants described in book VI, he underlined
and annotated 52 common plants, such as garlic, wormwood, borage,
watermelons, cabbage, dill, gentian, liquorice, melons, mallow, mint,
mandrake, nasturtiums and others. They are too many to examine in
detail. He seems to have chosen the commonest produce of the kitchen-
garden and the wild herbs most generally used as remedies in his day;
the same criteria were used for fruit-trees and bushes. He also seems
to have had some trouble with his horse, and underlined and annotated
the chapters on horse diseases (book IX, chaps. X and XI). After the
colophon he added a further note in French on an ointment to be rubbed
under the horse's hooves in the evening, so that it would be free of any
sign of lameness in the morning. But it is no accident that the herbs
mentioned above should have been picked out from de' Crescenzi's vast
fund of botanical knowledge. A sixteenth-century hand, perhaps that
same doctor Balan, an early sixteenth-century mathematician,[106] who
signed his 1481 Louvain copy, underlined and annotated fifty-two
chapters of book VI. Both annotators marked plants such as garlic,

---

[106] See Cambridge, UL, INC.3F.2.2. (3198), and *DNB, sub nomine.*

wormwood, mugwort, watermelons, cabbages, cumin, wild pink, lily, mallow, mint, mangold, parsley and plantain. But doctor Balan, or whoever was annotating the book, persisted in his labours and suggested a whole series of common English names for these plants; *dylle*, for example, or *wormwoode, sorel, betony, goord, cammolyll*. His reading of the *Liber cultus ruris* did not end with the herbal; on the first flyleaf, at the beginning of the volume, he compiled a list of authors whom he clearly considered to be connected with the work – Columella, Bartholomew Glenville, Pliny, then Paulus Aegineta, 'Leonardus Arretinus supra politica' (that is, the translation and notes on Aristotle's *Politics*, by Leonardo Bruni) and Cato. He had underlined the titles in the index here and there, adding the numbers of the chapters of book I, and underlining the prescriptions and medicinal properties connected with the cypress, the ash and the rose. Lastly, he added a long handwritten note in the margin of book IX, chapter VI, on how to teach horses to amble; corresponding quite closely to the example mentioned above. Here we have the case of a doctor who connected the medicinal properties of plants and herbs with the healthiness of the environment and a well-chosen house.

Thus the reader seems to have been eager to find a connection between the botanical studies of Pier de' Crescenzi and the social-economic world that lay behind him. It is an approach to the text that we come upon again, both in certain pages taken from book VI – all that remains today of a copy probably published in Louvain – and in a Latin manuscript of the fifteenth century annotated either by a certain Thomas T . . . or by a William Rishworth, but in any case in the mid-sixteenth century.[107] This is a dated copy (1563) which cannot be overlooked, for it was obviously treated like a printed copy at a time when the important point was to examine a text that came from the Continent, as we shall see later (chaps. 5 and 6). An older hand had already annotated a good deal of book II, chapters VIII, XIII, VII, XIV and XV, on manure, the transmutation of one plant into another, the benefits of ploughing. The second hand completed the underlinings, reading the text from the same point of view

---

[107] See Oxford, BO, INC.C.N.97 1 (2), and Cambridge, St John's College, ms 25. One cannot help thinking that 'Thomas T . . . ' (the missing letters were clearly erased later) stands for Thomas Tusser, poet, musician and agricultural writer, then well connected with Trinity Hall, Cambridge. In 1563 his patron Lord Paget died, leaving him once more in financial trouble, hence a certain Mr Carter was asked for the considerable sum of 20 shillings for this manuscript, as we learn from a note on the flyleaf. For Tusser see *DNB, sub nomine*, and also below, chap. 6, 4.

and adding to books III, V, VI the English names of the plants that were considered of most interest. The botanical knowledge of this reader was that of a man of culture but not of science; he did not aspire to erudite discussion concerning identification, but simply listed varieties and common names. Among his definitions are that of spelt, 'Small corn which is like to zea which we call spelt', and of bean, *phaseolus*, which to him was simply 'kidney beans or Garden similar'.[108] He proceeded in the same way for trees, setting beside a Latin name its corresponding name in English; and when he came to the fig-tree, he made a very careful drawing of a leaf and two figs. He also added a marginal note that southernwood, placed under the pillow, 'stimulat venerem', and in book VI gave some short notes on pharmaceutical prescriptions. From here he went straight to book IX, on horse diseases – the English gentry's skill in treating them was becoming proverbial[109] – and then to book XI, where the various parts of plants and their reproduction are described. This combined interest in plants, horses and prescriptions for increasing the sexual urge was not uncommon, as we have already seen. One very illustrious reader has left us delicate underlining in chapter IV of book III, where chick-peas are mentioned because they were believed to increase potency. This was young King Edward, aged fifteen, born into a family obsessed with the question of the royal succession, whose tutors selected this choice Italian text for him. The king was known to be a diligent scholar; besides Latin, Greek and French he read and tried to write Italian. Here and there he formulated a few short phrases in his rather unformed hand. He wrote his initials 'E[duardus] R[ex]' between the end of book II and the beginning of book III, drawing an oak-tree with acorns quite charmingly between them. His underlinings are of no particular significance, yet it is touching to see the ailing youth linger over the chapter on the sicknesses of the hawk, which was a symbol of the ruling class.[110]

---

[108] The beans were of the *Dolichos* species, which the sixteenth century inherited from the ancient world; the South American bean (*Phaseolus vulgaris*) belongs to a different species and found its way into European fields from the dining tables of European royal families.

[109] See above all G. Markham, *Cavelarice [sic] or the English horseman: contayining all the arte of horsemanship*, London 1607, and J. Thirsk, *Horses in early modern England: for service, for pleasure, for power*, The Stenton Lecture 1977, University of Reading, 1978.

[110] See London, BL, 169.I.11.VI 1490. It is part of the King's Library and is stamped with George III's initials. The autograph has been identified thanks to Oxford, BO, ms Autogr.e.2, *Liber sententiarum . . . Edwardus*, 1548; ms Bodl 899, fo. 14*v*: 'E[duardus]

4.2. A scholarly East Anglian farmer

It is in a 1548 Basle copy of de' Crescenzi, however, that we come upon the greatest effort to read and learn to be found in the whole of our sample. From the handwriting, not always of the clearest, and from the context, it would seem that this anonymous reader was living in the mid-sixteenth century and was familiar with the Classical texts. He wrote fluent Latin, while his English spelling was very erratic, typical of his day.[111] Besides the marginal notes, typical of so many other readers, as they recalled what had been said in other parts of the book, this reader made additions of his own. He used the text of the *Liber cultus ruris* as a framework to give shape to his experience as an agriculturalist. On looking more closely into his notes, we find that very few pages of book I escaped his notice. After reading the parts on air, water, the site of the house, and the construction of wells and cisterns, he made his first addition, explaining lagoons, marshes and wells; further on, while commenting on how courtyards and threshing-floors should be arranged, he mentioned that whitethorn and blackthorn were used to plant hedgerows, a clear reference to the agricultural landscape of his time.[112]

The chapter on the good husbandman goes beyond conjecture and the odd note, to give a real picture of life on the land. He took great satisfaction in recounting the right time of year for every task, which it will be useful to come back to when we are dealing with the relationship between work and time. He pointed out that the slack winter season should be used for collecting wood, gathering the sheep into folds, digging lime-pits, besides routine jobs like breaking the ice on the drinking troughs. Then, in Latin, he added the work to be done on rainy days, quoting Pliny[113] to the effect that the bad husbandman does during the day what can be done at night, that he who does on working days what can be done on a holiday is worse; and worst of all is he who stays at home on a fine day instead of going to the fields. It was Pliny once again who reminded him that it is a bad farmer who buys what he can produce himself. He also made reference to Cato, and probably owned an

---

R[ex]', probably written in 1550; see also J. G. Nichols, *Literary remains of Edward VI*, Roxburgh Club, Oxford 1857, which gives various samples of Edward's signatures and says that the young king took up falconry in 1552.

[111] See Cambridge, UL, N * 8.16.

[112] *Ibid.*, pp. 5, 17.

[113] Pliny too, in *Naturalis historia*, XVIII 6, was following the example of Cato, *De agri cultura, Officia patris familiae.*

edition of the *Rerum Rusticarum Scriptores*, since he quoted the number of the page that interested him. He listed a whole series of tasks in a footnote: how to make traps for catching rats; how to make ropes, ladders and sacks; how to thresh; to whitewash the walls with well-soaked clay; to kill a pig and salt and smoke its meat; to make and mend rakes and hay-forks, shoes and clogs; how to repair the horse's harness; make new draught-yokes; repair the flail, the harrow and the plough; tidy up the courtyard; and keep the thatched roof in good repair against wind and rain. The good householder is justified in calling on his dependents to work at any time of the year or day, because he guarantees the survival of those who live under his roof, all the year round. Hence he is the owner of their time and now makes use of it from a clearly capitalist point of view, that is, to conserve his fixed capital.

Chapter II was the starting-point for going more deeply into the question of grafting. Once again the experiment of grafting blackthorn or cherries on the willow to get stoneless fruit did not pass unnoticed. Our reader was a scholar who quoted Theophrastus where Pier de' Crescenzi's text made no mention of him. Columella, Pliny, the herbalist Turner (whose inclusion means that the notes must be later than 1551 but no later than 1568, cf. Chap. 6, 1) are named among the first quotations and comments on the chapter on manure and the growth of plants; he was particularly interested in the connection between the moisture of the plant and the heat of the manure, which in de' Crescenzi's biology were two vital principles. He quoted the *Georgics* and Polydore Vergil and was very interested in loam. A propos of this he inserted a phrase from Columella II 16 'Si letaminis copia desit', and continued, in English, 'laye Sandd, yf you lack dong and marle'. Green manuring, by ploughing in lupins (which he rightly terms 'a pulse corn') did not escape his notice. In commenting on the chapter on seed he made another long note entitled 'Experience teaches', saying that rich, heavy soil produced more straw and you could not get more than a bushel of corn from fifteen sheaves; while on light soil straw was less abundant but you got two bushels of corn. This brought him to the heart of field cultivation (chap. XVIII), a suitable point for the introduction of a long note on ploughs and ploughing. He paid close attention to the problems of shallow ploughing and advised the use of a wheeled plough for stony ground. In the margin of the next page he pointed out that land ploughed for sowing should not be lowered too much, and described how to harness the horse to the plough, how to regulate it properly, and how the plough should be set with respect to the share and coulter. What at first sight might seem a scholarly, bookish reading, with a bent for Classical quotation, reveals, in fact, experience of practical farming. Though Pliny, XVIII 17 was the point of departure for discussing corn smut and his advice about always buying the best quality seed was included, it was backed up by the reader's first-hand knowledge of the poor germination rates of old corn seed.[114]

The notes on cultivation stop here and only start again when the text speaks once more about grafting that was capable of producing stoneless fruit.[115] Amazingly, this anonymous reader passed over the whole of book III on field produce as well as book IV on the vine. The notes become frequent again when the text speaks of animals, particularly horses, in which he shared the interest of so many other readers; in their teeth and the physical marks of a good horse.[116] By this stage we have a clear idea of where our reader's interests lay and the fairly common economic background to which they belonged. The section on sheep-breeding prompted him to write down his own remedy for goitre and swollen spleen. He also advised keeping ewes and rams separate, except in the breeding season, and being careful to have enough grazing land for ewes and lambs. Then he passed on to pigs and bees, noting that the best bees swarm in May, describing how to collect and care for them, and the remedies against bee-stings given by Petrus de Abano in his *De cura venenorum*, another surprising quotation. This brings us practically to the end. The last notes on shooting the wild goose, the snipe and the plover with the crossbow, on how to catch birds with lime, or fish in ponds, tell us nothing of importance; they are mere hints of a kind we have met with elsewhere.[117]

The reading has already covered household management, the cultivation of the fields, grafting, sheep-keeping and the care of the horse. In comparison with the chapters underlined by some of this man's contemporaries, it is not an original reading and for this very reason it is perhaps more significant. It does not reveal outstanding botanical knowledge, Classical doctrine or experience in agronomy. Our reader does not even seem to have owned a large Renaissance country house, since he spoke about tying and strengthening the typical East Anglian thatched roof. Yet he had a very definite economic plan. He considered

---

[114] Cambridge, UL, N * 8.16, pp. 31, 37, 38, 40, 47, 50, 51, 54.
[115] *Ibid.*, pp. 163, 263, 264, book VIII, chap. vii.
[116] *Ibid.*, pp. 266, 267, 272, book IX, chaps. i, vii, viii.
[117] *Ibid.*, pp. 308, 311, book IX, chaps. lxxiii–lxxiv; p. 311, book IX, chap. lxxvii; p. 328, chap. xcvii; pp. 331, 332, chap. xcix; pp. 344, 348, 357.

it his duty to organize his servants' and workers' time day by day and year by year, outlining his plan according to the resources of the region, corn-growing, sheep, the inevitable pig, bees, the horse, feathered game and the wildfowl from the marshes (it was only in the seventeenth century that the marshlands between Cambridge and the sea were drained). All this was part of a refined Classical culture not restricted to the odd quotation, but searching systematically for examples of good agriculture. It may be that his daily work of supervision prevented him from making a more extensive reading, and that many other readers who have left us brief indications and underlinings followed the same routine as he did. The text of the *Liber cultus ruris* encouraged people to confront directly a system that was based on a greater variety of natural features, partly because it was older, partly because it was Mediterranean. This confrontation took the form of reducing the herbal to a minimum of familiar botanical plants, exclusively composed of cultivated species. Elsewhere, the rule on which to found future operations was shrewdly culled from the theoretical chapters. The classics from the Continent were enjoying great fame in the mid-sixteenth century and many were to seek to obtain a copy of the original texts or the translations made towards the end of the century (see Chap. 5). It was Pier de' Crescenzi's fate to appear beside more recent texts for several decades to come. While the information provided by these texts was largely different from his, the technique of reading and learning adopted by so many readers underwent no change. The times had brought great institutional, economic and social changes and the new class of landowners who achieved status and in some cases nobility after the dissolution of the monasteries had only one way of maintaining their new social position and high incomes, by good administration of their estates, the keystone of a very subtle balance of forces.

5. CONCLUSION

Pier de' Crescenzi served European readers as a point of reference for the Mediterranean tradition. In some cases, as in France, and in Germany (which we have not dealt with in this volume), he became almost a national author. Actually the period over which his book on agriculture was used was much longer than the period with which we have been dealing, though after it ended we no longer get the same sympathy between text and reader that can be found in the seventeenth century. Yet in Bologna, in the mid-nineteenth century, reference was still being made to Pier de' Crescenzi's suggestions for improving the productivity of Bolognese agriculture by creating a model farm. Many of the problems which we have presented out of their European context, only in relation to the use of Pier de' Crescenzi's text, will be brought up again in the following chapters (Chaps. 4 and 5, for example). It is partly the great volume of material examined here that has made this separation inevitable. As the Soviet writer Bulgakov would have said, 'off-the-cuff' history is necessary to reexamine and correct opinions that cannot stand up to close scrutiny. The readers of the *Liber cultus ruris* have left us a portrait of themselves in its pages. They also saw themselves in parts of it. For example, they generally agreed on the duties of the master of the house, while they read other parts in a spirit nearer to their own requirements (see the botanical nomenclature and manuring), and they expressed their relation to the natural world in various ways (focusing on the hawk, the house or pharmacopoeia as the case might be). There emerges from their readings a world very much more varied than that to be found in manorial accounts. It is a world that reflects more middle-class expectations; it is linked with the direct production and consumption of goods and the care of the family, seen as a collection of people and material possessions. It gives a glimpse of man's intervention in, and action upon, the surrounding environment through production and harvesting, while keeping the balance between the resources of the wild environment and the world of agriculture.

3. *Lucerne in Italy*

1.TOWARDS A NEW SENSITIVITY TO NATURE

In the fifteenth century plants were classified as wild or cultivated, more or less as they are now. Noble, yeoman, and peasant owners alike built up the knowledge required for the cultivation of field and meadow from a long tradition of tilling the flower and vegetable garden. Gardens tilled for pleasure or food presented the same problems as those that faced the farmer using highly intensive labour. Fertile soil is the product of irrigation, tillage and manuring, the growth of the plants is checked continually in the course of the year, seed-time and harvest follow hard on each other; the flower and vegetable garden acts as a laboratory for experiments which it would be reckless to carry out straight away in the field. The canons of medieval agriculture combined food and medicinal herbs with flowers and ornamental trees and shrubs, practical use with delight. Gardens became the experimental ground for plants that would later be transferred to large-scale cultivation. Concern for health had moved Pier de' Crescenzi to deal with both cultivated plants and the wild ones invaluable to the good householder and most of all to those living in country places, where medicines were hard to come by. It is not surprising that health care should have been a constant concern of people who were barely self-sufficient, at a time of demographic recovery. However, wider issues were involved; the body is the tangible mediator of relations between the public and private spheres. Leon Battista Alberti defined health as the foremost honour to be presented in public. According to this great Florentine Humanist, health is achieved by a good diet, fresh air, physical exercise and a harmonious relationship with the seasons, with seeds, plants, flowers, fruits, including grafted cultivars. In an age when disease could destroy whole families and cities, the health–wealth–honour sequence, in which Alberti included health care, the use of wild and cultivated herbs and plants was seen as a link between the private and public spheres. Health became an asset just as much as the estate, the household or the storehouse.[1]

De' Crescenzi introduced his readers to 217 wild and cultivated plants in one of the largest works of medieval botany, encompassing field produce and cereals, fruit trees, trees grown for timber and medicinal herbs. He added exotic plants like rice (an addition in the Italian translation, Book III, chap. XXIV), pepper, papyrus and the palm to the list of known plants; but left only the mandrake among the plants proper to the medieval tradition, such as chickweed and moonwort. The inventory was large. Classical writers had catalogued a heritage of 408 indigenous, cultivated, naturalized and foreign plants. To these should be added a further 189 described in the medieval herbaria, for the West never had a medieval botanist as widely travelled as the twelfth-century Arab Ibn-el-Beithar. Actually a smaller number was generally used and described, as appears from Pier de' Crescenzi and the extant herbaria listing herbs like chickweed, moonwort, or the mandrake itself, which botanists now rightly assign to popular botany and mythology, not considering them as part of scientific botany.[2]

This knowledge was qualified by its institutional context – the flower or vegetable garden of the bourgeois home, of the great country house, the simples plot of a hospital or monastery, or the Vatican gardens. The horticultural rules of cultivation were the same, but it was the capacity to distinguish one botanical species from another which enhanced their economic or pharmaceutical value. Thus the absence of illustrations, of accurate botanical descriptions, made Pier de' Crescenzi's text a closed book to all but those who had some training in botany. The function of the medieval herbaria was to make plants easier to identify; so the *Tacuina sanitatis*, the illustrated and pharmaceutical equivalents of Pier de' Crescenzi's work, became more numerous in the fourteenth and fifteenth centuries.

The most advanced illustrated surveys are to be found in Lombardy

---

[1] On Italian gardens see Sereni, *Storia del paesaggio, passim*, and A. Tagliolini, *Storia del giardino in Italia. Gli artisti, l'invenzione, le forme dall'antichità al XIX secolo*, Firenze 1988. On Leon Battista Alberti see R. Romano and A. Tenenti, *Introduzione* to L. B. Alberti, *I libri della famiglia*, Turin 1969, pp. vii–xlii; D. Bonamore, *Prolegomeni all'economia politica nella lingua italiana del Quattrocento*, Bologna 1974.

[2] On botanical studies in Pier de' Crescenzi see Societa' agraria di Bologna, *Pier de' Crescenzi. Studi e ricerche*, Bologna 1933; see also P. A. Saccardo, *Cronologia della flora italiana*, Padova 1909, p. ix and appendix, and H. Fischer, *Mittelalterliche Pflanzenkunde*, München 1929, p. 47.

and the Po Valley, where the courts of Milan, Ferrara and Mantua were the stimulus behind the naturalists' work and the production and use of these manuscripts.[3] In the following pages we shall endeavour to trace the links between these three components, and to see how the same factors are reproduced at the European level. From the contacts between botanists and travellers it will also be apparent how much information was exchanged between the Mediterranean area and Northern Europe. Towards the end of the fifteenth century, Leonardo da Vinci introduced improvements in the representation of Nature and botanical studies were the first to benefit from them. He achieved a link between figurative art, which reproduced physical matter, and philosophy, which enquired into its inner properties or *virtù*. The connection between drawing and the herbals describing the properties of plants is clear; for the outer form was considered to be not unrelated to those inner qualities. In practice, the sixth part of Leonardo's *Treatise on Painting* is a study of the outer forms of plants (branches, roots, bark and the ribbing of leaves). But Leonardo's work does not stand alone in the fifteenth century; painters like Paolo Uccello (the Santa Maria Novella frescoes), and Sandro Botticelli (*La Primavera*), the Verona School and Bellini, all depicted plants in greater detail than anything found in the herbals of their time or of the preceding generation.[4] The document that most fully reflects this advance in the representation of Nature, in the course of the fifteenth century, is unquestionably the herbal of Nicolò Roccabonella. It passed,

---

[3] See on orchards and gardens D. Faucher, 'Les jardins familiaux et la technique agricole', *Annales (ESC)*, 14, 1979, pp. 297–307; M. Coulet, 'Pour une histoire du jardin', *Le Moyen Age*, 73, 1967, pp. 239–70; H. Bresc, 'Les jardins de Palerme (1290–1460)', *Mélanges Ecole Française de Rome. Moyen Age–Temps Modernes*, 84, 1972, pp. 55–127; G. Lais, 'I due orti botanici che successivamente fiorirono in Vaticano', *Atti della Pontificia Accademia dei Nuovi Lincei*, 32, 1879, pp. 63–78. On the *Tacuina Sanitatis* see especially L. Cogliati Arano, *Tacuinum Sanitatis*, Milan 1979; on courts and Humanism see *Il Rinascimento nelle corti padane. Società e cultura*, Bari 1977, and *La scienza a corte. Collezionismo eclettico, natura e immagine a Mantova fra Rinascimento e Manierismo*, Rome 1979. Finally on the figurative value of this kind of document see O. Paecht, 'Early Italian nature studies and the early calendar landscape', *Journal of the Warburg and Courtauld Institutes*, 1950, pp. 13–47. Furthermore one should remember the analysis of the flowers in the most famous of Botticelli's paintings, M. Levi d'Ancona, *Botticelli's Primavera. A botanical interpretation including astrology, alchemy and the Medici*, Florence 1983, and the large catalogue of symbolic botanical illustrations of Renaissance painting, idem, *The garden of the Renaissance: botanical symbolism in Italian painting*, Florence 1977.

[4] See Leonardo da Vinci, *Scritti letterari*, edited by A. Marinoni, Milan 1974, pp. 22–3, A. P. Macmahon, *Treatise on painting [Codex Urbinas Latinus 1270]*, Princeton 1956, and G. B. de Toni, *Le piante e gli animali di Leonardo da Vinci*, Bologna 1922.

at the end of the century, into the hands of the Venetian doctor Benedetto Rinio, and is generally named after him.[5] It also appears from this document that until the mid-sixteenth century the manuscript herbal still gives the best representation of the species studied, clearly superior to printed reproductions. Nicolò Roccabonella's herbal surpasses the traditional *Tacuina sanitatis* not only in the illustrations but in the text too. All those details on domestic economy, natural products such as wool, honey and wax, and details on the seasons have been cut out, and the text is linked with the Greek works that humanistic philology had made more readily available. So as well as Pliny and Pier de' Crescenzi there appear Galen and Dioscorides, besides the less well-known Serapion and Rufinus, and in place of the hundred or so specimens of the *Tacuina sanitatis*, here we have about four hundred plants described and illustrated.[6] But even more important is the nomenclature referring to the illustrations. The text was written by Roccabonella between 1415 and 1458 and the illustrations executed by A. Amadio, with a skill praised by John Ruskin. Moreover, this herbarium seems to have been used in the Testa d'Oro pharmacy at Rialto until the second half of the sixteenth century, and so some additions may have been made at a later date. Although the Italian names of the herbs are not given, it contains the Latin, Greek and Arabic names, to which the German and Serbian-Croat (*slavonice*) were added while doctor Roccabonella held a practice in Zara and came into contact with Slav and German people; further additions were probably made when the manuscript passed to the library of the monastery of San Domenico in 1604. So the document, which was easily available for consultation, was used to identify the local and foreign plants with which the people of Venice were becoming ever better acquainted, through the travellers and botanists who passed their way. Travel, Classical sources and first-hand experience were the means by which sixteenth-century botany enriched its heritage and succeeded in

---

[5] See Venezia, BN, mss Lat., VI, LIX, 2548, and E. de Toni, 'Il libro dei semplici di Benedetto Rinio', *Memorie della Pontificia Accademia dei Nuovi Licei*, V, VII, VIII, 1919–25; M. Minio, 'Il quattrocentesco codice Rinio integralmente rivendicato al medico Nicolò Roccabonella', *Atti dell'Istituto veneto di scienze, lettere ed arti*, 111, 1952–3, pp. 7–64.

[6] On the latter see Thorndike, *The Herbal of Rufinus*; on Serapion see below, note 12. In the fourteenth century the Greek monk Neophyte had copied a book for the seminary of Padua from the Constantinople text: see E. Mioni, 'Un ignoto Dioscoride miniato: il codice greco 194 del seminario di Padova', in *Libro e stampatori in Padova. Miscellanea di studi storici in onore di Mons. G. Bellini*, Padova 1959, pp. 345 ff.

becoming a science in its own right, while still supplying information on the economic exploitation of plants.

2. PRIVATE BOTANICAL GARDENS

The growth of botanical knowledge in the late fifteenth and early sixteenth centuries is connected with two circumstances, the inclusion of plant study in the faculty of medicine and the widening of the geographical environment. Pier de' Crescenzi's treatise itself pointed out how far the cultivation of medicinal plants was seen as part of good husbandry. The garden that the householder set out for domestic consumption grew into the herb-gardens of herbalists, doctors, monasteries, hospitals and princely courts. We recall once more the Roccabonella–Rinio herbal, the monastery of Vallombrosa near Florence, the gardens of the Gonzagas in Mantua and of the Este family in Ferrara and Modena. Lorenzo de' Medici himself tried his hand at farming at Poggio a Caiano.[7] Moreover, private gardens often served their purpose in teaching about simples, in the fourteenth century, in Salerno, Naples and Rome, where the study of medicine had developed, thanks to the medical school of Salerno, and encouraged by concern for the health of the prelates of the papal *curia*.

One key to the growth of botany as a science, which at the same time reveals distinct signs of interest on the part of individuals, lies in the date when the study of simples was instituted in the principal universities and when botanical gardens properly so called were founded. In Rome, in 1514, Giuliano da Foligno set out the botanical garden in the *Giardini Vaticani* which precedes by several years the study of simples in Pavia carried out by Leonardo Leggi (1520), in Bologna by Luca Ghini (1527) and in Padua by Francesco Buonafede (1533).[8] These were only the first steps and we know very little of the study of simples itself, yet we cannot but relate it to the increased interest in Nature being shown by scholars and landowners of the sixteenth century. This relationship is

---

[7] See above, note 3, and add G. B. de Toni, 'Notizie bio-bibliografiche intorno a Evangelista Quattrani, semplicista degli Estensi', *Atti del R. Istituto veneto di scienze, lettere ed arti*, 77/2, 1917–18, and A. Rochon, *La jeunesse de Laurent de Médecis (1449–1478)*, Paris 1967, p. 287.

[8] See in the following order Lais, *I due orti botanici*, V. Giacomini, *Alle origini della lettura dei semplici e dell'orto dei semplici e dell'orto botanico nell'Università di Pavia*, Pavia 1959, and A. Chiarugi, 'Le date di fondazione dei primi orti botanici del mondo', *Nuovo Giornale Botanico Italiano*, 60, 1953, pp. 785–839.

extremely clear in the case of Venice, where a patrician of the calibre of Ermolao Barbaro – mentioned by illustrious botanists such as the Bauhin brothers, Gesner, Fuchs and Tournefort – was writing commentaries on Pliny and Dioscorides. His is not an isolated case; to him must be added Daniele Barbaro, the famous Pier Antonio Michiel, Lorenzo Priuli, Francesco Molino as well as Filippo Pasqualigo, Torquato Bembo, Domenico Moro, Gaspare Gabrielli, Giacomo and Nicolò Contarini (the greatest expert on plants in Venice at that time and a patron of botanists). They all had private botanical gardens, either in Venice or on the mainland, during the first half of the century. But men of letters schooled in Padua, such as Pietro Bembo and Lodovico Beccadelli of Bologna, also showed a keen interest in botany and agrarian studies, derived from the reading and imitation of the Classics. As the horizons of the sixteenth century were widened by geographical discovery, the physical and naturalistic perception of the old Continent was also extended. In Venice alone, the Venetian ambassador Andrea Navagero, who had a villa in Selva and a botanical garden on the island of Murano, speaks in his letters to Giovanni Battista Ramusio of new botanical species he has seen in Spain (1525); he is one of the forerunners of botany in Italy, together with Ramusio, the aforementioned Pietro Bembo, the doctor Girolomo Fracastoro and Pandolfo Collenuccio. Here we have a group of men of letters, politicians and landowners moving in the direction illustrated by Pier de' Crescenzi's chapters on gardening, the reference work for so many anonymous readers of the sixteenth century (see Chap. 2).

It was a complex juncture. The botanist, in his capacity as herbalist, was also doctor and pharmacist and his profession put him in touch both with the natural environment and with the scholars reproducing the Classical texts of scientific knowledge. In Pier de' Crescenzi, Corniolo della Cornia, Roccabonella–Rinio and in the *Tacuina sanitatis* the study of plants from a Classical perspective had already been made available to the non-specialist, the ordinary householder. The herbalists and doctors of the early sixteenth century became editors of ancient texts to increase their own knowledge, hence the Greek authors were translated and published. After Dioscorides was made more accessible by Aldo's clear edition (1499), Marcello Virgilio and Ermolao Barbaro also analysed his work. In France, first Jean Ruell and, towards the middle of the century, Daléchamps made careful commentaries, and turned themselves into philologists in order to correct, interpret and create definitive texts that had often been corrupted by manuscript copying and so had become incomprehensible (see Chap. 4). Towards the end of the century

Pietro Andrea Mattioli wrote his commentary on Dioscorides, the first step in a successful career which was to culminate in his appointment as doctor to Emperor Ferdinand I. First William Turner, then John Gerard, followed similar paths in England (see Chap. 5). Only in the middle of the century were the volumes on botany completed by illustrations on the model of French and German publications. For several decades printers made a clear distinction between herbals (Besançon 1486–8, Pavia 1485, Rome 1481, Mainz 1484, 1485, 1491), which had reproduced medieval manuscripts like the *Circa Instans*, and the editions and commentaries on the texts of Classical literature. With the growth of botanical studies and competition among publishers issuing similar works, illustrations became an indispensable way for readers to identify and utilize plants.[9]

But the road to some consensus concerning the interpretation of traditional plants was to be long, and soon everyone was expected to make the journey to the Mediterranean. The botanist, by now seeking a system of general classification of plants, maintained the mark of the old simples-gatherer – the personal, first-hand search for plants. The journey in search of herbs prompted the scholar to describe his natural surroundings – on the lines of the only model that seemed clear and complete to him, that of Classical culture; hence the effort to identify the already-known species and to describe the new plants.

Thus the Mediterranean area, the environment in which Classical culture developed, served as a living reservoir of Classical civilization. Through the examples of the ancient world, it supplied the means of identifying everything in the field that had been forgotten, and at the same time it acted as a databank. Nature in the wild was what interested the botanist, who knew how cultivation can change the phytological features of plants. The path of Classical botany was followed in the mountains, on the coast and along the wayside. Yet only the simplest details survive of the almost religious procedures of the old simples-gatherer (recommended even by Leon Battista Alberti in the mid-fifteenth century),[10] who collected the plants he needed following a set ritual, now digging them up with iron tools, now with wooden ones, at certain times of day, in certain seasons of the year and using certain formulae. The plants sought out were wild, and the best specimens preferably came from the mountains, and were not hybrids. The

---

[9] In general see W. Blunt and S. Raphael, *The Illustrated Herbal*, London n.d. (1979) for botanical illustrations.
[10] See L. B. Alberti, *Scritti volgari*, edited by C. Grayson, Bari 1960, *La villa*, pp. 357–63.

relationship between wild and cultivated specimens that lay at the basis of the agriculture of de' Crescenzi's *Liber* presented, on a larger scale, the problem of domesticating wild species, and consequently spurred the growth of knowledge of natural history.

In the sixteenth century interest in nature also stimulated an intense and continual exchange between scholars and the upper class, while the journeys and investigations of botanists brought the popular tradition within this cultural exchange. The valuable contribution of private individuals and botanists was to make available those elements of popular knowledge in the various European regions that had escaped notice in the written tradition, and to place them in a perspective in which the Classics were still the point of reference. The early inclusion of plant study in the faculties of medicine and the setting up of botanical gardens as institutions, apart from the hospitals, facilitated the exchange of information and specimens at a European level, lending uniformity to European flora at least among professional botanists, their patrons, local scholars and the nobles who supported them. It was more difficult when the time came for the economic utilization of the plants, to establish links with agricultural producers, with those who used plants for cultivation beyond the boundaries of the herb garden. Yet garden cultivation was still fundamental to planning and experimentation in the growing of those species that were to prove of the greatest value for the agrarian economy. In the second half of the sixteenth century, from Pier de' Crescenzi's *Liber cultus ruris* onwards, botany became the foundation of agriculture. Moreover, botanical studies of the Mediterranean area became the means *par excellence* by which uniformity in European flora was achieved. At the same time, Mediterranean agriculture gradually became the theoretical model and point of reference for writings on agriculture in the second half of the century.

3. THE EARLY FIFTEENTH CENTURY

We have already mentioned in the Introduction that lucerne (*Medicago sativa*) was well-known in Classical botany, and that all the fundamental texts (Theophrastus, Varro, Columella, Palladius, Virgil, Pliny and Dioscorides) gave descriptions of it, or rules for its cultivation which were always included unabridged in the printed editions. Despite the fact that the herbals of Northern Italy took their text and illustrations from previous copies or from drawings made directly from plants, they never included lucerne. The various types of clovers (*T. acutum, pratense* and *bituminosum*), vetch and peas are the leguminous species generally found between the thirteenth and fifteenth centuries. Even in the early fifteenth-century Carraresi herbal, with Jacopo Filippo of Padua's translation of Serapion's commentary on the text of Dioscorides, in which both text and illustrations are most complete, there is no illustration of lucerne, although the red and white varieties of clover were very accurately drawn from life.[11] Probably the herbal compiled by Nicolò Roccabonella (see p. 99 above), the doctor from Conegliano Veneto, between 1415 and 1458, with fine illustrations by Andrea Amadio, which passed into the hands of the better-known doctor and pharmacist Benedetto Rinio, gives the first illustration of lucerne. It is a complex document, the first attempt to go beyond the traditional herbaria and try to identify a hundred new or little-known species. Roccabonella still wavered somewhat in the index (but not in the text), attributing the name *medica* both to *Melilotus officinalis* and to *Medicago sativa*, carefully using the works of Dioscorides, Serapion, Avicenna, Simon Genuensis and Mundinus to clarify the medicinal use of these leaves.[12] The fact that Pier de' Crescenzi is excluded from this list of sources, while his name appears elsewhere in the text of the herbal, suggests that the great medieval agronomist was perused more critically by his contemporaries than by posterity, and that by the Middle Ages only doctors and pharmacists, who had access to the older manuscripts of Dioscorides, Theophrastus and Serapion, knew how to identify lucerne.

[11] The so-called Carrara herbal (produced for Francesco Novello da Carrara, lord of Padua) was housed in Venice for some time after the Venetian conquest of Padua; then it passed into the library of Ulisse Aldrovandi and only in 1866 was it bought by the British Museum (where it is still kept: London, BL, Dept of Mss, Egerton ms 2020): the text quoted here was edited by G. Ineichen, *El libro agregà de Serapion. Volgarizzamento di Frater Jacobus Philippus de Padua*, Venice–Rome 1962, part I, text, I pp. 23 and 89.

[12] See Venice, BN, ms Lat. VI, LIX, 2548, cc. 152, 296 c.r. The herbal, which belonged to doctor Roccabonella and later to Benedetto Rinio, is a manuscript of 459 paper pages in quarto, praised by Ruskin and other art historians for the quality of its illustrations. Paecht, *Early Italian Studies*, pp. 30–1 was at times very scathing about it because of its evident (few) debts to the Carrara herbal. It should however be emphasized that the two documents are almost contemporary and that doctor Roccabonella illustrated and described at least one hundred new or little known plants. Apart from twenty plates which were copied from the Carrara herbal, the rest were drawn from life by Andrea Amadio and were much admired first by Pandolfo Collenuccio, then by Ulisse Aldrovandi, for their excellent quality. A third contemporary herbal was produced in the Veneto region, the Codex Bellunensis, XV s., London, BL, Add. ms 41623 (a page is reproduced in Blunt and Raphael, *The Illustrated Herbal*, pp. 78–9). These drawings are slightly inferior, but it too was copied from life: more than one plant is illustrated on each page, however lucerne does not appear on any of them.

It was not by accident that this plant was rediscovered in the Veneto region, for, as Servius mentioned in his commentary on Virgil, lucerne was very plentiful there. Moreover, when Venice conquered Crete in 1418 she became more interested in agriculture, as a necessary adjunct to the exploitation of the island, where the only forage crops grown were cultivated grasses. Taking this situation together with the semantic transformation of *medica* into *melica* (sorghum) – for which there is evidence from the ninth to tenth centuries in France, confirmed in Italy at least by the fourteenth-century translation of Palladius, which, as we have seen, continued sporadically until the mid-sixteenth century (see Chap. 1, 2.4) – we can reasonably suppose that lucerne had disappeared from large-scale cultivation in Italian agriculture. Pier de' Crescenzi may even have mistaken it for melilot; it was Roccabonella, who gathered simples in the fifteenth century, and was able to consult texts unknown to de' Crescenzi, who correctly established the difference between melilot and lucernes and eventually clover. Nor can we suppose that lucerne was known to de' Crescenzi simply because the Italian translation gives *cedrangola* (a Tuscan word for lucerne) where the Latin text, quoting Varro on bees, speaks of *cytisus*, for this is no more than a bad translation.[13]

Lucerne also appears regularly in unpublished texts of fifteenth-

[13] The Dizionario dell'Accademia della Crusca of 1605, brought out by 'Nferigno' (Bastiano de Rossi) also kept 'cedrangola' for *cytisus* (*Liber cultus ruris*, IX, xcviii) without describing it as a grass. Corniolo della Cornia, the first to correct the text of Pier de' Crescenzi, realized that 'cedrangola–citrangola' was not the *cytisus* of the ancients. Corniolo correctly associated 'cedrangola' with the *Citrus* species and other fruit trees (*Divina villa*, V, xiv) and added another chapter on *cytisus* (*ibid.*, lii) drawn from the *Geoponics* and Varro, in which it was clear that he understood that this new plant was used as litter and fodder. Gianvettorio Soderini wrote to the same effect, see *Il trattato degli arbori, inedito della fine del XVI secolo* (Bologna 1904, edited by A. Bachi Della Lega) pp. 354–5, explaining that 'cedrangolo' was a kind of citrus tree. Probably the Italian translator of de' Crescenzi mistook *cytisum* for another herb mentioned by Soderini as 'cetronella or melissa', see idem, *I due trattati dell'agricoltura e della coltivazione delle viti*, Bologna 1902, vol. II, pp. 83–4. Melissa was not mentioned by de' Crescenzi. The *cytisus* of the ancients was identified for the first time as *Medicago arborea* by Bartolomeo Maranta, *Methodi cognoscendorum simplicium libri tres*, Venice 1559, and then taken up by S. Switzer, *A dissertation on the true cytisus of the ancients*, London 1731. Both plants, *cytisus* and *cetronella*, as well as sainfoin, lucerne and clover, were known to produce excellent honey (see *L'abeille, l'homme, le miel et la cire*, Musée national des arts et traditions populaires, Paris 1981, pp. 191–4) and probably this led to more confusion between the two. However in more recent times too O. Penzig, *Flora popolare italiana*, Genova 1925 and L. Palma, *Le piante medicinali in Italia*, Turin 1964 repeated unquestioningly this transformation of *cedrangola*, a citrus tree, into *cedrangola*, a grass.

century agronomy. Corniolo della Cornia, the patrician of Perugia, who wrote in the first half of the century, devoted a whole chapter of his *La Divina Villa* to it (VII, 4). And this careful author did not repeat the error of taking it for sorghum. Examination of the text confirms our suggestion that the author was a cultured man setting out to complete and correct Pier de' Crescenzi's agricultural system, with Columella's *Res rustica* at his disposal, in one of the many fifteenth-century manuscripts (see p. 67). His chapter on lucerne follows the text of Pliny almost literally (*Naturalis historia*, XVIII 144–48) to about the middle of the chapter, then it passes to a summary of Columella (II 10–25) and finally to Palladius. The only personal contribution Corniolo made was in the nomenclature ('La medica . . . vulgarmente dicta silla'), but he made an error of enormous interest, since he gave the correct name of the grass (*Hedysarium coronarium*) which had probably taken its place and for which we have evidence in the Siena region in the second half of the sixteenth century.[14] He quoted Serapion, Avicenna and Isidore of Seville, as Roccabonella did. The development of botany and agronomy derives not only from direct experience, which in the case of lucerne seems to have been non-existent (for example, he made no mention of seed-gathering, essential as it is to plant reproduction), but also from texts which Humanists and translators were making ever more widely available.

Michelangelo Tanaglia, writing at the time of Cosimo de' Medici, in verses which seem to have been based on Palladius or at most on Columella, said simply 'In that month (April) lucerne seed used to be cast onto the land . . . ' (lines 1092–3). This Florentine official, another erudite gentleman, a connoisseur of ancient matters, as the times required, used the past tense intentionally, to indicate that this cultivation had fallen into disuse. Even a poet-official who imitated the *Georgics* in honour of the Medici family was capable of avoiding the common pitfall. Knowing his Classics, he did not turn *medica* into *melica* as the translators and copyists of the time of Andrea Lancia did, though he kept his distance from the ancient text and put his readers on their guard.[15]

In short, the herbals of Rinio, Corniolo della Cornia and Michelangelo

---

[14] See Bonelli Conenna, *La Divina villa*, *passim* and pp. 386–7. Around 1560 P. A. Michiel (see below, note 33), used the name 'sulla' for lucerne when he mentioned fodder crops in the Siena district. On the 'sulla–medica' substitution see below, note 56. On the life-span of a lucerne field in the province of Perugia see A. Vivenza, *Stazioni sperimentali agrarie italiane*, 47, 1914, pp. 97–117.

[15] M. Tanaglia, *De agricultura*, edited by A. Roncaglia, with an introduction by T. de Marinis, Bologna 1953.

Tanaglia have left us fascinating evidence of contemporary attitudes to a plant which could still be found in its wild state, while it had obviously once been cultivated and held in great regard. All three proceeded in the same way, comparing the best texts of Greek botany, which led to the identification of a botanical species that had gone wild and been forgotten. The simples-gatherer merely identified and collected the wild plant; the agronomist had to fit it into an economic system wherein he foresaw its use and hence also had a rough idea of the costs and returns its cultivation would involve.

4. BOTANISTS, SIMPLES-GATHERERS AND LANDOWNERS

This difference in the approach of simples-gatherers and agronomists was to become more evident in the early sixteenth century. The gap between the two categories was to some extent bridged by de' Crescenzi's widely read text on agriculture. His book VI, on herbs, was a reasonable substitute for the *Tacuinum sanitatis* so long as the number of plants described remained within certain limits. But no sooner did the critical study of Greek and Latin botany begin, and with it the procedure for the identification of the species described by Dioscorides, Theophrastus, Serapion and Pliny, than a new kind of text sprang up. Rinio's herbal was the first to appear. Fifteenth-century publishers produced herbals such as the *Platearius, Apuleius Platonicus, Hortus sanitatis* and the *Grand herbier* (Rome 1481; Meinz 1484, 1485, 1491; Besançon 1486–8) to name only a few. Though they appeared in quick succession and sold well, they were of little scientific consequence. Then, in the early sixteenth century, a good number of illustrated, printed herbals and editions of Dioscorides were brought out, in line with the new Humanist studies. Once the Aldine edition of Dioscorides (1499) was available, scholars from Northern Europe were no longer forced to go to Italy to study Classical botany.[16] The old practice of gathering

---

[16] Erasmus made a similar comment to Aldo Manuzio with regard to the editions of Euripides and Sophocles: see E. L. Eisenstein, *The Printing Press as an Agent of Change*, Cambridge 1979, vol. I, p. 180. On foreign students in Italian universities see L. C. Bollea, 'Gli studenti ultramontani nell'Università di Pavia', in *Universitatis Ticiniensis Saecularia undecima*, Pavia 1925, and idem, 'British Professors and Students at the University of Pavia', *Modern Philology*, 23, 1925, 2, pp. 236 ff. On the medieval and Renaissance translations of Dioscorides see C. E. Dubler, *La Materia Médica de Dioscorides. Transmission medieval y renacentista*, Barcelona 1953–9, 6 vols.

fresh specimens of herbs to 'explain the simples' at university lectures was quickly dropped after students began to collect their own herbaria, under the guidance of Luca Ghini in Bologna.[17] Leonardo had already made detailed studies of the characters of botanical species using physiotypy (that is, pressing specimens on blackened sheets of paper to produce a 'negative' of the plant). He was followed by sixteenth-century artists who drew plants from life. Better printing methods and woodcuts brought further progress. The engravings of Otto Brunfels (1532) and Leonard Fuchs (1542) provided a model for Pietro Andrea Mattioli (1554) and many others throughout the century.[18]

Besides featuring as a part of the development of botany as a science in its own right, these works also served to illustrate the texts of Classical agronomy published in those years in cheap editions in Venice and Lyons, and the many editions of Pier de' Crescenzi. The description of the principal botanical features of wild and cultivated flowers was more complete in the new botanical texts than in those on medieval agronomy. The text and illustrations, drawn from life, from the Roccabonella–Rinio herbal to the early sixteenth century, showed how necessary it was to bring botanical studies up to date in agricultural treatises too. Their common origins (Classical science) and the Mediterranean environment made it easier to assimilate this information. It should be remembered that the physical world known to, and controlled by, man was growing in the sixteenth century. At that time the botanist and naturalist had the fundamental task of defining the natural environment, as the physicist, chemist and geographer have today. It was a complex period, because, as we have already pointed out, their spheres of action overlapped and it

---

[17] See De Toni, *Le piante e gli animali in Leonardo*, p. 25. On the first herbaria see J. Camus, 'Histoire des premiers herbiers', *Malpighia*, 5, 1895. It is said that an English student, John Falconer, showed the Portuguese Amatus Lusitanus the first collection of dried plant specimens glued on paper. The technique was also described by G. Targioni-Tozzetti, *Notizie sulla storia delle scienze fisiche in Toscana cavate da un manoscritto inedito*, Florence 1852, pp. 105–6 in his comment on a late fifteenth-century herbarium, the property of the Biblioteca Riccardiana.

[18] The practice of physiotypy consisted in producing a negative copy of the venation of the leaves, which were covered in soot and then pressed on paper. See T. A. Sprague, 'The herbal of Otto Brunfels', *Journal of the Linnean Society, Botany*, 48, 1928, and T. A. Sprague and E. Nelmes, 'The herbal of Leonard Fuchs', *Journal of the Linnean Society, Botany*, 51, 1931. On Andrea Mattioli see below, note 24. See also in general G. Olmi, 'Osservazione della natura e raffigurazione in U. Aldrovandi', *Annali dell' Istituto storico germanico in Trento*, 3, 1977, pp. 105–82 and Blunt and Raphael, *The Illustrated Herbal*, pp. 141 ff. For a catalogue of illustrated species in Italian painting see again Levi d'Ancona, *The Garden of the Renaissance*.

would be too easy to relegate botanists and simples-gatherers to the wild environment and agronomists and agriculturalists to that of cultivation. Both groups depended on wild plants, one to reproduce the ingredients for medicines, the other for grafting and cultivation. For nature in the wild is a huge reserve of botanical species and varieties uncontaminated by cultivation, humus or moisture. The growth of our botanical heritage in the course of the sixteenth century was so great that at least a reorganization of the system became imperative:[19] 1,171 native Italian, natural and domesticated species were identified and 127, cultivated and domesticated, brought in from abroad.

This great mass of data to be checked and classified meant that botanists and herbalists had to produce a new framework for their studies. They were aware of the limits of the old nomenclature, in reality popular nomenclature taken over by the scientists, and the lack of any real classification made by individual scholars on the basis of external features or the various uses to which the plants were put. Andrea Cesalpino introduced the first binomial nomenclature, of genus and species, to supply this want. Agronomists and landowners increased the number of cultivated plants, chiefly by using local varieties, best suited to the climatic and pedological conditions in their region, but also by bringing new, exotic plants into the country; maize, tomatoes, potatoes, tobacco and the American bean (*Phaseolus vulgaris*) to name only the most widely known among them. These plants were imported as rarities and grown in private and botanical gardens before they were used in the field. When botanical gardens became public institutions a vast botanical heritage was preserved and made available for study, while exchanges and discussion with European institutions and scholars were much improved. Just as travel was the commonest means by which new species were imported, so journeys were made by all the botanists of the century, in the first place to find and describe the local flora, then to compare them with the Classical texts. As we have already pointed out, it was by comparing the wild species with the ancient texts that the limits of Classical botany were recognized and the vast number of new, indigenous species was understood. By looking more closely into the phases by which lucerne was identified in Italy, we get an insight into the relations between ancient and modern, wild and cultivated plants, local and foreign ones, and between botanists and agriculturalists of the sixteenth century. Thanks to the writings of the botanists we shall be able

---

[19] See Saccardo, *Cronologia della flora italiana*, p. ix.

to reconstruct a chronology of this reintroduction of lucerne into Italy with some certainty.

5. LUCERNE RETURNS TO ITALY AS SPANISH GRASS

Lucerne never actually disappeared. It would be truer to say that it went wild and its phytological characters were forgotten until, with the development of botany described above, it could be rediscovered and recognized once more. How many people were capable of or interested in recognizing lucerne in the early sixteenth century? Ermolao Barbaro first tried his hand at growing it between the late fifteenth and early sixteenth centuries. He recalled how widespread it had been in the Venezie regions in late Classical times, how it disappeared, and told of his own efforts to reintroduce it. He insisted that very few people in Italy had seen it in his day and that no one really knew what it was. Finally he claimed that it had been brought into the Campania region from Africa (*sic*). Perhaps he was thinking of the Arabs who brought lucerne from North Africa into Europe when they conquered Spain, and who had continued to grow it with care until the early sixteenth century.[20]

Lucerne escaped the notice of even the observant Andrea Navagero, who should be numbered among the forerunners of Italian botany, though not a botanist himself. In 1525 this Venetian patrician travelled, as an ambassador, on horseback from Barcelona to Seville, through countryside where lucerne was commonly grown as forage by the Arab farmers, without noticing it. Yet he did note that carrots (*zanahorias*) were used to feed horses in the area round Toledo. He promised to bring back specimens of herbs and rare fish for his correspondent Giovanni

---

[20] On Ermolao Barbaro see *Dizionario biografico degli italiani, sub nomine*; his comment on Dioscorides, idem, . . . *P. Dioscoridis A. de medicinali materian ab eodem Barbaro latinitate primum donati* . . . , Venice 1516, 2 vols. in folio, was often published outside Italy: see Ioannes Ruellius, *P. Dioscoridis libri VIII, una cum Ermolai Barbari Corollarij et Marcelli Vergili* . . . , Strasbourg 1529, fo. 133*v*, or else Ermolao Barbaro, *In Dioscoridem corollariorum libri V* . . . , Cologne 1530, fo. 40*r*; and the critical edition *H. B. Castigationes Plinianae* . . . , Patavii 1973. Marcello Virgilio or rather Marcello Adriani son of messer Virgilio, was urged by Lorenzo il Magnifico to make an Italian translation of the copy of Dioscorides brought to Florence after the fall of Constantinople. Although he was not a doctor, he dealt expertly with the subject (see Targioni-Tozzetti, *Notizie*, pp. 107–10). Marcello Virgilio had also owned the Latin-Longobard version of Dioscorides that we have mentioned above (see Introduction, p. 7, and note 10). On cultivation in Spain and Arab-Andalusian treatises see Bolens, *Les méthodes culturales*, pp. 124 ff.

Battista Ramusio and to look out for ancient names (Toledo, 20 February 1526). Nevertheless, at least in the notes that have come down to us, he makes no mention of lucerne.[21] While in Venice the pharmacist Rinio was the first to offer his customers an illustration of lucerne, it was from Bologna that botanical interest in it was spread.

For it was Ludovico Beccadelli of Bologna, another traveller, cleric, diplomat and man of letters, who brought lucerne seeds to Italy from Spain. He went there early in 1539 as secretary to the English Cardinal Reginald Pole, envoy of the Pope to Charles V. Pole had been sent to negotiate conditions for breaking off the trade agreements between the Empire and the England of Henry VIII, then in open conflict with the papacy. After the failure of this mission, Pole and Beccadelli stole away from Spain, stopping at Carpentras, the administrative capital of the papal enclave in Provence, where they were the guests of Giacomo Sadoleto, then bishop of Avignon. As he visited the spots associated with Petrarch, Beccadelli's eye probably fell on lucerne, which was already beginning to spring up in gardens along the Rhône. It was no accident that lucerne returned to Italy from Spain via Provence and Avignon. On his return to Italy Beccadelli did little to spread his discovery. He certainly sowed it in the grounds of his villa at Pradalbino. He gave a few seeds to Luca Ghini, who was then lecturing on botany in Bologna (1527–44) and was the recognized master of the whole Italian school of botany in the first half of the sixteenth century; he grew it until the middle of the century.

In 1551 Pietro Andrea Mattioli was working on the second edition of his commentary on Dioscorides, which had come out in Latin in 1548, without illustrations. The edition was far from complete, for he was to work on it for the rest of his life. Mattioli needed a note on various specimens, including lucerne, described by the Greek botanist. He must have written to Luca Ghini for help, for in 1551 Ghini answered him, recalling Beccadelli's role in the rediscovery of lucerne. From the seeds Beccadelli brought from Spain in 1539–40 he had grown a plant still alive in 1551. A contemporary reader added in the margin of this letter, 'Tempore mirabiliter generat'. Mattioli was less fortunate. He got seed from friends, perhaps from Ghini himself, but nothing grew, though he

---

[21] See A. Navagero, *Lettere scritte dalla Spagna a Giovan Battista Ramusio*, Venice 1563; the original manuscript is in Venice, BN, ms it., VI, CX, 5902; see also M. Cermenati, 'Un diplomatico naturalista del Rinascimento', *Nuovo archivio veneto*, n.s., 13, vol. 24, 1912. On lucerne, called alfalfa in Spanish, see below, note 37.

sowed them with care. As a partial excuse, he added that truly in his day very few people had seen lucerne, or got results after sowing it.[22]

The Englishman William Turner called Ghini 'my master' and spoke of his teaching in several places. Turner was one of the young European botanists for whom the journey to Italy was a fundamental stage in their professional training. In 1548, the same year when Mattioli's second edition was published, he compared the European nomenclature of various medicinal herbs, gave some information on lucerne and added that it grew in many places in Italy. However he was not in great disagreement with Mattioli. Like Ermolao Barbaro before him and Luigi Anguillara after his time, he said that it grew, not that it was cultivated. His evidence is further complicated since, when writing about the same plant at greater length in 1568, he no longer remembered having seen it in Italy, but in Germany, near Speyer and, what is more, that it had yellow flowers.[23]

To sum up: the Roccobonella–Rinio herbal showed us lucerne with blue-mauve flowers. Luca Ghini said the flowers of the plant grown from the Spanish seeds were deep red, Turner claimed that lucerne flowers were yellow. At first sight it seemed as if the problem could never be solved. According to Dioscorides, lucerne looked like clover with horn-shaped pods (the English 'horned clover'), but he said nothing about the colour of the flower. The good sixteenth-century botanist had to base his identification on two certain features, leaving agreement on the third to chance, or else he had to rely on his own experience and faith in his master. He abandoned the system of textual criticism to lean on knowledge guaranteed by the esteem in which the master was held. This

---

22 On Beccadelli see *Dizionario biografico degli italiani, sub nomine*; G. Fragnito, *Memoria individuale e costruzione biografica Beccadelli Della Casa Vettori*, Urbino 1978; idem, 'Per lo studio dell'epistolografia volgare del Cinquecento: le lettere di Ludovico Beccadelli', *Bibl. d'Humanisme et Renaissance. Travaux et documents*, 43, 1981, pp. 61–87; idem, *In museo e in villa. Saggi sul rinascimento perduto*, Venice 1988, pp. 65–108. Copies of the correspondence between Mattioli and Ghini are in Bologna, BU, ms Aldrovandi 98 vol. II; see also G. B. de Toni, *I Placiti di Luca Ghini intorno a piante descritte nei Commentari al Dioscoride*, Venice 1907, pp. 9, 12, 13; P. A. Mattioli, *Commentarii secundo aucti in libros sex Pedacii Dioscoridis*, Venice 1554, p. 305. Beccadelli might have got a supply of lucerne seeds in Carpentras, but the colour of the flowers, red rather than purplish-blue like Provençal lucerne, warns that it must have been what was known at the time as Dioscorides' true lucerne.

23 See W. Turner, *The names of herbes in Greeke, Latin, English, Dutche and Frenche* . . . , London 1548, and idem, *The second part of the Herbal*, London 1568, pp. 51*v*–53*r* (see pp. 265–7). The plant with yellow flowers probably was *Medicago lupulina*, trefoil in more recent English; see below, n. 31 on the herbal of Pietro Antonio Michiel.

happened in Ghini's case, then in the case of Mattioli and Aldrovandi. What is more, Dioscorides himself was often seen as too restrictive. Luigi Anguillara, director of the Botanical Garden of Padua, another of Luca Ghini's students, wrote frankly, 'I know many species of lucerne, but not that described by Dioscorides . . . The species with the purplish seed is called alfalfa in Spain today'.[24] By now it was clear that Classical nomenclature could only be used to classify geographically determined plants from the area where the ancient botanists had been active, while different species existed in other European regions, especially in the Mediterranean area. Thus Anguillara considered that the colour of the flower was not relevant to the definition of lucerne, but focused on the presence of seed, and hence on the specimens capable of reproduction, which did not merely spring up from runners of the bushy plant.

The point of contact between the botanist and the agriculturist of the sixteenth century, when they were confronted with a new plant, lay in the chances of controlling its growth and fruit-bearing and introducing it into an organic scheme of cultivation. Misunderstanding might arise between the two groups because of the terminology they used – that of the botanist being precise, scientific, without alternatives, that of the agriculturalist using everyday expressions, which underwent all the variations common in such language. Indeed, it is to the botanists' credit that they recorded the imprecise regional language of European agriculture and thus left us a very important testimony of the new economic organization of nature that sixteenth-century man was endeavouring to establish.

6. PRACTICE AND THEORY, SOME POINTS OF CONFLICT

Problems concerning the identification of botanical species brought out, more and more, the botanists' conflict of opinion with, and distancing from, the cultured but non-specialized reader. Throughout the century botanical writings were addressed to men of science, doctors, pharmacists or young botanists rather than directly to landowners in search of a printed text which would help them to come to terms with nature. This

---

[24] See L. Anguillara, *Semplici dell'Eccellente L. A. li quali in più pareri a diversi nobilihuomini scritti appaiono*, Venice 1561, p. 118. Anguillara had little success partly because of the fierce competition from Mattioli, who had called him 'eel-skinner', a mocking reference to his name. A second edition of his work came out only in 1611, in fact nothing but a reprint with a new frontispiece.

needs to be pointed out, to put the problems connected with the spread of lucerne into perspective. A wider range of grasses existed, with certain characters in common, which must be kept in mind. When speakers were not scientists, but had an approach based on the utilization of a species rather than its definition, the metonym became very common.

Lucerne, cytisus, laburnum, melilot, clover, vetch and *onobrychis* can be used as alternatives to grass, according to the quality of the soil. Columella placed them in the following order – lucerne, vetch, barley, oats, fenugreek, lentil and wild pea (II 10). Most of our information on the spread of lucerne dates back to the second half of the sixteenth century. When Ulisse Aldrovandi made his famous journey with other botanists to the Sibilline Mountains in 1557 he found neither lucerne nor trefoil; and he only found cytisus and melilot in the private botanical garden of Giulio Moderato, a pharmacist of Rimini. Later, when Aldrovandi made his catalogue of herbs from the Bologna countryside, he did not include lucerne, though many specimens of clovers and melilot were included. A decade later, when the Frenchman Jean Pona was herb-gathering on Monte Baldo, he only found cytisus and birdsfoot trefoil, which Dioscorides had described.[25] The difficulty of finding lucerne is apparent from its virtual absence in herbaria and illustrated herbals; the uncertainty of its naming and identification is evident from the inclusion in the herbals of similar leguminous plants. It is to be found in the herbals of the Biblioteca Angelica in Rome, but not in the older volume (Erbario A), nor in the herbarium made in Ferrara for Alfonso d'Este, which focuses on ornamental plants and horticultural species. Andrea Cesalpino wrote that lucerne was sown in Spain and often deteriorated (1582). Nos. 437, 440 of the Cesalpino herbarium are specimens of various kinds of lucerne, placed next to clovers, *onobrychis* and other forage crops. It is above all in the volumes commenting on Ulisse Aldrovandi's herbarium that we find, together with a great variation in nomenclature, the problems of identification posed by the

---

[25] See G. B. de Toni, 'Spigolature Aldrovandiane. Il viaggio e le raccolte botaniche di U. Aldrovandi ai Monti Sibillini nel 1557', *Memorie della R. Accademia di scienze, lettere ed arti di Modena*, 3/8, Appendice; Bologna, BU, ms Aldrovandi 143, tomo II, cc. 2r–20; Joannes Pona, *Plantae seu simplicia quae in monte Baldo et in via ab Verona ad Baldum reperiuntur*, Antwerp 1601: the journey was made in the company of Francesco Calceolari, who left his own account in 1566. See also G. Olmi, 'Ulisse Aldrovandi. Scienza e natura nel secondo Cinquecento', in *Quaderni di storia e filosofia della scienza*, 4, Trento 1976, and idem, 'Natura morta e illustrazione scientifica', in F. Zeri and F. Porzio (eds.), *La natura morta in Italia*, Milan 1989, vol. I, pp. 69–91.

great Bolognese scientist. It was only in 1591 that the lucerne described by Dioscorides, which Anguillara declared he had never seen, was sown in the Botanical Garden in Padua, together with other specimens of the species, by G. A. Cortusi, Anguillara's successor.[26] At that time lucerne was popularly known as 'erba Spagna' ('Spanish grass') in the country-side round Siena and Bologna, a clear indication of its foreign origin.[27]

Such cases of erroneous geographical attribution were not uncommon in the sixteenth century. French disease and Turkey corn, for syphilis and maize are the two best-known examples. Once again it was Aldrovandi's papers that cleared up the mystery, showing that Spain was the constant source of supply for lucerne seed. The first time he got in touch with correspondents in the Spanish peninsula he seems merely to have been writing on behalf of Luca Ghini, to ask for a list of grasses and seeds, lucerne among them. In response Brancion, gentleman at the court of Spain and later director of the Botanical Garden of Malines, sent many lists of seeds, specimens of plants, carefully prepared packets of seeds with written instructions on how to grow them, on many occasions in 1567 and 1568. There was practically no communication between Brancion and Aldrovandi without the dispatch of some variety of lucerne, besides many species of clover and cytisus. With regard to *trebol real* and lucerne, the quoted correspondent wrote, 'they are to be sown at the end of February, in not very wet soil'; and went on to give the general rule about sowing in good, well-manured soil and to regulate the watering according to the severity of the winter.[28] Thus Brancion was

---

[26] See O. Penzig, *Contribuzioni alla storia della botanica*, I, *Illustrazione degli erbari di Gherardo Cibo . . .* , Milan 1905; on the complex story of the attribution of these herbaria see also E. Chiovenda, 'Francesco Petrollini botanico del secolo xvi', *Annali di botanica*, 7, 1909, that summarizes the whole question. J. Camus and O. Penzig, 'Illustrazione del ducale erbario estense', *Atti della Società Naturalisti di Modena*, ser. III, 4, 1885. Andrea Cesalpino, *De plantis libri XVI*, Florence 1583, and Th. Caruel, *Illustratio in hortum siccum Andreae Cesalpini*, Florence 1858. G. B. de Toni, 'Illustrazione del secondo volume dell'erbario di U. Aldrovandi', *Atti del R. Istituto veneto di scienze, lettere ed arti*, 67/2, 1908; idem, *Illustrazione del terzo volume . . .* , Genoa 1908; idem, 'Illustrazione del quarto volume . . . ', *Atti del R. Istituto veneto di scienze, lettere ed arti*,71/2, 1911, G. A. Cortusi, *L'Horto dei Semplici dove si vede primeramente la forma di tutta la pianta*, Venice 1591.

[27] See E. de Toni, 'Luigi Anguillara e Pietro Antonio Michiel', *Annali di botanica*, 8, 1910. In the summer of 1983 the present writer did hear 'erba spagna' for 'erba medica' at Romena, a village in Casentino, Tuscany.

[28] See Bologna, BU, ms Aldrovandi, 56, II, cc. 453*r*–458*v*, 458*r* on the quotation, cc. 460–61 on Ghini and Mattioli; see also *ibid.*, letters 136, I: April 1567, 22 September 1567, 17 February 1568, 16 March 1568; *ibid.*, III: 15 April 1568, 22 July 1568; *ibid.*, 143, II, cc. 56*r*–72*v*.

passing on valuable information, which came down from the grand days of Andalusian agronomy – that the quantity of water given to plants should be in proportion to the heat of the soil. Thus it appears that lucerne spread in the Mediterranean area where irrigation could best be carried out, and this was connected with a climate which heated the soil to varying degrees, so that irrigation regulated the heat of the soil and encouraged plant growth. Other Spanish correspondents of Aldrovandi were a pharmacist called Bergaso, the papal envoy to Philip II, Bishop Rossano, in Madrid, and a doctor called Micon de Viez in Barcelona.[29] But these seeds sent from Spain must merely have supplied Aldrovandi's needs as a collector and scholar, since lucerne was not among the species sown for Cardinal Paleotti in March 1568, or for Francesco Bolognetti. It was only later, from 1576–8, that Aldrovandi gave it away among his friends, after his own plants had produced seeds.[30]

It is Pietro Antonio Michiel's herbal that gives the clearest idea of the ambiguity and complexity of botanical knowledge in the second half of the sixteenth century and shows the relation between the development of scientific thought and that group of landowners, nobles and scholars who were contributing to a common scheme for the organization of the natural environment. This Venetian patrician, born in 1510, preferred study to business or politics, travelled throughout the Venezie and the bordering provinces, in search of plants and herbs, and cultivated a garden on the island of San Trovaso, in Venice. He was a correspondent of the greatest naturalists of his time, including Ghini, Anguillara, Guilandin and Aldrovandi, and received a great many botanical specimens from Venetians scattered from Constantinople to Alexandria, as officials and consuls of the Republic. He also kept in touch with French, German and Flemish travellers and merchants, who passed through Venice carrying seeds and dried specimens of plants in their bags. In short, Pietro Antonio Michiel's contacts ranged throughout the economic and political network of the Republic of Venice, to Dalmatia, the Levant, Crete, Constantinople, Egypt, France and Germany.[31]

[29] See *ibid.*, 56, II, cc. 455–6.
[30] See *ibid.*, 136, II, cc. 290–5; *ibid.*, 138, cc. 83–94. On Cardinal Paleotti see P. Prodi, *Il Cardinale Gabriele Paleotti*, Rome 1959, 1967, 2 vols.
[31] See G. Marsili, *Di Pietro Antonio Michieli botanico insigne del sec. xvi e di una sua opera manoscritta*, Venice 1845; E. de Toni, *Notizie su P. A. Michiel e sul suo codice erbario*, *L'Ateneo veneto*, 31–2, 1908; idem, 'Il codice erbario di P. A. Michiel (Introduzione e Libro Azzurro)', *Memorie della Pontificia Accademia dei Nuovi Licei*, 26, 1908; idem, *I cinque libri di P. A. Michiel Codice Marciano, trascrizione e*

Michiel was a discriminating observer of plants and identified and described about a thousand. From the drawings made for him by Domenico Dalle Greche it is easy to see which were copied from life, and which from other drawings or else invented from verbal or written description. In his text, Michiel gave a whole series of details on the places where the plants grew, which he took from the Classics, contemporary writers, or from the travellers who had collected them. The foreign and Italian nomenclature that he added to the description of the plants and herbs was very important. Michiel was endeavouring to rediscover the plants of the ancients. He realised that the Classics, by leaving us a nomenclature, had enabled us to identify them, albeit incorrectly and partially, because the botanists of those days tended to recognize the flora of their own central-European region from plants native to the central and eastern Mediterranean.

What we get from Michiel, even more than from the huge work of Ulisse Aldrovandi, is an idea of the effort made by the individual to catalogue and recognize the environment, places, and conditions of reproduction of European flora. Within this framework, ever greater attention was being given to regional floras, their similarities and differences. Mattioli's effort to describe European flora as eminently Mediterranean, on the pattern of Dioscorides, led to a withdrawal, a retreat from the confrontation necessary to research. Mattioli's violent reaction, in his later years, against anyone who expressed opinions contrary to his own, demonstrates how sterile this position was. Personal contacts were as necessary as travel to the study of plant life, to reconstruct the flora of a region, and so replace existing printed books where these were in disagreement. Michiel advocated the study of plants for the benefit of the human body, for the embellishment of gardens, to facilitate the discovery of rare plants, but he made it clear that this process of identification of the natural environment was to be achieved only with great effort and expense. For identification was only the first step towards the organization and transformation of nature, and effort and expense were essential to both.[32]

What Michiel actually achieved is clear. He rightly identified Dioscorides' polygala (*Onobrychis* sp., Lam.) with *sainfoin*, 'which is

---

commento, Venice 1940. However the published text does not reproduce the complete document, see Venice, BN ms Ital., II, XXVI, 4860: quotations in the text are from the original manuscript. Plants were identified by E. de Toni.

[32] See *ibid.*, *Libro rosso secondo*, f. IV.

called sain foin in Provence', saying he had received a sample from near Lyons, sent to him by the simples-gatherer Antonio Tolomei, who had let him have many other specimens from France and Corsica. His name for lucerne, large trefoil, was also correct in the European usage of his day; the French called it *grand treffle* and *foin de Bourgogne*, the Germans *burgundisch Gras* and the Spanish *alfalfa*. Fenugreek grew all over Italy, there was a variety of lucerne (*Medicago lupulina* or *Trifolium agrarium*) in the mountains round Belluno, Spanish sainfoin in the Siena countryside, round Pisa, in the Maremma, the Abruzzi and Apulia regions. He also claimed that polygala, sainfoin, now called *lupinella* in Italian, grew on the mountains round Bologna and in the Abruzzi, recalling that it was grown from seed and used as forage in Provence. At the same time he noted that lucerne as forage was quite forgotten in Italy, though common in Spain. He always dwelt on the question of reproducing the plants, on how vulnerable to frost were the seeds, which needed warmth and moisture. In sharp contrast to this, fenugreek 'grew all the better, the worse it was stored'; which explains why it survived in medieval Europe while lucerne disappeared. Clover, polygala, fenugreek and Spanish sainfoin were hardier species and might even become weeds infesting the lucerne field; when lucerne was left uncultivated, they soon choked it. For all varieties of lucerne 'love clean, rich soil with all the weeds pulled up. And moist soil'.[33] So with careful cultivation essential to the ripening of its seeds, and the threat of the icy winters of the Middle Ages, lucerne was at a disadvantage.[34] Lucerne seeded and reproduced only where irrigation was practised, as in Moorish Spain;[35] and only where cultivation and regulation of water once more proceeded side by side, as in Provence and the Po valley, did lucerne spread again in the sixteenth century. Not surprisingly it was in Venice that Agostino Gallo published his text, giving ample space to the cultivation of lucerne in the country round Brescia.

---

[33] *Ibid.*, *Libro rosso*, fos. 215v, 216r–v, 233r–235v, 312r–v, 345r–347v, 384r–v, 400r–v. The forms *sainfoin* and *sainctfoin* (in Italian *sanofieno* or *santofieno*) were common in Europe until *sainfoin* prevailed towards the second half of the seventeenth century (see below, chap. 6).

[34] A recent work on infesting flora and the effects of cultivation in a lucerne field is H. Marsili, 'Ricerche sulla flora infestante delle colture in Italia, V, La flora infestante di un podere della regione collinare della Val d'Elsa', *Nuovo Giornale Botanico Italiano*, 60, 1953.

[35] See L. Bolens, *Les méthodes culturales*, pp. 129, 136.

7. BRESCIA AND AGOSTINO GALLO

While botanists spend their lives observing the natural environment, landowners, peasants, sharecroppers, labourers and agronomists transform it by their daily work. Agricultural work implies biological choice concerning which plants to cultivate, which to consider as weeds, which land to leave fallow; and it is always interfering with the spontaneous pedological processes produced by the decay of plants. This was already happening in the sixteenth century and earlier, so that all the descriptions of a so-called traditional society, founded on agricultural routine and tending to be static, are fundamentally wrong. They take no account of the fact that producers were working under the pressure of diminishing returns and that much of their effort was spent merely on renewing the conditions with which they started. Agricultural land represented capital, and its renewal demanded a price in terms of the labour expended on it. In ancient times Columella had shown a definite tendency to count the costs of production; Pliny had insisted that the shrewd farmer should work together with the plants to obtain the best possible agricultural land.

Fundamental as the experience and knowledge of the botanists are to the reconstruction of the history of the spread of forage crops and fertile land in sixteenth-century Europe, they must be set against the literature on the new agronomy, if we are to achieve a full understanding. Once again it is in central and northern Italy where the two sides joined hands, when Venetian publishers printed the work of landowners who did not merely annotate Pier de' Crescenzi's text, but also wrote down the practical results they achieved in agriculture. All sixteenth-century Europe eagerly read and clamoured for publications to provide the new class of large landowners with a knowledge of agronomy presented from a regional point of view. Publishers from Paris, Lyons, Venice, Basle and Antwerp were quick to take up the challenge and, with very few exceptions, were to remain foremost in the field throughout the century.[36]

The position of Pier de' Crescenzi and the Classics was undermined not by any new Italian work, but by the Latin and Italian translations of

---

[36] At present there is still no general study on European agricultural writings in the sixteenth century: some account will be found in G. E. Fussell, *The Classical Tradition in West European Farming*, Newton Abbot 1972; C. Beutler, 'Un chapitre de la sensibilité collective: la littérature agricole en Europe continentale', *Annales (ESC)*, 1973, and E. Casali, *Il villano dirozzato*, Florence 1984 is useful as a general introduction for Italy.

Gabriel Alonso Herrera's *Book of Agriculture*, which came out in Venice in 1557, two years before the Treaty of Cateau-Cambrésis established Spanish supremacy over Italy. This book, which had already been published in Madrid in the early sixteenth century, listed lucerne (*mielga* or *alfalfa*) among horticultural crops, the description being based on Theophrastus and the rules for its cultivation taken from Columella. Actually Arab-Andalusian agriculture kept up the cultivation of lucerne because it was based on irrigation, knowledge of the soil, deep ploughing and crops suitable for green manure. Herrera was prompted to write his book to conserve the heritage of agricultural knowledge which was threatened when the Christians conquered Granada, and which later disappeared under Philip II. Herrera, a Churchman who had travelled in Italy after 1503, had nothing to say about methods of cultivation in that country; he probably felt that Arab-Andalusian agronomy had little to learn from Italian agriculture.[37]

The *Book of Agriculture* was printed three times in 1557 and six times between 1568 and 1633. On 1 December 1558 Agostino Gallo wrote from his villa near Brescia to a patron who wished to remain unnamed but who can easily be identified with Alfonso Capriolo, the founder and inspirer of the *Accademia degli Occulti* in Brescia, to let him know how his work on the *Giornate di agricultura* was progressing.[38] In his letter

[37] In general see G. A. Herrera, *Obra de agricultura*, ed. J. U. Martinez Carreras, Madrid 1970, pp. xlvii–lxviii and lxviii–lxxiv, *passim*. His agricultural book was published in Madrid in 1513.

[38] On the life of Agostino Gallo we will quote only G. B. Pagani, *Vita di Agostino Gallo*, Brescia, B. Queriniana, ms L. 1.28, misc. 11; G. M. Mazzucchelli, *Gli scrittori d'Italia*, Brescia 1753–63, 2 vols.; O. Rossi, *Elogi historici di Bresciani illustri*, Brescia 1620, pp. 286–7; B. Martinelli, 'Agostino Gallo: una vita per l'agricoltura. Traccia per una nuova biografia', in A. Gallo, *Le tredici giornate della agricoltura* (Venice 1566), Brescia 1986, photostatic reprint; M. Pegrari (ed.), *Agostino Gallo nella cultura del Cinquecento*, Brescia 1988. On the Accademia degli Oscuri and intellectual life in Brescia see *Storia di Brescia*, Brescia 1963, vol. V, pp. 591–3. In different editions Agostino Gallo published his books as *Le dieci giornate dell'agricoltura et dei piaceri della villa*, Brescia 1564; *Le tredici giornate . . .* , Venice 1566; *Le vinti giornate . . .* , Venice 1567. The complete list of the numerous Venetian editions is to be found in F. Pirro, 'Il lessico delle Giornate d'Agricoltura', *Lingua Nostra*, 30, 1969, pp. 1–5; M. Nervo, 'Le edizioni torinesi delle 'Venti giornate di agricoltura' di M. Agostino Gallo', *Studi piemontesi*, 1985, pp. 122–5; about dating the early editions including the pirated editions, see C. Poni, 'Struttura, strategie e ambiguità delle 'Giornate': Agostino Gallo fra l'agricoltura e la villa', in Pegrari (ed.), *Agostino Gallo*, pp. 73–7. The timely French translation by Belleforest, *Les secrets de la vraie agriculture*, Paris 1576, and the many copies with readers' marks and marks of ownership show the interest and fame achieved by A. Gallo's treatise. The edition published by the Accademia di Agricoltura of Brescia 1775 may serve as a critical edition. Our page

he said the work would include some pages on the cultivation of lucerne and how to gather lucerne seeds. Another letter, of 4 February 1560, from Gallo to Giovan Battista Romano, a landowner of Padua, once more announced the work on lucerne and gave a short description of the plant. On both occasions Gallo mentioned Herrera, while in the first letter he recalled how lucerne was neglected in Italy, though still cultivated in Spain. These were the same years when Aldrovandi's Spanish correspondents were sending him alfalfa seeds, and Italian botanists all agreed that lucerne had disappeared in Italy in the Middle Ages. From this letter of Agostino Gallo's we glean two very important points: that it was difficult to obtain a lucerne-field free of weeds, and that Gallo belonged to a group of landowners who used to meet in Rezzato near Brescia, to talk informally but regularly about agriculture, technical problems and religious and social issues[39] under the auspices of Cardinal Reginald Pole. The group included gentlemen of note in Brescia at the time, such as Giovan Battista Avogadro, Vincenzo Maggi and Lodovico Barigrano, who all figure in the dialogues of Gallo's *Dieci giornate*, first printed in 1564.

In that group, besides Gallo, we find scions of the Gambara, Avogadro and Martinengo families, all of whom had links with the *Occulti* of Brescia and were representatives of the Ghibelline party in that city, the dull communications at their meetings being mainly a cover-up for their political interests. For when the Venetians came back to Brescia in 1516, many of them had been burdened by heavy taxes, despite the promises made to them before they surrendered, and they were forced to withdraw to their manorial estates to practise agriculture or, in some cases, to become bandits. The most enterprising of them passed to the service of Charles V or Philip II, Camillo and Giovanni Brunoro Gambara, for example, while Gian Giacomo Chizzola travelled with Cardinal Pole on his mission to Mary Tudor in 1554. Pietro

numbers refer to the useful photostat edition (Percaccino, Venice 1569) published by A. Forni, Sala Bolognese 1978. A useful up-to-date bibliography is given in F. Grasso Caprioli, 'Camillo Tarello, Agostino Gallo, Giacomo Chizzola e l'Accademia di Rezzato', *Rivista di storia dell'agricoltura*, 1982, 2, pp. 37–122. The letters referred to were published by Gallo himself in the various editions of his work. The Accademia degli Occulti was founded in 1540 by Alfonso Capriolo 'prince' of the Occulti and spokesman for the town of Brescia on various missions in Italy, France and Flanders. Agostino Gallo's letter supports that date, though the Accademia was really active only from 1564–5; see M. Maylender, *Storia delle Accademie d'Italia*, Bologna 1926–30, vol. IV, pp. 87–91. Gallo's pseudonym in the Accademia degli Occulti was 'Incognito'.

[39] See *Storia di Brescia*, vol. II, pp. 455, 551, and Grasso Caprioli, 'Camillo Tarello'.

Avogadro passed into the service of another famous ally of the Empire, Emmanuel Philibert, Duke of Savoy, who won the important battle of Saint Quentin. It was to the Duke that Agostino Gallo dedicated the 1566 Venice edition of his *Giornate di agricultura*.

Though the minor group round Rezzato never reached the status of an academy, the *Occulti* having more to do with Imperial sympathies than with agriculture,[40] Emmanuel Philibert did actually take some interest in horticulture and natural history and set up some fine gardens in the Royal Park of Turin.[41] It is not surprising that Gallo and Tarello, the two great agronomists of Brescia, did not move in the same circles, though they lived a mere twenty miles from each other, since Agostino Gallo leant towards the Empire and the House of Savoy, while Camillo Tarello was openly on the side of Venice.[42] Tarello even applied to the Venetian Senate for support in defending the originality of his agricultural memoir, published in 1567. This was in line with the tradition of his family, for the Tarellos belonged to the class of medium-sized farmers that the Venetian Republic counted on to oppose the great feudal families who had received their titles from the Empire. When Giovanni Lezze drew up the Brescia land register in the early seventeenth century, the Tarellos were still mentioned among the best farmers in their district.

---

[40] See C. Pasero, *Francia Spagna Impero a Brescia, 1509–1516*, Brescia 1957, pp. 386, 388, 389; Rossi, *Elogi historici*, pp. 373 ff.; *Storia di Brescia*, vol. V, pp. 591, 593. Banditry among the nobility was mainly a seventeenth century phenomenon: see J. M. Ferraro, *Family and public life in Brescia, 1580–1650: the Foundation of Power in the Venetian State*, Cambridge 1993, pp. 133–54. Poni, 'Struttura', p. 77, argues that most likely the new dedication to the Duke of Savoy, Emmanuel Philibert, had been suggested by the Venetian publisher, Nicolò Bevilacqua, who was negotiating with the duke to transfer his firm to Turin.

[41] See O. Mattirolo, 'La frutticultura in Piemonte nella storia dell'arte', *Annali della R. Accademia di Agricoltura di Torino*, 59, 1917, and idem, 'L'opera del duca Emanuele Filiberto in favore della botanica e dell'agricoltura', in *Studi pubblicati dalla Regia Università di Torino nel IV centenario della nascita di Emanuele Filiberto*, Turin 1928. See Turin, AST, Archivio Camerale, art. 179, 252, 253. See also the collections of drawings of flowers and animals that Duke Charles Emmanuel I (1620) had made, now housed in the Biblioteca Reale di Turin: see A. Griseri, 'La natura morta in Piemonte', in Zeri and Porzio (eds.), *La natura morta in Italia*, pp. 154–5, 158. The *XX giornate* were published a number of times in Turin.

[42] See C. Poni, 'Un privilegio di agricoltura. Camillo Tarello e il senato di Venezia', *Rivista Storica Italiana*, 72, 1970, pp. 592–610, and M. Berengo, 'Introduzione' to C. Tarello, *Ricordo di agricoltura*, Turin 1975, *passim*.

8. LUCERNE-GROWING

The distinguishing mark of Agostino Gallo's work, as compared with Tarello's, is that Gallo recommended lucerne-growing even before his manual was published. Otherwise, they both seem to have agreed on repeated light ploughing, to clean the ground and make it more fertile by airing the soil well and so improving the productivity of the seed; and on the fertilizing effect of clover or *pabbio* (bristle grass, *setaria viridis*).[43] These are the chief rules on which the agronomy of the two Brescian authors was based, not so very different from the principles of the best agricultural practice in their district in the late fifteenth century. But while Gallo declared openly that his ideas were in line with the best agriculturalists in the region, Tarello was not so ready to recognize debts to anyone and took his claim to originality before the Venetian Senate. An old biographer of Agostino Gallo wrote that he liked to talk about agriculture with 'a certain old peasant, most expert in field cultivation'. If these conversations took place in the 1550s, when Gallo was at the height of his powers, his 'old peasant' must have begun working at the end of the previous century. The same source tells how *cavalier* Luzzago, also a great expert in agriculture, maintained that the whole secret of agriculture could be summed up in the practice of 'mucking the fields well and cleaning them well'.[44] Gallo seems to have held the same principles with regard to the cultivation of lucerne.

In writing about lucerne Gallo recalled Columella, how lucerne disappeared from Italy after the Barbarian invasions and how this plant was still grown in Spain. He suggested that it was brought back into Italy via Naples and from there to Volterra, Scandiano and to Brescia. Further on in the volume, in the section on the nineteenth day, which deals with a variety of subjects, he also mentioned that Gianfrancesco Gambara was the first to plant lucerne on his estate in Pralboino. Gianfrancesco did not spend all his time on hunting and poetry, his literary activity included the correction of Pier de' Crescenzi's text.[45] Unfortunately his work, which

---

[43] The late Signor Francesco Grasso Caprioli kindly suggested to the present writer that the grass 'papulo' should be identified with *setaria*. This plant had been illustrated and described in the Roccabonella–Rinio herbal: see above, note 12.

[44] See Rossi, *Elogi historici*, p. 287.

[45] See Gallo, *Le vinti giornate*, p. 444. The Latin manuscript on de' Crescenzi's agriculture (Brescia, BQ, ms E II.5), with the first pages missing, belongs to this tradition. Once kept in the Santa Faustina Monastery, for the personal use of Giovanni Ludovico Luchi, it was written and corrected in the early sixteenth century.

rightly belongs to the history of the diffusion of de' Crescenzi-style agriculture in the sixteenth century, has been lost. Nonetheless it testifies to the great attention still devoted to the Bolognese agronomist and to the work of individual readers in perusing and annotating his text. We have already examined this for the 1474–1560 period, leading directly to Agostino Gallo's circle.

It is difficult to find proof of the route suggested by Gallo. We shall see later that Giovan Battista Della Porta, the only Neapolitan writer on agriculture at the end of the sixteenth century, was rather unreliable. For Volterra, among the volcanic, tufa hills, evidence is totally lacking. As for Scandiano, a few miles from Reggio Emilia, it was a fief of the Boiardo family until the mid-sixteenth century (the poet Matteo Maria was born there) and this connects up with the Bolognese circles of Beccadelli and Aldrovandi.[46] Gallo also mentions Ercolano Cucco, one of the Brescia growers who got the best results with lucerne. We shall return to him later.

The cultivation of lucerne started from a well-ploughed and harrowed field, left completely fallow from June to the following February, to get rid of the weeds. When the field had been manured and ploughed again, lucerne was sown together with panic grass or millet. When the seed had been covered using a wooden rake (following Columella's advice, to avoid damaging it), the panic grass choked the weeds and then, being an annual, died away after the first mowing. In this way the lucerne had a chance to grow thickly and easily, assisted in its struggle against weeds by the panic grass. It was thought that at least twenty-five pounds of seed per *jugerum* (equal to about 12 kg per quarter of a hectare) were needed to produce a good lucerne field free of weeds. The lucerne had to be sown early in the morning so that the dew would help it to strike root; it had to be irrigated, or at least manured, from September to April, to keep the soil friable. Harvesting the seed was a very complex operation. The second-year harvest was preferable, as it was stronger than the first. You had to wait for the second growth of hay, when the pods were well

---

[46] On G. B. Della Porta see below, note 93; a local Spanish sainfoin (*sulla*) from the Volterra region was mentioned by Pier Antonio Michiel when he wrote on sainfoin and Spanish Sainfoin in the regions round Siena and Pisa (see above, note 33) and later by D. Sbrozzi, *La sulla*, Casale 1899. Corniolo della Cornia mistook *sulla* (Spanish sainfoin) for lucerne (see above, note 14). On Scandiano see G. Tiraboschi, *Dizionario topografico degli Stati Estensi* (1821–5), Bologna 1963, *sub nomine*, and M. Martilli, 'Origini e sviluppo della mezzadria in provincia di Reggio Emilia', *Rivista di economia agraria*, 12, 1957, pp. 532–44. Scandiano was, and still is, a centre of high farming: it was also the birthplace of Filippo Re.

ripened by the heat of the summer, before cutting them, at dawn after a good dewfall, so they would not open in the process; lastly they were beaten by hand to get rid of the chaff. The second-class seed could be harrowed over the best quality later. Around a hundred pounds of seed per *jugerum* (a quarter of a hectare) could be collected. The hay could be used like clover hay. Gallo emphasized the importance of drying it quickly, because it was more nourishing and palatable to the cattle. Gallo's section on lucerne aimed at creating a lucerne-field that would last a considerable time, in cases where the owner was farming his own land and could afford the by no means negligible expense of laying it down.[47]

8.1. Ercolano Cucco

At this point we should take a look back. In the third edition of the *Vinti Giornate*, Gallo mentioned a fellow-citizen of his, 'Hercolano Cucco, a very exceptional agriculturalist', praising him for his success in cultivating lucerne. This name was added, like many others in the course of the various editions, to complete the text and persuade the reader.

Ercolano Cucco was probably born in Brescia in 1522, into a family that was only registered among the nobility at the beginning of the century. The Cuccos belonged to the guild of 'gardeners and carpenters' and had the right to keep two retainers in their service. Theirs can hardly have been the only case of a family who moved on from the gardeners' guild to produce a good farmer in the next generation. Gardeners' corporations had sprung up in Rome, Florence, Brescia and Viterbo and it may well be that this highly labour-intensive sector contributed very considerably to the expansion and renewal of agriculture in the fifteenth and sixteenth centuries. His newly acquired nobility did not prevent Giacomo Cucco, Ercolano's father, from dealing in illicit contracts or even in usury, next door to the local Franciscan friary; not surprisingly, since it was the friars who set up pawn-broking (*Monti di Pietà*) in Italy. Giacomo died in 1540 and was buried in consecrated ground, though in great haste, as if to forestall possible objections from the townsfolk.[48] But

---

[47] Gallo kept the Latin *jugerum* (0.25 ha) to indicate the local land measure (*piò*, 0.32 ha). Gallo believed that direct management by the owner was the best way to farm one's land, see Gallo, *Le vinti giornate*, pp. 12, 14, 18.

[48] See Brescia, BQ, C.I.15, *Pandolfo Nassino, Cronaca*, fo. 299*v*; A. Valentini, 'Di Pandolfo Nassino: della sua cronaca e di alcune lettere storiche in essa contenute', *Archivio veneto*, s.II, 30/1, 1885; F. Lechi, *Le dimore bresciane in cinque secoli di*

Giacomo's speculations had not passed unnoticed by the city Tax Office, and in their 1548 estimate they placed a burden 'greater than honesty required' on his son Ercolano, who complained in those terms in his tax returns for 1568. In that year Ercolano declared real estate of 804 *piò* (256.64 hectares), which he valued at 46,200 lire in view of the 'very sad condition' of the land; to this he added 3,000 lire as the value of houses in Brescia and credit for the sum of 14,655 lire. On a total capital of 63,855 lire he had debts of only 5,870 lire. Most of the property was in Porzano, a hamlet in Leno where, despite the unfortunate condition of the land, the Cuccos had a country house, ploughed land, vineyards, pastures and an irrigation channel. All in all, the 670 *piò* (214 hectares) yielded 130 *somate* ('loads') of winter corn (wheat and rye), 52 'loads' of spring corn (7,600 litres of panic grass, millet, etc.), 10 *carra* of wine, 40 loads of hay, timber worth 105 lire, and a little flax, which was only sown occasionally. The land was managed by tenants, who paid rent partly in money, partly in produce; labourers (there were five cottages on the estate rented at 5 lire and a couple of capons a year); and herdsmen.[49] Ercolano Cucco was in a position to lend money both in Brescia and in the neighbouring countryside. He was owed various sums by the noblemen Gerolamo Luzzago, Giovanni Fenarolo, Costanzo and Baldessar Baitello, Alessio Brunello, Annibale Martinengo, all designated as 'signore'. Then came a group of middle-class debtors, known as 'messere', Evangelisto Cavallo, for example, Giovanni Paolo Zanetto, Urbano and Zuane Pilotto and others. After these came the tenants who were deeply in debt. The Pozzanos owed 700 lire, a Francesco Moretto 1,000 lire, Giacomo and Gerolomo, 'former' tenants, 700 lire and lastly Paolo Maistrino 400 lire. It is a pity that the tax return sent by Ercolano and his relatives Francesco and Michele in 1588 to the Brescia tax office is lost, because the development of the family property could have been deduced from it. However, we still have the 1557 contract laid down between Ercolano and Francesco Zamboni, by which Zamboni rented, for seven years, barely 100 *piò* in Porzano, together with the house, barn and dovecote 'where the Madonna appeared' for 375 lire (3 lire 15 soldi per *piò)*. Besides the rent in money, Zamboni undertook, among other things, to feed cows, but not sheep, with the

---

storia, IV, *Il Cinquecento nel territorio*, Brescia 1975, pp. 296–7, 434. On the forgotten relationship between agricultural growth and the development of trade guilds see T. Cuturi, 'Le corporazioni delle arti nel comune di Viterbo', *Archivio della Società romana di storia patria*, 7, 1884, pp. 55 ff.

[49] See Brescia, AS, Estimo, 1568, mazzo 187, n. 612, 'Polizza domini Hercolano Cucho'.

hay gathered on the land, to keep the irrigation channels in good order (flowing freely), to deliver, as a gift, a *soma* (load) of spelt or oats or a load of rice (if he grew any) for his master's horses. The tenant had a clause added to the effect that 15 lire 4 soldi should be taken off the rent for any improvements made, while the master was to keep the rent of a small room to be let to a labourer.[50] There is no trace in the contract of the lucerne mentioned by Agostino Gallo. Perhaps it was grown on some land apart under direct management; in any case Ercolano's name only appears in the third edition of the *Giornate* (1569). This was a good ten years after he let to Francesco Zamboni, who was not even required to grow clover, which was specified in many other documents of the same or earlier years. Nevertheless he must have been quite an expert farmer, since the contract laid down a compensation for any improvements made that did not come under the formula of 'well-farmed land'. But by 1557 Ercolano seemed very careful about the care of his horses and the tenant Zamboni did not neglect varieties of spring corn, spelt, oats, even rice, thanks to the master's irrigation channel. Lucerne may even have been substituted for rice in the years 1557–69. The conditions necessary for the improvement of the Porzano estate already existed. It was divided into four farms of three 'units' each. A channel dug by Ercolano's ancestors ensured good irrigation of almost all the land. A close network of channels and springs had been constructed during the second half of the fifteenth century in the country between the Oglio and Adda rivers, and water had become one of the most important factors in the improvement of the land in the Po valley.[51] With so many clauses in their contracts imposing obligations which took up their time and ate into their produce, it is not surprising that the seven tenant farmers of Porzano and Leno each owed 100 lire after ten years and were probably on the way to losing their capital. By these contracts the benefits of the

---

[50] See *ibid.*, Estimo, 1588, C.IV.460, f. 29, missing; *ibid.*, Notarile, Leno, G. Domenico Bonomini, filza 1193, 14 dicembre 1557.

[51] Of the vast bibliography on the subject see only C. M. Cipolla, 'Ripartizione delle colture nel pavese secondo le 'misure territoriali' della metà del '500', *Studi di economia e statistica*, ser. I, 1, 1950–1, pp. 252–61; G. Coppola, 'L'agricoltura di alcune pievi della pianura irrigua milanese nei dati catastali della metà del secolo xvi', in *Contributi dell'Istituto di storia economica e sociale*, Milan 1973, vol. I, pp. 185–286; V. Ilardi, 'L'allevamento del bestiame e la diplomazia in Lombardia nel xv secolo', *Rivista di storia dell'agricoltura*, 27, 1987, pp. 151–63; G. Chittolini, 'La pianura irrigua lombarda fra Quattrocento e Cinquecento', *Annali Cervi*, 10, 1988, pp. 207–21, with extensive bibliography. On Brescia, see *Storia di Brescia*, vol. II, p. 212.

improvements remained strictly in the hands of the landowners, leaving little for those who actually worked the land.

8.2. Structural problems and cultivation

Lucerne only became part of a regular crop rotation in the long term. The lucerne-field might last at least ten years and cover the cost of the initial outlay and cultivation by yielding six or seven crops of hay per year. Meanwhile, more generally, the fields would be put down to clover. Clover seed, which had previously been sown in March, was harrowed over the harvested wheat or rye fields between August and 10 September, a fortnight or so before Michaelmas, so that by early November (St Martin's Day) there would be a heavier crop of hay to last through the winter. This is another practice that Gallo advised and most Brescian farmers preferred. Like lucerne, clover also had to be thickly sown; either 60 kg of loft sweepings or 6 kg of very clean seed to the *jugerum*. Most people seem to have harvested their own seed; the corn merchants in Brescia, as well as Milan and Piacenza, always seem to have been well supplied with it towards the end of the century.[52] Clover also served to lay down permanent pastures. Gallo suggested sowing clover and oats together in order to clear the ground of weeds and so that the fine clover seed would take root more easily. The oat harvest would benefit the hay crops. Otherwise, irrigation or manuring would enrich the soil and give a heavy crop of hay. He also advised special attention to cleaning the cowhouses, threshing floor, courtyards and dovecote, to collect the manure for meadows, not for the fields or vineyard, because it produced too much grass. Manure was also collected from the streets of Brescia and the country roads, sold and spread on the neighbouring fields. The combined action of irrigation and manure gave high yields from poor, infertile land. Land fertility was rightly considered as a product of agricultural labour (and thus not an independent variable, as Ricardo's theory of rent would suggest). It was

---

[52] See Berengo, '*Introduzione*', pp. xl–xli; we should also quote Brescia, AS, A. Bucellini, filza 653, 18 dicembre 1533; *ibid.*, T. Boschetti, filza 963, 10 luglio 1547; *ibid.*, S. Raimondi, filza 2965, 10 maggio 1570 (Marino Berengo helpfully pointed out this material to me). On clover seed supply see also Gallo, *Le vinti giornate*, pp. 26–9; see also Tarello, *Ricordo di agricoltura*, pp. 99–100; G. Falcone, *La nuova vaga et dilettevole villa* (1577), Venice 1628, p. 235; N. Poggi, *Tariffa delli daci et imbottati di Brescia e suo territorio*, Brescia 1591, p. 59: duty was paid to the city of Brescia 'at value' for clover seed; in 1616 large supplies of clover seed were bought on an estate in the neigbourhood south of Milan: see Sella, *L'economia lombarda*, p. 296.

preserved by various agricultural practices, especially by keeping the turf thickly covered with grass, so as to protect the soil from the heat of the sun. Farm contracts in the region were designed to defend the old leys, while meadows were seeded, manured and levelled regularly over the years.

Putting cattle and sheep out to graze was not always easy in such carefully tended meadows. Vincenzo Maggi, one of the speakers in Gallo's dialogues, complained of continual quarrels with shepherds and cowherds over the mouldy, rotting hay they claimed a right to without paying for it. He declared himself so desperate that he was almost forced to plough up old meadows, which meant threatening the system that kept them fertile.[53]

The pasture was never meant primarily as a basis for stock-breeding, which was considered as a by-product. The chief aim of production was still corn-growing and fodder for draught horses and oxen. The large quantities of dairy products were the property of the tenants and cowherds, who sold them to pay the rent for the fields. It was no accident that Gallo put Scaltrito, the canny shepherd and cowherd, as the chief expert in the dialogue for the eleventh day, on cows, calves and bulls. It was this humble man, not a well-off person, who explained the subject. Despite his modest appearance, Scaltrito was the owner of his herd. He bought cows in the Valcamonica or the Grisons district, where they cost less because pastures were plentiful, he never risked buying cows in calf or sucking calves. He explained his procedures in purely monetary terms.To keep heifers for at least three years meant using six or seven cartloads of hay, besides the cost of renting meadows and the risk that the animal might not turn out well. He brought his herds down to the plains from September to the following May, so they could graze in the meadows, after the hay had been got in. Finally he suggested that the cattle should not be kept shut up in the sheds on hot days because this reduced the milk yield. Scaltrito-Gallo also suggested a different diet,

[53] See Gallo, *Le vinti giornate, giornata seconda*, pp. 38–9. The real Vincenzo Maggi owned land in various places near Brescia, at Mairano, Frontignano, Quinzano, Codignano, a castle with farms and five barns at Pampiano, and more lands with vineyards and flax at Seniga. He had a sound literary education, including Greek and Latin: see *Catasto bresciano*, Brescia 1973, vol. II, p. 383; Rossi, *Elogi historici*, pp. 289–90; *Libraria bresciana*, Brescia 1694, pp. 202–3. In the early nineteenth century sharecroppers in the Bolognese area were still expressly forbidden to allow shepherds and flocks onto the farm, so that none of the forage should be damaged or eaten: see C. Poni, *Gli aratri e l'economia agraria nel bolognese dal xvii al xix secolo*, Bologna 1963, p. 246; see now idem, 'Struttura', p. 87.

reducing the hay ration and supplementing it with linseed cake and salt. The working oxen should also be given less hay and, to make up for this, should not be expected to work so hard; they should also be kept cleaner. The landowners in the plains benefited from the cowherds and shepherds because their animals consumed large quantities of hay, but also left large quantites of manure in the sheds; this, together with the dust and manure collected from the roads, explained the high yield of the lowland farms.[54]

Farmers were very unwilling to allow sheep and cattle to graze on their well-kept meadows; shepherds and cowherds generally fed mown grass and hay to their animals. The lowland farmers only needed the hay mown in spring and summer to be transformed into manure; a careful check had to be kept on the cattle from October to May, so that by continually treading the pastures during the cold, wet season, they did not damage the soft turf, thus increasing the effect of erosion in the hot summer season. Although sheep dung was considered the richest manure, much of it was lost, at least when the sheep (especially the Brescia breed) were not kept indoors. On the other hand it was dangerous to let them graze in the water-meadows, as the grass was too rich and damp and could too easily cause bloat in ruminants, endangering their lives.

The sixteenth-century agronomists were really describing the ideal farm, on which all the crops suitable in their region were grown. They were doing more or less what Arrigo Serpieri did in the first few decades of the twentieth century. The farm Agostino Gallo portayed, on the basis of what farms round Brescia were really like, aimed at producing a large variety of good quality crops. So in the fields imagined by Gallo we find, in the following order, oats and vetch, clover, lucerne, wheat of various kinds, millet,[55] panic grass and sorghum, beans, chick-peas, wild peas, lentils, lupins and rye, flax and Calabrian flax. The problem of storing was important for other products as well as wheat. The farmer had to aim at producing lucerne and clover hay, which would not lose its goodness in the months before it was fed to the animals in the winter. It had to be

---

[54] See Gallo, *Le vinti giornate, giornata undecima, passim* especially pp. 219, 223 on the relationship between dung and meadows. The relationship between dairy products and milk production on a larger area and over a longer span of time is studied in M. Ambrosoli, 'Produzione casearia nel Basso Saluzzese tra xv e xvi secolo: il caso di Caramagna', *Quaderni storici*, 25, 74, 1990, pp. 588–604: figures from Gallo and the region of Saluzzo, bordering on the Dauphiné, compare well with Dutch data of the Napoleonic period.

[55] Millet, 'manzaro', was so called probably because it looked like the legs of cows, called 'manze' in dialect.

well dried for the draught animals but fed as green forage to the milking cows.

Although Classical literature, particularly Varro and, later, French agricultural writers, gave the Italian peninsula a reputation for being highly fertile, Gallo realized that, in fact, the scarcity of agricultural land in Italy[56] meant continuous cultivation and relatively low yields. The agricultural systems of northern and southern Europe are clearly distinguished by this difference; hence the importance of the role of lucerne in the evolution of European agriculture in the following centuries.

9. AGOSTINO GALLO, PLOUGHING, SOWING AND NICOLÒ TARTAGLIA

At the end of the best editions of the *Vinti giornate* there are illustrations of a whole series of agricultural implements and two pages of ploughs. These include the wheel plough, the foreign wheel plough and foreign plain ploughs (*pertegato* and *roversone*).[57] In practice, all these implements are quite similar, with iron coulter and share, the rest being made of wood, with light mouldboards to right or left; all of them are intended to be used with the plough wheel. Their chief feature lies in the design of the share, a flat iron tip, which cuts the earth without actually turning the clod; above this is the coulter, set very far back in comparison with the ploughs of the last century or present-day ones, which are placed so as to cut the lump of earth lifted by the share into two parts. These instruments are very similar to the ones described in a well-known book by Carlo Poni, on farming near Bologna. But while the double-tipped share of the ploughs illustrated in Gallo's book are not very different from the wheel plough (*piò*), the plain plough (*roversone*) is much smaller, rather like the Bolognese plain plough (*ravagliatore*). The different design certainly does not reflect any technical backwardness (the iron industry of Brescia produced first-class agricultural tools), but corresponds to the ploughing technique recommended by Agostino Gallo: 'Truly you can never go wrong by always taking up a small

---

[56] See Gallo, *Le vinti giornate, giornate prima e seconda*.

[57] See *Vocabolario della Accademia della Crusca*, Florence 1601, *sub voce*; other examples of Italian ploughing instruments and wheelploughs are found in P. Scheuermeier, *Bauernwerk in Italien in der italienischen und rätromanischen Schweiz*, Erlenbach–Zürich 1943, and discussed in A. Haudricourt and M. J.-B. Delamarre, *L'homme et la charrue à travers le monde* (1955), Paris 1986.

quantity of earth with the plough' (p. 22). Gallo's chief concern was that the plough should not make furrows too deep, so that together with the top layer of soil it would not turn over the layer of inert subsoil beneath it. Moreover, light ploughing, carefully done, was labour-saving. Instead of two ploughmen with four oxen to plough six or eight perches a day badly, one ploughman and two oxen were enough to plough three perches perfectly. In this way, the land would yield more wheat from four quarts of seed than badly ploughed land from twelve quarts. Gallo was taking up the Classical tradition of careful ploughing and thinly scattered seed, correcting the mistake of many farmers of his time, who went over the ground first with a deep ploughing, sowed straight away, then covered the seed by light harrowing. When the first frosts came, they ploughed again, burying the seed under several inches of earth. In this way the corn grew stunted, choked by the heavy lumps of earth.

Actually, according to Gallo, the ground should be ploughed four times, along and across the field alternately, then after a fifth ploughing, though in some cases only three ploughings would be enough, the seed could be sown along it. Every ploughing should be followed by harrowing along and across, the better to break up the soil. In this well-tilled, broken-down soil the corn would produce longer roots, which would protect the seedlings from the rain, and above all each grain of corn would have more chance of taking root and growing. In practice, Gallo was against broadcasting seed in the furrows and then ploughing it in, because the share pushed the seeds into heaps and they choked each other. According to Gallo, the well-tilled, well-sown field should look like the product of the system described by Dal Pelo Pardi and other Italian agronomists of the early twentieth century, who were against deep ploughing.[58] This produced a level field of finely broken-up soil, with irrigation channels lined with willows, like the landscapes of the *piantata*. But it could be a short field, irrigated more regularly, from which the water would run off more easily; and where the ploughing and cross-ploughing could be done more quickly, lightening the work of the

---

[58] See Poni, *Gli aratri*, chaps. i, ii *passim*, especially table 3; see also Haudricourt and Delamarre, *L'homme et la charrue*, figs. 131–2, p. 280; the question of the number and manner of ploughings to be given to a field is discussed by Gallo, *Le vinti giornate*, especially in the *giornate prima e seconda*, pp. 22–5; see also A. Oliva, *Le sistemazioni dei terreni*, Bologna 1958, pp. 142–3 on the Dal Pelo Pardi system; see idem, *Agricoltura e civiltà*, Turin 1971.

oxen, as they could rest more often, every time the plough was turned and cleaned at the end of each furrow.[59]

In practice the system which Gallo wished to improve was worse. As we have already mentioned, only some of the seeds scattered randomly over the ploughed fields germinated, especially in the case of those ploughed in when the first autumn frosts came, so that, instead of being scattered, they were crowded together and choked each other. To demonstrate his case, Gallo made a complicated but extremely interesting statistical calculation. Poor quality land round Brescia was generally sown with 6 quarts of wheat (c. 73 litres) per *piò* and yielded on average not more than 30 quarts (360 litres, or 1,080 litres per hectare) of grain, a yield of five to one. To get this result, if all the seed germinated, every ear of corn would have had to bear five grains. Actually the ears could bear ten, twenty or forty grains each and so the grain produced should have been 120 or 140 quarts respectively. Moreover, it has to be taken into account that every seed sown produced more than one stalk and hence the number of ears should have been greater than the 30 quarts actually produced. Gallo explained this by the damage caused not so much by birds, worms and mice, as by the peasant's wrong procedure, by broadcasting the seed and then ploughing it into the soil.

At first sight there seems to be nothing special about this. Gallo had a good example and explained it with his usual clarity. But on reading the figures carefully and writing them as ratios ($1:5 = 6:30$, $1:10 = 6:60$, $1:40 = 6:240$) we note that Gallo set up an equation above the second degree, in which the unknown factors were $x = n$ grains per ear and $y = n$ ears per seed sown, while the number of grains that made up the 6 quarts of wheat sown represented a positive whole number by which the equation could be solved. But the solution of an equation above the second degree was the great question being discussed by Italian mathematicians in those decades. The Brescian mathematician Nicolò Tartaglia had suggested a particularly ingenious solution for it. This is not the place to go into the history of the personal relations and mathematical challenges between Tartaglia, Gerolamo Cardano and Lodovico Ferrari, but it should be remembered that Tartaglia was teaching at the so-called Accademia di Rezzato before the publication of his most important results (1556–60), almost twenty years after he first wrote them. The fact is that Gallo and Tartaglia moved in the same

---

[59] On the *piantata* landscape and Renaissance agriculture in Italy see Sereni, *Storia del paesaggio*, pp. 115–81 especially 125–35.

circles and the *Vinti giornate* and Tartaglia's *Generale trattato* came out in the same years. If we write down the figures suggested by Gallo as part of his statistical calculation we find a perfect correspondence with the form of the triangle suggested by Tartaglia – 1, 11, 121, 1331, 14641, 15101051, . . . Which are none other than the numerical coefficients to be attributed to the solution of an equation of the $(x + y)n$ type, which is what Gallo was proposing when he multiplied the number of the ears of corn by the number of the grains on every ear. This is not surprising, since many of the mathematical problems which Nicolò Tartaglia dealt with attempted to solve practical problems of the society of his day (measuring of land or corn, valuing land, mortgages and so on).[60]

Gallo took up this question again briefly in his dialogue for the ninth

---

[60] Of the vast bibliography on Nicolò Tartaglia see A. Masotti, *Studi su Tartaglia*, Brescia 1962. Here we will mention only *Storia di Brescia*, vol. II, pp. 598–617; his main work – *La prima parte del generale trattato de' numeri et misure . . .* , Venice 1556, which was followed by five more parts, Venice 1556–60 – was dedicated to the English gentleman Richard Wentworth, one of the sons of Thomas, 1st Baron Wentworth of Nettlestead, father of sixteen children in all (see *DNB*, vol. XX, *sub nomine*) and younger brother of Thomas, 2nd Baron, to whom Turner dedicated his *Second Parte of the Herbal . . .* , see p. 266. This is a branch of the larger Wentworth family, later Earls of Stafford: see *The Complete Peerage*, London 1959, vol. XII, pp. 497 ff.; W. Wentworth, *Wentworth Papers, 1597–1628*, edited by J. P. Cooper, Camden Society, 3rd ser., 12, 1973: see also J. P. Cooper, 'The fortune of Thomas Wentworth, Earl of Stafford', *Economic History Review*, ser. 2, 11, 1958, pp. 227–48. Tartaglia's writings were translated into English as *Three Bookes of Colloquies concerning the Arte of Shooting in Great and Small Pieces of Artillerie . . . and now translated into English by Cyprian Lucar Gentleman . . . , and three Bookes of Colloquies named Lucar Appendix*, London 1588. It should be remembered that Tartaglia's formula was only one brilliant contribution to the solution of an equation above the second degree, which was solved by Newton: see L. Amerio, *Analisi matematica con elementi di analisi funzionale*, Turin 1977, pp. 23–6, and M. Kline, *Mathematical Thought from Ancient to Modern Times*, New York 1972, Chap. 13 *passim*, Chap. 16 *passim*. In any case Gallo's proposition was not a real equation, but only an exponential function, $y = a^x$, where y = crop expressed in grains of wheat, a = grains of wheat sown, x = (ears $\times$ n grains of every ear). Moreover Gallo had omitted a stage which he considered as known or else he could not solve, that is how to establish the number of grains of wheat sown that made up the four intial quarts. The equation 1 hl = n . v + n_1 . v_1, where n and n_1 are the number of grains and v and v_1 the average volume of each space (see F. Crescini, *Piante erbacee di grande cultura*, Rome 1951, p. 49), is the present starting point for calculating the weight of a hectolitre of wheat, in which the grains have different specific weights. In Gallo's time the problem was how to calculate the different quantities of wheat and other cereals without suitable scales. It was solved by using cubic formulas, with which the procedure could be carried out more rapidly without using containers: see N. Tartaglia, *La prima (-sesta) parte del general trattato dei numeri et misure*, Venice 1556–60, parte I, fo. 39r–v.

day, when he mentioned that it had been learned from experience that poor fields should not be thickly sown. Four quarts of seed were enough, as compared with six sown on average soil and seven on rich soil. This is one of the rare occasions when Gallo based his evidence explicitly on that of the Classics, in this case Columella.[61] Rich soil produces stalks much longer and juicier than those produced on other soil. No more than a certain quantity can be produced on poor fields, so it would be a waste to increase the quantity of seed, just as reducing the quantity sown on the rich fields would not repay the saving by a further increase in the ears produced.[62]

9.1. Agostino Gallo and Camillo Tarello: aspects of ambiguity

But Agostino Gallo was not the only writer in those years to deal with the problem of the sowing and yield of wheat and its relation to the culti-vation of forage crops. On 18 November 1565, Camillo Tarello of Lonato, one of the best-known farmers of Gavardo, on the hills over-looking Lake Garda, presented his *Ricordo d'agricultura* (Agricultural memoir) to the Doge and Senate of Venice, asking to be granted a 'privilege'. After rather complicated procedures, the 'privilege' was granted and the short work was printed in 1567. What happened is well known. It appears that the Senate guaranteed Tarello a royalty payable on the increased income of those who followed his system of cultivation. Tarello's system consisted mainly in alternating wheat and clover, since it was proven that clover roots enriched the soil; hence, the land on the farm under clover ought to be increased at least twofold; the ploughings of the field to be sown with wheat ought to be doubled; and lastly the quantity of wheat seed used ought to be reduced. Camillo Tarello's *Ricordo* is generally considered as the starting-point of modern agronomy, because it connects the impoverishing effect of wheat-growing with the renewed fertility of the ground through growing clover.[63] It is certainly an intelligent work, written by someone with great experience of agriculture, to which was added a good knowledge of the Classical writings on agriculture, though it was certainly less original

---

[61] On Gallo and ancient agricultural writers, mainly Columella, see also Poni, 'Struttura', pp. 77, 85.

[62] See Gallo, *Le vinti giornate*, p. 188; see Amerio, *Analisi matematica*, pp. 23–6.

[63] A bibliography on Tarello is given in the already mentioned Grasso Caprioli, 'Camillo Tarello'; the text quoted here is from M. Berengo's edition of the *Ricordo di agricoltura*.

than its author claimed. Even the alphabetical order in which the *Ricordo* is arranged recalls that of certain medieval herbals, and had already been used in unpublished notes that other careful readers in Italy, France and England had taken on books on agronomy over a considerable period of time.[64]

Tarello himself must have felt indebted to the literature on agronomy and the experience of others, since he concludes rather arrogantly ' . . . this *Ricordo*, made up according to my judgement, of things taken from the sayings of others, is not, must not be, and cannot truly be said to belong to any of them or all of them together, but must be said to be mine'.[65] The author's almost obssessive insistence on the originality of his system of agriculture is a real *excusatio non petita*, since in his day study was based mainly on *excerpta* and *exempla*, ready to respond to any accusation of plagiarism from his numerous enemies. It is, however, useful to clarify the conditions under which the *Ricordo* was published. From Tarello's point of view, since the Venetian Senate had already shown an interest in regulating river waters on the mainland, it was only natural that it should grant every consideration to agricultural reform and that some honour or at least prestige or money should be awarded to the author of this project. But the project could only be carried out by a direct decree of the Venetian government, not by means of a petition, the only way by which a 'most faithful servant' of the Serenissima could make his request known. Did Tarello really think that the judges of the Venetian courts could verify the increased incomes of those landowners shrewd enough to adopt his method? Tarello had some experience of the law and was probably not ingenuous. The key to an understanding, not of the publication of the *Ricordo d'agricultura*, but of the public and political context in which it belonged, lies in the fact that in 1542 Tarello had been exiled for some years from the city and territory of Brescia, for a crime unknown to us, but certainly not negligible. He probably sought the protection of the Venetian government for the publication of his *Ricordo* to show his enemies in Brescia and Gavardo that he was much esteemed by the Venetian Senate. He had already been prepared to serve Venice by reporting tax evasion in 1543 and 1545 and now he was presenting an

---

[64] See the extracts from the Italian translation of Palladius' text (see pp. 16–17), the unfinished commonplace book of Sir John Prise (see pp. 36–8), the horticultural notes to the French version of Agostino Gallo by Monsieur Barrier, a notary in Avignon (note 86), the long unpublished manuscript produced at Wentworth Castle in 1666 (London, BL, Sloane ms 3815).

[65] See Tarello, *Ricordo di agricoltura*, pp. 23–4.

agricultural project of importance to the whole state. Not unintentionally, in the last paragraph of the memoir that he presented in Venice he quoted ' . . . the experience of exiles who do not hesitate to risk their lives to serve their country . . . ' This reference seems to sum up the 1542 episode, when he was exiled, and the attack made on him in 1552.[66] In short, since he could not secure entry into the circle of Brescian notables (he did not belong to any of the literary academies of his city, though he had a good knowledge of Classical literature and was clearly familiar with Petrarch and Bembo) or even get the 1542 sentence revoked (on the contrary, in 1552–4 he again got into a violent quarrel with three inhabitants of Gavardo who were supported by Marcello Zamara, the most important solicitor in Brescia), Tarello openly declared himself on the side of Venice; in this case, he set himself against the group that centred round the Accademia di Rezzato. He also asked in his memoir how it was that the farmers of the Venetian Dominion did not emigrate onto the lands of the Duke of Savoy (*sic*) ' . . . where you can get good land for no more than four ducats a field [*campo*, 0.34 hectares]', suggesting that patriotism was a more powerful motivation in their lives than personal profit. He also suggested calling home 'our subjects who have gone against the Most Gracious Rule [of Venice] and entered the service of other Princes'. We have already seen that Agostino Gallo dedicated his work to the Duke of Savoy and that many of his friends were in the service of foreign princes.

The *Dieci giornate*, published first in Brescia in 1564, then in Venice in 1565, did not appear among the books on agronomy used by Tarello and quoted widely in his text (Virgil, Cato, Varro, Columella, Palladius, the *Geoponics* and Pier de' Crescenzi). Yet at the beginning of the book we find the following comment on the ratio of corn sown and harvested: ' . . . we should get fifty grains from every grain, which would be fifty quarts or *stare* for every quart or *stara*, yet we do not get them'. This was supposed to convince the Venetian Senate of the excellency of Tarello's method. What follows is too near to Gallo's argument to escape suspicion, including the part played by bad weather, by animal parasites (mice, birds, moles and worms) and the example of lupins, which do not germinate completely, although, because they are bitter, they are not eaten by animals. Lastly, he too commends the solution of repeated

---

[66] On the life of Tarello see Berengo, *Introduzione*, pp. x–xiii; on Tarello's memorial to the Venetian Senate see Tarello, *Ricordo di agricoltura*, appendix, p. 139.

ploughing and manuring.[67] It is true that Tarello makes some original points, such as the difference between the grains that always germinate and those which produce an irregular number of fully developed plants; in this he was two hundred years ahead of Jethro Tull's experiments on sowing sainfoin and the invention of the seed-drill (see Chap. 7). However, the points of contact with the *Vinti giornate* are not restricted to those given here; they also concern flax and clover (pp. 19 and 60), keeping very close to the whole paragraph on flax in the *Vinti giornate*. Tarello also insists that one fourth of the meadows on a farm ought to be burn-baked, going on to describe how to burn the old turf, cutting it with a spade and burning it slowly, another procedure mentioned by Gallo (pp. 25 and 38). Other points on which he is close to Gallo are the use of flower seeds from haystacks to be scattered on the fields, road dust (with horse and other dung) to be used as manure and clover to renew wheat-fields (pp. 98–9 and 26). In short, where Tarello reports the practice of Brescian farmers he seems to have Agostino Gallo's words in mind, and his system is based on the Brescian method of enriching the soil.

What is most striking and yet has gone strangely unnoticed by the various scholars who have so far studied Tarello's system, is that lucerne is completely overlooked as a plant for use in laying down meadows. It is true that it was ill suited to Tarello's theory that the pasture should be part of a rotation system, yet it is strange that a careful reader of the Classics, as Tarello was, did not show the least curiosity about lucerne, which was so highly praised by Columella and Pliny. Perhaps this constitutes further confirmation of how far lucerne in the Brescia area was an experimental crop at that time and had not yet gone beyond the social sphere from which Tarello was excluded, that of the Martinengos and the Cuccos portrayed by Agostino Gallo. Italian agronomists of the 1930s praised the wheat–lucerne rotation, which they saw as an improvement on the wheat-clover variant formulated by Tarello.[68] Lucerne leaves a larger deposit of nitrogen in the soil and yields a heavier crop (120–30 kg from lucerne fields 4–5 years old), hence more cattle could be fed on it. In the farming system of the sixteenth century, in Italy and elsewhere, lucerne could ensure high levels of production on relatively small fields. According to Columella, the crop from a *jugerum* of lucerne

---

[67] See *ibid.*, pp. 12–15, and Gallo, *Le vinti giornate*, pp. 41–4; see also idem, *Le dieci giornate*, fos. 36r–38v.

[68] See E. De Cillis, *Trattato delle coltivazioni*, Portici 1937, vol. II, pp. 115 ff., vol. III, p. 344.

was enough to feed three horses for a year, and perhaps Tarello, like Gallo, for lack of first-hand experience, might have taken the agronomist of Cadiz at his word, since he agreed with him about so many other things. Sixteenth-century farmers, who had small room for manoeuvre and tended to be suspicious of innovations unless they were proved to increase production, could have improved their forage crops by growing lucerne, without any dangerous reduction in the cultivation of cereals. The scarcity of lucerne seed may have prevented the crop from spreading.

Another puzzle is that Tarello's library contained not a single copy of the many herbals being produced in the mid-sixteenth century; illustrated books were always costly and probably Tarello was forced to use Pliny book XVI and Pier de' Crescenzi book VI for his study of botany, for lack of anything better. Or perhaps it seemed a luxury to plant a novelty like lucerne on the poor soil of the Brescian hills, and he thought the triumph over poor soil would be achieved by insisting on the cultivation of clover (the decay of the roots and leaves would gradually enrich the soil until it was more suitable for growing cereals).[69]

On the other hand, Tarello's project was risky and involved too drastic a reduction of the seed. Even on perfectly ploughed land, rendered more fertile by clover and by spreading animal manure, not all the corn seed would germinate or grow fully. It is well known that Tarello himself did not succeed in applying his system completely on his estate, La Marcina, which, surprisingly, he did not manage himself. In 1564 he quarrelled with his sharecropper over a series of tasks that had not been carried out, chiefly ploughing and sowing poorer land left to grass, which would have yielded a good crop of millet. It appears that the tenant had been unwilling to adhere to the contract because it was too burdensome (it included heavy work like hoeing the vineyard, gathering and dressing stone and hauling sand for masonry work) and probably because he was not given a share of the produce of the meadows. It is not surprising that Tarello's system was infrequently adopted among farmers of the time, although the memoir was reprinted three times in fifty years. He wrote of large profits but actually gave no figures to support his claims. A comparison between Tarello's method, which we will call the 'new system', and the traditional system with guaranteed yields, backed by Gallo's experience, which we will call the 'old

---

[69] See Tarello, *Ricordo di agricoltura*, p. 101.

system', shows at once that the advantages of Tarello's system, which he praised so highly, were not easy to achieve.

Old system: 10 fields (*campi*, 0.34 hectares) × 6 quarts of seed per field (traditionally sown on average quality land according to Gallo and Tarello) = 60 quarts of seed × 5 (average yield of land round Brescia) = 300 quarts.

New system: 5 fields × 4 quarts ($2/3$ of the seed traditionally sown on average quality land) = 20 quarts of seed × 10 (double average yield) = 200 quarts + 40 quarts (saving on seed sown on 5 fields) = 240 quarts.

or: 20 quarts of seed × 15 (a high yield for Europe at that time) = 300 quarts + 40 quarts (saving on seeds sown) = 340 quarts.

In practice, Tarello's system would only have been advantageous if it had yielded 15 to 1 for every quart sown; this was not a very likely yield on average quality land or land still to be improved by growing clover on it. The real advantage was that the land could rest between one five-year cycle and the next period of cultivation. As for the 'codega vecchia' meadows of the Brescia district, the best guarantee for farmers in the Po Valley against dispossession by marauding armies, taxes and military demands for hay was to defend the fertility of the soil under a thick layer of grass. Tarello's system could have been put into practice only if the grain production, half what they used to grow, had been enough to support the labourers' families. It was calculated that every adult needed x quarts of wheat, hence a family of 5 needed $5x$ quarts of wheat and y fields (n cornfields × 4 grassfields). Tarello's system could only work for medium-sized owner-occupiers or for larger landowners who managed their own farms. Between 1440 and 1542 the inhabitants and the villages of the Brescia district lost one third of the two thirds of the land they had owned, while land ownership was gradually concentrated in the hands of townspeople. This trend in the Brescia countryside was characteristic elsewhere in Europe.[70] The average property was no longer owned by the peasants; by 1548 the peasant class had lost 80 per cent of the grain production; in 1564 alone 19,000 *piò* (6,333 hectares) of land changed hands. By the early seventeenth century only a quarter of the whole province still belonged to the peasants. Ninety-seven of the 163 estates round Brescia, the best ones, were owned by private citizens and

---

[70] See Poni, '*Struttura*', p. 101, and B. Scaglia, 'Note sull'agricoltura bresciana nei secoli xvi–xvii', in *Atti del Convegno su Camillo Tarello*, Lonato 1986.

institutions, only 66 were left to the peasants, and over half of them (35) were of very poor quality.[71]

Given this state of affairs, Tarello's work was clearly of more theoretical than practical value. For all his knowledge of the Classics, he ignored Agostino Gallo's advice that the owner should live on his own land and manage it himself, so that he need not share either responsibility or profits with anyone. Instead he followed the general tendency in Italy at that time, making his tenants work even harder than before. The weakness of Italian agriculture consisted in the harsh terms of the contracts imposed on tenants, who had no hope of getting them changed.[72]

10. STRUCTURAL PROBLEMS AND HAY

No clear picture of combined livestock and cereal production emerges from the contracts of the day or from the work of Gallo or Tarello. There is certainly a connection between the two sectors, but it is at the regional level rather than on the same farm. Tarello, for example, gave no indication of the number of animals that could be kept by adopting his system, while Gallo has Scaltrito the cowherd speak as the expert on livestock, not one of his landowner friends. Tarello's agricultural system looked back more to the Roman way of growing vegetable produce than ahead to the high farming of the nineteenth century. The landowner tried to increase production on his farm by improving farming methods without using more capital to increase the number of labourers. On the contrary, the peasants had to pay for their own labour, through the sharecropper system. The adoption of rough grazing or even of trans-humance for livestock in the fifteenth and sixteenth centuries prevented closer interaction between cattle and meadows. Historians who attribute the pre-industrial agricultural failure exclusively to lack of manure are mistaken, since they overlook other ways of restoring fertility to the soil. Often scholars of the late medieval agricultural crisis attribute the recovery of productivity during the sixteenth century agrarian revolution to the lands reclaimed after neglect during the decades of depopulation and forget that the fall in population stimulated labour-saving systems

---

[71] See C. Pasero (ed.), *Il Catastico bresciano di Giovanni da Lezze (1609–1610)*, Brescia 1969, 3 vols., *Introduzione*, pp. 62–4.
[72] On Italian agrarian contracts see G. Giorgetti, *Contadini e proprietari nell'Italia moderna*, Turin 1974, pp. 33–137.

and the decision to suspend work on the most inconvenient, poor or outlying land, where the process of plant decay gradually renewed it. Much of the dung from the great flocks and herds was dispersed on the upland pastures or at most collected by the shrewdest farmers with the dust on the roads, as Agostino Gallo mentioned.

Had it not been for the resources of the mountain pastures, the lowland farmers would not have been able to keep their herds and flocks throughout the year and at the same time feed the working animals and deliver the required consignments of hay to the cavalry. In 1528, the city of Brescia owed its rural district the equivalent of 275 loads of hay to pay for its share of the consignments of hay to the army. The year after, it was the district which owed ninety-three loads. The quotas were divided as follows:[73]

	1528	1529
From the Steward of the district	1,008	815
From the peasants	480	632
Deducted from the city's share	808	722
Deducted from the district's share	1,212	1,083
The city owes the district	275	0
The district owes the city	0	93

A century later documents concerning the *Consignment of hay* for 1625 give us more information on the sheep and cattle belonging to landowners in Brescia and the surrounding district. In Algise, a village with a population of 4,000 in the fertile lowland area 11 miles from Brescia, on an estate of Count Annibale Gambara, who had a castle and palace there, a total of 150 head of cattle and 100 horses was declared by the community in the tax returns for 1609–10. Then, on 26 August 1625, 606 loads of hay (equal to 6,545 cubic metres) were calculated as the forage necessary for 70 pairs of oxen and 70 farm horses, besides Captain Romanello's 50 horses; they alone consumed 250 loads of hay per year (50 loads each, equal to approximately 2,500 m³); to these were added 200 sheep reared for the butcher, which consumed an unspecified quantity (perhaps deliberately so, to avoid tax). The total requirement for draught horses, cavalry and working oxen was 880 loads, as against the 660 declared – a debit of 274 loads of hay, not counting the sheep.[74]

[73] See Brescia, AS, Arch. Terr. ex-veneto 265, 1528, 1529.
[74] *Ibid.*, Consegna dei fieni, 1625, fo. 154*v*.

The data collected for Ospitaletto on 3 August 1625 show that there was little connection between the high output of hay and the large number of livestock. Ospitaletto was also near Brescia and half its land belonged to city-dwellers, the other half to local peasants. We have information on 21 landowners, including the number of *piò* they owned, the hay they produced and the number of their oxen and horses. Eleven people owned from 10 to 25 *piò* and produced an average of 1.98 loads of hay for 3.72 oxen. Eight owners with 30 and 50 *piò* produced 4 loads of hay for 3.62 oxen. The 2 largest landowners, who had 80 and 160 *piò* respectively, produced 6 and 22 loads of hay, but had no oxen. No owner had more than 2 horses. Deviations from the mean were considerable. One man had 15 *piò* and produced 7 loads of hay to keep 8 oxen, another had 15 *piò*, getting only one load of hay for 8 oxen. We have already mentioned the cases of owners who did not keep cattle. The largest landowner had 10 oxen on 40 *piò* and produced 3 loads of hay. The number most often found is 4 oxen (7 cases), then 8 oxen (5 cases), followed by 3, 5, 6 and 10.[75] In conclusion, it could be said that these farms certainly produced a large quantity of manure (on average one adult head of cattle produces 12 cubic metres of manure per year), but this was produced by recycling the straw from cereals as litter and by using green cereals (oats and millet) as forage. But if this was the case, Gallo's advice does not seem to have been followed very closely and fresh manure was preferred to old manure, which was known to produce less grass.[76]

---

[75] *Ibid.*, Arch. Terr. ex-veneto 266; see also *Il Catastico bresciano*, vol. III, *sub voce*.

[76] The chief difference between cattle and horse manure lies in the greater amount of water contained in the former (81 per cent as against 67 per cent) and the smaller amount of nitrogen (0.34 per cent as against 0.67 per cent). The weight in water is also considerably greater in fresh manure than in old (75.4 per cent as against 66.1 per cent). The higher percentage of nitrogen is harmful rather than useful on most Italian soils, which are already acid, hence it increases oxidation. Gallo listed ten ways of making soils fertile: leaving them fallow for at least a year or two, mud taken from cleared ditches, beans and wheat rotation and green manure, fresh rather than old manure, irrigation of corn fields in February, burning the stubble and spreading ash, lime, and waste from saltpetre production: see Gallo, *Le vinti giornate*, pp. 32, 177. It should also be remembered that saltpetre was manufactured around Gottalengo every two or three years: see Pasero (ed.), *Il Catastico bresciano*, vol. III, *sub voce*. The Brescia custom differed from that of the ancients mainly, as Gallo stressed, in the use of fresh rather than old manure, despite the fact that it produced more grass, weeds and corn-stalk in proportion to the ears of wheat. Probably the fresh manure used by the more informed farmers came from cattle that had grazed on meadows and fallow fields where white clover grew spontaneously, as it did on irrigated fields in Lombardy: see Crescini, *Piante erbacee*, pp. 451–2 (see below, Conclusions). Tarello advised similar measures

Thus the animals mentioned in the Ospitaletto land register were plough- or draught-horses and oxen, and in two very rare cases cows. Nothing even hints at a connection between animal husbandry and the cultivation of cereals in the modern sense. The animals were used for land work and to produce manure; preferably old manure to reduce excessive leafy growth in crops. Agostino Gallo and Tarello also describe farming practice round Brescia as using small amounts of good quality manure, together with dust and manure from the roads, lime and a thick layer of grass to renew the fertility of the land. Rather than trying to combine the two sectors, animal husbandry and cereal-growing, owners made agreements with their tenants to ensure that the land would be kept fertile, by protecting the humus with clover-covered turf, with crops like vetch and lupins to improve it, and by irrigation. Gallo's advice about ploughing the fallow as the first step in the cultivation of cereals might seem to ignore the fragile, alluvial soil round Brescia, where the humus had been created by the plant deposits of crops and the turf of the meadows. However, it was justified by the need to destroy the roots of weeds, especially in summer. Since this left the layer of humus exposed to the scorching sun, Gallo (and Tarello) preferred light-tillage ploughing and harrowing to a deeper break-up of the ground. Modern agronomy explains this as a procedure necessary to prevent the loss of moisture from the soil.[77] Actually, farmers preferred protecting the moisture with a thick cloak of grass and manuring, not acid enough to burn the soil. Heat and dryness, as against coolness and moisture, were the two criteria that correctly explain the agricultural process and the effort to renew the fertility of the fields.

In studying the technological interdependence of Mediterranean and Northern Europe one has to take into account this path to learning and the adaptation of Classical agronomy by growers working in damper climates, where pastures and forage crops served a different purpose on the farm. The meadow and stock-keeping were to take on a different meaning when the northern farming pattern was imitated in some Italian regions and indeed became dominant from the early nineteenth century to the present day.

In the mid-sixteenth century, the Italian Wars had forced peasants and

---

in his *Ricordo di agricoltura*, pp. 56–61, with different priorities. He favoured old manure produced on clover fields, straw and leaves left to decay with manure, lupins ploughed into the vineyards, and road dust.

[77] See De Cillis, *Trattato*, vol. II, p. 120; G. Haussmann, *La terra e l'uomo*, Turin 1964, pp. 134–8.

owners to change their agricultural practices, so as to be able to deliver the consignments of hay which were to distort the productive system of the farms until the Napoleonic Wars. Perhaps this explains the great number of meadows in Italian land registers and the small number of cattle kept on the farms, as well as the extent to which transhumance was practised in all the regions bordering on the Alps, in the Maremma and in Southern Italy. What tithes did to other countries, France in particular, the consignments of hay imposed by the cavalry did in the war-torn regions of Italy. Farmers were not free to choose the best rotation, their hands were tied by the consignments they were bound to make, an extremely important factor never recalled in the economic and social history of Italy under the old rule. Paradoxically, in the example of Ospitaletto mentioned above, while leaving land to grass enabled the farmer to deliver his due consignments of hay, it had the advantage that it defended poorer soils from the summer heat and made use of a natural system for renewing fertility. The fertility of the soil is not a constant factor, as David Ricardo claimed, but the result of saving, in this case saving made by not producing cereals or other crops. The sixteenth-century Italian farmer was constantly working for diminishing returns; he was quite aware of this, and tried to calculate the cost of increasing production in the middle term. At first sight, this seems a contradiction. The period was noted for increased production, the reorganization of farm structures, the rearrangement of the landscape, land reclamation and so on. These improvements were achieved by an increase in the daily labour of tenants or owner-occupiers. Terms of exchange for agricultural products improved, but not necessarily the terms of tenancies. The increase in population meant that tenants and their families could easily be replaced by others. The new landowners followed the rules of the old and new agriculture of the century quite strictly, forcing tenants to do tasks like ditching, caring for trees grown for timber, and repeated ploughings. Generally speaking, they tried to turn the peasants' labour into their fixed capital, so that it would not be taken away from the farm at the end of the contract. The tenant who had been productive would certainly have his rent put up. Not without cause, while returning to the subject of tenants' cunning, Agostino Gallo gave the very rare advice that tenants should be adequately paid and that those of proven experience should be encouraged not to leave the farm.[78] Virgil's precept

---

[78] See Pasero (ed.), *Il Catastico bresciano*, p. 64, and Giorgetti, *Contadini e proprietari*, pp. 33–137; a few examples of local contracts are given above, note 49; Brescia, AS,

of small-scale cultivation (*exiguum colite*) took on new meaning, for it was the only way to increase labour productivity; small, intensively cultivated holdings gave higher yields. Moreover, in the Italian situation, peasant ownership was the only way to guarantee to the man who actually farmed the land the right to consume his own produce, to be free to sell it[79] and, in the medium and long term, to enjoy the slow but not costly effect of the renewal of natural fertility.

11. AGOSTINO GALLO'S RECEPTION IN EUROPE IN HIS OWN DAY

The many editions of the *Vinti giornate* show that, at least in Northern Italy, this publication rapidly established a position that Pier de' Crescenzi's agriculture had held unchallenged for 250 years. It is more difficult to follow the relations of this work with its readers, as the greater number of new books on agriculture made the market less uniform and the farmer-reader's approach to the manual easier. However, a few indications can be found which it would be a pity to omit.

David Odasio, of Brescia, did not overlook the pages on lucerne-growing in his copy of the 1564 first edition, published in Brescia, making a marginal note of the quantity of seed needed. His annotations appear almost throughout the book, suggesting careful study. They confirm that the care Gallo himself devoted to lucerne, mentioning it twice in the letters published in the appendix, found immediate response in the city of Brescia.[80] The references in the margin of a copy published in Venice in 1565, which came from Contarini's family, are more general. The reader noted the improvement obtained by hoeing not only millet, panic grass and leguminous plants, but wheat as well; and the need to take into account the different qualities of soil when ploughing. Other points he marked were the advantages of cultivating the hillsides intelligently and the new rules on sowing; ploughing to get higher yields from cereals; while the note on the manuring of vineyards and the cultivation of fruit-trees is another instance of the interest of the

---

filza 3145, Gerolamo De Como, 4 October 1558, lease between Geronimo and Achille Raineri on the one hand and Antonetto and Giovanni Savoldi on the other at Pralboino, is also of interest. See also Gallo, *Le vinti giornate*, p. 13.

[79] Tenants were compelled to sell any surplus they had to the landowner at current prices, see Brescia, AS, filza 3145, Gerolamo De Como, 15 February 1558, lease between Gabriello Albertini and tenants.

[80] See Brescia, BQ, O.XIII.3, fos. 36, 37*r*.

Venetian aristocracy in the administration of farms on the mainland.[81]
Two other copies published in Venice, in 1578 and 1591, the latter once
the property of the Franciscan friary of Pietrasanta, are less interesting.
No detailed plan of reading can be deduced from them, though they
provide a general indication of current interest in agriculture.[82]
Moreover, the criteria of Pier de' Crescenzi's readers can be traced in
Gallo's readers too; the parts of the work read and annotated are those
nearest to the interests of the owner. Even a Humanist like Belisario
Bulgarini confined his many notes and questions to wine, the garden and
the kitchen-garden, livestock, hunting and bees. Nor did his method of
annotation differ from that of the majority of readers. He replaced
Brescian with Tuscan vocabulary, and noted in the margin what
interested him in the text. Additions and comment proper were always
brief. In one illuminating comment he pointed out that the protection of
Princes could do little to raise the fortunes of Italian agriculture, which
was in serious difficulty because absenteeism was so common among
landlords. He agreed with Gallo that land did not produce as much in
their day as in the past, but considered this was the fault of the masters,
who exploited it with their tenants and labourers. It is significant that a
Humanist and a man of letters should have shared Pliny's opinion on this
matter, to which Gallo also subscribed in practice, condemning those
who tried to increase production by making contracts harsher. Pliny's
opposition to Columella's planned, commercialized administration
could still make itself felt at the height of the sixteenth century.[83] The
many editions of Gallo's work travelled far from his native Brescia and
the Veneto environment. Aldrovandi's secretary annotated it, with an eye
to the different varieties of millet and limes 'various and marvellous in
form'. The volume was also used by an anonymous Florentine or Tuscan
reader, who was compiling his own notebook on agriculture in the
seventeenth century, including a calendar, fruit-trees, flowers, many
products of the kitchen-garden and, lastly, Gallo's suggestions on wine

---

[81] Venice, BM: see Gallo, *Le dieci giornate* (*ex libris* Girolamo Contarini, 1843), fos. 11,
     18, 19, 20–2, 36–7, 61, 64, 77, 83–4, 102–3, 116, 118, 222.

[82] See Venice, BM, 151.D.228 e 44.D.291.

[83] See L. Dal Pane and C. Poni, 'Le annotazioni manoscritte di Belisario Bulgarini
     alle Vinti Giornate . . . di Agostino Gallo', in *Ricerche storiche in onore di Corrado
     Barbagallo*, Napoli 1970, pp. 348–59. On Gallo's suggestion for humane treatment of
     the tenantry, see Casali, *Il villano dirozzato*, and also Poni, 'Struttura', pp. 85–8, and in
     general G. Benzoni, *Gli affanni della cultura. Intellettuali e potere nell'Italia della
     Controriforma e barocca*, Milan 1978.

and vines. Taking into account that Gallo described a method of wine-
making 'alla franzese' (by which the must was only fermented for a short
time) much before this became general practice, one gets the impression
that the light Tuscan wines were an imitation of those produced by
the nobles of Brescia, who came into contact with the French before the
Tuscans did.[84] Another early seventeenth-century indication of the extent
to which Gallo's text was put to practical use, and this same technique of
wine-making was practised, is to be found in a pamphlet on Turin wines
by Giovan Battista Croce, a Milanese goldsmith who worked at the court
of Emmanuel Philibert of Savoy. The inventory of his assets in the will
of *cavalier* Carlo Felice Maletto of Turin is an extremely clear, though
unfortunately rare example of what has been pointed out concerning the
relationship between the private library, the manual on agronomy and the
choice of farm produce. In 1672 this gentleman had a copy of Agostino
Gallo's book on agriculture in his large library, which also included
such important volumes as the *Constitutiones Sabaudiae* and Sardi's *De
Alimentis*; while in his granary there was rye, maslin, sorghum and beans
and various kinds of hay, carefully kept separate. These included 12
Spanish doblas' worth of the third mowing of hay (*ricetto*), 13 loads of
green millet hay, 5 loads of the same, gathered on the Dros, and 5 loads
of clover. The date of the document is rather late, but the connection
between Gallo's book and the good quantity of clover-hay cannot be
passed over.[85] Lastly, all of Gallo's thinking on agronomy, ploughing,
meadows, pasture and cattle is implicitly based on the written rules that
Bishop Innocenzo Malvasia sent to the bailiff of his estate in Panzano di
Castelfranco Emilia in 1609. We shall refer to these in section 12 of this
chapter.

Agostino Gallo was not unread outside Italy. He was translated into
French by Belleforest, a Parisian lawyer, at a time when there was no
lack of French publications on this subject. Indeed, the monopoly
enjoyed by Estienne and Liebault's *Maison rustique* did not make it easy
to sell the Italian work, which was perhaps only read by people of Italian
sympathies. Among these was a certain Barrier, a lawyer of Avignon,

---

[84] See Bologna, BU, mss Aldrovandi 143.2, cc. 171*r–v*, 172*r*, 174*v*; Florence, BN, ms
Palatini Targioni 148, cc. 65 ff. See also Brescia, BQ, Carteggi Gambara, 25 July 1564,
Louis Martinengo to Bartolomeo Della Torre, asking the latter for a small vat for
making wine in the new French manner.

[85] Vedi G. B. Croce, *Della eccellenza e diversità de i vini che nella montagna di Torino
si fanno e del modo di farli*, Turin 1606 (photostat reprint edited by Ada Peyrot, Turin
1970), pp. 48–53. See Turin, AS, Notarile, Min.851, 1672, Lib.2.

who marked a copy between 1625 and 1635 with just a few strokes of the pen where gardens are dealt with, in the section on the sixth day. To these Barrier added a small notebook of twenty pages in all, entitled 'Useful instruction for all those who enjoy gardens. To know when, in which month and moon, one should sow and plant.' The pages, in the lawyer's hand, dealt first with vegetables such as pumpkins, melons, onions, cabbage, white cabbage, Milanese cabbage, lettuce, green lettuce, horseradish, leeks, parsnips, endive and so on. A second part, in the form of a calendar of work, was on peas, artichokes, borage, hyssop, spinach, panic grass, burnet, basil, Flanders peas, Normandy peas, chicory, garden cress, Roman lettuce, red and streaked cabbage, to name just a few. This attention to varieties of vegetables and seeds was typical of Provence, very ready to import from Italy (Roman lettuce was a 'must' in the Avignon neighbourhood), and in Northern France. Barrier's incomplete manuscript ended with some notes on some other products typical of the region, such as fennel, figs and pomegranates. One might wonder why the good lawyer should use Gallo rather than the excellent text that Olivier de Serres wrote not so many miles from Avignon. In c. 14*v*, tucked away among the notes on seeds, he wrote 'Louué soit Dieu et sa toussaincte Mère'. Obviously, as a good Catholic and subject of the Pope, Barrier would not be tempted by a book which, if not actually forbidden, had been written by one of the Huguenot leaders of the Vivarais region.[86] For his part, the great Olivier de Serres did not ignore the Italian work; we shall be indicating elsewhere some points of contact between the two writers.

Not surprisingly, the *Vinti giornate* also came into the hands of a few Elizabethan gentlemen, hungry for Italian culture. There is a copy published in Brescia in 1564, in the Bodleian Library, unfortunately without any mark of ownership or signs of its having been read; whereas John Arscher, William Lilly and Robert Leyestet left their signatures on the frontispiece of a copy published in Venice in 1575. A volume published in Turin, purchased at once by a certain Stefano Rumi of Genoa, was marked by the pen of an anonymous English reader during the seventeenth or eighteenth century. This person was very interested in fruit-trees. He compared Gallo and Virgil's method with the English

---

[86] See Avignon, MC, 1482.4°.313, A. Gallo, *Secretes de la vraie agriculture . . .* , Paris 1571, cc. 1–2, 3–14, 14*v*, 19. Another Italian copy (Turin 1579) is at Carpentras, BI, E.1175, Ex Dono Dn. de Bove 1697. On the fortunes of Gallo in France see A. Tenenti, in Pegrari (ed.), *Agostino Gallo*, pp. 9–21.

practice of turning trees to the north when transplanting them. He took note of the layout of the vineyard, the grafting of cherry, peach, fig and mulberry trees, adding 'white mulberry thrives best in fat, rich ground'. Nor did he neglect the olive, lemon, chestnut and a few others.[87] The most interesting English library to which Agostino Gallo's text soon found its way was that of Edward Coke, the eminent barrister and judge, Attorney General in 1606, who played such a great part in English institutional and intellectual life. Unhappily, this copy is unmarked. Yet it is significant that it was inherited with the library by the famous agriculturalist Thomas Coke (1754–1842), known as 'Coke of Norfolk'.[88] In the following chapters we shall explore in greater detail this continual connection between Mediterranean agricultural technology and the English economic world.

12. LUCERNE IN THE REST OF ITALY

Late nineteenth-century Italian writers on agriculture speak of leguminous forage plants as a recent acquisition in Italy. In their opinion it was only the integration of agriculture and livestock-rearing that prompted the cultivation of forage crops. They are thought to have become common after the spread of model farming from Northern Europe.[89] This would explain the delay in the spread of lucerne, clovers and sainfoin in leys in the sixteenth and seventeenth centuries. At the same time, more traditional plants like lupins, vetches and broad beans were used in green manure, while the other leguminous plants, chick-peas, peas and beans, were sown in rotation with grain crops. Spanish sainfoin (*Hedysarum coronarium*) alternating with wheat also deserves special mention as part of an early but effective form of crop rotation.

The cultivation of leguminous plants was, in fact, a heritage of

---

[87] See Cambridge, UL, U*.5.109 (Turin 1580); another copy, Adams 6.57.3, signed first by Baron John Maule, then by Johannis (*sic*) Couch Adams, is in the same library; for a third English commonplace book containing a few extracts from Gallo, see S. A. J. Moorat, *Catalogue of Western Manuscripts on Medicine and Science in the Wellcome Historical Medical Library*, London 1962, vol. I, n. 215, pp. 60–2.

[88] See in the following order Oxford, BO, art.4°.G.10 e 70.e.2 (18); on Edward Coke see chap. 5, 3.3. On Thomas Coke see R. A. C. Parker, *Coke of Norfolk. A financial and agricultural study, 1707–1842*, Oxford 1975.

[89] See V. Niccoli, *Saggio storico e bibliografico dell'agricoltura italiana*, Turin 1908, pp. 286 ff.; Poni, *Gli aratri*, pp. 169 ff.; C. Pazzagli, *L'agricoltura toscana nella prima metà dell'800*, Florence 1973, pp. 267 ff.

peasant farming, although it was only talked of when the need for forage crops on the large farms increased to such an extent that it could no longer be satisfied by natural pastures or age-old meadowlands (the so-called 'codega vecchia' meadows named in contracts in the Brescia region). Hence it is not so much the presence of forage crops, wild or cultivated, which made good sixteenth-century agronomy an important phase in the transformation of Italian agriculture, as the trend of general economic development in the following centuries, within which this transformation took place.

Lucerne was to return to Italy from Spain via Naples, and from there it was to follow the path we have already traced – at least this is what Agostino Gallo reported. The other sixteenth-century writers either repeated this version or embroidered on it a little, but without adding clear information on its origins. Mattioli also mentioned the part played by the Spaniards in bringing lucerne back to Italy,[90] not in his first but in later editions. Books on agronomy and botany had become so common in Italy that it is not difficult to discover the source of what other texts on agriculture were repeating during the last years of the century. Castore Durante, who wrote that lucerne was taken to Rome by Cardinal Carlo Montigli of Casale Monferrato, Bishop of Viterbo from 1576 to 1594, seems initially not to be connected with the Brescia route. Actually, when we come to read the biographical sources on Montigli with care, we realize that he had only been bishop suffragan of Cardinal Gambara in the see of Viterbo, and so we are brought back to the castle of

---

[90] See P. A. Mattioli (or Matthioli), *Il Dioscoride dell'eccellente dottor medico A. M. da Siena coi suoi discorsi*, Valgrisi, Venice 1548 (in Italian without illustrations), pp. 323 (lucerne or *medica*), 462–3 (clover or *trifoglio*), 582–4 (*loto* and *citiso*); idem, *Commentarii secundo aucti in libros sex Pedacii Dioscordis anazarbei de medica materia*, Venice 1560, pp. 305, 410–11, 440–1; idem, *I discorsi di P. A. M. senese medico cesareo . . . nelli sei libri di Pedacio Dioscoride . . .* , Venice 1568 (with illustrations), pp. 576–7, 1220–1, 1224; of the many translations we would point out only the following: idem, *Commentaires de P. A. M. revenues et augmentés en plus de mille lieux par l'autheur . . .* , Guillaume Roville, Lyon 1572, pp. 329, 472, 616–17 (illustrated with prints taken from the Valgrisi edition, 1568); idem., *Kreuterbuch mit den aller schönsten und artlichsten Figuren . . .* , Georg Melantrich von Quentin, Prag 1563 (once more illustrated with prints from Valgrisi, 1568, however the text is much abridged and there is no discussion on plants, just plant descriptions and properties), pp. 350–3 (*Klee*), 303–5 (*Steinklee*, which correspond to the Italian chapters on *loto* and *citiso*), 508–9 (*Weissklee*), chapter on lucerne has been omitted. See also J. E. Gilibert, *Concordance des noms de Linné avec ceux de Matthioli appliquée aux figures de l'édition de G. Bauhin*, in idem, *Histoire des plantes d'Europe*, Lyon 1798, vol. II, nn. 385, 1075, 702–4, and G. von Sternberg, *Catalogus plantarum ad septem varias editiones commentariorum Matthioli*, Prague 1821.

Pralboino and the words of Agostino Gallo.[91] Some further indications of the older origins of lucerne are furnished by the Neapolitan scientist Giovan Battista Della Porta, landowner and agriculturalist in the village of that name, who had travelled between 1559 and 1579 through Calabria and Apulia, had seen Venice and gone beyond the Alps through France and Spain 'visiting most scholarly men and famous libraries'. The results of these agrarian interests went into his pamphlets *Pomarium* and *Olivetum* issued in Naples, into his books on the *Villa* published in Latin in Frankfurt, and to a lesser degree into the more famous *Magia naturalis*. According to Della Porta the plant was brought to Italy from Spain and was called *farfara* by the Neapolitans. Elsewhere Della Porta follows Pliny, Varro, Palladius and Columella; but although his Latin is far superior to that of the compilers, he too adds nothing personal, apart from the nomenclature. Yet he was enquiring and well informed. After lucerne he gives us a long chapter on cytisus (*Medicago arborea*), a bush that might have improved herbage on tracks along the transhumance routes, and in general on the uncultivated southern pasturelands impoverished by fire and flocks.[92] To these major forage crops he adds others, in the order recommended by Pliny and Columella – red clover (*T. pratense*), vetch, *ocimo* and green spring corn. Here again, Della Porta's main contribution is in the nomenclature; to the Neapolitans, 'meadow' apparently meant clover.[93] But the term *farfara* for lucerne

---

[91] See C. Durante, *Herbario nuovo*, Rome 1585, *sub voce*; on Carlo Montigli see F. Ughello, *Italia sacra sive de episcopis Italiae*, Venice 1717, vol. I, p. 1421, and G. Signorelli, *Viterbo nella storia della Chiesa*, Viterbo 1940, vol. I, part II, pp. 273 ff. on Giovanni Francesco Gambara (son of Brunoro Gambara, mentioned above p. 121) and pp. 292–336 on Montigli. It is questionable whether 'signor conte Fabio, nipote di S. S. molto illustre' introduced lucerne to Paris (*sic*) whence it spread into Lombardy, as Durante himself said. On Viterbo see T. Coturi, 'Le corporazioni delle arti nel Comune di Viterbo', *Archivio della società romana di storia patria*, 7, 1884, pp. 1–114, and A. Cortonesi, *Il lavoro del contadino. Uomini, tecniche, colture nella Tuscia tardo medievale*, Bologna 1988.

[92] On slash-and-burn husbandry see E. Sereni, *Terra nuova e buoi rossi e altri saggi per una storia dell'agricoltura europea*, Turin 1981, pp. 45 ff.; on a more favourable appreciation of fire husbandry see D. Moreno, *Dal documento al terreno. Storia e archeologia dei sistemi agro-silvo-pastorali*, Bologna 1990.

[93] See G. B. Della Porta, *Pomarium, Olivetum*, Naples 1583; idem, *Magiae naturalis libri XX*, Frankfurt 1591; idem, *Villae Io. Baptistae Portae Neapolitani libri XII*, Frankfurt 1592, pp. 908–14; F. Fiorentino, *Studi e ritratti della Rinascenza*, edited by his daughter Luisa, Bari 1911, *passim*, especially pp. 244, 246, 253, 256–7, 266; L. Muraro, *Giambattista Della Porta mago e scienziato*, Milan 1978; G. Belloni, *Conoscenza, magia e ricerca scientifica in G. B. Della Porta*, in G. B. Della Porta, *Criptologia*, edited, with a biographical note and translated by G. Belloni, Rome 1982, pp. 17–19: Rudolph II granted a privilege to print *Villae* on 15 May 1582. Della Porta's

makes us want to know more about the etymological background. *Cot, alfasasat, falsasat, alfalfa, falfala* are the names given in the Arabic texts from Avicenna onwards. Alfalfa is one of the names commonly used for lucerne in sixteenth-century Spain (together with *ervaje, mielga* and *trebol*),[94] and by this time it recurs in many European texts on botany, and is used very occasionally in Italy too. Farfara is merely the falfala of the Arabs resulting from the phenomenon of dissimilation (l/r) common in the Neapolitan dialect; hence, perhaps the legend of the introduction of lucerne into Sicily, thanks to the Arabs, and its return to the Neapolitan area, thanks to the House of Aragon. This version, couched in the cautious terms of Filippo Re, has come down to us via the agronomists of the second half of the nineteenth century. It will be discussed more fully below.

The issue, however, is not simple. If *falfala* is the Arabic for lucerne, the Italian *farfara* is also a plant well known to botanists (*Tussilago farfara*), which has always kept this name. Sandro Botticelli painted it at the feet of his *Primavera*, and it is used too in the first edition of the *Vocabulario* of the Accademia della Crusca. So it remains in the sixteenth-century herbaria and herbals. Thus Della Porta's *farfara* is certainly a dissimilation for *falfala*, but a real slip of the pen for the scientist to have left in the text, written in excellent Latin, but obviously conceived in Neapolitan;[95] in the same way that the Longobard copyist of Dioscorides kept the inversion of b and v typical of the dialects of the Campania region.

In those same years Gian Vettorio Soderini, author of one of the many unpublished works on Tuscan agronomy, also reported a similar nomenclature – lucerne was called 'falfala amara' or 'Burgundy hay' (*fien di Borgogna*) or, by some, more simply *trifoglio maggiore*. Soderini had no doubt that it was widespread in Europe, in the Spanish peninsula, France and Germany (he probably meant the Netherlands) and

words should be assessed with reference to Domenico Grimaldi (see below, note 99), who said that lucerne was probably unknown anywhere in the kingdom of Naples and surely in Calabria, however he had seen red clover growing luxuriantly around Naples.

[94] See G. A. Herrera, *Agricultura general corregida segun el testo original de la primera edicion publicada en 1513 por el mismo autor y adicionada para la Real Sociedad economica matritense*, Madrid 1818, 1819, fo. cxliiiir–v, with supplements by C. Boutelou.

[95] See F. Re, *Saggio sopra la storia e il coltivamento dell'erba medica*, Milan 1816, p. 9; *Vocabolario della Accademia della Crusca, sub voce*; S. Battaglia, *Grande dizionario della lingua italiana*, Turin 1968 and 1975, *sub voce*; Levi D'Ancona, *Botticelli's Primavera*.

later in Italy, though he actually only spoke about Lombardy. He took greater note of the French sources, which is not surprising in late sixteenth-century Florence. He seems to have known lucerne at first hand but not to have cultivated it himself. His description reads like a combination of Columella on cultivation and Agostino Gallo on seed-gathering. He was probably more familiar with the cultivation of clover sown in March in cornfields or in August and September in newly harrowed rye-fields. When grown together with winter corn, clover, like lucerne, has to be sown deep enough to avoid frosts. Otherwise it can be planted in March after light harrowing of the fallow. The kind of advice Soderini gives on clover (above all combined with other crops) suggests that the hay produced on Tuscan farms was partly clover hay, though often mixed with the straw of cereals or perhaps with green millet.[96] While setting a lucerne field was costly and hardly useful on small Tuscan farms, these were the chosen home of the humbler and more adaptable clover mixed with corn crops.

In the last few decades of the sixteenth century the nomenclature and identification of lucerne no longer presented any difficulty for those who wished to cultivate it. It is likely that lucerne is underestimated in estate records, since it was generally used in the traditional way (that is to say, it grew wild in permanent meadows) and was rarely found in rotation with wheat or other cereals. The only exceptions were the regions of Lombardy, the Po Valley and certain areas of Tuscany and Calabria. The documents in the land-registers (see for example the so-called 'Charles V' estimate) and farm documents record all the fodder produced simply as hay, and any piece of land not used, even temporarily, for cultivating cereals, was described as meadow or pasture.[97] Lucerne probably remains hidden in the nooks and crannies of everyday language and, it must be said, is given little space even in the unpublished writings of landowners, some of which have already been mentioned. Indeed, even the documentary sources make no mention of the cultivation of lucerne and, except for Lombardy, they never had much to say about the presence or absence of sown grassland.

From Mattioli and Gallo onwards, those who mentioned lucerne recalled Naples, the Spaniards and then the Arabs in Sicily, perhaps

---

[96] See G. V. Soderini, *Trattato della cultura degli orti e giardini*, edited by A. Bacchi Della Lega, Bologna 1903, pp. 193, 222–7, 378–81.

[97] See Chittolini, 'La pianura irrigua lombarda', pp. 209–16, and Coppola, 'L'agricoltura di alcune pievi', *passim.*

depending more on intuition than on documentary evidence. Indeed, if the Arabs ever did take lucerne into Sicily, it went wild there and never became part of the agricultural system of the island. From the Sicilian Vespers onwards, cereal-growing and sheep- and cattle-rearing and grazing took two different directions, though they both depended on the wide availability of land, grass and flowing water. The Crown had huge possessions in the centre of the island, made up of rights and lands which quickly deteriorated in the fourteenth and fifteenth centuries. Husband-men and shepherds came from the town and exploited the land in different ways. Sheep-rearing was based mainly on the low cost of grass, which enabled owners to make a good profit on the money they invested in terms of the number of animals and the quantity of dairy products. Despite these good profits, the methods used were primitive – the veterinary art was reserved for mules and horses; there were no farm buildings; and no hay was gathered. It was no accident that cattle diseases raged. Of one hay harvest alone we do know that it consisted of Spanish sainfoin (100 *salme* sold in Messina on 10 January 1442). In that case it was a wild leguminous crop which took the place of the delicate lucerne (*Medicago sativa*) in the Pisa area, in the Abruzzi, around Benevento, in Calabria and Sicily (as Michiel carefully noted), and spread whether cultivated or not. We suspect the high yields of milk from cows in Sicily in the fourteenth and fifteenth centuries depended on the presence of this wild forage-crop, at least on the low-lying land.[98] Fifteenth-century Sicily was a less peripheral area of the Mediterranean than it became later, and the growing (or at least the harvesting) of selected fodder was taking place at the same time as sainfoin was being grown in Provence (see Chap. 4, 1–2), and can well be compared with the clovers of the irrigated plains of Lombardy.

Beyond the Straits of Messina, near Palmi in the Seminara territory of Calabria, Spanish sainfoin was used in a two-year but fruitful rotation, described only in the second half of the eighteenth century by Domenico Grimaldi. After the wheat was harvested, the podded seeds of the sainfoin would be thrown onto the stubble-fields, which were set on fire immediately, so that, thanks to the heat, the hard pods containing the seeds proper opened. The autumn rains and the ashes helped them to germinate and the turf made an ideal seedbed, producing a regular

---

[98] See H. Bresc, *Un mond méditerranéen: économie et société en Sicile, 1300–1400*, Rome 1986, vol. I, pp. 103–7, 133–8, 141, 156–9, note 157 p. 157; M. Lojacono, *Monografia sui trifogli in Sicilia*, Palermo 1878, pp. 82 ff.

forage-crop in the following May. Later this was ploughed into the soil, ready for the sowing of the wheat, which grew all the better for the nitrogen deposited by the leguminous plants. The main disadvantage of this rotation was the poor tillage of the soil, which was not cleared completely of the clumps of wheat and sainfoin roots. In practice, the formation of white clover leys in the Lodi area, and of Spanish sainfoin meadows in Calabria, took place as a result of the spontaneous regrowth of tufts of the leguminous plants.[99] It is very difficult to establish how far this simple type of no-tillage agriculture, forerunner of the agricultural techniques of today, was also adopted in the areas where Spanish sainfoin was already growing in the sixteenth century. It should be emphasized that the cultivation of Spanish sainfoin in the nineteenth century spread in precisely those areas where the above-mentioned documents provide evidence that it had previously been grown. Might this indicate a return to its chosen soil of this forage crop that used to grow wild in Italy?

When Filippo Re wrote on lucerne at the beginning of the nineteenth century, the type of cultivation he advised was the same as that recommended by Gallo – in rich, friable, deep soil. The soil was prepared by slash-and-burn husbandry, deep digging and manuring; then it was dug over again. He advised sowing in the autumn, after the first rains, to get three or four crops, as against the two that could be obtained from spring sowing (but, obviously, he was speaking of the higher parts of the Po Valley and the Appennine region). He considered spreading manure or chalk necessary to encourage growth; harvesting seed-lucerne brought in a by no means negligible income (seed was sold at 80 cents per *libbra piccola* in the Reggio area) and it was done by cutting off the tops of the plants and leaving them to ripen on the threshing floor. Not knowing the Roccabonella–Rinio herbal (which, together with various works of art, had been transferred to Paris in honour of Napoleon after the Treaty of Campoformio) and probably solely on the basis of Servius' commentary on the *Georgics* and Ermolao Barbaro's *Castigationes plinianae*, Filippo Re suggested that lucerne might have been preserved in some remote

---

[99] See D. Grimaldi, *Saggio di economia campestre per la Calabria Ultra*, Naples 1770, p. 103, and De Cillis, *Trattato delle coltivazioni*, vol. II, pp. 361–8. Strangely enough this type of fire husbandry was not discussed by Sereni in *Terra nuova e buoi rossi*; only a paleobotanical study might reveal whether Italian *sulla* – a term derived from North African *syllak* and not from Greek, as in the case of lucerne (*medike*) and clover/trefoil (*triphullon*) – was a plant foreign to Italy. It might have crossed the Sicilian Channel with imported African wheats, since it was a weed common in the wheatfield.

place along the coast of the Veneto region. Again, in the early nineteenth century Ottaviano Targioni Tozzetti thought that lucerne had not completely disappeared from Italian agriculture, but had only been forgotten and its traces lost.[100] Behind this reasoning probably lay an attempt to explain why the cultivation of lucerne met with so little favour, and why the role of the forage crops in the system of rotation was restricted to so few regions three hundred years after it had been rediscovered.

Generally speaking, the agriculturalists of the sixteenth century had explored the practical problems of how to increase production and improve techniques at a time when prices were rising, thus coming into conflict with the sharecroppers (*mezzadri*), who refused to do the heavier work, such as digging, or to accept the unfair division of the tax burden and of the produce, which was laid down by contract. This harshening of the conditions of contracts came about because so many small owners were ousted from their land and transformed into *mezzadri* and tenants. The writings of Bishop Malvasia share this managerial tendency of the more informed landowners, who took careful note of the agronomists' advice, in this case in the *Vinti giornate*, while adapting it to the requirements of their property. Innocenzo Malvasia of Bologna wrote a long memorandum to his steward Pietro Rangone concerning the administration of his estate at Panzano. It was compiled for private use but published by the family two centuries later.[101] As we have pointed out elsewhere, writing on agriculture is always prompted by a practical situation. In this case Malvasia's views stand somewhere between the agronomic solutions of de' Crescenzi (the tradition of Bologna) and those of Gallo (the innovator of Brescia). Innocenzo Malvasia had to take a stand on three issues – whether the estate should be managed directly or on the *mezzadria* system; which farm produce should be given priority (hemp, silk, animal husbandry or cereals); and what policy to pursue on livestock and manure. Actually the property was not suitable for direct management as the estate was too large, and the land, in the Romagna and Polesine regions, too uneven in quality. He turned his workers into partners of his enterprises and his partners into mere

---

[100] See Re, *Saggio*, pp. 1–9, see over p. 153, and O. Targioni Tozzetti, 'Prospetto della flora economica fiorentina', *Società italiana delle scienze*, vol. XIV, 1808.

[101] See A. and E. Malvasia (eds.), *Istruzione di agricoltura dettata da Mons. Innocenzo Malvasia pel fattore delle sue terre a Panzano di Castel Franco*, Bologna 1871; to know more about this document see R. Finzi, *Monsignore a suo fattore. La 'Istruzione di agricoltura' di Innocenzo Malvasia (1609)*, Bologna 1979, pp. 5–6.

workers, by the very fact that he imposed a system of priorities for work and crops.

In practice, as happened throughout the agricultural area round Bologna, Malvasia subordinated the whole productive cycle of his farms to the production of hemp. Hence horses and oxen became machines for the production of manure. He also ordered dovecotes to be built on all the farms, and calculated large quantities of pigeon-droppings to be delivered to the steward. He described to the latter how lucerne was to be cultivated, almost as if it were a subject that, at least in theory, could no longer be neglected. He followed Agostino Gallo's instructions very closely. Lucerne was to be cultivated together with panic or millet; he added an inessential suggestion about manuring it, mentioned the beneficial effects of irrigation, saying it could take the place of leaves gathered as forage in spring and summer. He made no mention of seed-gathering, but wrote a great deal on better-known crops such as vetch, oats and clover. The fact that irrigating the Panzano estates was out of the question seemed to be the greatest obstacle that Malvasia had to over-come in applying the two-year rotation, one year wheat, one grass, used in the Brescia and Cremona areas. Giving priority to the hemp crop forced him to increase the production of manure, and hence his recourse to lucerne greatly helped to solve the problem. Malvasia seems to have been aware of this, although in practice the choices he made led him elsewhere. He forbade the *mezzadri* to keep livestock of their own, allowing them just oxen for ploughing. On the other hand he did not reduce the number of stock bred (bulls, cows, steers, horses, mares, colts or donkeys imported from Apulia), but sent his herds off on a complicated itinerary along the borders between the Bologna and Modena areas, then up towards Ferrara and the Polesine and along the Po delta back to the Romagna region.[102] In this way he certainly made his peripheral land more productive, but he lost the manure (litter was only given to the landlord's own animals, not to the second-class cows and mares). It appears from the aforementioned documents that the number of livestock actually kept on the Brescia farms was mostly restricted to animals needed to do the farm work, without reducing the quantity or quality of the crops by so doing. Subordinating the choice of crops found in Italian agriculture to consumption and the needs of urban industry probably goes back very much further than the subordination of

---

[102] See Malvasia (ed.), *Istruzione di agricoltura*, p. 118; Finzi, *Monsignore a suo fattore*, pp. 55 ff., 79 ff., 110–11, 133 ff., 169 ff.

agriculture to the chemical industry in the second half of the nineteenth century. The Bologna case might be interpreted as a significant example of this early specialization in agricultural production that had to face a European market. In this case, however, the connection of Bologna hemp with late sixteenth- and seventeenth-century Northern Europe, which was the centre and propelling force for the social-economic transformation that followed the system propounded by Wallerstein,[103] did not encourage a movement towards more modern relations with the producers.

Malvasia might have exploited his property to greater advantage by intensive production of lucerne, in some cases grown instead of lupins; but also by selecting and reducing livestock in favour of the larger breeds and individual animals. As they were better fed, they produced more manure than those that depended entirely on grazing. The straw which Malvasia recommended as food for the second-class animals was certainly of lower nutritional value than lucerne, oats, vetch or clover-hay. Moreover, even the dung of horses fed in this way was less effective as manure. Gallo, using the words of the Alpine herdsman Scaltrito, had insisted several decades earlier on good, rich feed for larger animals; whereas the bishop only cared about increasing the production of manure, whatever the quality, mixing the 'fats' of all his animals and only keeping the pigeon-droppings separate. And yet all this manure produced very little in terms of the grain crops (furnishing a yield ratio of between 3.48 and 4.95 grains for every seed sown); it produced only just as much as the poor land round Brescia and in any case much less than the 6.30–6.95 ratio from the lands owned by the Santa Maria della Scala hospital in Imola in 1612, and the 8–10 ratio calculated for the best land at the time of the 1740 Boncompagni land-register.[104] Perhaps a good deal of the seed sown went to feed the pigeons, bred for their droppings. Perhaps digging, back-breaking job though it was for the farm hands and part-time labourers, did not rid the soil of weeds so well as cross-ploughing and harrowing. Perhaps the rotation Malvasia planned had excluded the essential alternation of leguminous plants and wheat (even the hemp would have benefited from green manuring with leguminous plants, which Malvasia included later in his rotation system).

---

[103] See I. Wallerstein, *The Modern World-System. Capitalist agriculture and the origins of the European World-economy in the sixteenth century*, New York 1974, vol. I, *passim*.
[104] See Finzi, *Monsignore a suo fattore*, pp. 80–1, 122–5, 132–42; C. Rotelli, 'Rendimento e produzione agricola nell'imolese dal xvi al xix secolo', *Rivista storica italiana*, 80, 1968, 1.

And perhaps all that that abundantly and scrupulously spread manure did was to cover the land with weeds that sprang up from seeds eaten on the rough pastureland, and gave it an overdose of nitrates, which made the clay soil of the Bologna area, already poor in lime, too acid. In short, in terms of the grain produced, his efforts were ill rewarded; but the bishop, in line with the dominant economic pattern of Bologna, preferred hemp to grain.

Could Bishop Malvasia have done better and obtained the same produce with less effort? Perhaps he could, by asking for information from the Beccadelli family, whose land bordered his own at Panzano; or, at least, by studying the local natural environment as indexed and described by the Classics. Though lucerne was not among the wild species that grew around Bologna, there were other leguminous forage plants, melilots and a great many clovers. Even Aldrovandi had started out very simply to collect information for his *Syntaxis plantarum* by studying the Latin agronomists, among whom he included Pliny and Virgil. The pages that these authors wrote on meadows include more varieties and species than Gallo's work on lucerne and clover. We have already recorded how Aldrovandi sowed various leguminous plants, including red clover (*T. pratense*), fenugreek and lucerne, in Camillo Paleotti's garden as early as 1568, whence, we can imagine, they found their way to the fields.[105] Filippo Re had already mentioned the poor quality of the forage from the Bologna valleys, which only provided litter for the cowsheds and stables. But the species collected by Aldrovandi in the Bologna countryside is proof even today that local wild flora could already provide indications for more profitable cultivation, based on the diversification of the species rather than hemp-growing to the exclusion of other crops.

Innocenzo Malvasia's *Instructions* served to show how unwilling the great landowners were to take up the idea of forage crops, a novelty for those times. They understood their importance but restricted their use, in deference to the dominant economic model. Perhaps, for the economic

---

[105] See Bologna, BU, ms Aldrovandi 81, *Syntaxis plantarum*, cc. 250v–255v; *ibid.*, ms Aldrovandi 143, vol. II, *Bononiensis agri catalogus*, cc. 7v, 10v, 11v; see also O. Mattirolo, *L'opera botanica di Ulisse Aldrovandi*, Bologna 1897, pp. 55–6. See Bologna, BU, ms Aldrovandi 136, vol. III, cc. 3–5v. Moreover Bolognese agronomy of the mid-nineteenth century pointed out this road to agricultural improvement: see for example C. Goretti, 'Sul bisogno di coltivare i prati stabili e asciutti dell'agro bolognese', *Annali accademia agraria*, 18, 1873, pp. 227 ff.; D. Bourgeois, 'Della coltivazione della lupinella', *Rendiconti società agraria*, 1, 1841, pp. 84 ff.

outlook of the day, a yield of 4–5 grains for average soils and 8–10 for good quality ones was already sufficient to reward the efforts made to cultivate them, and the city-dwelling landowners made up for unsatisfactory yields by the number of farms in their possession.

Moreover, commercial production was hampered by widespread self-sufficiency. That same early sixteenth-century Italy which was setting up the first Academies of Science, which proved how necessary the artisan's work was for experimental research, which was still visited by so many foreign scholars, whose goods and agricultural products were imitated and copied throughout central and northern Europe, quietly retired from the scene of these innovations. The gap between the everyday reality of Italy's economy and these advance-guards of production grew ever wider. The great landowners abandoned the way of technological innovation in favour of a safer and more effortless increase in their families' capital, based on marriage alliances and purchase.[106]

The model of development that historians have so far applied to sixteenth-century Italy has emphasized the fall in the production of cereals after 1620, the return to rough grazing, the victory of uncultivated grasslands over ploughing, until the agricultural recovery of the mid-eighteenth century, despite some previous local improvement.[107] Behind this convenient interpretation lie hidden certain complexities that are now coming to light. Even now studies on Lombardy under Spanish rule are showing that a more dynamic force was at work in economic life, and craftsmen were setting up on their own in the rural areas. Two recent studies of seventeenth-century Liguria also emphasize the emergence of well-ordered estates among common lands (*comunaglie*) in that region.[108] Hence the history of agricultural innovations (even such unsuccessful and belated ones as the spread of scientifically studied forage-crops in sixteenth- and early seventeenth-century Italian agriculture) helps to demonstrate on the one hand the greater dynamism of what is generally considered as traditional agriculture, and on the other the

---

[106] As an example see G. Delille, *Famille et propriété dans le Royaume de Naples (xvᵉ–xixᵉ siècle)*, Rome–Paris 1985.

[107] See Sereni, *Storia del paesaggio*, pp. 183–225; A. De Maddalena, 'I bilanci dal 1600 al 1647 di un'azienda fondiaria lombarda', in C. M. Cipolla (ed.), *Storia dell'economia italiana*, Turin 1959, vol. I, pp. 557–604; idem, 'Il mondo rurale italiano nel Cinque e nel Seicento', *Rivista storica italiana*, 76, 1964; Rotelli, 'Rendimento e produzione agricola'; P. Villani, *Feudalità, riforme, capitalismo agrario*, Bari 1968.

[108] See Sella, *Crisis and continuity*, pp. 135 ff.; L. Faccini, *La Lombardia fra '600 e '700*, Milan 1988, pp. 137 ff., 201 ff.; Moreno, *Dal documento al terreno*, pp. 181 ff.; O. Raggio, *Faide e parentele*, Turin 1990.

control over the land of the city-dwelling landowners, who forced their subordinates to cultivate crops such as wheat, hemp and flax which, while highly remunerative from the commercial point of view, were costly in terms of production.

4. Forage-crops in France: advance and retreat

1. FROM *ERBA SANA* TO *SAINCTFOIN*, FROM THE THIRTEENTH TO THE EARLY SIXTEENTH CENTURY

The French names for forage-crops, *sainfoin* (*Onobrychis sativa*, Lam.) and *luzerne* (*Medicago sativa*), are currently used in modern French, English and German. *Esparcette*, a word which originated in the Dauphiné and spread through Provence, is no longer in use; it was a kind of *Onobrychis*, now a synonym for *sainfoin*. The everyday language of our time reflects a hundred and fifty years of production and sale of seeds on both a national and an international scale (France was still the largest producer of seed for forage-crops until the Second World War), the linguistic predominance of Paris, and Tournefort's influence in giving uniformity to French botany. The path that led to this uniformity is extremely significant, since it started from a series of conflicts that reveal how deeply the kingdom of France was split, socially and economically, and how the violent effort to regulate provincial differences was brought about by the political power of the capital and the centralized market. Rolland's *Flore populaire*[1] gives a good idea of the variety of provincial nomenclature, but only explains it up to a point. By studying these words in their historical context we can get an idea of the spread of forage-crops in France more quickly than from the traditional sources in the archives. What at first sight appear to be mistakes of the uneducated classes, in reality give precise indications of local history.

Unlike psychologists and experimental scientists,[2] historians have

---

[1] E. Rolland, *Flore populaire ou Histoire naturelle des plantes dans leur rapports avec la langue et le folklore*, Paris 1896–1914, see especially vols. III, IV *sub nomine*.

[2] In general see S. Freud, *The Psychopathology of Everyday Life* (1901) (transl. by J. Strachey, A. Freud, A. Strachey and A. Tyson), London 1960, the standard edition

so far paid very little attention to the mistakes with which human communication is fraught, or the ambiguities of the spoken and written word, deriving, as they do, from changing situations and common misunderstandings. Yet such variables are of great interest when we come to study the evolution and diffusion of technological innovations, and take into account the fact that they are the product of tension between everyday experience and scientific language.

In Chapter 1 we pointed out a mistake, the phonetic change of *d* to *l*, which turned *medica* into *meliga* (*Medicago sativa* into *Surghum volgare*) in a wide range of romance languages. This change took place the more easily because lucerne was no longer cultivated and the former lucerne fields had been overgrown by weeds. Those capable of cultivating this plant did not always have access to the books that described it, and stewards, bailiffs and administrators had lost interest in the crop. The books that preserved the memory of, and rules for cultivating, the plant were available but very little consulted, while the new references to these crops in the vernacular came from different sources.

In the Provençal translation of the Gospels, made at the time of the crusade against the Albigenses at the beginning of the thirteenth century, we find a reference to the pods (*espars*) of the *esparcette* (wild sainfoin) or of other plants (similar to the wild everlasting pea, *Latyrus silvestris*). The pods, *espars*, were generally fed to pigs, but in Luke 15: 16 it is men who fill their stomachs with them.[3] Both *erba sana* and *espars* also

of the complete works of S. F., vol. VI; Lakatos' criticism on falsification (*The methodology of scientific research programs. Philosophical Papers* vol. I, Cambridge 1978) is also illuminating.

[3] See E. Levy, *Provenzalisches Supplement Woerterbuch . . . zu Raynouards Lexique Roman*, Leipzig 1892, *sub nomine*, and L. Cledat, *Le Nouveau Testament traduit au xiii s. en langue provençale*, Paris 1887. See also 'espars', 'ersparsette' in F. Mistral, *Lou Tresor dóu Felibrige ou Dictionnaire Provençal-Français*, Aix-en-Provence–Avignon–Paris 1875, and the *Trésor de la Langue Française*, Paris 1971. The consumption of *Lathyrus* pods (hence *lathyrism*) by human beings in time of dearth is extremely harmful but can still be found in poor countries such as Nepal. 'The peas contain an alfa-amino-beta-oxalylaminopropionic acid and this produces a variety of nervous irregularities in which motor symptoms predominate. The legs are particularly affected . . . then [the patient] walks dragging the body on both hands in sitting positions': see Don R. Arthur, *Survival. Man and his Environment*, London 1969, p. 165. This extremely unfavourable opinion concerning the food value of *Lathyrus* needs reconsideration following C. Regnault Roger, 'La culture du Lathyrus en Aquitaine: passé, présent et perspectives', *Journal d'Agriculture Traditionelle et de Botanique Appliquée*, 34, 1987, pp. 89–94, and the more recent bibliography contained therein, which takes a positive view of its properties as a rustic plant resistant to heavy rainfall, flooding or drought, which can be used by human beings and animals in various ways and which only becomes toxic when no other food is available.

appear in a manuscript of pharmaceutical prescriptions, written in Fréjus in the thirteenth century, as ingredients in medicines for constipation.[4] *Erba sana* almost certainly meant *sainfoin*, in the Provençal sense of lucerne, and *espars* meant either *esparcette* or the wild sainfoin of the Dauphiné. But were the herbs mentioned in these writings cultivated or were they picked wild? That is a difficult question to answer, since the documents of the medieval manors and the manorial accounts never recorded meadow-grasses accurately. Yet some important information can be gleaned here and there from the place-names in the documents of the time. Again in the thirteenth century, among the Vercors mountains, in the neighbourhood of the old Roman colony of Die (Dea Augusta), the bishop used to receive tithes from a variety of lands, one of them called 'Vercheira Ersparsois', or sainfoin garden, which leaves no room for doubt. In this case, the place-name gives vital information about the history of the cultivation of this plant, since *esparcette* in an enclosed garden is not the same as a meadow crop. Sainfoin was not the only forage-crop to leave its name in the Dauphiné Alps (one seventeenth-century document mentioned a piece of land called 'Esparcelet'). Along the old Roman road through Valence–Die–Gap, which led to Mongenèvre and Italy, there is a little village called Luzerand, probably connected with the name *luzerne*.[5] The two plants must have been quite widely grown, to deserve mention in place-names.

The situation in northern France is less clear. It is hard to understand whether Thiercy d'Hireçon, an agent of Philip the Fair and official of Henri II of Artois, who was a careful manager of his own property, sowed sainfoin on the estate for which he kept careful accounts until 1328. Products such as hemp, flax, turnips, colza, horse-radish, carrots and *sainfoin* were generally grown on the enclosed land of the region (*warison*); at least, this was the custom in the early eighteenth century. Whether or not *sainfoin* was included in the produce grown in Thiercy's time is unclear. He certainly had the necessary techniques available. In March 1314 he sowed oats, *paumelle*, *scurion*, vetch, peas, beans,

[4] See G. Brunel, 'Recettes médicales du xiiie siècle en langue de Provence', *Romania*, 83, 1962, pp. 154, 159, 177. In general see also M. Moulon, 'Recettes médiévales', *Annales (ESC)*, 1964, pp. 933–7.
[5] See J. Brun-Durand, 'Censier de l'Évêché de Die, a Die, Montmaur et Aurel. Document du xiiie siècle en langue vulgaire', *Bull. de l'Academie Delphinale*, ser. 4, 3, 1890, p. 71; P. Guillaume, 'Le livre de raison de la famille Souchon des Praux (xviie–xviiie s.)', *Bull. Soc. Etudes des Hautes Alpes*, 13, 1894, pp. 202–17; T. Sclafert, 'Le Haut Dauphiné au Moyen Age', Thèse pour le doctorat ès Lettres, Paris 1926, p. 263.

bisaille (a crop of mixed vetch and beans harvested while still green for use as forage). He had improved his land by marling and manuring and kept his meadows well watered. We have accurate details of all this work and tillage because they were carried out beyond the boundaries of the lord's estate, and so Thiercy had to pay cash for them.[6]

However, there are no references to lucerne or sainfoin in the texts on botany or agronomy written for the upper classes, such as Anne de Bretagne's *Book of Hours* or the French version of the *Circa Instans*, the *Livre des simples médecines*, the encyclopaedia of Bartholomew of Glenville or Pier de' Crescenzi's *Proffitz champestres*.[7] Nor can we find any reference to Burgundy hay, or anything more than common hay in other types of document for use in the upper classes, such as the accounts of the stables of Philip the Bold, Duke of Burgundy. Margaret of Flanders' head groom tells us that in her stables, between 1384–5, a poultice of fenugreek, sometimes mixed with honey, was used for sick horses. Normally the administrator's jargon, using everyday words such as hay or meadow, conceals more than it reveals; in this case the mention of fenugreek (a field plant which adapts to very different kinds of soil) is a warning note from which we learn that we shall soon be coming across lucerne, the more refined, cultivated species.

It is no accident that these early references to forage-crops, and their cultivation in France and Provence, should be found among private documents and writings for personal use, particularly in Provence. From 1471–1507, Fazy de Rame, a gentleman from the Alps, kept a diary, like many other people. Fazy shared the lordship of the village of Embrun with his brother and cultivated his land in the upper Drôme valley. As the

---

6 See M. Richard, 'Thiercy d'Hireçon: agriculteur artésien (13..–1328)', *Bibliothèque de l'Ecole des Chartes*, 53, 1892, pp. 383–416, 571–604, especially pp. 392, 401, 403, 404, 405–6. To understand the term *warisons* see Maillart, *Coutumes d'Artois*, Arras 1749; more recent research points out that fallow disappeared from the thirteenth to fourteenth century on and that these crops spread into Artois during the seventeenth and eighteenth centuries: E. Le Roy Ladurie, 'De la crise ultime à la vraie croissance', in *Histoire de la France rurale de 1340 à 1789*, Paris 1975, vol. II, p. 415, and p. 593, note 50.

7 See J. Camus, 'Les nomes des plantes du Livre des Heures de Anne de Bretagne', *Journal de Botanique*, 19–23, 1894; C. Maury, 'Un herbier en français di xvᵉ s. Le livre des simples médecines', *Ecole nat. des Chartes. Positions des Thèses*, Paris 1963; M. Haven, *La vie et l'oeuvre d'Armand de Villeneuve*, Paris 1896. The same is true of the manuscript books: see Paris, BN, ms fr 19081, Platearius, xv s., Nouv Acq fr 6593, Simples medecines, 1452, ms fr 12322, Platearius, xvi s., ms fr 12322, Livre des propriétés des choses; Bibliothèque Nationale, *Le livre des simples medecines*, Paris 1985, for Pier de'Crescenzi see Chap. 2, 3.

corvées due to him were insufficient, he had to harvest wheat, grapes, hay and sainfoin at his own expense. He noted in his diary that he had had two fields tilled and later sown with *esparcel* and *poulz de foin* (dust from the haystacks), which had cost him twenty florins. On another occasion, he had bought a *salmée* and a half of *esparcel* for his horse, probably before he harvested his own, and this had cost him twenty-two and a half *gros*. Sainfoin was not merely cultivated, it was also kept separate from ordinary hay, to gather the seed for sale.[8] In 1507, the land-register of Bourdeaux, a canton of the bishopric of Die, reported that the land of Las Rotas and La Cort could be farmed 'either as *luzerne* fields or as leys'.[9]

A few years after Fazy finished his diary, lucerne started to be grown in gardens and in the bends of the Rhône near Avignon. In 1517 Pierre Firmin Vachier rented a farm in the Orange district, agreeing with the owner, by contract, 'to grow some *luzerne* on enclosed land'. As early as 1527, the statutes of the city of Orange laid down that lucerne fields were to be kept closed between the Feast of Carmentras (Shrove Tuesday) and St Martin's Day (11 November).[10] There had been social and economic links between the Alps and the fertile Rhône valley for a great many years and the Comitat Venassin (Papal Possessions) enjoyed a privileged position even after the Popes returned to Rome. In 1473 Fazy's young son also left Embrun and went to study in Avignon.

A scholarly printed account of lucerne in France was published a few years later. Then in 1536, thanks to the patronage of François I, the Parisian botanist Jean Ruell, who had already published the first Latin version of Dioscorides' text in 1516, brought out his own research. Ruell belonged to the first generation of sixteenth-century botanists, for whom the analysis of Dioscorides was an essential stage of training, before starting on the study of the flora, first of their own region, then of the whole of France. His work was quickly and unjustly forgotten by his contemporaries; besides which, the botanists of the second generation were much more skilled as philologists (Daléchamps, for example) than he was, and more adventurous as traveller-collectors (L'Ecluse). It was to Ruell's advantage that he began work on the description of French flora before the political and religious split between Catholics and

---

[8] See G. De Manteyer, *Le livre-journal de Fazy de Rame, 1471–1507*, Gap 1932, vol. I, pp. 15, 57, 84; vol. II, p. 216.

[9] See J. Brun-Durand, *Dictionnaire topographique du département de la Drôme*, Paris 1891, *sub nomine.*

[10] See Arch. Dep. Vaucluse, fonds des notaires, n. 309, f. 131, and Arch. Comm. Orange, FF7.

Huguenots took place. He based his research on the work of Marcello Virgilio, the first Italian annotator of Dioscorides; the comparison with the Florentine doctor is quite amazing. Ruell's comment on lucerne is clear, exhaustive and leaves little room for further observations. In his day lucerne ('medica' in Ruell's Latin text) was very common ('trivialis') in France, while it was unknown to Italians. French speakers of the time called it *grand trefflon*, Burgundy hay (*foin de Bourgogne* or, in Latin, *foenum burgundiense*), or *fenasse* (from *foenacia*, a term that suggests that it grew among other grasses used as hay). Ruell lived in Paris and worked for the Chapter of the cathedral of Notre-Dame. He gathered his specimens in the Paris area and north-eastern France and never referred to lucerne as sainfoin or luzerne. He realised that the plant did not originate near Paris and that seeds had been brought there a generation or two before, from Burgundy, which explained the name given to it. He did not suffer from all the uncertainties of Italian botanists in identifying this species so highly valued by the ancients. His chapter on the subject went into great detail. He observed accurately that while lucerne often grew wild in grassfields, something – perhaps the fact that it was foreign to the Paris area – prevented it from growing or spreading unless it was cultivated. In practice, at least a generation before Italian botanists, Ruell understood that lucerne would only develop fully and produce ripe seeds, when it was cultivated.[11]

---

[11] See J. Ruell, *De natura stirpium libri tres*, Basle 1537 (Paris 1536), pp. 393–6, and also his earlier book *Dioscoridis De medicinali materia*, Paris 1516. Like many other scholars of his times Ruell was a Humanist as well as a botanist. Hence when he wrote that ' . . . allatum a Burgundionibus semen avorum nostrum memoria . . . ' (p. 394) the word 'avus' must be understood in the classical meaning of an ancestor two generations older than the writer. Elsewhere in the introduction (*Epistula ad Galliarum Regem*) Ruell spoke correctly of 'antiqui', 'veteres', with reference to the ancients. For general background see K. M. Reeds, 'Renaissance humanism and botany', *Annals of Science*, 33, 1976, pp. 519–43. For a positive assessment of Ruell's work as a scientist see E. L. Greene, *Landmarks of Botanical History* (1909), edited by F. N. Egerton, Stanford 1983, pp. 598–656; on Marcello Virgilio see *ibid.*, pp. 569–82. Some information on Marcello Virgilio and Ruell is also found in *Firenze e la Toscana dei Medici nell' Europa del Cinquecento, La corte il mare e i mercanti. La rinascita della scienza*, Firenze 1980, pp. 196, 200. According to Le Roy Ladurie, *Paysans de Languedoc*, vol. I, p. 78, lucerne came to France from Italy in the same way as other horticultural species in the early fifteenth century. But Ruell openly disclaimed this hypothesis. P. Chorley, 'Early evidence of sainfoin cultivation around Paris', *Agricultural History Review*, 29, 1981, pp. 123–4, has recently suggested that the plant described by Ruell was really *Onobrychis sativa*, Lam., that is sainfoin not lucerne. The identification is supported by a reading of the text which selects the few words which would enable us to recognize the sainfoin pod in the pod of Ruell's lucerne. Very probably the specimen that Ruell was examining was simply a specimen of *Medicago* that had run wild and

Although a very brisk demand for books on natural history and agriculture built up from the 1530s onwards, Ruell's death and the great size of his book prevented it from reaching a wider public. To satisfy that demand, Charles Estienne, publisher and man of letters, began to bring out some small volumes in octavo, on the vineyard, the kitchen-garden and tillage, from 1536 onwards.[12] Actually, Charles Estienne's work was not very different from Ruell's. He presented the agricultural practice of the Paris area from the point of view of Classical agriculture. He wrote in Latin, making an effort to explain agricultural tools, work and plant-life in a clear, simple way, almost as though French alone were insufficient to deal with the problem and one could hope for some success only by comparing the present-day French situation and Ruell's plants with the past, with Columella and Pliny. He obviously felt that agricultural practices could only be improved by imitation. The ancients cultivated meadows with great care and sowed mainly vetch, lucerne and fenugreek, whereas in the early fifteenth century no attention was paid to the choice of fodder seeds. 'Lentils and vetch were mixed together'; to these were added oats; unspecified legumes (*fourrage* in the original) were cut and fed green. Yet even at this time of experiment and confusion, there is clear reference to 'medica, which our folks call sainfoin (*foenum sanctum*)', which was cut as a forage-crop for horses; thus certainly it was kept separate from other grass if not actually sown.

Estienne's source on the subject was partly Ruell, while he himself

---

developed different features in the pod; what in the literature throughout the century is known as Burgundy hay (*Foin de Bourgogne*). The name *fenacia* (*fenasse*) mentioned by Ruell is still used on the southern slopes of the French Alps to refer to mixed sainfoin hay used for local consumption see J. Miège, *La vie rurale du Sillon Alpin. Etude géographique*, Paris 1961, and idem, 'La culture et le commerce de la fenasse dans le Sillon Alpin', in *Mélanges offerts à M. Zimmermann*, Lyon 1949, pp. 119–27. To trace the medieval evolution of the term see W. von Wartburg, *Französisches Etimologisches Wörterbuch*, Tübingen 1949, vol. III, p. 455.

12 See C. Estienne, *De re hortensi*, Paris 1536; idem, *Vinetum*, Paris 1537; idem, *Seminarium*, Paris 1536; idem, *Pratum, Lacus, Arundinetum*, Paris 1554, which were later collected in a single volume: idem, *Praedium rusticum*, Paris 1554. The French translation was an outright revision of the text made by Estienne's son-in-law, Jean Liebault, published as *L'agriculture et la maison rustique*, Paris 1564, 1570, 1573, 1583 ff.; this was part of a more extensive plan of the Estiennes to free themselves of the debts encumbering the publishing house, which had been caught in the upheaval of the wars of religion. On the Estiennes and Robert see E. L. Eisenstein, *The Printing Press as an Agent of Change*, Cambridge 1979, vol. II, pp. 387, 509, 541, 566–7, and F. Schreiber, *The Estiennes. An annotated catalogue of 300 highlights of various presses*, New York 1982, p. 182 and nn. 58, 61, 116, 117, 119, 120, 134.

added the name *sanctum foenum*,[13] for the first time in print. He wrote *sanctum*, not *sanum*, noting that the plant's power to restore exhausted, sick animals to health was like a divine gift (his source was Columella here). But did the *erba sana* of the medieval document become *sainct foin* as the result of a phonetic corruption in its passage from Provence to the Ile-de-France? Or did the popular nomenclature perhaps triumph over the correct Latin name because the plant had obvious beneficial effects on the thin livestock of the peasant short of grazing? The fact is that *sainfoin* and *sainctfoin* were used without making any distinction in French or English towards the middle of the seventeenth century. Moreover, in certain regions, the word sainfoin was used for quite a long time both for *Medicago* and for *Onobrychis*.

Ruell and Estienne have led us into a continued state of confusion, a real conflict between scholarly and popular botany, grafted onto the larger conflict between *langue d'oc* and *langue d'oïl*. As we have already seen in the case of Italy, popular botany was not strict about the use of words; while sixteenth-century botanists used everyday or vernacular words to translate Dioscorides' nomenclature, which served them as scientific terminology. To name a plant by one term of Dioscorides rather than another is often arbitrary, unless there is some correspondence with the everyday language. The scientific struggle went on over the rarer plants and herbs, or those about which there was already some disagreement in the Classical sources. In this case, in the nomenclature of Ruell and Estienne, *sainfoin, fenasse, foin de Bourgogne* and *grand treffle* only meant *Medicago*, never *Onobrychis*. Thus, by looking it up under the right entry, we come across the old term of Dioscorides, *polygalon* or *cicercula*, which Pliny used to indicate a plant that looked like vetch, with an unusually red flower, for which there appeared to be no local name. It is very probable that these names hid various kinds of *Onobrychis* (*O. viciaefolia*, *O. hedysarum*, Scop., and *Hedysarum glomeratum*), which are all vetch-like legumes with red flowers; and all of the same family as the legume now commonly called sainfoin.[14]

Actually, Charles Estienne's real addition to the botany of Pliny and

[13] See C. Estienne, *Praedium rusticum*, pp. 452–3.
[14] See J. Ruell, *De natura stirpium*, p. 640: it should also be remembered that Ruell did not associate the name *sainfoin* with any particular plant. Fifty years later Jacques Daléchamps (see below, note 25) associated it with lucerne. Born in Bayeux (Caen) and working mainly in Lyon Daléchamps got to know both the French and Provençal nomenclature.

Ruell was his description of the practice, common among farmers, of intentionally mixing seeds and grasses when they sowed new grassfields; vetch and lucerne seeds were added to those swept up from the floor of the barns.[15] This practice, which might seem risky, had the advantage that it kept down the number of weeds by mixing several botanically related forage plants. However, as far as lucerne was concerned, it had the drawback that it produced a wild variety, Burgundy hay, and not exclusively lucerne, which was much more nourishing for the cattle. Moreover, the confusion of the nomenclature of the species may well depend on the practice, for in this way the farmer was really producing *sanum foenum, sainfoin,* healthy hay properly so called, and not a specific crop. Hence the name of the plant derived from the technique adopted, since, by sowing a variety of forage-grasses, the different species in the same field were competing with one another and the quality of the hay varied from year to year. Under these conditions it was difficult to collect pure lucerne-seed, which could only have been done if the lucerne had been grown alone, separate from other forage-crops. Otherwise, seed had to be brought from Provence, where lucerne was not sown mixed. The names used by Ruell and Estienne were rapidly reproduced in other contemporary translations of the *Geoponics* and Columella's *Res rustica. Grand treffle, medicque, saintfoin, foin de Bourgogne* were printed without the wavering that had characterized Italian translation in the same decades.[16]

The French translation of the *Praedium rusticum,* given the title *Maison rustique,* was a success throughout Europe, due in part to the personal surveys carried out by Charles Estienne and his son-in-law Jean Liebault on the farms in the Paris area. The chapter on meadows gave a crop of first-hand information not included in the previous edition. In that region, meadows were preferred to gardens and fields, as they were less damaged by torrential rains. Along the Marne, Aube and Viselle rivers or between Bar-le-Duc and Vitry-en-Perthois, and further north, in the Beauvais region, water- and other meadows were known to be a good investment. On comparing the new edition with the 1544 *Pratum,* we find that Estienne and Liebault were more careful about advising that lucerne should be sown with vetch and mixed hayseed. They suggested

---

[15] See C. Estienne, *Praedium rusticum,* p. 447.
[16] See Cassianus Bassus, *Les XX livres de Constantin Cesar ausquels sont traictés les bons enseignements d'Agriculture,* Poitiers 1545, I, p. 1; XVI, p. 10; XVII, pp. 8, 117; XVIII, p. 2. L. I. M. Columella, *Les douze livres des choses rustiques,* Paris 1551, pp. 83 ff.

renewing the old meadows with lucerne (now called *sainctfoin, or soupe en vin*, because of its purple blossoms); it was described among the plants cultivated in the vegetable garden, and this time instructions were given for harvesting it. The methods described in the *Maison rustique* are now believed to be closely connected with documents in the archives of the Parisian region of Hurépoix.[17]

2. FROM WILD SPECIMENS TO DELIBERATE CULTIVATION

Obviously, in France in the mid-sixteenth century there were two kinds of forage-crops, *Medicago* and *Onobrychis*, which were often mistaken one for the other. Looking back over the scene, we realise that the local nomenclature had the advantage that, although variable at any one time, the object corresponded to its name, and that this could be proved on the basis of the Classical texts. Moreover, it was particularly difficult to identify *sainfoin* as *Onobrychis*, since there was no officially recognized nomenclature and when cultivated there were often morphological differences between different specimens of the same species.[18] Now, while lucerne was a plant that had been so accurately described that a careful botanist could harbour no doubts about it, polygala (which later became *Onobrychis*) was unsatisfactorily described in Dioscorides' text. Besides this, polygala was illustrated very briefly in the oldest manuscripts of Dioscorides, which had been available to scholars of the second half of the sixteenth century in Vienna and Padua.[19] What is more, although French and Flemish botanists had travelled and gathered herbs in the Mediterranean regions, they were beginning to have difficulty in describing the flora of central and northern Europe on the basis of the eastern-Mediterranean flora described by Dioscorides. In the second half of the sixteenth century all botanists, but above all those

---

[17] The following are the translations of the *Maison rustique*: in Italian, Venice 1581; in German, Strasbourg 1598; in English, London 1600; in Dutch, Dordrecht 1627. In general see also C. Beutler, 'Un chapitre de la sensibilité collective: la littérature agricole au xvie siècle', *Annales (ESC)*, 28, 1973, pp. 1280–1301; see on meadows the *Maison rustique*, Paris 1564, pp. 278–80. In general see also J. Jacquart, *La crise rurale en Ile-de-France, 1550–1670*, Paris 1974, pp. 289–90, 292, 296, 317 ff., 328 ff.

[18] See P. Saccardo, *Cronologia della flora italiana ossia repertorio sistematico delle più antiche date e autori del rinvenimento delle piante*, Padua 1909, p. iv.

[19] See H. Gerstinger (ed.), *Dioscurides. Codex Vindoboniensis Med. Gr. 1 der Österreichischen National Bibliothek*, Graz 1970, 2 vols., and E. Mioni, *Un ignoto Dioscoride miniato* .

outside Italy, were endeavouring to define regional flora and create national schools, so as to free themselves from the predominance of the universities of Padua and Bologna.

Rembert Dodoens, the Flemish botanist from Malines, was the first to associate the Classical name *Onobrychis* with the plant, still often called polygala, that would become universally known as *O. sativa*, Lam. In 1557 he could only say that this grass was being sown in botanists' private gardens. In an edition published much later than his main herbal, Dodoens added that sainfoin grew in many places in Northern Germany, near the city of Cureghem (Brabant) and in Bohemia, in fields watered with abundant rain. Besides this, a second *Onobrychis* was beginning to appear in the specialists' gardens; from the illustrations it can be identified with *Hedysarium coronarium*. Dodoens, who came from Flanders, a country of small farms and well-developed horticulture, left some keen observations on sown forage-crops. He noted that clover (*T. pratense*) grew in both dry and marshy natural meadows and was also sown in the fields of Brabant. Actually it was sown as lucerne by the uninformed, while specialists had grown it separately in their gardens. Cytisus (*Medicago arborea*) was grown exclusively in gardens, while another kind of lucerne (*M. scutellata nigra*), which Dodoens called 'Trifolium cochleatum', had already been grown in gardens in Belgium and Germany for some time. Outside his own circle, Dodoens was given little praise or support by his contemporaries; indeed Johan Bauhin made a personal attack on him, accusing him of confusing things in general and lucerne in particular.[20]

His fellow countryman, Charles de L'Ecluse, did give him some support, mainly while they were both working in England for a time, and during the journeys that L'Ecluse made to Portugal and Moravia, to collect specimens that had now become necessary to describe European flora. From these studies it began to emerge that many plants were merely regional varieties and that Dioscorides' nomenclature applied at

---

[20] See R. Dodoens, *Histoire des plantes*, Antwerp 1557, pp. 338, 341; idem, *De stirpium historia . . .* , Antwerp 1563, 1564, vol. II, pp. 32, 45; idem, *Stirpium historiae . . . ab auctore aucti et commendati*, Antwerp 1616, pp. 548–9, 565, 568–9, 574–6. On the corresponding modern nomenclature see P. J. d'Avoine, *Eloge de Rembert Dodoens suivi de la concordance des espéces végétales . . . avec . . . Linné*, Malines 1850, nn. 546, 549, 565, 569, 575, 576. On small botanical gardens in the Low Countries see C. Petrus, *Annotatiunculae aliquot Cornelii Petri Leydensis Phisicii, in quatros libros Dioscoridis Anazarbei*, Antwerp 1533, II 5. On Bauhin's comment see J. Bauhin, *Historia plantarum universalis*, Basle 1561, vol. II, p. 760 ('hic praetera nullum certum ponit discrimen inter Medicas sed suo more commiscet').

most to species. In our case, the name *Onobrychis* could be attributed
to a larger number of legumes that grew in dry meadows in Hungary,
Austria, Styria, Moravia and Bohemia. One specimen gathered in 1580
in Znai, in Moravia, and transplanted into a garden, did not change
morphologically and continued to produce seeds. This did not happen
with another specimen, gathered in 1574, which stopped producing pods
after a couple of years. A very rare specimen was growing in London in
1581, in the garden of Dr John Riches, pharmacist to Queen Elizabeth.
Other plants, known by names ranging from *Onobrychis, galega
officinalis, cicer silvestre* and *foenum graecum silvestre*, grew in
L'Ecluse's garden, from seeds sent from Spain; originally they had
grown wild in a wide area between the Drave river and the town of Mor.

L'Ecluse was among the first to think that the colour of the lucerne
flower was not an essential feature for the identification of the species.[21]
From their journeys Dodoens and L'Ecluse brought back a quantity of
information on *Onobrychis*, in the wild and growing spontaneously in
meadows and fields. On the other hand, it was already clear by that time
that wild specimens transplanted or sown in botanists' gardens did not
always produce seed. The domestication of *Onobrychis* presented greater
problems than lucerne did. Once more it should be remembered that
while lucerne was one of the first plants ever to be cultivated, *Onobrychis*
was still a weed (as were *Trigonella* and *Hedysarum*), which took the
place of lucerne whenever it was left uncultivated or when environmental conditions were unfavourable.

The cultivation of forage-crops in sixteenth-century France provides
a very definite example of how wild varieties were transformed into
cultivated products at that time. Dodoens and L'Ecluse showed the great
effort made by northern botanists to become familiar with wild, southern
species and to grow them as crops. Matthias de L'Obel and Pierre Pena
carried out a similar operation, moving in the opposite direction; they
introduced the northern variety of *Onobrychis*, appropriately called
caput gallinaceum Belgarum, into the Montpellier area; it had grown

---

[21] L'Ecluse published the results of his travels in 1576 (Spain and Portugal) and 1580
(Germany, Austria, Hungary and other regions of the Habsburg empire): we have
mentioned above his main work *Rariorum plantarum historia*, Antwerp 1601,
pp. 232–3, 238, 240, 243. L'Ecluse also edited some illustrated editions of the *Histoire
des plantes* by Dodoens (Antwerp 1557). A bibliography on him is listed in F. W. T.
Hunger, *Charles de l'Escluse (Carolus Clusius) Nederlandsch Kruidkundige,
1526–1609*, The Hague 1927, 1943, 2 vols. His relationship with Italian botanists
were studied by G. B. De Toni, 'Il carteggio degli italiani col botanico Carlo Clusio',
Memorie della R. Accademia di Scienze, Lettere e Arti di Modena, ser. 3, 10, 1912.

wild on the coasts and in the fields of Holland and Zeeland.[22] It is significant that Dodoens and L'Ecluse met with success in Elizabethan England, in part an even more northerly area, where local botany developed late (see Chap. 6, 3). On the other hand, they met with little interest south of Paris (see below, 2.1.). This is a striking contrast with the situation in Provence and the Venice area, where botanists like Daléchamps and Michiel and an agronomist like de Serres were thoroughly familiar with these plants, which were already being cultivated.

The Venetian Pier Antonio Michiel, the extremely scrupulous botanist who had collated the sixteenth-century printed sources with the dried specimens and with information sent to him by Venetians in the consular service, and others in his vast network of contacts, harboured no doubts. In his opinion, *grand treffle* and Burgundy hay were synonyms of lucerne, while Dioscorides' polygala was *sainfoin* ('which means sainfoin in Provence'). Antonio Tolomei, an Italian botanist who gathered herbs in France and Corsica, had sent him specimens from the region round Lyons.[23] Actually Tolomei might have been expected to call this plant 'esparsette', the local name, or polygala, the erudite name. *Sainfoin* rarely meant our sainfoin in the mid-sixteenth century.

Jacques Daléchamps was the most outstanding botanist of Lyons, working in the middle decades of the sixteenth century. He was a correspondent of Gesner and many other scholars of his time, himself a sedulous Humanist who had written an unpublished criticism and commentary on Theophrastus; he was particularly interested in tracing the wild features of the species and the local nomenclature.[24] Theophrastus already knew that plants improve and change their appearance when cultivated, hence Daléchamps could not ignore the fact. One of the tasks of the botanist was to record the nomenclature and regional use of the species. Daléchamps wrote that the French called lucerne *sainctfoin, foin*

---

[22] See L. Legré, *La botanique en Provence au xvie siècle. Pierre Pena et Matthias de L'Obel*, Marseille 1899, pp. 216, 218.

[23] See chap. 3, notes 31, 32, 33.

[24] See on his unpublished works Paris, BN, ms Lat. 13.063, Daléchamps epistulae, fos. 27–30, to C. Gesner, 27 March 1561; fos. 31–3, 35–9, 257–62 (they were all concerned with ancient and modern plant nomenclature). *Ibid.*, ms Lat. 11.857, Theophrastus, *De plantis*, translated by J. Daléchamps. A biographical note is published in *Dictionaire de biographie française*, Paris 1961, vol. IX, *sub voce*, and C. B. Schmitt, 'Some notes on Jacobus Dalechampius and his translation of Theophrastus (ms BN Lat. 11.857)', *Gesnerus*, 26, 1969, pp. 36–53; idem, 'The Correspondence of Jacques Daléchamps (1513–1588)', *Viator*, 8, 1977, pp. 399–434.

de Bourgogne, herbe aux limassons (from the shape of the pods, which looked like snail-shells); moreover this legume was sown by some farmers in Provence, the Languedoc and Guienne (especially near Secteriens) in water-meadows which were mown three times a year and produced very rich forage. Locally they called it *lucerne* or *lucert* and there was a wild variety that grew in the fields and under the hedges near Montpellier. The chapter on polygala is also full of surprises. Daléchamps used the same words as Ruell did to describe the plant to which Ruell had never given a vernacular name. After clarifying the confused text of Dodoens and L'Obel, he gave it the name used in the Dauphiné region, *sparse* (that is, *esparsette*) and told how it was grown on the mountains above Die. *Esparsette* was sown where there was no pasture. The steep, stony slopes were dug with the spade, to make terraces which were carefully manured, but irrigated only with rainwater. The plant took three years to produce a crop, but in the end gave rich pasture, 'laetissimi prati', for sheep on land originally very poor, 'squalidissimo solo'. It grew particularly well on poor, sandy soil.[25] We cannot help thinking of the 'sainfoin garden' (*Vercheira Esparsois*) described in the rent-roll of the bishop of Die in the thirteenth century and the accuracy with which it reported the same practice that Daléchamps described. Until very recently, Die was still one of the foremost areas for the production of lucerne seeds.[26]

Daléchamps' botanical scheme was supported in many of its details by Olivier de Serres, lord of Pradel, the greatest agronomist of the century. De Serres was an illustrious figure, a politician, soldier and Huguenot of the Dauphiné, who went over to Henri IV's side when the king's peace

---

[25] See Jacobus Dalechampius, *Historia generalis plantarum in libros XVII per certas classes artificiales digesta*, Lyons 1587–8, pp. 444–6, 489–90, 502–3. The work, written twenty years or so before it was published, was interrupted on the death of Daléchamps and published without being revised. It contained a number of errors, mostly attributed to the publisher Guillaume Roville. Roville had dedicated the volume to Charles Emmanuel I of Savoy, a sign of the split in the French scientific world during the wars of religion. Johan Bauhin was the commentator most hostile to this work, but he never attacked the chapters examined here. It should be remembered that Bauhin and Daléchamps had collaborated for some time, until Bauhin was obliged, for religious reasons, to leave France and seek refuge in Basle. The French edition of the *Historia plantarum* came out as *Histoire generale des plantes*, Lyons 1653, translated by Jean de Moulins, who rendered the Latin *medica* coherently as 'sainfoin ou foin de Bourgogne'. See also A. Magnin, *Prodrome d'une histoire des botanistes lyonnais*, Paris 1898.

[26] See M. Gérard and M. Cheyssière, *Monographie agricole de Die. Hiver 1967–1968*, typed copy, pp. 51–5, kept in Valence, AADD.

brought relief to a war-stricken country. Even now there is still no recent detailed study of this writer on agriculture.[27] Despite the wars of religion, and the fact that he lived in the Dauphiné, the region where they raged most violently, Olivier de Serres found the time to compose a voluminous, up-to-date treatise on agriculture. His *Théâtre d'agriculture*, published in Paris in 1601 and dedicated to Henri IV, was intended to play the same role as the *Prouffitz champestres* had played in the dark age of the Hundred Years War. The lord of Pradel's work suggested that, in the decades following the Massacre of St Bartholomew, agriculture and managing one's own business was a more profitable occupation for landed nobles than tearing one another to pieces. But unfortunately, since the king was assassinated and war broke out again, since the book was so voluminous and circulation was restricted outside Huguenot circles (no editions were printed in Paris after 1617, though reprints were made in Rouen and Geneva), the *Théâtre d'agriculture* made little impact on French and other European readers of the time, except when it was first published.

In the dry climate of southern France, meadows, pastures and woods were an important part, as much as two thirds, of a farm. The former had to be kept closed to animals to allow irrigation and let the grass grow thick, sheltered from seeds borne on the wind and from the close cropping of sheep. 'Le près clos est dite la pièce glorieuse du domaine . . . dont ils tirent le plus de commodité.' The ground had to be prepared by careful ploughing, sixteen months before the clean, well-ripened hayseed was broadcast. Mixed hayseeds with 50 per cent of oats were sown in March, to ensure full germination and to pay for the costs of tillage with the first harvest. The rules for the cultivation of the meadow

---

[27] See A.-H. Vaschalde, *Olivier de Serres seigneur de Pradel: sa vie et ses travaux*, Paris 1886 (with unreliable extracts from the *Livre de raison*), and M. Lebaudy, *Olivier de Serres*, Paris 1963, are the most useful works. See also J. Meuvret, *Le problème des subsistances à l'époque Louis XIV. La production des céréales dans la France du xviie et xviiie siècle*, Paris 1977, vol. I, *passim*, and Bourde, *Agronomie*, vol. I, pp. 51–7. A more up-to-date bibliography on Olivier de Serres is to be found in M. Boulle, 'Bibliographie sur Olivier de Serres', in *Information regionale, CRDP Grenoble*, 40, 1982, pp. 33–4, and idem, 'Olivier de Serres (1539–1619)', Bourgeois, huguenot, agronome et humaniste et son Théâtre d'agriculture et mesnage des champs', *Etudes Drômoises*, 3–4, 1984, pp. 3–32. The unpublished papers of Olivier de Serres are kept in Paris, Société pour l'Etude du Protestantisme en France, ms 950, *Livre de raison*; see *ibid.*, ms 9954 for notes and corrections of H. Vaschalde's transcriptions. Many editions of the *Théatre d'agriculture* were brought out: eighteen in Paris (never, after 1617, until 1803–4), Rouen and Geneva. In Grenoble, 1695, a summary of the whole work was published as *Agriculture et ménage des champs et de la ville*, 250 pp.

were completed by careful hoeing of the growing grass, manuring every two or three years, as well as irrigation with cold water from the mountains or warm water from the springs and fountains, according to the season and the temperature of the soil. This method might be chosen by the farmer for growing clover, vetch or the other 'exquisites semences', such as sainfoin and lucerne.

Olivier de Serres was writing for all French readers and could not afford to be misunderstood with regard to nomenclature. *Sainfoin* in France, *sainfoin* and *luzerne* in Provence and the Languedoc, *erba medica* in Italy, all referred to the same plant, he explained. De Serres confirmed that lucerne was well cultivated in Spain and France, but almost unknown in Italy and Piedmont. The French regions where it was most widely grown were the Languedoc, Provence, the Dauphiné, Orange and the Comitat Venassin. It was usually cut five or six times a year, but even eight or nine times where it was looked after well. Lucerne was given, freshly mown, to horses in spring for no more than eight or ten days, then oats and hay were given; or else it was mown as hay for the cattle. Lucerne was a plant that did not take root or flourish easily during the first year, when the scorching sun might destroy the seedlings. Once it was growing well, it might serve for ten or fifteen years. After that the farmer could choose between breaking up the lucerne-field (*luzernière*), and so reaping the benefit of the fertility that had accumulated in the soil, by planting a number of cereal crops, or he could turn it into permanent pasture by letting water run through it; if he did this, the lucerne went wild and became *grand treffle* or Burgundy hay (*M. falcata*).[28] Lucerne was seldom sown alone in the time of Olivier de Serres; vetch, oats and barley seeds were mixed in equal parts, so that the annual plants provided protection against weeds and gave the farmer immediate income from the first cut. This practice was typical among Provençal farmers, who

---

[28] De Serres' sources included the French translation of Agostino Gallo: see A. Tenenti, in Pegrari (ed.), *Agostino Gallo*; but it should not be imagined that he had a mere bookish knowledge of the situation in Italy, for the flocks from the southern valleys of Piedmont came to graze as far as the mouth of the Rhône, see T. Sclafert, *Cultures en Haute-Provence: deboisement et pâturages au Moyen Age*, Paris 1959. The Dauphiné valleys, famous for their wealth of botanical species, were commonly included in the itineraries of the Italian herbalists in search of simples, see N. Chorier, *Histoire générale de Dauphiné*, Grenoble 1661–Lyons 1672, vol. I, p. 49. This is probably the plant Ruell had described under the name of lucerne (see above, note 11) with bean-shaped pods that grow on stalks that branch from the main stem, in a very different way from *Medicago sativa*. A fine illustration was reproduced in Daléchamps, *Historia generalis*, p. 503. For a modern description see H. Coste and C. Flahault, *Flore descriptive et illustrée de la France*, Paris 1937, vol. I, p. 322.

had found that cereals grown together with lucerne produced more abundant crops 'pour certaine secrète vertu de la dite plante'. Like all legumes, lucerne enriched the soil with the nitrogen necessary for growing cereals. On the other hand, the mixture of plants had the drawback that it required costly hoeing to keep down the weeds and prevent the lucerne-field from becoming contaminated. Olivier de Serres gives a very clear example of the practical difficulties that were met with in setting a new crop in a Mediterranean climate. Human intervention as a factor of change has to be uninterrupted and the whole process of selection and innovation has to be backed up by appropriate practices. De Serres was clearly aware of this when he advised collecting only the best seed, from the best flower-heads, cut in the second year of growth, in the month of August, when it was fully ripened; the cutting had to be done at dawn, the pods dried out completely on the threshing floor, and they had to be threshed gently.

Lucerne was not the only forage-crop that Olivier de Serres valued highly. For three hundred years after the first document on the cultivation of *esparcet*, Die was still the centre of sainfoin growing and selling. The price of sainfoin seed there was double that of oats and it could be bought on the market. Yet de Serres spoke of sainfoin as a novelty that had the advantage of growing on light soils. As with lucerne, there was no yield from sainfoin in the first year, while from the second year on it gave three crops of healthy hay. In any case it was advisable to keep the sainfoin-field for three or four years and then use it as arable land, for winter or spring wheat. In practice de Serres was suggesting a regular rotation, always keeping a certain number of fields for hay, and ploughing them up in turn to sow wheat.[29] As Tarello showed, local practice (in this case a practice centuries old) was ahead of agricultural experiment and had demonstrated the favourable correlation between legumes and cereals grown in rotation.

At this stage, the chronology of events and their documentation grow very complicated. How did it come about that *sainfoin*, the name for lucerne in the sixteenth century, was used for *Onobrychis* in the eighteenth century? In view of the fact that many seeds from Provence were exported to northern France, with its different climate and soils, this is no idle question. The success of the innovation depended mainly on the quality of the seed. As we have seen, it was no accident that so many owners in Italy, France and England were studying the nomenclature of

---

[29] See De Serres, *Théâtre d'agriculture*, pp. 262–5, 270–4, 274–5.

herbs and plants. Accuracy was a necessary step on the way to agricultural improvement and more intensive cultivation. The old proverb 'C'est cuellir chardons pour luizerne / C'est marcher la nuit sans lanterne' was no doubt based on bitter experience.[30]

2.1. Books in print and competition on the book market

The differences of terminology that we have mentioned indicate the depth of sixteenth-century scientists' concern for nomenclature, and their continual comparisons with, and references to, erudite and popular language. Actually, the language of the scientists was poorly equipped for its task and even the publication of Theophrastus' *Historia plantarum* (1495–8, by Aldo Manuzio), did little to develop terminology, perhaps because ancient botany had been seen merely as a branch of knowledge preliminary to the study of medicine. The problems connected with the identification of central-European varieties and comparison with those of Theophrastus and Dioscorides could only be faced by studying the language of the unsophisticated, and comparing it with the remains of Classical culture. For this reason, the work of re-identifying forage-crops in northern and southern France in the sixteenth century was no empty academic exercise; the great variability of everyday language and the continual interchange of *sainfoin* and *luzerne* made it imperative. One of the problems of sixteenth-century culture was that just when regional differences attained dignity in the press, with the books published in the first decades of the century (Quimpereau Le Beaujeu's *De laudibus provinciae*, for example), publishers found that their local markets were too small for them to bring out only works dealing with a regional culture. Expensive books on botany, and sometimes on agriculture, had to be translated into French, Latin and Flemish, and had to cater for a wider market, to meet the high cost of the engravings.[31] This problem

---

[30] See Rolland, *Flore populaire*, vol. IV, pp. 121–57, 242–54, which reproduced all the popular nomenclature of the species *medicago, melilotus, onobrychis, trifolium, trigonella*; the proverb quoted is on p. 125. See also in J. Gillieron and E. Edmont, *Atlas linguistique de la France*, Paris 1909, maps 722, 733, 784, 793, 1705 for *sainfoin* and 789 for *luzerne*. The *Théâtre d'agriculture* made an important contribution to the understanding of sixteenth-century French, see *Dictionaire de la langue française du seizième siècle*, Paris 1925 ff., and K. Adernacht, *Der Wortschatz in Olivier de Serres*, Erlangen 1917.

[31] On the relationship between technical language, scientists and the lower classes see H. Busson, *Les sources et le développement du rationalisme dans la littérature française de la Renaissance, 1553–1601*, Paris 1922; L. Febvre, *Le problème de*

was especially acute in France, where Tournefort's nomenclature was still used, even after European botanists elsewhere had completely accepted the Linnaeus system. Italian botanists had also leapt into the fray, bickering angrily over the most hotly debated attributions. Mattioli was a master in these practices, with his attacks on the unfortunate Luigi Anguillara, guilty only of being too much in the public eye as director of the Botanical Gardens of Padua, and eventually forced to give up his post. In this way Italian botanists gambled for the positions most sought after, as chief doctor to the Pope (held by Andrea Cesalpino), or physician to the Emperor (Pietro Andrea Mattioli), or director of one of the Botanical Gardens – in Padua, Pisa, Florence, Modena or Ferrara – or reader, teaching about simples in the universities of those cities. They were posts that conferred prestige and a regular income, which the profession of medicine or pharmacy or the small market for printed herbals did not ensure (especially at a time when it was monopolized by Mattioli's books, leaving little room for other writers).

The social divisions created in France by the Reformation had repercussions in the scientific world too.[32] The book market grew, the boundaries between the French, Flemish and German worlds were more uncertain, religious conflict more violent. So far we have shown how linguistic differences made communication between France properly so called and Provence and the Languedoc difficult in various ways. There were times when communication between botanists was restricted to a few individuals. While Ulisse Aldrovandi, Pier Antonio Michiel and Conrad Gesner corresponded regularly with many specialists, the majority were shackled by haughty defence of their own nomenclatures, deaf to any attempt at discussion. As we have mentioned elsewhere, European botanists were creating national schools and, in a science for which specific institutions had not yet been created, a veritable power struggle was under way. So we find greater division between northern France and the Languedoc–Provence area, despite the fact that the

---

l'incroyance au xvi⁺ siècle. La religion de Rabelais (1942), Paris 1962, pp. 418 ff., 455, 457; in general P. Lacombe and A. Claudin, *Histoire de l'imprimerie en France au 15ᵉ et 16ᵉ siècles*, Paris 1900–14, vols. I–IV; on the role of the printed book in bringing about change see E. L. Eisenstein, *The Printing Press*, pp. 599 ff.

32 The bibliography on French botanists is rather large: a biographic sketch and a bibliography for each author are to be found in the *Dictionary of Scientific Biography*, New York 1970– , *sub voce*; see also A. Arber, *Herbals: their origin and evolution* [1938], Cambridge 1986; on French botanists besides Magnin, *Prodrome*, see also L. Legré, *La botanique en Provence au xviᵉ siècle*, Marseille 1899–1904, vols. I–IV; A. Davy de Virille (ed.), *Histoire de la botanique en France*, Paris 1954.

French botanists, or those whose field of action lay in the French–Flemish world, all came from the same school. Moreover, those who were confronting each other, in the best academic tradition, to gain pre-eminence, were all from the North: Daléchamps from Caen, L'Ecluse from Arras, Dodoens from Malines, L'Obel from Lille and Jean and Caspard Bauhin from Amiens. Daléchamps, L'Ecluse and L'Obel all studied in Montpellier under the great Guillaume Rondelet. Practical experience was foremost in the teaching of botany and medicine at Montpellier, unlike the Faculty of Medicine of the University of Paris, which was still attached to the tradition of book-learning; the discord between them was to last for another century. But the Languedoc, Provence and the Dauphiné were also the home of many 'heretics'. Some of them kept afloat very ingeniously; L'Ecluse and L'Obel worked for both Maximilian II and Elizabeth I. Others were forced to emigrate to Basle or elsewhere, like the Bauhin brothers.

One group gravitated not to Paris but to Antwerp. The Estiennes, the great Parisian publishing family, who brought out Ruell's Dioscorides in 1517, were deeply in debt. Robert openly adhered to the Reformation and fled to Geneva; Charles transformed his *Praedium rusticum* into a best-seller, the *Maison rustique*, but his funds were insufficient to produce an illustrated herbal that could compete at European level. Christophe Plantin, who emigrated to Antwerp from his native Touraine, rose from book-binding to become a successful printer. His was the mind that directed the largest and best collection of botanical engravings of the century. They were produced under the guidance of L'Ecluse from 1566 to 1573, were used for the herbals of Dodoens, L'Ecluse and L'Obel too and published with French, Flemish, Latin and English texts. It was a large market that endeavoured to meet the demand from France as well as from some provinces of the Empire and even from Anglican England, an avid consumer of new books.

Daléchamps, on the other hand, was left isolated in Lyons, unable to complete his philological endeavours. His annotated translation of Theophrastus' *De plantis* remained unpublished and his printed herbal was brought out after his death without due revision. Strangely enough, Guillaume Roville, the publisher from Lyons, published it in two folio volumes, dedicated to Charles Emmanuel I, Duke of Savoy; compared with Plantin's publications, they were too large and cumbersome to handle. Roville probably hoped the work would win him some favour in nearby Savoy, but an edition of this kind could not compare with the publications of Antwerp and Basle.

The brothers Jean and Caspard Bauhin emigrated to Basle for religious reasons. Fuchs' and Gesner's books with extremely accurate illustrations of plants and animals, drawn from life, had been brought out there in the 1530s and 1540s and the Bauhins hoped to compete with the Catholic printing houses in the north. The illustrations of the many books they published were perhaps not quite up to the standard of those of Antwerp, yet they constituted a successful attempt not only to foster a discussion on plants, but to list the synonyms used by botanists of the time, and provided a valid aid to the specialist and the general reader anxious to go more deeply into the subject. While Cesalpino's attempt to give a binary nomenclature to plants was confined to Catholic Italy, the work of the Bauhin brothers gave Protestant Europe an overall view of that great work of discovery and identification of the flora of Europe and the new worlds that had arisen before the eyes of sixteenth-century man.

3. CULTIVATION TECHNIQUES IN EMBRUN, DIE, AVIGNON AND CARPENTRAS

The documents show that lucerne and sainfoin had not disappeared in France, as happened in Italy in the Middle Ages. It was not, however, the part of medieval France still tied to feudal property or the inaccurate, hesitant vocabulary of medieval scribes that kept their memory alive.[33] From the descriptions of the botanists and agronomists mentioned in the paragraphs above, we have chosen to examine three neighbouring areas, Embrun, Die and Avignon-Carpentras, which preserved considerable cultural and ecological unity, though administered in different ways. Moreover, Provence is the region where the clearest signs of Roman colonization can be traced. Besides the famous architectural remains, there are contracts based on Roman private law, strictly connected with economic and urban development, which came back into fashion in the mid-thirteenth century.[34]

Die was a Roman colony, on the road from the Alps down to Lyons. Pliny the Elder spoke of the quality of its Clairette, a white wine which,

---

[33] See R. Fossier, *Polyptyques et censiers*, Brepols 1978, p. 63. Actually Olivier de Serres did not describe his crops in full detail in his *Livre de raison*, but used the vague terminology of the cadastres such as: ' . . . chanabievre . . . vergier d'ollivier . . . oultre vergier d'ollivier a la croix . . . le jardin et pre': see Paris, Société pour l'Etude du Protestantisme en France, ms 950.

[34] See M. L. Carlin, *La pénétration du droit romain dans les actes de la pratique provençale*, Paris 1967.

local tradition has it, was four hundred years ahead in the technique of re-fermenting wine in bottles, to be perfected later in the Champagne area. Embrun is also on the road from Mongenèvre down to the lower Dauphiné. Although the region was administered by the Pope until it became part of France once more in 1791, its real capital was Avignon, where considerable economic development took place during the great schism. Even after 1409, Avignon, Villeneuve and Carpentras, the administrative capital of the Papal Possessions (Comitat Venassin), still lay at the heart of the urban growth of cardinals' palaces, hospitals and monasteries, supplied by a fertile plain with gardens and kitchen-gardens watered by the Rhône, which produced first-quality early fruits and vegetables for the tables of the high-ranking clergy and for northern France. From the fifteenth century on, Provence exported trees from its nurseries, agricultural products, including cereals and wine. The mountains of Provence also had an interest in the specialized crops. Oranges appeared for the first time in 1411 in Seyne (Basses-Alpes), on the table that the consul of the community had laid in honour of illustrious guests.[35] In short, the whole region, variously administered by the counts of Provence, the Papal legate and the Dukes of Savoy, shared in the development of specialized crops started in carefully cultivated gardens. Italian gardeners were the first to grow fruit and vegetables for the bishops' tables, laying out gardens for the purpose. However, their contribution was limited. The French were not without horticultural experience, their gardens were already very famous, as Brunetto Latini and John of Garland clearly tell us.[36] Nor were gardens the prerogative of lords in France or Provence. Documents and research on medieval agrarian history are full of references to gardens and vegetable-gardens round the homes of the peasants in many regions of France. In Forez, in the sixteenth century, vegetables and fruit-trees were grown in well-

---

[35] In the following order, see E. Lavisse, *Histoire de France*, Paris 1905, vol. I, pp. 198, 205 note, 209, 345, 420; Pliny, *Naturalis historia*, XIV 83. On the export of crops see Le Roy Ladurie, *Paysans du Languedoc*, pp. 60–73; M. Venard, *L'Eglise d'Avignon au xvie siècle*, Lille 1980, vol. I, p. 45. On oranges see P. Meyer, *Documents linguistiques du Midi de la France, Ain, Basses-Alpes, Hautes-Alpes, Alpes Maritimes*, Paris 1909, pp. 192, 208.

[36] See B. Latini, *Li livres du Tresor*, ed. P. Chabaille, Paris 1863, I cxxvi–cxxx, p. 180: 'Mais li Francois ont maison grant . . . et vergiers et pomiers entor lor manoir . . . '; John of Garland, *Magistri Joannis de Garlandia Dictionarius*, in H. Géraud, *Paris sous Philip le Bel*, Paris 1837, Appendix, pp. 585–612, nn. LXXIII–LXXVII; see also *Notices et extraits des manuscripts*, Paris 1879, XXVII, pp. 1–86, esp. pp. 36 ff. and John of Garland, *DNB*, sub nomine.

manured gardens and orchards (*verchères*). In the Bordeaux region the peasant's home was centred on the garden, vegetable-garden and vineyard; sometimes there was a small field or meadow too. In the late Middle Ages, in the Gâtinais region (Poitou), the vegetables grown in the *ouches* (allotments, the extension of town gardens) included turnips and rapes. The 1461 land-register of Embrun often mentions *viridaria*, *pulchra viridaria*, where fruit-trees of various kinds were grown (plums, pears, apples, almonds and peach-trees being recorded from 1325 on); meadows and gardens were watered by irrigation channels, from the many streams in the region. In Gap, in 1444, gardens situated near tanners' yards may even have used waste products from the hides as a fertilizer.[37] At the end of the fourteenth century, the gardens of Aix-en-Provence were made within the city walls, on the site of districts that had been destroyed. They were marked out by irrigation channels supplied by water from the thermal baths and let out to expert gardeners, who grew peach-, plum-, fig-, pomegranate- and nut-trees, besides spinach, white and black cabbage and leeks, all well manured. In the Vivarais area, the waters of the Rhône were used to irrigate the gardens. In at least one case, a greengrocer rented an area greater than necessary to supply his own family's needs.[38]

Marc Bloch's writing on the role of new crops in French agrarian development and the recent description of agriculture in the last centuries of the old regime, according to the *Histoire Rurale de la France*, advance two conflicting theories.[39] The second work insists that French agriculture was incapable of change in the sixteenth and seventeenth centuries. It is a theme that has been taken up many times in local and

[37] See in the following order M. Gonon, *La vie familiale en Forez au xive siècle*, Paris 1961, pp. 228–31; R. Boutruche, *La crise d'une société, seigneurs et paysans du Bordelais pendant la guerre de Cent Ans*, Paris 1947, pp. 27, 30–1, 60; L. Merle, *La métairie et l'évolution agraire de la Gâtine poitevine de la fin du Moyen Age à la Révolution*, Paris 1958, e.g. p. 104; Sclafert, *Le Haut Dauphiné*, pp. 675 ff.; see also *Inventaire sommaire des Archives Départementales ant. à 1790 Hautes Alpes, Archives Ecclesiastiques*, vol. II, série G, Clergé séculier – Archidiocèse d'Embrun, Gap 1891, G 4, 6, 19, 29, 187, 191, 192, 216, 219, 229, 236, 238, for the years ca. 1332–1616; *ibid.*, *Archives Communales*, vol. II, séries BB–CC, Ville de Gap, Gap 1913, CC 5, 1444.

[38] See N. Coulet, *Pour une histoire du jardin*, *Le Moyen Age*, 73, 1967, pp. 239–70; R. Grand and R. Delatouche, *L'agriculture au Moyen Age*, p. 323.

[39] See M. Bloch, *Les caractères originaux de l'histoire rurale française* (1931), Paris 1952, vol. I, pp. 201 ff.; G. Duby and E. Le Roy Ladurie (eds.), *Histoire de la France rurale*, Paris 1975, vol. II; J. Jacquart, 'Immobilisme et catastrophes, 1550–1660', in Duby and Le Roy Ladurie, *Histoire*, and E. Le Roy Ladurie, 'De la crise ultime à la vraie croissance', in Duby and Le Roy Ladurie, *Histoire*.

regional studies carried out during the past twenty years. According to this research, agriculture could not guarantee the survival of the rural population or the urban masses. In this view, the new crops, which were taken into consideration again after 1750, only became important when they were introduced, at the beginning of the nineteenth century, into large-scale cultivation and really increased the productivity of the land. Actually, what were taken to be new crops (the forage-crops, textile and industrial plants, even potatoes) were products already known in the sixteenth century, which had fallen into disuse and were then presented as a novelty in the second half of the eighteenth century. It was a very different picture that Bloch drew over sixty years ago, for he included the new products, and above all the cultivated forage-crops of sixteenth-century agronomy.[40] The question of fodder in France centred round two issues; the abolition of *vaine pâture* and common rights. The first assault on common rights seems to have begun in Provence and Normandy in the fourteenth century.

The former region is of special importance because the earliest information we have on lucerne in France concerns the area between the Vercors mountains and Avignon. But fourteenth- and early fifteenth-century Provence is also the region where the spaces left empty by man were filled by huge flocks, which reduced the land to dust (*pulverage*) on their way to the Dauphiné pastures. It was not until 1540 that the region became inhabited once more, settled by poor people, 'pauvres hommes', since there was no lordly authority or pressure of population to introduce new families; in practice the villages were abandoned but not the land. On enclosed land it is difficult to replace intensive by extensive cultivation; and once flocks have begun to dominate the scene, crops have to be protected from the ravages of wandering sheep. Horticultural products were grown in the irrigated gardens of Grasse, and grass was mown all the year round on the well-manured *viridiaria*. But though land-ownership and common customs defended the rights of the individual in Provence, his crops and fruit-trees, pastures and wasteland were still subjected to common grazing, and transhumance continued along well-defined tracks. Consequently, there was continual conflict between farmers and landowners and the graziers, who trespassed onto private

---

[40] Bourde, *Agronomie*, pp. 55, 92–4, gives indications for a reassessment of sixteenth- to seventeenth-century agronomy, which was the basis for developing the more traditional practice of the eighteenth century. Bloch, *Les caractères originaux*, p. 219: lucerne, sainfoin and clover crops not grown in natural meadows came to be known as *fourrages artificiels*.

meadows, thus depriving working animals of fodder. In Forcalquier in May 1476 it was decided that pastures should be reserved for the community's working animals from mid-April to All Saints' Day.[41] In practice, where crops were not grown, the land was unstable, harsh and bare on the higher slopes (the so-called *garrigue*), fertile in the irrigated plains, but continually scorched by the wind. Here again, the labour of man brought fertility and retrieved spaces for cultivation from waste land.

During and after the time when the Popes were in residence there, Avignon was a city of about twenty thousand inhabitants, who consumed a great deal of meat of all kinds, and of cereals. It was also the seat of grasping clergy who exacted tithes down to the last penny, a point which Bloch takes partly into account. The bishopric of Avignon grew to great importance under Pope Julius II, politically and also because of its revenues; the Chapter had a right to income from at least six parishes, high-ranking prelates received stipends from a dozen parishes, and then there were the manors that belonged to the people of Avignon, the Archbishop first among them. In 1543 the property of the people of Avignon was exempt from duties from the river Durance to the Alpilles. Wheat yielded sixteen to one when grown on the best, well-drained land; the waters of the Rhône were diverted to irrigate gardens and vegetable gardens; fields not suitable as arable land were turned into vineyards; hemp fields were created on land threatened by flooding from the Durance.[42] At this time it became easy to sell crops of madder, the red dye plant (*Rubia tinctorium*) which was grown in the gardens and fields of the region. Land was often rented out; the Grange of Cassanet, near Courthezon, was let from 1561–6. The 75 *salmées* (35 hectares) of arable land could be 're-stubbled', that is cultivated without intervals of fallow, provided it was well manured and half of it was left in stubble at the end of the contract. The tenant had to look after the meadows and ditches, plant fifty willows or poplars every year, prepare a saffron field, a lucerne field, a garden or a vineyard on the impoverished land. The

---

[41] See Sclafert, *Cultures en Haute-Provence, passim* and p. 113; P.-L. Malaussena, *La vie en Provence orientale aux xive et xve siècles. Un example: Grasse à travers les actes notariés*, Paris 1969, p. 79; N. Coulet,'Encore les villages disparus; dépeuplement et repeuplement autour d'Aix-en-Provence (xiv–xvie s.)', *Annales (ESC)*, 1973, pp. 1463–83.

[42] See L. Stouff, *Ravitaillement et alimentation en Provence aux xive et xvie siècles*, Paris–La Haye 1970, pp. 111 ff., 190–2; Venard, *L'Eglise d'Avignon*, vol. I, pp. 44, 47, 51, 59 ff., 83. Bloch too had noted that cultivated grasses were grown after hemp (*Les caractères originaux*, p. 219, note 27).

mulberry leaves were to go to the owner; there were only four cows and two or three calves, but to these were added sixty sheep, with their lambs. A tenant with a lease of only six years must have had to work very hard, between one crop of cereals and another, on various constructive tasks from which he reaped very little benefit. The first year was almost lost on getting the lucerne field ready, saffron was a bulb which could not be grown for more than three years on the same field; while a vineyard took three years to produce a harvest. Besides all this, the owner took the mulberry leaves, which meant that the tenant could not keep silk-worms, excluding another ready source of income. Under such conditions it was almost compulsory to keep the production of grain high, for family consumption but also for sale; so pastures had to be restricted, without cutting down on the hay for the cattle too drastically; no doubt the sheep were kept away from the gardens by taking them along the transhumance tracks.[43]

As elsewhere, the cultivation of lucerne in Provence was closely connected with the leys, meadows and permanent pastures available, and the laws regulating the vexed question of introducing forage crops into the rotation scheme.[44] The meadows round Avignon were managed in much the same way as those on either side of the Alps. The first crop was mown in May (*foin majenc*), the second (*revioure, revoire*) in June–July and then the August crop; after that they were used as pasture until early February, when they were closed, so as not to spoil the first crop of hay. St Valentine's Day marked the end of the grazing season in Carpentras. Whenever possible, the meadows were irrigated. Generally meadows and pastures managed in this way were let (or their hay sold) to the butchers, who formed a very important guild in Avignon. In the sixteenth century a change had already taken place; instead of mowing twice, in May and June–July, as they did in the fourteenth century, and then using them for pasture, the meadows were mown three times and then left for grazing, a sign that they had become more productive. Even more

---

[43] See Venard, *L'Eglise d'Avignon*, vol. I, p. 48.

[44] The history of agricultural products and the economic institutions of Provence has become much easier to research since Mr Henri Chobaut, chief archivist of the Archives Départementales de Vaucluse, selected and catalogued under various headings the content of so many records in the 1930s and 1940s. These invaluable, painstaking labours were largely carried out during the dark years of the Vichy regime. The Fonds Chobaut are now housed in the Musée Calvet in Avignon: as a mark of appreciation of the high quality of Mr Chobaut's work (that is too often forgotten), I have quoted them as Fonds Chobaut, followed by the manuscript number, serial number of the document, date and place of the original document when necessary.

noteworthy is the evidence that meadows were being included in the rotation scheme involving arable land. A meadow of two *émynes* and a half in Bosco Domini was let for six years on 5 January 1564; it was laid down in the contract that the meadow should be made into a garden, vegetables should be sown and fruit-trees planted, ditches should be dug all round it and willow trees planted. In exchange for this work, the tenant was not to pay rent for the first three years, but undertook to pay twelve florins for the last three; the new garden was to be valued when the contract terminated. On 7 March 1556, the priory of Nôtre-Dame of Chèze and Sigoyer was let for three years; the tenants could plough, cultivate and sow the meadow known as 'Verdant', but they were to give it back sown with sainfoin, according to custom. Lastly, on 27 September 1595, the grange of Gallias was let for four years at seventy-two *écus* and a half a year. Permission was granted to plough and sow the field, but lucerne was to be planted in the fourth year. The owner was insuring himself against the fact that lucerne fields only produced a yield in the second year and that sowing and hoeing entailed considerable expense in the first year.[45]

Meadows, enclosure and lucerne were closely connected. When Etienne Saunier and Pierre and Firmin Vachier's property in Orange territory was let in 1517, it was clearly specified that 'the said lucerne field, growing under the fruit-trees' was to be kept closed and no animals allowed to graze on it. In the same Orange community the meadows and lucerne fields were to be kept closed from Ash Wednesday to St Martin's Day, according to the statutes of 1527.[46] But it was in the middle decades of the century that lucerne appeared more frequently in notaries' documents. Lucerne-growing spread the more easily because there was a market for seed. On 22 August 1545, Loys Conte, a husbandman of Orange, sold four *émynes* of seed to a fellow-citizen for ten florins, which were paid for with two Venetian gold ducats. The seed was to be gathered by mid-August of the following year. A few years later, on 2 August 1550, Pierre Gautier, stocking-maker of Orange, let to Jean Guichet, a husbandman, an *émyne* of land sown with lucerne, for seven years at a yearly rent of eleven florins, expressly forbidding him to grow other crops on it. In another case, on 19 December 1550, Thibaut de Lastic, his wife and her sister let the grange of Croc, in Caderousse, to

---

[45] See in the following order Fonds Chobaut, ms 5955 Prés, nn. 20–151 Avignon; 218–30 Carpentras, 1358, 1362, 1570–80; 253, 22 April 1409; 92, 7 March 1556; 311; 103.

[46] See *ibid.*, ms 5956 Luzerne, nn. 417, 419.

Jean Lusin, a husbandman, for six years. The grange consisted of 130 *saumes* of land; wheat could be grown in the meadow in the first year, then the land could return to grass and be sown with lucerne.[47] There are many contracts of this kind, which lay down that lands rented and used for growing grain should be returned after sowing with lucerne during the last year. Leases generally lasted three, four or nine years, in some cases requiring a third of the land to be manured every year. The hospital of Champfleury let five measures of land for six years, from 6 August 1599, at twenty five florins a year. No rent was due for the first year, since the tenant undertook to make a lucerne field and to manure the land once. If the crop were to prove unsuccessful, he could plough the field and sow another crop.[48]

From what we have seen so far it is obvious that lucerne was not only a forage-crop, intended to produce a high-quality meadow to be kept permanently enclosed; it also became part of the rotation scheme. Expressions like 'permission to mow the ley and lucerne field' (1450, Caromb), 'a closed ley or lucerne field' (1566, Aubignan), 'ley called lucerne'(1566, Bedoin), or 'ley or lucerne field' often appear in documents to define the context to which the crop belonged. Thus, to prevent animals from wandering over and spoiling it, it was agreed in Malémont, in 1577, that the surrounding walls should be built 'straight and enclosed'. In Baulme, the statutes of 1632 established that lucerne fields should be enclosed the year round; in Aubignan, in 1652, closing the lucerne fields was allowed for the first crop and while the second was growing, but after 20 July they had to be opened for free grazing and even sheep could be taken there from Christmas to Lent.[49] These different regulations reflect different situations within the communities. Probably where lucerne fields were grown on private property owners insisted on their being exempted from common grazing, while when it was grown on common land, it could rarely be withdrawn from this obligation.

Two other important factors, however, encouraged the cultivation of *luzerne*; the link with small-scale cultivation in gardens, and seed production. We have already mentioned the lucerne that grew under the trees in Etienne Saunier's garden in Orange in 1517, and the case of a

[47] See *ibid.*, ms 5956 Luzerne, nn. 429–30; 431–2; 235.
[48] See *ibid.*, ms 5956 Luzerne, nn. 83–7; 90–2; 94–6; 105; 112; 115–16; 121; 122; 131; 136; 142.
[49] See in the following order *ibid.*, ms 5956 Luzerne, nn. 214–15; 261; 66; 262–71; 205; 362–5 Mazan 1553, 1556, 1557; 358, Malemort 1577; 67.

lucerne-field turned into a garden. In January 1559, Esprite Arnaude of Serignan came into possession of half a garden called 'le jardin de la luzerne', which bordered on two meadows. In Sainte Cécile in 1568 lucerne was growing behind a garden next to a hemp field, while in Sablet in 1581 a small patch of lucerne was growing among gardens and hemp. The list does not end there. Lucerne grew next to meadows and gardens in Violes in 1618, among arable fields and hemp in Visan in 1578, and in a place known as 'aux jardins' in Bouchet in 1613.[50] It happened repeatedly that new crops were first acclimatized in the garden before passing to field production. We have seen how lucerne grew accustomed to local conditions in the garden of the Assyrian king Merodachbaladam, then in the 'sainfoin garden' of the mountains round Die, or again in the gardens of lower Provence in the sixteenth century. It was a constant custom that died hard, for the garden afforded the right conditions for transplanting seedlings. In the Avignon region, where horticulture was highly developed, it made it easier to introduce a specialized crop such as lucerne, which was much in demand. Around 1580, patches of lucerne were let at about 4 *livres* 10 *sous*, which became 7–8 *livres* on average around 1600 and even reached 15 *livres* in the middle of the century.[51] Even today certain characteristics are still the same; though extensive lucerne-growing in the Rhône valley and on the hills of the Drôme region, favoured by sprinkler irrigation, can scarcely be compared with the sixteenth-century technique, numerous patches of lucerne still appear along the river banks in the bends of the Drôme, among vegetable gardens and orchards kept for family use. The mountains still harbour a reserve of technology and unselected seed, as in the past they were a source of local botanical varieties that could profitably be transferred to the large farms in the plains.

It is always the small plots which, on the one hand, confirm interest in a specialized crop that is only highly productive when grown intensively (a bad lucerne-field yields no more than a permanent pasture), while, on the other, they reveal a social picture in which artisans, husbandmen and butchers were loath to give up small cultivated patches of ground and small quantities of produce which could be profitably exchanged in an urban setting. They enhanced the value of certain crops. The increase in the cultivation of this crop certainly depended on the fact that it was easy to procure the seed. We have already mentioned how Loys Conte, a

---

[50] See in the following order *ibid.*, ms 5956 Luzerne, nn. 257; 491; 487; 563–4; 230.
[51] See *ibid.*, ms 6376 Luzerne, n. 154.

farmer of Orange, sold four *emynes* of seed in 1545. In Avignon in 1555 a tenant had to procure seed at his own expense for the lucerne field to be planted before his lease ran out.[52] Lastly, from 1630 on, the authorities of Carpentras were to record the price of lucerne seed placed on the market (see below, 3.2.). Even in the older documents, a greater confidence concerning cropping schemes can be attributed to this regular supply of seed, which enabled a tenant to pass from lucerne to grain crops, generally for a period of three years, and then go back to lucerne. The best seed was often produced in gardens, especially prepared, since to obtain it the pods needed to be fully ripened and the flower-heads picked by hand so that no weeds were included. Moreover, since the nutritional value of the plant is greatest a fortnight before ripening, seed production and fodder production were incompatible.

3.1. Tithes and economic institutions in Provence

Though the rules for the cultivation of lucerne remained constant at least until the early nineteenth century, no steady increase in lucerne-growing occurred in French agriculture under the old regime. In France, as in Italy, farmers were not free to choose the crops they grew, but were bound by political and economic institutions, both local and regional. The statutes of Bédamide (Var) of 29 March 1543 made no mention of *luzerne*; they did mention it in 1598 and in a third document of 1609 a municipal official recalled that lucerne had been widely cultivated in those years, though it had not been so in the past. This was of considerable importance when the time came to pay tithes, which in that area ranged from 4 to 25 per cent. The tithe was due only on the first hay mown, which involved a great loss to both the farmer and the tithe collector, for if lucerne had remained in the field and been consumed on the farm the yield of grain crops would have been higher.[53] Information gathered by Chobaut also shows an increase in data for the 1550–1600 period, a considerable number of observations up to 1650, growing progressively fewer in the second half of the century, to reappear in the eighteenth century. Thus, while the technique remained the same (the lucerne-fields could be ploughed up and wheat sown only provided lucerne was sown again in the last year of tenancy) the type of document changed. While up to 1650 contracts were generally private, from 1600

---

[52] See *ibid.*, ms 5956 Luzerne, nn. 70–1.
[53] See *ibid.*, ms 5955 Prés, n. 162; ms 5956 Luzerne, nn. 207, 213.

on the number of legal disputes between the religious authorities and local communities and individuals concerning the payment of tithes increased steadily.

Tithes due to the religious institutions of Avignon made up the greater part of their revenue, as in the case of the Chapter of Saint-Agricol, or of the monasteries of the Celestine Order and of Chartreux, and of great landed properties. The tithe generally exacted was a twentieth or a thirtieth, due on grains, grapes or wine and generally also on hay, hemp and flax. The tithe on livestock, being difficult to levy, was generally paid in cash. The requirements of the tithe-gatherer even included garden produce. There was bickering over cabbages, leeks, onions, the new crops such as saffron, madder and lucerne; even the crops from the fruit-trees were subject to haggling. The tithe was paid at harvest-time, the rule being that everything was subject to it, even products that were innovations, provided the land was already being taxed.[54] There were various differences between tithes in the Papal States (and hence the Comitat Venassin) and the Kingdom of France. In practice fruit, vegetables and everything that came under the definition of minor tithes was regulated according to local custom, and so was quite different from place to place. Woods, meadows, ponds and enclosed gardens were generally excluded, except for certain regions, where grass and hay were already subject to payment. In reality all products that could be consumed or eaten, everything for use in the home or produced for industrial use, was subject to tithe, and that included the produce of livestock, wool and cheese. During the years of rebellion against tithes in the Paris area (1563–7), the Languedoc states confirmed the obligation to pay according to local custom (1564), and the whole question of tithes was brought up to date by the Council of Trent (1563), which had established that tithes should also be paid on all land ploughed up for the first time, irrespective of who owned it. Tithes were partially suppressed in 1567 and then in 1607 Henri IV exempted new lands from payment. The situation for new forage-crops varied considerably, with continual differences in regulations and exemptions, from the Alps to the English Channel. The Comitat Venassin, for example, applied criteria nearer to

[54] See Venard, *L'Eglise d'Avignon*, pp. 100–2. The administrative situation in Avignon had some points in common with that of the Lazio region, particularly the lands of the so-called Patrimony of St Peter, which passed from being let, to direct management by selling grazing rights to shepherds and landowners: see J.-C. Maire Vigueur, *Les pâturages de l'Eglise et la douane du bétail dans la province du Patrimonio, xive–xve siècles*, Rome 1981.

the Kingdom of France than did the Duchy of Savoy, whose subjects enjoyed greater exemption.[55]

The better cared-for meadows and the lucerne-fields, built up with toil and patience in the course of the sixteenth century, had not gone unnoticed. As in the case of Bedarrides, already mentioned, the collectors complained that the greater part of the production was exempt from tithes. In Vaison in 1581 and Aubignan in 1598 a twentieth part was levied on hay and *luzerne*, but this was a novelty, since in 1561 in Vason, and in 1567 and 1589 in Aubignan, meadows and lucerne-fields were exempt. In Vason in 1638 the tithes were farmed out for six years, at 962 *écus* and 23 *sous* a year, giving the right to charge on grain, hemp, flax, May and June–July hay and lucerne. But the picture is extremely varied. In Carpentras in 1554, the twentieth part could be levied only on hay mown in May, and a century later (1640) the tenth part was levied before the twentieth, but only on May hay. The same happened in 1613 at Mormoiron.[56] A lawsuit between the community of Caumont and the Charterhouse of Bonpas lasted fifty years and was finally decided only by the Sacra Rota tribunal in Rome. In 1621 a good many local owners purchased irrigation rights from Monsieur d'Oppède and made many new meadows which they claimed were exempt from tithes. Traditionally, there were only seven or eight places in the Comitat Venassin where tithes were paid on hay, and in 1657 the tribunal of Avignon declared that the community was in the right. The monastery appealed to Rome, where the monks' claim was approved, and a compromise was reached in 1677 which took account of the meadows that had been old-established before 1621 (these would have been subject to tithes only if ploughed up, but not if transformed into lucerne-fields). On new meadows and on lucerne-fields tithes were to be levied on the whole production. Moreover, spring cereals grown for fodder were to be subjected to tithes only if reaped as grain.[57] It is clear from the context that the local farmers had had to wait until irrigation was avail-

[55] See R. Benoist, *Traicté des dîmes*, Paris 1564; Le Roy Ladurie, *Paysans du Languedoc*, p. 382; R. Doucet, *Les institutions de la France au xvie siècle*, II, *La seigneurie. Les services publiques. Les institutions ecclésiastiques*, Paris 1948, pp. 821, 824–5; R. Mousnier, *Les institutions de la France sous la monarchie absolue, 1598–1789*, Paris 1974, vol. I, p. 239; R. Devos *et al.*, *La pratique des documents anciens*, Annecy A.D.H.S. 1978, p. 174.

[56] By far the most valuable information is that collected by Henri Chobaut: see in the following order ms 6383 Dîme, nn. 573 (Aubignan, Vaison); 355 (Vaison); 377, 380–1 (Carpentras); 379 (Mormoiron).

[57] See Fonds Chobaut, ms 6383 Dîme, n. 296.

able to increase the productivity of their meadows. These were turned into lucerne-fields and back to meadows and then converted to arable land, according to the practice described above, which was still common in the seventeenth century. The intervention of the Charterhouse of Bonpas and the Sacra Rota of Rome increased the cost of the innovation, and slowed down the spread of the rotation by interfering unduly, thus holding up developments at the fifteenth century level, when they introduced regulations applied to pastures in the Campagna Romana, the so-called Patrimony of Peter. The tithes lost on meadows and lucerne-fields would have been gained on the increase in grains produced from arable land; for the sake of a few extra loads of hay, the spread of lucerne-growing was restricted, and consequently the possible increase in grain and livestock reared in years when prices were high, as in 1649 and 1678, was foregone. This pattern of procedure persisted throughout the seventeenth and eighteenth centuries and indeed was dangerously imitated in Vauban's project. Hence in the agreement between the tithe-collectors of Montamajour and the community of Bedoin, stipulated at Avignon in 1680, the tithe on lucerne was valued at ten *sous*, half in cash and half in produce, or else a fifteenth part of all the hay was to be collected. So the producers could choose between paying for the hay at market-price and using it on their own farms, or else giving up part of it and restricting the number of livestock they reared.[58] The lifting, and then the renewed imposition, of Church authority also made itself felt in the Comitat Venassin.

3.2. Die and Carpentras: local decline, seventeenth-century expansion and market connections

The French economy was hampered by tithe-collection before the Revolution, and recent agrarian history has produced some interpretation of that event. In the early eighteenth century Vauban proposed imitating the Church's system for providing revenue by instituting a Dîme Royale; a project which shows how rigid the political situation had grown, applying state intervention merely to levy taxes and provide a check on private initiative. The seigneurial reaction was foreshadowed by monarchic and Church reaction. These institutions attempted to regain

---

[58] See *ibid.*, ms 6383 Dîme, n. 216; J. Goy and A.-L. König, *Une expérience. Les revenus décimaux en France méditerranéenne xvie–xviiie siècles*, in J. Goy and E. Le Roy Ladurie (eds.), *Les fluctuations du produit de la dîme*, Paris–La Haye 1972, pp. 256–72.

incomes that they had enjoyed before the wars of religion and the Fronde. What happened in Die is symbolic of this situation, which had an adverse effect on the development of agriculture and the spread of forage-crops in particular.

There were many Protestants in the Die community, as in many others in the Dauphiné, while nearly all the inhabitants of the Drôme valley were Protestants; hence they were able to get the most fertile land in the Die district out of the hands of the Bishop and Chapter and avoid payment of tithes.[59] Charles-Jacques de Leberon d'Ambres, bishop of Die and Valence, never released his hold on the parish and persisted in collecting his rights and defending his privileges. His pastoral visit of 1644 marked the beginning of Catholic moves to question the advantages gained by the local Protestants. In May and June of that year he listed, to the last detail, the tithes due to him from the parishioners, and registered the number of Catholic and Protestant families. Actually, the latter were concentrated in hamlets such as Brette (with forty or forty-three Huguenot families as against one Catholic family) or Estoblet (twenty families to two), whereas in other communities they were clearly a minority group (Eusage, Omblèze, Savel and Rimont) and in others not represented at all. The tithes were never negligible; a thirtieth part of their grain, barley, spelt, legumes and wine, plus an annual 100 livres in cash in Suze and Chosséou. Eusage's due was paid in cash, 60 livres for grain and legumes, the burden of a further 13.10 livres for the *décime* (the tax paid by the state to the Church) was placed on the parishioners, as well as 5 livres in money and twenty-five pounds of cheese. In Savel and Rimont, Church revenues amounted to 300 livres for tithes on grain and lambs and 140 livres, the value of a grange. Because of the large number of Huguenots in Estoblet, the tithe had been lowered from one sixteenth to a twenty-fifth part of the grain to be paid. Besides exacting these taxes, the deacon of the cathedral of Die took the consuls and community of Poyols to court. He wanted the tithes to be exacted on grapes and wine and his request was granted. The community's claim that they should not have to pay tithes on wine was annulled, by an appeal to the customary law. Notre-Dame of Die managed to have an old decree of the *Parlement* of Paris (1547) applied; this decree declared that wine belonged to the category of *gros fruits* (basic necessities of life, hence always subject to tithe), because, together with bread, it formed an integral part of the

[59] See B. Urien-Causse, 'Die communauté reformée, 1600–1685', Thèse III cycle, Paris 1979, 2 vols., *passim.*

Eucharist. As a result, all traces of the forage-crops that had made an early appearance there in the thirteenth century disappeared from the lands that came under the Chapter of Die.[60] Since farmers could not fully dispose of their produce, it was not worth while for them to make innovations to increase production. By the late seventeenth century local contracts foresaw only the most ordinary crops. Preference was given to the traditional hay crop, grown on natural pastures and meadows, not cultivated in any way and so generally not subject to tithes.[61]

Only in the last decades of the eighteenth century did an explicit interest in *sainfoin* and *luzerne* reappear, though it never took the form of a regular series of references, such as was published for products registered on the 'price-currents' used in contemporary market quotations. Hemp seed appeared on them occasionally in the eighteenth century, but never forage-crops. Paris increased its control over the border regions by the 1793 law on the *maximum*, which fixed 5 livres as the price of the old quintal of hay from old cultivated fields, but this did not persuade the municipal officials of Die to register any forage-crops apart from ordinary hay before 15 January 1830. In the same decades, the authorities advised farmers to grow cotton, sugar-beet, sumach shrubs, fruit-trees and potatoes, and to use a Machon harrow for weeding grain and forage-crops and for sowing lucerne and sainfoin.[62] In nearby Romans, the cultivation of meadows and lucerne was only introduced under the first Empire, following the example of Dedelay d'Agrier, a cavalry officer of the Royal Army before 1784, and later a farmer and mayor of the small town. It took over forty years for forage-crops to become widely grown in the Drôme valley but, by 1835, 5,000 of the 12,00 hectares of pastureland were being irrigated and a further 5,000 cultivated. In 1814 the latter had yielded 239,000 quintals as against

[60] See Mons du Faur Saintaraille, *Le prélat courageux ou Discours sur la vie et la mort de Mons. de Leberon d'Ambres*, Lyon 1654; J. Chevalier, *La diocèse de Die en l'année 1644*, Valence 1915, pp. 7, 34, 38, 48, 50, 73, 91, 95, 101–2, 159. See also for example Valence, AADD, serie G, Terriers de la Chapitre de Die, Jombères 1616, Aoustc 1624, 1662, 1682; 1 MI.486 R 8, Doyen de Die . . . contre Comm. de Poyols, 1644.

[61] See *ibid.*, E 2254, not. Joseph Bonnet; 1690, 29 September; 1697, 27 October; 1697, 7 November: lease between Thomas Merand *laboureur* from Beauforêt and Claude Eschinard, by which the former was obliged to deliver 70 *quintaux* of the first cut of hay (*maienc*) and 90 *quintaux* of the second (*regain*) and to sow 17 *sestiers* of wheat and 20 of rye; however the lease did not mention cultivated grasses. The old *quintal* was equivalent to a third of the metric quintal.

[62] See Die, AACC, 4 F 2, Mercuriales, Gros fruits, 1738, 1824, 1853; printed notice, 1818. On the 15 January 1830 hay was valued at £7, straw at £4, lucerne hay at £6, clover at £5. 60s and sainfoin at £5. 30s per load.

214,000 from natural water-meadows and 190,000 from the dry meadows. Although straw and roots (carrots, turnips and beetroot) were grown for fodder, the Département needed a further 27,000 quintals. So farmers were advised to use tree-leaves to make up the fodder, as was customary in Tuscany; John Symonds had written of this in English fifty years earlier, in an article translated into French at the end of the century and published together with the writings of Arthur Young.[63] A steady increase in lucerne- and sainfoin-growing was beginning in the Département and particularly in the Die district; lucerne for fodder had recently been grown on 40 per cent of the sown fields.[64] Amazingly, just when the cultivation of legumes was spreading throughout a region that had preserved the memory of this technique during the Middle Ages, farmers were advised to use forage trees, while in early nineteenth-century Tuscany they were trying to restrict this custom by growing more forage-crops. Pre-capitalist agriculture was obviously a very flexible system, with sophisticated practices like cultivating legumes existing unhindered alongside more primitive customs. Actually, all the crops on which the so-called agricultural revolution hinged were very ancient, and so could easily co-exist. The trends indicated in the Die price-currents are in some sense completed by those of Carpentras (see Appendix, table 2). This capital of the Comitat Venassin was more important as an administrative centre than as a town. In the mid-fifteenth century it had about 3,200 inhabitants, many of them Jews (it is, in fact, the oldest Jewish community in France) and quite an important hospital, or *Hôtel-Dieu*, was set up there in the eighteenth century. Carpentras also had a large cattle market and slaughter-house, as did many other communities in the Comitat. Between 1400 and 1500 the consumption of meat was as high as 26 kilograms per head of the population, higher than that found three or four hundred years later in other European regions.[65] It was the market centre for a vast area, though the produce sold was quite severely taxed. Besides the manorial due, called *sextier*, payable to the Bishop (a

---

[63] See A. Gosson, H. Michel and G. A. Roch, *Grands notables du premier empire*, Paris 1980, p. 192; M. Delacroix, *Statistique du département de la Drôme*, Valence 1835, pp. 328–33. On John Symonds see M. Ambrosoli, *John Symonds. Agricoltura e politica in Corsica e in Italia (1765–1770)*, Turin 1974, p. 143: a French translation of this letter was published in A. Young, *Voyage en Italie pendant l'année 1789*, Paris 1796, edited by F. Soules, pp. 366–8. On trees for fodder in Italian and Mediterranean farming see now Moreno, *Dal documento al terreno*, pp. 181 ff.

[64] See Valence, AADD, M. Gérard and M. Cheyssière, *Monographie agricole de Die*, 1967–8, typewritten copy, p. 55.

[65] See Stouff, *Ravitaillement et alimentation en Provence*, pp. 114, 190, 192.

thirty-second part), there was the *leyde*, an excise on all the grains that came into the town. The only exemption granted was for grain brought into the town by producers for their own consumption. The *sextier* was finally ceded to the town authorities in 1784, in return for a hundred *salmées* of wheat and 3,600 livres in cash annually. Lucerne-seed was quoted on this market for the first time in 1634, so the product was obviously widely grown and easily saleable.[66]

The records were not always kept carefully, and we cannot be sure that lucerne-seed was not sold more often than would appear from them. A brief account needs to be given of the indications provided by this source. Lucerne-seed generally appears together with hemp-seed and such minor products as beans and spelt, and was generally recorded, as happened with other products, only when the price changed. There can be no doubt about the species sold; *Medicago s.* was always called *graine de luzerne*. Sainfoin only appeared, under the heading *esparcet*, in 1777 and 1778. Table 2 in our Appendix clearly shows that lucerne-seed tended to appear only at certain times of the year, generally in spring; sometimes, however, it also appeared in autumn or early winter, obviously coinciding with sowing times.

The price variations in question correspond to a considerable extent with the Paris price-lists, particularly with regard to short-term cycles.[67] The peaks of the 1630s were followed by the trough of 1640 and the recovery of the early 1640s, as shown in the March 1644 price. There is spectacular evidence of the fall and recovery of prices in Paris in the 1648–51 cycle, with the price of seed falling again only in May 1654 and January 1655, after reaching very high levels, as, for example, 21 livres in March 1651. In the same period, 1654–6, seed was sold on the Carpentras market almost every month, thus confirming a general interest in this product. Lucerne-seed was also on the market for most of

---

[66] See R. H. Bautier, 'Feux, population et structure sociale en milieu du xve s. Carpentras', *Annales (ESC)*, 1959, pp. 255 ff.; R. Caillet, *Foires et marchés de Carpentras du moyen âge au début deu xixe siècle*, Carpentras 1953, pp. 55, 58, 59. Avignon, AADD, B 3289–92 (= III G 232–6), *Premier livre et mercurial du prix des graines qui se vendent le mardyt et vendredit sour le marche de Carpentras* (1597–1650, 1650–75, 1676–1711, 1712–61); Carpentras, AC, HH 18 (1761–6), HH 19 (1773–8). Some yearly averages (1640–1777) were collected by Mr Chobaut (Fonds Chobaut, Luzerne 5956, nn. 49–50, 1–2).

[67] See A. P. Usher, 'The general course of wheat prices in France: 1350–1788', *Review of economic statistics*, 12, 1930, pp. 159–69; H. Hauser, *Recherches et documents sur l'histoire des prix en France de 1500 à 1800*, Paris 1936; M. Baulant and J. Meuvret, *Prix des céréales extraits de la mercuriale de Paris (1520–1698)*, Paris 1960, 2 vols.

1658, during the following upward trend of the 1658–63 cycle. The favourable situation in 1678–81 was again reflected in both Paris and Carpentras, with another fall at the end of the decade and the beginning of the 1690s, followed by a recovery only in April 1692 and a sustained price-rise in April and May 1696. Prices remained high in Carpentras, with peaks of twice the usual figure in the spring of 1698 and 1699, going down to the usual 8–10 livre level only in 1702. Throughout the period, the correlation between the price of lucerne in Carpentras and grain prices in the Dauphiné markets was marked only when the trend of prices in Grenoble and Romans corresponded to that of Paris.[68] Prices did rise in an appreciable manner in 1709 and again in 1714. For the following years the data become so rare that no regular comparison can be made with the capital (perhaps in part because lucerne was being replaced by sainfoin on the Paris market; see section 4 below). It can however be pointed out that the peak years of 1725, 1766 and 1773 can be connected with the rise in Paris prices. The clear correspondence with the rise of grain prices in Paris supports the hypothesis of a link between seed production in Provence and the growing of grain in the Paris area. An increase in grain prices would suggest that lucerne-growing was becoming widespread on arable land, to slow down the loss of fertility of fields regularly under wheat. The Abbey of Saint-Germain-des-Prés enlarged its property in Thaïs in 1648; besides 196 *arpents* of arable lands, it had 4.33 *arpents* of meadowland and two planted with *sainfoin*. Between 1667 and 1684 Mathurin Degas, a burgher from Paris, rented various pieces of land from the same Abbey, to which he added a series of purchases from petty landowners who were in debt. After considerable haggling, he managed to add, to the 50 *arpents* of arable land already let, a further 7 *arpents*, exclusively for growing *sainfoin*, for which he undertook to provide the necessary seed. His was not the only case in which the owner provided good-quality seed. It was something that could happen in hard years, such as 1709, but it also happened with other owners, in 1682 and 1688.[69] Since it was a costly business, sowing lucerne was justified only in years when there was a relative increase in the price of wheat. When Clément Bouchère let his estate in Beauvaisière in 1673, he made the tenant sow oats and lucerne on one field in March

[68] Meuvret, *Le problème des subsistences*, vol. III, part I, p. 183.
[69] See M. Venard, *Bourgeois et paysans au xviie siècle. Recherche sur le rôle des bourgeois parisiens dans la vie agricole au Sud de Paris au xviie siècle*, Paris 1957, pp. 25, 60, 82–4.

1674 and in exchange offered to provide the seed. He had not foreseen the rapid increase in the price of seed in Carpentras, from 8 livres in April 1673 to 12 livres in the following February.[70] Lucerne only becomes really productive as a forage-crop in the second year, but from the start it deposits a large quantity of nitrogen in the soil (208 kg of nitrogen per hectare accumulates after about four years) and it also rids the ground of weeds. Under these conditions, it was more profitable for the farmer to adopt green manuring, taking advantage of the brief cycle of three or four years of rising prices, than to risk investing in cattle, which meant not using the land for growing cereals, so as to produce manure to spread on the fields (a much more costly operation; see below, section 5).[71] The presence of seed on the local market, to which more regular price quotations bear witness, was related to the need to keep a reserve, wherever the local harvest, both in Provence and the Paris area, could not satisfy the corn-growers' demand. For the latter did not specialize in seed production, much less were they prepared to wait for the crop to get a good hold on the ground for a couple of years before they could begin to harvest the seed. Similar conditions were to be found in England from the mid-eighteenth century on (see Chap. 7).

Hence the price-current for Carpentras seed may point to a crop chronology in disagreement with the better-known version. The spread of lucerne before 1750 was not restricted to the fashionable period of the 1620s and 1630s; whenever there was an increase in the production of grains, and prices took off again, as can be deduced from the tithes of 1630–50 and 1660–70, a parallel increase took place in sales in Carpentras.[72] There was greater flexibility in the old agricultural system, which also demonstrated that legumes could be integrated with the growing of cereals without any need to keep livestock.[73] But the exaction of tithes, together with government taxes and lords' dues, and obligations to enforce common grazing rights, are partly to blame for the slow diffusion of this important crop. The fact that price quotations were so rare in the eighteenth century may, of course, also mean that the seed was easier to find around and after 1750.

---

[70] See *ibid.*, p. 83.
[71] See *ibid.*, pp. 88–9: Venard, too, suggests that oxen were raised as draught animals.
[72] See Jacquart, '*Immobilisme*', pp. 251 ff.; Goy and Le Roy Ladurie (eds.), *Les fluctuations*, pp. 21–3, 356 ff.
[73] This may be why one farm at Beaulieu kept 86 *arpents* of wheat, 85 of oats, 106 left fallow, of which at least 9 were sown with sainfoin in 1656: see Venard, *Bourgeois et paysans*, p. 84.

The link between the Carpentras and Paris markets was much strengthened by the behaviour of *sainfoin* prices on the Paris market during the last decades of the seventeenth century (see Appendix, table 3). The product concerned was clearly the seed, not the hay; it appeared only from 1683 on and maintained the typical features, already described for Carpentras, which were to be found again on the London market in the eighteenth and nineteenth centuries. The seed generally appeared in the last weeks of February, in March and April, and sometimes in May. It was quoted much less often in the summer and autumn months, when the prices were generally considerably lower. Moreover the Paris market, though disguised by a nominally lower price-range, followed the 1683–98 trend of Carpentras very closely. The correlation values between the two are very high (r = 0.979 and r² = 0.958) and it even seems as if the price in Carpentras influenced that of the following month in Paris. A hundred years later, Arthur Young was told on the Liancourt family estate that seed from Provence was commonly sold in northern France, though it did not always give good results. Even if we take into account that the *sainfoin* of the Paris market was not the same as the *luzerne* of Carpentras, there is still a connection.[74]

It is interesting to note that Arthur Young, who was generally not very ready to appreciate French agriculture of the late eighteenth century, praised the cultivation of lucerne, as 'one of the principal features of French husbandry', though he continued to be more critical about sainfoin. Lucerne was widespread throughout the kingdom in Picardy, the Ile-de-France, Gascony, Roussillon, Languedoc, Poitou, Touraine, Provence and the Dauphiné. It generally lasted ten or twelve years; on the best, well-drained soils, up to twenty. After lucerne, wheat could be grown for three years running (as was done in the Roussillon region) or else oats for two to five years and then corn (as was the practice on the Liancourt estate in Pontoise). Sown in March in the country round Avignon, mown four to six times a year if irrigated and manured, lucerne improved the soil to such an extent that grain could be grown for six to eight years running. Yet the splendid French lucerne was not of such

---

[74] See in the following order M. Gilbert, *Traictée des prairies artificielles*, Paris 1789, p. 75; Paris, AANN, KK 1000–2; M. Baulant and J. Meuvret, *Prix des céréales extraites de la mercuriales de Paris*, Paris 1960 (they published one monthly quotation of the best wheat for each month of the period 1564–1698); I warmly thank Mr Gilles Postel-Vinay who pointed out that sainfoin could be traced in this Parisian price-current; the price correlation between Carpentras and Paris prices for the month of March is r=0.910, r² = 0.829.

good quality as that grown in Catalonia (which Young visited in 1788) or the little he had seen in Italy (where he went in 1789).[75] Sainfoin was not grown so regularly, though it was common in Picardy, Quercy, Roussillon, Languedoc, Touraine, Ile-de-France, Artois, Normandy, Lorraine, Alsace and the Dauphiné. Good and bad crops alternated on a patchwork pattern that Young explained by the length of time it had been growing (he said twelve to fifteen years), which was longer than the sharecroppers' contracts, which only lasted nine years. Side by side with bad sharecroppers were found bad landlords. But where the owner farmed his own land, *sainfoin* was always grown before grain in the rotation scheme. Yet, while Young continued to admire *luzerne*, he was openly critical of the way sainfoin was grown in France, saying that French farmers did not generally trouble to clear the fields of weeds, except during the fallow before wheat was to be planted. Moreover, the advantages of the forage-crops were restricted because there was no intermediate winter crop.[76] But after this uncommon praise of lucerne, Young contradicted himself. For he had written that lucerne and sainfoin would of themselves rid the soil of weeds. In any case, sainfoin may have been used in France as an alternative to lucerne on soil not suited to the latter; while in England *sainfoin* was grown on limestone and chalk land because English growers had not learned how to cultivate lucerne (see Chap. 7, *passim*); therefore they also chose clover, another crop neglected by the French, for their rotation schemes on arable land.

[75] See A. Young, *Travels in France During the Years 1787, 1788 and 1789*, 2 vols., London 1794, vol. I, pp. 384–9; idem, *Voyages en France en 1787, 1788, 1789* (translated and published by H. Sée), Paris 1931, vol. III, pp. 662 ff.; Meuvret, *Le problème des subsistences*, vol. I, pp. 36–40, 137 ff., and vol. II, pp. 46–53, 177 ff., which provides new data on the diffusion of forage-crops in France and discusses Young's comments and explanations on this question. Of the explanations suggested by Meuvret for the dispersion of cultivated grasses the most convincing is that lucerne cultivation forced farmers to till arable fields flat (*en plat*) and not in furrows (*billon*) so that the forage-crop could be mown. This point had been made first by the English farmer and agricultural writer Richard Bradley in the 1740s (*ibid.*, vol. II, p. 51); see below, chap. 7, notes 7 and 61. The famous Tuscan landowner and agricultural innovator of the mid-nineteenth century, Cosimo Ridolfi, held the same opinion (see his *Lezioni orali di agraria date in Empoli negli anni 1857 e 1858*, Florence, 1868, vol. I, pp. 364–5) and his convictions on this matter were shared in our century by A. Oliva, *Le sistemazioni dei terreni*, pp. 94 ff.

[76] See Young, *Travels in France*, vol. I, pp. 390–6.

4. FROM JEAN ROBIN TO TOURNEFORT, SCIENTIFIC INSTITUTIONS AND BOTANISTS

The French people endured great suffering during the years of misfortune from 1630 to 1650; yet miraculously, in the midst of so much
despair, with the collapse of social structures, revolts and the military
suppression of revolt, some good agrarian practices managed to spread
and increase the productivity of arable lands. Fundamental changes are
often brought about in unusual times, when the normal routine is upset
by the course of events; thus, the very crisis that threatened to destroy the
monarchy drove the king to take measures which at last encouraged the
diffusion of forage-crops.

In the first place these measures led to the creation of the Jardin des
Plantes, in Paris. Lucerne, *onobrychis* and *polygala* had already been
grown as early as 1601 by Jean Robin, botanist to the king, in the garden
that he tended for Henri IV in Paris.[77] The king's botanical garden and
the herb garden of the Sorbonne were institutions which catered for the
needs of the royal household, or provided specimens for lectures on
herbs, but they could not stand comparison with the most famous
foreign botanical gardens.[78] In France the standards of the Sorbonne in
botany were mainly challenged by the School and botanical garden of
Montpellier, which, though it had only been founded in 1594, boasted a
tradition and teaching experience linked to the much older Faculty of
Medicine.

It is well known that the regional divisions between Catholics and
Protestants continued to be reflected in scientific institutions and book
production. As we mentioned in connection with the previous century,
Parisian botanists lost the contest against the Flemish of Antwerp and the
Bauhin brothers in Basle. Nor did Lyons emerge unscathed from
the struggle for supremacy. Although it had no printing industry, the
University of Montpellier, the Huguenot stronghold, enjoyed unques-

---

[77] See J. Robin, *Catalogus stirpium quae Lutetiae coluntur* . . . , Paris 1601, medica,
onobrychis, poligala, *sub nomine* (a very rare pamphlet consulted in Oxford, BO,
Sherard 237, a copy with a series of French common names of the plants listed);
according to Guy de la Brosse Jean Robin's garden might have been made around 1580
(see below, note 78). Both the profession and office often remained in the family:
on Jean Robin's son see E. T. Hamy, 'Vespasien, arboriste du Roy, premier sous-
demonstrateur de botanique du Jardin royal des plantes (1635–1662)', *Nouvelles
archives du museum d'histoire naturelle*, ser. 3, 8, 1896, pp. 1–24.
[78] According to Guy de la Brosse Jean Robin's garden was never larger than three
hundred teses of land (see above).

tioned fame, not only in the Languedoc region. Its graduates worked throughout the kingdom, stealing the limelight from the Faculty of Medicine of the Sorbonne. The quarrel was bitter even in the years when Henri IV sought pacification. The Sorbonne refused to allow graduates of Montpellier to practise medicine, claiming that they took their degrees in six months. It is true that, besides degrees in the *grande mode*, after a full-length course of study and practice, the Montpellier School of Medicine also conferred degrees in the *petite mode*, after a six-month course, for students who did not intend to practise in Montpellier after graduation. It was mainly this system that offended the pompous doctors of the Sorbonne.

The partly private, short-lived garden set up by Jean Robin was unable to provide for the needs of practical teaching or to supply fresh specimens, with their pharmaceutical properties intact, from which good remedies could be extracted for the sick in the overcrowded city of Paris, in the early seventeenth century. As we mentioned above, medicinal plants must be picked in specific months, according to whether the leaves, seeds, rhyzomes, buds or petals are to be used. That is why the old hospitals used to keep a small garden to meet their daily needs. But strangely enough, because of the dogmatic, bookish way in which medicine was taught in Paris, the capital had no institution comparable to the botanical gardens of Padua, Pisa, Florence, Leyden and Basle, and was incapable of meeting its pharmaceutical requirements adequately. In contrast, Languedoc, Provence and the Dauphiné were famous for the fine quality of their horticultural products and medicinal plants. The chief botanists whom we have mentioned had all gathered herbs in those provinces and Italian doctors went to the Dauphiné mountains to gather the rarest ones.

Lucerne and sainfoin, both very ancient plants, had proved quite capable of adapting to the climatic and pedological conditions of the limestone soils round Paris and were able to stand up to the bouts of cold weather that swept over Europe from the early decades of the seventeenth century onwards. But the species required for pharmaceutical purposes required greater care; they also needed to be made easily available at a time when new illnesses, connected with famine, war, the colder climate and contagion, were spreading like wildfire. Neither the private botanical gardens of Paris, nor those connected with the hospitals, of which little now remained, could satisfy the need for medicines and pharmaceutical products for the sick; nor were they up to the standards of provincial institutions, such as the *Hôtel-Dieu* in Lyons, where Daléchamps worked.[79] The quality and freshness of the medicinal plants was a requisite that could only be met by a specialized institution, which extracted medicaments using the most advanced method, that of Theophrastus of Hohenheim, the famous Paracelsus. The Parisian doctor Guy Patin went to the lengths of calling him 'the great and most pernicious braggart, Cacofrastus Paracelsus, master at murdering folk with chemistry'.[80]

The idea of founding an institution to supply the means of caring for the sick took root in Paris among the followers of Paracelsus. The result was the Jardin des Plantes in Paris, completely outside the pale of official medicine as it was taught at the Sorbonne. In 1628, Guy de la Brosse, son of one of Henri IV's doctors, himself Louis XIII's personal doctor, and a protégé of Richelieu, published a project for a botanical garden, with the declared aim, not of providing specimens of herbs, but of cultivating medicinal plants. The dedication addressed to the king, the true patron of his subjects' health, gave a brief summary of the problem. The medicinal plants sold on the Paris markets were poorly developed, forced, or else withered and out of season.[81] On the other hand, in response to those who maintained that the medicinal plants of the Languedoc were superior to those of the north, de la Brosse argued that the local flora of each region was best for the region in question. The Paris area had its own special plants, which were difficult to grow in the south. The real problem was to gather the right specimens at the right time for transforming them into pharmaceutical products. Lectures and practical courses should also be held twice weekly on the growing, gathering and use of medicinal herbs. Lastly, de la Brosse appealed to Richelieu, insisting that a large garden should be set up, to serve both for teaching and for cultivating the specimens necessary 'for use in great quantity, so that recourse can be had to them whenever they are needed'.

Guy de la Brosse, who had gathered herbs in the Paris countryside, openly defended Paracelsus' practice of pharmaceutical chemistry. He

---

[79] See M. M. Eug and E. M. Haag, *La France Protestante*, Geneva 1966 (reprint), *sub voce*, and on the Aumône general and the Hôtel Dieu in Lyons see N. Zemon-Davis, *Society and Culture in Early Modern France*, Stanford (CA) 1975, chap. 2 *passim*.

[80] Of the rather extensive bibliography on Paracelsus note only A.-M. Schmidt, *Paracelse ou la force qui va*, Paris 1967; W. Pagel, *Paracelsus. An introduction to philosophical medicine in the era of the Renaissance*, Basle 1982.

[81] See G. de la Brosse, *Dessin d'un Jardin Royal pour la culture des plantes médecinales a Paris . . .* , Paris 1628, pp. 685–8; R. C. Howard, 'Guy de la Brosse and the Jardin des Plantes in Paris', in *Essays in the history of science in honour of H. Gerlac*, Ithaca 1981, pp. 195–224.

had no qualifications from the Sorbonne and his many enemies often spoke of him disparagingly as a doctor from Montpellier. Clearly, the official institutions, in this case the Faculty of Medicine of the Sorbonne, held in the utmost contempt these so-called doctors, who went back to folklore and to distilling potions, and they tried to put every possible obstacle in their way. What is more, in a century when corruption was rife and few were sensitive where public services were concerned, de la Brosse's idea of producing inexpensive medicines must have sounded like an undisguised challenge to the powerful body of Parisian doctors.

The project was at last carried out in 1633 and the king purchased a house and some land in the suburb of St Victor. It was meant to include a building where lectures could be held and laboratory tests done. But although he was openly supported by the sovereign and his powerful minister, the fight against de la Brosse did not stop. The Faculty of Medicine forbade him to teach botany because he was not a graduate of the Sorbonne. Under these conditions, the publication of the first catalogue in 1636 was a great achievement. *Medica, onobrychis* and *polygala* were not forgotten, although only the rarest species were cultivated (*m. arabica, m. altera . . . , polygala valentina*). Perhaps in the hope of gaining more approval from the Parisians, he did not hestitate to set up in competition with the botanical garden of Montpellier, which had no pharmaceutical laboratory attached to it. He reminded his readers that the importance of the Jardin des Plantes lay not so much in the novelty of the initiative, as in the fact that a more complex institution had been created.[82] Although the garden was set up, the practical tests of medical chemistry were restricted to the lectures of William Davidson, a Scotsman from Aberdeen, follower of Paracelsus, who taught at the garden from 1633 to 1635, but had to wait until 1648 to be officially nominated professor of chemistry and supervisor of the garden.[83]

The garden was only opened officially in 1640. Unfortunately Guy de la Brosse was not to live long to see the fruits of his work. He died on 31 August 1641, and within two years his patrons, Richelieu and Louis XIII, were also dead. The Faculty of Medicine seized this opportunity to get control of the institution that they had opposed so doggedly.

---

[82] See G. de la Brosse, *Description du Jardin Royal des plantes médecinales . . .* , Paris 1636, pp. 13–14, 70, 80, 85, 98.

[83] See Schmidt, *Paracelse*; H. Guerlac, 'Guy de la Brosse and the French Paracelsians', in A. Debus, *Science, Medicine and Society in the Renaissance. Essays to honour Walter Pagel*, London 1972, pp. 189, 191; W. Pagel, *From Paracelsus to van Helmont. Studies in Renaissance Medicine and Science*, edited by M. Winder, London 1986.

The Jardin des Plantes was prevented from harming their interests further. Incompetent administrators removed the new practical work from the syllabus, only a little theoretical teaching was done, and, what was worse, the botanical collections were allowed to perish. The garden ran sadly wild for about fifty years and it was only in the 1690s, when even the memory of Guy de la Brosse and Paracelsus had been wiped out, that the garden was given a new lease of life, ready for the assault that would place European botany under the control of France and Paris.[84]

In these same years another person was organizing a new institution, also intended to make a practical contribution to solving the problem of the poor and the sick. Théophraste Renaudot was born in Loudun (Poitou) in 1586 and had attended the Montpellier School of Medicine. He graduated in the *petite mode* in 1605–6 in only eight months. Renaudot wisely practised in small provincial towns until 1609 (the worst mistakes were more easily kept quiet there). When he returned to Loudun, he married Marthe Dumoustier, who belonged to one of the most famous Protestant families of the place. While he was practising at the Loudun Hôtel-Dieu, he entered the entourage of Armand du Plessis, then bishop of Luçon and later Cardinal Richelieu, after treating him successfully for syphilis. In 1612, as Richelieu's 'créature', he took part in the conference on poverty organized by the future cardinal. Although he still belonged to the Reformed Church, he became doctor to the king in 1617, with a salary of 800 livres a year, and in 1618 he was nominated general commissary for the poor. His conversion to Catholicism was inevitable; it took place when his daughter, born of his second marriage in 1626, was baptized. Shortly after, in 1628, he opened his *Bureau d'Adresse*, for which royal patents were granted and confirmed.[85]

The Bureau d'Adresse was a complete novelty in the society of that time, yet surprisingly few documents have come down to us concerning the activities of this agency. In the course of his work as commissary for the poor, Renaudot had noticed that a great mass of workers, artisans and servants from the provinces were wandering around Paris daily, in search of work, and realized the great delay that occurred before the many people needing workers were able to take advantage of this supply. The growing numbers of unemployed people were quickly transformed into

---

[84] See Howard, 'Guy de la Brosse', p. 223; J. Pronteau, 'Etude sur le Jardin Royal des Plantes médecinales à Paris (1626–1788)', *Annuaire 1974–75 Ecole Pratique des Hautes Etudes*, sez. IV, Paris 1975, pp. 651–64.

[85] See H. M. Solomoń, *Public Welfare, Science and Propaganda in 17th Century France: the Innovations of Théophraste Renaudot*, Princeton 1972, chap. 1, *passim*.

paupers and beggars and urgent measures, more effective than the distribution of alms, were needed. The Bureau d'Adresse was conceived as a veritable labour exchange, where the new immigrants to Paris were registered, and those who needed a worker, an artisan or a servant could leave their addresses. Demand and supply of work were thus linked up through a centralized agency and not through the slow process of mediation and wandering from door to door to which the itinerant artisans were accustomed. The Maison du Grand Coq, in the Ile-de-la-Cité, the very heart of Paris, was swarming with so many people that Renaudot had to rent extra rooms nearby for his many activities.

Besides filing the names of those looking for or offering work, town houses, farms, merchandise, or any other asset that could be put on sale or let, Renaudot also published monthly extracts from his registers. He complained of the iniquity of the *colporteurs*, who refused to publish his notebooks, full of information of use to the public. To supply this need he had been forced to organize a printing house, which had four presses and at least thirty employees at the height of its success. He regularly published the 'Prix courants des merchandizes' and the 'Mercure françois' and later the 'Gazette de France' (1635–44). In all, eighty thousand people used his labour exchange between 1630 and 1644, an average of five thousand seven hundred transactions were carried out every year, not to speak of other services. But unfortunately we know nothing about the vast clientele of this extremely original institution and the enormous amount of business done there. All that has come down to us are two notices of September 1633, loose sheets published for distribution in haste and destroyed when they were no longer of use, which did not become collectors' items.[86] Perhaps envy, or the very slight interest that the *colporteurs* had in publications which definitely lay beyond the confines of their business, restricted their distribution to the Paris area.[87]

But Renaudot did not deal only through advertisements. His old profession as a doctor, and the calamitous times the country was going

---

[86] See *ibid.*, pp. 53, 55, 56, and *passim*. E. Hatin, *La Maison du Grand Coq et le Bureau d'Adresse* . . . , Paris 1885, p. 41. *L'ouverture des ventes, trocques et achats du Bureau d'Adresse en exécution de l'Arrest des Nosseigneurs du Conseil du Mars 1637* . . . , Paris 1637. *Le Mercure françois* . . . , ed. T. Renaudot, Paris 1635–44.

[87] According to R. Mandrou, *De la culture populaire aux xviie et xviiie siècles: la Bibliothèque bleu de Troyes*, Paris 1964, pp. 56–8, 64, 67 ff., *colporteurs* were very reluctant to favour the distribution of booklets on technical subjects or to introduce innovations in their range of publications.

through, made him decide to give public lectures on medical matters, as well as on all kinds of scientific and technical subjects, excluding only religion and matters of state. Five volumes of these lectures were published; those on medicine, diet, and the connection between illness, the weather and astrology interested his public most. His malignant enemies claimed that libertine doctors, heretics, Huguenots and tramps met in his rooms. To this were added his loans at low rates of interest, the foundation of a real pawn-broker's office and a scheme for keeping poverty under control, which could only make him unpopular among those who were speculating on the disastrous economic situation to get rich. Théophraste's activities did not go unnoticed on the other side of the Channel. In the troubled years of the 1630s and 1640s Samuel Hartlib was to take the Bureau d'Adresse as his model, when facing similar problems (see Chap. 6, 5–5.1).[88]

Renaudot and Guy de la Brosse came from the same kind of background. They were both men from the provinces, from prominent Huguenot families and complete strangers to the political and Catholic world of Paris. They entered Richelieu's entourage by virtue of the practical experience on which scientific knowledge was based. This was what the cardinal needed, to organize some kind of social measures. Unfortunately the two institutions to which they devoted their energies have left only slight traces of their work, and the part they played in spreading the technical knowledge necessary to encourage the cultivation of forage-crops can be grasped intuitively rather than demonstrated by facts. We shall gather more information on this point from the contacts with English botanists of the early seventeenth century. For the moment we can only mention that the two surviving samples of the *Petites affiches* show great interest in agricultural matters; manorial lands, fee-farms and freeholds were put up for sale; and, among the miscellaneous advertisements, appear an invention for a new trap for catching wild animals, and a method of keeping poultry and other farmyard animals. These notices sound like the first and last chapters of treatises on agriculture, such as the *Prouffitz champestres* or the *Maison rustique*, another indication that the sections into which books on agriculture were divided really corresponded to categories adopted in

---

[88] See Solomon, *Public Welfare*, pp. 58–9, 64, 68, 76, 79, 89, 94. T. Renaudot (ed.), *Première centurie des questions traitées . . . depuis le 22 jour d'Aoust 1633 jusques au dernier julliet . . . Avec une table des matières*, Paris 1638; E. Renaudot, *Recueil général des questions traitées des conférences du Bureau d'Adresse sur toutes sortes des matières . . .*, Lyons 1666.

everyday life. Very probably, among all that information that Renaudot put across to his readers, there was good advice on how to grow lucerne and sainfoin and prices from the Paris market for seeds of these species. From the English observers that Hartlib sent to France to collect first-hand information we learn of the trade between the capital and the *Midi* (see above, 3.2). They brought back evidence of widespread cultivation of *sainfoin* and *luzerne* in the early decades of the century. It would have been strange, had a southerner like Renaudot, interested in the development and welfare of his country, done nothing to make these products better known.

The change in meaning of the word *sainfoin*, which until then had been used for *Medicago* and sometimes became the name for *Onobrychis* in the seventeenth century, still has to be demonstrated. It has been mentioned that Jean Robin and Guy de la Brosse used Latin names like *medica, onobrychis* and polygala in the early decades of the century and although they approached botany 'from below' they kept Latin as the scholarly language for scientists. By now, Renaudot himself questioned the use of Latin. Like other writers, he had his lectures distributed in French, so that they would reach a wider public. As early as 1634 Cureau de la Chambre was writing that scientific results should be published in French; the task of science was, he said, to convey clearly the secret and specific virtues of natural philosophy. But science might well prove useless and harmful because it made the clearest things seem obscure, and authors should write their texts in French and avoid making obvious statements. A little later Louis Le Laboureur took up the subject again, maintaining that the French language was not without the appropriate terms for discussing all subjects worthily and hence could free itself from the dominance of Latin.[89] And the French which was clamouring so vehemently to set itself free from Latin was the French of Paris, which in those very decades became the capital, the real centre of the kingdom, under Louis XIII and even more so under Louis XIV. So it is clear that the change of *sainfoin* into *Onobrychis* took place at the level of everyday language. Olivier de Serres' message had been heard. A new southern product, *esparcet*, was cultivated directly on arable land because it increased the yield of grains, but the capital did not take over

---

[89] See M. Cureau de la Chambre, *Recueil des épistres, lettres et préfaces de . . .* , Paris 1664, pp. 267 ff. (*Preface pour . . . ecrire les sciences en François*, 1634), pp. 280–1; L. le Laboureur, *Les avantages de la langue française sur la langue latine*, Paris 1667, pp. 123 ff., 138, 164, 253 ff. In general see F. Brunot, *Histoire de la langue française des origines à 1900*, vol. V, *Le français en France . . . au xviie siècle*, Paris 1947.

its original name, as happened in regions bordering on the Alps. Then, as always, Paris refused to copy others, she launched her own fashions and new words. *Foin de Bourgogne*, by then known for several generations, continued to be grown on old meadows, *sainfoin* (sometimes also called *luzerne*) in the water-meadows, and sainfoin (*Onobrychis*) most extensively on limestone and chalky soils, but also on arable land, where the three-year rotation course was convenient and linked grain-growing to the Paris market.

Only towards the end of the century did botanists take up, once again, the question of a single system of nomenclature acceptable to all European scientists, which had been left unsolved in the sixteenth century. Once again the initiative was taken in Montpellier, and Pierre Magnol brought out the first of his works on flora growing in the neighbourhood of the city, describing not only those growing spontaneously, but also plants foreign to the region, which were carefully cultivated in gardens. He was following the Bauhin brothers' system of nomenclature, as given in their work *Pinax*, and so, despite a few formal references to polygala, he only recognized that it corresponded to *Onobrychis foliis viciae*, which flowered abundantly in the Tarral *garrigue* and the infertile meadows near Saint-Martin. But Magnol was writing in Latin and so cared little about the French nomenclature. He suggested classifying lucernes as *trifolium cochletatum*, as others had done unsuccessfully before him, which also meant swelling inordinately the number of varieties of clovers. Besides this, Magnol was very careful to point out the varieties of lucerne that grew spontaneously at the edges of fields, along the roadsides or among the crops. It was certainly the most frequent species, which could not by any stretch of the imagination be made to correspond to *Medicago sativa*. It was a question not of a selected variety but of the spontaneous spreading of a species that grew in various micro-environments, more or less suitable for reproducing it.[90] The work further confirmed the difficulty that farmers of the day had in maintaining their crops within the boundaries of meadows and fields and preventing them from spreading where they were not meant to grow. Hence every crop grew alongside its specific range of weeds, which reproduced according to the nature of the soil.

Paris responded without delay and the catalogue of the Jardin des

---

[90] See P. Magnol, *Botanicon Monspeliense sive plantarum circa Monspellium nascentium index . . .* , Montpellier 1686, pp. 150–1, 191, 267–8.

Plantes, the royal botanical garden, came out in 1689. It was signed by Jean Tournefort, Paul Hermann and a certain Simon Wharton Anglus, who was none other than William Sherard, the future professor of botany at Oxford. He had taken notes during Tournefort's lectures in 1686–8, in the three years he had spent studying in Paris. At this stage, the two schools, which used the same classifications, were drawing nearer. Here too the varieties of lucerne were classified among the clovers, while *Onobrychis*, Caspard Bauhin's term for sainfoin, had by now triumphed over other variants. Another work by Pierre Magnol came out in Montpellier in the same year. Ahead of other authors, he dealt with classification, taking up the discussion where Andrea Cesalpino and Fabio Colonna had left off. For a catalogue of the species, he referred to the work of the other Oxford botanists, Robert Morison and John Ray, so lucerne, sainfoin and Spanish sainfoin all ended up among the leguminous plants.[91] By now Tournefort and the Paris circle were certainly not willing to give up their aspirations to re-organize botany, and they brought out the *Eléments de botanique* in 1694. These were written in French, with Latin only for the nomenclature, while the common names of the plants were also given. This is the work in which the correspondence between *sainfoin* and *onobrychis* and between *luzerne* and *medicago* was officially confirmed. The scientist had simplified the situation by using the two principal names, one Provençal and one French, for the two main forage-crops. It was, however, a choice made only for the sake of convenience, keeping in mind how often these terms were used in the Paris area. But it was also partly arbitrary, and confirmed the inversion from *sainfoin–lucerne* to *sainfoin–onobrychis* which had come about in ordinary usage. John Ray, another English scientist active on the Continent in those years, mainly in France, noted that *onobrychis* was 'commonly but falsely' called *sainfoin*; and, with regard to lucerne, explained that it was called 'Trifolium Burgundiacum seu Medica legitima Saint Foine dicta'.[92] The constant English interest in

[91] See J. Pitton de Tournefort, P. Hermann and S. W. A. (Simon Wharton Anglus), *Schola Botanica sive Catalogus Plantarum quas ab aliquot annis in Horto Regio Parisiensis studiosis indigitavit*, Amsterdam 1689, pp. 231 ff., 244: the preface was dated London, 15 November 1688 and signed by Simon Wharton, which was the pseudonym of Sherard. Paul Hermann, Dutch physician and botanist was the director of the botanical garden in Leyden. P. Magnol, *Prodromus historiae generalis plantarum in quo familiae plantarum per tabulas disponitur*, Montpellier 1689, pp. 44 ff.

[92] See J. Pitton de Tournefort, *Eléments de Botanique*, Paris 1694, vol. I, pp. 310–11, 320, 327. J. Ray, *Synopsis methodica stirpium Britannicarum tum indigenis, tum in agris cultis, locis suis dispositis*, Londini 1696, 2nd edn, pp. 193, 197; no corrections were

the history and life of the Continent, especially in the natural environment and the Mediterranean system, was to produce the most radically innovative system of the whole of pre-industrial agriculture. It was elaborated by Jethro Tull on the basis of the seed-drill and the horse-drawn hoe (see Chap. 7, 1). In the earliest years of the eighteenth century, Tull, who was an observant traveller in Continental and Mediterranean Europe, from Calais to the Languedoc and Calabria, recorded that in gardens, right up to the walls of Paris, on land compacted by the rains, lucerne-fields were broken up, to be sown with *sainfoin (Onobrychis)*. This was unquestionable evidence of how sainfoin was taking the place of lucerne in the late seventeenth century, while keeping its name.[93]

The patronage of Louis XIV had by now been extended to the botanical garden of Montpellier and Pierre Magnol was obliged to pay homage to him, by recalling the great number of plants that adorned and swelled the collections of the Montpellier garden, in the same way as military glory and the perfecting of all the sciences were an ornament to the great king. He also insisted on the pharmaceutical outlook of that institution and declared that he would religiously carry out His Majesty's orders; at least, this is what he said in the French dedication to the king. The Latin preface was very different, pointing out that the successes of the great king lay in having restored splendour to the Paris School of Medicine, while the royal munificence had enabled Montpellier to expand in size. He took up his stance on the question of classification, warning that it would be preferable to reduce the number of categories and families into which plants were divided anthropomorphically, and that these categories could not be inferred only from flowers, seeds and pods; and he reasserted the medical and utilitarian view that had made the School of Montpellier famous in the past. In short, even after the Edict of Nantes had been revoked, and in a work formally dedicated to Louis XIV, the doctors of Montpellier continued to keep their distance from their colleagues in Paris (indeed, they would have preferred to deal with

made in the third edition, London 1724, pp. 327, 333. The copies used for this work (Oxford, BO, mss Sherard, 454–7), interleaved, fully annotated and corrected by Sherard himself, do not in any way invalidate the definitions given above. Hence Sherard, who had worked with Tournefort in Paris, must also have agreed on the use of *sainfoin* for lucerne and sainfoin. On Ray and Sherard see chap. 5.

[93] See J. Tull, *A Supplement to the Essay on Horse-Hoing Husbandry containing Explanations and Additions both in Theory and in Practice*, London 1740, 2nd edn, p. 94; for more information on the various editions of the *Horse-Hoing Husbandry* see chap. 7, note 14.

the Oxford botanists) and Pierre Magnol reaffirmed the classification he had made several years earlier.[94]

With a procedure so similar that it cannot but arouse some suspicion that they were imitating each other, Tournefort also published the results of his herb-gathering journey in the Paris countryside in 1698. Lucerne (*sylvestris* and its varieties) was the forage-crop most frequently found in the vicinity of the Bois de Boulogne, and in the meadows of Versailles, Palasieau and Montmorency, eight times more often than *sainfoin*, which could only be picked outside the gate of the Conférence.[95] Late in the day, but not uselessly, he confirmed that the specimen described by Jean Ruell as far back as 1536, and the *sainfoin* mentioned in many seventeenth-century documents, probably also belonged to the *medicago* family.

4.1. Scholarly terminology and everyday language

Tournefort's system, guaranteed by royal authority and upheld by the central role played by Paris, provided the opportunity to prevent eighteenth-century specialists from allowing excessive multiplication and overlapping in their scholarly nomenclature. One might expect rapid growth, but surprises lie in wait. In 1732 a certain Pascal, known as 'Pascal de la lieutenance colonelle', was compiling a small herbarium in Rocroi, where he was stationed, for his friend Roland Miffre. Actually it is more like a bilingual list, in French and Latin, than a herbarium, as it contains no reference to botanical works. Pascal must have had quite a good knowledge of the subject, as he called hound's tongue *cynoglossa* and chervil *charephyllum*; melilot and clover certainly presented no problems; but to our surprise we find 'sain-foin ou trefle dou. haec medica'.[96] Hence, a generation after Tournefort, *sainfoin* was still associated in everyday language with lucerne and was a synonym for sweet clover. But the extent of a writer's knowledge is to be measured by the profession he practises. François Nicolas Marquet, a botanist and

94 See P. Magnol, *Hortus Regius Monspeliensis sive Catalogus plantarum quae in Horto Regio Monspeliense demonstratur*, Montpellier 1697; there is an older manuscript version based on a Lyons edition of 1676, see Oxford, BO, Sherard ms 40. L. Granel de Solignac and M.lle L. Bertrand, 'Les herbiers de l'Institut de Botanique de Montpellier', *Naturalia Monspeliensia, série botanique*, 18, 1967, pp. 271–92.

95 See J. Pitton de Tournefort, *Histoire des plantes qui naissent aux environs de Paris avec leur usage dans la médecine*, Paris 1698.

96 See Carpentras, BI, ms 2.384, Livre de Raison.

doctor to the French king, composed three volumes of historical research on the plants of Lorraine in 1737. It was a herbarium, so there could be no possible mistakes. The true lucerne was the one with the purple flower and corresponded to Burgundy hay. It looked like clover and was found in damp, fertile fields. In Marquet's opinion, and in agreement with what Daléchamps wrote, lucerne was a slightly different plant and was also to be found on almost all sown fields. Lastly, *sainfoin* corresponded to *onobrychis viciaefoliae*, or to *caput gallinaceum belgarum*, and also grew in fields, meadows and damp places.[97] There is an obvious difference between these two contemporary documents. The author who was a doctor or botanist by profession always followed Tournefort's nomenclature, but the one who was of a lower professional status, or merely an amateur, paid greater attention to popular nomenclature.

Tournefort's work was followed by a whole series of studies on regional flora named strictly according to the new nomenclature; they all agreed that *Onobrychis = sainfoin* and lucerne = *luzerne = treffle de Bourgogne*. The greater or lesser accuracy found from one author to another lay in the description of the varieties (*medicago silvestris, sativa, lupulina* and *orbicularis*), the conditions under which they developed, and their usefulness or the harm that they caused to agriculture. In any case they were by now common plants. Only authors from the Alpine regions still mentioned that *sainfoin* corresponded to *esparcette*, which was used less and less because it was essentially a local term.[98] Jean-Jacques Rousseau noted how widespread *esparcette* was, from the Dauphiné region across to Switzerland, where this name was kept. From the late seventeenth and throughout the eighteenth century, botany was studied more and more assiduously by European upper-class amateurs and *virtuosi*; as a hobby it was recommended mainly to ladies; Rousseau himself, deeply attached to nature, gathered herbs on many occasions, in particular along the road from Lyons to Paris in 1768, putting together a well-organized collection of two thousand plants. Provincial terms and scientific nomenclature were interchangeable for an amateur of the stature of Rousseau, who was won over at once by the Linnaeus system. Thus it is clear that he knew and used *sainfoin* and *luzerne* according to

---

[97] See Paris, BN, mss fr.8.685–87, *Dictionaire historique des plantes en Lorraine*, Nancy 1737, vol. II, fos. 270*v*, 271*r*; vol. III, fo. 25*r*.

[98] The many writers on regional flora include G. Gauthier, *Introduction à la connaissance des plantes ou catalogue des plantes usuelles de la France*, Paris 1760, pp. 215, 231; M. Villars, *Histoire des plantes de Dauphiné*, Grenoble–Lyons–Paris 1786, vol. I, pp. 339, 342; vol. III, pp. 390 ff., 400 ff.

the custom of his time, not following the everyday language of the Swiss, who used them as synonyms, but used *sainfoin* in its old meaning of lucerne.[99]

5. SOME CONCLUSIONS

By now the advantage of growing *lucerne* and *sainfoin*, for fodder and for the nitrogen it deposited in arable land, was clear not only in the Paris area and Provence, where it was widely grown and where information spread rapidly, but in the west of France and other regions where economic change was slower. In September 1576, two hundred years earlier than the date generally given, a small field of *sainfoin* reserved for the use of the lady-owner, made its appearance on the sharecropping farm of Bois Dousset, in Haut-Poitou. The *noues*, small plots of land among the meadows, and *pâtis* (second-class meadows where the animals were put to graze), which gave plentiful fodder for mowing, were common in this region and suitable for *sainfoin* crops. There were lucerne patches in gardens and vineyards in Privas, in the Ardèche region, between 1658 and 1687; and we have notice of other meadows sown with lucerne and sainfoin, always carefully enclosed, again in the Poitou area, at the end of the seventeenth century.[100] However, the new crops were grown here and there, tucked away in odd corners of estates and farms, in gardens and vegetable gardens, where it was hoped they would escape the notice of the ever more vigilant collector of tithes. For while the high price of hay encouraged the cultivation of these crops, as happened in the Paris area after 1630,[101] it was discouraged in some

---

[99] See A. François, 'Les provincialismes suisses-romands et savoyards de J. J. Rousseau', *Annales de la Société J. J. Rousseau*, 3, 1907, pp. 37–8; J. J. Rousseau, 'Dictionnaire de botanique', in idem, *Oeuvres complètes*, Paris 1969, vol. IV, pp. 1201–47; idem, *Ecrits botaniques*, *Oeuvres complètes*, vol. IV, p. 1888.

[100] See P. Raveau, *L'agriculture et les classes paysannes en Haut-Poitou au xvie siècle*, Paris 1926, p. 141: since meadows were also reserved for the owner's use and were not usually included in the lease (*bail à ferme*, p. 142), some innovations not shared with the tenants may have been made there. See L. Merle, *La métairie et l'évolution agraire de la Gâtine poitevine*, pp. 103–4 for a more traditional view of farming in the region. Besides the allotments known as *noues*, the *ouches*, also used for cultivating cereals for green fodder, recall the practice already described by Estienne in the *Praedium rusticum*, pp. 453–5, of cultivating cereal crops analogous to lucerne. See also the important bibliographical references quoted by Meuvret, *Le problème des subsistances*, vol. II, part II, p. 49.

[101] See *ibid.*, pp. 59–60 quotes the ruling on tithes on sainfoin made by the Parliament of Paris in 1647, which complained that arable land had been laid to grass in about thirty parishes in the Paris region.

parishes where the Church authorities complained of the loss of income when arable land was put to grass. In other cases, lucerne and other forage-crops were subject to tithes even when grown in enclosed gardens, not only in the instances we have seen in Provence. On 12 March 1643, a royal decree confirmed the right of the dean of Saint-Mellon of Pontoise (Oise) to collect all tithes from the enclosed land of two tenants, the widow of Jean Prevôt, and Simon Le Thieu. This meant small tithes on horticultural products and lambs, while the decree also preserved the right to the tithe on the fallow lands and lands ploughed up in the previous forty years. On 7 September of the same year 1643, the tithe of the curate of Saint-Siméon of Meaux (Seine-et-Marne) was confirmed for barley and oats, sown separately or together with peas, beans, vetch, lentils, turnips, buckwheat, millet and other grains known as *tremois*. Lastly, on 6 March 1712 the parliament of Rouen settled the dispute between F.E. Poussin, tithe-collector, and Paul Pellot, curate, concerning the tithe of Burgundy hay, peas, beans and lentils in the parish of Aubervoye; the curate was considered to be the legitimate owner of all the so-called green tithes on legumes and greenstuffs.[102] Elsewhere, as in the area south of Paris, tithes did not weigh too heavily on rural incomes. Once again, however, one cannot exclude the hypothesis that in France, too, as in Provence, the recorded estimates for lucerne and sainfoin were undervalued to avoid payment of the tax.

In short, the economic policy of Sully, first of all, then institutions such as the Jardin des Plantes and the work of Renaudot and Colbert, would seem to have been of some importance in the spread of forage-crops in France. There is a continuity in the data presented here, not unbroken in the decades after 1618, when the Thirty Years' War and then the Fronde reduced the provinces of the eastern frontier and the Paris area to ruins. They were decades in which the French army claimed ceaseless daily supplies of green forage and dry fodder and straw for litter.[103] It has

---

[102] See *Recueil des Edits et d'ordonnances royaux*, Montalant 1720, vol. II, pp. 679, 685, 859–60.

[103] See Bloch, *Les caractères originaux*, pp. 215–16; Meuvret, *Le problème des subsistances*, vol. I, pp. 107–9, and vol. II, pp. 55–66; H. Neveux, 'La production céréalière dans une région frontalière: le Cambrésis du xvᵉ au xviiiᵉ siècle. Bilan provisoire', in Goy and Le Roy Ladurie (eds.), *Les fluctuations*, pp. 61 ff., maintains that the impact of war can be studied for the region involved, from the fifteenth to the seventeenth century. The fall in tithes on oats between 1550 and 1700 may also reflect the fact that oats as the main food for horses had been replaced by the more widely grown lucerne and sainfoin.

been calculated that the horses and mules of an army of 30,000 consumed daily the hay produced on 133 hectares of land, not to speak of that for rearing 35 quintals of livestock to be butchered for the daily rations of the men themselves.[104] The war of the old regime, which often extended its fury to distant provinces, was very profitable for a host of middle-men, speculators, tax-farmers, quartermasters (not to speak of the looting of the enemy and, in times of necessity, of friendly provinces too). The demand for supplies was not limited to requests for provisions, but extended to the French monarchy's growing need for money. The 33 million *livres* of 1624 had become 208 million in 1635; the figures for 1644 and 1647 were also very high, 118 and 142 million respectively. This draining of finances was reduced only in the last years of the Fronde (1648–50), but went up again in 1651. The increase in taxes concerned new and old income (*taille, taillon, subsistances, aides, sol pour livre* paid at 3 per cent).[105] The French farmer was crushed on the one hand by the Church, on the other by the State. Under such conditions, it was best to reduce production to a minimum (or hide the better part from the tax-collector). Besides all this, in most cases the farmer was forced, by customary right, to leave his arable land open after harvest and his meadows after the first and second mowing, so that the cattle and sheep of the community (or those who had purchased grazing rights) could graze freely. Apart from the indications given by Bloch, Meuvret and Bourde,[106] the history of the enclosure of common land in France still has to be written. It is clear that while tethering or movable fences would have allowed the diligent farmer to sow legumes in fields and meadows, his rights were greatly restricted by the community, or rather by social groups and entrepreneurs who ran local political life and the lands of the community. The butchers were notorious for renting pastures and the rights to finish fattening their animals before they were slaughtered. The butchers of Troyes appealed against the agreement of 10 November 1642, between the mayor of Troyes and the nobleman Jacques de la Motte-Hodancourt, by which the latter had usurped a total of 145 *arpents*

[104] See L. André, *Michel le Tellier et l'organisation de l'Armée monarchique*, Paris 1906; G. Parker *et al.*, *The Thirty Years War*, London 1984.
[105] See R. Bonney, *The King's Debts. Finance and Politics in France, 1589–1661*, Oxford 1981.
[106] See M. Bloch, 'La lutte pour l'individualisme agraire dans la France du xviiie siècle', *Annales d'histoire économique et sociale*, 1930, pp. 329–83, 511–56; idem, *Les caractères generaux*, pp. 201 ff.; Meuvret, *Le problème des subsistances*, vol. II, pp. 22 ff.; Bourde, *Agronomie*, vol. I, pp. 509–95; vol. III, *passim*.

of pastureland in several places, used alternately as meadowland and pasture (2.5 *arpents* were even sown with turnips).[107] The right of *vaine pâture* was used to curb the most enterprising individuals, unless they belonged to a sufficiently powerful local pressure group. As in England, enclosure of commons was the cheapest way of getting extra land, provided the beneficiaries could get round the considerable legal obstacles.

Generally, however, historians of agricultural improvement tend to approve of the cultivation of lucerne and sainfoin only when grown on arable land in rotation with cereals. They do not consider as a positive sign the enclosed gardens or plots where small quantities of lucerne were reproduced.[108] Yet forage-crops could never have passed so rapidly to arable land after 1750, had so many farmers not had experience of growing them in previous centuries. It was this fact that enabled large-scale cereal-growers to risk introducing a crop costly in seed, manure and labour, and make a success of it. This laborious sequence was repeated, again successfully, in England, where these crops were not grown before 1600 (see Chaps. 5 and 6). In France, too, as in Italy, valuable crops disappeared whenever farmers lost the habit of growing them. In the Gâtinais, for example, the sharecropping system excluded all but grain crops. When the Intendent enquired about cultivated meadows during the drought of 1785, he was told that vetch and lucerne had never been sown in the region, nothing but a few fields of buckwheat. The good practice of growing lucerne, even in small patches, for which there is evidence in the previous century, had disappeared.[109] French agrarian history is not strewn with the same failures that occurred when lucerne and sainfoin were introduced into England; under favourable economic and political conditions, they were quickly adopted where soils were suitable, since seed was available and many farmers already had the necessary knowledge to grow them properly.[110] Seed production is a forgotten chapter of the history of agrarian innovations. The seed exported from France to London and the English countryside, in the last quarter of the

---

[107] See L. le Grand, *Coutume di Baillage de Troyes avec les commentaires de Mr. ****, Paris 1737, p. 292.

[108] For example see both Meuvret, *Le problème des subsistances*, vol. II, pp. 33 ff., 37 ff., and Jacquart, *La crise rurale*, p. 328.

[109] See Merle, *La métairie et l'évolution agraire*, p. 137: obviously the farmer had the option of feeding his cattle or his family with spring grains, according to the quantity of wheat harvested.

[110] As an example see Gilbert, *Traitée des prairies*.

eighteenth century, is evidence of the lively exchange between southern and northern Europe, small peasant producers and capitalist land-owners.[111] France's outstanding success in producing the seed of forage-crops, which she maintained until the second half of the twentieth century, started from the small quantities of seed produced on patches of garden, little esteemed as they were by the theorists of *la grande culture.*

It was by imitating the techniques of *la petite culture* that rules and rotations could be formulated, so as to cut out dead periods in the agrarian cycle on large farms and increase productivity. The model to imitate was that of the regions of northern France, from Calais to Liège, the French and Austrian Low Countries, where large landowners and small peasant owners were variously distributed, leaving some enclaves for middle-class owners, but very little Church property. Although the old regime held full sway until 1789, the small peasant owners (of up to 3 hectares) elaborated a system of cultivation in which the land was never left fallow. The ground was divided into three equal parts, for wheat, then *hivernage* (rye and vetch sown together and mown green), clover, lucerne and sainfoin according to the type of soil. Turnips and carrots, oil-seeds, hemp and flax were commonly grown in the peasants' gardens. These crops were grown by using sewage and later peat-ash and oil seeds (after extraction of the oil) as fertilizers, but mainly by adopting the more traditional rotation of clover and wheat. Clover was generally preferred to lucerne and sainfoin (though there is evidence that it was used from the early sixteenth century on; see section 2, above) for the annual cycle of cultivation and for undrained land. This system of intensive production was very flexible and could be integrated with the domestic textile industry, horticultural production and early urbanization. It was the southern model of farming that Olivier de Serres presented in France, which in the long term proved extremely sound, and applicable to other situations. It was the large estates of the nobles, who defended the economic institutions of the old regime, the large-scale growing of

---

[111] See *Arrêt du Conseil d'Etat du Roi du 2 mai 1676 concernant la levée des dîmes de colzats et autres graines en Flandre*, Paris 1676; P. Bonnassieux and E. Lelong, *Ministère de l'Instruction Publique et des Beaux Arts. Conseil de Commerce et Bureau du Commerce 1700–1791. Inventaire analytique des procès-verbaux*, Paris 1900, p. 450 b: '3 avril. M. l'Intendant de Flandre propose pour user de représailes envers l'Empereur, d'interdire la sortie des pierres blanches et des graines de trèfle et de luzerne que les sujets de ce prince tirent du royaume'.

cereals, fallow years, and *vaine pâture*, by which the owner's flocks were fed on common and private land, at the expense of the community.[112]

The solutions put forward in the mid-eighteenth century to increase the productivity of capitalist agriculture had by now been tested out on both sides of the Channel for at least a century. To them should be added the struggle of the individual landowner to wrench the commons and common pasture from collective use and the search for more efficient ploughs and ploughing implements.[113] The increase in the production of cereals and of agricultural produce, generally witnessed in the whole of Europe from 1750 to 1850, was achieved in part by exploiting the fertility accumulated in the soil in previous centuries, thanks to the efforts of generations of peasants. Evidence of this in the documents has too often been passed over by scholars bent only on transforming the practical achievements of nineteenth-century farming into a historical model.

[112] See F. de Neufchâteu *et al.* (eds.), *Le Théatre d'agriculture et mesnage de champs d'Olivier de Serres*, Paris 1804; T. Radcliffe, *A Report on the Agriculture of Eastern and Western Flanders*, London 1819; G. Lefebvre, *Les paysans du Nord pendant la Révolution française* (1924), Paris 1972, pp. 191, 194, 195–8, 211 ff.; M. Hocquette, *Histoire générale des jardins: jardins flamands et lillois*, Lille 1951; Le Roy Ladurie, 'De la crise ultime à la vraie croissance', pp. 414–17; M.-J. Tits-Dieuaide, 'L'évolution des techniques agricoles en Flandre et Brabant du xive au xvie siècle', *Annales (ESC)*, 36, 1981, pp. 367–8; idem, 'Les campagnes flamandes du xiiie au xviiie siècle, ou le succès d'une agriculture traditionelle', *Annales (ESC)*, 39, 1984, 3, pp. 590–610.

[113] Haudricourt and Delamarre, *L'homme et la charrue*, pp. 343–70.

5. Tradition and innovation in sixteenth- and early seventeenth-century England

1. THE GREAT LANDOWNERS AT A CRITICAL JUNCTURE

In the chapter on Palladius, we saw how at least the upper reaches of English culture had some features in common with the economic culture of the medieval Mediterranean world. Vineyards, orchards, gardens, protected by high castle or abbey walls, were common to both northern countries and the South. Though direct contact between the two cultures was always difficult, these features of upper-class agriculture were deemed essential to the administrative needs of the great religious and lay properties on which the social and economic power of the aristocracy was built.

The history of late medieval English agriculture generally starts from a serial analysis of manorial accounts, the kind of document produced by the abbeys of Winchester and Westminster. Emphasis is laid on the connection between food shortages and the demographic crisis, which became apparent in the years 1315–17, before the plague broke out in 1348. The Black Death was to halve the population of England, which had reached a peak of five to six million inhabitants, a point to which it would only return three hundred years later. During this period the owners of great estates had become absentee-landlords, content to let others shoulder the responsibility for cultivating the land, given the serious labour shortage.[1]

---

1 Of the extensive bibliography on the subject we will mention only M. M. Postan (ed.), *The Cambridge Economic History*, vol. I: *The Agrarian Life of the Middle Ages*, Cambridge 1966; idem, *Essays on Medieval Agriculture*, Cambridge 1973; idem, *The Medieval Economy and Society*, London 1972; J. K. Titow, *English Rural Society, 1200–1350*, London 1969, and idem, *Winchester Yields: a study in Medieval Agricultural Productivity*, Cambridge 1972. H. E. Hallam, *Rural England, 1066–1348*, Glasgow 1981, presents an interpretation which constitutes an alternative to Postan's

The English situation differed from that of Italy and France during the period in question because of the sparse population in England and the quantity of agricultural land, both arable and pasture, albeit of uneven quality, on offer. Recent research has been evaluating the role of peasant farmers in facing the crisis of the fourteenth to fifteenth centuries, and their capacity to economize on labour by substituting horses for oxen as draught animals and making wide use of the harrow to complete the work done by the traditional plough.[2] It is clear from this research that the necessary technical changes came about more swiftly in East Anglia, which was to serve as the model for agricultural improvers throughout Europe from the eighteenth century on, because horses and iron harrows had already been used, and sheep reared there in the late Middle Ages, and turnips were grown there first, before anywhere else, in the seventeenth century. There were two easily accessible markets for the produce of this region, the city of London, which had a population of around a hundred thousand in the fourteenth century and half a million in the seventeenth; and Norwich, with its great wool market, the second manufacturing centre of England in those days. It should also to be emphasized, more than do the authors quoted here (in the footnotes), that the soils of East Anglia are very light and easy to till, and that the fall in

and Titow's views. E. A. Wrigley and R. S. Schofield, *The Population History of England, 1541–1871. A Reconsideration*, London 1981, has now become the standard reference work. Some good points on the history of the vine in England are made in H. Phillips, *Pomarium Britannicum: an Historical and Botanical Account of Fruits Known in Great Britain*, London 1823, pp. 177–207; G. Ordish, *Vine growing in England*, London 1953. On gardens see T. Mclean, *Medieval English Gardens*, London 1981. See also B. F. Harvey, 'Introduction: the Crisis of the Early 14th Century', in B. S. M. Campbell (ed.), *Before the Black Death*, Manchester 1991, pp. 1–24.

[2] See especially R. H. Britnell, 'Agricultural technology and the margin of cultivation in the fourteenth century', *EcHR*, ser. 2, 30, 1971, pp. 53–66; idem, 'Minor landlords in England and medieval agrarian capitalism', *Past and Present*, 89, 1980, pp. 3–22; M. Mate, 'Profit and productivity on the Estates of Isabella de Forz', *EcHR*, ser. 2, 33, 1980, pp. 326–34; idem, 'Medieval agrarian practices: the determining factors', *Agricultural History Review* (hereafter *AHR*), 33, 1986, 1, pp. 22–31; B. M. S. Campbell, 'Agricultural progress in Medieval England: some evidence from Eastern Norfolk', *EcHR*, ser. 2, 36, 1983, pp. 26–46; idem, 'Arable productivity in medieval England: some evidence from Norfolk', *Journal of Economic History*, 43, 1983, pp. 379–400; idem, 'Towards an Agricultural Geography of Medieval England', *AHR*, 36, 1, 1988, pp. 87–98; G. H. Dury, 'Crop failures on the Winchester manors, 1232–1349', *Transactions Institute British Geographers*, n.s., 9, pp. 401–18; H. Osmaston, 'Crop failures on the Winchester manors, 1232–1349 AD: some comments', *Transactions Institute British Geographers*, 10, pp. 495–500; see also J. Langdon, *Horses, Oxen and Technological Innovation: The Use of Draught Animals in English Farming from 1066–1500*, Cambridge 1986; B. M. S. Campbell and M. Overton, *Land, Labour and Livestock*, Manchester 1991.

human population favoured the use of horses instead of oxen for farm work, bringing about a reduction in the arable land growing wheat for human consumption and an increase in oats for horses. They were also fortunate in that, in the damp English climate, the practice of substituting fallow by another crop, which would rid the soil of weeds, did not entail any reduction in the land under cultivation, as it did in Italy or Provence. In practice, the late medieval fall in population enlarged the area of land which was farmed extensively, and the productivity of English peasant labour increased simply because the ratio between the unit of labour and the area cultivated had improved. In the meantime, until further research on the geography of these innovations is available, it must be noted that higher yields were obtained in areas where cultivation procedures connected with grain-growing were most intensive, as in East Anglia.[3]

However, it is obvious that the low yields of the late Middle Ages can be attributed to various factors, such as the need to keep the fields tilled in order to prevent both weeds from taking hold and the formation of scrub, which had to be cleared later by hard and costly labour. Devonshiring was not common in the fifteenth century and applied only to old pastures that were being cleared to grow arable crops, an infrequent requirement in the fifteenth century. The heavy plough or *caruca*, which was essential for breaking up heavy land, was only used in districts that had open fields, where Anglo-Saxon colonization had been strongest. Those who already used horses instead of oxen and had adopted lighter ploughs found it very hard to rid the land of weeds.[4] Institutions such as the manor favoured extensive cultivation and had a tendency to keep cereals on unsuitable land, as happened on Winchester Abbey property. The creation of fields was a tangible sign of political power (*potestas*); therefore territory was not abandoned lightly in times of civil strife.

So far, agrarian history has focused principally on the study of the great Church estates, such as those of Winchester Abbey, because they are better documented, providing a better model of administration (Henry VII, for example, got most of his officials from the Church). The

---

[3] Especially Campbell, 'Arable productivity'.

[4] See Postan, *The Medieval Economy and Society*, p. 51; on English ploughs, a rather neglected subject in recent British historical writing, see J. B. Passmore, *The English Plough*, London 1930, and E. Kerridge, *The Agricultural Revolution*, London 1967, pp. 33–7, 67–8; on the iconography of medieval weeding see B. Andreoli and M. Montanari (eds.), *Il bosco nel Medioevo*, Bologna 1988, especially M. Baruzzi and M. Montanari, *Silva runcare*, pp. 126–36.

smaller estates of the lay nobles are only now receiving due attention.[5] But between the thirteenth and the early sixteenth century, there grew up a whole school of bailiffs and stewards, whose technical knowledge was largely drawn from legal treatises on management and the collection of feudal dues according to the rights of lordship. It was no accident that the philosopher Robert Grosseteste, Bishop of Lincoln, dictated what came to be known as the *Rules of Saint Robert*, the first treatise on farm management. The other writings, including the *Sénéchaucy* or *Husbandry* of Walter of Henley, do not seem to have come from such a scholarly background.[6] Actually, the *Rules* were inspired by the *regulae compoti*, which the great abbeys, such as the Cistercian abbey of Beaulieu, used to insert in their rolls as a model for book-keeping. They were treatises that took into account the requirements for managing the property of the great nobility and Church dignitaries, who employed a number of bailiffs, and of the small landowners who had to be content with only one. So the *Rules*, written in French for the Countess of Lincoln, were divided into two parts, one concerning the land and one the home of the feudal lord. The text was translated into Latin and adapted to the requirements of Church property; it became part of the legal literature of the time and was translated into English at the end of the fifteenth century, when this class of manorial employees grew more numerous. The most famous of this group of treatises is certainly the one probably written around 1286 by Walter of Henley, a monk who had gained practical experience as a bailiff on some great estate in the West Midlands. It was intended more as a supplement to and comment on the text of the *Sénéchaucy* than as a text that could stand by itself. Perhaps it owes its fame to the clear organization into divisions and paragraphs and the confident demonstration of ideas on costs and work. After the prologue, in which the reader is advised to live by the tenets of divine and human law, the text deals first with the administration of the master's house; then come the *extenta manerii*, a detailed report of the size and productive capacity of the estate, then the duties of the bailiff, the supervision of work and the famous discussion on the advantages of ploughing with oxen or horses. From here it passes to grain-growing, its costs, ploughing, seeding and harvesting, and ways of increasing yields; and lastly, the administration of money, buying, selling and keeping

---

[5] See now Britnell, 'Minor Landlords in England'.

[6] See D. Oschinski, *Walter of Henley and Other Medieval Treatises on Estate Management*, Oxford 1971.

accounts. The importance of the treatise lies not only in the technical information and in the explanations about cultivation that no other source manages to give, especially concerning production costs, but also in the large number of copies that have survived, providing evidence of how widely it was used.

Walter's treatise and the so-called *Husbandry*, which best depict daily farming life in England in the days of the open fields, were later printed in very incomplete form. His original treatise was wider in scope; lawyers copied extracts from it in preference to others, as it made their work easier. It made no difference whether the treatises were copied in Latin or French, since both were spoken by the ruling class and their officials. Anyone who could read was capable of reading both languages, while the application of Palladius and Pliny was part of a wider context, presenting feudal administrative problems on the one hand, and the Mediterranean model with a wider range of economic choices on the other. Middle English translations of treatises on farm management date from the fifteenth or sixteenth century, and their fate and relationship with the book market were different from those which the translation of Palladius enjoyed. The *Boke of Husbandry*, published in 1523, has been variously attributed to the brothers John and Anthony Fitzherbert.[7] It was based in part on the text of Walter of Henley, but it solved the traditional problem of the quality of work on the lord's home farm, with regard to ploughing with oxen and horses, in a very different way. It was the quantity of pasture available to the owner that decided the choice. Like John Prise, William Lambarde and John Smyth, Sir Anthony Fitzherbert certainly belonged to the group of royal officials and administrators who had had legal training and knew how to deal with the administrative and legal problems arising on the great estates of the nobility. He used Walter's text as a point of reference and took into account the economic changes concerning property that followed the sale of Church lands (1536–9), which was rapidly creating entirely different conditions in the land market from those under which Walter and the

---

[7] No detailed study on the two brothers Sir Anthony and Sir John Fitzherbert has been produced so far. The elder brother, Sir John, a wealthy country gentleman, inherited the family estate and probably wrote both the *Husbandry* and *Boke of Surveying*; Anthony, the younger brother, became a judge and was author of the famous law treatise. This was probably the reason why the anonymously published *Surveying* was attributed to Sir Anthony, against all the old family evidence: see R. H. C. Fitzherbert, 'The Authorship of the "Book of Husbandry" and the "Book of Surveying"', *The English Historical Review*, 12, 1897, pp. 225 ff.

others had worked. In the early sixteenth century, but above all after the dissolution of the monasteries, two economic models came face to face: the traditional one, in which the manor was the administrative centre of a whole series of economic and personal relations between the lord, his tenants, copyholders and freeholders and townships incorporated in the estate; and the modern one, which afforded the landowner an opportunity to set up a new estate on land that had either belonged to the monasteries, or was rented from the Crown, or from old feudal families now in decline, and which included common lands that might be disputed and extorted from the village communities. Here lay the seeds of the great movement which eventually transformed English rural society, and which, for the sake of convenience, we still call the Agricultural Revolution; it constituted a continuing struggle between new economic forms and existing institutions, during which the new landowners looked elsewhere for economic models that were adaptable to the English situation.[8] The 1586 edition of Walter's treatise and *Husbandry*[9] was published more to meet the demands of the late sixteenth-century book market, which was greedy for printed texts on agriculture and good administration, than for the practical value that texts, by now three hundred years old, could have in such a different epoch. John Smyth, steward of the Berkeley estates (1596), consulted them when he was looking for a point of reference from which to understand how the estate he was managing had been built up; so did the more famous William Lambarde, anxious, like so many Elizabethan gentlemen, for social and economic advancement and at the same time ready to introduce himself into the European culture of his century (for both, see section 2, below).

English booksellers were surprisingly quick to seize their opportunity, as feudal English institutions confronted the Classical literature brought out by Continental publishers. They produced the first editions of Fitzherbert, together with a translation of Xenophon's *Oeconomicon*

---

[8] Of the vast bibliography on this subject we will mention only J. Thirsk (ed.), *The Agrarian History of England and Wales* (hereafter *AHEW*), 4, *1500–1640*, Cambridge 1967: only more recent contributions will be mentioned. E. Kerridge, *Agrarian Problems in the Sixteenth Century and After*, London 1969, is very useful for an understanding of the difficult legal problems concerning the difference between tenure and estates, manorial rights and freehold: a work addressed polemically to the more famous R. E. Tawney, *Agrarian Problem in the Sixteenth Century*, London 1912; see below chap. 6, note 39.

[9] Published by James Bellot as *The Booke of Thrift*, London 1586.

(1534), later adding Torquato Tasso's dialogue on the householder (1588).[10]

1.1. *John and Anthony Fitzherbert and the English translations of Xenophon*

A sharp contrast is apparent between English texts and those produced in Italy and France in the same period, but this is not the point that needs to be emphasized; rather it is the contrasts among English readers that enable us to define the context in which the learning of new agricultural methods was introduced. John and Anthony Fitzherbert's books, on *Husbandry* and *Surveying*, were probably addressed to two different kinds of reader.[11] In the *Husbandry*, the ideal landowner was a noble, knight or gentleman in theory, while in practice he did not disdain to follow the plough; his wife deigned to deal with chickens, hens, eggs, pheasants, ducks and pigeons; besides which she did the milking, got the meals, made butter and cheese, looked after the garden, sowed and harvested flax and hemp, sieved the grain, ordered the hay and, in case of need, helped her husband with ploughing, hay-making and so on. It was the woman's duty to take the produce to market and superintend the sale of cheese, milk, eggs, poultry, pigs and corn. In short, the *Husbandry* was advocating a frugal, decorous well-being (not a search for social status for noblemen and -women). As the prologue to *Surveying*[12] urged, this could be achieved by careful control of every manor, field and possession, measured and valued from every point of view, so that nothing should be lost to the lord.

Recent historical studies on medieval English agriculture rightly insist that the increase in population contributed to the maintenance of high cereals yields, by providing labour for hoeing and weeding the fields while the corn was growing. The techniques of ploughing, sowing and harrowing described by Sir Anthony in *Surveying* were quite rudimentary, and only additional manual labour and constant manuring, while the land lay idle, were able to improve yields. He recommended

---

[10] See the English translations of *Xenophon's Treatise of Household*, London 1534, 1537, 1544, 1551, 1573, 1727, 1767, and T. Tasso, *Il padre di famiglia*, translated by T. K. [Thomas Kyd] as *The Householders' Philosophie*, London 1588.

[11] The following quotations are from J. Fitzherbert, *Booke of Husbandry* (London 1598), photostat reprint Amsterdam–Norwood (NJ) 1979, and idem, *The Boke of Surveying and Improvements* (London 1523), Amsterdam–Norwood (NJ) 1974.

[12] See Fitzherbert, *Husbandry*, pp. 175–8; idem, *Surveying*, fos. V, vii Prologue.

sowing four bushels of seed per statute acre, and sowing thickly to try to counterbalance the loss of seed before germination. For ridge and furrow ploughing, broadcasting seed and then ploughing it in, produced the same disastrous effects that Agostino Gallo described for Italian fields. Better results were obtained in Essex, where the seed was covered by harrowing, very tiring work for horses and oxen that had to break up the clods of earth left by the plough, which was still an extremely rudimentary, wooden implement. Two bushels of corn or rye per acre were sown on this land, which meant considerable saving.[13] Sir Anthony did not consider it necessary to give further elucidation on the care of arable land, apart from the need to weed fallow land thoroughly, the best method of weeding and how to recognize the commonest weeds.

His brother, John Fitzherbert, was much more painstaking. He devoted eighteen chapters of his small treatise to the improvement of soil, not only of arable land but of pasture, permanent meadows, leys, old arable land no longer under cultivation, moorland that had never been cultivated, marshlands, brushwood and untilled wasteland. A great deal of land around the deserted villages of the early sixteenth century could quite easily be turned into arable land, since the natural process of re-afforestation had not gone beyond the undergrowth and brushwood stage. The cornfields that had been abandoned during the previous century had turned into neglected meadows, marshes or various combinations of meadowland and scrub; in any case, grassland was on the increase and the feudal lord frequently took this course to give him an extra source of income.[14] The technique was relatively simple – cutting, ploughing, manuring, marling (or spreading sand) or flooding (never devonshiring), in a much simpler sequence than the procedures adopted on the Continent; simpler, for example, than in France, where meadows were irrigated with cool spring water or warm water from cisterns according to the season.

---

[13] See idem, *Husbandry*, chaps. 12, 15. For a very convincing discussion of competition amongst badly sown seeds see Osmaston, 'Crop failures'; see also chap. 3, 9. E. Boserup, *The Conditions of Agricultural Growth. The Economics of Agrarian Change under Population Pressure*, London 1965 is the well-known anti-malthusian formulation of population growth and agrarian development.

[14] See Fitzherbert, *Surveying*, chaps. xxiv–xxxviii, the text speaks generically of bushes and other wild plants such as gorse (*Ulex europeus*), broom (*Sarothamnus scoparius*), moss, heather (*Erica vulgaris*), fern (*Filix sp.*). On plants and soil deterioration see G. Haussmann, *L'evoluzione del terreno e l'agricoltura*, Turin 1965, pp. 200–70, *passim*. See also M. Beresford, *The Deserted Villages*, London 1954, and M. W. Beresford and J. G. Hurst (eds.), *Deserted Medieval Villages*, London 1971.

The two texts are generally considered as models of the English agronomic system, before it came into contact with the Continental system. This is certainly true of the book on *Surveying*, which is set within the clearly defined limits of the English manor. That judgement is less applicable to *Husbandry*, in which by no means trite and formal references to classical agriculture are hidden here and there. John Fitzherbert chose to cross swords, not with Palladius, as one might have expected, but with Virgil. On the vexed question of whether to use oxen or horses to draw the plough, Fitzherbert dwelt on Virgil's preference for the ox, while he himself left the matter to be decided according to the quantity of pasture that the owner had available: oxen needed good pasture, while horses were content with common grazing, though they were more expensive to keep in the winter, when they needed oats or other cereals. Horses, he pointed out, worked faster on flat land, but were no use for food if they had to be destroyed. He concluded by agreeing with Virgil that the ox-drawn plough was cheaper than the horse-drawn plough.[15] Later, when dealing with harrowing, he mentioned Virgil's advice about going over fields sown with oats with a heavy roller. In chapter 20 he discussed the quality of various kinds of manure, considering slurry from pigsties very bad, and sweepings from granaries and barns unsuitable, because they produced weeds; road sweepings were better, especially for barley; horse dung was poor and manure from all the ruminants excellent. Pigeon-droppings, he added, 'burnt up' stubble-fields; Virgil thought that setting fire to them was better, as it nourished the soil. At this point he quoted a passage of the *Georgics* (I 83–93) literally.

In 1534, Geoffrey Pole, a member of the famous Catholic family, asked Gentian Hervet to translate Xenophon's *Oeconomicon* from the Greek original; he was convinced that the Classics were not, after all, so foreign to the Northern world. Xenophon had composed this Socratic dialogue between Critobulos and Iscomachos in the fourth century BC. The two interlocutors of Socrates discuss household management, land, the simplest agricultural rules and the virtues necessary to keep people and property united. They reveal the economic and social ideas of the lesser nobility or middle class of Athens, who felt a certain admiration for Sparta. Household management, the economy of the Greeks (*eikos*

---

[15] See Fitzherbert, *Husbandry*, I, 7. On the role of draught horses see Langdon, *Horses, Oxen and Technological Innovation*, pp. 86–127, 176–229.

nemein), could be made to correspond quite naturally to English *husbandry* (house, fields, members of the household united in the service of, and at the orders of, the householder or husband), advancing a point of view typical of the pre-industrial world. The tendency of sixteenth-century readers to equate the two cultural situations is reflected in the fact that the two works were bound together, thus associating Xenophon and Fitzherbert both conceptually and physically.[16] Direct observation of the life of his times, rather than interest in Socratic teaching, prompted an early reader to change the title of the work from *Of Household* to *A farmer*, and to note in the margin themes such as lord, bull, carpenter, carrier and so on. However, the simplest agricultural rules of Xenophon's treatise (burning the stubble left on the field, ordering vines and olives, but particularly sowing less seed on poorer land) did not pass unnoticed, though they were far removed from English agricultural practice. Two readers, one anonymous, the other a certain Thomas Rowland (or Roland), underlined this principle in the two 1537 volumes. This means that the old method of medieval agriculture, based on the conviction that high yields could only be got from large amounts of seed, was beginning to appear unfounded in the light of writings from the Mediterranean area, where men were used to taking into account the different qualities of the land, and shortages of manure, and so used seed sparingly where soil was poor. The large amount of manure produced on late medieval English farms, and spread generously on arable land, was not an indication of good farming, or even a guarantee of high yields. Indeed, the greater fertility of the soil only created competition between all the seeds scattered, so that many of them choked one another and died. The quantity of manure spread only served to compensate for the poor ploughing technique, which choked seed, and wasted land tilled on the ridge and furrow system.[17] The problem had been dealt with by the Classical agronomists, who had shown that it was useless to sow seed too thickly on poor soil, on which only a limited number of plants would ever develop fully. Agostino Gallo had taken up the same issue (see Chap. 3, 9). Farm management was a question of payments received and

---

[16] See the edition of the Greek text of Xenophon, *Economique*, ed. D. Chantraine, Paris 1949, pp. 8–9. A few examples of books bound together are Oxford, BO, Douce XX 3 (1.2), London 1534; Antiq. f. E.85 (1.2.3), London 1534, 1537; 70.c.103, binds Xenophon 1544, *Glasse for Householders* 1542, Fitzherbert 1534, 1536, and *Court Baron* 1544.

[17] Similar problems have been studied by Poni, *Gli aratri e l'economia agraria*, pp. 32–6.

payments made. 'Levis est labor cum lucro', as one William repeated three times at the end of his copy of *Surveying* (1523).[18]

Thomas Rowland made a mass of marginal notes and footnotes in his volume (in which the Fitzherbert text was bound together with that of Xenophon), giving us a clear, accurate picture of the new interest in agriculture, which even at the beginning of the sixteenth century was wholly commercial.[19] Rowland comes to the point at once, declaring his intentions as follows: 'At Bartholomew or Stourbridge Fair buy what is needful [for] thy house . . . sell to thy profit both Butter and Cheese . . . Thomas Roland his Boke'.[20] The two fairs he mentions were held in London and Cambridgeshire. Thomas probably lived at some distance from both places, in Oxfordshire or Hampshire. Both fairs drew purchasers and merchants from all over the country, to buy and sell anything from horses, cattle and wool, to hardware and hops. This explains his notes on goats, the age and class of horses, on quadrupeds in general and on turkeys.[21] But he also took careful note that the best seed 'for profit and tillage' was that grown facing south. He advised sowing wheat after barley, to guarantee a good crop; hemp or flax should be sown in May and it should be remembered that there were two kinds of hemp seeds, male and female, both of which bore flowers; also, hemp should be sown in rich, damp soil and dried in the sun. In the margin of the section on sowing peas and beans, he pointed out that chick-peas (*circerculas*) were better than 'our [English] pease' and could be ground. Tares (vetch) should be sown when the moon was on the wane, in January or March, and wheat and peas after a fallow period. These notes are followed by details of the quantities of peas, beans and barley to be

[18] See Oxford, BO, C 9.3 (8) Linc.
[19] See *ibid.*, Antiq. f.E.85 (1.2.3); the annotations are in three different hands: the oldest, now almost illegible, were probably written by a relative of Thomas Rowland (see the signature 'Ro:st à Gun: Rewland', in the frontispiece of Fitzherbert's *Husbandry*); Thomas Rowland himself wrote very extensive annotations throughout the volumes and the flyleaves; the others are by an anonymous hand, written around the mid-seventeenth century. The notes examined here are by Thomas Rowland unless otherwise indicated. Other sources confirm that it was customary to hand down husbandry books from father to son: see the notebook of Robert Carpenter II and III in Oschinsky, *Walter of Henley*, p. 89.
[20] Oxford, BO, Antiq. f.E.85 (1.2.3), cover page *v.* On these two fairs see A. Everitt, 'The Marketing of Agricultural Produce', in *AHEW*, 4, pp. 61, 511, 535–7, 539.
[21] Oxford, BO, Antiq. f. E.85 (1.2.3), fo. 1r–v. 'Turkey' probably means guinea fowl, of African origin, and the American turkey proper, which was believed to be a variety of the former, when it was first brought into England at the beginning of the sixteenth century: see *OED, sub nomine.*

sown, commenting on those given in the text; other, older notes are now illegible.[22] Ahead of the most up-to-date methods of his day, Rowland showed an interest in fallowing, harrowing, manuring and weeding arable land. 'Harrow your Ridges before you strike oates, barley and pease . . . Rie Oates Lupines refuse no grounds. Sow Rie ye latter end of August or ye beginning of September. Sow wheat in October or Hallowmass Eve [All Saints] two bushels of an Acre if ye ground be drie if not two bushels a perch'.[23] The notes on the text of the *Husbandry* continue with a series of prescriptions for sick cattle, horses and swine; they also show his interest, mentioned above, in grafting and in fruit trees, though on these points he added nothing to the text.[24] As a good Christian, he did not miss the opportunity to underline the part on the moral duties of the householder.

Surveying gives much more information on the various feudal obligations by which the land was bound. It is extremely interesting to see how carefully a landowner set out his worries. For example, the acres he owned in common pastureland were not worth 'the hay they were made of', while the pastures he used in severalty were only worth half the hay they were made of.[25] All the following chapters are annotated in the same way, telling what kinds of land were held in common, if and when the lord could sell the residue of a wood; specifying grazing rights and the right to pass through towns, discussing mills and fisheries, the freeholders who lived within or beyond the boundaries of the manor, which tenants were freemen, how to let land to a stranger, whether in demesne or in service; and enumerating various ways of rendering homage and showing loyalty.[26] Further on, the reader focused on improvements; the centre of the selion should not be too high or its sides too low. Manuring and sheep-folding were important; cross-ploughing should be done three or four times, then three furrows made where before there were two. Arable land to be turned into leys should be left fallow; overgrown land should be improved and turned into arable land; yet other points have already been mentioned.[27]

[22] Oxford, BO, Antiq. f.E.85 (1.2.3), *Husbandry*, fos. 1v, 6, 7r–v.

[23] *Ibid.*, fos. 7v–17v.

[24] *Ibid.*, III, 13, 14.

[25] *Ibid., Surveying*, fo. 5. Lands held in 'severalty' were free of communal rights, consolidated into a single property by the same owner, but were subject to grazing rights after the harvest: see E. Kerridge, *The Agricultural Revolution*, pp. 16–19; *OED*, *sub nomine.*

[26] Oxford, BO, Antiq. f.E.85 (1.2.3), fos. 8r–13v, 33r.

[27] *Ibid., Surveying*, fos. 41v–52.

What Thomas Rowland seems to have appreciated most in Xenophon's *Oeconomicon* were the parts concerning the organization of the home, women's duties, bees given as an example of an organized microcosm, how to make out a leasing contract, how the contract is undermined by the absence of love and goodwill (underlined in the text) or, to paraphrase Aristotle, the social contract is rooted in distributive justice. He read the pages more directly devoted to agriculture very carefully, noting that good quality land could be recognized by the quality of the wild fruit growing on it, and adding in the margin that ploughing should be done in spring and seeds should not be sown when the soil was dry.[28] But above all, he made a marginal note where the text dealt with the quantity of seed sown in relation to the fertility of the land. He emphasized the need not to cut crops too close to the ground, so as to leave stubble to be burnt and enrich the field; and he quoted Fitzherbert's principles of land improvement, concerning moorland, combining the breaking up of the soil, burning and manuring.[29] He devoted most of the last pages to annotations on growing trees, developed the idea of growing trees on land under cultivation, 'set trees in ground yt is occupied', and shared an interest in the vine that we have already noticed in some of his contemporaries (see chap. 1, 3, 3.1.1.). He marked a long passage that suggested it was better not to buy fields that were already well cultivated, but to choose land that could be improved by labour, because it yielded more profit.[30] On the following pages he wrote long notes on astrology, the days when it was dangerous to bleed cattle, to take medicines, to graft (grafting should not be done during leap years, because the tree would not bear fruit until the following year), adding a long weather forecast for the whole year and some notes on the calendar for agricultural work. Lastly came three closely annotated flyleaves on cultivation ('Sow not in adverse sunne nor when the wind is in ye East . . . Pull Broome till out it to kill'), agricultural measures ('To a load of hay there is 36 lbs'), on animals ('ffodder cattle with Rie straw then wheat straw and oats the oate straw and Barly then Hay if you please ffresh threshed . . . In May buy the Hay for your Cattle to eat'), and the sale of produce ('Let Wheat to sell be unthreshed till March').[31] He wrote his signature again at the end of the page, Thomas Roland 'his booke', but then went on with the notes, on the penultimate cover-page 'Suffolk

---

[28] *Ibid.*, *Xenophons Treatise of Householde*, fos. 22–47.
[29] *Ibid.*, fos. 49, 50v, 51–3. [30] *Ibid.*, fos. 54r–59r.
[31] *Ibid.* (flyleaves are not numbered).

calves are best to weane. Hempe seed sown will kill ye nettle.' Next there was a long note on how to plant trees, mentioning not only the willow, walnut, chestnut, birch and quince, but the mulberry and almond as well, confirming his interest in southern trees. The earlier notes on hemp, flax, manure, age of calves, rye, oats and lupins were repeated here.

On the whole, few writers on these subjects were ever as clear as Thomas Rowland, who pointed out the differences between the three texts and used the agronomic differences to his own advantage, especially as far as differences in soil were concerned. But above all he was interested in agricultural practice, in sowing, manuring and improving the fields and in the sale of the produce, cereals, butter and cheese; he fattened cattle, owned a flock, but took little interest in horses. He read Xenophon more from a middle-class than from an aristocratic point of view; indeed, like many others, he made almost no mention of hunting. He had probably already freed himself from communal bonds, though not from feudal ones, and so needed the legal support of the *Surveying*. He wrote very fluent English but does not seem to have known much Latin, unlike Sir John Prise or the anonymous annotator of Pier de' Crescenzi (see chap. 1, 3.3; chap. 2, 4.1).

1.2. The Rerum Rusticarum Scriptores, *a gateway to the Mediterranean*

However, the translation of Xenophon was not the only text which enabled the enquiring farmer to become familiar with Mediterranean techniques and crops. Annotations on the *Rerum Rusticarum Scriptores* are so plentiful that a complete survey of the surviving copies is out of the question. Various owners have left their mark on them; generally it was the older readers who made comments and left signs of reading indicative of an effort to learn. In the middle of the century, the English were reading Columella in the cheap Lyons and Venice editions. One Bartholomew Dodington purchased his copy for eight shillings and left some rather slight but quite coherent marks of his reading. He was interested in the site of the *villa* and which way it faced, in water, the duties of the householder (where Columella advised against letting the estate), the duties of shepherds, the fact that the farmer should live on his farm ('villicus non sit ambulator'), the careful execution of farm work, the choice of labourers according to the work to be done (Columella's slaves worked in chains). He studied the kinds of soil and noted their characteristics – lowland, hilly or mountainous, which corresponded perfectly with English uplands and lowlands. In particular, he underlined the description in the text of how, as the ploughman walked back along the furrow he had just made, he would split up the strips of tightly pressed soil between one furrow and another.[32] The fact of the matter is that the way square fields were ploughed in Mediterranean countries was completely different from the method used on the long strips of the English open field. In Columella's opinion (II 2.25) furrows should not be made longer than a hundred and twenty feet, to avoid overtiring the oxen. Unfortunately, Bartholomew Dodington interrupted his reading at this point. Another reader of Columella made simpler markings, though they were connected with one another; he noted a passage on sheep (VII 5); then, in the index, the sowing of cytisus and lucerne (VII 3, where Columella speaks of putting rams and ewes on a field of lucerne or cytisus); and rock salt, which was used in various veterinary prescriptions.[33] These were not the only annotators. In 1561 a certain H.L. closely underlined his copy of the French translation of Columella in red ochre; for, as we shall see later, in mid-sixteenth-century England good books were read in all European languages.[34]

Side by side with so many partial readings, one that shows evidence of a wider plan of study can always be found. Peter Lauerbeck, a figure who moved in court circles, had read Cato's *Agriculture*, besides Varro, Columella and Palladius.[35] He underlined practically the whole volume, noting in the margin some chapters that he found particularly interesting. He noted, for example, the one on how to buy a field and prepare it for sowing; what to sow on arable land; the characteristics of a good farm; the suburban estate; where to build the *villa*; the duties of the householder and those of the farmer. Then he noted how the land was to be used, with reference to the commercial value of the produce; the olive grove and the

---

[32] See Cambridge, UL, Hhh175, L. I. M. Columella, *De re rustica*, Paris 1543, bound together with Cato, Varro, Palladius: see pp. 21, 26, 28, 29, 31, 33, 35–6, 38–9, 44.

[33] See *ibid.*, L.12.57, L. I. M. Columella, *De re rustica*, Lyons 1541: three different hands left comments in the frontispiece, one finds the initials of the first owner, a second hand dated 1655, the signature of 'Joe. Atartyn, 6 December 1727': see pp. 257, 377, Index.

[34] See *ibid.*, R*10.44, *Les douze livres de L. I. M. Columella des choses rustiques*, Paris 1555.

[35] See London, BL, 450.d.1 (1–4), M. Cato and M. T. Varro, *De re rustica libri per Petrum Victorium . . . suae integritati restituti*, Lyons 1549: on the frontispiece are the signatures of Petrus Laurbecchius, the name of a second owner carefully erased, the stamp of Jos. Banks; on Peter Lauerbeck see *DNB*, *sub nomine*. The above quotations of Cato, pp. 14–15, 17–18, 20 ff., 42 ff., 48 ff.; Varro, I 43; Columella, pp. 61–3, 254; Palladius, pp. 106, 138–9.

production of oil, how the press was built, the oil jars, the vineyard and wine; seeds and sowing, crops, the manure suitable for cereals, problems of the seed-bed; the manures for meadows, the pastures for cattle and many chapters on remedies for sick animals and the cultivation of the fields. In short, he used Cato's simplest text as an intensive preliminary course of instruction and turned to the others to go more deeply into what obviously interested him most, the subject of forage-crops. When he read Varro, he skipped the chapter on lucerne, but did not miss that on cytisus (I 43). He read, carefully, everything that Columella had to say on the subject – the kind of meadow, lucerne that fattens cattle, adding its Latin name in the margin; then the rules for sowing lucerne and vetch. He underlined the text on the other forage-crops (*farrago*, oats, fenugreek and lentils cut while green) and finally jumped to where the farmer is advised to feed sheep on lucerne or cytisus, fresh or as hay, during the winter (VII 4). Clearly he had more than a casual interest in lucerne, for he marked the main passage that Palladius devoted to it (V 1) and went back to vetches and fenugreek later on, and to the laying down of new meadows (X 9–10). In short, Peter Lauerbeck had read the whole of Cato's text carefully and was certainly not the only one to be enchanted by the beauty of olive groves and vineyards; but then he chose to make a thorough study of meadows and plants that would improve the diet of his cattle. This suggests a movement away from a rhetorical interest in Mediterranean plants and species bordering on the exotic, to a capacity to read ancient texts for the purpose of learning the features in which Classical agriculture was superior to early sixteenth-century English farming. It is significant that 85 per cent of the examples given in the Latin–English dictionary for schoolboys, published in those very years, came from Pliny or Columella and dealt with agriculture (land, fields, cattle, farmers, corn, meadows, cow-houses, houses, markets and so on).[36]

2. WILLIAM LAMBARDE: AN ENGLISH GENTLEMAN STUDIES AGRICULTURE

William Lambarde was trained as a lawyer in preparation for entering into administrative service at court in the time of Elizabeth I. At the end

---

[36] See J. Whithals, *A short Dictionarie for younge Beginners gathered of good Authors specially of Columella, Grapald and Plinj* [*sic*], London 1556: 73 of the 86 pages deal with agriculture.

of a long and very substantial career as an officer of the realm and a writer he became keeper of the royal archives in the Tower of London. His friendship with Matthew Parker, Archbishop of Canterbury, no doubt contributed to this success. His fame, however, rests on his writings. The library of the Chapterhouse of Canterbury, to which Matthew Parker himself had devoted great care, provided an excellent basis for Lambarde's training as an expert on the ancient legislation of the realm and a specialist on the local history of Kent. In 1570 he dedicated the first version of his main work, *Perambulation of Kent,* to the archbishop, who promptly made a few corrections. William Lambarde was presented with a copy of Walter of Henley's treatise, in French, by the archbishop and made the best and most complete English translation of it that we have.[37] This translation formed part of his studies on local antiquities and his interest in agriculture, common at that time. His training in law enabled him to interpret a text by then obsolete, which could only be explained by someone who had had the same legal and administrative education as Walter. His translation was most useful in preserving the meaning of the text for those of his contemporaries who were crying out more and more for translations of texts not originally written in English.

Lambarde's personal interests can be discovered in a small book of notes that he made for his own use, which show how far he shared the general enthusiasm of his day for agriculture and what he thought was the right way to approach a text like that of Walter.[38] The notebook probably dates from the very years when he was working on his history of Kent and translating Walter into English. It is obvious how anxious the Elizabethan gentleman was to acquire knowledge on the agriculture of his time and how scrupulously he undertook to complete it by consulting the many European sources. William Lambarde's notes on agriculture become a document of exceptional importance to grasp the gap between the local English tradition and European agrarian culture, and the attempts being made to fill it by judicious textual collation. The content and structure of the manuscript are quite simple. It consists of passages

---

[37] On William Lambarde see *DNB, sub nomine,* and Oschinski, *Walter of Henley,* pp. 42–3; W. Lambarde, *A perambulation of Kent, containing the description, Historye and Customes of the Shyre,* London 1576.

[38] See London, BL, Add. ms 20709, *Commonplace book of agricultural rules and veterinary presciptions . . .,* 12°, 48 ff.: a few brief notes by Nulton Lambarde, O. Wood, W. Mills, William Molins have been added to those by William Lambarde. Printed volumes and commonplace books were used by various owners.

from various authors, collected under various subject headings. Briefly, the subjects included are ploughing, sowing, and harrowing (fos. 1–18), cultivation of cereals (fos. 9–10), meadows (fos. 11–12), quantity of seed per acre (fo. 13), vetch (fo. 16), sheep-rearing (fos. II, 18), cattle (fos. 22–5), treatment of cattle, horse and ox diseases (fos. 28–34), miscellaneous subjects (fos. 34–8), hemp (fo. 39), 'from an old book written in French, entitled gain from land' (ex libro vetusto gallico conscripto cui titulus est du gainage des terres; fo. 41), marling (fo. 42), fruit-trees and dovecotes (fo. 43), two- and three-course agriculture (fo. 43), 'Letter from the Blessed Bernard to Sir Raymond' (Epistula Beati Bernardi ad Raymundum militem; fos. 44–5), 'On the office of bailiff or sénéchal and of provost and clerk of the manor' (Du bayle ou sénéschal et de provost du manor et de clerke; fos. 46–7), and weather forecasting (fo. 48). The items that did not form part of the feudal tradition can be seen at a glance – weather forecasting, hemp and vetch, for example. But it is mainly the inner structure of the manuscript that brings out the gap between local English tradition and the agronomy of the European continent. Every paragraph begins with a quotation from the manuscript of *Du gainage des terres* (one of the titles that masked Walter of Henley's text), followed by important quotations from authors far removed from the English medieval tradition: Virgil, Palladius, Columella, Cato and Varro for the Classics, and the Pier de' Crescenzi, Conrad Heresbach and Charles Estienne, chosen from more recent Continental works.[39] Obviously the author wanted to integrate Walter's text on the points where in the local English tradition knowledge was most limited, that is, concerning the natural history of plants. So, beside Walter's passage on sowing wheat, rye, beans and peas (fo. 5'), he copied the passage on the same subject from the first edition of Conrad Heresbach's *Libri Quatuor Rei Rusticae*.[40] The German author also quoted Pliny and Dioscorides on the quality of oats, fallow land and sandy and impoverished land; next came Virgil on how flax, oats and poppies impoverished the fields, then Heresbach again on how wheat degenerates into oats (according to Pliny),[41] and lastly, Columella could

---

[39] See *ibid.*, fos. 6, 12, 16, 17, 24, 36, 37, 39, 42.

[40] The works of this official from the duchy of Cleves were translated and published in England more often than in Germany itself, see C. Beutler and F. Irsigler, 'Konrad Heresbach, 1496–1576', *Rheinische Lebenbilder*, 8, 1980, pp. 81–104.

[41] See G. Plinius Saecundus, *Naturalis historia*, XVIII 149: Pliny was the only Classical writer to believe that both barley and wheat degenerated into oats.

not but be quoted on the use of oats sown in autumn, as hay or pasture or to be used for the seed.

Walter's remarks with regard to the most typical features of two- or three-course agriculture are rather slight, and Lambarde felt they somehow had to be supplemented from other works which the book market had to offer. It took a very assiduous reader to examine, along with the Classics and Pier de' Crescenzi, whose work had been easily available in print for a century, the work of Conrad Heresbach, published in Cologne only the previous year. The quotations from these non-English writers are always used to fill some gap concerning the natural history of plants, their agricultural value completely omitted from English texts on agronomy and botany. It was not a matter of chance that English herbals of that time were of poorer quality, in both text and illustrations, compared with the editions, first of Jean Ruell, then of Plantin or Mattioli. On the whole, however, the context is quite similar. On the one hand, there is the connection with the local tradition, which was quite normal, especially for anyone studying local history, who, like so many intellectuals of the Elizabethan era, emphasized his country's past for political reasons. On the other hand, Lambarde was in touch with what were then the most vital cultural centres – Italy, Paris, the Rhineland – and drew from them the information necessary to supplement the local tradition. This is not a case of an Elizabethan popularizer,[42] simply imitating foreign fashions, but of someone seeking factual details about Mediterranean culture, which was still pre-eminent in the science and technology of Europe. In any case it is important to remember that the process of innovation was based on the study of agricultural tradition, the only true point of departure for the transformation of local structures.

In line with this, William Lambarde gathered information based on local experience, under the heading 'vox cantianorum' (the voice of the people of Kent). For example, ploughing after a barley crop (fo. 5), care of lambs on cold land (fo. 17), treatment of diseases in livestock and the prescription given daily by a certain Philip Yewell in 1571 (fo. 23), other remedies for horses (fos. 29, 31, 31', 32'), the above-mentioned marling and the use of pigeon-droppings as advised by vicar Brock. In a

---

[42] See H. R. Palmer, *List of English Editions and Translations of Greek and Latin Classics Printed before 1641*, London 1911, for example pp. 38, 86, 110, 114, 118; C. H. Conley, *The first English Translators of the Classics*, New Haven 1927, pp. 34–8, 41–8, 58, 69, 77, 106–7, 109 ff.; F. O. Matthiessen, *Translation and Elizabethan Art*, Cambridge (MA) 1931; *Cambridge History of English Literature*, IV, chap. 1.

pre-scientific age, when only personal experience could prove whether a method was sound or not, it was essential to get information from someone directly engaged in agriculture. Thus, while medieval English writers of treatises on husbandry had no need to declare their sources, since they themselves constituted tradition and source, the sixteenth-century scholar had to choose and declare the reasons for his choice; William Lambarde provided a fine example of this changed relationship between source and experience. The fact that there are so many blank pages in the notebook is evidence of work in progress, and shows how carefully Lambarde was seeking out the passages to serve as a comment on Walter's text. Hence, where the English tradition was particularly weak, in the care of meadows, Lambarde filled his notebook with quotations from Virgil, Columella, Varro, Cato, Pliny, Pier de' Crescenzi, Charles Estienne and Heresbach. The same is true for plants like vetch and hemp, or for marl, where Heresbach's text is adapted to local requirements; it is not so much summarized, as seeking the relation between the marling system in Kent and that in the Moselle region described by Heresbach. But this qualitative change could be made only through acquaintance with the knowledge of soils proper to the Classical tradition, in which they were classified first of all by their colour; this enabled Lambarde to identify French marl from its colour.[43] Though we do not know what the ultimate purpose of the notebook was, there can be no doubt that it constitutes a keystone in the reconstruction of a new economic outlook in its initial stages. It should also be remembered that this outlook was formed through the discussion of texts made available by Continental publishing. It followed naturally, once it was understood,

---

[43] See for example L. I. M. Columella, *Res rustica*, II 2–2.21, II 4, and C. Plinius Saecundus, *Naturalis historia*, XVII 25–41 on soils suitable for vines and XVII 42–8 on marl. This passage has been forgotten by English historians: Pliny insisted that Britons and Gauls had discovered the soil-improving qualities of marl (the Greeks of Megara had done the same using *leucoargilla*, white clay). Gauls and Britons used white and red limestone, tuffstone, clayey and sandy marls to improve both arable land and pastures, their fertilizing effects lasting for fifty years. The kind most commonly used in Britain seems to have been silvery clay (*creta argentaria*). The Ubii, a Rhineland people, the Eduin and Pittavian Gauls made their fields very fertile with lime. In his comment on book XVII, André (Paris 1964) preferred to read *marga* (a fertilizer containing phosphates) instead of *marna* (marl). These chapters were abridged by Robert Cricklade in his Latin epitome of Pliny's *Natural history*, produced at the beginning of the fourteenth century (to him *marga* plainly meant marl) and advised the white variety, to be spread with the help of the plough, the dry one on wet fields and vice versa, see London, BL, Royal ms, 15, fo. 54*r*. Hence marling dates from pre-Roman times, however the Classical tradition has left the oldest written evidence of it.

after the dissolution of the monasteries and the upheavals of the first half of the sixteenth century, that the relationship between man and nature did not depend on the landlord's control over agricultural work, but was being changed according to the requirements of the crops and of production in general.[44]

3. A NATIONAL MODEL OF AGRICULTURAL LEARNING

We have so far picked out many signs of interest in Mediterranean agriculture shown by sixteenth-century English gentlemen, but how widespread this acquisitive movement was can only be ascertained by examining a wider sample. Just how great was the effort made to learn a new way of exploiting the natural environment can be measured by studying the catalogues of the private libraries and the sale of foreign books in England. Of course, the fact of owning a book does not necessarily mean that it was read and absorbed uncritically, with no consideration for local conditions; but from the moment the book market came into existence, and the monopoly of the manuscript had been broken, together with the whole system that bound it to certain archetypes, a choice could be made between two distinct streams of thought, namely that of the Fitzherberts and that of Charles Estienne. The purchase of one rather than the other is indicative of the great interest in Continental agriculture. This preference may have been prompted mechanically by the example set by Queen Elizabeth's court, or by the London booksellers, who urged customers to buy Continental work.[45] Not only were books, particularly Italian, French and German books, still rare and costly, and not only were Continental or Classical works translated in great quantity by the Elizabethans, but texts on agronomy properly so called were added to, and sometimes took the place of, texts of the new sixteenth-century natural science. This was the result of the neo-Aristotelian outlook, with its constant classification, based on experience and direct contact with plants and animals, which had so little to do with the English medieval tradition of the bailiffs of lay and

---

[44] In general see G. Batho, *Landlords in England*, in *AHEW*, 4, pp. 256–305.
[45] See H. R. Plomer, *Abstracts from the Wills of English Printers and Stationers from 1492 to 1630*, London 1903; H. Fetherstone, *Catalogus librorum in diversis locis Italiae emptorum anno 1628 qui Londini in officina Fetherstoniana prostant venales*, London 1628.

Church lands.[46] It was the first step towards intensive agriculture, founded on knowledge of the biology of the plant cycle.

When all is said and done, the gentleman who adopted the cultural fashions of the European Renaissance for the sake of appearances, bowing to the fashions set at court, and then approaching the themes of European science, was taking a big step forward. For while dancing or fencing, Italian style, and reading Ariosto and Baldesar Castiglione, merely gave proof of a formal, courtly acceptance[47] of a new relationship between man and society, reading the Classics and consulting the treatises on the technology of the Classical period meant being aware of the issues of one's own century, establishing a new relationship with nature, storing up already elaborated knowledge and hence preparing to transform one's natural environment on a new basis, on foundations different from those of the preceding generation.

It is extremely useful to look at the English private libraries of 1500–1650, especially for the years 1550–1650. A sample has been chosen (cf. Appendix, tables 4–6) to show not so much the relation between book-owners generally speaking and owners of books on agriculture (since the subject of this survey is not the history of the treatise on agriculture and its market), but rather the model of economic and technical agricultural knowledge produced in the Mediterranean area and the extent to which it could be adapted elsewhere. We are endeavouring to show how that model, previously restricted to individual instances, was spread. For, however precise they are, the examples of the translation of Palladius, John Prise's notes on Palladius' text, the readers of Pier de' Crescenzi, and William Lambarde's notes are all single examples. Moreover, we must keep in mind that agricultural processes react on a wider natural environment. The possible alternatives to the agricultural text proper need to be traced, to show the owner's adherence to this or that cultural model. The time-span examined here corresponds to the Tudor and Stuart periods, since books bought in the 1640s still belong to the previous 'generation', to the years when works of a new school of agronomy were beginning to come out, rapidly outdating the type of agricultural treatise produced by sixteenth-century culture.

Of course few of these sixteenth- to seventeenth-century catalogues are accurate enough for all their contents to be fully assessed. Denomi-

---

[46] In general see G. Sarton, *The Appreciation of Ancient and Medieval Science during the Renaissance*, Philadelphia 1956, and Eisenstein, *The Printing Press*, II, chaps. 5, 6.

[47] See for example J. R. Hale, *England and the Italian Renaissance*, London 1954.

nations such as *latine, graece, English, ffrench* may serve to indicate the language of the volume and show, were that still necessary, a receptive attitude, or at least the will to be receptive to a culture not principally Anglo-Saxon. At the same time, when comparing English and Continental publications of the period, we realize that there is a great difference in quality between them. From the point of view of the printing, English books could hardly compete at all with Continental ones.[48] This perhaps explains the rough-and-ready cataloguing of the larger volumes and the loss of small, aesthetically more negligible ones or their description as 'pamphlets of trivial value'.

In 1509 Martin Collins, canon of York, owned a printed copy of Pier de' Crescenzi, valued at two shillings, as well as a book on animals, by Albert the Great, bishop of Ratisbon, worth five shillings, part of a considerable collection of 150 volumes. Another figure of this first half of the century, the ninth Earl of Kildare, Gerald Fitzgerald (1487–1554), owned ninety-two printed books, among them a *Regimen Sanitatis* and four editions of Virgil, with commentaries. One can certainly suppose that the *Georgics* were numbered among those works. In 1549 John Clement, a protégé of Sir Thomas More, who married his niece and who accompanied him on the journey to the Low Countries in 1515, left a good collection of books, very important for the history of medicine. Among them there were various herbals not otherwise specified, the *De Venatione* by Gratius and a comment by Theophrastus on Aristotle's *Animals*. On his death a few years later, in 1556, Henry, first Baron of Stafford, owned quite a fine collection of 302 volumes, in part correctly identified. Among the various dictionaries, grammar books and books on rhetoric, we find two copies of the short works by the Fitzherbert brothers, *The book of husbandry* and *The book of surveying*. This section of the library is completed by *The assize of ales and bread*, a short manual on duties levied by towns, the famous *A booke of hawking and hunting*, published by Winkin de Worde in 1532, and then four herbals, which were practically all that was available on the subject in English, *The great herbal* (London 1525), *The newe herball*, by Turner (London 1551), *The properties of the herbes* (London 1544), and *The names of the herbes*, also by Turner (London 1548). Three small works concluded this section on the natural world – Lloyd's *The judgement of urines*, *The regiment of health*, and *The castell of health*. The principle feature of this

---

[48] In general see H. S. Bennet, *Oxford History of English Literature*, Oxford 1947, vol. II; C. Clair, *A History of European Printing*, London 1960.

choice of books is that they are all, without exception, in English. It is true that there is a *Cato cum commento*, published in London by Winkin de Worde in 1508, but this is the well-known work on education in rhymed couplets, attributed to Cato, and not the treatise on agriculture. To these were added another edition of Cato, in English (London 1550), and *Xenophon on household* (London 1537), both in Thomas Berthelet's edition. Plutarch and Polydore Vergil were also read in the abridged English form. Socially, the Staffords belonged to a group beneath the peers of the realm, that is those who received rents of between £500 and £999 from their lands in 1559 and in 1602; Edward, the brother who succeeded to the title when Henry died, was driven to the lengths of confiscating cattle belonging to a farmer who had refused to lend his son a sum of money. In 1591 he was to write to Lord Burghley, to enquire whether a marriage could be arranged between this son and some sole heiress of a rich merchant family in London.[49] But to return to Henry, owner of the books: there is something provincial about his choice. He read nothing but English, but he paid great attention to the natural world, which was perhaps typical of his class or of anyone whose social prestige depended on his yearly income from land. At that time the Continental treatises and their subsequent translations had not yet come onto the book-market. He had to be content with the work of Fitzherbert. Of this, however, he had as many as three copies, which shows that he did not take a merely passing interest in agriculture, while to supplement the text he purchased the herbals mentioned above. In the end, the collection covered every aspect of the natural world that was meaningful to a nobleman – the fields and household management, the herbals and the imitations of the medieval *Regimina sanitatis*, real encyclopaedias of the individual relationship between man and his environment. Hence, while foreign books were scarce, at least in this section of his library, Henry Stafford clearly made an effort to bring the knowledge supplied by the Fitzherberts' texts up to date, by adding herbals and books on medicine and completing his acquaintance with the natural history of plants and their use, though with a slant towards consumption rather than agricultural production.

---

[49] Henry Stafford, 1st Baron Stafford (1501–63) only son of Edward Stafford, 3rd Duke of Buckingham: see Batho, *Landlords in England*, p. 259, and L. Stone, *The Crisis of the Aristocracy, 1558–1641*, Oxford 1965, pp. 230, 630, 760, 794.

3.1. The private libraries, 1550–1650

In the examples given so far we have found two trends reappearing regularly down the years: on the one hand, the Classical tradition, on the other, the tradition of works written in English. Our survey of the 1550–1650 period will be carried out on the lines of this finding, looking first at the Classical authors who recur most often. Virgil appears frequently, of course, though he cannot be placed in the forefront, since the catalogues do not always specify whether the volume contains the complete works or only the *Aeneid*, in which case it must be excluded, since only the *Georgics* are relevant to the present study. Nevertheless, it is true that interest in Virgil, and through him in the agriculture of the ancients, developed to a very considerable extent in England, with highlights such as Dryden's translation of the *Georgics*, Dickson's essay on Roman agriculture, John Symonds' study of the connections between Italian and Classical agriculture, not to mention Spenser's *Shepherd's Calendar*. Thus Pliny's *Naturalis historia* seems to have been the volume most anxiously sought after. There are fourteen copies, besides a manuscript and a printed edition with the date 1500 entered by its owner. It is to be found constantly in the years 1560, 1574, 1592, 1598, 1634, 1640, 1643 and 1650.[50] Obviously its encyclopaedic form, which encompasses the whole range of ancient science, made it much more sought after, and in the end less expensive, than a number of single volumes. Columella comes a close second, with eleven printed copies owned between 1550 and 1650,[51] except for a manuscript found among the belongings of a Cambridge student towards the end of the fifteenth or the beginning of the sixteenth century.[52] Naturally, anyone who owned the works of Columella often owned the works of Cato, Varro and Palladius as well, as these were commonly bound together in late fifteenth-century editions. While the French and Italian editions of the *Rei rusticae* authors are often found separately, when they are published in one volume they are always in Latin. Actually, Xenophon's short treatise *Oeconomicon*, to be found in various copies in the 1556, 1583, 1597, 1598 and 1643 catalogues, outnumbers Cato, Varro and

---

[50] See nos. 9, 12, 16, 18, 44, 54, 56, 73 (for a key to these sources please see tables 4–6, pp. 423–5 in the Appendix).

[51] See nos. 9, 11, 18, 27, 30, 45, 68, 71. William Cecil's library reveals a strong interest in Ermolao Barbaro's comments on Pliny and those of Filippo Beroaldo on *Rei rusticae auctores* (nos. 52, 112, 117).

[52] See n. 1.

Palladius:[53] and it probably owed its success to the fact that the Greek
'Oeconomicon' corresponds exactly to the English word 'husbandry'. It
is interesting to note that it was owned in English translation or in Latin,
never in the original.

Readers of Virgil's *Georgics* and *Bucolics* were also numerous,
although these books might be read for a literary rather than an agricultural interest.[54] However, Virgil's text is often found bound together
with other texts on agriculture. This is true of the collection of Michael
Ormer, who was a great reader of Italian texts. His bequest (1604) to the
Bodleian Library included Palladius (Venice 1538), the *Geoponics*
(Venice 1543), the *Vineto*, by Carlo Stefano (one of the Italian
translations of the frequently mentioned Charles Estienne, Venice 1545),
in addition to Alberti's *Descritione d'Italia*. William Crashaw, too,
owned two copies of the *Georgics* and a manuscript of Pier de'
Crescenzi, a treatise on birds and animals by Robert Grosseteste, Bishop
of Lincoln (author of the rules of agriculture). Lastly, the Oxford scholar
Brian Twyne owned both an incunabulum (Daventry, 1496) and a
sixteenth-century edition of the *Georgics* (Basle, 1539), together with a
series of texts, the most outstanding among them being the remedies of
Dioscorides and Mattioli (Basle 1579), Conrad Gesner's history of plants
(Paris 1541), the four books on agriculture by Heresbach, in English
(London 1578) and Turner's herbal (London 1548).[55]

Next comes Palladius, who had obviously lost his medieval fame,
though evidence of it can be found in the fact that two or three of the six
copies of the *Opus agriculturae* were still in manuscript. One or two
copies belonged to John Dee, the well-known Elizabethan scientist, and
another to George More, a knight from Surrey, who made a small bequest
of twenty-nine volumes, partly printed, partly in manuscript, to the
Bodleian Library in 1604. Cassianus Bassus' *Geoponics* is rarer. It had
been reintroduced into Europe only through Renaissance philology and
was probably read in Greek, perhaps in the Basle edition, like the one
owned by Thomas Kerry, an official of the Privy Seal. He too left his
books on agriculture to the Bodleian Library, in 1604. Otherwise it was
read in Italian, in the 1542 Venice edition.[56] A good number of nobles left
their collections to the Bodleian Library, especially between 1603 and

---

[53] See nos. 7, 13, 17, 18, 59, 60, 61, 63.
[54] The traces of Virgil in Fitzherbert's *Husbandry*: see chap. iv, I, should not be
overlooked.
[55] See nos. 29, 36, 71. On Conrad Heresbach's agricultural textbook, see chap. 6, 2.
[56] See nos. 13, 30, 31.

1605, following the example that Sir Thomas Bodley set with his munificent donation of 200 books, which led to the radical reorganization of the Oxford library from 1603 on. This small group within the more general one indicates great sensitivity to Italian and French practical and scientific studies. Philip Scudamore, for example, bequeathed Choppinus' legal treatise *De agrorum conditionibus* (Paris 1554); William Allen left Carlo Ruini's *Anatomia del cavallo* (Bologna 1598); Thomas Docwra donated the first edition of Conrad Heresbach (Cologne 1570); and Thomas Kerry left 145 printed volumes, among them some important Italian books (see below, 3.3).[57]

Lastly, almost negligible with respect to the whole sample, there are just a few copies of Aristotle's works, the small tract on economy and the larger work *De natura*, as well as one copy of Cicero's *De lege agraria contra P. Servilium Rullum.*[58]

3.2. The Classical world as a metaphor of the Mediterranean

In the years 1550 to 1640 readers were in constant touch with the Latin and Greek Classics; the former particularly were being bought for libraries all the time, both in the reign of Queen Elizabeth and under the Stuarts. Varro, for example, appears in private libraries in two copies for 1566, then for 1583, 1598, 1603, 1611 and 1637.[59] Similarly, there do not seem to be any great variations in the languages read. The Latin Classics were mostly read in the original, while Greek seems to have been accessible to people in some way connected with the universities; sometimes Italian appears as a substitute for both. William Lambarde's commonplace book provides the basis for our hypothesis that the intellectual movement towards Classical culture served as both foundation and support for local agronomy, linking it up with the mainstream of European writings. By examining private libraries, we can grasp the fundamentally dichotomous nature of the system of knowledge in the books possessed by this sample of readers, all English landowners. In these libraries we find a real chain of knowledge, a series of links connected up with one another, of which the essential feature was that ancient and modern, Classical and new sixteenth-century thought were put on the same plane. The result of this continuity was the need to make a choice, to break out of the stalemate created by medieval, even late

---

[57] See nos. 22, 24, 25, 28, 30.
[58] See nos. 18, 30.   [59] See nos. 11, 14, 18, 27, 35, 49.

medieval, man's dependence on his natural environment. Thus nature was no longer seen as a phenomenon beyond human control; scholars and laymen aimed to create a link between nature and the work of man, through the natural history of plants and animals.[60] This effort becomes clear if we do not consider the owners' choice of purchase as purely fortuitous, but trace the hidden structures that lie behind the use of certain key words. In this context husbandry was not only a synonym for agricultural work, but encompassed a vast range of issues connected with the production, transformation and consumption of the produce of the home and farm. 'To be a good husbandman . . . To achieve good husbandry', wrote Leon Battista Alberti; and the sixteenth-century Italian expression spoke of 'cultivation of the estate', a translation from the Latin 'agriculture', where *ager* plainly meant estate (*fundus*), as it was understood in Roman private law.[61] Hence husbandry meant regulating social-economic relations within the farm and with the outer world; it was halfway between economics and politics, according to Aristotle's definition.

Among the personal belongings bequeathed by five students resident in Cambridge about the end of the fifteenth and the beginning of the sixteenth century, there were not only manuscripts of Columella and Pliny, but also Apicius' *De re culinaria*, and some manuscripts described simply as being on birds, botany and plants (there were four copies of the latter), perhaps summaries of Aristotle's better-known works.[62] We have already seen that the canon of York, Martin Collins, owned the work of De' Crescenzi and Albert the Great's *De animalibus*. Later in the century Sir Thomas Smith, ambassador and statesman, classified under the heading 'Philosophica' a long list of scientific works, such as Aristotle, Gesner, Dioscorides, Galen, Ruell, Mattioli's commentary on Dioscorides, Nicander, besides two editions of Cato, Varro, Columella, Cassianus Bassus' *Geoponics* (probably in Greek) and Charles Estienne and Jean Liebault's *Maison Rustique*. To this quite considerable

---

[60] Similar problems have been discussed by K. Thomas, *Man and the Natural World. Changing Attitudes in England, 1500–1800*, Harmondsworth 1984, pp. 51 ff., 81 ff., 192 ff.; the sample discussed here shows that the seeds of scientific revolution fell on the fertile ground of practical interests, see C. Webster, *The Great Instauration. Science, Medicine and Reform, 1626–1660*, London 1975.

[61] See Alberti, *I libri della famiglia*, l. III, *Oeconomicus*, and Bonamore, *Prolegomeni, passim*. See also the Italian version of the *Liber cultus ruris* by Pier de' Crescenzi, translated in Italian as 'coltivazione della villa', a version also accepted by Cardinal P. Bembo, *Prose della volgar lingua al cardinale De Medici*, Florence 1549, p. 138.

[62] See n. 1.

collection he added, under the heading 'Medica et Chirurgica', Galen on the properties of food and a whole series of treatises on the veterinary art in French but written by authors such as Lorenzo Ruso, Vegetius and Grison.[63] In short, all the publishers of the time were reissuing works on veterinary matters, a sector near and necessary to agriculture, which had had even closer links with Greek and Arab culture in the Middle Ages. The categories that Sir Thomas suggested are extremely important to trace the criteria adopted for subject division and the links between the different subjects. He put Gesner's quadrupeds and Charles Estienne's *Maison Rustique* together, though there was no real connection between them. He placed Georg Bauer's famous treatise on metallurgy beside certain *Icones avium*, not otherwise specified, and the *Rerum Rusticarum Scriptores*. On the other hand, he divided philosophy and medical-surgical works merely on the basis of the traditional social distinction, the farrier being considered an outstanding figure in the still feudal hierarchy of monarchy, and surgery still being an ambiguous art; not many years had passed since Vesalius broke the rule forbidding doctors to dissect corpses.[64] Other authors gave a rather different picture. To take but one example, Conrad Gesner's large volumes provided information on the lion, the elephant and other exotic, fierce and wild animals, besides the densely packed pages on the cow and the ox, the calf, the goat and the horse, and often quoted Cato, Varro, Columella, Pier de' Crescenzi and so on. Gesner did not omit ancient tradition, but placed beside it direct observations on the treatment of diseases in livestock. It cannot be denied that the sixteenth-century English landowner attributed a very different value to a page on cattle or horses from one on animals he could hardly expect to meet with in his locality. Similarly, in the text of Mattioli, such a reader would find information on the therapeutic properties of plants side by side with natural history. Or, again, in works like the *Maison Rustique* the reproduction of the natural environment is described in such a way that it goes well beyond the boundaries of farm production (see, in particular, the pages on the renovation of the meadow, in chap. 4, 1). Man's relationship with nature changed when plants and animals, agriculture and animal husbandry, were dealt with in the same space; these readers' outlook seems to stem from the wish to go

---

[63] See n. 11 and M. Dewar, *Sir Thomas Smith*, London 1964. On horses in early modern England see J. Thirsk, *Horses in early modern England: for Service, for Pleasure, for Power*, The Stenton Lecture, University of Reading 1978.

[64] See Thomas, *Man and the Natural World*, pp. 51–69.

beyond the divisions of the various disciplines concerned in scientific research and the attempt to gather together the information that scientists were making available, from an economic viewpoint. The classification adopted for the library of Sir Thomas is especially meaningful because he was one of the foremost figures among the gentlemen anxious to acquire all kinds of useful information, but who never became Humanists or academics; in his pragmatism he went to the lengths of setting up a society, with other noblemen, for turning iron ore into copper.

3.3. The great private libraries

Among the 221 volumes owned by Francis Russell, second Earl of Bedford, in 1584, was the text of Dioscorides in Italian (which we can reasonably suppose was one of the twelve books that he purchased himself during his journey through Italy from 1555 to 1557) and the English translation of Heresbach's work on agriculture, the text most often found in noblemen's libraries, apart from Estienne and Liebault's *Maison Rustique*. Among the books of Richard Stonley, sold in 1597 to repay the sum he transferred to his own funds from the Exchequer while he was treasurer there, we find Pliny, Virgil with the commentary by Servius, Xenophon, William Turner's Herbal, besides Torquato Tasso's *The householder's philosophy* and Thomas Hill's *The gardener's labyrinth*.[65] The list of books in the possession of William Cecil, Lord Burghley, who was perhaps Elizabeth's most efficient and trusted minister, is too long to examine in detail.[66] Even though the volumes in the catalogue may not all have belonged to him (many of them date from the eighteenth century, whereas he died in 1598), there is a uniformity of interest in the additions made which show that they belong to the same cultural background. Indeed, his son Robert was also a servant of the state and used to sign himself Roberto Cecilio when writing to Italy. Hence, to the texts of Pliny, Columella, Xenophon,

---

[65] See nos. 15, 17; on the origins and the initial fortunes of this important family see D. Willen, *John Russell, First Earl of Bedford. One of the King's Men*, London 1981, pp. 101 ff.; on the translation of Torquato Tasso's text see above, note 10; T. Hill, *The Gardener's Labyrinth*, London 1577; see B. Henrey, *British Botanical and Horticultural Literature before 1800*, London 1975, I, pp. 60 ff.

[66] Of the vast bibliography on William Cecil see especially C. Read, 'Lord Burghely's Household Accounts', *Economic History Review*, 2nd ser., 9, 1956, 343–8; idem, *Mr Secretary Cecil and Queen Elizabeth*, London 1955; idem, *Lord Burghley and Queen Elizabeth*, London 1960; Stone, *The crisis of the aristocracy, passim*, and idem, *Family and fortune*, pp. 3–91.

Aristotle, Gesner and Mattioli, frequently mentioned above, were added those of De' Crescenzi and the other Latin agronomists, with commentaries by Filippo Beroaldo (in the 1548 Basle edition), the first editions of Charles Estienne's pamphlets, *Pratum . . . silva, frutetum* (Paris 1545), Battista Confalonieri's volume on oenology and the medicinal properties of wine (Basle 1535), and the rare little treatise on the silkworm, by Corsuccio da Sassocorbaro (Rimini 1581). Here, too, the veterinary section is well furnished, focusing on the horse, since English nobles were paying great attention to horses and horse diseases. We find Giordano Ruffo's famous text (Bologna 1561), Cesare Fiaschi's *Il cavallerizzo* (Venice 1575), another work with the same title, by M. Claudio (Venice 1562) and Pasquale Caracciolo's *La gloria del cavallo* (Venice 1589). *Le infermità del cavallo*, by Carlo Ruini (Venice 1599) and the very famous text of Antonio Ferraro, *Il cavallo frenato* (Naples 1602), which must have been added after William Cecil's death. There were works of note in French too. Before coming to the *Histoire des plantes* by Jean Daléchamps (Lyons 1663),[67] we find *La maréschalerie françoise*, by S. de la Brove (Paris 1602), suitably illustrated; the French translation of Mattioli's commentary on Dioscorides (Lyons 1620); and another veterinary text, *La castramentation*, by Simon Stevin (Leyden 1618). Such a carefully chosen, well-furnished library could not be without that masterpiece of French agronomy, the *Théâtre d'agriculture*, by Olivier de Serres, just published in Paris in 1600; actually this work met with very little success in England, for the market was by now flooded with translations of Estienne and Liebault's *Maison Rustique* and Heresbach's book on agriculture, already brought out in many reprints and new editions which had nothing really new about them except the frontispiece.[68] At least in this section of the Cecil library, English texts are very rare, nothing but a manuscript copy of Bartholomew of Glenville's famous medieval encyclopaedia, *De proprietatibus rerum*; and John Norden's more recent dialogue on land surveying. Norden was the famous expert who personally surveyed the property of Lord Burghley's sons, Sir Robert

---

[67] This is the French translation of a text originally written in Latin: see chap. 4, 3.

[68] G. E. Fussell, *Old English Farming Books from Fitzherbert to Tull, 1523 to 1730*, London 1947, gives an incomplete list of these editions: the printed catalogues of the Goldsmith Library, University of London, and of the Rothamstead Experimental Farm point out many editions. On the many volumes published by Gervase Markham, see F. L. Poynter, *Gervase Markham: an annotated bibliography*, Oxford Bibliographic Society Publ. 1962.

and Sir William, Earls of Salisbury.[69] Perhaps William Cecil's library portrayed all too exclusively the interest in everything that was being published on the Continent, to the detriment of English writings. But it should not be forgotten that it was William Cecil himself, as minister to Elizabeth I, who issued decrees to encourage foreign inventors, technicians and experts in every field to migrate to England, and so his library inevitably reflects this effort to modernize technology in the country, by learning everything useful and more advanced that was to be found in Europe.[70]

Though the case of William Cecil was perhaps exceptional, the general pattern also tends to recur in the second half of the period under examination. So in 1604 Thomas Kerry, whom we have already mentioned, left a total of 145 books to Oxford; all those concerning agriculture were in Italian. There were Agostino Gallo, in the rare edition of the *Dieci giornate della villa* (Brescia 1564), the Italian translation (Venice 1568) of Gabriel Alonso Herrera's *Agricultura*, the *Geoponics* of Cassianus Bassus' in Greek (Basle, undated), an Italian text on land surveying, Girolomo Cataneo, published in Brescia in 1572, and finally Columella, in the Italian translation of Venice 1564. This same interest in foreign agriculture prompted the gentleman William Petre to purchase a not otherwise specified book on agriculture in French, with a French–English dictionary to understand it better. In those same years the 2,300-acre demesne of Petre's family property, which had been managed by the landlord in 1536, had gradually decreased to a mere 1,000 acres in 1636; the rest had all been let.[71] Interest in the agriculture of the Continent, where estates and farms were smaller, was not just a matter of curiosity. Sir Edward Coke, Lord Chief Justice under Elizabeth, had founded the family fortunes at the time of the dissolution of the monasteries, by purchasing great estates, including that of Holkham, which was to become famous in the history of English agriculture in the eighteenth and nineteenth centuries. In the year of his death, 1634, he owned a vast library of 1,227 volumes.[72] It is strangely

---

[69] See note 66.
[70] See London, BL, Lansdowne mss 14.15, 17.3, 26.55, 28.18–22, 24.63, 63.20–2, 64.33, 101.8–9, 118.1–75; and J. Thirsk, *Economic Policy and Projects: The Development of a Consumer Society in Early Modern England*, Oxford 1978.
[71] See n. 34: the volume in question is not fully described, dating from 1610 it might have been either the *Maison rustique* or the *Théâtre d'agriculture*.
[72] See n. 44: on Sir Edward see C. Hill, *Intellectual Origins of the English Revolution*, Oxford 1965, and on the Coke family in the eighteenth and nineteenth centuries see R. A. C. Parker, *Coke of Norfolk: A Financial and Agricultural Study, 1707–1842*,

prophetic that the ancestor of one of the most famous English land-owners, Thomas William Coke of Norfolk, owned almost exclusively Continental books on agronomy. He had the Italian translation of Charles Estienne's work, published in Venice in 1581, the already mentioned Italian edition of Gabriel Alonso Herrera (Venice 1577) and then the *Vinti giornate* by Agostino Gallo, in the 1567 Venice edition; to which he added Columella, for good measure. As a useful supplement, there was Pliny's *Natural history*, in the Italian translation (Venice 1580) and the by no means easy volume of Gian Battista Della Porta, *Magia naturalis*, in the French translation. It is of special interest, in the sample examined here, that Edward Coke also owned the *Five Hundred Points of Good Husbandry*, by Thomas Tusser, one of the few English writers who had been endeavouring, since the second half of the sixteenth century, to counterbalance the flood of Continental texts with local writings.[73]

The number of volumes owned by a collector like Lord Conway does not put his library in the medium-sized group; he had about 4,700 in all, of which only 3,000 titles can be described with certainty. This is not surprising, since his prestige rested more on his support for the king than on his personal wealth; in 1641 his annual income was between £1,100 and £2,200, well below the average of £3,930 for each of the seventy-three new peers of the realm. Yet it is worthwhile taking a look at his books on agriculture. It should be said at once that the catalogue of Lord Conway's books was not made as a tool for finding one's way among the collection, but to establish the value of each volume when a special committee put them up for auction, together with the assets of twenty-four Catholic Royalists of London, in 1643. So it was a question of valuing and selling these volumes and not of classifying them correctly. This is why the descriptions of the titles are often very poor and incomplete. Despite these shortcomings, it is at once evident that Lord Conway's collection was particularly well furnished with works in Italian, French and Spanish and that the greatest number were on the subjects of military art and cavalry.[74] By the mid-seventeenth century,

---

Oxford 1975. Coke's private library has been donated to the Bodleian Library, under the Holkham shelf-mark: very sadly none of the books mentioned here present any marks or proof of reading.

[73] See Fussell, *Old English Farming Books*; recently the text has been reissued as T. Tusser, *Five Hundred Points of Good Husbandry*, edited by G. Grigson, Oxford 1984; see chap. 6, 4.

[74] See J. Roy, 'The Libraries of Edward, 2nd Viscount Conway and others: an inventory and valuation of 1643', *Bull. Ins. His. Res.*, 41, 1968, pp. 35–46.

the ideal of the Elizabethan gentleman had been substituted by a more Spanish model, based on arms and cavalry, something similar to the models of the Italian Francesco Birago.[75] Very probably these features were purposely emphasized by the fact of Lord Conway being a supporter of the king, but they probably depended equally on the modest dimensions of this lord's estate.

On examining the titles we at once come across an Italian work, *Le delitie et frutti della villa*, an unknown text rather similar to Giuseppe Falcone's *La nuova vaga et dilettevole villa* (Brescia 1577); only by checking all these titles could one hope to identify such works.[76] *Le vinti giornate della vera agricultura e piaceri della villa* by Agostino Gallo, is more easily recognizable in the title *Dialogo del Gallo*; while *Dell'agricoltura Italiana* (bound with seventeen other works) might in reality be Sansovino's work of the same name, published in Venice in 1560 and later reprinted. *La Agricultura fr.* [*sic*], in octavo, is more difficult to identify; it might mask one of the editions of Estienne–Liebault, perhaps in Italian translation, for it could not be the work of de Serres, which was never published in octavo. Besides these there was a not otherwise specified *Discorso di arte coquinaria* and a *Trattato delle carni et sapori*. Should it be thought bold to put together the examination of a bibliography on agriculture and texts on food, we would point out that in those very years Vincenzo Tanara dealt at great length with the preparation of food in his *Economia del cittadino in villa* (Bologna 1640); it was concerned not only with bread and wine, but with garden produce too. For the consumption and growing of this produce provide an important indication of agricultural progress, not only in pre-industrial times. Butler's text on bees can also be connected quite easily with the many treatises on the subject, certainly influenced to some degree by the Classics. The *Nature and quality of chocolates* was

---

[75] On military questions see H. J. Webb, *Elizabethan Military Science: The Books and the Practice*, Madison 1965, and C. G. Cruickshank, *Elizabeth's Army*, Oxford 1966. On English Catholics M. J. Havran, *The Catholics in Caroline England*, Stanford 1962; J. A. Bossy, *The English Catholic Community, 1570–1850*, London 1975, A. J. Loomie, *The Spanish Elizabethans*, New York 1963, and idem (ed.), *Spain and the Jacobean Catholics*, London 1978, contain important contributions on questions indirectly related to the main theme of this book.

[76] Notwithstanding the very important contributions of F. Re, *Dizionario di opere di agricoltura e veterinaria*, Reggio 1808–9, O. Niccoli, *Saggio bibliografico sulla storia dell'agricoltura italiana*, Turin 1911, the very useful Lord Westbury, *Handlist of Italian Cookery Books*, Firenze 1963, and the recent contributions by G. Benzoni, M. Berengo and E. Casali, mentioned above, we still have no complete list of all the early modern editions of Italian agricultural books.

addressed to those with a taste for exotic products, which, because they were rare, expensive and foreign to traditional eating habits, were of interest only to the privileged classes.[77] A panorama of the botanical interests of Lord Conway is completed by a *Traité de jardinage*, a *Plantarum historia* and a *Hortii dissertatio*. His fondness for horses is reflected is such titles as *The breeding of horses*, the *Disciplina del cavallo*, *De natura equorum*, *Markham's cavalry* (that is, the book on veterinary science written by Gervase Markham), and a *Discourse of horsemanship*, also by Markham (1593). The subject of Norden's *Surveyor's dialogue* and an *Answer of surveying*, directly connected with measurement of his land, was best dealt with in English, the lord's own language.

3.4. Learning as a means of intervention in a changing economic situation

It is typical that there should be translations of Charles Estienne and Heresbach, and more so that there should be work by popular writers such as Markham, Googe and Surfleet now available to the English public.[78] We are not speaking here of Fitzherbert or Tusser, to be found neither here, nor in 90 per cent of the cases examined. The model of knowledge of the natural world closely reflected the outlook and economic structures that had been formed in the course of the sixteenth century on the continent of Europe; and the Grand Tour had become a powerful means for transmitting this knowledge.[79] After a journey to London and France for purposes of study, young William Drummond also retired, from 1610 on, to the small property near Edinburgh owned by his family for generations. He had brought home books like the *Res Rustica*, by Columella, the *Maison rustique* by Estienne–Liebault, the *Geoponics*, together with *La compagnia della lesina* and, the most unlikely, given the climatic conditions of his home, *Trattato sulla*

---

[77] Imports of coffee, sugar and cocoa rose considerably during the seventeenth century: see J. A. Chartres, 'The Marketing of Agricultural Produce', in *AHEW*, 5/2, *1640–1750: Agrarian Change*, Cambridge 1985, pp. 407 ff., *passim*.

[78] See in the following order B. Googe, *The Foure Bookes of Husbandry*, London 1572, a translation of C. Heresbach, *Libri quatuor de re rustica*, Cologne 1570; R. Surfleet, *The Countrie Farm*, London 1600, translated C. Estienne and J. Liebault, *L'agriculture et la maison rustique*, Paris 1572; Gervase Markham published both of them under his name adding a few pages here and there: see Poynter, *Gervase Markham*.

[79] See J. W. Stoye, *English Travellers Abroad, 1604–1667: Their Influence in English Society and Politics*, London 1952, 1988.

coltivazione degli ulivi by Pietro Vettori.[80] In this, as in so many other
cases, we are not dealing with imitation, or habit or the requirements of
the book market, which was actually quite varied, or with an obsequious
acceptance of cultural fashion set by the court of London, but with
the wish to learn, to seek out novelties, to adapt foreign species to the
climatic conditions of the British Isles. These interests of the nobility in
agriculture and Continental plants, from constituting a single stream
around Palladius throughout the fifteenth century, divided up into
so many rivulets suitable for the owners, now very different and indi-
vidualist, of great, medium and small noble estates in the sixteenth and
seventeenth centuries. Within the limits of a rather inflexible book
market, there were, however, certain outstanding alternatives. The
favourite work became Charles Estienne's treatise, which appears no
fewer than thirteen times in the private libraries, in its provisional
pamphlet form and then in the final collected volume in Latin, in Jean
Liebault's later French adaptation, and in Surfleet's English translation
(also once even in Italian). In second place comes a strange pair, Pier de'
Crescenzi and Heresbach, which confirms once more how vast was
the fame of the Bolognese agronomist in sixteenth-century Europe. The
fame of Heresbach's text was more recent, being no doubt connected
with the fact that the author, an official of the Principality of Cleves, took
part in the mission to England in 1571. On that occasion he probably met
Barnaby Googe, poet and protégé of Lord Gray, who at once agreed to
translate the *Quattuor libri rei rusticae*. The copies of the other texts that
we have considered as equivalent to agricultural treatises proper, given
the quality of the information they provide, are much less numerous.
Conrad Gesner's animals (four specimens) barely outnumber the three
copies of Olivier de Serres, a text of great value which met with very
little success between 1600 and 1650. As we have already mentioned
(Chap. 4, 3), his work seems to have been hard to sell in England, as the
market was monopolized by the great trio *Maison Rustique*, Heresbach
in Googe's translation, and Markham. The size of the work must also
have discouraged would-be translators (pirated books were common in
the seventeenth century and it was certainly more profitable to reproduce
an old text, with the convenient formula 'newly enlarged and enriched'
in the frontispiece). Then we have all the Italian authors, Mattioli,
Agostino Gallo, Sansovino, Herrera (though a Spaniard, he was read in
Italian), Vettori and Falcone, which, although while taken singly do not

[80] See n. 72: he was the only Scotsman in this sample.

go above one to three copies, taken together form a group only just below the *Maison Rustique* (eleven copies), without counting the de' Crescenzi, which was written in a different age. Yet the sense of the past may have been lost in England because of the different social-economic structures, so that the *Liber cultus ruris* and the others were all read simply as examples of Mediterranean agriculture. Just as to say France was to say the Continent (after all, French was still the scholarly and administrative language of the nobility in the early sixteenth century), so interest in Mediterranean agriculture at that time was often equated with de' Crescenzi, and quite easily went so far as to introduce Palladius again, together with the lofty tradition of Columella and the great scholars of the Classical age. Seen in this perspective, authors like Charles Estienne and Conrad Heresbach were partly responsible for that levelling out of the centuries between the Classical age and the sixteenth century, since they used the Classical texts as sources of their knowledge of the Mediterranean world and presented Varro's evidence of the fertility of Italian soil as if he were speaking of contemporary matters. Moreover, this uniformity in the reading and purchasing of texts on agronomy and their alternatives was enhanced by the fact that the majority of the sample of seventy-one private libraries considered here belonged to nobles (thirty-five cases) and only ten to scholars. Thirteen and five belonged respectively to members of the professions and the clergy. On the whole, the clergy and scholars showed very little interest in questions of agriculture. It could hardly have been otherwise, since the Church had just been deprived of much of its land, while scholars were generally supported by the universities and hence were mostly prevented from owning land. Nobles and members of the professions, on the other hand, showed a very tangible interest in rural economy. Members of the professions showed the greatest interest in the works of Elizabethan translators;[81] this is consonant with the new opportunities being afforded to government officials and members of the professions to become landowners, and even to aspire to the title of nobleman within three generations.[82] At the same time it should be emphasized that none of the nobles in our sample was among the great landowners of Britain; their libraries reflect a time when the reorganization of medium-sized farms was being planned. These were the farms where Continental models

---

[81] See nos. 64, 66, 67.
[82] See Stone, *The Crisis of the Aristocracy*, pp. 65 ff., 335 ff., 424 ff.; Batho, *Landlords in England*, pp. 280–5.

could be adapted more easily, and intensive agriculture developed by channelling knowledge of the natural history of plants and animals into productive processes. The great estates of the peers of the realm, owned more as status symbols and for the political power they conferred than as a direct source of wealth, were run on the principles of extensive farming and the relation between labour and product was not even taken into account. Little did the lord care about knowing the best quantity of seed to be sown per acre when the losses due to bad administration could always be counterbalanced by a mortgage or favours from the king.

4. THE GREAT NEW ESTATES AND THE MODEL OF THE RENAISSANCE VILLA

The new family dynasties that were making a name for themselves in the country districts or the counties, after the purchase of lands that had belonged to the monasteries, needed a visible sign of their prosperity to place at the heart of their estates. The great country houses and mansions of the Elizabethan age were the result of this eager quest for social prestige. However, the high cost of keeping an array of servants in livery, such as the small private armies which the great aristocracy of the North and West of England could afford, put a display of this kind quite beyond the means of the new landowners. It was precisely this class, after rising at the expense of the old noble families and the monasteries, which became the staunchest supporters of the political power of the Tudors.

The new buildings, which proclaimed the new social status achieved by the families of merchants, professional men and, very rarely, yeomen, were the hall or house, no longer the manor. Moreover, the surest way of maintaining this new social status was by good administration of the land. Hence the cultural model became a model of economic administration and the texts printed on the Continent of Europe provided this model ready made. The new relationship with the environment, and cultivation founded on natural history and the new plants, served to exploit the land more successfully. An economic institution like the Italian Renaissance estate could not be transferred unmodified to England, where the economic cycle linked with sheep-rearing entailed a rapid fall in the rural population and the enclosure of whole villages. Much less was it possible to adopt outmoded contracts like share-cropping, on which the Italian villa was founded. The learning process that took place in the 1550–1640 period was creative, not a mere slavish imitation. The decades of hard times following 1620 forced owners to achieve marked improvement in the organization of farm work and to forge direct links with their sources of information.

6. The new crops and English agriculture

INTRODUCTION: READERS AND PRINTED BOOKS, THE NATURALIZATION OF FOREIGN CROPS

In the previous chapter we saw how the advent of printing and the work of Elizabethan translators extended cultural relations between the upper classes of English society and the Mediterranean world to a wider group of readers. Whereas an unbroken relationship existed between man and his natural and agricultural environment in Italy and France, a greater split divided upper- from lower-class culture in English society. Those able to read and use the Classics also owned a private garden for their experimental crops, which was at once an ornament to their homes and a source of greater variety on their tables. On the other hand, growers whose produce was intended for the market simply needed to fill in the slack periods in the agricultural year. We also saw in chapter 5 that the English book-market was part of the European publishing scene, and technical books, in Italian, French, Spanish, Dutch, Flemish and German, not to speak of Latin and Greek, were used a great deal by cultured but not necessarily erudite readers. In Elizabethan England, relations between scholars and ordinary people were more fruitful than elsewhere. The proportion of the population with some schooling was very high, considering that the number of inhabitants fluctuated between three million (1551) and a little over five million (1651). Standards of literacy varied, from those who only knew English to those who could read and write in several foreign languages. It can be estimated that, of the adult male population, over half a million (1551) and over a million (1651) were capable of acquiring information from printed matter.[1] In view

---

[1] See. E. A. Wrigley and R. S. Schofield, *The Population History of England, 1541–1871. A Reconstruction*, London 1981, p. 528: to estimate the potential readership of agricultural books we have taken into account only the adult male population in

of this, two factors need some explanation: firstly, the naturalization of better-quality forage-crops, which mingled with those growing wild in the British Isles, and their adaptation to the local agricultural cycle; and secondly, the final triumph of the humbler clover over the more productive grasses favoured on the Continent, particularly lucerne or sainfoin.

1. WILLIAM TURNER

The oldest evidence of lucerne being grown in England is provided, in at least one case, by archaeological findings dating from Roman times. But whereas plants like garlic, celery, laurel, parsley and the vine became acclimatized for good, lucerne disappeared, and perhaps no serious attempt was ever made to cultivate it.[2] The fact that a cornfield in the county of Essex was called 'lucerne field' in the fifteenth century is no proof at all that lucerne was grown in England; it is more likely that the field was connected with some lamp (*lucerna*) dating from Roman times.[3]

Nonetheless the Englishman William Turner, who studied under Luca Ghini in Bologna, described lucerne before Andrea Mattioli did. After studying at Pembroke Hall, Cambridge, Turner obtained financial help from Lord Thomas Wentworth to pursue his scientific interests, proceeding to study flora and fauna and other medical subjects, while continuing his training, using Classical texts[4] (then annotated by Ruell and Marcello Virgilio), and making many of his own personal observations. He combined his interest in the natural sciences with an

the 25–59 age group (41.72 per cent of the entire male and female population divided by two). In the whole of this study only one woman was found to have signed her name in her husband's commonplace book (see Moorat, *Catalogue*, vol. I, n. 212: 'Corbett Arthur, Collection of practical receipts', signed on the cover by 'Alice Corbett her book', seventeenth century). On different degrees of literacy see. L. Stone, 'The Educational Revolution in England, 1560–1640', *Past and Present*, 28, 1964, pp. 41–80. See also note 106.

[2] See Sir H. Goodwin, *The History of the British Flora. A Factual Basis for Phyto-geography*, Cambridge 1975, p. 177.

[3] See J. Field, *English Field-names. A Dictionary*, Newton Abbot 1972, p. 131. In France and Italy too most of the place-names like 'Luserna' stem from the Latin *lucerna* (lamp) and not the Provençal *luzerne*.

[4] Like so many others, Turner, too, started out from Pliny and mentioned his edition corrected by Erasmus and published by Frobenius, as well as by other commentators of the *Naturalis historia* such as Ermolao Barbaro, Filippo Beroaldo, Guillaume Budé and Jean Caesarius.

intense interest in the Protestant cause. He was an early follower of Latimer and Ridley at Cambridge, was committed to the support of the Protestant cause in England, and linked philological criticism with criticism of the Church of Rome. He was trying to repeat, in England, the role of Jean Ruell and Otto Brunfels in the field of natural sciences. Turner certainly went to Italy, spurred by his interest in Classical science, though it was at an unfortunate time for one of his radical religious convictions, which he expressed as a preacher and commentator on the Scriptures. He had been involved in the struggle between Stephen Gardiner, a personal enemy, and Thomas Cromwell, besides which he was openly hostile to Henry VIII's religious policy. Turner left England in 1540. From his herbal we learn that after Calais, Dunkirk and Flanders, he visited Cologne, Bonn, Basle and Worms and finally crossed the Alps. The island of the Certosa in the lagoon of Venice, Ferrara (where he briefly followed the teachings of Antonio Musa Brasavola), the Po between Ferrara and Cremona, and finally Bologna, where he encountered the teachings of Luca Ghini, repeatedly described as 'my master', were the main stages of his visit to Italy.[5] Between Bologna and Ferrara, Turner was in touch with John Falconer, the Englishman who, so tradition has it, compiled the first modern herbarium, sticking dried and pressed plants to the pages of a book. Turner himself mentioned the dried botanical specimens that he carried with him.[6]

Since lucerne does not appear in the *Libellus de re herbaria*, written while Turner was at Cambridge, he must have become acquainted with it during his stay in Italy.[7] In 1548, before Mattioli and Anguillara (but it is hard to say how far independently of Ruell and Estienne), Turner wrote that lucerne did not grow in England, where he had never seen it, though it could be found in many places in Italy.[8] He also suggested that it should be called *medic fodder*, obviously after the Latin term. He associated with lucerne the *lotus urbana*, a cultivated clover (foreign to the English flora; the name could be rendered *gardine Claver*), to be seen

---

[5] See C. E. Raven, *English Naturalists from Neckam to Ray*, Cambridge 1947, pp. 52–70, full of information on William Turner. We shall deal only with Turner's writings on botany, leaving aside his important religious writings (such as *The Huntynge of the Romysh Wolf*, etc.) and those on the natural history of birds and fish.

[6] See Camus, *Histoire des premiers herbiers*, p. 13.

[7] London 1538.

[8] See W. Turner, *The names of Herbes in Greke, Latin, Englishe, Duche and Frenche with the common names that Herbaries and Apotecaries use*, London 1548, *sub nomine*.

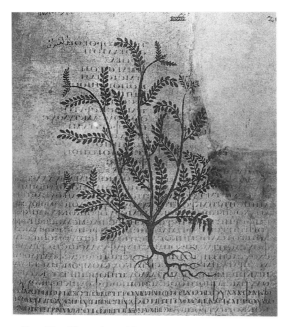

1 The oldest illustrations of forage-crop plants, Poligalon (poligala, *onobrychis*); in Dioscorides, sixth century, facsimile, Graz 1965–70, fo. 265r, Turin, Biblioteca Nazionale.

2 The oldest illustrations of forage-crop plants, Trifullon (*trifolium bituminosum*); in Dioscorides, sixth century, facsimile, Graz 1965–70, fo. 265r, Turin, Biblioteca Nazionale.

3 Melica (*Surghum vulgare*) replaced *medica* (*Medicago* sp.) on poor soils; *Tacuinum sanitatis*, Rome, Biblioteca Casanatense.

4–5 Clover (*T. pratense*, bottom left) appears together with other meadow plants in paintings. Gentile da Fabriano, 'Saint Dominic' and 'Saint Mary Magdalen', panels from the polyptic of Valle Romita, Milan, Pinacoteca di Brera. By permission, Ministero per i Beni Culturali e Ambientali, Milan.

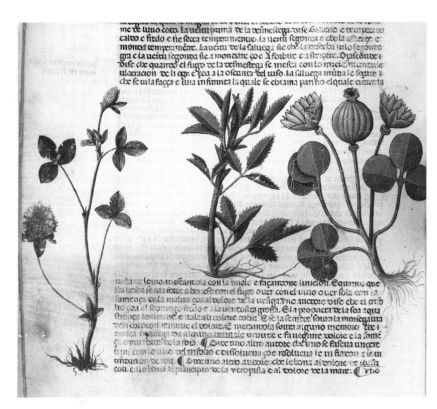

me te limo coto. La ueti panna te la tesmestega vise Sa ueno e tempera
calto e sitto e ne seca tempera mente. la ueti segona e cte la asterige e
moncoa tempera mente. la ueti te la saltega ne cte la enseca ento seguno
gra e la ueti segona ne a mon cone coe A fotbut e a strigere. Oiase out e
vise cte quarto el sugo te la tesmestega se mesca con to miele maute
ulceraciou te ti ogi. e goa a la oscanta tel uiso. la saltega muta le segue
cte se ula saggere e una infunta la quale se cbtama pan no el quale caueta

un ta te lomo a mescantola con la miele e sagantone iunicion. Equa ma que
ita beaba se ula touce o betese con el sugo ouer con el uuto ouer sola con ta
somengu tela malina con al uolote te la uesiga Yno auctone vise cte el aub
tio goa al stomego stoto e a la uetutosita grosta. E la propuett te la soa agua
stempe tomenote e uale a lu uolote cotta. E se la semete soura la monegauta
teta couxon tenuue el tolote. E metantola soura alguno membuo tte t
no sea hautega te alguna animale uoure e sa negune uolote e la some
ge e nur tte te la sou. Oue uno altro auctore cte uuo se saseua uncete
ti pu con le ulto tel ntsolio e ctssolueta coe tsolueta se ut sucon e te ut
unuoa uo te tott. Oue uno altro auctore cte te bona al uolote te ttesta
coti. e tte bona al puncpto te la uetopista e al tolote te la mate. Yno

6 A new sensitivity to nature: clovers from the illustrated manuscript of Serapion, British
Library, Egerton ms 2020, fo. 7v.

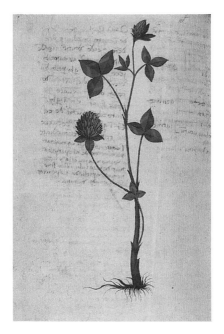

7–9 Lucerne and clovers were recognized and represented with their distinguishing features.

7 Red clover (*T. pratense*), from the Roccabonella, later Rinio Herbal, Venice, Biblioteca Marciana, Lat. ms VI, LX, 2548, fo. 152v.

8 White clover (*T. repens*), from the Roccabonella, later Rinio Herbal, Venice, Biblioteca Marciana, Lat. ms VI, LX, 2548, fo. 153v.

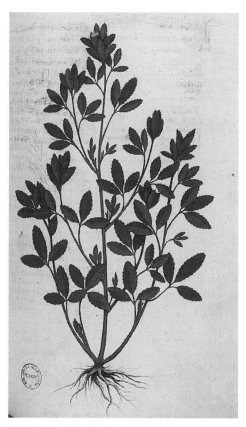

9 Lucerne (*Medicago* s.),
from the Roccabonella, later
Rinio Herbal, Venice,
Biblioteca Marciana, Lat. ms
VI, LX, 2548, fo. 396v.

10–11 Sixteenth-century
botany identified many
varieties.

10 Polygala (*Onobrychis
sativa*), P. A. Michiel, *Erbario
o Istoria generale delle piante*,
I, Red book, Venice, Biblioteca
Marciana, Ital. ms II, XXVI,
4860, fo. 216r.

11 Lucerne (*medica* s.).
P. A. Michiel, *Erbario o Istoria generale delle piante*, I, Red book, Venice, Biblioteca Marciana, Ital. ms II, XXVI, 4860, fo. 345r.

12 Reader's markings of famous texts. A copy of Croniolo della Cornia's *Divina Villa*, made, with corrections, by ser Giorgio, son of Jacopo Di Bonaparte; mid-fifteenth century, Florence, Biblioteca Nazionale, cod. Magl. XIV 3, fo. 1r.

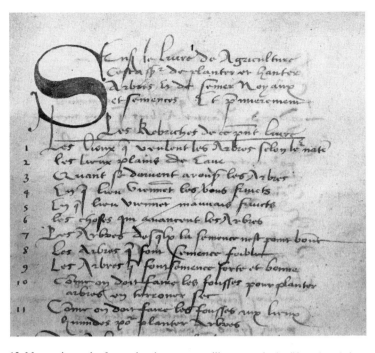

13 Manuscript copies from printed texts were still common in the fifteenth and sixteenth centuries, Turin, Biblioteca Reale, Varia ms 271, fo. 1r.

14 Ancient Mediterranean economy was carefully studied in Elizabethan England. Xenophon's *Oeconomicus*, London, 1544. Oxford, Bodleian Library, Antiq. F.E. 85(3), fo. 50v.

Xenophons treatife

grene newely ryfen oute of the erthe, if he ftyrre and turne it in ageyne, it is as if hit were a fuftinaunce to the ground, and get-teth as moche ftrength by it, as if it hadde ben donged. But if ye fuffre the grounde continually to bring forth fruite of the fede it is harde for a weake grounde to brynge forthe moche fruite ftyll, lyke wyfe as it is harde for a weake fowe to gyue fucke and fuftinance to many pigges, and kepe them fat and in good plite whan they waxe gret. Socrates. Ye fay good Ifchomac. that ye muft fowe leffe fede on a weaker grounde. Ifcho. So I do in dede good Socra. and ye alfo did graunte it vnto me a littel afore, whan ye faid, that ye thought that the wea keft fhuld be leaft charged. Socr. But for what reafon good Ifchomac. do ye make diches in the corne fieldes? Ifchoma. Ye wotte well, that in wynter are many fho-wers. Socra. what therof? Ifchomachus. Mary therof chaunce many hurtes: for a great part of the fielde is furrounded with water, and the corne couered in mud, and the rootes of moche of the corne ar worne and wafhed away with the water, and fur-ther oftentimes by reafon of the great a-bundaunce of water, there cometh moche wides and other harlotry, that fuppreffeth and

15 An Elizabethan gentleman studies agronomy. William Lambarde, *Agricultural Common-place Book*, 1571, London, British Library, Add. ms 20709, fo. 16r.

16 The book on agriculture as a means of collecting personal observations. A. Gallo, *Secrets de la vraye agriculture*, Paris 1572, with manuscript notes on the end papers, Avignon, Musée Calvet.

minis libro quarto in sylucstris loti capite, dum ita scribit. Sylucstris lotus plurimùm in Libya gignitur, caule bicubitali, & sape maiore, alis multis, folijs trifolij pratensis. Ex quibus utique Dioscoridis uerbis liquet, eos maximè hallucinari, qui recenter contendunt Trifolium pratense esse lotum sylucstrem, uel urbanum. Plinius lib. XXI. cap. IX. de tribus trifolij generibus differit in hunc modum. Folio coronat & trifolium. Tria eius genera. menyanthes uocant Graci, alij asphaltion, maiore folio, quo utuntur coronarij. Alterum acuto, oxytriphyllon cognominatum. Tertium ex omnibus minutissimum, hactenus Plinius. Trifolij acuti meminit quoque Scribonius Largus, qui ita scriptum reliquit. Trifolium acutum, quod oxytriphyllon appellant, nascitur in Sicilia plurimum. nam in Italia regionibus nusquam eam uidi herbam, nisi in Luna portu, cùm in Britanniam peterem cum Claudio Cæsare. Est autem folijs, & specie communi trifolio similis, nisi quod pleniora sunt folia, & quasi lanuginem quandam super se habent, & in extrema parte uelut eminentem
10 *aculeum. Sed frutex huius duûm pedum, interdum altior conspicitur, & odorem grauem emittit, quorum nihil circa pra-*

TRIFOLIVM PRATENSE.

Aaaa 4 *rense*

17 Competition and disagreement among European botanists: P. A. Mattioli, *Dioscoride*, Venice 1565. Turin, Biblioteca Nazionale.

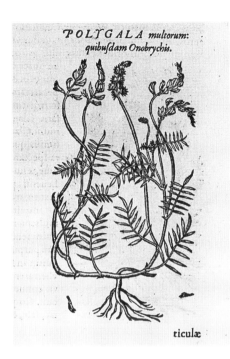

18 Jacobus Dalechampius,
Historia generalis plantarum,
Lugduni 1587–8. Turin,
Biblioteca Nazionale.

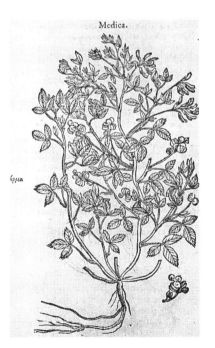

19 'Medica', from Rembertus
Dodonaeus, *Stirpium Historiae*,
Antwerp 1616, Turin, Biblioteca
Nazionale.

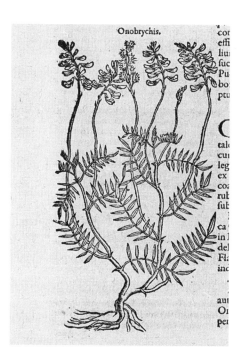

20 'Onobrychis', from Rembertus Dodonaeus, *Stirpium Historiae*, Antwerp 1616, Turin, Biblioteca Nazionale.

21 'Trifolium majus', from Carolus Clusius, *Rarorium Plantarum Historiae*, Lugduni 1587–88, Turin, Biblioteca Nazionale.

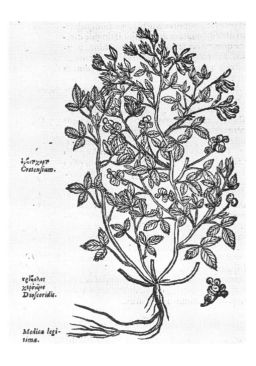

22 From Carolus Clusius, *Rarorium Plantarum Historiae*, Lugduni 1587–88, Turin, Biblioteca Nazionale.

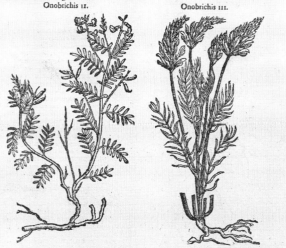

supra Posonium, arido solo, apud Petronellam oppidum (quod nonnulli, ex loci situ, rude-ribúsque antiquis Carnútum veterum esse coniiciút, à Plinio numeratum inter Pannoniæ urbes) ad viarú margines, & frequentissimé toto illo itinere ad Badenses thermas tendente, multísque alijs circa urbem Viennam Austriæ locis, tam citra quàm ultra Danubium.

Flores proferebat Maio, Iunio, & Iulio, interdum etiam Augusto, quo etiam tempore semen maturum legebam.

Onobrichis II.   Onobrichis III.

MVLTOS ex eadem radice promebat Altera vimineos cauliculos, pedales, nonnun- *Onobri-*
quam etiam longiores, humi fusos, crebris nodis distinctos, & in his alata folia, hoc est, tre- *chis i k.*

23 'Onobrychis', from Carolus Clusius, *Rarorium Plantarum Historiae*,
Lugduni 1587–88, Turin, Biblioteca Nazionale.

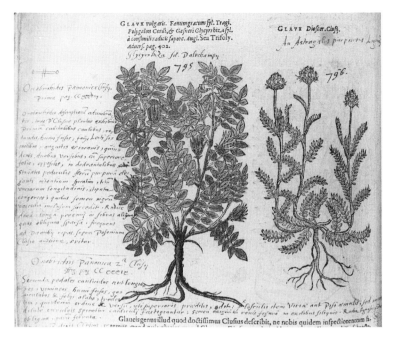

24 Collation of old prints and new texts: the preparation of a new edition. Matthias L'Obel, *Sirpium adversaria nova*, late sixteenth century. Oxford, Magdalen College Library, ms 328, fos. 795, 796.

25 C. Bauhin, *Pinax*, Basileae 1651.Turin, Biblioteca Nazionale.

26–27 Handwritten and personal letters concerning experiments and innovations offered a preferential channel of communication.

26 Letter from E. Ashmole on Sir R. Weston's experiments, c. 1650. Oxford, Bodleian Library, Ashmole ms 358 (IX), fo. 18r.

... now [?] ... [?] [?] ... to [?]
fully all yt [s]had learned will in this, will
plead excuse for my [er]

Another lre From a Friend
concerning Esperate or Clovergrass

The Country where Esperate or Clovergrass is
most in use at this day is Daphine, towards
ye Quarters of day it is a grass very hardy, not
much inferiour to Luzerne; it renders abundance of very exquisite Hay, very great &
substantiall & much desired, proper to nourish &
fatten all sorts of 4 footed beasts young &
old; Calves & lambes, makinge theire Damms
exceedingly to abound wth milke; it also endureth
seed every yeare, yt serveth ye Cattell in stead
of oats, and fattens poultry & make ym to prove
quickly to lay eggs, it will growe well in a

27 Letter from E. Ashmole on Sir R. Weston's experiments, c. 1650. Oxford, Bodleian Library, Ashmole ms 358 (IX), fo. 18r.

in the gardens of the Dominican friars in Ferrara or Chiavenna. We have already dealt with the problems concerning the probable route along which lucerne spread through Italy and how Anguillara insisted on the various species to be found growing wild in Italy. Turner also spoke of the plant growing, never actually saying that it was cultivated. Having attended Ghini's lectures and studied the works of Ruell, he was able to recognize and describe lucerne in the 1540s, while Mattioli, who was only Ghini's friend, never his pupil, had to ask for his help on this point (see Chap. 3, 5). Information communicated orally and by letter played a greater role in the first decades of printed books.[9]

Attacks on the champions of the Reformation in England did not cease until after the death of Henry VIII (1546). Only then did Turner return home and, thanks to his friendship with the Wentworths, he entered the service of Somerset, as a doctor, without, however, receiving the recognition he expected as a supporter of the Protestant cause. His degree in medicine was recognized by the University of Oxford and he rented a house belonging to Lord Somerset, in Kew. On his return he had submitted his *Latin Herball* for publication, but the work depended too heavily on Continental sources and nomenclature to be immediately useful. Hence, while a compendium on botanical nomenclature came out in 1548, he only began to revise the herbal after checking the sites and wild flowers of England.[10] Being too closely linked with the uncertain fortunes of the Lord Protector, he did not obtain a post that took account of his scientific merits. In 1550 he appealed in vain to Robert Cecil, the Home Secretary, for the post of President of Magdalen College, Oxford, which had fallen vacant. There was nothing for it but to set out for Germany again, to complete the research necessary for his herbal. In the same year he returned to England with a group of German Protestants and was elected superintendent of the Church of the Strangers in London. For a short time, things took a happier turn for him. He was elected Dean of Wells Cathedral and the first part of the herbal came out in 1551.[11] Then the premature death of Edward VI and the accession of Mary Tudor brought the collapse of Turner's fortunes. Fearing for his life, he crossed the Channel once more with his wife and three children, and sought refuge in Cologne. He spent the following years in North and South

[9] Similar problems are discussed by Eisenstein, *The Printing Press*, pp. 453 ff.
[10] See Raven, *English Naturalists*, pp. 95–7; see note 8.
[11] See *ibid.*, pp. 95–6, 101–5; W. Turner, *A new Herbal, wherein are conteyned the names of herbes in Greke, Latin, English, Duch, Frenche . . .* , London 1551.

Germany, travelling, gathering herbs and attacking those who had robbed the Church of Christ of her wealth and humiliated her ministers, depriving the people of all chance of improvement. In 1557 he composed a treatise on thermal waters. On the death of Mary, his safety guaranteed since Robert Cecil was a member of the government, he came back to England. He still had to wait until 1561 to be reinstated as Dean of Wells and became rector of Wedmore in 1563. In 1562 the second part of the herbal had come out, dedicated to Thomas Wentworth, son of the patron who had helped him at Cambridge and put him in touch with Somerset and Cecil. The Italian mathematician Nicolò Tartaglia had dedicated his main work to the younger brother of this Thomas, perhaps in the hope of making useful contacts in England (see Chap. 3.9, note 60), since, just at that time, Robert Cecil's government was welcoming Italian science and technology and encouraging direct contact between the two countries.[12] We shall look later at the evidence of the family's interest in agriculture and botany, including a long, anonymous manuscript produced in their great country house.

The lucerne described in Turner's 1562 herbal was probably a specimen of *Medicago lupulina*, L., with its characteristic yellow flower. He may have seen it growing wild between Speyer and Worms. The Italian specimens must have faded from his memory in the meantime. The novelty, with respect to 1548, was that lucerne could then be found in English gardens. Albeit restricted to the circles of those who had a botanical garden, read the Classics and imitated foreign treatises, lucerne had spread rapidly in England. Turner felt obliged to describe it and compare it with the more ordinary clover, and also to compare lucerne seed with fenugreek. In this description of lucerne, Turner followed Pliny, Dioscorides, Palladius and Columella. In little more than a couple of pages, he gave the reader all the information he needed to attempt to grow the plant. It was typical of his time, and the circles with which he was connected, that he was most interested in the growing of lucerne and its use as fodder. Twice he repeated that a Roman *jugerum*, a little less

---

[12] See Raven, *English Naturalists*, pp. 106–8, 114–15; W. Turner, *The second parte of the Herbal* . . . , London 1562, reprinted as *The first and seconde partes of the Herbal William Turner lately overseene corrected and enlarged with the Thirde parte lately gathered and now set oute* . . . , London 1568 (edition dedicated to Queen Elizabeth I). The following quotations in the text are from this edition (hereafter referred to as *Herbal*), which is more a reprint than a new edition. On Cecil's interest in foreign technology see London, BL, Dept. of mss, Lansdowne Papers, Cecil Manuscripts nn. 17.3, 24.9, 26.55, 28.18–19, 28.21–2, 53.63, 63.18–24, 64.33, etc.

than an English acre, would produce enough to keep three horses for a year. He rendered the essence of Palladius and Columella faithfully and with understanding, though he did not suggest any innovation. To encourage readers to adopt it, he mentioned that he had personally grown three types of lucerne, the best variety, the sweet variety and the large, rough variety. He was almost certainly speaking of *Medicago sativa* and Burgundy hay. He advised keeping a bush or two and gathering the seed before the winter, taking care to cut the stems with the pods and allow them to go on ripening in pots, watering them twice a day. He said he had tried out this method himself several times. In these words of his are contained all the problems connected with the more widespread use of lucerne for the next hundred years. In practice, Turner advised separating the production of seed, following the rules of horticulture, from the cultivation of the forage crop, which he had not attempted. Obviously, in times when a continual supply of seed could not be guaranteed, he rightly turned his attention to the production of seed, endeavouring to make up, by inventiveness, for the adverse climate and lack of local experience which might easily lead to failure. While on many occasions Turner displayed a willingness to give details of his sources of information and his correspondents, in the case of lucerne he was silent on both heads. While he obviously had knowledge of Continental specimens, it is also probable that they were only to be found in a few gardens.[13] How poor in species and varieties the English natural environment was can be seen even in the apparently ordinary field of clovers. Turner deals at length with the characters of the one that was known at the time as *trifolium bituminosum*, quite a common variety even in medieval herbaria. He says that he saw it for the first time in Conrad Gesner's garden and then in that of Master Riches, the famous pharmacist and herbalist of London.[14]

1.1. After Turner

Turner was not alone in reading the writings of the Continental botanists with an eye to the needs of English agriculture, to increase the range of its botanical species. In the same years, Thomas Francis, a medical

---

[13] See Turner, *Herbal*, pp. 51*v*–53*r*.
[14] *Ibid.*, pp. 157*v*–158*r*. On Turner's correspondents see Raven, *English Naturalists*, p. 116.

doctor, made ample marginal notes in his copy of Ruell's herbal.[15] In the same copy of Ruell an earlier owner had already made notes in red ink, now faded; then a certain John Pullan wrote a long series of plant names in the margin of the first book. Lastly, Thomas Francis made a group of notes, a commentary collating the work with other sources, Theophrastus, Columella, Platearius, Gesner, Boch (Tragus) and Mattioli among them. These are all books which came out around the middle of the century. Francis was a famous doctor in those years. A graduate of Christchurch, Oxford, he practised in Silver Street, London, where he died in 1574. Like Turner, he paid great attention to the German literature on botany and drew continual comparisons between Ruell's Latin and French nomenclature and the German. He underlined a long chapter on lucerne, adding 'Burgundische Heu, medica Kraut' in the margin. Further on, he read the chapters on *lotus sylvestris* (which he grouped with a series of melilots or German trefoils) and then *cytisus* (a still-mysterious species to be identified with the *trifolium maius Romanorum* or with a *gross weyss klee* (white clover) or the two varieties of *cytisus* described by Columella).[16]

It is fairly certain that this interest in lucerne dates back to the mid-sixteenth century. Before that time only general interest was shown in Mediterranean culture.[17] The relation between printed English texts and the annotations in Latin or English in foreign books, which precede, take up again, or go more deeply into the themes of the vernacular literature, can be reconstructed with a little patience. Even individuals who were not connected with one another shared an interest in certain books, which goes to show that what may at first appear to be individual and exotic interests, in the end are supported by the individual work of others. As we have already seen, Peter Lauerbeck purchased a second-hand copy of the Lyons edition of the *Rerum Rusticarum Scriptores* in the mid-sixteenth century and carefully underlined and annotated practically every page. Here we can give only a few indications of his interests. Oil, figs, wine, the vineyard and grape harvest, but also the meadow and

---

15 See London, BL, Dept. of Printed Books, 440 m.1, J. Ruell, *De natura stirpium*, Basle 1537. The volume belonged to: A, illegible signature; B, John Pullan; C, Thomas Francis; D, Tobias Martin, in this order.

16 *Ibid.*, pp. 394, 629–30. On Thomas Francis, see *DNB*, *sub nomine*.

17 See for example London, BL, Dept. of Printed Books, IB 34043, *Opera agricolationum Columellae Varronis Catonisque nec non Palladij . . . ,* Reggio 1498, with many fine annotations by two hands, one probably English, which however include no comment upon meadows and lucerne.

oxen, are the subjects that he read with greatest interest in Cato (actually, he cannot be said to have selected, for he was studying all the text). The novelty of lucerne and *cytisus* did not escape his notice in Varro; he went more deeply into the subject when he read Palladius. He underlined the part about lucerne enriching the soil and strengthening lean cattle and about mowing six crops a year. He left out the cultivation of sesame (book X, chap. VIII), but underlined the chapter on the role of vetch and fenugreek and the following one on laying down new meadows (book X, chap. X). In his copy of Columella he read the whole chapter on meadows very carefully, writing clearly in the margin 'medica herba, medicae satio', and adding 'vicia, farraginem, avena, foenum graecum, ervuum'.[18] Thomas Francis and Peter Lauerbeck were definitely two of the most careful readers.[19] And the current interest in new plants, foreign varieties and seed was no mere bookish curiosity. In the mid-sixteenth century, among other goods, caraway seeds, cucumber, fenugreek, hemp, onion and other unspecified garden seed passed through the port of London. For example, the boat *Cock*, from Bruges, arrived on 29 April 1568 with a barrel of all sorts of seed, valued at £4 13s 4d; and the ship *Samson*, arriving from the same port, had unloaded fifty pounds of garden and vegetable seed for the sum of £72 13s 4d. And these are only a few examples. Together with seed, exotic goods such as oranges and lemons, almonds, nutmeg and aniseed, were imported. Slowly but steadily they transformed the diet and agriculture of the Elizabethan era.[20] In this case, too, fenugreek appeared several decades before lucerne.

[18] See London, BL, Dept. of Printed Books, 450 d 1 (1–4), Marci Catonis, M. Terenti Varronis, T. R. A. Palladi, J. M. Columellae, *De re rustica Libri. Per Petrum Victorium . . . suae integritati restituti*, Lyons 1549, especially pp. 14, 15, 17, 18, 20, 21 (Cato), 106, 138–9 (Palladius), 61–3, 254 (Columella). This volume was later bought by Joseph Banks.

[19] See Cambridge, UL, L.12.57, Columella, *De re rustica, de arboribus*, Lyons 1541, had three owners (n.d., 1655, 1727), perhaps it was the first of them who marked the passage on cytisus and lucerne; *ibid.*, H.h.h.175, idem, *De re rustica*, Paris 1543, signed by 'Bartholomew Dodington, praecium s. viii', with a few underlinings in the first two books; *ibid.*, R*10.44, idem, *Les XII livres des choses rustiques*, Paris 1555, signed 'H. L. pret [?] 1561', with many underlinings throughout the text.

[20] See B. Dietz, *The Port and Trade of Early Elizabethan London. Documents*, London Record Society, London 1972, pp. 63, 78, 138 ff.

2. ENGLISH TRANSLATIONS

By now it is clear that in England, more than elsewhere, bodies of botanical and agronomic knowledge differed from one social group to another. The reading of the botanists proper was aspired to not only by doctors and pharmacists, but by the wider public, of landowners who needed some pharmaceutical knowledge to keep their families healthy, of farmers and agronomists who wrote and published in English on practical problems of agriculture, and of translators who took the great works of the Continent as their model. Nor is that phenomenon which continues to be called the 'Agricultural Revolution' something that concerns only English society. It belongs, root and branch, to the European scientific and economic culture of the mid-sixteenth century.

In the previous chapter we spoke of the great number of texts on agronomy published on the Continent, and offered on the English book market between 1550 and 1640. But while books published in Italian or Latin were read in the original editions, various English translations and expanded versions of French and German texts were available to a different kind of reader, though the translations never drove the original editions from the market. The fact is that these publications were produced rather hastily and cheaply. Only those who owned the work in the original and also had access to a Continental herbal could fully understand certain crucial chapters such as that on forage-crops and particularly on lucerne. Even Turner's herbal, which was certainly one of the most advanced works on the subject, had come up against the greater efficiency of Continental printers, who saw the English public as an easy market to capture.

2.1. Barnaby Googe

In 1577 Barnaby Googe, poet and protégé of Lord Grey, translated the *Libri quatuor rei rusticae*, which the German Humanist Conrad Heresbach had compiled and published a few years earlier. The translation met with success and many reprints were issued. Then, in 1631, Gervase Markham produced a new edition with some very slight variations in the text, presenting it as his own work.[21] Fortunately, the

---

[21] See the edition and translation of the text (C. Heresbach, *Libri quattuor rei rusticae*, Cologne 1573) edited by Wilhelm Abel, and Beutler and Irsigler, 'Konrad Heresbach'; Heresbach also wrote a book on hunting, *Thereutices*: J. Blusch (ed.), *Conradi*

entire section on lucerne was left intact for about fifty years. Googe had seen the novelty of this crop in the original text and had been careful to add the Spanish name *alfalfa*, probably drawn from Turner's herbal. He was aware that in doing this he was mediating between North and South. In his epistle to the reader, he mentioned the recent English texts of Fitzherbert and Tusser, comparing them generously to Latin authors, but he insisted that the reader could benefit from the rules of the farmers of ancient times, the truth being that the most expert modern farmers had borrowed 'knowledge and skill' from them. This is a courageous admission, forgotten by many scholars, which brings us back to the question of Tull's agriculture in relation to the learning of Classical agronomy (see Chap. 7). On the other hand Googe was aware that he had introduced the reader to many new seeds, plants and trees unknown to his contemporaries, which could be acclimatized with care and attention. He pointed out that the cypress, almond, walnut, cherry, fig, apricot and so on were by then acclimatized in England. The successful cultivation of the vine continued to be meaningful as a symbol of the capacity to get the better of the hostile British climate. Googe spoke with satisfaction of the designs on the ancient windows at Chilwell House, near Nottingham, as evidence that the vine could adapt to even more northerly climates and of how, in his time, Lord Williams and Lord Cobham (who had two private botanical gardens, at Calais and Winchelsea, duly visited and mentioned by Turner) had planted vineyards for commercial production.[22]

The translation of a recent work was thus set against the more complex scene of Elizabethan translations as a whole. It formed part of the rapid process by which all English Renaissance culture was brought up to date by borrowings from abroad. In this way, a definitely wider public, less attached to the court models, became acquainted with the results of the agronomic experience of the Continent. Once again the marginal notes tell us something of how foreign technology was interpreted and used. At the end of the sixteenth century, an anonymous author, probably

---

Heresbachi Thereutices hoc est de venatione aucupio atque piscatione Compendium ... (Veröff. zur Humanismusf., 2), Boppard am Rhein 1977. On the English translation see Fussell, *Old English Farming Books*, and *DNB, sub nomine.* F. N. L. Poynter, *Gervase Markham. A Bibliography*, on the editions published by him. A total of seven editions were printed in English (1577, 1578, 1586, 1601, 1614, 1631, 1658).

[22] The following quotations from Heresbach–Googe are taken from the London 1586 (pp. 37*r*–38*v*, 43*v*–46*r* for lucerne, cytisus, melilot and pastures in general) and London 1614 editions.

connected with Peterborough Cathedral, left long annotations ('Directions to Husbandmen') in which he advised keeping to the number of ploughings traditional in the region, choosing seed with care and soaking it in rape-seed oil, which would mean a saving of at least a quarter of the amount usually needed for sowing.[23] The benefits which would derive from this procedure were a saving in the expense of folding with sheep, liming and manuring, the aforementioned saving of a quarter of the seed, the protection of the seed against mice and parasites, an increase in the amount of arable land in proportion to pastures and meadows, a reduction in the number of poor farmers forced to fatten cattle to increase their income while reducing arable land, and an increase of tithes on grain. It should not be forgotten that Peterborough Cathedral had a direct interest in improving its cereal crop for tithe purposes. This was clearly an attempt to escape from the vicious circle in which the production of cereals depended on costly manuring and liming, at the same time forcing the farmer to keep a large part of his farm under grass. The really positive aspect of lucerne-growing, even when it was not included in the grain-growing rotation, was its high productivity, by dint of which the proportion of grassland to arable land could be kept low, without reducing the number of working animals. The real difficulty in achieving this lay in starting the cultivation of a crop which had only just been tried out in botanical gardens. Some readers took the advice of Heresbach–Googe and chose the humbler spurry, following the practice of German farmers, in preference to lucerne.[24]

2.2. Gervase Markham

The *Maison rustique* published by the Estiennes, a book quite frequently used, translated into English only in 1600 by the London doctor Richard Surfleet, had a more complicated history.[25] As we have seen, the *Maison*

---

[23] See Cambridge, UL, Peterborough D.6.18, Heresbach-Googe, *Foure Books of Husbandrie*, London 1596, manuscript pages found between fos. 32*v* and 33*r*.

[24] See *ibid.*, Rel.d.61.1, idem, *The Whole art and trade of Husbandry*, London 1614, p. 26*v*, coat of arms of the Rich family. Spurry was occasionally tried out with success in the following decades, see J. Thirsk, 'Agricultural Innovations and their Diffusion', in *AHEW*, 5/2, p. 556.

[25] See *Maison Rustique or The Country Farme compiled in the French tongue by Charles Stevens and John Liebault Doctors of Physicke and translated into English by Richard Surfleet Practitioner in Physick*, London 1600; *Maison Rustique or The Country Farme compiled in the French tongue by Charles Stevens and John Liebault Doctors of Physicke and translated into English by Richard Surfleet Practitioner in Physick.*

rustique was to be found on the English book market in the first Latin pamphlets, later collected under the title *Praedium rusticum* (1543). Actually, readers of one of these volumes and of the latest English version *Countrey Farm* (1616) were reading very different texts. In the French version, many of the quotations taken from Classical literature on agronomy had disappeared, to leave room for a quantity of information drawn from French farming practice (see Chap. 4). The terminology concerning lucerne was based on the experience of Northern France and the nomenclature, *foin de Bourgogne, sainfoin, foignasse* all described plants of the same species (*Medicago vulgaris, M. sativa*). The English reader thus came face to face with the Paris area and the nomenclature collected by Charles Estienne and his son-in-law Jean Liebault. His botanical knowledge, however, would not have been sufficient for him to understand the Latin or French text fully. Besides the *Maison rustique*, the average reader would have needed a good herbal, preferably with illustrations of the new plants, though it is true that Surfleet's translation did try to take into account the novelties introduced into English botany during the last decades of the century and to give a full botanical explanation to the average farmer.[26] But instead of making the text clearer, the translation tended to oversimplify; *meadow clover* and *snail clover* were not synonyms but demonstrated the more complex French nomenclature. Surfleet, the English translator, was probably following the herbal of Gerard, one of the commonest English texts on the subject, rather than Turner's more accurate description. For lack of a native nomenclature, he explained by literal translation ('three-leaved grasse', or 'Soup in wine' referring to the purple colour of the flowers); he made no attempt to give his readers precise indications of how to identify these new, highly praised forage-crops, nor even to suggest a source for the supply of seeds. Yet a few people did have small stocks of seed available in those years. In London, the hub from which so many novelties spread, the doctor and pharmacist John Gerard described eleven varieties of clover – including lucerne in the *foin de Bourgogne = sainfoin* variety

---

Newly Revised, Corrected and Augmented, with divers large Additions out of the works of Serres his agriculture, Vinet his Maison Champestre in French, Albyterio in Spanish, Grilli [sic] in Italian; and other authors and the Husbandrie of France, Italie and Spaine reconciled and made agree with ours here in England by Gervase Markham, Adam Islip for John Bill, London 1616. The Italian author Grilli is an obvious misreading of Gallo in the gothic script.

[26] The evidence from chapter 5 shows that landowners generally found that one book on agriculture was adequate to cover their interest in the subject.

and snail clover – and he himself cultivated no fewer than five varieties of lucerne.[27]

In 1616 Gervase Markham, in one of his many publishing ventures, brought out an enlarged version of the *Countrey Farm* (with his notes in the margin or at the end of every chapter). It contains a long discourse on housing cattle and folding sheep; on sweepings from barns used as seed for new meadows; on the advantages of folding; on water-meadows in England and France; on salt marshes; on oats as fodder; on the saxifrage, 'a great friend to meadows'; on how repeated mowing is good for meadows and pastures; and on the best time for mowing.[28] But despite these honest efforts, yielding evidence of a new interest in meadows, he still left, untouched, all the information that would confuse the careful reader who wished to discover the real lucerne among the wild plants of his home district. This publishing venture of 1616, and the similar one of 1631, showed that however aggrieved Markham felt about foreign texts, saying as much in other publications, he still managed to make money on the reprints of the *Countrey farm* and the *Four books of husbandry*. This linking up of Continental and English agronomy was preferable from the commercial point of view to the translation of the large volume of Olivier de Serres, which had just come out in 1601.[29] In the decades between 1570 and the Civil War, the agricultural technology available in England cannot be considered as an integrated body of knowledge. What knowledge there was, was very fragmentary and even practical information was disconnected. The texts produced on the Continent reflected their regional origins only too clearly, and in many cases local conditions were too unlike those found in Elizabethan England. Hence much more than mere translation was needed to make the rules of Classical or

---

[27] See J. Gerard, *The Herball or General History of Plants*, London 1596–7, II, pp. 1017–33; B. D. Jackson, *A Catalogue of plants cultivated in the garden of John Gerard in the years 1596–1599*, London 1876, pp. 34, 41: *Medicago sativa, scutellata,* Lam., *spinosa, arabica, Camerarij, marina*. On John Gerard see B. Henrey, *British Botanical and Horticultural Literature before 1800*, London 1975, I, pp. 36–54.

[28] See *Maison Rustique or The Country Farme . . . Newly Revised*, pp. 491–516.

[29] The short treatise on silk and silkworms published in Paris, 1599 by Olivier de Serres did not escape the notice of English printers. It was translated into English by Nicholas Gesse, *The Perferct Use of Silk-wormes*, London 1607. Local rearing of silkworms would have made London silk manufacturers independent of the Lyons market and foreign production. On this and other points of political economy in the reign of Elizabeth and James I see J. Thirsk, *Economic Policy*. On other English attempts to import Italian techniques of silk production see now G. Chicco, *La seta in Piemonte 1650–1800. Un sistema industriale d'ancien régime*, Turin 1995.

Continental agronomy applicable in England. The necessary effort would be accomplished in the years 1620 to 1640 and thereafter.

3. DODOENS AND LYTE, LUCERNE VERSUS *ONOBRYCHIS*

In these decades of transformation many conflicts emerged even at the level of language. Clover, a fodder-crop native to England, was rediscovered and soon rivalled foreign grasses (by then variously known as *Burgundy hay, sainfoin, snail clover, meadow clover or medick fodder*). What until then had seemed mainly a cultural movement, founded on the curiosity and interest of a select few, gradually proved able to bring about change. Meanwhile the spread of foreign technology was restricted by the serious risk of making mistakes. At this point local substitutes had to be found. For as long as mistakes could only be avoided by consulting foreign books, Continental agricultural practices were bound to be limited to Englishmen who could afford to buy books and knew foreign languages. Such was the case of a pharmacist from Reading who annotated his Dutch herbal. Those who depended on local intermediaries often purchased inadvisedly, and their mistakes discouraged the further spread of the crops involved. The battle over the respective merits of *sainfoin* and *lucerne*, which lasted so long in France, formed part of this learning process.

With a printing industry of modest proportions compared with Europe, but with a growing demand for up-to-date texts on botany and agronomy, the book market of Elizabethan England seemed to invite competition from the most enterprising French and Flemish printers and their outstanding authors Pierre Pena, Matthias de L'Obel and Rembert Dodoens. After attending Rondelet's lectures in Montpellier, Pena and L'Obel travelled through the British Isles from 1569 on, preparing the edition of *Stirpium adversaria nova*, dedicated to Elizabeth I, which introduced readers to a number of plant specimens unknown to Turner. Plantin himself purchased eight hundred copies, using them to prepare a new edition which came out in 1579. Matthias de L'Obel had been physician to William the Silent before the latter was murdered in 1584. He settled permanently in England in the service of Baron Edward Zouche, becoming superintendent of the gardens of Hackney, then, in 1607, herbalist to James I. On his death, his papers, in particular those which he used to write a new edition of the *Stirpium adversaria*, were left to the young botanist John Goodyer, fellow of Magdalen College,

Oxford. The translation of the *Cruydeboeck* (1554), the herbal of Rembert Dodoens, doctor and pharmacist of Malines, was also made in this Anglo–Flemish–French circle. For it was Henry Lyte, one-time student of Oxford and amateur botanist, quite a cultured Somerset landowner, who had travelled at length on the Continent, who translated the French version of the herbal by Dodoens, which Charles de L'Ecluse had published a few years previously.

Henry Lyte took great pains in preparing the herbal, to which Dodoens himself added some new specimens. All this care should have provided an opportunity to notice the two possible meanings of *sainfoin*, *Onobrychis s.*, Lam., or *Medicago s.*; but, out of haste or ignorance, the name *sainfoin* was used, although it was meant to indicate only our *onobrychis sativa*, Lam. What happened was this. To distinguish his work from that of his colleagues, Dodoens had started to use the name *Onobrychis* for the plant that his contemporaries called *polygala* (on the strength of a poor description of both in Dioscorides' herbal) and for which they were unable to find a name in the French northern dialect. The Flemish name *hanetammeten* did exist, translated as cockscomb in English, which led to the term *onobrychis caput galli* in the Linnean system.[30] Meanwhile, thanks to the known Don Brancion, Dodoens had seen lucerne growing in Malines and Charles de L'Ecluse had sent him some seed from Spain. At this point he identified it with the German *steinklee* or Flemish *steenclavern*. In this he was mistaken, or at least was grossly oversimplifying, since Brunfels had already given the name *steinklee* to melilot or fenugreek. What is more, in a Latin edition of his herbal, Dodoens stated that while *onobrychis* was sown in the gardens of the herbalists, lucerne, that is *Italienische Claveren*, was unknown even to pharmacists, and those who sowed clover on pastureland often gave it the Latin name of lucerne (*medica*) twisted into *perpera*.[31] Like all mistakes, this one reveals more of the truth than it conceals. Quite probably, in Flanders as in Lombardy, where clover-growing was not always intentional and preceded the introduction of lucerne by a couple of generations, natural selection favoured the growth of lucerne on some land at the expense of clover itself and so farmers mixed up the two

---

[30] See R. Dodoens, *Frumentorum, leguminum . . . historia*, Antwerp 1569, pp. 166–7; L'Ecluse, *Rariorum plantarum historia*, p. ccxxxii supported the new nomenclature for legume crops.

[31] See R. Dodoens, *De stirpium historia*, Antwerp 1563–4, II, pp. 32, 45; idem, *Stirpium historiae pemptades sex sive libri XXX, varie ab auctore . . . aucti et emendati*, Antwerp 1616, p. 565.

plants. This shows, once again, how difficult it was to identify species which did not always grow spontaneously, each of them being considered a weed in fields planted with the other. The Bauhin brothers had already attacked Dodoens, a doctor and pharmacist rather than a botanist, for being inaccurate on the subject of lucernes (see Chap. 4). Dodoens and L'Ecluse worked in England, where they had no one to oppose them, and so they left their mark, errors included, more deeply impressed there than elsewhere.

Lyte started to translate Dodoens' herbal from the French version made by L'Ecluse in 1557. The copy he used has come down to us. He corrected and made marginal notes, as did so many less illustrious or anonymous readers.[32] It is difficult to establish whether all the notes were written by Henry Lyte, though his old biographer says they were, or whether the various languages used, French, English and Latin, hide different hands. Lyte travelled widely on the Continent, and there was nothing more usual for an Englishman of his day than to be well acquainted with various European languages. The crucial point lies in a number of manuscript additions in chapter XXVII, which were retained in the definitive, printed edition. Where Dodoens–L'Ecluse spoke of

---

[32] See idem, *Newe Herball or Historie of Plants . . . and now translated out of French into English by Henry Lyte*, London 1578: on p. 345 someone (i.e. Lyte, see below) refers to the book with the corrections he made as 'my French copy the which is in divers places newly corrected by the Author himself'; the copy with these handwritten corrections is in London, BL, 442 h 9, R. Dodoens, *Histoire des plantes . . .*, Antwerp 1557. The identification of the marginal notes of what Lyte called 'my French copy' is of vital interest. According to Raven, *English Naturalists*, p. 200, who quotes Lyte, they were made by Rembert Dodoens, 'the Author himself'; Henrey, *British Botanical and Horticultural Literature*, p. 36, makes no hypothesis, while F. W. T. Hunger, *Charles de l'Escluse (Carolus Clusius) Nederlandsch Kruidkundige, 1526–1609*, s'Gravenhage 1927, 1943, vol. I, p. 117, believes that they were in the hand of Charles de L'Ecluse, even though they do not look at all like the samples of his writing reproduced in the volume. P. Chorley, 'Early Evidence of Sainfoin Cultivation around Paris', *AHR*, 29, 1981, 1, p. 122, agrees with this hypothesis. But an old article by a descendant, H. C. Maxwell Lyte, 'The Lytes of Lytescary', *Proceedings of the Somersetshire Archeological and Natural History Society*, 37, 1892, p. 44, maintains that the French notes to Charles de L'Ecluse's text were Lyte's first work on botany. Furthermore, in the top margin of the frontispiece, London, BL, 442 h 9, next to an old shelf-mark, somebody had written in ink: ' . . . Manuscript notes by Henry Lyte'. Below, almost as a conclusion to his own labour, Lyte himself wrote: 'Henry Lyte ~~made~~ [a line was drawn through the word] taught me to speake Englishe' (meaning that Henry Lyte had taught me, French book, to speak English). It is as if the book were speaking directly to the reader, as happens in so many frontispieces. Hence Lyte probably made some corrections in French, so that Dodoens and L'Ecluse could revise those points. On Lyte's other manuscripts see J. Britten and G. S. Boulger, *Biographical Index of Deceased British and Irish Botanists*, London 1931, p. 197.

vetch, they added a species of *onobrychis*, which was in accordance with some writers' nomenclature. And the illustration they gave is a good rendering of *Onobrychis s.*, Lam., drawn from life. Both on and below the illustration Lyte wrote 'onobrychis sorte, Medica Ruellij, Saint foin; Medick fitche or yellow fitching, saint foin; de Ruellius pone [*sic*]: Medica: on la nomme en François Saint foin. On la sème aux Prez à l'entour de Paris. Et y croit aucune fois de soi mesme'[33] (Medica is called Saintfoin in French. It is sown in the meadows round Paris. Sometimes it grows wild).

Now, it would have been difficult to mistake lucerne, with its purplish flowers, or *sainfoin*, with its red flowers, for the 'yellow fitching' clearly specified by William Turner when describing *medicago lupulina*. Moreover, the *Maison rustique* may have been another source of information. However, the agreement between the *sainfoin–onobrychis*, illustrated by Dodoens and L'Ecluse, and the *medica* described by Ruell, is still interesting. If we follow this version, we must admit that, without realising it, Ruell, and above all Estienne and Liebault who followed him, were speaking of *onobrychis* and not *medicago*, despite the fact that all the other indications (description and agronomy of the plant) would suggest otherwise.[34] If it was a mistake this could be explained by the fact that, by the mid-sixteenth century, the two forage-crops were already competing, in the field and linguistically as well, and thus the less well-informed were confused. Lyte was to be the first of a long series of English writers to be taken in by the equivalence in meaning of *medicago* and *onobrychis* in French dialects. But this point was not made clear in the French texts of Dodoens, L'Ecluse or L'Obel, and so it remained, far from fortuitously, unclear in English.

In the margin of chapter XXVII of Lyte's *Newe Herball*, William

---

[33] See London, BL, 442 h 9, Dodoens–L'Ecluse, *Histoire des plantes*, pp. 331–2.

[34] This is also the opinion of Chorley, *Early Evidence*, pp. 122–4: Lyte's translation would explain Ruell's text and why we should read *onobrychis* where *sainfoin* was mentioned around Paris in the mid-sixteenth century. But none of the subsequent French editions of the *Histoire des plantes*, which faithfully reproduced the version prepared by Dodoens in 1563, takes up what would have been an important amendment to the 1557 text. Daléchamps, *Historia generalis*, p. 502, had already shown how the corruption of Dioscorides' text made it more difficult to identify the plant (the term 'sperm' apparently referred to the seed and not the whole pod, as was usual in the sixteenth- and seventeenth-century botanical tradition). Moreover, Ruell's description of lucerne is very near to the drawing reproduced in the *Historia plantarum* by Daléchamps; or what is now called *M. folliculo spinoso*. L'Ecluse also speaks of it in his *Histoire des plantes*, p. 342. For an appreciation of Ruell's work see Greene, *Landmarks of Botanical History*, chap. iv, note 11.

Browne, fellow of Magdalen College, Oxford, and one of the curators of the botanical garden set up by the university, reiterated Lyte's conclusion: 'Medica Ruellij'.[35] As we have already seen (see Chap. 4, 4), at the end of the seventeenth century another Englishman, William Sherard, who studied under Tournefort in Paris and then became professor of botany at Oxford, cleared up once and for all the overlapping of the term *sainfoin* with lucerne and sainfoin. But for at least a century, the use of the same name for two different species was to create not a few difficulties in the introduction of an important forage-crop into England.

The contributions of Dodoens, L'Ecluse and Lyte regarding lucerne are less interesting. Lucerne or Burgundy hay, they wrote, grew in Italy and Spain (they said nothing of France or Provence); in Flanders they only grew in herb-gatherers' gardens.[36] The most complete part of the work of the three botanists, Dodoens, L'Ecluse and L'Obel, produced with the support of Plantin's printing house and by collating the work of all three, are the unpublished volumes collected by L'Obel and left to the young Oxford botanist John Goodyer.[37] Among the various kinds of lucerne, L'Obel had spoken of the variety called *lauserdo* in Provence, saying that it indicated the lucerne of the ancients better than any other. He definitely confirmed that where the French used the term *foin de Bourgogne* they meant lucerne. But the volume published posthumously in Lyons under the name of Daléchamps illustrated three different elements in the same plant, which in point of fact was the variety known to a very few people, under the name of *perpera*. Lastly, lucerne was

---

[35] See Oxford, BO, 50 d 25, R. Dodoens, *Newe Herball or Historie of Plants . . . and now translated out of French into English by Henry Lyte, Esq., corrected and augmented,* London 1619. For the identification, see the printed note by G. C. Druce on the flyleaf: the author visited Padua and other Italian cities during the years (c. 1620) when the Botanic Gardens were being set up in Oxford. In Druce's opinion it was probably William Browne, one of the compilers of the 1658 Catalogue. R. T. Gunther, *Early British Botanists, Based on Unpublished Writings of Goodyer, Tradescant and Others,* Oxford 1922, pp. 80–8, does not share this opinion, merely pointing out that the anonymous writer was attached to Magdalen College.

[36] See Dodoens–L'Ecluse, *Histoire des plantes,* pp. 342–3; Dodoens, *Newe Herball or Historie of Plants . . . translated . . . by Henry Lyte,* pp. 358–60.

[37] See Oxford, Magdalen College Archives, mss 326–28, L'Obel, *Stirpium illustrationes.* On the death of L'Obel, these three volumes containing much information both printed and in manuscript were left to John Goodyer, Fellow of Magdalen College, himself a botanist (see below). The first volume contains the classification of 223 herbs as against the 45 described in the *Historia plantarum* by L'Obel. Volumes II and III describe a total of 835 plants, with corrections and additions from his *Observationes* (1576) and illustrations taken from the *Icones stirpium* printed by Plantin (1581). On L'Obel's manuscripts in general see Gunther, *Early English Botanists,* p. 253.

sown in Flanders, but only in botanical gardens; it had not yet been planted in the field. The analysis of *onobrychis* given in this last work is longer and more accurate. It was doubtful whether *caput gallinaceum Belgarum* was Dioscorides' *onobrychis*, but L'Obel gave it as certain that it corresponded to Daléchamps' *polygala*; it was a very healthy forage-crop and greatly increased the yield of milk. It was said to have been sown in the fields of Picardy, as spurry was used in Brabant. In the plate accompanying the text, beside the usual illustration, L'Obel added in ink 'Saint foin Gallis, Anglobritannis Medick fitcheling'. There followed the description of three varieties of *onobrychis pannonica*, taken from L'Ecluse, who had noticed them on a journey through central Europe, the first along the Danube towards Pressburg, the second between Schwechat and Götzendorf, near Vienna, the third seen once near Hamburg and again north of Pressburg.[38] Probably L'Obel too, as a man of the north, was more familiar with the fields and meadows of regions where lucerne was difficult to grow and the legume preferred in its place was the humbler *sainfoin–onobrychis*, which grew well in the sandy and calcareous soils of Picardy and southern Germany. But even L'Obel's writings provide evidence of the ambivalence of the term *sainfoin*, which in Northern and Continental Europe and in the British Isles more commonly stood for *onobrychis*. The difficulties were to come later, when information and seed from the Mediterranean regions began to be used.

4. LUCERNE VERSUS CLOVER, THE LOCAL ALTERNATIVES TO FORAGE-CROPS, MARL AND MANURE

So long as the new agriculture had yet to take shape satisfactorily, landowners who, in the years from 1540–1640, were building splendid new homes as the hub of the estates they had acquired after the dissolution of the monasteries, or by enclosing common land, or by purchasing the estates of old, noble families seriously impoverished in the early sixteenth century, applied the traditional farming practices more or less wisely.[39] A brief list of the procedures for the improvement of land, printed in those decades, will show what efforts some owners

---

[38] See Oxford, Magdalen College Archives, ms 328, fos. 215 ff.
[39] See M. W. Barley, 'Rural Housing in England', in *AHEW*, 4, pp. 698–724; W. Hoskins, 'The Rebuilding of Rural England', *Past and Present*, 4, 1953, pp. 45–57.

made to replace time-worn practices by improvements, or at least to introduce new methods side by side with old ones. Clover, the natural forage-crop in the British Isles, did not appear as a way of revitalizing old meadows and pastureland until the end of the sixteenth century. Even the most widely read agricultural calendar of Elizabethan England, the one published by Thomas Tusser, first in 1557 and in a larger edition in 1573, made absolutely no reference to clover.[40] The author prepared various lists of herbs and seeds grown in pots, in kitchen gardens, such as medicinal herbs or decorative plants. He also included plants important in the new agriculture, such as roots and turnips (*Februaries Husbandrie*), but these were recommended only as human food. This was a strange omission, when we have recently had documentary proof of early, if not general use of turnips in the counties of Suffolk and Norfolk in the sixteenth century. Roots were grown in the fields and given as winter fodder to the sheep kept on the fold courses to enrich the initially poor and sandy soils of the eastern counties. But this was the only practice mentioned by Tusser, a Suffolk farmer who knew the eastern counties well. The commonest remedy that Tusser recommended to restore vigour to exhausted land was rest.

> Otes, rie or else barlie, and wheat that is gray,
> brings land out of comfort, and soone to decay:
> . . . Still crop upon crop many fermers do take,
> and reape little profit for greedines sake.

While three crops running could be produced on good lands held in severalty, this could not be done in the open fields, the champion lands. Tusser advised growing a crop of peas between two crops of cereals, barley and wheat. It was better still to enrich the soil with two crops, one of them peas; whereas the rule on open fields, in Middlesex for example,

---

[40] Thomas Tusser (1524?–80) went to Eton, then to Trinity Hall, Cambridge; became a tenant-farmer at Rivenhall, Essex; was musician to Lord Paget for ten years and an unlucky farmer at Cattiwade, Suffolk. Being no more successful in his wife's village, West Dereham, Norfolk, he returned to Fairstead a sick man, before moving to London, where he died in the plague of 1580. The poor rhyming of his *Hundredth Good Points of Husbandrie*, London 1557, enlarged in the *Five Hundreth Points of Good Husbandrie united to as many of Good Housewifery*, London 1573, turned out to be his most successful production. On the whole they show that he followed the agricultural practice of Eastern England with care, though with very little profit. On Tusser see Fussell, *Old English Farming Books*; T. Tusser, *Five Hundred Points of Good Husbandry* (with an Introduction by G. Grigson), Oxford 1984, reproduces the 1580 text, published by the author, and the notes by Hillman 1710, Mavor 1812, and the English Dialect Society 1878. The quotations below are taken from this recent edition.

was 'drink before bread corn . . . ', that is, spring barley (for beer) before wheat (winter cereal), while some land needed to lie fallow after every crop. Where there was stagnant water, he advised sowing oats, grey peas, ronceval peas and vetch during the winter.[41] He especially recommended vetch, saying that cultivating it would lighten the dependence of the oxen or draught horses on fodder from the pasture. He also expressly recommended threshing the seed, as was done by the best farmers in Norfolk (*December's and Februaries Husbandrie*). According to Hillman, the first commentator on Tusser, vetch in Tusser's time was the only plant that helped the farmer to lay a field to pasture. The great variety of trefoils, clover and nonesuch-grass, as well as ray-grass and sainfoin, were to follow only in the early eighteenth century.[42]

Current opinion had it that the success of crops in mid-sixteenth-century English agriculture depended on the amount of manure spread on the land. Tusser also devoted many pages to the subject:

> Who laieth on doong er he laieth on plow,
> such husbandrie useth as thrift doth alow.
> One month er ye spred it, so still let it stand,
> er ever to plow it, ye take it in hand.

But the great quantity of manure, especially horse-dung, collected throughout the year in a corner of the farmyard, encouraged the growth of weeds (wild camomile, thistles, vetch [*sic*], bracken and burdock); and this negative correlation between manure and weeds was not clear to the English agronomists of the time. Indeed, recent research has connected the increase in agricultural productivity in the fifteenth and sixteenth centuries with the greater labour expended on cleaning and weeding the fields, which Tusser also advised.[43] The practice most often recommended by Tusser, for destroying the greatest number of weeds, was summer fallow, with tillage. The plough and manure were the pivots of cultivation, but ploughing in furrows, manuring at the bottom of the furrow and casting seed on the ridge (for barley, oats and rye), or in

---

[41] See *ibid.*, *October's husbandrie, Digression concerning tillage*; see also pp. 231–3. The 'roncivalle' variety (perhaps from Roncisvalle: see *OED, sub nomine*) was the most widely used pea in field cultivation.

[42] See Tusser, *Five Hundred Points*, p. 242.

[43] See Campbell, 'Arable Productivity'; idem, 'Agricultural Progress'; Tusser, *Five Hundred Points*, pp. 93, 106, 115, 265 6, 272, 284, 299, 301. Vetches were seen as destroyers of weeds and weeds themselves (pp. 83, 105): ploughing in, like summer fallow, would have rid the field of them before sowing the new crop, as well as enriching the soil.

the furrow (for wheat) covered by what Fitzherbert called a second stirring, which was recommended by Tusser, fostered, unawares, the growth of weeds, the loss of seed and the problems already dealt with by Gallo and Tarello. So the problem was to produce enough hay and fodder to feed the working animals, and then reclaim the land suitable for making meadows, since in those decades whole communities had enclosed pastures for sheep rearing.[44] Tusser and other tenants and owners who depended on the corn or wool market were to obtain an increase in productivity by changing from the open-field system to enclosures. We shall see later how the two compared in economic terms. In any case, while the difference between Fitzherbert's and Tusser's agronomy lies in the advice to sow vetch in old, impoverished pastures (*April's Husbandrie*), Tusser did not mention clover and seems not to have known what *sainfoin* was,[45] although the botanists of his generation had already acquired a good knowledge of it. But Tusser's verses provide an account of agricultural practices rather than an explanation of them.

In the last decades of the century, phenomena such as the rise in prices, increase in the population, the growth of urban society and of rural industries, regional specialization and the spread of enclosure, had increased the call for new land to satisfy the demand for food supplies in the new commercial society.[46] In England, at that time, agricultural land was obtained by disafforestation, by reclaiming marshy land and by soil improvement. The English obssession with manure may perhaps be explained by the need to warm the soil when the climate had grown colder, so that wheat and grains, which fetched the highest prices on the market, could be grown, and for want of more varieties of wheat, could be made more resistant to harsh winters. Even the smaller farmers

---

[44] On sixteenth-century enclosures see J. Thirsk, 'Enclosing and Engrossing', in *AHEW*, 4, pp. 200–56; E. K. Gonner, *Common Land and Enclosures* (with a new Introduction by G. E. Mingay), London 1966; J. A. Yelling, *Common Fields and Enclosures in England, 1450–1850*, London 1977.

[45] See Tusser, *Five Hundred Points*, pp. 242, 275–6: Hillman wrote this note in 1710 and knew very well that the use of new fodder-crops was very recent. It is an open question whether Tusser knew sainfoin at all. He mentioned *Sops in wine* (*Marches abstract*) among grasses grown in pots for decoration. According to the *English Dialect Dictionary* and the *OED* it was a purplish-red carnation. Dodoens–Lyte, *Niewe Herbal*, p. 154, also called them *pinks* or *soppes in wine*. Amongst the plants sown in the vegetable garden, the *Maison rustique* listed the *sainfoin* (*Medicago*) under the local name of *soupe en vin*. It may be noted here that the question of Tusser's literary sources has never been dealt with.

[46] The growth of market society in Elizabethan England is discussed by Everitt, 'The Marketing of Agricultural Produce'.

preferred wheat to other cereals, as a cash crop. A combination of wheat and barley gave the highest income for small producers. A wider range of cereals – rye, barley, oats and maslin (a seed mixture of rye and wheat) – was grown on larger farms, where greater attention could be paid to differences in soil. The agronomic practices adopted on these farms had something in common with the rules of Classical agronomy. It is important to emphasize this point, for it was in contrast with the dependence on a single grain crop which limited the choice of produce possible for the weaker social groups. They managed to make a small profit only by selling the wheat produced in average years.[47] What was happening in sixteenth- to seventeenth-century England was to happen later in Italy. The widespread cultivation of wheat on unsuitable land lowered the yield and raised costs, made heavier mainly because of the expense of manuring and marling. What was lacking in England was above all a crop to be alternated with wheat, like the sorghum and later the maize grown in Italy, so that small farmers or those who kept livestock could be more self-sufficient. This would only come about with the introduction of the potato (the poor man's food, almost always combined with livestock rearing) and the early adoption of roots and turnips on the light soils of East Anglia. These first appeared in the inventories of the late sixteenth century as garden products, food for the peasants, and later became cattle food. It was a successful attempt to get round the bottlenecks of wheat monoculture.[48] The tendency of English agriculture to develop specialized regional markets imposed a limit to technical solutions, forcing the farmer to compute the monetary value of his annual harvests and not their agronomic value over the medium term.

Of all the forms of land improvement, that which made use of manure was by far the most popular. According to Hugh Platt, alternate layers of manure and mould or else a mixture of marl, manure and soil, would produce not only first-class pasture but also very sweet hay. Although Pliny the Elder already knew that Britons were adept at improving their land with marl and there were also plenty of examples of the practice

[47] See W. G. Hoskins, 'The Leicestershire Farmer in the Sixteenth Century', in *Essays in Leicestershire History*, Liverpool 1951, pp. 123–83; P. Bowden, 'Agricultural Prices, Farm Profits and Rents', in *AHEW*, 4, pp. 650–63.

[48] See *ibid.*, pp. 653, 658 (I have placed the emphasis on the costs of grain production); H. Salman, *The Social History and Introduction of Potato*, Cambridge 1987; M. Overton, 'Estimating Crop Yields from Probate Inventories: an Example from East Anglia, 1585–1735', *Journal of Economic History*, 39, 1979, pp. 363–78.

throughout the Middle Ages, in the late sixteenth century Platt himself preferred to quote widely from the French author Bernard Palissy, giving the example of Flemish peasants using marl and then again Flemish and Lombard examples of soil fertilization with soap-ashes.[49]

The writings of John Norden should be seen against this background. Norden was the most famous agronomist and surveyor of early seventeenth-century England, the man with most practical experience, employed for years in measuring the estates of Robert Cecil. In the course of the sixteenth century, the surveyor became progressively more important as the specialist responsible for the economic development of the manor by increasing rents and improving unused land within the boundaries of the estate.[50] Getting rid of alders (*Alnus glutinosa*), which were excellent as timber and for making agricultural tools but which impoverished good quality land, removing the commonest weeds on wet, swampy ground (fox-tail (*Carex repens*), myrtle (*Myrica gale*), sedge (*Acorus calamus*) and rushes (*Juncacea*)) by draining, were the first steps towards reclaiming land and turning it into pasture. After being thus transformed into pastures and meadows, these fields might be ploughed, and such improvement was warmly recommended as a way of retrieving the lord's demesne.[51] Even an author so fully immersed in provincial life as Norden, who knew the southern counties of England at first hand and is generally quoted as an example of the practical English farmer, had an unexpected range of Classical quotations at his fingertips.[52] It should not be forgotten that when Norden wrote his most famous

---

[49] See in the following order H. Platte, *Diverse new Sorts of Soyle not yet brought into a publique use for manuring both of pasture and arable ground*, London 1594, pp. 34–6; idem, *The Jewell House of Art and Nature*, London 1594, pp. 50, 52; H. P. (Hugh Platte?), *Sundrie and new Artificial Remedies against Famine*, London 1596; B. Palissy, *Discours admirable de la nature des eaux et fontaines . . . des metaux, des sels et salines . . . plus un traité de la marne . . .* , Paris 1580, recently reprinted in the collection 'Travaux d'Humanisme et Renaissance', Paris 1988; see also Bourde, *Agronomie*, vol. I, pp. 38–40.

[50] See, on Norden: R. Tawney, *The Agrarian Problem in the Sixteenth Century*, London 1912, *passim*; Fussell, *Old English Farming Books*; Stone, *The Crisis of the Aristocracy*, pp. 241, 303, 307, 311–12; idem, *Family and Fortune*, pp. 39, 131; Kerridge, *The Agricultural Revolution*, especially pp. 79 ff. Of the writings of Norden *The Surveyor's Dialogue*, London 1601, 1610, 1618 is of interest here. The following quotations are taken from the third edition, 1618.

[51] See Norden, *The Surveyor's Dialogue*, pp. 192, 194–5.

[52] Norden had also produced a number of geographic descriptions of some southern counties, Middlessex and Hertfordshire (1593, 1598), Essex (1594), Norfolk (posthumously printed), Cornwall (posthumously printed in 1728). On the beginnings of geographical studies in England see F. V. Emery, 'English Regional Studies from

work he had already been in the service of Lord Burghley and so had easily been able to consult the many volumes of the Classics in the library at Hatfield (cf. *Sources*, no. 18, p. 424, in the *Appendix*). He used Cato's saying 'pratum quasi semper paratum' to introduce a digression on some good natural meadows, in particular some not far from Salisbury, and how grasslands of very poor quality had been improved by art. The *levis putredo* (in Latin in the text) left by the water which was made to run through these fields, was the first source of improvement. Unfortunately not all land could be reclaimed by irrigation. Meadows were divided into two categories, the low, wet ones, recommended by medieval specialists, and the dry ones on higher ground. Norden said the former never changed their natural role, while the latter were not essentially different from arable land and could be ploughed and sown at any time. In practice, as Norden stated, meadows were introduced into a rotation system, by which they passed to pasture and then to ploughing, according to the state of the turf and the need to interrupt the cycle by ploughing several times and sowing grains.[53] In this way the intelligent farmer tried to use the land in accordance with the composition of the soil. Cold, wet clays had to be treated with ashes and sand, the hot, dry soils needed correction with marl, a rich, cold substance.[54] In practice, a principle had been established that there was no land that could not be cultivated in some way. With the sequence permanent pasture–temporary pasture the land could regain fertility and produce cereals. From this viewpoint Norden suggested that the land available should be rationally organized, by increasing the number of plants cultivated, whether trees or various kinds of cereals (rye, barley and oats, but also several varieties of wheat). Thanks to this greater attention devoted to meadows and pastures and to the botanical species, it was pointed out that meadows in poor condition used to be sown in spring with clover or other seed gathered from the best hay, being careful to mix it with fine mould, not overly wet. In the worst cases it was advisable to plough the meadow in summer, leave it fallow until autumn, plough it a second time and sow peas and vetch; the following year it should be sown with wheat

Aubrey to Defoe', *The Geographical Journal*, 124, 1958, pp. 315–25. Surprisingly Norden quotes Varro on meadows and Virgil, Horace, Theophrastus on fishponds (pp. 199, 201, 223, 225, 217).

[53] See Norden, *The Surveyor's Dialogue*, pp. 198–204.

[54] See the list of soil-fertilizing techniques in Kerridge, *The Agricultural Revolution*, pp. 240–50, decidedly optimistic about their diffusion and results. A more cautious view is that expressed by Thirsk, 'Farming Techniques', in *AHEW*, 4, pp. 179–85.

and then again with vetch and chaff from hay. In the course of a couple of years the grass would be plentiful again and of good quality. Another method of improvement, little practised in reality, was to pare the turf of old meadows and burn-bake it.[55] This whole process of cultivating the meadow is very near to what Agostino Gallo recommended for land in the Brescia region (see Chap. 3, 2).

The idea of reclaiming land, which Fitzherbert had already dealt with at the beginning of the century, was put forward once again, for unproductive, neglected land of various kinds, covered with bracken, bushes or moss, and was deemed the quickest way to get extra land until the time of Parliamentary enclosures. Manuring together with marling was the main technique adopted, as it modified the acidity in soil that had been left uncultivated. Norden, too, used the dominant Aristotelian division into classes, hot, cold, dry and wet,[56] and it was perhaps not by chance that he mentioned Theophrastus (and Horace) on the effects of manuring and the destruction of bracken. These botanical indicators suggested to him that cultivation had once been more general than it was in his time and that what had once been arable land had turned into undergrowth and woodland.[57] The work of the ploughman was the first step in reclaiming abandoned land, to be followed by greater attention to growing the right species in the right soil; oats on clay, barley on sandy soil, 'light red rush wheat' on light soil, and white grain on heavy soils.[58]

By dealing with the issue of sowing old meadows, Norden (and those farmers who had begun this practice) brought about a great improvement in the cultivation of meadows and pastureland in England. The great amount of cold land (that is, predominantly alkaline in present-day terminology) forced farmers to manure land when growing grains frequently. Animal husbandry and sheep-farming were the two sectors of growth, not only independently, but in connection with grain-growing.

---

[55] See Norden, *Surveyor's Dialogue,* p. 224: this is the well-known practice called *devonshiring* or *denshiring*, after the county of Devon where it developed, otherwise known as *burn-baking*. Kerridge, *The Agricultural Revolution, passim,* is again very optimistic about the extent to which it was used.

[56] See G. E. Fussell, 'Soil classification in the 17th and 18th centuries', *Pochvovdeniya*, 1933, 5; N. Hilton, *An Approach to Agricultural Land Classification in Great Britain*, Institute of British Geographers, Special Publication, I, 1968, pp. 127–42; L. Bolens, 'Engrais et protection de la fertilité dans l'agronomie hispano-arabe, xie–xiie siècles', *Etudes rurales*, 1972, pp. 34–60.

[57] See Tawney, *The Agrarian Problem*, pp. 85–9, Beresford, *Deserted Villages, passim.*

[58] See Norden, *Surveyor's Dialogue*, p. 222.

For the first time, the grass covering the turf was taken as an indication of the pedological condition of the soil and no distinction was drawn any more between meadows and arable land, insofar as drainage made it possible to grow cereals. The natural fertility so necessary to their growth was built up again below the grass covering. The three ways of using grass-covered land, as pasture, meadow or water-meadow, and ley, became interchangeable and were subjected to the same rules of cultivation as rotations with arable land. If we compare these practices still described by Fitzherbert with the earlier ones found in Walter of Henley we realize that the influence of Classical and Mediterranean agronomy was at work. The meadow-pasture became a reserve of arable land to be sown with cereals in case of need. From 1350 to the Second World War, in times of depression, the leys reverted to meadow, then turned into pastureland, and then into wasteland covered with bracken, peat and moss.[59] Every time there was an agricultural recovery in England, it started with the reclamation of these lands.

Next to manuring and marling, the method that met with most success in transforming pastures to meadowland and in increasing their productivity, was irrigation. The system of irrigating and flooding low-lying meadows along the rivers in the winter months was an old medieval practice, as was the transformation of common pastureland into enclosed meadows.[60] But in sixteenth- to seventeenth-century England, which had never known any shortage of pasture, the practice was used to increase the productivity of the meadows and so reduce their extent with respect to arable land. Meadows were irrigated with clean, running water from November to March, then drained off in March and April, manured in May and irrigated again before the summer mowing. There were by now many successful examples, mainly in the western counties of Somerset, Devon and Hereford, at least from 1582. The most famous expert in the field, Rowland Vaughan, wrote, among others, of Lombardy (where grass was said to spring up twice a day!). He also spoke of his legal tussle with a master carpenter who boasted that he worked in the Venetian style [*sic*], making constructions that proved more costly and

---

59 See for example H. I. Moore, *Grassland Husbandry*, London 1943.
60 See R. Grand and R. Delatouche, *L'agriculture au Moyen Age de la fin de l'empire romain au xvie siècle*, Paris 1950, pp. 291–314. According to D. Berra, *Delle marcite*, Milan 1811, and C. Cattaneo, *Notizie naturali e civili su la Lombardia*, Milan 1844, 'prato marcitoio' or 'marcita' might have derived from 'March' when the first cut of hay is ready after the winter irrigation.

less sturdy than the ones which he himself had planned.[61] This conflict between the upper and lower classes is interesting, showing the craftsman adopting a foreign technique, in this case the Venetian fashion, while the specialist now declared he could surpass that model. It should also be remembered that land improvement by means of irrigation was a recent innovation in the Venetian countryside, dating from the mid-sixteenth century, though based on the much older Lombard model.[62] Nor can it be merely fortuitous that the counties where most water-meadows were introduced were those near Southampton, traditionally the port for Anglo-Italian commerce. Vaughan specialized in channels that took water to the upper slopes of hills (here the Venetian model worked better than the Lombard one) so that waste and arable land of very little value could be turned into rich meadowland. Vaughan boasted that by spending an initial £2,000 his capital had increased four- to sixfold in four years. However, these water-meadows, for that is what they were, could only be established by those who could wait for a return on their capital and at the same time invest in livestock, especially sheep. In some regions of England the best land was used preferably for pasture, so that all the manure produced could go to the arable land. The Vale of Belvoir, in Leicestershire, and the whole county, which passed from high-quality arable land to pasture in the hundred years following 1630, is an example of this. On the other hand, even modern agronomists consider it fundamental, if they are to increase the weight and strengthen the breed of cattle, for calves to be suckled and the cows' milk to be enriched by fresh fodder rich in proteins, which can be obtained by improving meadow grasses.[63] In this way the English farm tended, as far

---

[61] See R. Vaughan, *Most approved and long experienced water works*, London 1610, fos. 36*v*–67*v*, especially fo. 40*r*. Such a polymath as G. Markham, *Markham's Farewell to Husbandry, or the Inriching of all sorts of Barren and Sterile Grounds*, London 1625, also took up the subject of water-meadows. The most commonly used Venetian mechanisms were the waterwheels, see S. Ciriacono, 'Irrigazione e produttività agraria nella Terraferma veneta tra Cinque e Seicento', *Archivio Veneto*, ser. 5, 112, 1979, pp. 110 14 and his newly published *Acque e agricoltura. Venezia, l'Olanda e la bonifica europea in età moderna*, Milan 1994,

[62] See A. A. Ruddock, *Italian Merchants and Shipping in Southampton, 1270–1600*, Southampton 1951; J. Georgelin, 'Une bonification dans la "bassa" friulane', *Studi veneziani*, 13, 1971, pp. 623–46; Ciriacono, *Acque e agricoltura*, pp. 29–102.

[63] See J. Thirsk, *English Peasant Farming: The Agrarian History of Lincolnshire from Tudor to Recent Times*, London 1957, and H. C. Darby, 'The Age of the Improver', in idem (ed.), *A New Historical Geography of England*, Cambridge 1973, p. 325. Moore, *Grassland Husbandry*, pp. 56–80. W. Davies, *The Grass Crop*, London 1952, pp. 168–89. This was known to late eighteenth-century agriculturists, see Kerridge, *The Agricultural Revolution*, p. 260.

back as the sixteenth century, to employ a disproportionate amount of capital in cattle, while retaining the chance to alternate meadows with arable land.

The system worked in England, as it did not in Italy or southern France, because of the better ratio between cultivated land and the number of inhabitants. This ratio had been kept high because common and waste land had been reclaimed in the early seventeenth century, with enclosure reaching 50–70 per cent, and in many cases more than 70 per cent, in the counties of East Anglia (Essex, Suffolk and parts of Norfolk), in Central–Southern counties (Hampshire and Wiltshire), the West Country (Somerset, Devon and Cornwall), the counties on the borders of Wales (Cheshire and Lancashire) and parts of the north, Yorkshire, and counties on the borders of Scotland (Northumberland and Durham). Open-fields and commons were defended from enclosure in the Midlands, where privatization only really started after the mid-eighteenth century.[64] With enclosure, much arable land had been turned into pastureland; at best, it facilitated the spread of up-and-down husbandry, alternating arable land and leys. Woodland, too, had been noticeably reduced. The value of enclosed land went up but the volume of grain production did not always follow, and food shortages were not unknown even in those decades of agricultural development.[65] At the regional and national level, the protest of the poorer classes was genuine, when they complained of the high price and scarcity of food. Despite regional differences the individual farmer insisted on the need to encourage enclosure and disafforestation and to substitute trees of little value with fruit-trees and timber. At best, the emphasis was placed not so much on the increased value of the land as on land reclamation and the creation of work for the whole community (a purpose which historians have commended). The problem lay in the loss of the right to gather wood and put animals to pasture, which the poorer farmers and tenants held on common lands. Protection from the Crown and outspoken

---

[64] See F. Emery, 'England circa 1600', in Darby (ed.), *A New Historical Geography*, p. 256: see also E. C. K. Gonner, *Common Land and Inclosures*, H. L. Gray, *English Field Systems*, Cambridge (MA) 1915, and J. A. Yelling, *Common Fields and Enclosures*.

[65] See W. G. Hoskins, 'Harvest Fluctuations and English Economic History, 1450–1619', *AHR*, 12, 1964, pp. 24–86; A. B. Appleby, *Famine in Tudor and Stuart England*, Liverpool 1978.

opinion in their favour, though rare, were not completely lacking in those decades of rapacious expropriation.[66]

4.1. John Smyth, Robert Loder and others

The above-mentioned issues feature regularly in comments on farm accounts and in books of memorials written in the decades before the Civil War. The texts in question, well known as they are, cannot be passed over.

John Smyth entered the service of the powerful Berkeley family in 1584, when he accompanied young Thomas to study law at Magdalen College, Oxford, and later became steward of the Berkeley estates. His main duty was to preside over the court baron of the manor, where minor trials were held and debts of under 40 shillings were dealt with. In this post, having access to the oldest documents of the Berkeley family, from the thirteenth century on, and following the sixteenth-century fashion of stewards of great households, he compiled a chronology of the administration of the manors. The first lords of Berkeley did not pay much attention to administrative problems, preferring to strengthen their manorial rights. When Thomas, the second Lord Berkeley (1281–1321) took over the administration, the traditional open-field system became part of a well-run administrative order. Although military campaigns, jousting, tournaments and hunting were his favourite occupations, Thomas personally noted the fruit-trees, pears and apples, to be planted and grafted; a large amount of cider was also made from the abundant apple crop. Yet by the end of the sixteenth century, only two or three trees had survived in the great orchards of Slimbridge and a place called Hunt in the documents (Hinton?). To improve the arable lands Thomas allowed marl to be dug from the pits and soil taken from the commons of Alkington, Ham and Cowley. He allowed enclosure and arranged for the exchange of strips to obtain larger areas of pasture. In the years before and after the Black Death, the enormous increase in the number of sheep (every manor had a flock of from 300 to 1,500) and farmyard fowl (pigeons, ducks, geese, peacocks) did not bring about a reduction in the cultivation of cereals, though more barley was transformed into malt and

---

[66] Of the vast contemporary literature on enclosures see only: A. Standish, *The Commons Complaint . . . Two special Grievances: the First is the General Destruction of Waste of Woods . . . the Second the Extreme Dearth of Victuals*, London 1611, and R. Chambers, *An Olde Thrift newly Revived*, London 1612, pp. 32–43; in general see Thirsk, *Enclosing and Engrossing*, pp. 200–56.

more alms were given to the needy, in preference to distributing food. Neither were fruit or cider reduced. Indeed, the fourth Lord Maurice (1361–68) even planted a vineyard at Berkeley, probably remembering his journeys to Spain or his years of imprisonment in France. Shoots of this vineyard were still growing among the grass in the early nineteenth century.[67] The administration changed with the fourth Lord Thomas (1368–1417). Instead of cultivating and caring for the demesne himself, he started to let his pastures to the local livestock rearers, getting substantial heriots and entry fines from his tenants. In these years of change the Berkeleys extended their patronage to men of letters, and John Trevisa, vicar and chaplain to Lord Thomas, formerly a member of Christchurch, Oxford, dedicated to him his English translation of Bartholomew of Glenville's *De proprietatibus rerum*, the epitome of Pliny's *Natural History* (1398). Once again, interest in nature in the Mediterranean area coincided with interest in orchards and the vineyard, and good local farming with marling. Between 1417 and 1523, the first Lord James and the sixth Maurice of Berkeley merely collected rents, taking no interest in the administration of the estate. Only Thomas, the fifth Lord (1523–32), made it his direct and detailed concern once more, going round with an auditor and lawyer to visit all the manors once a year and above all keeping a direct and personal account of his immense and valuable flocks. Like so many English landowners, the Berkeleys, too, had passed from arable farming to sheep farming.[68] Being a good steward, John Smyth observed in his final considerations that various marl-pits had several times been used by the men of Berkeley to improve the land. The second Lord Thomas had already granted lands in fee simple, with a clause in which the holder undertook to improve pastures and arable land. In his own day (1639) John Smyth was still recommending that marl should be spread in narrow furrows, to be widened later. He recalled that Peckham field was fertile for ten years after marling, that people came from as far away as Coventry to get marl from the pits, and marl had also improved the cherry orchard he had planted

---

[67] See J. Smyth, *The Berkeley Manuscripts. The Lives of the Berkeleys from 1066 to 1613 with a Description of the Hundred of Berkeley and its Inhabitants*, ed. by Sir John MacLean, Gloucester 1888, vol. I, pp. 156–60, 187, 302, 365; Phillips, *Pomarium britannicum*, p. 187; Stone, *Family and Fortune*, pp. 243–67.

[68] See Smyth, *The Berkeley Manuscripts*, vol. II, pp. 5, 22, 222, 227. On the English aristocracy's renewed interest in farming see J. Thirsk, 'New Style Demesne Farming in Early Modern England', The Neale Lecture in English History, 9 December 1982, University College of London, quoted with the author's consent.

with his own hands. He considered it his duty to teach and to make sure that the farmers were not ignorant on agricultural matters and that every meadow and field was improved with salt, marl and fresh water, as Markham's books on farming instructed. In his opinion, the business of planting, ploughing and manuring was the only one that still had something innocent about it, and for this reason was to be encouraged.[69] Smyth's manuscripts follow the long evolution of an agricultural system severely taxed in the late fourteenth century by shortage of labour, in which grain production was replaced by sheep-farming and animal husbandry and was only taken up again with great difficulty in the second half of the sixteenth century.

Robert Loder's farm accounts for the years 1612–21 have often been used to demonstrate how quickly English farmers responded to the incentives of the market.[70] In the village of Harwell, halfway between Oxford and Reading, Loder probably had 150 acres of open field land, another hundred enclosed in a single block, besides some small, enclosed pieces of land, an orchard and a small meadow. He tried to keep account of everything, sometimes without quite succeeding in identifying the sources of his profits or the causes of his losses. Yet he was definitely practising commercial farming on a monetary basis. Most of his income came from arable land, a total of 120–39 acres, according to the year, divided into East and West Field, two open fields of equal size. Being bound to a two-year rotation, Loder had simplified his system to the utmost. It comprised barley, vetch and legumes, fruit, pasture and sheep. He had stopped growing minor cereals for domestic consumption or as fodder, and tried to produce as much wheat and barley as possible, as they fetched a better price on the market. The two-field system meant that he could not completely avoid leaving the land fallow and could not grow a second crop. But he generally managed to keep part of his land from being used as common pasture, and grew a little vetch and legumes for fodder on it. Notwithstanding this, he had quite a high ratio of yields to seed for his times, between 7.9 and 14.6 for wheat and 5.2 and 11.5 for barley (that meant about 20 to 35 bushels). They were decidedly lower in 1613 (5.5 and 4.6 respectively) because of bad weather. His good results probably depended on the unusual amount of work spent on the land, which he ploughed four times and harrowed twice before sowing. He

---

[69] See Smyth, *The Berkeley Manuscripts*, vol. III, pp. 40–3.

[70] See G. E. Fussell, 'Robert Loder's Farm Accounts', *1610–1620, Camden Society Publications*, ser. 3, 53, 1936, pp. xxxi ff.

took great care in preparing the furrow before putting in the seed. All this must have compensated for the less than average amount of manure he could spread, since he owned few large animals. As he regularly sowed no more than two and a half bushels per acre, the very high yields for 1618–20 can only be explained by his careful ploughing and the effect of the vetch and legumes grown on the fallow.[71] Loder manured his arable land with a mixture of horse and cattle dung and mud dredged from his pond, to which he added indefinite quantities of the waste from his malt production, pigeon-droppings and ashes. He also had trouble with manuring his meadows, both enclosed and in lots. Besides taking the usual precautions (thorough weeding and mole-catching) in 1618 he managed to spread sixty loads of manure on his lots in South Marsh and the following year spread about forty on his lots in Town Meade. But while all the green forage was consumed by his horses and cattle and went back into the farm, droppings from his sheep on the open fields could not all be retrieved, nor could any radical improvement of the pastures be ensured. During the winter months the fodder given to the livestock was of very poor quality, often they got nothing but straw. Under such conditions, Loder obviously could not assess the value of his flock accurately. The poor diet produced weak lambs, which easily fell sick.[72] Loder's main purpose was to increase the profit he made on wheat and barley, varying the amount that he grew according to current prices. In the ten years under consideration, he managed to make a constant profit of between £181 15s in 1613 and £292 10s in 1619. Examination of the national average for all cereals does not bear out the saying that years of higher prices (1612 and 1613) are years of greatest profits. The considerable grain yields of 1618–20 coincided, as was to be expected, with years of lower prices, but the noteworthy profits are connected with merely average yields, in cases where the cultivation costs were kept reasonably constant (between £104 17s and £146 2s).[73] To sum up, Robert Loder's results confirm that an average farmer could very well make a profit under the open-field system. The solution to the question of yields lay rather in the quality of the tilling than in manuring and hence

---

[71] See *ibid.*, pp. vii–x, xii–xviii.

[72] See *ibid.*, pp. xviii–xxiii: it should be noted that the emphasis that G. E. Fussell places on the lack of manure is not the same as that pointed out in the text above.

[73] See *ibid.*, table iv: the costs of ploughing, seeds, harvesting, threshing, manuring and interests have been added for the years 1612–17 for comparison with the single figure for the years 1618–20. For the index numbers see 'Statistical Appendix', in *AHEW*, 4, p. 820.

in the possession of a large herd.[74] The real trouble with Loder's farm was the insufficient botanical variety of his crops – wheat (white, red and cone-wheat), barley, peas, beans and vetch. Had he sown maslin (wheat and rye mixed) in 1613 he would have halved the risk of losing his harvest because of the hard winter and would have made a higher profit.

This insistence on two basic crops, wheat and barley, was common in southern England. Robert Wansborough of Shrewton, in Wiltshire, produced for the market in a countryside of open fields, where the production of cereals and sheep-rearing predominated. After the bad years for cereals in 1630–1, Wansborough's main worry was to get good seed from clay soil and from the hills. He visited a number of markets (Easterton, Imber, Market Lavington, Salisbury and others) in the six years between 1633 and 1639, alternating the seed that he purchased with his own.[75] This use of seed from poor soil, or soil from upland areas, on fields in the plains, was a practice recommended by the Classical agronomists and mentioned by Leon Battista Alberti and others.

The notes written in 1641 by Henry Best of Elmswell, Yorkshire, show a different attitude to pasture and fodder.[76] The care of sheep and lambs, of meadows, and problems connected with hay-making, came before the cultivation of cereals. The favourable wet weather of the spring of 1641 had produced a great quantity of fodder, thick and luxuriant, from healthy turf. Sheep and calves liked short grass with more leaves best. Poppies and daisies, short, thick plants, hindered mowing; seeds were often full of thistles. Hay-ricks should be built large and well packed. The outer layer served as a protection and should be removed, while the inside of the rick fermented and the hay was sweeter and more nourishing. In rainy years, fodder rotted if left in the furrows; it should be placed on the ridges or taken to the top of the field. These are the most significant comments to be found in Henry Best's notes. Most of the pages are taken up by lists of the value of the grassfields or meadows, open or enclosed, belonging to the family, and the calculation of the hay they produced and the number of days' work each required. The

---

[74] Campbell, 'Arable Productivity'; idem, 'Agricultural Progress'; and Overton, 'Estimating Crop Yields', bring out the importance of weeding although they do not underestimate the importance of manure in open-field grain production.

[75] See E. Kerridge, 'The Notebook of a Wiltshire Farmer in the Early Seventeenth Century', *Wiltshire Arch. and Nat. His. Magazine*, 197, 1952.

[76] See D. Woodward (ed.), *The Farming and Memorandum Books of Henry Best of Elmswell, 1642, Records of Social and Economic history*, New series VIII, London, 1984, pp. 33–7 *passim*.

language Best used was much more detailed than normal manorial accounts and the many provincial expressions bring out, rather than conceal, points that were to be developed only in the modern science of meadow cultivation. Grazing of livestock depended on the growth of grass on pastureland and meadow. However, Best noted, the needs of cattle and sheep were very different, cattle eating tall and sheep short grass. Adequate drainage was essential to get good pastureland, but if the ridge and furrow system on arable land was kept in the leys, the fodder crop would be poor. It is difficult to say how far Best's ideas on agronomy were still based on southern European models. However, there are some points on botany in his notebook which show that, though his struggle against weeds was far from being won, he had made considerable progress, having reduced the weeds to a few species, and rooted out with the plough the bushy varieties mentioned by Fitzherbert and Tusser, and even later by Norden. Henry Best's endeavours were not unique in the northern counties of England. In 1640 Walter Stonehouse, fellow of Magdalen College, Oxford, and vicar of Darfield, in West Yorkshire, drew a very detailed plan of the vicarage garden. It consisted of five beds, laid out in the French manner, within a surrounding wall, which extended into a vegetable garden where he grew saffron. On the north side and on the east side it opened out into an orchard, also enclosed. Here grew plums, peaches, apricots, cherries of various qualities, and white *moscato* grapes, various kinds of apples and pears, which were grafted on 25 February 1644. In all, there were 866 varieties, few of which were alive in 1652. Probably the vicar's age, and the severe frosts of several previous years, had undone the labours of the early 1640s.[77]

4.2. Botanical gardens and private gardens (1600–40)

The great drawback was that just when English agronomy was looking towards the Continent, prepared to put into practice the ideas gleaned from books and increase the number of plants to be grown in the field, the farming system was unable to produce the necessary seeds. British wild flora did not produce plants which could be bred selectively to produce these new crops and increase the farm produce for sale, while reducing the unproductive periods under the prevailing system of grain cultivation. We have already seen that seeds for pharmaceutical use (fenugreek) and fruit-trees for domestic use (apples and pears, apricots

[77] See Oxford, Magdalen College Archives, ms 239.

etc.), hemp, onion and various other horticultural seeds appeared among the goods unloaded in the port of London towards the middle of the century. They were destined for the gardens and kitchen gardens of private individuals or pharmacists, counterpoint to Shakespeare's Forest of Arden. The taste for a fine, well-ordered landscape, tamed by cultivation, was beginning to make headway and was to predominate until the Romantic Age.[78] Only by examining the scanty documents concerning the few private gardens of the time can the contribution of the few experts on foreign plants and crops be appreciated.

The gap between theory and practice was bridged by the efforts of private individuals, landowners like Robert Cecil and Edward Zouche, pharmacists like John Gerard, gardeners like John Tradescant and Jacob Bobart, scholars and botanists like John Goodyer, William Coys or Walter Stonehouse, who owned and studied so many books on Classical agronomy and botany. The cultivation of new species in the private garden and botanical garden was not carried on for profit. It enabled those who organized it to become familiar with the cycle of a plant's life and to distribute the specimens cultivated through the network of their social relations, who would produce it in their turn.[79] It is mainly the medicinal plants (cornflower, common mallow, lady's mantle, knapweed and shepherd's needle) of the oldest gardens that are mentioned; then, suddenly, in the garden of the pharmacist Henry Cross of Oxford, a specimen of *Hedysarum aut securidaca* (*Coronilla varia*, L.) appears. Or in Norton's garden in Hampshire, we find the *trifolium odoratum* (*Melilotus officinalis*, L.). Both species are widely used in the treatment of heart diseases. The *coronilla* is a poisonous plant to be used with caution and both are closely connected with lucerne.[80]

---

[78] In general on the different aesthetic and moral approaches to the environment see K. Thomas, *Man and the Natural World. Changing Attitudes in England 1500–1800*, London 1983, pp. 254 ff.

[79] The following pages are largely based on the documents published in Gunther, *Early British Botanists*, pp. 302–63. The botanical gardens and the private gardens dealt with here are those of Hugh Morgan, Coleman Street, London, working 1569–87; Henry Cross, Oxford, and John Watson, Winchester, 1570–2; Sir John Salusbury (*sic*), Lleweni, 1596, 1607–8; Simon Forman, 1597–1608; Robert Cecil, Lord Salisbury, Hatfield, 1611; Richard Shanne, Methley, 1615; William Coys, Stubbers, 1604, 1616, 1621–2; the botanical gardens of John Parkinson, 1618–20; John Goodyer, 1622; John Tradescant, Lambeth, 1629–34; George Gibbs, 1634; Walter Stonehouse, Darfield, 1640–4; Edward Morgan, Westminster, 1662; Robert Morison, London, 1661–2.

[80] In the dialect of the Veneto region lucerne is called 'coronilla', 'erba spagna','erba cavallina salvadega', or 'jàrbe-mèdiche-zale' (*T. agrarium*); in French *Melilotus officinalis* is also known as 'luzerne bâtarde'. See Gunther, *Early English Botanists*, pp. 305–6, and De Palma, *Le piante medicinali*, pp. 293, 304.

William Coys was the most enterprising amateur botanist at the turn of the century. Having organized a very well-stocked garden, he has left us a wealth of information. His garden at Stubbers, Essex, was known to his contemporaries because it was there that the white yucca flower bloomed for the first time in England in 1604. It had also become an important source for the Spanish plants which the traveller William Boel had brought him. On collating the Latin nomenclature of Coys with the English of John Gerard, we find many species missing in the latter, perhaps undeservedly considered as the greatest English botanist of his time. William Coys had planted 342 species. In the list made on 24 and 25 March 1616/17 we find cytisus (*cytisus maior semper vivus*), two melilots, and *Hedysarum coronarum*, that is Spanish sainfoin, an obvious contribution by Boel from Spain. The 1621/22 list gives a greater number of legumes then cultivated – *cicer rubrum*, the bean of the ancients, fenugreek, six different kinds of vetchlings (*Lathyrus pratensis*), Spanish sainfoin again, two varieties of *securidica* (wild *luzerne*), four varieties of melilots and five varieties of lucerne. Coys had not begun to collect the foreign specimens merely as a curiosity; he was focusing on plants of economic interest, such as turnips, lentils, panic-grass, barley and peas. At the end of his list, he stated that 136 of the 1621 specimens and 70 of those of 1622 came from the garden of Baron Zouche, directed by Matthias de L'Obel. Edward Zouche, a politician of the first order, had personally gathered many specimens during his travels. Coys also distributed his own seeds. On 22 March 1622, Goodyer received twenty-two different kinds of seeds of flowers and fruit-trees from him, including crimson clover ('trefoyle with a crimsen bush'). Common red clover was also a species considered worthy of the botanical garden, to be carefully selected. There was nothing eccentric in this, since in those years it was very difficult to get seed of this valuable forage-crop for agricultural use.[81]

The library of Robert Cecil, Lord Salisbury, provides examples of a series of interesting practices, and his garden at Hatfield was the arena for their practical application. Lord Salisbury had received the estate of Hatfield from James I in exchange for Theobalds, and there Cecil had planted a vineyard of 30,000 vines on the banks of the river Lea. He had the help of Madame de la Broderie, wife of the ambassador of France, and Maria de' Medici herself, who had let him have the necessary varieties and specimens. In 1611 Cecil had set the gardener John

[81] See Gunther, *Early English Botanists*, pp. 316–25.

Tradescant the task of supplying Hatfield with the best specimens of fruit-trees in France and Holland, to be sent by Cornelius Helin of Haarlem and Jean Robin of Paris.[82] Fruit-trees and botanical species were sent to Hatfield straight from Louis XIII's botanical garden, directed by Jean Robin. The collaboration of Tradescant and Robin continued after the creation of Hatfield (and had perhaps preceded it). While annotating a copy of Parkinson's *Paradisus soli*, published in 1629, Tradescant added a list of plants he had received that year.[83] Among other things, Monsieur Robin had sent him from Paris four kinds of rose, an unusual vine, a specimen of *Red honny succle*, which might be identified with Spanish sainfoin. This was a plant that Robin had not included in his 1601 catalogue and very probably Tradescant's translation simply designates *sainfoin*. Moreover, in the catalogue that Tradescant made out in 1634, which was never printed, he had listed eight varieties of lucerne, *Hedysarum clypeatum* Lob., and two varieties of *Polygala valentina*, Clus., what we call Spanish sainfoin. As we have seen (in Chap. 4), in England and in France too, the already-mentioned disagreement continued over nomenclature and the identification of *sainfoin*.[84] Tradescant's papers show that the spread of foreign plants, even those commonly used in farming, was quite often linked with court circles. A few years later, Jacob Bobart, curator of the Botanic Garden of Oxford, used the catalogue of the botanical garden of Blois, which included all the agricultural species studied here, to compare it with the Oxford garden.[85] Links with France and a tendency to imitate French things were very marked in the early seventeenth century, when James I came to the throne and the marriage of the future Charles I to Louis XIII's sister Henrietta Maria seemed to have eased the traditional conflict between the English and the French. In 1617, among Goodyer's

---

[82] John Tradescant probably made drawings of fruit at this time, adding the date of ripening of each species: see Oxford, BO, ms Ashmole 1461. See also M. Allan, *The Tradescants, their Plants, Gardens and Museums, 1570–1662*, London 1964.

[83] See G. S. Boulger, 'A Seventeenth Century Botanist Friendship', *Journal of Botany*, 1918, p. 197, on the notes in the margin of J. Parkinson, *Paradisi in sole Paradisus terrestris*, London 1629.

[84] See Gunther, *Early English Botanists*, pp. 328–46; J. Parkinson, *Theatrum botanicum: the Theater of Plants or an Universall and Complete Herball*, London 1640, 1650; Robin, *Catalogus stirpium* (*medica, onobrychis, polygala*); whereas J. Pitton De Tournefort, *Elements de botanique*, Paris 1694, pp. 310, 320, showed that certain varieties of *Hedysarum* and *Onobrychis* were sometimes confused. *French Honeysuckle* meant *sainfoin-onobrychis-hedysarum* in everyday French, too: see note 97.

[85] See A. Brunyer, *Hortus Regius Blesensis Auctus*, Paris 1635, with manuscript notes by R. Morison (Oxford, BO, ms Sherard 28).

many suppliers, he also dealt with a family of merchants of Cambrai, Jean Franqueville and his son, who also had a nursery in London. The Franquevilles in their turn were in contact with Jean Robin and with correspondents in the Pyrenees who had supplied Gerard and L'Obel with plants. The trade in seed, whether rare or of the ordinary varieties, must have been more extensive than is generally thought.[86]

Nor was it only in southern England, thanks to London circles, that the novelties were spreading. As early as 1577, near Methley, in Yorkshire, Richard Shanne had begun to keep a herb and flower garden. His list of 1615, besides ornamental plants (tulips, narcissi, peonies and so on) and the more traditional species of the herbalists (wild angelica, borage, calamint, motherwort, hyssop and marjoram) included horticultural varieties (fennel, endive, asparagus and artichokes) and industrial plants like madder and saffron. We have already mentioned the Reverend Walter Stonehouse, of Darfield in the same county, who had made a very careful list of the species in his garden and orchard, which included sainfoin, Spanish sainfoin and lucerne, all the forage-crops examined here, and all grown from seed.[87] For whereas in early seventeenth-century Italy, the naturalist's research was at once channelled into the academies, such as the spectacular collection of Aldrovandi, in England the academic world lagged far behind the initiatives of minor figures, unattached to any institutions, who proved most efficient in supporting the wider distribution of the botanical species. Marginal notes in books were still the form of study chosen by practical botanists like Tradescant, who were too busy to keep a systematic account of their labours (it was fitting that Tradescant should be portrayed with a gardener's spade in his hand). Collectors and scholars like Goodyer, on the other hand, preserved the memory of the work of others who, but for him, would have remained unknown. In this phase, when little professional training was available and information and specimens passed from hand to hand, the simplest thing was to learn by imitating others. In the first half of the seventeenth century botanists no longer copied from texts, but from the gardens of friends and acquaintances.[88]

---

[86] See Raven, *English Naturalists*, pp. 252–5; Gunther, *Early English Botanists*, pp. 325–6; seeds and horticultural novelties from Provence found their way into Northern France at an early stage, see Le Roy Ladurie, *Paysans de Languedoc*, pp. 74–6.

[87] See Gunther, *Early English Botanists*, pp. 311–12, and Oxford, Magdalen College Archives, ms 239, fos. 31 ff., 'plantae annuae et hiemes ex seminibus oriundae'.

[88] See for example Raven, *English Naturalists*, p. 262.

John Goodyer (1592–1664), of Hampshire, had two small botanical gardens, one at Droxford and one at Petersfield, even before he became a fellow of Magdalen College, Oxford. It was an important juncture in the history of the university. The botanical garden of the University of Oxford was created in 1621, on five acres of land that Magdalen College had donated for the purpose. The funds for the buildings were offered by Henry Danvers, Baron Danvers of Dauntsey (Wilts) and Earl of Danby. The chair of 'Regius Professor in Botany', however, only dates from 1669. The close connection between Magdalen College and the botanical garden was maintained until the early twentieth century. Hence the beginnings of systematic botany and its teachings in England were linked more with practice than with theory. The German gardener Jacob Bobart (1600?–80) was the real head of the organization and compiler of the first printed catalogue.[89] In the building on the other side of the street, John Goodyer put together a large collection of books on Classical and European botany, necessary to transform the endeavours of the experts into a discipline, and was in contact, personally and by letter, with the botanists and landowners engaged in broadening the range of English flora. One of the first things Goodyer did was to translate Theophrastus' history of plants from the Greek. He completed this work in February 1624 and then started on years of study, keeping up the contacts mentioned above. Between 1652 and 1654 he at last took up translating again, this time choosing the five books of Dioscorides. To complete the subject, he also translated the comment on Dioscorides by Antoine Sarrasin of Lyons, published in 1598.[90] Goodyer played an important part as assistant to Thomas Johnson when Gerard's herbal was revised in 1633; he was also in touch with John Parkinson. Perhaps the most important scientific contribution that Goodyer made was to realise

---

[89] See [J. Bobart], *Catalogus plantarum Horti medici oxoniensis*, Oxford 1648; A. A. Wood, *The History and Antiquities of the University of Oxford*, Oxford 1796, vol. II, part 2, p. 896; S. H. Vines and G. C. Druce, *An Account of the Morisonian Herbarium*, Oxford 1914, p. xiv; Henrey, *British Botanical and Horticultural Literature*, vol. I, pp. 96–97.

[90] See Oxford, Magdalen College Archives, mss 222 a, b; ms 229, *The Scholia or Animadversiones of Antonius Saracenus Lugdunens upon ye 5 Books of Dioscorides*; mss 238–9, *Catalogues of Plants*; mss 316–28 (properly speaking these are mss Goodyer 1–15 followed by R. T. Gunther in his *Early English Botanists*); mss 316–21, *Of Pedachius Dioscorides of medicinal matter, translated by John Goodyer*, published by R. T. Gunther (ed.), *The Greek Herbal of Dioscorides Illustrated by a Byzantine AD 512. Englished by John Goodyer AD 1655. Edited and First Printed AD 1933*, Oxford 1934; ms 322, *Theophrasti de historia plantarum*; mss 329, 330, 345.

the difficulties of describing English on the basis of Continental flora, especially that of southern Europe. Turner, Gerard and L'Obel, to mention only the most illustrious authors, had worked on Continental publications and the illustrations, copied from those made for Fuchs (Basle 1545) or Plantin (Antwerp 1576 and after) were misleading. His contacts with local amateurs were necessary both to introduce them to novelties and to obtain local information from them. In 1620 Goodyer sowed, in Droxford, a series of legumes that Boel had sent from Spain (*aracus maior* = *vicia sativa var.*, *faba veterum* = *vicia faba var.*, *ervilia silvestris* = *lathyrus var.*, *lagopus trifolium* = *trifolium var.*). In July 1624, as he was herb-gathering in Wiltshire, he noticed sainfoin in flower at Langford and Stapleford. He also worked on the description of lucernes, vetches and vetchlings (*lathyri*), but they were almost always foreign specimens.[91] The compilation of a complete account of British flora was a task beyond the powers of a single individual, mainly because it was being carried out at least fifty years later than the analogous Continental works. This meant that problems of nomenclature of the kind already mentioned had to be solved and at the same time adaptations were needed for the foreign specimens. The institution of public and private botanical gardens was essential, not only to spread information about the new plants, but to identify the varieties in the British Isles correctly.[92]

In the course of a few years, in the short distance between Oxford and London, many attempts were made to describe British flora. Taking as their model the herb-gathering tours organized by Aldrovandi and Pena, a group of people connected with the Apothecaries' Society planned a long journey through Kent and along its coasts. Thanks to Thomas Johnson, who had the scientific results of the journey published, we learn that various kinds of clover (*T. fragiferum*, Clus., *luteum minimum*, Lob., *corniculatum*, Dod., *luteum majus*, *pratense album*, *p. purpureum*,

---

[91] See Gunther, *Early British Botanists*, pp. 34 ff., 36–7, 45, 51, 67 ff., 101–2.

[92] Gunther, *Early British Botanists*, thought very highly of Goodyer's discoveries of local flora and Raven, *English Naturalists*, p. 291, rated him a good deal lower as a scientist. He certainly shut himself up within the sheltering walls of Magdalen College too early and never produced a complete work, even in manuscript. However he built up a specialized botany library for his College, which was necessary to sort out with great care and patience the many errors that had sprung from haste and competition between English and Continental botanists during the late sixteenth century. After the Civil War, a King's man like Goodyer was at a disadvantage with respect to the intellectuals who sided with Parliament.

acetosum, pes leporis) were found in the neighbourhood of Thanet, Margate, Nash and Sandwich. Along the road from Canterbury to London, one plant was even identified as *medica minor, medica arabica,* Cam. The good botanists, satisfied with their discoveries, did not, however, consider it useful to record the cultivated plants, thus depriving posterity of a precise picture of the varieties and species grown in the fields, meadows and orchards of Kent, the garden of England.[93] Johnson had already been herb-gathering in other parts of the country (in the North, including Yorkshire in 1626) and was to make other journeys round London, where he worked as a pharmacist. With the help of the specimens gathered during these journeys, and of Tradescant's garden, an inexhaustible source of specimens, Johnson and Goodyer produced a new, fully revised edition of Gerard's herbal. It constituted a step towards an account of British flora, which, for lack of more complete previous collections, provides poor evidence of the period of transition through which wild and and cultivated plant-life was passing in the middle of the seventeenth century. The interest in foreign plants displayed in private botanical gardens favoured the spread of certain species beyond their growers' intentions.

The already-mentioned royalist, Anglo-French bond reappears clearly in the works of Parkinson, dedicated to Henrietta Maria (1629) and to Charles I (1640).[94] The London botanist was trying to bring writings on the subject up to date in England, where they still swore by the works of Matthias de L'Obel, by taking into account what had been published in the first decades of the century. The result was a striking medley of English plants, some described for the first time, and of European and exotic plants which could fulfil a useful purpose. The first work dealt mainly with horticultural species and the renewal of their cultivation in England at that time. The volume was dedicated advisedly to Henrietta Maria, and emphasized the gender connection between the Queen and gardening as a womanly task. Tusser and Markham had also spoken of horticulture as essentially an occupation for housewives. There are other iconographical and literary indications too that this economic sector was

---

[93] See Raven, *English Naturalists*, pp. 276–7; T. Johnson, *Descriptio itineris plantarum investigationis ergo suscepti in agrum Cantianum AD 1632*, London 1632, pp. 6, 14, 18, 21, 24, 29, 31, 33.

[94] See Parkinson, *Paradisi in sole*; idem, *Theatrum botanicum*. On Parkinson see Raven, *English Naturalists*, pp. 248 ff.; Henrey, *British Botanical and Horticultural Literature*, pp. 79 ff.

run by women and probably underestimated in the farm accounts until men took it over.[95]

The *Theatrum botanicum* also kept to the practical approach, the horticultural species were still given importance and the comparison with Continental varieties continued. Parkinson was trying to bring L'Obel's writings up to date, using works published in subsequent decades without neglecting the hard task of identifying the new local species.[96] He pointed out new varieties of *onobrychis* in the class of legumes. Only the first, *onobrychis vulgaris*, grew under the hedges and sometimes in the open fields in several places in England. All the others were foreign and only grew in botanical gardens. Following L'Obel, he gave the French name as *sainfoin*, the English as medick fetchling. Later Parkinson was able to identify ten varieties of *hedysarum*, including the one called French Honeysuckle in English.[97] The chapter on lucerne also contained a good discussion of the subject. Parkinson pointed out Gerard's mistake, identified the variety from the shape of the pod, announcing that his correspondent from Spain, the above-mentioned Boel, had a dozen different specimens available. He described the different colours of the flowers very accurately, recalled that it grew wild in Spain and Provence, was used as fodder in Spain, the Low Countries, France and Germany, and finally suggested that there was some in the fields and marshes around Woolwich and Deptford, south of London. Despite this accuracy, his account of where it grew was rather sketchy – from Italy to Belgian Gaul and thence into Burgundy. He was not even disturbed to learn, from his sources, that the French called it both lucerne and sainfoin, without making any distinction between them. We suspect

[95] A number of specialized horticultural booklets were produced expressly to promote ladies' interest in gardening, for an example see W. Lawson, *The Housewife's Garden, together with the Husbandry of Bees* (London 1617) reprinted with an Introduction by R. Verey, London 1983; see also Henrey, *British Botanical and Horticultural Literature*, vol. II, pp. 577–84. However after Tusser, Markham and other male writers, horticulture became progressively a man's trade. It has been noted, see above, note 1, that only one English woman signed her own commonplace book on husbandry: C. Merchant, *Death of Nature. Women, Ecology and the Scientific Revolution*, San Francisco 1980, has dealt with the role of women in seventeenth-century natural studies.

[96] Twenty-eight of the species had never been described before: see Henrey, *British Botanical and Horticultural Literature*, p. 82.

[97] See Parkinson, *Theatrum botanicum*, pp. 1081 ff.; I believe that *Hedysarum clypeatum vulgaris* was the same as *French Honeysuckle*, whilst Parkinson thought it corresponded to *Hedysarum onobrychis*, L., that is *sainfoin*, however *Onobrychis vulgaris* was the variety now called *O. caput galli*. Spanish sainfoin, requiring a Mediterranean climate, does not grow wild in England.

that the English specimens that came into his hands grew wild in the fields. By the 1640s, English farmers were experimenting with lucerne and sainfoin and so these plants very likely spread spontaneously, where ploughing and manuring of the fields created a habitat favourable to their reproduction. Grain bought on the Continent in the famine years (1622, 1623 and 1629, for example) and used as seed, could easily have had seeds of lucerne or sainfoin among it, which would have sprung up spontaneously in southern England. Of course, such spontaneous spreading of the two plants coincided with their diffusion in French agriculture in the early seventeenth century.

5. SAMUEL HARTLIB AND RICHARD WESTON

During the Civil War and the Protectorate there was a great deal of propaganda about agricultural improvement, which Parliamentary intellectuals considered to be part of a general plan for improving the economic situation and reducing social conflict. The history of those years, and the relationship between the Puritans and the scientific revolution, have been dealt with from many points of view. We shall touch on these discussions here only in connection with the diffusion of the new forage-crops.[98] The personal contacts and exchange of letters, which in the previous decades had been the favourite means of communication between botanists and landowners, also became the means of spreading and discussing the agricultural innovations. The story of the French horses sent as a gift to Charles I, which were dying of exhaustion when they got to the English Channel, but picked up strength to face the crossing after grazing in a lucerne field, aroused the curiosity and interest of the Duke of Newcastle and Sir John Walters of Sarsden, Oxfordshire, who had those seeds sent to them from France. In 1636 Bulstrode Whitelocke, who wrote a long diary during the reign of Charles I, recalled his own experiments with lucerne or sainfoin. And again in the 1630s and 1640s, the Duke of Lennox used his family connections with France to obtain the same seeds.[99] Lord Zouche's garden and the Botanic Garden of Oxford also played a leading role in

---

[98] See C. Webster, *The Great Instauration. Science, Medicine and Reform, 1626–1660*, London 1975, and Thirsk, 'Agricultural Innovations', pp. 533–89, especially pp. 542–59.

[99] See F. Emery, 'The Early Adoption of Sown Grasses in England and Wales: Evidence from Probate Inventories' (I am able to quote this unpublished paper thanks to the generosity of the late Frank Emery); Thirsk, 'Agricultural innovations', pp. 555–6: the

the spread of the seeds within certain groups of English high society. In these circles there was no lack of ideas, curiosity and interest in putting into practice the foreign customs read, and heard of, over and over again, for decades. What was most lacking was an agency to provide accurate and concise information, and above all to co-ordinate so many partial experiments. The model was not far to seek. Samuel Hartlib, a Pole who had fled from the horrors of the Thirty Years War and anti-Protestant persecution, had been living in London for thirty years. With the help of a group of Puritan intellectuals, he organized something like Renaudot's Bureau d'Adresse. In 1647 he put forward the idea of an Office of Address for Accommodations, which was to follow the Paris model of a labour exchange; while an Office of Address for Communications was to deal with religious and educational problems and the discoveries useful for the material conditions and intellectual life of man. Though they did not succeed in creating a permanent institution, being divided amongst themselves and without sufficient funds, the group round Hartlib acted with great moral and political fervour in the decade following 1646.[100] It was mainly Samuel Hartlib, through his work as a publisher and journalist, who helped to establish contacts between the reformers and innovators and the wider public.

In 1650 Hartlib published an anonymous text, the brief account of a journey made for agricultural purposes through Flanders and Brabant, by an English gentleman. The first edition was sold out within a few months and Hartlib brought out a second one after gathering more information about its author, Sir Richard Weston. The story of this edition and the content of the travel diary is well known, but it never ceases to afford new ideas and new information.[101] Sir Richard Weston, of Sutton, West

story of the horses takes up, almost literally, a passage from Columella: 'lean cattle of every kind grow fat on it; it has medicinal value for an ailing beast', II.x.25 (see L. J. M. Columella, *On agriculture,* transl. by Harrison Boyd Ash, Loeb Classical Library, Harvard–London 1960, vol. I, p. 172). It is doubtful whether the plant in question was really *sainfoin-onobrychis,* which was generally grown on arable land, not in meadows. It is however probable that Sir John Walters grew *sainfoin-onobrychis* successfully on the light, chalky soil of his estate in the Cotswolds.

100 See Webster, *The Great Instauration,* pp. 67–77.

101 See for example the two most recent discussions by A. R. Mitchell, 'Sir Richard Weston and the Spread of Clover Cultivation', *AHR,* 22, 1974, pp. 160–61, and Thirsk, 'Agricultural innovations', p. 549, which outline considerable differences in the relationship between Hartlib and Sir Richard. The editions and reprints are as follows: 1. [R. Weston], *A Discours of Husbandrie used in Brabant and Flanders . . .* , London 1605 [but 1650], Introduction by Samuel Hartlib, 26 pp.; 2. *Samuel Hartlib His Legacie or an Enlargement of the Discours of Husbandrie . . .* , London 1651, 131 pp.;

Surrey, began farming by experimenting with sainfoin and water-meadows. When the Civil War broke out he sided with the Royalists and in 1643 or 1644 his property was confiscated and he was forced into exile in the Low Countries. Here, in 1645, he wrote the brief account of his agronomic observations, using the literary mode of a spiritual testament to his sons. When he returned to England he continued his experiments on the cultivation of clover. He exhorted his fellow-citizens to make the stretch of the river Wey leading into the Thames navigable, to give producers easier access to the London market. He died in 1652. A King's man, Sir Richard remained on the margins of Hartlib's group, without being any the less disposed to collaborate with visitors or to correspond with anyone who asked him for information, as did John Lloyd of Woking. Moreover, such outstanding figures as William Petty and Elias Ashmole visited Sir Richard's estate, linking his name forever with the experimental growing of forage-crops in England.[102]

In those years at least four of Hartlib's correspondents and collaborators were discussing the cultivation of clover – Cressy Dymock, Colonel Hutchinson, Robert Boyle and Sir Cheney Culpeper. Boyle sent Hartlib an anonymous manuscript on the subject, which was very likely Richard Weston's *Discours*.[103] It should be said at once that in the hard years of the Civil War and the Protectorate, farmers' attention was shifting from crops that were of great value but were unusual, like lucerne and sainfoin, to those that transformed plants native to the British Isles into specialized crops, like clover. In the years 1652 and 1653, Hartlib was engaged, among other things, in answering correspondence about the cultivation of clover.[104] This intense activity left its mark on the accounts for the publication of the second edition of the *Discours*. It was

---

3. *A Discours of Husbandrie . . . The second edition corrected and enlarged*, London 1652, 30 pp.; 4. *Samuel Hartlib His Legacie or an Enlargement of the Discours of Husbandrie . . . Wherein are bequethed to the Commonwealth of England . . . in reference to Universal Husbandry. The second edition augmented with an Appendix*, London 1652, 131 pp. and appendix; 5. *Samuel Hartlib His Legacie of Husbandry . . . several Augmentations and enriching Enlargements in this Third Edition*, London 1655, 303 pp. (quoted hereafter). To these should be added two later editions, which are pirated or anonymous editions: London 1670, ed. by G. Reeve, and London 1726. Hartlib's complete bibliography is in G. H. Turnbull, *Hartlib, Dury and Comenius. Gleanings from Hartlib's Papers*, London 1947, and Webster, *The Great Instauration*, pp. 562–3.

[102] Mitchell, *Sir Richard Weston*, p. 160; Thirsk, 'Agricultural innovations', p. 554.

[103] See *ibid.*, pp. 553–4.

[104] See for example Sheffield, UL, Hartlib mss 7/114, 26/87/1–3, 67/23/4–8. The Hartlib manuscripts are quoted here with the permission of the owner, Lord Delamare.

sent to press in April 1651 and entailed an expense of £11 for forty reams of paper, a total of twenty thousand sheets, sufficient for the fifteen thousand pages of text alone, without counting the flyleaves. The bill from the printer Richard Wodenoth calculated a variable number of copies, 527 or 627, to be distributed among himself, Cliffe, Florence and Hartlib. Elsewhere, by adding up the number of volumes that had been divided, for sale, between Cliffe, Francis, Dury and Coxe, only 447 copies were calculated. From this scanty documentation we can surmise that the group calculated the costs of publication of the short treatise to divide the profits. Some difficulty had arisen between the printer, who considered the price of twelve pence a copy too high, and William Dugard, schoolmaster, journalist and himself a publisher, who had not received his share of copies for sale. Wodenoth wrote out a bill of £12 2s 9d on 6 July 1651, for books sold to Samuel Hartlib, most striking among them being Hobbes' *Leviathan*, a history of chemistry, a book on rhetoric and one on shorthand.[105] It is unclear how much profit they made, but obviously the little group of subscribers undertook to sell the pamphlet, using the same way of circulating information that we have already seen used when communicating by letter. The large number of reprints of this and other works on agriculture in a very short space of time confirms the importance of the press in spreading innovations and the almost exponential growth of the readership.[106]

---

[105] See *ibid.*, mss 31/20/1–12. On Dury, Cliffe, Dugard see *DNB*, and Webster, *The Great Instauration.*

[106] The following formula may help us to estimate the ratio of printed copies to readers:

Copies (1650–55) =

$$[C_1 + (C_1 + C_2) + (C_1 + C_2 + C_3 + C_4) + 0 + 0 + (C_1 + C_2 + C_3 + C_4 + C_5)] \cdot n,$$

Where $C_{1, 2 \ldots 5}$ is the number of copies printed in the years 1650, 1651, 1652, 1652 . . . , 1655; n = readers per copy, unknown factor. Keeping the approximate number of copies per work constant at 600, we should get a total of $(600 + 1200 + 2400 + 0 + 0 + 3000) = 7200$ copies available for the whole five-year period. Of the 5,281,347 English people only the 25–59 years age-group in 1656 was greatly interested in reading the *Legacy*, that is only 2,204,962 people: of this group we have taken into consideration only the male population, 1,102,481 people, roughly 50 per cent (see above, note 95). Counting literacy at about 40 per cent, the number of potential readers goes down to 440,992, equal to 61 readers for each of the copies available up to 1656. The above figures are taken from Wrigley and Schofield, *The Population History of England*, p. 528; R. J. Sullivan, 'Measurement of English Farming Technological Change, 1523–1900', *Explorations in Economic History*, 21, 1984, p. 280. On diffusion of agricultural information through the press see also T. Kiaergaard, 'Origins of Economic Growth in European Societies since the xvith Century: The Case of Agriculture', *The Journal of European Economic History*, 15, 1986, pp. 591–8.

Richard Weston addressed his memoir of agricultural travels to his sons, going straight to the point after a couple of implicit references to Cicero and Xenophon. As he travelled from Dunkirk to Antwerp he noticed that poor, sandy soil, on which wheat, barley and peas could not be grown, produced rich crops of rye, oats and buckwheat. Moreover, between Antwerp and Ghent the main crop was not wheat but hemp, of which an acre was worth four or five of grain, producing hemp to the value of £40 or £50 on the Antwerp market. It was followed by turnips and in April of the following year clover seed was scattered on the field and harrowed in lightly, together with oats. Under these conditions the field yielded three crops of hay per year and was left under clover for four or five years.[107] A similar rotation was applied on another farm that Weston visited in the following spring. The fallow field was broken up with a heavy plough, then cross-ploughed and the stubble and weeds burned. After this it was well manured, ploughed, and sown with rye. This was followed by oats; it was later harrowed and finally sown with clover. Once the land was tilled, it was fertilized with half the usual amount of manure and sown with hemp, together with clover. At this juncture an acre of clover was worth £12 and was enough to keep four cows for a year; alternatively, it produced seed after the first mowing, worth sixpence a pound, a total gain of £8.[108] The priorities of Robert Loder and so many other farmers changed considerably in those decades: they no longer alternated grain and barley on the basis of the prices of the previous season, but planted a larger variety of products, hemp, grains with good nutritional value (though not suitable for making bread), turnips, and clover as fresh fodder for the cattle. It was a continuous cycle, which kept the workers employed throughout the year and had transformed the peasants of the Low Countries into the best-off social group in the countryside of Europe.[109]

---

[107] *Samuel Hartlib His Legacie.*

[108] *Ibid.*, pp. 7–14.

[109] On farming in the Low Countries see B. H. Slicher Van Bath, 'The rise of intensive husbandry in the Low Countries', in J. S. Bromley and E. H. Koззman (eds.), *Britain and the Netherlands*, London 1960; J. De Vries, *The Dutch Rural Economy in the Golden Age, 1500–1700*, New Haven–London 1974; H. Van Der Wee and E. Van Cauwenbergh (eds.), *Productivity of land and agricultural innovation in the Low Countries (1250–1800)*, Louvain 1978; S. Schama, *The Embarrassment of Riches. An interpretation of Dutch Culture in the Golden Age*, New York 1987, pp. 129–220. Actually relations between the Low Countries and English farmers were confined to the 1660s–1680s and the years after 1730, when the Dutch were spared or less affected by military operations against Spanish rule or against local rebellions: see M. P. Gutmann, *War and Rural Life in the Early Modern Low Countries*, Princeton 1980.

The sequence recommended by Weston to reclaim the heath and wastelands seems to have been as follows – devonshiring (paring and burning of the grassy turf) followed by treatment with a mixture of manure, lime and marl: the soil thus prepared would be equal to the best land of England or Flanders, capable of producing hemp, turnips, clover and then wheat and barley. Contrary to tradition, the idea was advancing that good land was of the poor variety, but loose and easy to till, and so was preferable to soil that was rich but only suited to a limited number of crops. Weston's methods broke away from the idea of self-sufficiency on the farm and calculated the relative prices of crops with a high market value, which grew well on quite poor land. Alternatively, he advised following the practice of the sheep-farmers of St Leonards Forest in Surrey, who collected by day the sand where they had folded their sheep by night, producing a great quantity of manure. By following these practices, an acre sown with hemp yielded £40 worth of beaten hemp when sold on the market of Ghent. Calculating rents, taxes and losses at £750 per 25 acres, the income amounted to £1,500. Moreover, to the harvest of hemp he added the income from the production of turnips for the same year and from the crops mentioned above for the subsequent years. Adding one to the other, in the short space of five years 100 acres of land so treated would give the owner-occupier over £7,000.[110]

There was, however, a weak point in the system that Weston recommended, and he was aware of it. It was seed production. Every farmer not only had to have sufficient seed to continue production but needed to be particularly careful to use only the best quality, from Eastern Europe for hemp, from Flanders for clover. Each product could also be sold as seed, the cost of which was always entered in the detailed accounting. The neighbours, filled with admiration at the successful improvement, would be the farmer's first customers for the new seed, especially for clover seed. Historians have never really given Weston his due for the attention he paid to seed. He said the hemp should be changed at least every four years, regardless of the expense. Although hemp, turnips and clover were already grown in England, there was the same difference between them and the Flanders varieties that existed between wild and garden plants. Lastly he pointed out, accurately and in agreement with recent observations on grassland management, that white clover would get the better of red clover, in a field planted with the latter, in the course of five years. This effect was produced by the cattle

[110] *Samuel Hartlib*, pp. 14–22.

put to graze in the field. Weston's readers, among others, at once had difficulty in dehusking clover seed. In response to a letter of enquiry, in February 1651, Weston gave the name of a certain Sadler, with a shop in Bucklersbury, London, who supplied him in the last three or four years.[111] In the 1651 edition, in which Hartlib published Weston's text, together with a collection of letters and comments on the subject, he had already given the name of another London merchant, James Long in Billingsgate, who was prepared to get clover, lucerne and sainfoin seed from Flanders and France at a fair price.

Weston and Hartlib knew of each other, but were not in direct contact, and this is further proved by the data collected by Hartlib, included, at least in part, in the issues of the *Legacy*. Among other things, as often happened, Hartlib received an undated, anonymous letter, written just after the publication of the *Discours*, an extract of which had been published in the first edition of the *Legacy*. In it the author, perhaps a fellow exile in Flanders, reported that Richard Weston had told him that he had produced a good field of clover on what had once been moorland. He answered 'without any other helpe than my owne memory', but actually often giving Weston's opinion, calling him simply 'the Gentleman', that he did not consider sowing clover after the last harvest to be an improvement, but he thought forage crops were good for cultivation on any soil, all the better if deep and light, at an initial expense of only five or six shillings an acre. The clover-field was excellent for grazing cattle and sheep, which would manure the soil directly, following the practice at Godalming, in Surrey. However, it was better not to let over-heavy cattle graze on it, so as not to destroy too many plants. To this he added details on the risk that bad weather might damage the blossom and the production of seed.[112]

These issues reappear in another unpublished letter that shows how welcoming and helpful Weston was to enquiring visitors, and that accounts of these visits circulated in several manuscript copies before being partially published.[113] Weston had thirty or forty acres of clover, of which he later sowed ten acres with barley, and made a series of

[111] See *ibid.*, pp. 8, 12, 15, 23, 26; Moore, *Grassland Husbandry*, p. 32; Mitchell, *Sir Richard Weston*, p. 160.

[112] See Sheffield, UL, Hartlib mss 26/87/1–3.

[113] See Oxford, BO, Ashmole ms 358 (Ix); London, BL, Add. ms 33509; letters partially published by A. Speed, *Adam out of Eden, or an Abstract of divers excellent experiments touching the Advancement of Husbandry*, London 1659 quoted here from Oxford, BO, Ashmole ms 358 (Ix).

experiments to solve the seed problem. Presumably in the years, or year, before his death, he had divided his land into two fields. He sowed one with seed from Flanders, the other with seeds he had gathered himself and left in their husks. This was an attempt to avoid the task of threshing and winnowing. Sixteenth-century Italian books also recalled that clover and lucerne could be sown in their husks, provided a larger quantity was used. Of the two fields, the first had grown normally by mid May, the second had not taken hold so well. In Weston's opinion, it was difficult to tell whether the husks were full or empty. Notwithstanding this, he had decided to use the second meadow for grazing and keep the first for seed, because it had grown on much wetter soil; or else because of the shortage of hay and its high price, £3 a load for ordinary quality, he intended to mow his water-meadow (he had known about watering meadows for some time). Should the drought last (he was probably referring to the famous drought of 1652),[114] he would cut the flower-heads of the clover and leave them to ripen in the sun, thus saving the hay crop too. In fact Weston was imitating the method of gathering seed recommended by Agostino Gallo for lucerne, and still used in very recent times in central Italy. He said that he would never master the cultivation of clover until he had managed to produce the necessary amount of seed himself. Indeed, foreign imports tended to be mixtures of old, new and not fully ripened seed. He repeated the advice about sowing clover alone to get the best results. Certain difficulties about supplies of seed remained unchanged for the next two hundred years. Besides formulating English experience of clover theoretically, Weston was the first to discover the structural difficulties which English farmers met with in adopting foreign crops in the field.

After speaking of the yield and soil, Weston recalled that another plant, 'saintfoyne', was extremely profitable and could be mown six or eight times a year, but needed rich soil. Like some English and many French farmers of his time, Weston was using *sainfoin* in its common meaning of lucerne. Then came another letter on 'esperate' (for *esparcette*), presented as a species of clover. The text follows, very closely, the only known source on the subject, the pages of Olivier de Serres that had already been published by Hartlib in the *Legacy*. Once again problems connected with harvesting the seed and how easily sainfoin would reseed the meadow, as well as its inclusion in the cycle of

---

[114] See J. M. Stratton and J. H. Brown, *Agricultural Records AD 220–1977*, London 1969, p. 50.

cereals grown, aroused the author's interest. But these pages take us back to the problem created by having two plants, lucerne and sainfoin, with the same name (*sainfoin*), but with very different uses, growing together. This is not the only case where Weston appears to be directly responsible for reporting his own experiments. In February 1651 he had written to John Lloyd of Forest Glyncoth, Carmarthenshire, explaining the difficulties of harvesting the seed, mentioning the name of a London merchant and advising him to sow clover together with barley. Weston and Lloyd became neighbours, when the latter married the widow of James Zouche, Welsh like himself, and moved to the estate at Woking, near Sutton Court. The lucerne seed used by Weston probably came from the Hackney garden owned by the Zouches, already mentioned as a private botanical garden (see above, 4.2.). These family connections provided a channel for the spread of the cultivation of clover in Wales in the following decade.[115]

5.1. Hartlib and his correspondents

In 1651 Hartlib had published a collection of letters on the subject of the shortcomings of English farming and ways of remedying them, under the title *His Legacy, or Enlargement of the Discourse of Husbandrie*. Hartlib listed the main faults of English farmers. They did not improve their meadows, they neglected plants like clover, lucerne and sainfoin, did not irrigate meadows in the Lombard manner to increase production, did not sow the best forage-crops on fields to be turned to pasture. He went on to list ninety species of grass for fodder and twenty-three varieties of clover.[116] The efforts of the botanists who had preceded him had not escaped his notice. The most clear-cut point he made concerned lucerne and sainfoin, known abroad but little used in England. Weston was well known before 1644 for his experiments on water-meadows and on *sainfoin–onobrychis*, which English historians always interpret as sainfoin, not knowing the ambiguity of the term.[117] Actually, as we have seen above, Sir Richard worked on lucerne, not sainfoin, which was a by

---

[115] See F. Emery, 'The Mechanics of Innovation: Clover Cultivation in Wales before 1750', *Journal of Historical Geography*, II, 1, 1976, pp. 36–7.

[116] See *Samuel Hartlib*, p. 39.

[117] See E. L. Jones, 'Agriculture and economic growth in England, 1660–1750: Agricultural change', *The Journal of Economic History*, 25, 1965, pp. 1–18; Kerridge, *The Agricultural Revolution*, pp. 278 ff.; Thirsk, 'Agricultural innovations', pp. 556 ff. G. E. Fussell, *Jethro Tull: His Influence on Mechanized Agriculture*, Reading 1973.

no means negligible factor in his successful use of the species. The constant risk of misunderstanding was pointed out at once by Hartlib, who published a long letter on the subject, which Arnold Boate had sent him from Paris, where he resided.[118] The information that Parkinson had collected proved to be accurate. *Sainfoin*, in English, could be called medick fetchling, a plant very similar to the one called French Honeysuckle, which grew in many English gardens and was used for fodder in France, especially in the neighbourhood of Paris. According to the data collected by Boate, *sainfoin* had been cultivated for seven years in the countryside round Paris. It had already spread to southern England and could be found in Cobham Park, near Gravesend, Kent. Boate suggested that land should be carefully ploughed more than once, that weeds should be pulled up before they were fully grown, and warned against economizing on the quantity of seed sown, particularly because that imported from the Continent contained a proportion of old seed. It was an excellent plant for improving poor, dry soil, but for rich damp soils it was better to use large clover (the literal translation of *grand treffle*, one of the French names for lucerne, it should be remembered). *Luzerne*, another plant recently brought to Paris from southern France, had shown at once how valuable it was for producing fodder and how much better it was than *sainfoin–onobrychis* for improving soil. This, too, had already crossed the Channel and was working wonders in England. On the whole, Boate seems to be speaking from hearsay. The written source that he followed was the work of Olivier de Serres, the *Théâtre d'agriculture*; he did not notice that the *sainfoin* mentioned there was not the one called by the same name in the plain of Paris.[119]

Boate's letter started up a lively correspondence between Hartlib, the readers of the *Legacy* and Boate, from Paris, on the differences between *sainfoin* and *luzerne*: where to purchase the seed, at what price, how much to sow per acre, at what point in the rotation system to introduce it, on what soils to plant it and whether to feed it green. After some initial hesitation, not overly damp, light and loose soil was advised, to be ploughed three times from October on, and not too heavily manured. April sowing was to consist of a sixth of the quantity necessary for the ground in question (otherwise, 12–15 pounds of seed per acre were advised, very little in comparison with the 35–40 kg per hectare used in northern Europe today). Oats as a cover crop would protect lucerne

---

[118] Webster, *The Great Instauration*, p. 431; *Samuel Hartlib*, pp. 1–4.
[119] See De Serres, *Théâtre d'agriculture*, pp. 271–3.

during the first few months. Climate, of course, played an essential role. Lucerne was cut five or six times a year in the southern provinces of France, while in northern France and in England only two crops could be expected, in June and September. They should be dried as quickly as possible. Lucerne was excellent for all kinds of cattle, for fattening or milk production, and splendid for horses. After the second mowing, the animals could graze on it during the winter, until late March. The seed should be harvested before the second mowing, using the method described several times above. The hay would keep two or three years and the crop from an acre would be enough for three horses for the whole year, according to Columella's old reckoning. Other information came from a doctor of La Rochelle, resident in London in the middle of the century. He considered most of Boate's information was correct, except for the date of sowing, which should be changed from April to March, and the amount to be sown. Boate's final advice, based on information gathered from seed merchants, was to sow ten pounds per English acre; he added that the difference between *sainfoin* and *luzerne*, as found in the plain of Paris, tended to diminish when they both grew on very similar dry, wet or poor soils.[120] Such imprecision was largely responsible for the two plants being mistaken for each other and became crucial once the seeds were no longer used by the producer but were mixed by merchants and even sold abroad. Obviously the selected, botanically well-defined plants that grew in the various private botanical gardens of England constituted an essential point of reference but unfortunately were unable to supply a sufficient quantity of seed to satisfy the growing demand for the product.

In 1652 and 1653 the problem of French seed was faced once more. In some French provinces the name *sainfoin* was applied to *luzerne* and Sir Cheney Culpeper expressly asked to have specimens of the three species in question, to test which was most suited to the English environment. The Paris seed market also depended partly on the *Midi*, and so could not guarantee a constant supply of this crop, which, as a result, had highly variable prices (see below). Little by little, light was thrown on the ambiguous presentation of de Serres, which suggested that in Provence and some other regions *sainfoin* and *luzerne* were the same thing and that the *esparcet* of the Dauphiné corresponded to *sainfoin* in the rest of France. Anxious to get correct information, someone, perhaps Boate, wrote to Die to get clarification of what Olivier de Serres had not

[120] See *Samuel Hartlib*, pp. 98–104.

explained very well: that is, that *esparcet* did not grow alone but mixed with other varieties and so was difficult to distinguish from *onobrychis*. But it had to be accepted that there were minute differences between the seeds and only the expert's eye could distinguish the different species.[121]

This confrontation between seventeenth-century English improvers and Continental peasant farming is of great interest. On the one hand was the advantage of a great number of species, and the fact that ordinary people were used to recognizing at once those differences which, in England, were the subject of discussion between groups of intellectuals and agricultural improvers. On the other, there was muddle and inaccuracy on the part of farmers who were not using their productive capacities fully. The work of choice and experiment seemed at first to bring a broader outlook, because it encouraged study and made new agricultural species available, but since its aim was to increase production to the utmost, it carried within it the dilemma of selection. This point of view was to be found in the pages of the *Legacy*, which showed an interest in other botanical varieties used as fodder in France – vetch, *romayne* or *vicia aphaca* vetch, or spurry (*Spergula arvensis*) in Brabant – but which were being studied to obtain a selection of the species most suited to the English environment.[122] The discussion on the productive potential of clover, a less sought-after and less productive plant, but simpler to use, was introduced with this in mind.

Clover-growing was at an advantage initially, because it grew spontaneously in England, it was a plant that adapted better to all kinds of soil, acid or alkaline, and could stand badly drained soil better,[123] while lucernes could not stand stagnant water round their roots (the so-called wet-foot, as it was called, even in the late seventeenth century). The quantity of seed recommended was also more correct (10, 12–14 lbs per acre, not too much below the 25–35 kg per hectare used today), but in some cases much lower quantities were advised (4–5 lbs an acre, obviously to save on seed). On seed alone the farmer spent 11s 6d at 12–14d a pound, or 5s 9d when seed cost only 6d. To this had to be added the cost of preparing the ground (three ploughings), manuring, irrigation

---

[121] See *ibid.*, pp. 250–5. This practice had been described by Estienne, *Pratum* (1554), and again mentioned by J. Miège, *La vie rurale du sillon alpin*, Paris 1961, pp. 538 ff. in our times.

[122] See *Samuel Hartlib*, pp. 255–8.

[123] On modern seeding ratios see F. Crescini, *Piante erbacee di grande cultura*, Rome 1951, pp. 408–65, *passim* and Davies, *The Grass Crop*, pp. 270–4.

if necessary, hoeing and haymaking. In the end, the profits were quite considerable, despite some serious failures. A certain R.H. cultivated two acres of clover, sowing 15 lbs per acre after barley. At the end of May, he got a first crop of two loads, worth £5 and a second in August of three loads, worth £9; he also harvested seed, sold at 1s 4d a lb, making a total profit of £30, without counting the income from winter grazing. Sir Thomas Payton wrote that, from April to October, his six acres of clover had kept thirteen cows, six oxen, three horses and twenty-six pigs, giving an income of 30s a week or £40 for the six months. The harvesting of the seed by the producer was certainly the right way to solve the problem of keeping it unadulterated and those who had tried to grow clover before the publication of Weston's text had solved the issue for themselves. A letter from Upton in 1653 told how, after sowing Dutch seed once, the farmer had managed to produce enough to sell some in London, at 8–10d for the new and 6d for the old. He only managed to thresh three gallons of seed a day, however. An anonymous owner in Kent obtained clean seed by using repeated threshing and fine sieves. A certain Stoughton, a gentleman of Norfolk,[124] who had been an expert on clover-growing for years, used a millstone to separate the seed from the husks, a process which only cost him 3d a pound. Sir Cheney Culpeper campaigned actively for the cultivation of clover in Ireland, newly subdued by the Parliamentary troops. He had sent seed to Robert Wood, with instructions to distribute it among the officers of the English army, to bring about agricultural improvement. Over there they were posing the same questions as English farmers, though in a generally more backward setting. Actually, the seeds were two years old when they arrived, and in any case using the pasture for grazing was the best way to avoid destroying the green sward, which was the final product of the investment, not a stage in convertible husbandry.[125]

The practical details of all that wealth of information and knowledge, accumulated between 1550 and 1650, which had formerly only been applied here and there in eastern England, began to be discussed and spread in certain circles of farming people, through their personal contacts in London. On 23 June 1652 Robert Child, one of Hartlib's most active collaborators on the agriculture and natural history of Ireland,

---

[124] The Stoughtons, Puritan gentry with links in the colony of Plymouth, Massachusetts, were also in contact with Hartlib: see Webster, *The Great Instauration, passim.*

[125] See *Samuel Hartlib*, pp. 236–7, 240–1, 245, 248–9; Webster, *The Great Instauration*, especially pp. 431–3.

wrote from Lisneygarvey, in the county of Antrim, saying that he had received a parcel of seed, probably sent to him by Anthony Morgan, and wished to carry out some agricultural experiments. He looked forward to receiving any new book on agriculture, or some novelty from Walter Blith (see below) and told of the great endeavour the English were making to drain the Irish bogs. The arrival of another parcel of seed in the winter of 1653 brought a second long letter from Child to Hartlib, telling of the progress being made on the natural history of Ireland, of the experiments on the effect of nitrates on the growth of cereals and on the grafting and domestication of fruit-trees.[126] Having first-hand experience of these things, since his brother owned a farm in Gravesend, Kent, Child let slip his conviction that agricultural method in Kent was superior because there were no furrows running the length of the fields there and they were constantly being cross-ploughed and harrowed. To this important comment Child added the suggestion that manure should be used very sparingly and substituted by peat.[127] In short, the experimental farmer who wanted to increase the botanical resources of English agriculture had first of all to fight against the two technical causes that continually hindered any attempt at innovation, the loss of seed due to ploughing in furrows and the competition from weeds, contained in seed form in cattle dung. Child may never have read Agostino Gallo or Olivier de Serres, but points of contact had by then been established between the best English practice and Continental literature on agriculture in the Classical tradition, circulating for so long in the previous century.

The same approach was also adopted for other plants introduced into the commercial farming recommended by Weston and already practised by a few farmers. In 1658 Sir William Boswell recommended the use of turnips in various ways, either boiled as fodder, or for the extraction of oil from the seed, since London was becoming the chief market for this product; or else an attempt could be made at growing hemp with seed imported from Flanders and Holland. Though he was away from Huntingdon on a visit to Coventry, Boswell kept discussing recent methods. He would have liked to make a decision with his tenants on the use of carrots and potatoes for fattening cattle, following Richard Weston's idea of boiled turnips. He was also determined to try growing potatoes and turnips on some marshy ground after laying it a foot higher

---

[126] See Sheffield, UL, Hartlib mss 15/5/12, 15/15/18–19.
[127] *Ibid.*, mss 15/15/19.

by ploughing, a system described by Walter Blith in 1649.[128] But the new enthusiasm for the Low Countries never quite ruled out the old Classical and Continental model of agriculture, which at times was actually strengthened by comparison. Peter Smyth, a correspondent of John Beale and a farmer of Dyffrin in Wales, began a long letter comparing English and advanced Dutch agriculture, recalling Virgil's pre-eminent position in the study of the physics, politics and mathematics of agriculture. The nectarines, almonds, apples, pears and vines in his garden had yielded greater profits than twenty acres of pasture. The idea of dividing the pasture and arable land into three parts and leaving one to grass for ten years, thereby increasing the productivity of the arable land with a greater quantity of manure, inevitably calls to mind Tarello's method. As with land reclaimed by irrigation, this method allowed spontaneous germination of fallen seeds and the natural selection of forage crops, which need water to develop and predominate in the pasture. The practice of using a mixture of marl and waste vegetation, as was common in Kent and Hampshire, and the use of nitrates for dressing seed, come very close to Robert Child's letter. But Smyth found the key to success in Virgil's forgotten precept, which taught that spontaneous products of the region should be studied. Spreading lime in Cheshire and Staffordshire and growing clover and Dutch hemp were examples. He maintained that blackthorn made the best hedgerows because the sloes and thorns kept the cattle away from them, and he did not miss Virgil's note on cytisus, the best bush to provide forage for goats, though he honestly admitted that he did not know it. Once again it was the voice of Virgil that recommended growing trees on pastureland, for the extra fodder and for the timber. Smyth backs all this up by saying that Cato valued the *salicetum* above the best pasture. Virgil did not furnish Smyth with a merely literary example, but with an agricultural model comparable with that of Holland. There are other marks of Continental agronomy as well. In 1650 Cressy Dymock took, quite literally, Gallo's and Tarello's lesson on how the number of grains per ear can be increased by good husbandry ('by the blessing of God, the native fertility of our English ground . . . will bring forth').[129] This was the great age of experiment, which would lead to man's dominion over nature, yet

---

128 *Ibid.*, mss 26/50/1–2; 67/23/1–2; on Boswell and drainage projects see Webster, *The Great Instauration*, pp. 372–3.
129 See Sheffield, UL, Hartlib mss 66/23/1–2; Thirsk, 'Agricultural innovations', pp. 552, 559; *Samuel Hartlib*, pp. 104–5.

they had to use old-fashioned forms of communication by letter, since the *Transactions* of the Royal Society were not yet available. It constituted no break with the accumulated experience of previous decades, though it had to be verified personally, by experiment.

5.2. From Hartlib to the Restoration

The middle decades of the seventeenth century were not only characterized by great admiration for the agriculture of the Low Countries. The farsightedness and broad mind of Hartlib were never equalled by the many who had supported the cause of Parliament in the English Revolution, modernization of modes of production and the colonization of Ireland. They believed that the causes of poverty were to be found in prejudice and in the enemies of the Gospel. Walter Blith, one of the most fervent supporters of the alliance of Bible, sword and plough, considered that idleness, improvidence and the old agriculture were all one.[130] Let us look at the six methods of improvement that he proposed in his book: clover and sainfoin; design and loading of the ploughshare; woad, dyer's weed and madder; hops, saffron, and liquorice; turnips, colza, hemp and flax; and fruit-trees. He warned his readers at once that, of the many varieties of clover, the really useful kind was the red Flanders clover, far better than those that grew wild in England. Unfortunately, the seed imported from the Low Countries on sale in London was of poor quality, either spoilt by the journey by sea or adulterated because Dutch merchants were cunning and jealous. He himself was sold a bad lot and so warned buyers to send a trusted expert to purchase on the spot. Consequently the seed gathered in the second year, from Dutch clover grown in England, was preferable because one knew where it came from. But English growers could not rival Flemish skill in threshing and winnowing and even Blith could only offer the methods already familiar. He was equally vague on the quantity of seed to be sown per acre, which he connected with the quality of the seed. His suggestion about mixing seed and sawdust, to weigh the seeds down, and to use the harrow to cover them without burying them too deeply, was more realistic. He also recommended sowing oats together with barley, as a cover crop, to

---

[130] See W. Blith, *The English Improver or a New Survey of Husbandry*, London 1649, pp. 7, 9, 10. On Blith see J. Thirsk, 'Plough and Pen: Agricultural Writers in the Seventeenth Century', in *Social Relations and Ideas. Essays in Honour of R. H. Hilton*, Cambridge 1983, pp. 306–14.

protect delicate seeds before germination. But the real chance of success lay in the preparation of the field with manure, good ploughing, lime and marl or chalk, according to the requirements of the soil, which had to be enriched and warmed before it received the seeds. Unfortunately, it was often forgotten that manure produced before cattle were put to graze on clover contained a large quantity of seeds from weeds, which at once began to compete with the clover. The secret of farming, as Weston described it, lay in these procedures, even though Flemish and Dutch cattle already produced manure with a high percentage of white clover seed in it (since white clover predominated on natural pastures). Under these excellent conditions, Blith suggested sowing nine to ten pounds of seed and considered any land suitable for wheat and all the work of preparing the soil for cereals excellent for cultivating clover. The rule was to practise intensive agriculture and not to cultivate more land than one could cope with satisfactorily. Whether or not he was aware of it, he was adopting the Italian practice of having proportionately more hands than land. English improvers of the mid-seventeenth century also believed that the land had to be tamed by tillage. It is obvious from the context that the idea was still a novelty and that, in spite of everything, the abundance of land and the open-field system had favoured extensive cultivation to the detriment of the quality of the work. The yields foreseen from clover were also a little less optimistic than those given by Weston. The yield of the first year was scanty, that of the second better (even today the clover-field doubles its production in the second year), giving three crops and good winter grazing, while there was a falling off in the third and fourth years.[131] In practice, it was not worth growing it beyond the fourth to fifth year. The English, too, had discovered with surprising rapidity that the clover-field did not last long. The land soon showed signs of rejection and repeated sowing did not give good results.

Blith also dealt with sainfoin and lucerne, without adding anything new to what Hartlib had already written in the *Legacy* and even shortening by a considerable amount what was already known.[132] He even seems to have mistaken one plant for the other, and considered *luzerne* more suitable for improving poor, dry soil, when exactly the opposite is true. The same dependence on precise manuscript information was shown again by Adolphus Speed a few years later. The

---

[131] Blith is quoted here from the second enlarged edition, *The English Improver Improved*, London 1652, pp. 177–85.
[132] See *ibid.*, pp. 185–6.

unpublished writings already used, coming from the papers of Ashmole and Thomas Stringer, on clover, turnips and *esparsette*, were published again, not altering the technical side too much, but toning down the political starting-point from which experiments and information stemmed.[133]

The *Legacy* had certainly not exhausted the demand for new publications. The rapid succession of books, which often ran into two editions or printings in the course of a few years, shows that technical and practical writing for the general public sold very well; this encouraged the production of new works giving an account of practical experience rather than re-establishing the fame of a new Classical text.[134] The experience of Andrew Yarranton of Astley, in north-west Worcestershire, is a good illustration of how even the counties a long way from London fell into line without delay, on the new agricultural front. Outside the Hartlib circle, but still connected with the Puritan movement, Andrew Yarranton, a captain in the Parliamentary Army, actively organized the spread of the cultivation of clover in Worcestershire, his home county, and in the neighbouring counties, Staffordshire, Shropshire and Herefordshire.[135] Yarranton examined a series of causes that had delayed the spread of the cultivation and frustrated the endeavours of many. The technical reasons lay in the soil, seed and wrong time of sowing, a too-rigid observance of old farming practice, irrational fear of anything new, and the attempt to cultivate too much land. Moreover, he considered the practice of ordinary people much superior to the writings of the experts. The cause of many failures was to be found in the quality of foreign seed, in its high price (2s per pound), which made farmers sow too sparingly (5–6 lbs instead of 12 lbs per acre), sowing on over-wet and clayey soil, and putting animals to graze on it too soon. While mistakes left slight trace, failure left an even

---

133 See Speed, *Adam out of Eden*, pp. 33, 38–44.
134 R. K. Merton's early appreciation of the role of scientific pamphlets (*Science, Technology and Society in Seventeenth Century England* (1938), New York 1970) is shared by Webster, *The Great Instauration*, pp. 487 ff. On popular booklets see now M. Spufford, *The Great Reclothing of Rural England: Petty Chapmen and their Wares in the Seventeenth Century*, London 1984, and L. C. Stevenson, *Praise and Paradox: Merchants and Craftsmen in Elizabethan Popular Culture*, Cambridge 1984.
135 On Andrew Yarranton see P. E. Dove, *Account of A. Y. the Founder of English Political Economy*, Edinburgh 1854; *DNB*, *sub nomine*; A. Yarranton, *The Improvement improved by a second edition of the great improvement of Lands by Clover*, London 1663; the date of first edition is unknown, it was probably a privately printed letter with local circulation.

slighter mark. In the decade in question, many farmers tried to grow clover, persuaded by the enthusiastic but inaccurate writings of Weston. The attempt to get quick profits from poor, neglected land had probably made farmers sow fodder crops on the wrong soil, hurriedly prepared. The plant alone could not work wonders, it was the work of preparation that transformed wasteland into highly profitable leys. So sparing seed prevented the victory of clover over weeds and early grazing destroyed the meadow. Yarranton advised trying out clover on arable land where wheat and rye had been grown for six or eight years running, well limed, perhaps stony or sandy, but dry in the winter, on waste land where bracken and broom grew; or on mixed, clayey soils, without stagnant water. Between twelve and sixteen pounds of seed should be sown in a well-enclosed field, between mid-March and the end of April, according to the year; cattle should not be allowed to tread on the pasture before mid-April. Barley was a better cover-crop than oats, it could be consumed fresh or mown with the first crop at the beginning of June. The second crop was to be mown in August and winter grazing followed. It was excellent for cattle, for fattening sheep quickly, and for horses, especially sick ones. A list of twenty-eight Worcestershire villages where good local seed could easily be bought[136] shows that the problem of threshing seed could be solved satisfactorily where cultivation had spread successfully, and where local conditions were quite unlike the rest of England. In Worcester, a high standard of horticulture obtained, summer rainfall was low and small farms predominated. Fifteen years later Yarranton published a large volume in which, polemically, he compared the Dutch with the English system and advised a series of economic reforms which would lead to the setting up of public granaries, a land register, and an agricultural bank which could provide loans for new investment on the strength of bills guaranteed by the quotas of grain deposited in the public granaries.[137] A decade ahead of the constitution of the Bank of England, and inspired by the Dutch banking system, Yarranton had an insight into the structural weakness of the English social system, which needed to defend the lower agricultural classes from the ups and downs of the economic cycle, if they were to stand up to competition from the more aggressive Dutch economy.

The newly founded Royal Society also undertook to encourage the

---

[136] See *ibid.*, pp. 1–8, 14–15, 21–7, 46.
[137] See idem, *England's Improvement by sea and land, or to outdo the Dutch without fighting to pay Debts without Money*, London 1677, 2 vols.

spread of new crops. In 1664 a Georgical Committee was set up for the purpose of gathering information on the history of agriculture, of gardening and the general situation of the time, by means of a question-naire, to be distributed among members and other farmers of proven experience in the counties of England, Scotland and Ireland. Lord Brereton, John Evelyn and William Petty, among others, were elected to the committee and a series of reports was compiled between 1665 and 1666. In practice, the survey was restricted to a series of questions on arable land (soils, tillage, manure, products and seed of cereals, diseases and parasites) and on meadows (soils, weeds, reclamation work, grasses found on pastureland and meadows).[138] Although the answers were obtained from the most advanced sector of the farming community and only for a limited number of counties (Dorset, Devon, Cornwall, Yorkshire, Kent and Gloucestershire) they provided good information on farming standards, which can give an idea of how far the new technology, elaborated up to the mid-seventeenth century, was being applied. Most of the questionnaires mention wheeled implements and mixed teams of oxen and horses for breaking up fallow land and the use of lighter ploughs and teams on land that had already been well tilled (East Riding of Yorkshire, Devon and Cornwall, and Kent). The number of times the fields were ploughed was above the traditional number, four or five times in Yorkshire, and three ploughings, one harrowing, plus the ploughing in of the seed in the district of Berkeley. The more modern system of cross-ploughing recorded for Ripon, Yorkshire and for Devon and Cornwall co-existed with the more traditional one of ploughing in furrows in Kent, Devon and Cornwall. The communications of the Georgical Committee clearly show that the advice found in agronomic literature that was frequently adopted was that on the manuring of arable land and the use of any organic material, waste products from tanning, from soap-making, algae, horse-dung from the roads, as well as sand and shells gathered on the shores, not to mention the commoner marl and lime. All these things were used in variable quantity to correct the characteristics of the soil and keep it productive, as if prolonged fallow were a sign of abandon. The same happened on the pastures. Manure was spread ready for the next crop of cereals, ashes and fresh mud were put on the old meadows. In practice, farmers of that time avoided the costly operation of paring and burning, preferring to correct the acidity of the

---

[138] See *Philosophical Transactions*, I, 1665–6, n. 5, pp. 91–4; R. V. Lennard, 'English Agriculture under Charles II', *EcHR*, ser. 1, 4, 1932, pp. 23–45.

soil, produced by the ageing of the grasses of the pastureland by weeds, bracken, broom and reeds, without any real cultivation of the pasture. Beside a general tendency to favour manure, there were signs of an adverse opinion developing wherever the system of leaving land fallow every three years had been used for as long as thirty or forty years; while some farmers saw that manure, particularly when fresh, transferred weeds from pasture to arable land. In East Yorkshire open-fields and the fact of not manuring produced grain free of smut (much sought after as seed by more careful farmers). In Yorkshire common fields were left fallow every three or four years, and on the better ground a rotation of one ploughing, then barley, three ploughings then barley again, one ploughing, then wheat, without manuring, gave good harvests with a fallow every seven years. Indeed, in that county, enclosure was synonymous with bad farming. There were no turnips among the new crops, but this was mainly because there was no report on East Anglia in the survey. However, there were legumes in Kent (wild white and red clover) and in Gloucestershire (where sainfoin was preferred to cultivated red clover, which was accused of impoverishing the soil). Elsewhere clover seems to have enjoyed greater popularity. In Exeter even the seed was on sale (at 2d or 3d a pound); sown with oats as a cover crop, it lasted three or four years at most.

In the last decades of the seventeenth century, ready-made innovations began to spread, thanks to the new Newtonian philosophy of science. However, practical research in agriculture was still founded on the mass of experiences by which it had hitherto been regulated. The agricultural pamphlets brought out very clearly how fragmented practical knowledge became, since it was linked to a varied social group of occasional writers. Hence it is not surprising that the question of the cultivation of legumes was not always dealt with in every printed pamphlet after 1650.[139] The fragmentary nature of the oral and written communication concerning the new techniques, side by side with their unbroken connection with the history of Classical times, was also emphasized by John Worlidge of Petersfield, Hampshire, the most famous agricultural writer of the Restoration. Worlidge was a successful landowner, mayor of the small town where he was born, deputy steward of Chalton Manor

---

[139] See for an example J. S., *Brief Discoveries of Divers Excellent wayes and meanes for the Manuring and Improving of Land*, London 1646; G. Plattes, *Practical Husbandry Improved*, London 1656; J. Shaw, *Certaine Plaine and Easie Demonstrations . . . for the Improving of . . . Barren Land . . .* , London 1657.

from 1689, and steward of the Earl of Pembroke's woods, probably from 1665. He had gradually built up experience in all those sectors in which seventeenth-century noblemen and gentlemen speculated, the cultivation of cereals, the management of meadows, fruit-growing, the new cider industry and timber. He generously made this experience available to the public in a series of quite long books, reaching a fair cultural standard, which he obviously hoped would find their way into the libraries of the new gentry of the 1660s to 1680s.[140]

Even in the frontispieces, these books contain many quotations from Virgil, which were no mere whim foreshadowing the fashion of the early eighteenth century, but confirmed the comparison between what had become the good English practice of Worlidge's days and Classical agronomy. Virgil, too, was of the opinion that the plough rendered the soil fertile with the help of the sun (' . . . glebasque iacentes/Pulverulenta coquat maturis solibus aetas'). A combination of rich, black soil could be improved by the plough 'nigra fere et pinguis . . . / Optima frumentis . . .' as the poet said.[141] Interest in Virgil was not an accidental, eccentric trait. A few years later Purcell was to set *Dido and Aeneas* to music and in the next generation Dryden would translate Virgil's works. Later, in the early eighteenth century, the whole agricultural system of Virgil and the Classical world would be carefully discussed (see Chap. 7, 2). Worlidge eagerly listed the innovations and changes to which traditional English agriculture had been subjected in the course of the previous century. He considered the division of arable land into small fields an improvement and he repeated his contempories' opinion that the smaller the fields, the higher their rent should be. Enclosures, he thought, should be made by replacing bushes that grew spontaneously with varieties of trees chosen according to the soil and the situation of the field. Water-meadows, on the other hand, should be left open. The only drawback produced by enclosure was smut in wheat,[142] whereas many benefits were attached to enclosure combined with ploughing. Arable land was defended from the excesses of winter and summer weather by the narrower furrows which produced the even distribution of humidity

---

[140] See Thirsk, 'Plough and Pen', pp. 314–18; J. Worlidge, *Systema agriculturae. The Mystery of Husbandry Discovered . . . to which is added Kalendarium Rusticum . . .* , London 1669, 1675 (quoted here); idem, *Systema horti–culturae: or the art of gardening . . .* , London 1677, 1683, 1688, 1700, 1719.

[141] See idem, *Systema agriculturae*, pp. 32, 33, as an example. Note that Worlidge, who came from Southern England, called the plough *sull*, from the Latin *sulcum*.

[142] See *ibid.*, pp. 12–14; also at pp. 201–2 he spoke about smut.

necessary for wheat. The London gardeners had begun to make narrower furrows in those years, while Worlidge himself, an expert horticulturalist, confirmed that peas grew better when sown on the south side of the furrow. He recommended three ploughings for wheat and four for barley, saying that well-tilled soil prevented smut and helped the root system of every plant sown to develop. Ploughing destroyed weeds, which competed with cereals, especially on heavy soil. Although the technique of ploughing in narrow furrows had been used for at least a hundred years, Virgil's descriptions were decidedly more time-honoured. Worlidge made full use of the scientific terminology of his time: devonshiring was the best way to turn pasture to arable land, because it reduced the acidity in the soil. Ploughing was also necessary for the healthy growth of a grass turf (modern agronomy also recommends the use of cultivators to aerate the soil). Lastly, the combination of enclosure and untiring work on the fallow to prepare it for crops, together with the alternation of two crops, then leys, ensured that the retrieved fertility of the so-called barren land would be maintained.[143] The best way to prepare the field was by two deep ploughings, along and across, followed by a third one, with a light plough, to make narrow, shallow furrows in which the seed would be sown and covered by harrowing. He was repeating exactly the method described in the late sixteenth century by Sir Hugh Platt, who was obviously following the ploughing technique advised by Agostino Gallo[144] and the practice of southern France.

With regard to pastures and meadows, Worlidge's knowledge did not go beyond the frequently quoted publications of Hartlib and Blith. However, something had changed his language. He often repeated that the problem of fertility was linked to the warming of the soil by such diverse means as irrigation, manuring, air and the sun. Water-meadows seem to have become the commonest form of reclamation, despite the mistakes made by the most ignorant farmers, who used stagnant water, and despite the mills commonly built beside the rivers to exploit the water power. Worlidge paid great attention to the mineral salts in the water, the real cause of many failures. Dry meadows, out of reach of irrigation systems, had to be cleaned by burning unwanted scrub or pulling it out, flattening the soil and destroying ant-hills, then finally manuring and improving the soil.[145] At this stage the new forage-crops

[143] See *ibid.*, pp. 31–4.   [144] See *ibid.*, p. 35.
[145] See *ibid.*, pp. 15–24.

could be used, clover, red clover, sainfoin, lucerne, spurry or trefoil. But the starting point was tilling the soil well with the plough and the right amount of seed (ten pounds of undressed seed, fifteen pounds if dressed, according to the theory of Richard Weston and the practice of many others). Worlidge, quite an expert on vegetable-gardens, devoted a considerable amount of space to dressing seed, comparing Weston's figure of five bushels an acre with the one he knew, of two bushels an acre. He mentioned a few novel agronomic points about sainfoin, saying it was excellent on poor, chalky hillsides, better sown thickly and hoed to destroy the weeds. It lasted longer than clover but it was better not to graze it in the first year so as not to weaken the crop. His advice on lucerne was very similar, but he does not seem to have grown it himself and was extremely hazy on soil, whether poor and dry or rich and damp. Three ploughings should be sufficient to prepare the field, but the yield was the same as for clover, two crops, plus winter grazing.[146] Though he was so keen on water-meadows, he did not think of increasing lucerne crops by irrigation.

Worlidge had an advantage over the previous generation; he was able to make better use of the German chemist Glauber's teaching and its application to agriculture. He also agreed with Willis' theory, according to which heat was responsible for the transformations in the natural world, and held that mercury was the active, warm element which governed the transformation of earth and water into sulphuric and saline elements. While, by means of heat, mercury caused the decay of vegetable matter and the creation of fertility, mineral salts, above all nitrates, the salt of the earth, caused the growth of plants in warmer climates, where they grew nearer the surface because of evaporation. Hence water was not a neutral element but worked in various ways, according to the salts it contained. The sulphuric principle was, in itself, the most fertile element, but the most difficult to control; the saline principle was less volatile and easier to use. These notes on the chemical nutrition of plants were confirmed by observations of barley and wheat where soil was thin, in meadows that had just been burn-baked and on rocks near the sea. They are not unlike Tarello's observations about plants growing on dry-stone walls. Salts could be utilized better if dissolved in water or liquids such as urine. As the path to agricultural chemistry began to be traced, Worlidge was not at a loss to find confirmation of the theory in the accumulated experience of centuries

---

[146] See *ibid.*, pp. 22–30.

expressed by the Latin poet, Virgil.[147] Worlidge held that manuring and improving the soil should be seen from this point of view. He considered that manure, above all horse dung, was the natural product that gave most heat, as market gardeners had found, but it often produced weeds in meadow and field. Hence it was better to use mixtures of soil, marl, clay, mineral salts, lime and sand. Or else one should use a mixture of cattle dung, sheep droppings and soil, left standing for a long time to make sure the seeds were no longer viable.[148] For the same reason, though Worlidge did not seem to realize this, the manure collected after cattle had grazed on clover meadows greatly increased the crop, just because it contained a large number of clover seeds. The problems Worlidge dealt with were the same as those that Jethro Tull was to face, and in part solve, with his mechanical inventions. Worlidge himself described, very roughly, a kind of seed drill, which he thought would solve the problem of sowing grain and legumes.

In these same years, Nathaniel Fiennes was a colonel in the Parliamentary army (and confidant of Cromwell), exiled in Geneva and Scotland, son of William, Viscount Saye and Sele of Broughton, Oxfordshire, and descendant of the founder of Winchester School and New College, Oxford.[149] Formerly a gentleman farmer, he wrote a pamphlet on the cultivation of sainfoin, printed posthumously in 1671 and 1674. Nathaniel died in 1669 and so the little booklet can be dated a few years earlier. It, too, was a starting point for many attempts at improvement, such as that of Roger Kenrick, steward of the estates of Sir John Trevor in Wales. After personally searching in vain, in London and northern Wales, for the information and seed he needed, Kenrick stopped

---

[147] See *ibid.*, pp. 3–7: this theory has obvious points in common with Aristotle's theory, *De generatione et corruptione*, and the theory of the four elements, earth, water, air and fire. Had Pliny still been read in his day, Worlidge would have admired his careful references to the retrieval of nitrates and phosphates from caves, wine jars and other natural deposits: see E. Crivelli, 'Dell'uso di nitrati e fosfati minerali nell'antichità classica', *Historia*, 4, 1930. It was C. Marani, 'Camillo Tarello e gli inizi della scienza agronomica', *Rivista di storia economica*, 6, 1941, p. 30, who pointed out this early observation on the chemical nourishment of plants. On Thomas Willis and Johann Rudolph Glauber see Webster, *The Great Instauration, passim*.

[148] See Worlidge, *Systema agriculturae*, pp. 58–71.

[149] The identification of the unknown author of the pamphlet *St. Foine improved: a Discourse shewing the Utility and Benefit which England hath and may receive by the grasse called St. Foine*, London 1671, 1674, with Nathaniel Fiennes is another debt we owe to Frank Emery, 'The Mechanics of Innovation', p. 39: Nathaniel was the father of the better-known diarist Celia Fiennes: see C. Morris (ed.), *The Illustrated Journeys of Celia Fiennes, 1685–c. 1712*, London–Sidney 1982.

at Woodstock, near Oxford, and got Sir John to send him the printed information (*St. Foine improved*, Fiennes' pamphlet) and the seed. Once again London and personal contacts between stewards and landowners brought about the spread of innovations even in remote counties.[150]

The author of the pamphlet insisted on the fact that forage-crops had been introduced into England about ten years previously and their use was still limited. The great amount of land on which the new crops could profitably be sown was still very expensive to reclaim and prepare (40s or 50s an acre). Even in the few cases where it had been grown, sainfoin had not made the farmer self-sufficient. There was resistance on the part of those who thought that a crop in theory so productive would lower the commercial value of natural pastures, which in part was false, because the fall in rents had begun before the arrival of the new sown grasses. On the other hand, an abundance of hay and grains, even when prices were low, would have brought great benefits. The cost of producing English crops could have been lowered, and only good quality pastures would have been able to satisfy the need for fertilizer, manure and compost necessary for the production of cereals. Growing good grain crops meant starting from better grass. The example of Northern England, Scotland and Devon showed that the fertility of the soil and the well-being of the people derived from agricultural labours that had transformed soil that had lain so long in a backward state. On this general economic basis, the cultivation of sainfoin presented various advantages: the fertilizing action of its roots, even in cases of crop failure, the defence of the lower layers of the soil, the increase in the number of draught animals and raw material for manufactured goods. Nathaniel Fiennes' agronomy was the product of many experiments. He suggested that sainfoin should be used on very poor, sandy soil but not on poor, wet clay soil. He advised four bushels to the acre, to be sown in autumn, which would produce a richer crop, and to some extent solve the problem of the low yield of sainfoin in the first year after planting. Barley and oats were to be used as cover-crops for spring sowing, wheat for autumn sowing. Before attempting cultivation in the field, it was important to test the soil by hoeing a small plot well and sowing the sainfoin in rows, a system that has echoes of Columella and foreshadows Tull. Enclosure was necessary to prevent cattle grazing on it in the first year; in the following years the crop could be fed green or as hay.[151]

---

[150] See Emery, 'The Mechanics of Innovation', pp. 39–40.
[151] See Fiennes, *St. Foine improved*, pp. 2, 5, 7–8, 14, 17–22.

In this case the relation between printed information and the time needed to put the innovation into practice can be accurately checked. Roger Kenrick began to take practical steps in October 1668, but not until the middle of April 1669 did he manage to get the thirty-two bushels of seed necessary to sow eight acres with barley and oats, according to the instructions in the text. The results were poor and in 1670 he was asking for better seed. He obtained it, together with the booklet afore-mentioned, and sowed sixty bushels in 1671. The harvests of 1672 and 1673 also gave poor results but owner and steward remained undaunted and tried again.[152] At this point one wonders whether the method of growing forage-crops adopted by English improvers came up to European standards and whether it was not the general conditions of farming which delayed the decision to adopt innovations in this sector.

6. HERBARIA AND LATE SEVENTEENTH-CENTURY COLLECTORS

But how did the practical farmers and the scientists interact? From notes made by Jacob Bobart and William Browne in those same years it appears that the *luzerne* of the French had not yet been described in the inventory of the Botanic Garden of Oxford, although it was already growing there, and melilot grew in abundance in the neighbourhood of Oxford.[153] Here too we note that melilot preceded lucerne. A rustic plant like melilot is favoured in the wild, whereas constant growing in the botanical garden favoured the spread of the more prestigious agricultural species.

English botany was wide open to French influences. Morison, Ray and Sherard all lived and worked in Paris. Botanists kept in touch with Montpellier and Florence too. Indeed, it was on Andrea Cesalpino's half-forgotten classification that they focused to move beyond Bauhin's *Pinax* and the bottleneck produced by casual classification until that time.[154] In the years of the Restoration, Robert Morison and John Ray

---

[152] See Emery, 'The Mechanics of Innovation'.

[153] See Oxford, BO, ms Sherard 31: *Catalogus Horti Botanici Oxoniensis Philippi Stephani M.D., Guilelmi Brounei A.M.*, Oxford 1658 (manuscript notes by Jacob Bobart), unnumbered pages bound before the printed text; Oxford, BO, 50 d 25, Dodoens-Lyte, *Newe Herbal*, London 1614, p. 358.

[154] See *ibid.*, ms Sherard 27, Andrea Cesalpino, *De plantis libri XVI*, Florence 1583, with numerous manuscript notes by Robert Morison, who also endeavoured to render the sixteenth-century Latin nomenclature on sainfoin (still called *polygala*) consistent with

were already aware that the ambiguity in the French terminology on lucerne and sainfoin was reflected in English. But it was not easy to explain the matter clearly. The first attempt was made by the Scotsman Robert Morison, who spent the years of the Civil War in France and became a friend, first of Jean Robin and then of those in charge of the botanical garden of the castle of Blois. Unfortunately his botanical Latin was not very grammatical and rather confused the issue.[155] Lucerne and Burgundy hay (*Medicago sylvestris* to careful scholars, now *M.falcata*) were all one to him. He noticed that it grew commonly, almost like a weed, beside the roads and fields of Montpellier, at Lunel (Hérault) and in Poitou. He saw a great deal sown as forage between Tarragona, Barcelona and Valencia, but it grew wild elsewhere. According to Morison, the French called it *sainct foin* or *foin de Bourgogne* and it was sown on well-manured, irrigated land, mown three times a year, while on rich, well-manured but dry land they sowed the *onobrychis*, described as *caput galli* by L'Obel, but which the French called *luzerne* [*sic*]. So a fundamental inaccuracy added to the difficulties of those readers who only knew the new forage-crops indirectly. To support his assertion, Morison recalled the journeys he made in the company of Gaston, Duc d'Orléans, younger brother of Louis XIII, through Burgundy, where lucerne grew in rich, damp meadows and *onobrychis* in the higher, drier ones. This information was absolutely correct. It is a pity that Morison insisted on calling the latter plant 'luzerne'. He had some reason to insist because, to his readers' misfortune, he had restricted his survey to that small area of central and eastern France where another exchange of terms was the norm – *luzerne* was sainfoin and *sainfoin* lucerne. Unfortunately, this was a linguistic habit strictly confined to a minority, still to be found in the early years of this century.[156]

All this was happening at the same time as the new forage-crops were spreading, causing a great deal of confusion for the non-specialist reader. Probably Robert Plott had addressed his natural history of the county

the Anglo-French usage of his time. Morison's most important work is his *Plantarum historia universalis oxoniensis*, 2 vols., Oxford 1680–99. Oxford, BO, ms Sherard 194, G. Baldi, *Index ommium plantarum in Orto Botanico Florentiae*, Florence 1686.

155 See Vines and Druce, *An Account of the Morisonian Herbarium*; Henrey, *British Botanical and Horticultural Literature*, vol. I, pp. 119–26. Ray had already expressed the opinion that Morison wrote poor Latin: *ibid.*, p. 127, note 9.

156 It is easy to understand the reason: in Burgundy *foin de Bourgone* and *sainfoin* already unquestionably meant lucerne, hence *onobrychis*, the new plant from the Midi, would be given the commoner southern name, *luzerne*. See also *Atlas linguistique de la France*, carte nn. 722, 733, 784, 793, 1705 on *sainfoin* and 789 on *luzerne*.

of Oxford to such readers. This was a work produced in the same cultural environment, but it was based on work carried out in the field. According to Plott, perennial plants were sown as fodder (*grass* in the agronomic terminology of the time) in the county, but so were polyannuals, such as clover and *onobrychis purpurea*, commonly called *sainct foin*, but in fact the real *luzerne* in Morison's explanation.[157] Plott's close adherence to the words of Dr Morison, in a work quite widely read, wiped out, or at least slowed down the effect of all Hartlib's and Boate's efforts to clarify the difference between *luzerne* and *sainfoin*.

In these same years, John Ray had begun to travel to collect information for what should have been an account of English flora, which had still not been written. He was following the fashion of making studies in the field, which had by then become obligatory, since the Royal Society emphasized a direct approach towards the natural sciences. For the first time, ahead even of Linnaeus, some people were avowedly studying flora in their natural habitat and not as dried specimens kept under glass. There were many varieties of clover (*T. subterraneum, glomeratum, squamosum, pratense*, etc.); some wild varieties of *medicago* (*hispida, maculata, minima*) were to be found; there was no trace of *onobrychis*. After his journeys through the home counties, John Ray went to France, then to Holland, Germany, Switzerland, Austria as far as Vienna, the Friuli region, Venice, Bologna and all the cities of the Po valley, as far as Turin; then Genoa, La Spezia, Leghorn, by sea to Naples, then to Messina, through Sicily and across to Malta. On his return journey he called at Catania, Naples, Leghorn, and Florence, Rome, crossed the Appennines to visit Rimini, Bologna, back to Venice, Treviso, the Brenner Pass, the Swiss cantons as far as Lausanne, then France and Provence until 1666, when Louis XIV ordered English subjects to leave the country within three months.[158] These journeys enabled him to gather a great deal of information, particularly concerning Switzerland, Italy, Sicily and Malta. The journeys and studies that he undertook in subsequent years formed the basis of volumes which outlined the developments in European botany in the late seventeenth century, and gave descriptions of the British species, never attempted before. Hence

---

[157] See R. Plott, *The Natural History of Oxfordshire*, Oxford 1677, pp. 153–5; on Plott see F. Emery, 'English regional studies'.

[158] See C. Raven, *John Ray Naturalist. His life and works*, Cambridge 1950, pp. 85, 92, 98, 126, 128, 130, 132–8, 141, 173, 227, 268. For the general background on Englishmen on the Continent see J. Stoye, *English Travellers in the Seventeenth Century*, London 1955 (New Haven 1989).

Ray was in a position to compare British and Continental flora and to recognize those new species and varieties which had been introduced into Britain in the course of the century. This work was going forward at the same time as Tournefort's attempt to create a general system of nomenclature and description for European botany. To our surprise, we find Ray writing that *medica silvestris*, yellow medick in English, called Burgundy hay, was the real lucerne, and was called *saint foine*; it grew plentifully and spontaneously in Norfolk, at Lenn (perhaps present-day Lenwade) and not far from Norwich. The *onobrychis caput gallinaceum* described by Parkinson and the Bauhins under this name and by Gesner as polygala, was commonly but erroneously called *sain foin*. It grew on the hills of Gog and Magog in Cambridgeshire, at the edges of fields and on the chalk soils of Newmarket and Salisbury.[159]

So much could be read in the books of a few scientists, as a result of long research and journeys. But what did they say in the herbals that eclectics and amateurs compiled in those decades? A careful anonymous writer, taking his cue from Flemish realist painting reproducing fruit and flowers and their parasites, placed the specimen of a common butterfly beside five varieties of lucerne, among which a *medica elegans Cataloniae* takes pride of place. To complete the study he stuck on six specimens of Burgundy hay; for lack of sainfoin, he added three sprigs of bird's foot (*Lotus corniculatus*) and sixteen more or less well-known varieties of clover.[160] Unfortunately, he did not always collect the flowers and seeds and the only real guide to their identity is his nomenclature. Another collection was left by Sir George Wheler, who travelled as far as Greece in the 1680s and followed L'Ecluse in part and in part the Bauhins, as well as Mattioli in his nomenclature of clovers, hedysarum, a species of lucerne with a very beautiful variegated flower, a marine lucerne, another one picked in Crete, a *medica falcata* (or Burgundy hay) and, lastly, a magnificent specimen of Spanish sainfoin. That he botanized in Greece is evident from the hedysara and the twig of fir picked on Mount Olympus.[161] Edward Morgan, curator of the garden

---

[159] See Oxford, BO, mss Sherard 454, 455, 456, 457, J. Ray, *Synopsis methodica stirpium Britannicarum, tum indigenis tum in agris cultis* . . . , London 1690, 1696, 1724, interleaved copies personally annotated by Sherard, Lightfoot, Sir J. Hill, Hudson. The above quotations are from ms Sherard 457, London 1724, pp. 327, 333, which enlarge the text of ms Sherard 455, London 1696, pp. 193, 197.

[160] See *ibid.*, ms Arch. Selden B 3, *Hortus Hiemalis*, ff. 190–91, 294, 342–5, 353–4.

[161] On George Wheler see Raven, *John Ray Naturalist*, pp. 221, 276; Oxford, BO, ms Ashmole 1800–4, vol. 2, fos. 37, 44–5; vol. 3, ff. 29, 68; vol. 4, fos. 24, 74, 84, 86.

of Westminster, was older than the others; he had accompanied Thomas Johnson to North Wales in 1639 and was still alive and active in 1685. The oldest collection is probably that in a single volume which includes *onobrychis*, hedysara, Guilandin and L'Obel's lucerne (*M. sativa*), Burgundy hay and other examples of legumes (*lotus urbana*, bituminous clover, cytisus). In the three volumes compiled between October 1672 and November 1682 the same plants reappear, but with a larger number of specimens; *M. sativa* and Burgundy hay are missing. There are very few forage legumes among the plants in the third herbarium, probably collected in Tradescant's circle for pharmacological purposes.[162] One of the herb-gatherers was the gardener of Hampton Court, who in 1692 sowed six varieties of bean and two of melon for the royal table and also added the very common Italian melilot and sainfoin. Jacob Bobart the younger continued his father's untiring work as keeper and propagator. On 30 November 1697 he was despatching lucerne and *onobrychis* from Oxford. A decade or so earlier he had published an advertisement for the sale of sainfoin seed in the *London Gazette*. In 1697 he was still collecting the seeds of sainfoin, various lucernes and a new Spanish clover with a particularly beautiful red flower.

7. CONCLUSION: FROM LUCERNE TO CLOVER

In chapter 4 we showed that the reduction in the cultivation of forage-crops in France was connected with the economic measures of institutions including the great estates of the aristocracy, with pasture rights and with tithes collected by the clergy or let to others. In late seventeenth-century Italy the decline in population after the plague of 1630, and the return to rough grazing, certainly reduced interest in the cultivation of forage crops. In Restoration England the price of cereals as well as other arable crops fell steadily until 1750, except for certain special years, like 1673, 1674, the 1690s, 1708–11 and a few others. The prices of butcher's meat, whether mutton, beef or pork, were steadier.[163] Under such conditions, large and small farmers alike were forced to set about diversifying their production. Fruit-trees (apples and pears) and

---

[162] See *ibid.*, ms Ashmole 1465, fos. 4, 10*r*, 21*r*, 30*r* 34*r*, 36*r*, 43, 71, 81, 132; mss Ashmole 1797–9, vol. 2, fos. 73–74, 91, 117; vol. 3, fos. 81–7; ms Ashmole 1502, fos. 187*v*–188*r*. On Morgan see Raven, *John Ray Naturalist*, pp. 150–1.

[163] See P. J. Bowden, 'Appendix III. Statistics', in *AHEW*, 5/2, pp. 843 ff., 847 ff., 851 ff., and idem, 'Agricultural prices, wages, farm profits and rents', *ibid.*, pp. 33 ff., 41 ff., 52–53, 55.

horticultural products, roots, farmyard cattle and livestock, sheep for meat and wool, all made their contribution, according to the specialities of the region, which took into account the local markets and the chances of selling the produce in London.[164] In practice, the astute farmer tried to have a range of crops which would make up for the effects of the variations in prices, which did not move in the same directions in the different regions. On 30 March 1692, to encourage commercial integration of the different regional markets, John Houghton, fellow of the Royal Society, began regular publication of the prices of the principal products on the English provincial markets. To these he added a quantity of practical information on fertilizing composts, proposals and improvements in the art of agriculture, reviews of the new treatises on agronomy and any other information on trade, manufacturing and movements of the population.[165] He was taking up one of the tasks already undertaken by Samuel Hartlib, who could not have carried it on for lack of adequate information and funds. The very first issue included the quotation for clover-seed on the three provincial markets nearest to the capital – Reading, Farnham and Colchester – giving a price of 24–30 shillings per hundredweight. A few years later Charles Davenant's reorganization of the English Customs House was to make it possible to trace the quantity of forage seed imported annually into England (see Appendix, table 7). The shift in the interest of the average farmer from lucerne and sainfoin to clover took place in the 1690s. The work of the keepers of botanical gardens, both academic and private, and the communications between owners did not fail to establish lucerne and *onobrychis* as widely cultivated plants. A number of years were to pass before their efforts were backed up by adequate seed production and a nation-wide commercial network.

---

[164] Of the vast bibliography, see especially A. John, 'The Course of Agricultural Change', in L. S. Presnell (ed.), *Studies in the Industrial Revolution presented to T. S. Ashton*, London 1960, pp. 125–55; E. L. Jones, 'Agriculture and Economic Growth in England, 1660–1750: Agricultural Change', *The Journal of Economic History*, 25, 1965, pp. 11 ff.; E. A. Wrigley, 'A Simple Model of London's Importance in Changing English Society and Economy, 1650–1750', *Past and Present*, 37, 1967, pp. 44–70; see now *AHEW*, 5/1, *1640–1750: Regional Farming Systems*, Cambridge 1984, and 5/2, *passim*.

[165] See J. Houghton, *A Collection for Improvement of Husbandry and Trade*, London 1692–1703.

7. From theory to seed-production: England and continental Europe in the eighteenth and nineteenth centuries

THE GENERAL ECONOMIC CYCLE

The question of modern agricultural technology in early eighteenth-century England has been dealt with in various ways. The date usually chosen as the turning-point is 1750, which marks the end of the long economic depression and the take-off of European and English demographic recovery, though in the agricultural cycle the situation was much less clear-cut. Two factors do not correspond to the upward trend: on the one hand, the stagnation in the price of grains, which is considered to have slowed down economic development; on the other, the general indifference of practical farmers to the very advanced research of Jethro Tull on plant nutrition and agricultural implements. By focusing on the price of cereals as a measure of national prosperity, scholars have often neglected both the diversification of agricultural production and the lively discussion on, and eager search for, intensive methods of grain cultivation which would reduce the labour required without reducing the quantity of produce. By connecting the literature on agronomy, cultural relations and economic factors we obtain a more complex and realistic interpretation of the period.

Around sixty thousand Englishmen went abroad on the Grand Tour in the seventeenth and eighteenth centuries, neo-classicism became the hallmark of the *pax Augusta*, basis of the new constitutional order, and Virgil became the official model of those who aspired to royal patronage. The translation of Virgil by the Poet Laureate, John Dryden, was not an isolated event. It formed part of the long history of practical interest in Mediterranean agriculture that we have already described, accompanied by a growing interest in archaeology and local history. On the other hand, the new experimental science, centred round the Royal Society, was eagerly followed by many of the landed élite, who were the pillars of the economic system.[1]

The principal economic problem in the first half of the century was the fall in the price of grain, mainly due to plentiful crops at a time when the population was stationary both in England and on the Continent. One of the first Acts of Parliament passed after the Glorious Revolution was the Corn Bounty on exported grains, to offset these low prices, as a compensation to the landed aristocracy for their support of the Protestant cause and for accepting the Land Tax. In practice, the government was encouraging an alliance between agricultural and commercial interests, maintaining a lively exchange between country and town.[2] Excess land was converted to pasture in the grain-growing Midlands, with their open fields, where a common farming system was still in operation and alternate husbandry could work so long as general agreement could be obtained within the community.[3] On the other hand, the productive system could not reduce arable land so drastically and guarantee the survival of the population, without importing grain from Amsterdam and Danzig in years of shortage. And this had the drawback of lowering monetary reserves. It was because corn-growing, together with rationally planned livestock rearing, remained profitable in the first half of the eighteenth century, that agricultural methods were improved much earlier in England than in the rest of Europe.

1. FROM VIRGIL TO INNOVATION: JETHRO TULL, THE SEED-DRILL AND SAINFOIN

The geographical distribution of the new forage-crops is closely connected with cereal growing, in the southern counties (Kent, Middlesex, Berkshire, Hampshire), in the eastern ones (Essex, Suffolk

---

[1] See for example P. Deane and W. A. Cole, *British Economic Growth, 1688–1959*, Cambridge 1967, pp. 1 ff., 40 ff., and C. Wilson, *England's Apprenticeship, 1603–1763*, London 1965; Jones, 'Agriculture'; Stoye, *English Travellers*; *AHEW*, 5/1–2, *passim*; D. A. Allen, *The Naturalist in Britain. A Social History*, Harmondsworth 1978; Thomas, *Man and the Natural World*; see now T. Corse, *Dryden's Aeneid. The English Virgil*, New York–London–Toronto 1991.

[2] See D. G. Barnes, *A History of the English Corn Laws from 1660 to 1846*, London 1930, pp. 11 ff.

[3] J. Thirsk, *England's Agricultural Regions and Agrarian History, 1500–1750*, London 1987, p. 42 and *passim*, J. Broad, 'Alternate husbandry and permanent pasture in the Midlands, 1650–1800', *AHR*, 25, 1980, 1, *passim*, and R. C. Allen, 'The Growth of Labour Productivity in Early Modern English Agriculture', *Explorations in Economic History*, 25, 1988, pp. 117–46, hold different opinions on this point.

and Norfolk), the Midlands, such as Oxfordshire, parts of Herefordshire and Worcestershire, and some areas of Yorkshire. This pattern repeats the ecological division between the English lowlands of grain-growing in the alluvial vales and the English highlands of permanent pastures, together with a few areas that specialized in fruit-growing and horticulture.[4] It has already been pointed out that the best cereal-growing areas were near to the commercial centres of London or Norwich, or to ports trading with the Continent, like Ipswich and Southampton. They were also the cities where the Flemish and Dutch Protestant refugees settled in the seventeenth century, as well as the French Huguenots, after the Revocation of the Edict of Nantes. Agricultural innovations in England were brought about by a combination of local and physical factors (soil, rainfall), economic and institutional factors (large estates, legislation, trade cycles), and social factors (cultural fashions, foreign refugees and the enquiring minds of scholars).

Thus acquaintance with forage-crops, alongside imports from Continental Europe, in the very first years of the eighteenth century, has nothing astonishing about it. The modernization of English agriculture was never a matter that concerned England alone. It was supported by the supply of low-cost technology, which provided first the cultural models and then the seed. The fundamental problem to be overcome, if the new forage-crops were to spread, was the difficulty in obtaining specialized seed, which the local market could not produce in sufficient quantities. In the agricultural literature, sainfoin and clover-seed were called *foreign* or *French seeds*. The former was known as *French grass* par excellence, the latter *Great broad clover* or *Dutch great clover*, to distinguish it from local varieties and was recommended for the improvement of pastures and meadows, according to the soil. Clover, especially, worked wonders in the transformation of pastures where broom and thistles warned of soil deterioration. With an eye to the market, farmers saw that by improving pastureland they would be able to keep more sheep and cattle and diversify their sources of income. But at a time when prices were falling, the greater quantity and quality of fodder produced from legumes had already brought about such a decrease in the value of traditional pastures that Timothy Nourse asked Parliament to intervene by levying a crown on every acre sown with foreign fodder crops. The same consideration made farmers wonder whether it was not better to produce one bushel

[4] See Thirsk, 'England's Agricultural Regions', and idem, 'Farming Regions', in *AHEW*, 5/1.

of corn and sell it at 5s than two bushels at 6s. Gregory King formulated this law on grain prices during the depression of the late seventeenth century.[5] The spread of the innovations cannot be said to have derived from linear growth; it should be borne in mind that there was continual conflict between producers who had access to the international grain market and reaped the benefits of the Corn Bounty and those who sold on the local markets, for whom the value of their produce depended on regional supply.[6]

Information was made available to farmers in leaflets, as well as in treatises based on first-hand experience, gathered by authors such as John Mortimer or Richard Bradley. In either case it was demonstated that the experiments of the previous decades could now be put to use on the farm. Hartlib's publications were still the source of much information, now, however, provided with more appropriate figures on quantities of seed (10–12 lbs per acre for clover, two bushels per acre for sainfoin), backed up by longer experience.[7] Imitation was still rife, and the subjects of Queen Anne and George I were less original than their predecessors; yet the new society of gossip-loving busybodies, depicted in the *Spectator* or in *Tristram Shandy*, had the advantage that information spread rapidly by word of mouth among those who haunted the coffee-houses. The country inns provided many seed-merchants with a base from which to sell their goods (see also below, 4.1).[8] Experience gained in the early eighteenth century put an end to the mistakes and failures

---

[5] On the nomenclature see London, BL, Sloane Ms 3815. See especially T. Nourse, *Campania Felix or a Discourse of the Benefits and Improvements of Husbandry*, London 1700, pp. 47–50, 55–6, 83–92, 86–8, 92; G. King, *Two Tracts*, ed. by G. E. Barnett, Baltimore 1936, and D. V. Glass, *Two Papers on Gregory King*, in D. V. Glass and D. E. C. Eversley (eds.), *Population in History*, London 1965, pp. 159–220; W. Abel, *Agrarkrisen und Agrarkonjunktur*, Hamburg and Berlin, 1966, pp. 23–6, 161–8. See also P. J. Bowden, 'Agricultural prices, wages, farm profits and rents', in AHEW, 5/2, pp. 1–54.

[6] John, 'The Course of Agricultural Change', and Bowden, 'Agricultural Prices', bring out how prices differed from region to region.

[7] See J. Mortimer, *The Whole Art of Husbandry, or the Way of Managing and Improving Land*, London 1708, pp. 28–37, 56–66: the second edition, London 1728, is really a reprint of the first (see pp. 29, 31–6); *The Gentleman Farmer or certain Observations made by an English Gentleman upon the Husbandry of Flanders*, London 1726. On this literature see G. E. Fussell, *More Old English Farming Books from Tull to the Board of Agriculture*, London 1950.

[8] See Spufford, *The Great Reclothing, passim*, and Thirsk, 'Agricultural Innovations', p. 570; Jacob Bobart had made arrangements with a certain George Sedleys, a saddler, to sell pure seeds of clover and sainfoin at the Golden Faulcon Inn, Fleet Street, London, in 1675.

which had dampened the enthusiasm of so many early converts to the new ideas. It became clear that forage-crops did not adapt easily to all land that was waiting to be improved, but had to be introduced into the agricultural cycle with considerable attention to detail. In the same years, the experience of English farmers served as a model for Anglo-Irish and Scottish landowners, who had strongly supported the Act of Union. The information gathered on farming methods, applied in a different social and political system, though in similar soil conditions, affords an accurate key to the understanding of those same events in English history. To prepare arable lands in the Scottish lowlands, farmers were advised in turn to till the fallow in order to destroy weeds, to grow turnips and hoe well to aerate the soil, to burn-bake, and to sow selected seed. The most urgent problem, generally neglected by scholars, was the fight against weeds; darnel (*Lolium temulentum*), the poppy (*Papaver rhoeas*) and silverweed (*Potentilla anserina*). Scottish and Irish land, like the land in some English counties, was still worked on the infield–outfield system, which restricted continuous cultivation, even if alternated with fallow, to the lands nearest the farmhouse, the best on the farm, the outlying ones being tilled intermittently or used as poor pasture. There was no suggestion of sowing lucerne or sainfoin on these half-abandoned lands, where they would probably not have taken hold. A mixture of Italian rye-grass and clover was sown there, after slowly burning the moss on the surface, and then ploughing. The study of the ecology of this transformation (through the action of rain, lime, manure, grazing and the dung of animals put to pasture) was carried out so carefully that it vies in accuracy with the texts produced between 1939 and 1945.[9] S. Pierson had in mind mainly the example of the English counties of Northumberland,

---

[9] See R. H. Campbell, *The Scottish Improvers and the Course of Agrarian Change in the Eighteenth Century*, in L. M. Cullen and T. C. Smout, *Comparative Aspects of Scottish and Irish Social History, 1600–1900*, Edinburgh 1977, *passim*. A considerable shift can be noted from J. Donaldson, *Husbandry anatomized or an Enquiry into the present Manner of Tilling and Manuring the Ground in Scotland*, Edinburgh 1697; J. Hamilton, *The Countryman's Rudiments and advice to the Farmers in East-Lothian how to labour and improve their Ground*, Edinburgh 1699; to works such as S. Peirson, *The present State of the Tillage in Ireland considered and some methods offered for its improvement*, Dublin 1725, which considered the use of clover, rye-grass and so on; T. Dawson, *The great Importance and Necessity of increasing Tillage by an Act of Parliament in Ireland*, Dublin 1755; *An Essay on Ways and Means for inclosing, fallowing, planting Scotland*, Edinburgh 1729, and especially [T. Hope], *A Treatise concerning the Manner of Fallowing of Ground*, Edinburgh 1724, pp. 11–32, to be compared with Davies, *The Grass Crop*, pp. 169 ff., 185; M. Hanf, *The Arable Weeds of Europe with their Seedlings and Seeds*, BASF, Ludwigshafen 1983.

Hertfordshire and the area round London. He explained that the failures of the previous generation in cultivating fodder-crops, and above all Flemish clover, occurred because the seeds had been cast onto the pastures without any preparation. By trial and error it became evident that the seed should be sown on arable land depleted in nutriment by growing cereals. In England farmers stopped planting cereals when they yielded less than five to one per grain sown (see Chap. 3, 9); only then, before the soil was completely exhausted, was clover sown. On the cold soils of Scotland better results could be got from a selected mixture of clover (*T. pratense*) and rye-grass (*L. perenne*) (12 lbs of clover and 3 bushels of rye-grass), rather than pure clover. Lastly, Pierson advised growing clover together with grasses harvested on the spot if the meadow was to be kept under grass for some years. This was because rye-grass and clover have different biological cycles, which would impoverish the pasture when the clover died, while animal dung would favour the growth of gramen grasses, without loss of fertility.[10] The problem constantly insisted on, was the preparation of arable land before sowing the fine (and expensive) clover seed. This meant ploughing in deep furrows to free the soil of water, but harrowing the surface several times, across the field, and then rolling well. After all this, the traditional ridges were completely flattened.[11]

The criticism levelled against Dryden because of the poetic license that he allowed himself with regard to agricultural terms and practices, in his translation of the *Georgics*, goes to show how seriously it was read. It brought to light the high standards of cultured people, who had read Virgil not only as a poet but as an agronomist. In 1725 William Benson published an alternative version, perhaps less elegant stylistically, but certainly more accurate. With his philological knowledge and practical experience of agriculture, he was able to demonstrate the flimsy basis of many passages in Dryden's work.[12] In the fifty years that followed, English agronomy once more assessed itself by the rule of ancient agriculture. The comparison with European practices, common in the early eighteenth century, became continuously more neglected; the real

---

[10] See [Hope], *A Treatise*, pp. 41–2.

[11] See *ibid.*, pp. 36–8.

[12] See W. Benson, *Virgil's Husbandry or an essay on the Georgics. Being the first Book translated into the English verse to which are added the Latin Text and Dryden's Version. With notes critical and rustick*, London 1725, for example pp. 22 (on lucerne), 23, 129–30. See now the very recent works by Corse, *Dryden's Aeneid*, and J. Farrell, *Virgil's Georgics and the Traditional Ancient Epic*, New York–Oxford 1991.

model to be examined, on questions of rotation and method, was the classical model, a metaphor of Mediterranean agricultural civilization. It was against this background that the agronomic and economic options of the English countryside in the first half of the century needed to be discussed. The question was, whether to increase the number of crops and consequently the amount of work on the farm, or else to specialize in rearing livestock, together with subsistence corn-growing.

Jethro Tull entered Gray's Inn after studying at Oxford, more as a preparation for politics than for practising as a lawyer. In 1701 he went back to Howberry Farm, in Oxfordshire. Here, when the farm labourers refused to sow sainfoin seed in rows by hand, he invented his famous drill to do the work. He had it constructed by a maker of musical instruments, who copied the mechanism of the organ. Ideas for a seed-drill had already been put forward in the past by Cavallini of Bologna, Joseph Locatelli, by the Englishmen Sir Hugh Platt and Edward Maxey in the late sixteenth to early seventeenth century and had been discussed by Hartlib and Cressy Dymock, among others, and later by Worlidge.[13] Gallo and Tarello had already provided a tentative solution to the problem by cross-ploughing (see Chap. 3, 9). Thirty years went by before Tull published an account of his invention, thirty years of experience and experiment, starting from a simple mechanical device and finally arriving at a new theory of cultivation.

Tull moved to a new farm near Hungerford, Berkshire, in 1709, continuing his experiments and receiving visits from supporters. Ill-health forced him to spend a long time in France and Italy from 1711 on. It was then that he observed the cultivation of the vineyard, between Frontignan and Sett in the Languedoc, and thought of applying sowing in rows to wheat as well. On his return to England, he built a second machine, the horse-hoe, to be used together with the seed-drill, and developed a theory of cultivation. We owe the publication of his *Horse-Hoeing Husbandry* to the insistence of friends and admirers of the new

---

[13] See Earl Cathcart, 'Jethro Tull: his life, times and teaching', *Journal of the Royal Agricultural Society of England*, s. 3, 2, 1, pp. 6, 15, 21–2, 36; *DNB, sub voce*; T. H. Marshall, 'Jethro Tull and the New Husbandry', *EcHR*, 2, 1929, pp. 41 ff.; G. E. Fussell, *Jethro Tull: his Influence on Mechanized Agriculture*, Reading 1973, pp. 5–26, 27–42; C. Poni, 'Ricerche sugli inventori bolognesi della macchina seminatrice alla fine del secolo xvi', *Rivista storica italiana*, 77, 1964, pp. 455 ff.; E. Maxey, *A New Instruction of Plowing and Setting of Corne*, London 1601; H. Platt, *The Newe and Admirable Art of Setting of Corne*, London 1601; Worlidge, *Systema agriculturae*, p. 47; Thirsk, *Agricultural Innovations*, pp. 582–5.

system.[14] Right from the introduction to his book, Tull openly challenged the so-called Virgilian husbandry which was embedded in the neo-classical sympathies pervading the cultured society of his day. Further on, he discussed the point where Virgil advised burning the stubble on light soils, a practice which makes the soil barren once and for all. Tull pointed out that farmers had given it up even in Italy. In the same way he derided the practice of harrowing arable land to complete the work of ploughing. He considered cross-ploughing a bad thing because it did not turn the earth over completely. These were mistakes commonly made in England and justified by quoting Virgil. According to Tull, Virgilian husbandry was practised more in England than in Italy.[15] His comment arouses doubts not so much on the accuracy of Tull's observations, as on the way Italian agriculture has been dealt with by historians in the past hundred years.

The principles on which Tull organized his agronomic system are as follows: plants grow because their roots extract particles of nitrogen, air, water, fire and earth (all the elements of the old Aristotelian system, plus saltpetre, the recently discovered *salis terrae*). To help the root system to develop, the soil should be broken up as finely as possible; sowing in rows allows weeding and hoeing to be done; hoeing destroys weeds and lets the air circulate in the soil; the horse-hoe makes this work easier; turnips can be grown in the spaces between the rows, breaking up the soil and providing supplementary fodder for sheep. In practice, Tull was applying to corn and other crops cultivated on arable land what he had seen done in the vineyard in the Languedoc, where they ploughed and hoed between the rows and used no manure on the vineyard, so as not to spoil the taste of the wine. Tull came to the conclusion, after making a

---

[14] No definitive biography on Tull and his work has yet been published. The complete list of his printed books is to be found in the British library, *Catalogue of Printed Books*, London 1975. Only the editions published by the author are quoted here: J. Tull, *The New Horse-Houghing Husbandry, or an Essay about the Principles of Tillage and Vegetation*, London 1731, 168 pp.; idem, *The Horse-Hoing Husbandry*, London 1733, 201 pp.; idem, *A Supplement To the Essay on Horse-Hoing Husbandry containing Explanations and Additions both in Theory and in Practice wherein All the Objections against that Husbandry, which have come to the Author's Knowledge are considered and answered*, London 1740. The following quotations are from the last edition published by the author. According to Earl Cathcart, *Jethro Tull*, p. 15, Tull had probably travelled on the Continent in the years 1693–9, whilst Tull himself declared that he had visited France and Italy from 1711: see below, note 23, and Fussell, *Jethro Tull*, pp. 11–13, 20–21.

[15] Tull, *The Horse-Hoing Husbandry*, pp. v, vi, viii, 40–4, 71, *Notes, passim*. About the use of fire in Italian agriculture see Sereni, *Terre nuove*.

series of experiments, that the beneficial effect of spreading manure on arable land lay in the tilling involved in getting it into the soil. What is more, three supplementary ploughings cost less (12s) than one manuring (£3) and the former gave a better grain harvest. It was ploughing that was needed, not surface harrowing of the field after sowing, for the horses' hooves transformed the surface of the field into a hard crust which prevented air from circulating. The impressive agricultural machinery that lords it over our arable land today is accused of having exactly the same effect. To support his observation, Tull quoted Columella (II, 4); for, it must be said, in agronomy he was anti-Virgilian, but not anti-Classical. Indeed, it was what Columella called *sarritio*, applied to lucerne-growing, that gave him the idea of the horse-hoe, for weeding the growing corn. Actually, hoeing of the young corn had long been practised successfully in some parts of Berkshire. What is more, sowing in rows meant a saving of seed and, as Columella argued, seed was lost when covered too deeply by the plough.[16] Columella's Latin served the same purpose in the eighteenth century as Gallo's Italian had done in the sixteenth. The readers of Classical and Italian agronomy probably came from the same social background, Lord Cathcart, Townshend, Walpole, Lord Ducie and Halifax being among Tull's supporters. Paradoxically, the lasting progress of English agronomy was made by following the technology of what from many points of view was an economically backward area, the peninsula of Italy.

Tull was not the solitary innovator, struggling against the barbarians, portrayed by the ideologists of the first agricultural revolution, nor the charlatan that his contemporary or more recent detractors have made him out to be. He was a careful farmer pervaded by the scientific spirit of his time and a profound commentator on Classical literature.[17] The English agronomy that Tull was attacking was not that of the open-field system, but the more advanced agronomy of the early eighteenth century, in which forage-crops were known and cross-ploughing was common practice. The way contemporary farmers perceived the technology they were using is important for defining the relation between routine and

---

[16] See Tull, *The Horse-Hoing Husbandry*, pp. 18–20, 21–5, 28–9.
[17] See D. Y., 'On the improvements in agriculture', *Gentleman's Magazine*, 1764, p. 524; Lord Ernle (R. E. Prothero), *English Farming Past and Present* (1912), ed. by G. E. Fussell and O. R. Macgregor, London 1961, pp. 169–75; Marshall, *Jethro Tull*; Kerridge, *The Agricultural Revolution*, p. 36, is his most recent detractor, while Fussell, *Jethro Tull*, pp. 110–21, presents a balanced judgement on Tull's merits, assessed over the long term and with reference to modern farming practice.

innovation. What at that time was held to be the best agricultural practice went by the name of 'Virgilian agriculture'. Though sometimes found on open fields, forage-crops, in this case sainfoin, were hampered by sheep left free to graze, cross-ploughing and strips of land that were too narrow. Tull was addressing the farmers who cultivated the enclosed fields of central and eastern England, where lucerne, sainfoin, clover and turnips had already been grown for years. Sainfoin and lucerne especially were appreciated much more than historians have realized so far. Tull's statement, that sainfoin sown in rows and hoed with the horse-hoe was more satisfactory, was made with respect to the traditional method of sowing broadcast, with eight or ten bushels to the acre, sometimes with a mixture of rye-grass, clover and barley, to destroy the weeds, but which had the disadvantage of creating competition between the various plants sown. He gave the example of a hill above Crotone, in Calabria, where wild sainfoin was reduced to a pitiful state, which suggested that forage-crops should be grown following the general rules for cultivation. In this way two or three non-metric tonnes (equal to 1,800–2,700 kilos) of good sainfoin hay, rather than the tough, fibrous grass on his neighbours' farms, could be produced. Although seed-gathering was a laborious task, sainfoin was a good source of income (the yield from one acre was enough to sow a hundred) and was also good instead of oats as fodder for horses. Some of his neighbours had obtained very large seed-harvests, from 150 acres in one case, and elsewhere the product of half an acre of sainfoin, counting seed, hay and chaff, had given a profit of £4 10s. Tull himself had sown fifty acres of sainfoin, to sell the seed. It was a crop that could be recommended for all kinds of soil, if sown and cultivated in the right way.[18] The cultivation of lucerne was more difficult, though the failures did not seem to have reduced interest in the crop and kept the import of seed high. In this Tull is supported by Customs figures. In 1725, 900 pounds of lucerne seed came from Italy, and throughout the 1720s and 1730s Italy continued to be the largest supplier of lucerne to English farmers (see Appendix, table 7).[19] The best feature of lucerne was its resistance both to heat and to cold, as shown in the Languedoc and the Swiss cantons. Unfortunately, it was not easy to find soil in England where it would establish itself easily. In spite of all his praise of

[18] See Tull, *The Horse-Hoing Husbandry*, pp. 75–92, 231–3, 251; the contemporary author who mistook *sainfoin-Onobrychis* for *sainfoin*-Medicago was Morison, *Plantarum historia universalis* (see chap. 6, note 155).

[19] See Tull, *The Horse-Hoing Husbandry*, p. 93, and London, PRO, Customs 3/26.

lucerne cultivated with ploughing and hoeing, Tull seems to have grown only a small patch of it in his garden.[20]

The greatest advantage obtained by cultivation in rows and the use of the horse-hoe was that it prevented weeds from spreading. By applying this method, the stunted crops of many farmers would be rid of couch-grass, coltsfoot, melilot, bracken, wild garlic and wild oats.[21] These were plants which were capable of surviving in very unfavourable conditions, which were made hardier by manuring and, besides being strong competitors of crops, infested the soil, their seed lying dormant and springing up suddenly with the slightest variation in climate or chemical composition, increasing costs and dashing hopes of gain. Even the work of weeding, carried out by hand using a bladed tool, which had been done more and more regularly from the earliest years of the sixteenth century in the more populous and productive parts of East Anglia, made the weeds spread faster from the severed roots. Tull describes the ecology of the arable field as an environment with an unstable equilibrium between the species within it, often bordering on wasteland, otherwise on meadows and pastures, which were a source of weeds, especially those transferred in cattle- and horse-manure, full of seed enriched with nitrates. It is an invaluable picture for the historian who wishes to understand the problems of cultivation in the early eighteenth century.[22]

The introduction and spread of new crops does not depend only on the economic factors of costs and productivity, but on the environmental and economic context and the extent of competition. Early eighteenth-century farmers who believed in the value of legumes were endeavouring to transform temporary crops of foreign origin into acclimatized English crops. Rather than explaining the delay in the spread of the innovations, historians would do well to call attention to the role of those farmers who understood the importance of liming, marling and repeated tillage to maintain forage-crops, which were by then widely known.

In his notes to the text that he published in 1740, when the agricultural depression was at its worst, Tull gave ample demonstration that, after a

---

[20] See Tull, *The Horse-Hoing Husbandry*, pp. 92–102; crops are still transplanted to-day to produce seed selected from the finest specimens, see Crescini, *Piante erbacee*, p. 438.

[21] In the following order: *Agropyron repens, Tussilago farfara, Melilotus officinalis, Polystichum sp., Allium ursinum, Avena fatua.*

[22] See Tull, *The Horse-Hoing Husbandry*, pp. 37–40, 131 note 1, 213–15; W. Harwood Long, 'The Low Yields of Corn in Medieval England', *EcHR*, ser. 2, 32, 1979, pp. 459–69; Campbell, 'Agricultural Progress', p. 39, and Langdon, *Horses*, pp. 266, 278–82.

lifetime of experiments and cost–benefit analysis, his ideas on the whole cycle of the new forage-crops were very clear. He maintained that clover was introduced into England at the time of Cromwell, much before it came into general use. Gentlemen could sow it as they liked; tenants, having to think first about paying their rent, could not afford to reduce the amount of land used for growing cereals (see above, Chap. 3, 9). It took tenants fifty years to learn to cultivate it. But in his time, after 1730, they could not pay the rent unless they sowed clover, although the profits were not as high as before. The same happened with sainfoin, which was already known around 1630–40, to those acquainted with the Continent, but it only came into general use among farmers and tenants later. The notes also contained another piece of forgotten information. The price of hay and sainfoin seed fell thanks to its widespread use and because farmers had gained so much experience in preparing the seed that they no longer depended on buying at the market.[23] Lucerne seed, however, was still imported regularly, though in limited quantities. Tull completed his theory with designs for a plough with four shares, fore-runner of all the cultivators that were to appear in subsequent decades, first in England and France, then in the rest of Europe.[24]

2. VIRGILIAN HUSBANDRY AND EARLY EIGHTEENTH-CENTURY ENGLAND

The problems dealt with by Tull were common in the first decades of the eighteenth century. Edward Lisle was also in the forefront of those trying to solve them, working in the same years but independently of Tull. In 1693–4, at the age of twenty-seven, he took possession of his farm at Crux-Easton, in Hampshire, managing it scrupulously until his death in 1722. Like many others, he kept a diary, in which he noted conversations with neighbours, with other farmers, observations on books he had read, on the harvests and on the weather. Towards 1713 he began to think of publishing these notes; actually it was his son who prepared them for the press in 1756. Edward Lisle was a well-informed farmer, always ready to help and advise others. He was at the centre of a system of information which ranged from Bobart, of the Botanic Garden

---

[23] See Tull, *The Horse-Hoing Husbandry*, pp. 251–3; G. Mingay, 'The Agricultural Depression, 1730–1750', *EcHR*, ser. 2, 8, 1955–6, pp. 156–67.

[24] See Tull, *The Horse-Hoing Husbandry*, pp. 131–8, table 1; Haudricourt and Delamarre, *L'homme et la charrue*, pp. 333 ff., 343 ff.; A. Bourde, *Agronomie*, vol. I, pp. 325 ff.

of Oxford, son of the already-mentioned Jacob Bobart (see Chap. 6, 4.2.), to the experience of his own farm-labourers, with whom he discussed the work to be done, to communications and meetings with other landowners, even in remote counties (from Dorset to Leicestershire). He was certainly more than an ordinary reader of Virgil, whose ideas on the rustic virtues he shared, and considered it an act of patriotism to urge the noblemen of England to adopt them too. But rather than Virgil, he preferred to quote Columella, Palladius and the scientists of the Royal Academy, Boyle, Ray, Evelyn and Mortimer.[25] He was interested in all aspects of cultivation, focusing mainly on the battle against weeds. Without Tull's plough with three shares or the horse-hoe, but with the guidance of the ancients and the practical experience of the best farmers in England that he knew, Lisle, too, constantly recommended work on the fallow, breaking up the soil finely, deep-ploughing to rid arable land of weeds by exposing their roots to the sun in summer and the frost in winter. On the arable land of the open fields of Leicestershire they ploughed as many as five times for barley, four for wheat, five for oats and one for peas; not many, perhaps, in comparison with the eight times recommended by Tarello, but certainly more than the average number in England in those days. His notes also provide a series of details, of tests made to satisfy Lisle's curiosity, and of discussions he had with other farmers on the cultivation of clover, lucerne and sainfoin and the ecology of these crops. According to Lisle, clover (*T. repens*) often failed to give the results hoped for on cold, damp, clay soils, because they were not manured in the winter. He advised keeping twenty to thirty acres of clover for the cattle, when the other, natural pastures had been thoroughly grazed; but the cattle should not be allowed into the clover field, so as not to ruin the plants with their dung. Clover was considered useful if sown thickly to destroy weeds and was generally kept for two years, in rotation with cereals. Lisle produced his own clover and sainfoin seed, while others had it sent from Sussex. Farmers discussed the relative economic value of Italian rye-grass and sainfoin, thought to produce a crop of equal volume, while clover was better as a soil-improver.[26] The main feature of Lisle's agronomy was a complete

---

[25] See E. Lisle, *Observations in husbandry*, London 1757, 2 vols., pp. iii–v, xii–xiii, xvii.

[26] *Ibid.*, vol. I, pp. 87 ff., especially pp. 89, 94, 103, 137, 319–20; vol. II, pp. 37 ff., 42–3, 45–6, 49–50, 54–5, 59–60, 61–5: the extracts from Tull were added by his son in 1756 (pp. 61–7); G. E. Fussel, 'Adventures with clover', *Agriculture*, 1955, pp. 342–5; on weeds in English fields in this century see J. A. S. Watson and J. A. More, *Agriculture. The Science and Practice of British Farming* (1924), Edinburgh–London 1956, pp. 150–7, 431–6.

absence of preconceived ideas. He also made experiments based on passages from the *Georgics*, for example on the practice of green manuring' and reported the advice of neighbouring farmers on the effect of hoeing. While on the one hand Lisle's experience confirmed that the best crop of sainfoin could be got on lighter, hilly land, and that lime and ashes were preferable to manure, he also confirmed the difficulty of obtaining a meadow exclusively of sainfoin, saying that at best it would be mixed with white and red clover, at worst with bent grass (*Agrostis tenuis*) and twitch or couch-grass (*Agropyron repens*). Nor did clover grow without difficulty, many failures being attributable to the natural grasses on the land chosen. Sowing thickly or thinly might each give good results, provided the soil had been carefully prepared.[27] The work of the botanist Ray was quoted, as it illustrated the association of certain weeds with pedological features that needed correction. The dandelion (*Tarassacum officinale*) and couch-grass, white flax (*Linum catharticum*) and moss were all signs of a poor soil. The battle against weeds was fought by the repeated use of clean seed on the ley and repeated ploughing for arable land. The procedure advised by Lisle, and tested by the best farmers, was not very different from that applied today – a good meadow was the basis of good arable land. He was not much persuaded by the manual hoeing of seeds, which he thought costly and ineffective when not harmful. Study of the relation between weeds and crops was the first step towards getting rid of weeds. Those that came up in the late summer were not too troublesome because they would not survive the winter; whereas the common red poppy (*Papaver rhoeas*), the lesser bindweed (*Convolvulus arvensis*), ox-eye daisy (*Chrysanthemum leucanthemum*), centaury and creeping thistle (*Cirsium arvense*) were a menace. Manual hoeing was not enough, it destroyed a number of the valued plants and made the weeds spring up again from the roots and rhizomes. The practice of Lisle and some of his neighbours foreshadowed Tull's advice – repeated ploughing was useful, harrowing useless if not harmful, since it, too, encouraged the growth of weeds. The same plants were useful in transforming the micro-environment in many different situations. Rye-grass, well manured, kept coltsfoot in check, but the manure in its turn limited the growth of clover and sainfoin.[28] The good eighteenth-century farmer needed extensive knowledge and a wide

[27] Lisle, *Observations in husbandry*, vol. I, p. 43, note, pp. 64 ff., 68 ff., 319; vol. II, pp. 57, 58, 72–5.
[28] *Ibid.*, vol. II, pp. 207–13, 285 ff., 289–91, 308, 312–13.

botanical background to transform the environment and render the transformation more lasting. Pliny, not Virgil or Columella, should have been his point of reference.

We have already mentioned that Tull's writings did not meet with the complete approval of the public. Actually, a group of people hostile to him set up a Private Society of Husbandmen and Planters, who published a fierce attack on his method. The compiler of the work, but probably not the sole inspirer of the dispute, was Stephen Switzer, a gardener, a seed merchant in Westminster, himself the author of good works on agronomy, frankly inspired by Pliny, Columella and, above all, Virgil.[29] The attack on Tull becomes more understandable if connected with the wish to maintain control over the seed-market and to avoid losing buyers of the illustrated booklets sold with the seeds. Like all his contemporaries, Switzer had found ample sources of information and inspiration in Classical and Continental literature, which he circulated among experimental farmers, including Admiral Hughes, the Earl of Halifax and Sir John Dalrymple, and others in Dorset, Sussex, Berkshire, Kent, Oxfordshire, Gloucestershire, Wiltshire, Norfolk and Lancashire. He complained, however, that failures in the cultivation of lucerne were the consequence of the idleness of farmers who did not break down the soil finely enough. This was a criticism quite similar to that of Tull, but it was the only point of contact between the two. Switzer kept to more traditional advice: 10–12 lbs of seed per acre on good soils,14–16 on poor ones. Lucerne was to be sown with a cover crop of barley and oats (six to seven bushels on poor soils, four to five on the better ones), covered by light harrowing. He considered sandy soils afforded the best chances of success (in fact, from the late nineteenth century on, lucerne was grown mainly in East Anglia). He also advised trefoil, less dangerous in cattlefeed, to be used alone (12 lbs on good soil) or mixed with rye-grass, as was the practice on the hard, stony soils of Wiltshire

---

[29] See S. Switzer, *Iconographia Rustica or The Nobleman, Gentleman and Gardener's Recreation*, London 1715, p. xiii; idem, *The Country Gentleman's Companion: or Ancient husbandry restored and Modern husbandry improved. Shewing I. The most expeditious manner of raising . . . foreign salads and other kitchen plants . . . II. The method of burning clay for the improvement of land . . . III. The great improvement of land by grass seeds . . . IV. The excellency of the Medicago or Cythisus Maranthae of the ancients . . .* , London 1732 (pamphlets already published separately in 1731); idem, *The Practical Husbandman and Planter; or Observations on the Ancient and Modern Husbandry – deduced chiefly from practice rather than books*, London 1733–4, 2 vols. See also Fussell, *Jethro Tull*, pp. 57 ff.; J. Harvey, *Early Nurserymen*, London–Chichester 1974, *passim*.

and Hampshire.[30] In the ten years from 1730–9, the import of lucerne seed alone, into the port of London, was 331 cwt 30 lbs, which at the price of 15s for every 10 lbs, gave an income of nearly £500. In the same period, clover-seed imports amounted to around 4,800 cwts; sold at an average price of 3d a pound, which gave a total income of £6,720, to be added to the sale of 'many thousands'(*sic*) of booklets of instructions, which Switzer sold at 1s 6d each. It is difficult to say how many of these booklets were actually printed, since Switzer himself might have exaggerated the number for commercial reasons. However the public responded immediately. In 1732 the nurseryman Henry Woodman sent to Henry Ellison, Esquire, a hundred bushes of cytisus (*Medicago arborea*), broccoli seeds worth 8s and lettuce seeds worth 4s 6d. It is clear that the point was to sell the instructions with every small sample of seed, which would mean receipts of over £700 a year on the seeds for forage-crops alone. If we then recall that only about five firms were dealing in seeds in London in those years, we can see why this merchant lobby was so openly hostile to Jethro Tull, who advised reducing the quantity of seed sown and producing it on the grower's own farm.[31]

The problems that Tull had tried to solve by using original, though not easily applicable technology, were difficulties that he had in common with other English farmers, who also tried to introduce more productive techniques on their farms. The more expensive seed was cultivated in rows, sown by hand in the furrow, covered with the Dutch hoe and weeded. Improving the land by sowing seed was considered preferable to manuring; anyone who did not grow cultivated forage-crops was by then considered a very bad farmer in the limestone region of Hertfordshire. Nor were forage-crops limited to farms with enclosed fields. Numerous strips of clover were sown on the open fields and commons of Taddington (Bedfordshire), later enclosed by movable fencing. And this happened more often on the fields of the south Midlands than contemporary writers realized. Sometimes they made up for the failure of lucerne or sainfoin by sowing vetch, which received the

---

[30] See Switzer, *The Country Gentleman's Companion*, pp. 28–31, 32–4.
[31] See idem, *A Compendious method for the raising of the Italian broccoli . . . La Lucerne, St. foyn, clover . . .* , London 1731, pp. 78, sold for 1s 6d; idem, *The Practical Husbandman and Planter*, p. 32, estimated the cost of 10 lb of lucerne seed at 15s; on seed imports, see Appendix, table 7; on seed merchants see Harvey, *Early Nurserymen*, pp. 47 ff., 75 ff., 182. In the introduction to his *The Country Gentleman's Companion*, London 1728, p. x, Switzer thanked Messrs Garroway, Turner, Sears, seed merchants in London, very warmly.

benefit of all the preliminary tillage. During the depression of the 1740s, many farmers went on trying to cultivate legumes, almost as if they all believed the old saying that clover was the father of a good crop of grain. Besides Tull's drill, the simpler but no less effective one of William Ellis, a farmer and agricultural writer of Little Gaddesden, Hertfordshire, had also been devised. Ellis declared in print that he was prepared to send it anywhere in England or Ireland.[32]

By now it was generally accepted that the productivity of arable land depended on the number of times it was ploughed and the quality of the seed. Even the poorest soils had to be ploughed several times and grain seed was generally purchased to prevent the spread of blight and smut among the crops. It was considered good practice to sow enclosed fields with seed gathered on open fields, as Henry Best had already done in the previous century. Around 1730 a gentleman whose name has remained unknown, who lived two hundred miles from London, used to sell eight qualities of wheat-seed and various kinds of unspecified forage-crop seed. Ellis did the same on his farm in Little Gaddesden. Other markets, such as Salisbury (Wiltshire) and Leighton (Bedfordshire) specialized in seeds selected from pasture that had been ploughed and planted with cereals for the first time. Otherwise seed was brought by sea from Scotland and northern England, where it cost less and was gathered on colder soils, in colder climates, and so gave a better yield when sown on the more fertile soil of the southern counties. The practice of sowing grain from a poor soil on more fertile land, rather than the opposite, had been recommended ever since ancient times. In fact, it constitutes confirmation, at regional level, of Vavilov's theory that agriculture started in the mountains of the Middle East, and not in the fertile Crescent (see below, in the Conclusion). Alternate crops like turnips or clover were also sown on fallow land to reduce the number of weeds such as corn marigold.[33] Otherwise the clover was broadcast in spring on the wheat-field, or sown together with barley and oats, and covered by light harrowing. While cultivation of alternate crops followed the rules already applied in the previous century, a new treatment was suggested

[32] See W. Ellis, *Chiltern and Vale Farming explained according to the latest improvements*, London 1733, pp. 260–3, 275, 279–81; W. Ellis, *The Modern Husbandman or the practice of Farming*, London 1744, 8 vols.: *January*, pp. 56, 62, 64, 141–46; *February*, pp. 31, 76–7, 113–17; *March*, pp. 16–21, 80–2, 94, 101–11; *May*, p. x. Ellis was a scrupulous, though unpretentious farmer, see Fussell, *More Old English Farming Books*, pp. 6–13.
[33] See *Calendula arvensis* or *Chrysantemum segetum*; see also above, notes 27 and 28.

for leys and pastures. The manure spread on pastures in winter stimulated the growth of spontaneous legumes. Alternatively, farmers were advised to improve impoverished pasture by ploughing and harrowing it as for arable land and then to sow selected seeds, such as wild clover or kidney vetch (*Anthyllis vulneraria*), and not the seeds commonly collected in handfuls from the hay already harvested (the practice that Norden described in the early seventeenth century) or clover, possibly irrigating it with good quality water.[34]

From the 1720s and 1730s, Scottish farmers began to follow the ways of English agriculture and duly studied Tull's method. Light seeding with clover (four pounds as against the twenty previously advised) often mixed with rye-grass (see below, 5), gave good yields on Scottish moorland, prepared by burning, and drained to free it of stagnant water. In this backward countryside Tull's method gave full proof of its value as a key to understanding the power of the new crops to transform the land, in England as well as Scotland. In the number of ploughings (more necessary than manure, to cultivate wheat where only oats had been grown before) conditions in Scotland were comparable to those in England twenty years before; Virgilian and Tullian systems alike had opted for frequent tillage to solve cultivation problems. As we have seen, the more perceptive farmers did not treat pasture and arable land very differently.[35] In the eyes of contemporaries, the fall in the price of cereals had not hindered the spread of the innovations, despite the fact that ploughing was still the most costly form of labour. Pasture did not spread as a definitive alternative to growing cereals. Permanent grass-lands became established on higher ground, while meadows based on a single species of grass or legume occupied the valleys.[36] The agricultural depression did not bring about a slackening in the drive towards the integration of the English with the Continental agricultural system. Founded on imitation, it was now well supported by the importation of essential agricultural input and mutual commercial exchange. Mid-eighteenth century growers could count on crops that were by now well

---

[34] See S. Trowell, *A New Treatise of Husbandry, gardening and other curious matters relating to Country Affairs . . .* , London 1739, pp. 42 ff.; idem, *The Farmer's Instructor or the Husbandman and Gardener's Companion . . . and now completed and supplemented by William Ellis*, London 1747, pp. 3, 13, 15–16, 24, 35, 80–4, 118–37.

[35] See R. Maxwell (ed.), *Select Transactions of the Honourable Society of Improvers in the Knowledge of Agriculture in Scotland*, Edinburgh 1743, pp. vii, 22 ff., 47–9, 52, 61–3, 174–9, 180–5. See also E. J. Hobsbawm, '*Capitalisme et agriculture: les réformateurs écossais au 18ᵉ siècle*', *Annales (ESC)*, 33, 3, 1988, pp. 580–601.

[36] See T. Hale, *A Complete Body of Husbandry*, London 1756, book XVII, *passim*.

rooted in local practice, though the individual farmer might still make mistakes because of the great variety of soils.

The destruction of weeds was a starting-point for the introduction of new crops. The importation of seed was held within certain bounds until the middle of the century, when even the literature on agronomy began to pay less attention to the weed problem. The expression 'Virgilian husbandry' continued to be used by contemporaries because it evoked a system that was foreign to traditional practice and was connected with Mediterranean agricultural experience. It involved the exclusion of manure, and cultivation in rows, which made it easier to control weeds in fields of cereals and also amongst turnips or forage-crops. When the price of grains started to rise steadily again, in the middle of the century, it became economically more worthwhile to follow in Tull's footsteps. Then the issue at stake became the spacing of rows for wheat; Tull's suggestion of two rows for every six feet of land, leaving room for alternate rows of turnips, was too far apart; thus a row every eighteen inches was introduced to exploit the land more fully. The new agriculture used intensive tilling to prepare the ground and alternated crops, such as turnips, to kill the weeds; Randall's semi-Virgilian husbandry used the same concepts without depending on Tull's drill. Good use of the traditional plough and sowing in rows, by hand, would, he thought, double production obtained by the old methods. Instead of the implements designed by Tull, which worked well on flat land and light soil, but were difficult for the less expert mechanics to make, two more traditional tools were introduced, the 'spiky' roller for covering seeds, and the heavy harrow for breaking up the surface clods.[37] To these were added the two-shared plough and the horse-hoe to replace hoeing by hand. While Tull generously published the designs of his machines, making them available freely, after 1750 every new invention concerning agricultural machinery was jealously defended with patents.[38]

The fashion of the Grand Tour and the fact that English wheat was ever more conspicuous on the Continental market had an unexpected effect. Tull's method met with real success in France, and from there

---

[37] See I. Randall, *The semi-virgilian Husbandry, deduced from various experiments or an Essay towards the new course of National Farming*, London 1764, pp. liii–lix, 103, 106–8; 'Some account of Mr. Randall's seed plow with Reference to the Plate', *The Gentleman's Magazine*, 1764, p. 460.

[38] See K. Boehm, *The British Patent System*, Cambridge 1967, and R. J. Sullivan, 'Measurement of English Farming Technological Change, 1523–1900', *Explorations in Economic History*, 21, 1984, pp. 270–89.

passed into Italy. English agriculture became fashionable as Italian and French customs had been in sixteenth- and seventeenth-century England. But Tull had already weighed technological imitation against the political conditions under which French farmers were working, and despite his deep interest in Continental agricultural practices, he confidently claimed the superiority of English political institutions. William Harte and John Symonds both travelled through Italy in the 1760s. The former published a long history of agricultural innovations in England, in which he traced many of the points that have formed the object of this study. Harte had a good knowledge of sixteenth- and seventeenth-century English and Continental literature on agronomy. He had observed the seed trade in Italy and the cultivation of lucerne for seed, especially when transplantation was used.[39] John Symonds undertook his journey to Italy with the declared aim of solving the moot point about Virgilian husbandry – whether the practice of Latin rustics was still adopted in his time. He returned to England five years later, was elected professor of modern history at Cambridge and only in the 1780s, on the insistence of his friend Arthur Young, agreed to publish an account of his agronomic wanderings. In his opinion there was no lack of good agricultural practice, but the political authorities were doing their best to hinder agricultural development in Italy.[40]

By the middle of the eighteenth century, English agricultural writers were no longer asking whether Virgilian husbandry was good or not. The best practices had quietly been adopted, transformed when necessary for introduction into high farming, while some large landowners formed a pressure-group to appropriate the merits of agricultural growth and to parade it before an admiring Europe. To them good farming was a question of cash. Once more the great landowners and the smaller owner-occupiers found themselves on opposite sides in the debate.[41]

---

[39] See W. Harte, *Essays on Husbandry: Essay I. A general introduction. Essay II. An account of some experiments tending to improve the culture of Lucerne by transplantation* [*sic*], London 1764, pp. xx, 214, 232, to which was added a *List of writers upon whose authorities the principal passages in this work are founded*, London 1770, pp. xx–xxvi.

[40] See Ambrosoli, *John Symonds, passim*.

[41] The standard work on these events is J. D. Chambers and G. E. Mingay, *The Agricultural Revolution, 1750–1880*, London 1966; see now G. E. Mingay (ed.), *AHEW*, 6, *1750–1850*, Cambridge 1990, and the literature quoted therein.

2.1. Huguenot refugees in England and the new agriculture in France

Tull's work and fame were not confined to England. Sainfoin, clover and lucerne were by now well known throughout Europe, though they were very little used outside the areas that we have discussed at length. Relations between England and France were never simple. As we have seen, the English botanists Morison, Ray and Sherard worked and studied first in Paris, and together with Tournefort. Yet the botanical garden of the University of Montpellier kept in touch to some extent with the Oxford botanists even after the Revocation of the Edict of Nantes.

It was this very revocation which revolutionized the cultural relations between the two countries. Beside the culture of the élite who made the Grand Tour and the discovery of England by French intellectuals, between 1660 and 1715 must be set the mass of people who took the northward road to England. Two hundred thousand Huguenots left France and made their way to Geneva, Holland, Prussia and England. The skilled workers and artisans are generally the ones mentioned, but there were also a great many farmers. Most of the latter came from the Dauphiné, or rather the Vivarais region, the Languedoc and the Cévennes, where the cultivation of lucerne and sainfoin was a time-old tradition.[42] There were already colonies of Dutch and Flemish immigrants in England, who had made their home there for religious reasons in previous centuries, and to these other French Huguenots had been added in the course of the seventeenth century. They had settled in eastern and southern England, in such places as Canterbury, Sandwich, Dover, the Cinque Ports, Norwich and Colchester, and in London itself, in the parishes of Southwark and Lambeth. Almost all these new communities had among them a market-gardener or a gardener, who took an active part in developing that sector and spreading such novelties as hops, hemp, liquorice and horticultural products, the consumption of which was increasing; carrots and other roots, cabbages, peas and the

---

[42] See D. C. A. Agnew, *Protestant exiles from France in the reign of Louis XIV or the Huguenot Refugees and their descendants in Great Britain and Ireland*, London 1871–4; W. C. Scoville, *The Persecution of Huguenot and French Economic Development, 1680–1720*, Berkeley–Los Angeles 1960, p. 133; R. D. Gwyn, *Huguenot Heritage: The History and Contribution of the Huguenots in Britain*, London 1985; B. Cottret, *Terre d'exil. L'Angleterre et ses réfugiés, 16e–17e siècles*, with an introduction by E. Le Roy Ladurie, Paris 1985; M. Magdelaine and R. Von Thadden, *Le Refuge huguenot*, Paris 1985, pp. 262–3.

like. Others, more fortunate, made a name for themselves in the laying out of formal gardens. Among these were the Salomon brothers (1576–1626) and Isaac de Caux, who worked on the Palatine Garden, later in Whitehall and at Woburn Abbey, or Daniel Marot (1650–1718), creator of the garden of Het Lo, William of Orange's favourite spot in Holland. Others went to settle in Ireland with the intention of civilizing the predominantly Catholic population through their useful knowledge, and there became the trusted tenants of the Anglican aristocracy, as happened at Portarlington from 1697.[43] Foreigners and Huguenots or their descendants were also found in the more limited world of the nurserymen. Charles Minier, first of a family still active in the late nineteenth century, Pierre Collin, Laurence de Coussin, John Bonnor from Montilly in Provence, Jacob de Ayde, John Cotterell, Bartholomew Rocque, Paul Dupin and Charles L'Anson were all owners of firms of some importance. The man who did most to spread forage-crops was Bartholomew Rocque, market-gardener and nurseryman of Fulham, London, who wrote two pamphlets in the 1760s, on lucerne, burnet and timothy grass (*Phleum pratense*), noteworthy for their contribution to the creation of permanent meadows, and ahead of the experiments made at Woburn Abbey (see below, 4.1).[44]

It was thanks to these Anglo-French connections that the alternate husbandry which had developed in England moved out of the learning phase and began to be taken as a model. In the eyes of the enquiring French reader, what seemed like social success for the English farmer between 1680 and 1750 was, in fact, based on a bad translation of 'farmer' as '*paysan*', the term 'farmer' having a social and economic status higher than the sharecropper, or the French or Italian peasant; and the fact that the English rural population drank tea was in reality a sign of poverty when compared with the traditional wholesome beer, whereas

[43] See W. D. Cooper, *List of Foreign Protestants and Aliens resident in England, 1618–1688*, London 1862, pp. 11, 12, 14, 15–17, 18, 25, 60 ff., 83, 95, 99; C. Thacker, 'Huguenot Gardeners in the Age of Gardeners', *Proceedings of the Huguenot Society of London*, 24, 1912, pp. 60–5; G. L. Lee, *The Huguenot Settlements in Ireland*, London–New York–Toronto 1936; A. Carré, *L'influence des Huguenots français en Irlande aux xviie et xviiie siècles*, Paris 1937; J. Floyd, 'The Huguenot Settlement at Portarlington', *Proceedings of the Huguenot Society of London*, 3, 1889, pp. 10, 13–14; see also M. Thick, 'Market Gardening in England and Wales', in *AHEW*, 5/2, pp. 503–32.
[44] See Harvey, *Early Nurserymen, passim*; B. Rocque, *A Practical Treatise on cultivating Lucerne Grass*, London 1761; idem, *Some Hints relative to Burnet and Timothy Grass*, London 1764; published again in the *Museum Rusticum et Commerciale*, 1764.

it was taken by the hasty Continental traveller as an illustration of the English countryman's efforts to follow upper-class fashion. Moreover, the comparison between French and English farmers was made in the years of the long depression, when the price of cereals was low and there was always white bread on the Englishman's table. Jethro Tull's agricultural system, indebted as it was to the Continent, aroused the interest of French agronomists, who had produced nothing original since the days, now far off, of Olivier de Serres.

Henri Louis Duhamel du Monceau was born in Paris in the year 1700, of a family rich in money and land, from whom he inherited half the estate of Denainvilliers (Gâtinais). He was a farmer, grower of trees and cereals, a naval engineer, and a high-ranking official of the realm. He had collected a mass of practical and experimental knowledge by mixing with artisans and practical people, managing to synthesize this knowledge into original agronomic thought based on English experience.[45] He began his research on agronomy in 1728 with a publication on the saffron of the Angoumois area, where this sixteenth-century crop was gradually replaced by the saffron produced in the Gâtinais area. The cultivation of saffron, then an industrial plant, required a great deal of labour and seriously impoverished the soil. Duhamel advised growing it on barren land in a four-year rotation with *sainfoin*. In 1739, after failing to obtain the post as director of the Jardin du Roi, which was granted to the naturalist Buffon, he was appointed Inspector General of the Navy. In this capacity he visited the ports of England and Provence. His most important works on agronomy came out in 1756 and 1762. The *Traité de la Culture des Terres* (1756) was inspired by Tull's *Horse-Hoeing Husbandry*, a copy of which he had received in 1748, and grew out of a discussion between him and Buffon concerning the quality of the French translation.[46] The *Traité* was something more than a guide to Tull's agricultural methods. In following Tull's model, Duhamel too continually compared common practice among cereal-growers in France, and the cultivation of turnips and sainfoin, with the new farming methods and the higher yields that could be obtained by adopting them. This was the system Charles Estienne had used at the time of the *Praedium rusticum*, when he explained the agricultural terminology of

---

[45] See A. Bourde, *The Influence of England on the French Agronomes, 1750–1789*, Cambridge 1953, on this question in general, and in particular idem, *Agronomie*, vol. I, pp. 253 ff., 287 and 290.

[46] See *ibid.*, pp. 256–68.

his times on the basis of Latin terminology. In this continual return to the past, Agostino Gallo once more appeared on the scene, after having been rather neglected, though not in Italy, where he was to make a rapid reappearance. The example which Duhamel gave of the greater productivity of ears of grain when grown in rows took up Gallo's idea again. With regard to sainfoin, Duhamel followed Tull very closely, giving a notable description of threshing seed with the flail and then winnowing it. He also gave a few recommendations concerning lucerne, his personal contribution being the description of how to harvest the seed. But the really original part of Duhamel's work lay in the drawings and illustrations of new machines, including the seed-drill and the plough with several shares. They were less innovative than Tull's ideas but were based on the first-hand experience of machines and tools which Duhamel acquired in shipyards and workshops.[47]

In those same years La Salle de L'Etang discussed the use of sainfoin to make artificial pastures not only for fodder but to improve the soil for wheat-growing. The creation of these artificial grasslands also brought up the problem of the common rights on arable land and the length of leases granted to tenants, too short for them to improve the land and get back sufficient compensation for the work they and their families had invested in it. The Scottish emigrant Henri Patullo took to France all the recent experience that Scottish farmers had acquired in those years by studying Tull's work (see above, 2). According to Patullo, enclosure and the rotation of leys and arable land in a long ten-year course, giving ample space to forage crops and turnips, were the key to increasing the productivity of cereals. In practice, Tull's system (never applied completely because it took up too much space), together with the discovery of English farming, constituted the basis of the agricultural movement on which were grafted the thought of the Physiocratic School and the debate on whether *grande culture* or *petite culture* was preferable.[48]

To the praises that the Anglophiles lavished on the recent inventions

---

[47] See H. L. Duhamel Du Monceau, *Traité de la culture des terres suivant les Principes de M. Tull Anglois*, Paris 1750, especially pp. 207, 256–9, 267, 289 ff. The work particularly connected with the problems mentioned above is idem, *Avis pour le transport par mer des arbres, des plantes vivaces, et des semences*, Paris 1753.

[48] See M. La Salle De L'Etang, *Prairies artificielles ou Lettre à M. de . . . sur le moyens de fertiliser les terrains secs et stériles dans la Champagne et dans les autres provinces du royaume*, Paris 1756; H. Patullo, *Essai sur l'amélioration des terres*, Paris 1758; Bourde, *Agronomie*, vol. I, pp. 338–48.

of English agriculture, others responded with praise for the rural tradition of the French provinces, of the *Maison rustique*, of Olivier de Serres, recalling that cultivated meadows of clover and sainfoin had long been common in France, not only in Flanders, Artois and Picardy, but in the Ile-de-France, the Languedoc and the Dauphiné as well as Burgundy, Normandy, Beauce and the Gâtinais; not to speak of the use of turnips, cabbages and carrots for fodder. La Salle de L'Etang's criticisms bring out clearly how certain features of the new agriculture could co-exist with the three-field system. Whether or not open-fields, subject to common grazing rights, were preferable to closed fields and individualism, formed part of a more general question on the social and economic control of the land, which transcended the terms of the technology employed.[49]

Obviously the first question to be solved concerned the fertility of the soil, how to renew it and maintain it even when cereals were grown. Véron de Forbonnais, author of many articles on economy in the *Encyclopédie*, had already spoken very highly of the improvement of the soil with marl and sand by the Norfolk farmers, whom he admired greatly for their methods. But the decisive factor lay in the sainfoin, lucerne and clover, to which they added rye-grass and turnips, which meant tilling the soil in depth and being able to rear twice the number of sheep. Comparison with the results obtained on open-fields, and allowing for the rights of common pasture, should have convinced many more large landowners than it actually did of the excellence of the new system.[50] Even then some people raised the objection that tilling by mechanical means did not wholly improve arable land and that tilling it too frequently accelerated the decay of vegetable mould, which is the essence of fertility. Then, as now, vegetable mould had to be treated with care. The Italian scientist Giovanni Fabbroni, whose writings circulated in Italy and France, wanted to substitute crop rotation and tilling with a series of plants grown together, as was done in China, and in his opinion in England too, in the case of wheat and turnips; and as had been recommended by Agostino Gallo (panic-grass and lucerne). The idea was suggested again by Duhamel du Monceau (sainfoin and barley, or another cereal) and by current practice in England, where oats were sometimes used as a cover crop for lucerne and clover. It was necessary

---

[49] See M. La Salle De L'Etang, *Manuel d'agriculture pour le laboureur, le propriétaire et le gouvernement*, Paris 1764; Bourde, *Agronomie*, vol. I, pp. 384–91, 394–5.
[50] See *ibid.*, pp. 302–9.

to study the order in which plants were grown, so that the plant residues would help to build up fertility again (by green-manuring, mainly with beans, lupins and so on).[51]

For centuries English commercial policy concerning France had been that it did not matter what was imported or exported, provided the trade balance of the kingdom was favourable. Rearing livestock was less costly than arable farming. Wages were lower, the work was less, the cost of transport was practically non-existent, and the size of flocks and herds could be adapted more easily to the market situation. But the fundamental choice, livestock or cereals, depended on the total demand for food, and was less critical in England than in France, since England had a population of six million, as against the twenty-two million inhabitants of France. But in mid eighteenth-century France, rearing livestock involved transhumance and common pasture, and became an extremely costly option for the consumer, without diminishing the country's grain requirements.[52] The immediate alternative, while the economists and physiocrats debated whether Duhamel's system or the traditional one was better, was to reclaim wasteland, plough up pastures and pass decrees on enclosure.

3. WHAT AGRICULTURAL REVOLUTION?

In the middle of the eighteenth century the situation was changed by demographic recovery. Historical research of the past twenty years has produced frequently divergent interpretations of the significance and impact of the innovations, of the social and economic transformation, and the continuity or discontinuity of the changes. Since the famous publications of R. H. Tawney and Lord Ernle there have been two conflicting positions. According to one view, the period of radical

---

[51] See G. Fabbroni, *Réflexions sur l'état actuel de l'agriculture*, Paris 1780; Bourde, *Agronomie*, vol. I, pp. 398 ff.; F. Venturi, 'Giovanni Fabbroni. Nota introduttiva', in idem, *Illuministi italiani*, vol. III, *Riformatori lombardi, piemontesi e toscani*, Milan–Naples 1958, pp. 1089–90, and on Italian problems, idem, *Settecento riformatore*, V, *L'Italia dei lumi*, vol. I, *La rivoluzione di Corsica. Le grandi carestie degli anni '60. Le riforme lombarde*, Turin 1987, pp. 220–423.

[52] See A. Goudar, *Les intérêts de la France mal entendus dans les branches de l'agriculture, de la population, des finances, du commerce, de la marine et de l'industrie*, Amsterdam 1756; P. O'Brien and C. Keyder, *Two Paths to the xxth Century: Economic Growth in Britain and France 1780–1914*, London 1978; J. L. Goldsmith, 'The Agrarian History of Preindustrial France. Where do we go from here?', *Journal of European Economic History*, 13, 1984, pp. 175–99.

change in the economic and social structure of the English countryside lay in the years from 1540 to 1640; according to the other, the revolution occurred between 1750 and 1850.[53] On Tawney's side were the radicals, the Fabians and in part the Marxists; Lord Ernle represented the Tory interpretation of the history of the countryside. Marxists could be expected to opt for one or the other version, according to whether the emphasis was placed on pre-capitalist accumulation or on the reduction of labourers to a rural proletariat. Two crucial moments lay at the root of this choice of dates: on the one hand, the sixteenth-century enclosures which favoured the change from arable- to sheep-farming, and the sale of Church property after the dissolution of the monasteries, which restricted the growth of peasant ownership; on the other, enclosure by Act of Parliament in the eighteenth and nineteenth centuries and the increase in the great estates of the nobility, which brought a growth in mixed farming, combining livestock and cereals. Tawney's line led to a series of studies, interrupted and then taken up again after the Second World War, which revealed the complexity of the social-economic situation and how it presaged the English revolutions of 1640–5 and 1688–9. Lord Ernle's interpretation gave pride of place to production seen from a liberal point of view – the history of technique as a peaceful solution to the problems of society. So much for the background.

It was not clear which social groups had drawn advantage from these changes, whether English society had benefited from the concentration of wealth in the hands of a few, and above all whether the social structure of the country as a whole was the better for the disappearance of the small farmer, for turning the smallholder into a wage-earner, and for the urbanization of the productive system. Furthermore, research on agricultural techniques brought to light the fact that once one got away from ready-made allegories of agricultural growth, many factors rendered it unsatisfactory to make clear divisions between periods. The fortunes of the nobility and the small farmers, alliances between social groups or vertical cleavages in society were all themes that still required investigation before the history of agricultural structures could be

---

[53] See R. H. Tawney, *The Agrarian Problem in the Sixteenth Century*, London 1912, D. M. Palliser, 'Tawney's Century: Brave New World or Malthusian Trap?' in *Ec. His. Rev.*, 2nd ser., 35, 1982, pp. 339–53; A. Wright, *R. H. Tawney*, Manchester 1987. On Rowland Prothero, land agent to the Duke of Bedford, politician, president of the Board of Agriculture, minister of Agriculture, later Lord Ernle, see DNB, *sub voce*; see also E. Richards, 'The Land Agent', in G. E. Mingay (ed.), *The Victorian Countryside*, London, 1981, pp. 449–50.

correctly assessed. The question of whether the 1540–1640 or the 1750–1850 period had more right to the title of 'Agricultural Revolution' was still unsolved. In 1966 Chambers and Mingay repeated the claim that enclosures sanctioned by Acts of Parliament between 1760 and 1830 were related to the creation of great farming estates and the spread of the Norfolk four-course (but also sometimes a five-course) rotation of turnips, barley, clover and wheat. This was combined with sheep-farming, which was essential for the increase in agricultural production and the maintainance of the population during the Industrial Revolution.[54] In 1967 Eric Kerridge tried to give this theory a serious jolt by showing that all the changes on which the English Agricultural Revolution of the eighteenth and nineteenth centuries was founded had already taken place by 1720 and many of them before 1673 [*sic*]. Moreover he denied the connection between enclosure and the new technology, which had been generally accepted by both Tory and Marxist critics. In this way he hoped to solve the question of the nineteenth-century proletarianization of agriculture, so dear to Marxists, relegating the great capitalist farm to a secondary role.[55] In the same year, the fourth volume of the *Agrarian History of England and Wales* examined the 1500–1640 period more deeply, showing the relation between the landowning classes – Crown, Church, nobility, medium and small landowners and copyholders – their behaviour in the face of the so-called price revolution and the market, the role of the new estates of nobility and gentry and the country homes of aristocracy and peasantry. It provided a solid mass of information, an aid and support for all further research, which demonstrated the mutual dependence of the country's many regional economies and of its social groups, and showed that the cleavages in society were of very limited dimensions when compared with the economies of the Continent. The next volume of the *Agrarian History* (1650–1750) answered questions posed by historians, by giving access to a mine of unpublished material, which once more illustrated the complexity of the situation and the variety of possible solutions. While the whole significance of the research of Joan Thirsk, general editor and author of many essays in the volumes in question, could hardly be conveyed in the framework of this study, it may be useful to note the

---

[54] See Chambers and Mingay, *The Agricultural Revolution*; see also J. D. Chambers, *Population, Economy, and Society in Pre-Industrial England*, Oxford 1972, and G. E. Mingay, *Arthur Young and His Times*, London 1975; idem (ed.), *The Agricultural Revolution. Changes in Agriculture, 1650–1880*, London 1977.

[55] See Kerridge, *The Agricultural Revolution*, and idem, *Agrarian Problems*.

emphasis placed on the value of the personal experience of those who faced the economic issues and the subsistence problems of their own generation.[56] The innovations came from many sides, from the Dutch and Flemish (turnips and fodder), from individual curiosity (which favoured investigation into new commercial crops such as madder and saffron and into agricultural tools), from the Americas (tobacco and potatoes), and from discussion and communication between individuals (the Hartlib group and others). Judging from these volumes, 1500–1640 and 1640–1750, the most fertile period for innovation and transformation liable to subsequent improvement seems to have been 1600–80. Again in the 1960s, Eric L. Jones produced a series of articles, focusing mainly on the years 1660–1750, which attempted to solve the problem of the dating of the Agricultural Revolution from a more general perspective.[57] In economic theory the growth of the basic agricultural sector is a fundamental factor in the creation of an industrial sector. English agriculture had to be able to increase the productivity of the farm-worker before it could afford industrial development, assuming that time to be after 1750. Productivity increased between 1660 and 1760 wherever mixed farming could most easily spread, on the light chalky and limestone soils of central and southern England, and the light, sandy soils of East Anglia. Production increased on the large estates that benefited from the European grain market while the small farmers of the Midlands could not compete because their heavy, wet, clay soils were too difficult to improve. The economic system brought about a division between the more fortunate groups, already part of the capitalist system, who went forward successfully, and the farmers of pastoral and traditional England, who were excluded. This is a statement of fact, rather than an explanation. In Jones' view, the will to innovate was shared by all, but if everyone had practised the new style of mixed farming, there would have been serious over-production and prices would have fallen drastically, whereas the introduction of the Corn Bounty restricted innovations to the privileged minority who had the means to introduce them. Recent research (M. Overton) has emphasized the early emergence of a model of transformation (turnips and clover already being found in the inventories of East Anglia in the late sixteenth century); it has recalled the low yield of cereals grown on the outfields (Outhwaite), and

---

[56] See *AHEW*, 5–6; Thirsk, *English Peasant Farming*; idem, *The Rural Economy of England. Collected Essays*, London 1985; idem, *England's Agricultural Regions*.
[57] Jones, *Agriculture*; idem, *Agriculture and the Industrial Revolution*, Oxford 1974.

discussed the effects of enclosure on the spread of innovation (Allen).[58]

Many points made in these recent contributions deserve careful consideration. The main emphasis is on the early diffusion of cultivation techniques like weeding, marling, manuring and vetch growing in privileged areas of England, such as East Anglia, all of which brought about the late sixteenth-century increase in grain productivity. Not until the early eighteenth century was there a return to such levels, after a continual fall in productivity registered over a hundred years. This seems to undermine any idea of an 'agricultural revolution'. It is also in line with Le Roy Ladurie's more conservative approach to French agricultural growth, which insisted on a recovery dating only from the 1750s. It should not be forgotten that any good techniques used in the late Middle Ages must very soon have been lost during the fifteenth-century downswing, and that agricultural improvements had to start anew from other sources after 1540, when manorial agriculture was no longer viable. In any case, this recent research proves one thing beyond doubt – the main problems in early modern English farming were ploughing and sowing. Ridge and furrow husbandry was a poor way of preparing the soil, and any 'improvement' (enclosure, clover, turnips, seed drill) was bound to produce a better field, with better drainage and better-aired soil. Moreover, a fuller understanding of the whole question of innovation and its diffusion can be achieved by placing agrarian development in its wider cultural setting.

Allen discusses the dating and the Tory view of the Agricultural Revolution. He believes that the great eighteenth- and nineteenth-century landowners increased their productivity by engrossing more farms and expelling farm labourers, but they never increased the yields in wheat. This came about thanks to the yeomen who worked on the open fields

[58] See M. Turner, 'Agricultural Productivity in England in the Eighteenth Century: Evidence from Crop Yields', *Ec. His. Rev.*, ser. 2, 35, 1982, pp. 489–510; M. Overton, 'Computer analysis of an inconsistent data source: the case of probate inventories', *Journal of Historical Geography*, 3, 4, 1977; idem, 'Estimating Crop Yields'; idem, 'The diffusion of agricultural innovations in early modern England: an example from East Anglia, 1585–1735', *Journal of Economic History*, 39, 1979, pp. 363–78; R. B. Outhwaite, 'Progress and backwardness in English agriculture, 1500–1650', *Ec. His. Rev.*, ser. 2, 39, 1986. See also *AHEW*, 6, pp. 134–47 and B. M. S. Campbell, 'Land, labour, livestock and productivity trends in English seignorial agriculture, 1208–1450', in B. M. S. Campbell and M. Overton (eds.), *Land, labour and livestock: historical studies in European agricultural productivity*, Manchester 1991, pp. 144–82. See also Le Roy Ladurie, 'De la crise ultime a la vraie croissance', and idem and J. Goy (eds.), *Les fluctuations de la dîme*.

and had managed to double the yield of their grains, especially in the seventeenth century, by expending a greater amount of labour, selecting the seed and increasing their crops of legumes, their livestock and manure. According to the data collected by Arthur Young, in the early nineteenth century, the yield per acre on enclosed farms was only five per cent higher than on open fields. Moreover, converting from arable land to pasture reduced the produce (from £4 to £2–3).[59] Allen's conclusions are not unfounded. There were, in fact, two parallel movements, two agricultural revolutions, in one of which the small farms were the dominant feature and small growers achieved greater productivity per head than on large farms. This is a hypothesis which diminishes the role of innovations such as enclosure, cross-ploughing, new crops, and in part returns to Jones' research on the division of land into light and heavy soils. It says little of innovations and does not explain why, in the second half of the eighteenth century, England was growing too few cereals and had to have recourse to importation, despite the fact that her production was continually increasing.

Epistemological issues continue to stimulate debate but they call for the clarification of terms in order to make empirical research clearer. The expression Agricultural Revolution continues to be a fruitful concept, but it is also extremely vague in content. Marc Bloch rightly suggested that we should speak of 'agricultural revolutions' and Allen's conclusions move a little in this direction. In my opinion, more careful examination of past technology serves to construct more soundly based historical hypotheses, and is preferable to hypotheses drawn from other contexts. Since there were various possible solutions to every situation in the England of 1550, 1680 and 1750, we need to explain what the alternatives were in those years, not to measure the total transformation achieved by 1880. In the preceding pages we have endeavoured to show that the innovators had to pass through various stages of apprenticeship on their long road to modernization. The efforts and successes of the yeomen in the second half of the seventeenth century would have been impossible without the enquiring minds of the lesser gentry, the travellers and the botanists. They made available many new elements which enriched England's slight botanical heritage, and filled the great

---

[59] See B. M. S. Campbell and M. Overton (eds.), *Land, labour and livestock*, especially the contributions by Campbell, Thornton, Glennie, Overton and now R. C. Allen, *Enclosure and the Yeoman: the agricultural development of the South Midlands. 1450–1850*, Oxford 1992, pp. 1–21, 141–9, 191–210, 303–11.

and small gardens where novelties were kept alive until agricultural work adapted them to the local environment. With an abundance of land suitable for cultivation, unequalled anywhere in Europe, it was fairly obvious that a population increasing slowly but steadily after 1500, of whom ninety per cent were workers on the land and had no alternative employment, could bring about an increase of fifty per cent in the production of cereals. Capital per head was quite high and there were plenty of books that taught how to reclaim waste land and transform moorish pasture into arable land, so long as long periods of fallow (which horrified nineteenth-century agronomists) were allowed. While the demographic history of England explains the growth in agricultural productivity, it explains neither the forms of production nor the ability to make certain foreign crops permanent. The history of technological learning is of great use for a more general understanding of the whole process of transformation.

The years 1680–1750 had produced some very subtle technical advances, of which Tull's method was the most advanced: cultivation in rows, without manure and with suitable machinery. The demographic recovery in Europe brought about a rise in grain prices after 1750, which started up a speedier capitalist transformation, simplifications in the agronomic model, the restriction of legumes to clover. The agrarian system was unable to change the economic system, which had adopted it, but restricted the spread of innovations to those that were simpler to introduce into the rotational scheme of the large farm. As was happening at the same time in northern France, the large farm imposed certain solutions which did not make for the best possible productive system but for the greatest possible profit (see Chap. 4, 5). The history of technical innovation and the history of the great estates and their organization into capitalist farms are two parallel stories. Agricultural innovations in the England of the mid-eighteenth century were unevenly distributed within the economic system. Not all producers had equal access to the market of the new technology. When they went on, from the books and oral or printed instructions to putting them into practice, the search for good seed became a problem that had troubled the first experimenters of the mid-seventeenth century as it continued to trouble farmers from 1700 to 1870.

4. THE QUESTION OF SEED

The production of seed developed alongside horticulture in areas like those around Sandwich, Evesham, Norwich and Colchester where, besides soil and climate favourable to this production, there were early settlements of Protestant immigrants from Holland and Flanders and later of French Huguenots, who had developed this sector. Apart from seed produced locally by horticulturalists, the London markets had always received a great deal of seed from the Continent, which was generally distributed by corn-merchants (see chap. 4, pp. 300 and 335). The years 1620–80 yield references to small lots of seed and some activity on the part of nurserymen, though these were really more interested in propagating flowers and fruit-trees. This forced farmers to make personal contacts for the purchase of forage-crop seed. In the following years, very active, specialized firms were set up, such as that of John Turner, which later passed to the Huguenot refugee Charles Minier, or that of Stephen Switzer.[60] The demands of a growing number of farmers widened the area of production of these seeds, hitherto restricted to the local market such as Exeter and Worcester. The major seed importers would have benefited from a limitation of local English production, which in fact was encouraged by information on how to produce clover and sainfoin seed. Instructions for harvesting seed never differed from those given by Yarranton for clover and by Tull for sainfoin, although the difficulties inherent in gathering such very fine seed were at once apparent. Some advised cutting the clover for seed after the second flowering in mid-September, others advised the June crop, before the first hay was mown. Both seed harvests were liable to be ruined by the late spring or late summer rains. In any case, harvesting the seed reduced, then as now, the nutritional value of the fodder. While the growth of the plant itself is not damaged by rain, few things affect the success of the seed harvest like full ripening of the seeds and leaving them out in the sun for a long time.[61] The series of imports registered

---

[60] See N. Riches, *The Agricultural Revolution in Norfolk* (1937), London 1967, p. 88; *The London Gazette*, 1675, n. 1073, and 1676, n. 1155: Jacob Bobart, G. Sedleys and W. Tand advertised clover and sainfoin seed for sale; see also the numerous names of gardeners and corn and seed merchants published by J. Houghton, *A Collection for Improvement of Husbandry and Trade*, London 1692–1703 (for example n. 121, 23 November 1694; n. 127, 4 January 1694/95; n. 136, 8 March 1694/95); Harvey, *Early Nurserymen*, p. 47, and Thick, *Market Gardening, passim*; J. M. Martin, 'The Social and Economic Origins of Market Gardening Industry', *AHR*, 33, 1985, *passim*.

[61] See Yarranton, *The Improvement, passim*; Tull, *The Horse-Hoing Husbandry*, p. 86; E. Laurence, *The Duty of a Steward to his Lord . . . to which is added an Appendix shewing the Way of Plenty*, London 1727, pp. 195–6, stated that 20–25 bushels of sainfoin seed could be threshed per acre, at 3s a bushel, equal to 80–100 pounds in weight; R. Bradley, *A general Treatise of Husbandry and Gardening*, London 1726, vol. I, pp. 175, 177; R. G. F. Stanes (ed.), 'A Georgical Account of Devonshire and

in the early eighteenth century (see Appendix, table 7) shows a correspondence between two factors; difficult seed, such as lucerne, was constantly sought after, while the market for clover seed was more erratic, though the quantities continued to get larger. After a very rainy June or September, figures were high in the 1690s (1692, 1693, 1694, 1696, 1697, 1698), while the first decade of the new century was hotter and drier (yet in 1707 and 1708 it rained heavily in June; the average temperature in central England was 9.85°C and 13.45°C in May and June 1691–1700, as against 11.33° and 14.26° in the following decade).[62]

Just as a technological model had spread from London through the press and through a network of personal relations among the great provincial landowners, so traders in remoter places had contacts in London. Arthur Clepham of Edinburgh corresponded with William Crombie and John Turner, the largest merchants in London, and with firms in Brompton, then just outside London. He also dealt directly with English firms in Amsterdam and Rotterdam and his clients' many complaints made him prefer Dutch to English seed. He sold mainly flower-seed and seeds of trees, but did not disdain those for improving land, among them Dutch and English red clover-seed, white clover and rye-grass, sold to three different gardeners in 1722, 1723 and 1724, in quite small quantities, probably used to produce seed in its turn and not to sow on pastureland. His clients came from a radius of fifty to sixty miles round Edinburgh, and the same pattern was repeated for other provincial firms; clover seed for Ireland, for example, was imported from Bristol and Worcester.[63] There was strong competition between seed from Holland (a term which should perhaps be extended to all the seed from the Low Countries, and that from Flanders to all northern France;

Cornwall. Samuel Colepresse (1667)', *Devonshire Association, Reports and Transactions*, 96, 1964, pp. 269–302; on modern seed production see Davies, *The Grass Crop*, pp. 139–67; A. Fenwick Kelly, *Seed Production of Agricultural Crops*, Harlow 1988, pp. 96 ff., 125–55; T. M. Wigley and T. C. Atkinson, 'Dry Years in South East England since 1698', *Nature*, 265, 3 February 1977, pp. 431–4.

[62] See Stratton and Brown, *Agricultural Records*, pp. 60–7; G. Manley, 'Central England temperatures: monthly means 1659 to 1973', *Quarterly Journal of the Royal Meteorological Society*, 100, 1974, pp. 389–405. On the variations in weather and crops over the centuries see E. Le Roy Ladurie, *Histoire du climat depuis l'an mille*, Paris 1967; H. H. Lamb, *Climate: Present, Past and Future*, London 1977, vol. II, pp. 178 ff.; T. M. Wigley (ed.), *Climate and History: Studies in Past Climates and Their Impact on Man*, Cambridge 1985.

[63] See T. Donnely, 'Arthur Clepham, Edinburgh merchant and seedsman, 1706–1730', *AHR*, 18, 1970, pp. 151–60; S. Peirson, *The present State of the Tillage in Ireland considered and some methods offered for its improvement*, Dublin 1725, pp. 15–25.

see Chap. 4, 5) and English seed. Some preferred the Dutch variety because of the high quality of the forage-crops, others the English because of its good rate of germination. Advertisements in the local papers, such as the *Kentish Post* of Canterbury from the 1730s onwards, offered selected seed, including clover and lucerne, of varied origin. This trade was often carried on by travelling salesmen, preferably in the country inns (see below).[64] Some maintained that even lucerne, which generally had to be imported from France, could produce good seed locally if cultivated on sheltered, sunny ground. Actually seed sold by the merchants could rarely be trusted. All the lucerne seed said to be imported from Italy in the first decades of the eighteenth century really came from Switzerland, from the cantons of Lucerne and Basle, and from the Languedoc. It was taken first to Leghorn and then sent on to England. The English Customs considered the last port of call before landing in England as the country of origin of the goods.[65]

In the middle of the century the general situation was changing, the volume of imports was not only more regular but also larger. Farmers were already being advised to use local seed in the lean years, being careful not to sow barley with clover harvested two or three years before, but with the seed of the latest harvest. Two hundred years before seeds were certified, it was difficult for everyone to find good seed. The salesman's word provided little guarantee of its origin; the only guide was that good seed sank to the bottom when dropped into water.[66] On a market that was becoming constantly larger and more specialized, and was separating products intended more specifically for agriculture from those for vegetable and ornamental gardens, some merchants tried to create a greater impression of trustworthiness by publishing clear and accurate brochures. Richard North, who had a shop in Lambeth, near Westminster Bridge, gave a far-reaching guarantee for the seeds sold under the name of Dutch red clover, common red clover, white clover, clover with yellow flowers, perennial clover (the so-called marl grass, *T. hybridum*), sainfoin, lucerne and spurry. As Switzer had done before him, North

---

64 See Ellis, *Chiltern and Vale Farming*, p. 269; see *Kentish Post*, 29 November 1729, 8 August 1753, 14 May 1757 (Dr Dennis Baker kindly provided me with this information).

65 See T. Hale, *A Compleat Body of Husbandry*, London 1756, p. 442; Switzer, *The Practical Husbandman and Planter*, pp. 131–2.

66 See Randall, *The semi-virgilian Husbandry*, p. 153; Anon., *A new System of Agriculture or a plain Easy and demonstrative method of speedily growing rich*, London 1755, p. 157.

recommended sowing thickly to destroy weeds, and sowing in rows only for lucerne. He also advised against using lucerne on open fields, as there were better forage-crops for use in this situation. He warned that the so-called marl grass was not a real perennial clover but a local variety, not worth trying, which had spread between Wells and Bristol ten years or so before and was sold in London at a very high price, three times more expensive than the best seed. From the context it seems that when seed was purchased from the seedsman, it was then used to produce more seed for the farmer's own use, but, in the event, had to be substituted regularly by more of the purchased varieties because the local kind was full of weeds after the first harvest. The Countess of Oxford paid the firm Perfect £15 10s in November 1755 for three bushes of cytisus and seed of seven different qualities of clover.[67] The real problem for many producers and clients was transport, particularly at a time when the search for new, high-quality varieties was becoming more extensive and lucerne was even brought from Turkey and Syria. The journey by sea, shut in damp holds infested with insects and microbes, was very harmful to plants and seeds.[68] Yet after 1750, when the collection and search for varieties to be imported into England was becoming world-wide and the home market was expanding rapidly, the seed trade was controlled more and more by the London merchants. Perhaps William Harte was exaggerating when he claimed that there was not a nurseryman or a seed merchant within sixty to eighty miles of London. The largest provincial cities, Bristol, Gloucester, Worcester, Oxford and Manchester and many others certainly had their own nurseries. Yet around fifty per cent of the firms of this kind had their main centre in London or its immediate vicinity between 1680 and 1840.[69] In practice this meant that the London firms and above all the seed importers had the monopoly and could dictate terms to the farming sector.

[67] See R. North, *An Account of the different Kinds of Grasses propagated in England for the improvement of corn and pasture lands, lawns and walks . . . and some remarks upon . . . saving haie seeds from fine meadows*, London 1760, pp. 1–16; Harvey, *Early Nurserymen*, pp. 97, 93, 202: his customers seem to have come mainly from Norfolk.

[68] See J. Ellis, *Directions for bringing over seeds and plants*, London 1770, pp. 13 (' . . . the Alpine strawberry was first sent to England in a letter from Turin to Henry Baker, Esq., FRS, by pressing the pulp with seeds thin upon paper . . . the paper mulberry from China was brought over much the same way . . . '), 14, 17; Switzer, *The Practical Husbandman and Planter*, p. 132; Ellis, *Chiltern and Vale Farming*, p. 281.

[69] See Harte, *Essays on Husbandry: Essay I*, p. iii; Harvey, *Early Nurserymen*, pp. 60, 264–6.

The spread of agricultural innovations and the transformation of the estates of the landed gentry on the neo-classical model had become a very remunerative business with the support of an entire subsidiary sector. The catalogues of these nurserymen generally had a section devoted exclusively to seeds for agricultural improvement. To these they added tools and products like liquid or solid fertilizers, and offered the services of gardeners and estate managers.[70] From the first printed catalogues, consisting of single sheets, in the early eighteenth century, to the booklets of the early nineteenth century, very few catalogues do not include forage-crop seeds or give information on the time of sowing and amount needed. Purchasers wrote their orders in the margins of the catalogue. In 1764 a Mr Pink ordered from Gordon James, who had a shop in Fenchurch Street, four kinds of cabbage, at 15s, and a quarter of seed barley. The same firm had in its catalogue two kinds of lucerne, eight different clovers, *luzerne* and *sainfoin*, trefoil, vetch, seeds gathered in permanent meadows in Yorkshire, Suffolk and Hendon. A certain Mr Christian of London ordered from Paul Dupin half an ounce of evergreen cytisus and the same amount of cytisus from Montpellier for 1s 6d. When rare and difficult seeds became available, there was an immediate response on the market. By now, the nurseryman's catalogue, bound in leather and with blank pages for making notes on plants, had taken the place of a copy of de' Crescenzi. John Hunter brought one out in 1795, 1805 and 1822.[71] At the turn of the century catalogues, too, bore witness to the ever more frequent practice of agronomists and

---

[70] See for example North, *An Account*; R. Edmeades, *The Gentleman and Lady's Gardener . . . with a Catalogue*, London 1776, pp. 63 ff.; W. Middlewood, *A Catalogue of Seeds . . . times of sowing and planting calculated for this part of the Country . . .*, Manchester 1776; Thomas, *Man and the Natural World*, pp. 192–241, 254 ff.; in the early nineteenth century the formal garden in Northern Italy was giving way to the new English romantic approach, see E. Silva, *Dell'arte dei giardini inglesi* (Milan 1813), ed. by G. Venturi, Milan 1976, pp. 108–28; G. Mingay, 'The Eighteenth-Century Land Steward', in E. L. Jones and G. Mingay, *Land, Labour and Population in the Industrial Revolution. Essays presented to J. D. Chambers*, London 1967, pp. 3–27; J. R. Wordie, *Estate Management in Eighteenth Century England*, London 1982.

[71] See the following catalogues in Cambridge Botanical Gardens: P. Lauder, Bristol n.d. (18th century); J. Gordon, n.p. c. 1767; R. Edmeades, London 1776; W. Middlewood, Manchester 1766; *Bill of Paul Dupin*, 14 April 1778; Dickson & Co., Edinburgh n.d.; F. & J. Dickson, Chester n.d. (c. 1830), p. 6; Oxford, BO, John Johnston Collection; J. Webb, London 1760; W. Bridgewater Page, London c. 1750; J. Webb, London c. 1750; Dickson, n.p. n.d. (c. 1750); see also S. MacDonald, 'The Diffusion of Knowledge among Northumberland Farmers, 1780–1815', *AHR*, 27, 1979, *passim*.

landowners of seeking out the most effective mixture of seeds to solve the problems of improving the soil and keeping the turf well covered with grass.

A century of experiment and trial had taught that pasture and meadow should not be considered as land undergoing a period of rest or a cheap alternative to growing cereals. Pedological and climatic conditions might produce growth of couch grass and legumes according to the year. Only a carefully prepared short or long ley introduced into the rotation scheme gave a constant yield and helped to build up the land for grain-growing. After the middle of the century the spread of mixed or alternate farming opened up the sheep-keeping sector to many farmers, partly reducing the area set aside for seed crops. On the other hand, the constant rise in the price of cereals made cereal-growing very remunerative with very little effort. The integration of the two sectors, meadows and arable land, was far from ideal even in the golden age of mixed agriculture. The difficulties no longer lay in getting information or seed, but were connected with the way agricultural method worked now that it had become a nation-wide system and the basis of the prosperity of a growing number of people.

William Marshall's analysis of farming in the English counties, which he made for the Board of Agriculture, provides a rapid synthesis. The economic advantages of the Norfolk rotation left no trace on the poor, sandy soils of the county, which were showing signs of fatigue, producing stunted, patchy clover, attributable to over-frequent harvests, the scarcity of lime in the soil and the choice of sheep- rather than cattle-rearing. It was customary to sow a mixture of half a peck of rye-grass and twelve to fourteen pounds of clover per acre or red and white clover mixed with oats. The seed was not harvested but purchased from the neighbouring county of Suffolk. Yet the official market for clover seed of all the varieties mentioned was Norwich, where it was bargained for in bags of sixty-six pounds, weighed and sold on the spot, or sold by sample by the corn merchants and local bankers. The price of red clover fluctuated considerably according to the quality, from twenty to thirty shillings a bushel, other seeds varied according to demand.[72] In Gloucestershire the cultivation of meadows was less usual, being limited

---

[72] See W. Marshall, *The Rural Economy of Norfolk*, London 1787, I, pp. 178–80, 301–2, 305–8; G. Swayne, *Gramina Pascua or a Collection of Specimens of the common pasture grasses*, Bristol 1790; Davies, *The Grass Crop*, p. 167.

by the sufficiency of open-field arable land and enclosed permanent pastures, which produced abundant crops of cheap hay. However, small plots of land were often sown with clover on open fields. Unfortunately, both hay and clover seed were gathered without any quality control, while old arable land would have been improved by a seed mixture chosen to suit the soil. In the Midlands too, although growing cereals after a clover ley was not common, it was more frequent on open fields, where clover had taken the place traditionally reserved for beans. Vast areas of permanent pasture surrounded the few cultivated meadows. William Marshall did not think that the cultivation of grass-fields went back more than fifty years in the west of England. Nonetheless it appeared frequently on two thirds of the enclosed arable land, though much less on common land, where it only lasted a few years. Generally speaking, the rotation of wheat, barley, oats and clover, laid down as obligatory in more recent contracts, lowered agricultural standards. The situation was better round Maidstone, Kent, where cultivation according to a Flemish scheme had been established years before, as the farmers themselves claimed. This meant three crops of cereals, then one of clover hay, and a second clover crop for grazing or for seed. This system produced a large quantity of seed, as happened in 1790, and it was winnowed mechanically. The cultivation of leys was more backward in the north of England. Red and white clover, rye-grass and occasionally trefoil were sown successfully in Northumberland and Cumberland. The rye-grass seed was usually bought on the London market. At the beginning of the nineteenth century the seed merchants replaced it by an annual variety, which did a great deal of harm. Permanent meadows were not cultivated in the Westmorland region. After three years of growing cereals, the land was left to return to natural grassland. In Lancashire the land was well manured before potatoes were sown, then in August at the latest they sowed hay seed mixed with white clover. Greater care was taken in the West Riding of Yorkshire, where red clover was sown to prepare the soil for wheat, white clover and hay seed for pasture. Quite a lot of saintoin was grown around Tadcaster and Ferrybridge. In the poorer areas of northern Yorkshire they waited for the second crop of grain to prepare the land by weeding, sowing hay seed and rolling. The quantity of seed sown in northern England was higher (8 bushels of hay and 10 pounds of clover per acre). There too they had difficulty in obtaining good quality seed from the nurserymen and travelling sales-men who did business at the inns. On the whole, Marshall found the state of the meadows and grasslands of England unsatisfactory at the end of the eighteenth century and his judgement was confirmed by his colleague and rival Arthur Young.[73]

London's key position with respect to population, consumption, sea-traffic, and supply of seed placed the countryside in her immediate neighbourhood in the forefront of the cultivation of long and short leys, permanent meadows and the production of hay. Lucerne was grown in small patches of one or two acres and heavily manured. It was cut four times a year and fed green to horses. Permanent meadows and pastures in the immediate vicinity of London were all run directly by farmers who kept milk-cows. Red clover was grown in rotation with wheat in all the enclosed fields of Middlesex, more rarely on open fields, except at Shepperton. From ten to twelve pounds were sown on the best land, larger quantities on poor soil. Red clover and barley were often sown together on heavy soils. The seed sold in London had to be pure, so as not to lower the price of the hay produced from it. The clover was mown in full bloom, rather early than late, when the plant was at its best. In August the best part of the permanant meadow was allowed to ripen for another few days, then mown and threshed and the seed sown at once in the autumn. To the hay seed harvested in this way were added 10 lbs of white clover, 3 lbs of yellow, 2 lbs of red, 5 lbs of timothy-grass (*Phleum pratense*), 3 lbs of burnet and 1 lb of plantain. Sainfoin was not grown in the county of Middlesex, but was brought in great quantities to the London markets of Whitechapel, Smithfield and St James from the chalky downs of Kent and Surrey.[74]

During the years of the Continental blockade the advanced sector of English agriculture continued to depend on foreign imports. Although the blockade did not restrain this trade, the problem of improving the quality of the seed put on sale at the Corn Exchange in Mark Lane, London, was only faced after 1815. Unfortunately, that sector of English farming was unable to become self-sufficient. If English seed was harvested at dawn, according to the custom of the peasants on the

---

[73] See W. Marshall, *The Rural Economy of Gloucestershire*, Gloucester 1789, I, pp. 154–5, 157–8, 167–69; idem, *The Rural Economy of Midland Counties*, London 1790, vol. I, pp. 263–6; idem, *The Rural Economy of the West of England*, London 1796, vol. I, pp. 202–4; idem, *The Rural Economy of the Southern Counties*, London 1798, vol. I, pp. 145, 147–8, 150; idem, *A Review of the Reports to the Board of Agriculture from the Northern Department of England*, York 1808, p. 88, note, pp. 88 ff., 116, 151, 192–3, 235–6, 304, 482 ff.; A. Young, 'Of Artificial Grasses', *Annals of Agriculture*, 32, 1798, pp. 329–39.

[74] See J. Middleton, *View of the Agriculture of Middlesex*, London 1798, pp. 217, 219, 226–30, 233, 416–18.

Continent, it stayed damp and went mouldy, while if it was harvested fully ripe, much of it was scattered on the ground. The cost of harvesting and threshing came to as much as 5–7s a bushel if cleaned by hand. One acre produced around 3–5 bushels from 2–3 cwt of hay, a good income though very uncertain as regards both price and the amount of the crop. Foreign competition greatly hampered local attempts to specialize in this sector, and the high price of seed slowed down the spread of leys planted exclusively with clover. The alternative would have been a new customs duty of twenty to thirty shillings a hundredweight, which would have meant a considerable saving on payments sent to Holland and France. In response to this need, pointed out in the *Annals of Agriculture*, Arthur Young asked whether a low price at the time of sowing were not preferable to a high price for the sale of seed. However, he agreed that some difficulty over supplies encouraged local production.[75] Seed production benefited from exactly the opposite meteorological conditions from those that benefited farmers who fattened livestock. The spread of meadows and pastures in the years 1750–1800 was due partly to the long cycle of wet weather. The relation between the cold seasons of the 1760s and early 1770s and 1782, 1784 and 1789, and the state of cultivation, did not pass unnoticed by contemporary writers.[76] The reduction of arable land and the increase in the importation of cereals from Europe was one of the most striking features of English agriculture, brought about by cycles of bad weather, despite the growth in the population. The profound technological and institutional transformations which took place between 1750 and 1850 diminished corn-growing, apart from the twenty years of the Napoleonic Wars. The economic policy of the great landowners was conditioned much more by the amount of their expenses than by the chance of gain.

Worcestershire alone had gone on producing seed, probably because it had an area of small farms and market-gardens. Fallow, wheat, beans, clover and seed clover, wheat or clover was the usual rotation scheme on its heavy soils. Between 1540 and 1599 barley was already the most

[75] See R. W. Dickson, *Practical Agriculture or a Complete System of Modern Husbandry*, London 1805, vol. II, p. 863; J. Sewell, 'Duty on Imported Clover Seed', *Annals of Agriculture*, 42, 1804, pp. 175–9.

[76] See J. Williams, *The Climate of Great Britain, or Remarks on the Change it has undergone, particularly in the last fifty years, accounting for the increasing humidity and consequent cloudiness and coldness of our springs and summers*, London 1806, pp. 203–7, 252–6; G. Manley, *Climate and the British Scene*, London 1972, pp. 298–300, 323; J. Glasspole, 'Two Centuries of Rainfall', *Metereological Magazine*, 63, 1928.

widely grown crop in the county (26 per cent), often associated with legumes, as appears from the inventories. Clover was less regularly recorded in the inventories, appearing in 1670 and subsequently disappearing. Used for grazing until the first week in June, it was then closed to stock, and manured and harvested in September, the seed being put on sale in the market held on Saturdays in Worcester. The harvests of 1805 and 1807 were particularly good. Great quantities of rye-grass, trefoil and hay seed were also to be found on the market. The local practice of mixing grass seeds (eight pounds of white clover, the same amount of red and two pecks of rye-grass) to be mixed in different proportions according to the soil they were to be sown on, was an obstacle to the production of pure seed.[77] It is doubtful whether the county could have supplied the whole of England with seed, for various reasons, among them the habit of mixing seed, the fact that the second crop, which was best for seed, was also best for grazing or hay, and that the rains could rarely be predicted. It would have been better if every farmer had been able to provide his own seed supplies, but the rapid decline of the independent class of owner-occupiers created a shortage of the cheap labour available on the family farm of the early nineteenth century.

4.1. Adulteration of seed in the first half of the nineteenth century

Eighteenth-century agriculture had always accepted the advice of the practical farmer on the best use of forage-crops in the agricultural cycle. With the beginning of the new century, the preparation of seed became crucial for the diffusion of capitalist agriculture, now competing with pasture and hay alike. Arthur Young's famous journal, the *Annals of Agriculture* (1784–1815) regularly devoted space to the results of practical trials carried out on the initiative of men with medium-sized farms.[78] The great landowners also experimented with selected seeds

---

[77] See W. Pitt, *General View of the Agriculture of the County of Worcester*, London 1813, pp. 70–1, 106–7, 135–7, 140–2, 276, 281; R. C. Gaunt, *A History of Worcestershire*, Worcester 1939, pp. 42–3, 97, 276; J. A. Yelling, 'Changes in Crop Production in East Worcestershire, 1540–1667', *AHR*, 17, 1969, pp. 24–43; idem, 'Changes in Crop Production in East Worcestershire, 1540–1867', *AHR*, 21, 1973, pp. 18–34.

[78] See for example T. Baird, 'House and Grass Land', *Annals of Agriculture*, 21, 1793, pp. 151–3; D. Price, 'On the Improvement of Grass Lands and Sheep', *Annals of Agriculture*, 21, pp. 466–94; J. T. Dillon, 'Translation from a Spanish Memoir on the Cultivation and Advantages of Lucern', *Annals of Agriculture*, 23, 1794, pp. 429–32; P. A. H. Drummond, 'A Substitute for Red Clover', *Annals of Agriculture*, 23,

on different soils, with a view to increasing the yield of meadows and pastures, and hence obtaining a greater live weight for livestock. At Woburn Abbey, centre of the Duke of Bedford's estate, famous for its yearly sheep-shearing trials, a series of experiments was carried out on the production of over two hundred varieties of forage crops, their yield green and as hay, alone or mixed, and their production of seed, in order to find the best rotation for the local soil. Lucerne proved to be the most productive, followed by red clover and then sainfoin. The results of these experiments were formulated as follows: a mixture of rye-grass and white clover for the best pastures on the uplands; pure red clover seed, sometimes sown together with grain, for soils of average quality, generally taken in from poor pastureland. An acre of clover gave a yield of two or three non-metric tons, which fetched fifteen shillings a ton on the London market, besides the hay from natural pastures. However it was worth sowing other grasses in clover meadows which were to be turned to natural pasture after the first year.[79] This was, and is, the practice of mixing seed for short and long leys and meadows, recognized as sound by modern agricultural science, since it provides grasses that grow well in constantly changing ecological conditions. In particular, the nitrogen produced by the white clover increases the growth of the rye-grass. Hence the early nineteenth-century farmer could choose the permanent meadow for his milk-cows, which produced a regular cash income, or leys, alternating with cereals to fatten sheep for slaughter.

Forage-crop management continued on these lines, clarifying once

pp. 533–35; Anon., 'Queries submitted to the Consideration of Intelligent Farmers regarding the Proper Management of Grass Land and Naked Fallows on strong or clayey Soils', *Annals of Agriculture*, 29, 1797, pp. 548–55; W. Belcher, 'On Grasses', *Annals of Agriculture*, 42, 1804, pp. 202–4; F. Gilbert, 'On Examination of the Respective Value of Artificial Grasses', translated from French, *Annals of Agriculture*, 42, pp. 145–73; Sewell, 'Duty on Imported Clover Seed'; W. D., 'Courses of Crops and Annual Profit on a Farm in Kent', *Annals of Agriculture.*, 36, 1801, pp. 119–32; G. Tollett, 'Proposals for the Separate Cultivation of the best British Grasses', *Annals of Agriculture*, 36, pp. 337–42; Anon., 'Couch Grass', *Annals of Agriculture*, 36, pp. 454–5.

[79] See G. Sinclair, *Hortus Graminaceus Woburnensis or an account of the results of experiments on the produce and nutritive qualities of different grasses and other plants used as food of the more valuable domestic animals*, London 1816, pp. iii, v, 104–7, 108–11, 196, 217, 290 ('comparisons with Trifolium pratense: produce per acre, herbage lbs 49005, ditto hay lbs 12251; Medicago sativa, herbage lbs 70785, hay lbs 28314; Hedysarium onobrychis, herbage 8848, hay 3539'): the seed selected at Woburn was sold by seed merchants; idem, *The Code of Agriculture, including Observations on Gardens, Orchards, Woods and Plantations*, London 1817, pp. 380–2, 386, 401.

and for all the fact that most of the past failures had been due mainly to two factors, the poor quality of seed and the wrong choice of soil. It was a mistake to plant lucerne on undrained soil, too impoverished by previous crops. Lucerne also reacted well to a dressing of lime and potassium in the early months of cultivation and again in the winter months. Sainfoin was more resistant and had won considerable success as a means of improving the poor chalky and limestone uplands of central and southern England. Apparently there were places where one could find specimens that had lived for nearly a hundred years. While plants such as plantains (*Plantago lanceolata*) and burnet (*Poterium sanguisorba*) were on the wane, the number of legumes that could be utilized was increasing. There was crimson clover from Italy, long used in gardens as an ornamental plant, another late variety which came from France, the purple or red clover in the variety from Normandy, the perennial, in the variety from Argovie or from Göttingen. Even broom, which had been rooted out tenaciously during the previous centuries, was suggested in the middle of the century as forage for sheep.[80] In practice, the mixtures of seeds seem to have been sown on meadows and pastures for produce to be consumed on the farm, while hay from the selected grass-fields was sent to market in town, particularly in London, where it fetched higher prices. Despite the high degree of specialization achieved in meadows and pastures, harvesting seed still presented considerable difficulties, because of its poor germination rate, and hundreds of tons were imported every year.

Free trade, which allowed the importation of raw materials into England for more than a century, forced entrepreneurs to face the question of quality control, a constant necessity for every economic sector. At the end of the Napoleonic Wars, the problem of the quality of imported goods, which had been brought up by a few lone voices in the *Annals of Agriculture*, was dealt with for the first time at Parliamentary level. In 1816 the Select Committee on seeds, wool and tobacco recommended that no measures should be taken to reduce the import of agricultural seeds, especially of flax and clover, while the revocation of the duty on linseed cake would encourage its consumption and ultimately

---

[80] See P. Lawson & Son, *Agrostographia. A Treatise on the cultivated grasses and other herbage and forage plants*, Edinburgh 1853, pp. 74–80: the Lawsons, father and son, were seedsmen in Edinburgh. J. B. Lawes and J. W. Gilbert, 'Report of Experiment on the Growth of red clover by different manures', *Journal of the Royal Agricultural Society of England*, 21/1, 1860, pp. 178–200.

the production of wheat. Average receipts at the Customs House had been £18,021 for an average weight of 52,382 cwt of imported clover seed.[81]

A few years later the much more important question of the adulteration of seed was raised. In May 1821 Mr Robert Felton, seed merchant of Southwark, and other traders were called to give evidence before the Select Committee. They told how old, impure seed was mixed with new seed, after being fumigated with sulphur, to restore the yellow colour that gave the impression that the seed was fresh. Seed worth 35s was resold at 60–70s by salesmen who supplied local seed shops. In their defence, they explained that this so-called 'doctored' seed was also produced in foreign warehouses when collecting the seed from Holland and France. Actually, more scrupulous merchants said that very little doctored seed came from abroad. In London, in the Southwark district, there were said to be six or seven firms that used this process, which was simple and cheap; three tons of seed could be doctored in twenty-four hours. The 'doctors' called to give evidence also declared that they knew very little about the life of seed, and they simply made the colour the same for all varieties to overcome the suspicions of farmers, who could not tell good seed from bad. Actually, this fumigation with sulphur completely prevented the seed from germinating. Finally, those who maintained that the duty on imported clover seed should be raised to 3d a pound, to encourage home production, were told that the duty of 20s per hundredweight was the highest that could be imposed, because an increase in duty would diminish the use of clover, and the accumulation of large stocks of old clover seed would slow down the production of fresh English seed. It was better to stamp out adulteration of seed than virtually to stop importation. Before the year was out Parliament had passed a law to that effect.[82] The fact was that in the face of the huge

---

[81] See *Third Report from the Select Committee on Seeds and Wool . . .* , in *British Parliamentary Papers* (hereafter *BPP*), 1816 (272), vol. 6, p. 209; gives an account of the clover and lucerne seed imported from Ireland and elsewhere, 1806–15: the average for the decade was 52,832 cwt of clover and 493 cwt of lucerne seed.

[82] See *Report from the Committee on the Adulteration of Clover and Trefoil Seeds*, in *BPP*, 31 May 1821, vol. 4, pp. 305–23, see especially pp. 307, 311, 315, 317, 321, 323; 1821 (611) 3. 1167, 2 George IV Sess. 1821, *A Bill to prevent the Adulteration of Clover and other Seeds*. A number of foreign species were imported into the British Isles unwittingly, as impurities in other seeds and foreign wares: see T. Johnson, *Agricultural Seeds and their Impurities: a Source of Ireland's Alien Flora*, Dublin 1910.

amount of seed being imported in that decade the merchant and farming lobby in Parliament felt they could not bring about a radical change. The need for imported seed was insistent because the home market was unable to produce in sufficient quantity. In the case of trefoil, for which demand was small, the home-grown supply was ample. Adulteration of seed did not stop completely, but took on various forms, since the unbending structure of the clover-seed trade hardly helped to reconcile the salesman's need to sell regularly with the farmer's unpredictable requirements. In partial compensation for the repeal of the Corn Laws (1846), Peel's government abolished the duty on the importation of clover seed, thereby increasing consumption on the home market.[83]

The seed trade was centred at the Corn Exchange in Mark Lane, London, where brief but intense transactions were carried out. In June 1869, since the law of 1821 had proved ineffective, a new Parliamentary Committee called together the representatives of the principal firms. The Royal Horticultural Society also held an enquiry. It emerged that good purple or white clover seed was mixed with seed of inferior quality. It should have deceived no one by its appearance at the time of purchase, but it had been dried and devitalized, so that the fraud would not be discovered when the plants grew. This adulteration was practised by at least four firms, two of which doctored exclusively clover seed. The good quality seed was collected from producers in the English countryside and on the international market, brought to London and then retailed throughout the country, in grocers' and hardware stores, in chemists' shops and those selling agricultural tools and the like. The shopkeeper bought from the wholesaler, who in his turn got supplies from the importers' middlemen; alternatively, the wholesalers had a number of salesmen who supplied the local market. A few important nurserymen, like Daniel Nash of London, sold directly to a select group of gentlemen clients. The farmer, on his part, tried to buy regularly from someone he trusted; the salesman's professional ethics consisted in selling 80 per cent viable seed at 10s a stone, rather than seed that was 40 per cent viable for 8s.

According to the evidence gathered by the Parliamentary Committee,

---

[83] See J. C. Loudon, *An Encyclopaedia of Agriculture*, London 1835, pp. 871–81; D. C. Mooris,'Corn Laws and High Farming', *EcHR*, ser. 2, 18, 1965, pp. 544–61; F. M. L. Thompson, 'The Second Agricultural Revolution, 1815–1880', *EcHR*, 21, 1968, pp. 62–77.

at least a thousand non-metric tons of seed were adulterated in this way in London, Liverpool and Hull every year. Viability of clover seed varied naturally from 50 to 92 per cent, but with adulteration it was lowered to average values of 70 to 80 per cent, so they said, while the merchants themselves admitted that in many cases it did not go beyond 40 per cent. The farmers bore the brunt of this fraud, which allowed the wholesalers to get rid of their old stock. It is true that the wide range of prices on the Corn Exchange was always an indication of the quality and freshness of the seed on sale, but the merchants expressly asked that the new legislation should not prevent the cheap seed from being kept out of the quotation lists. In practice, those who could get supplies directly from Mark Lane, where seed was brought from all over England and the Continent, could be sure of their purchases, provided they paid the highest price, but the less wary provincial farmers, who tried to economize on the price, were certainly buying poor quality produce. The principal firms on the London market (James William McKay of Dublin, John Thompson Burnell, Thomas Franklin of Hull and others) tried to defend their positions while never directly admitting that they were involved in adulteration. In reality they were justifying it because it gave high profits, because it could easily be done in France too, before importation, and because, after a bad harvest, the one- or two-year-old seed was mixed with the new, accompanied by the warning that it should be sown more thickly. In any case they complained of the high degree of natural variability of the seed from year to year to be found not only in seed produced in England, but in the imported seed, which was the greater part. Henry Cutler's estimate, that more than half, probably two thirds of the national requirement of red clover seed was imported and seven tenths of the white clover seed, is unique in showing to what extent nineteenth-century English farmers depended on the peasant farmers of the Continent. However, according to the same source, a good 50 per cent of imports from the Continent, especially those from Antwerp and Germany, were slightly adulterated, while the system of sale by sample, practised in London, enabled suppliers to deliver seed that did not correspond to the sample examined. Moreover, the best quality English clover was exported to Ireland, where it was sold at double the price, the second quality went to Scotland and the worst was used in England. At the end of the enquiry, Parliament passed a new law on the adulteration of seeds which was much more precise than the one in force. In 1869 the adulteration of any seed whatever, by any means whatever, including the mixture and sale of old seed with new, was declared a legal offence, to be punished by a fine of up to £50.[84]

5. THE IMPORT OF FORAGE-CROP SEED

At the beginning of the eighteenth century relations between gentlemen, the wider public, nurserymen and seed merchants were intensified, while curiosity concerning products from the Mediterranean, the number of people travelling for study and pleasure and the mediation effected by merchants and refugees had grown to the point of transforming the question of forage-crops, which had previously been a matter for highly educated people, into an economic relationship between England and the Continent. Imports of seed, initially rather erratic, now began to be registered regularly in the annual accounts of the Customs Records, bearing evidence of the reorganization that took place in the eighteenth century. For the years 1698–1870 the relationship between a gradually changing English agriculture and the agricultural systems of the Continent can be reconstructed from these records (see Appendix, tables 7 and 8). The critical phases of the long struggle between capitalist farming and the peasant economy, ending in the disappearance of the latter, can be traced in these documents. There is a wealth of data on the varieties of seeds imported, particularly in the late nineteenth century, including clover, sainfoin, lucerne, rye-grass, trefoil and unspecified hay-seed. For the sake of uniformity with the early years, only the figures for red and white clover seed, taken together, and lucerne are given here. For 1870 all the items are grouped together as grass-seed, without further specification. There are some late eighteenth-century published figures, but these refer to imports for the whole of the United Kingdom and do not take into account the quantities re-exported. Only by going back to the manuscript volumes, made out annually by the officials of His/Her Majesty's Customs, can one compile a regular series, from 1698 to 1870, of the quantity of seed really imported and used in England and Wales.[85]

---

[84] See *Report from the Select Commitee on Seed Adulteration Bill*, in *BPP*, 1868–69, vol. 9, pp. 619–727, especially pp. 629, 631, 633, 635–7, 644 ff., 652, 664, 666–9, 674, 679, 690, 698–701, 707; *The Adulteration of Seeds Act, BPP*, 1869, vol. 5, pp. 161–6.

[85] See G. N. Clark, *Guide to the English Commercial Statistics, 1696–1782*, London 1938, p. 211; E. E. Noon, *The Organization of English Customs System, 1696–1786*, New York 1938; R. C. Jarvis, 'The Archival History of the Customs Records', *The Journal of the Society of Archivists*, vol. 1, 1957, pp. 239–50. Printed sources: 'An

In such a long time series it is important to establish the years in which the increase in the quantities imported represent a change in quality, involving a larger number of farmers and widening the range of the traditional supply. In 1732 alone, imports rose to above 1,000 cwt; actually the figure was 2,372 cwt, enough to sow a total of 22,138 acres. Even with the few hundred hundredweights imported annually between 1698 and 1730 several thousand acres could be cultivated (3,229 in 1730, for example, and more in 1701, 1726 and 1731) if the recommended quantities of 14–16 pounds per acre were used, and much more if the foreign seed was mixed with local seed or rye-grass. This meant thousands of acres which not only made the crop more widespread but increased the amount of good quality germoplasm. Imports were lower in the 1740s than in the 1730s. It was of course predictable that in years of abundant harvests of cereals and low prices, little would be done to increase the production of grain by planting legumes. The year 1750 was a turning point; from then on, not only was there an increase in imports of cereals, but imports of clover seed rarely fell below 1,000 cwt (1750–3, 1755, 1761). In the decade 1770–9 the average was always above 10,000 cwt, and in the following decade it went up to 15,000 cwt. In 1787 Pitt's government reduced the number of articles subject to duty (from 1,700 to 1,200) as a way of reducing smuggling, but the same duty continued to be levied on clover seed as in 1758. From 1697 to 1757 imports had been taxed according to value, then they were subject to a tax varying between 2s 3d and £1, lowered to 5 shillings in 1846, to compensate for the repeal of the Corn Laws, then finally abolished in 1853 (see Appendix, table 9). Only then was the Customs' valuation substituted by current prices; hence it is impossible to calculate the monetary value of the imports and their cost for English agricultural

Account of all Clover Seed imported into Great Britain, 1797–1803', *Annals of Agriculture*, 43, 1805, pp 356–62; J. Marshall, *A Digest of All Accounts relating to the Population, Productions, Revenues . . . of the United Kingdom of Great Britain and Ireland*, London 1833, part 1, pp. 137, 140, 154 (years 1827–30); *Annual Trade and Navigation Returns, 1837–1870*, London 1838–71; Thompson, 'The Second Agricultural Revolution' (years 1806–91); M. G. Mulhall, *Dictionary of Statistics*, London 1899, pp. 476–8 (years 1861–89); M. Ambrosoli, 'Cloverseed imported into England and Wales and retained for home consumption, 1750–1850', in G. E. Mingay (ed.), *AHEW*, vol. 6, *1750–1850*, Cambridge 1990, *Statistical Appendix*. Unpublished sources: London, PRO, Customs Accounts, Cust 3 (years 1698–1780), Cust 17 (years 1781–90), Cust 14, 17 (years 1791–1808), Cust 4, 11 (years 1809–11), Cust 5 (years 1812–70).

production.[86] In the 1790s an average of 23,000 cwt was reached. On average an area varying from 93,333, 142,000 to 218,000 acres of leys or permanent meadow was probably sown according to the seed ratio. Despite the blockade inflicted during the Napoleonic Wars, the average doubled in the course of the decade 1800–9 (46,234 cwt) and an average of 52,000 cwt was easily reached between 1810 and 1815. Most of this seed was sent straight from France.

As time passed, the exporting countries also changed. For the first seventy years of this series Flanders and Holland continued to hold the lion's share of the market. Only after 1780 did French and German seed begin to find its way in larger quantities into English ports, until, from 1810 on, it definitely prevailed. The doubt remains whether seed dispatched by Flemish and Dutch merchants already contained some French and German produce, since until 1904, for customs purposes, the country of origin of all goods was defined by the last port of call before arrival in England. The series of imports of clover seed also gives an indication of the chronological order in which the cultivation of clover spread through Europe. The peasant producers of Continental Europe found an outlet in England for a slowly and laboriously produced commodity which spread definitively only in the first half of the nineteenth century. The importers do not seem to have shown any preference for one European country over another, as the produce imported tended to increase throughout the nineteenth century. Wholesalers seem rather to have built up stocks wherever they could find them, sure of being able to sell off what was left over from one year, mixed with the new harvest of the following year, in the way described above. The two foreign markets most closely followed by the English press that specialized in this sector were Antwerp and Bordeaux, but other ports, such as Le Havre and Hamburg, were regular exporters of seed.[87] Generally

---

[86] See N. Schlote, *British Overseas Trade from 1700 to the 1930s*, Oxford 1952, pp. 6–7. On grain imports see B. R. Mitchell and P. Deane, *Abstract of British Historical Statistics*, Cambridge 1962, pp. 94–6, 190–1; Deane and Cole, *British Economic Growth*, pp. 62 ff.

[87] See Schlote, *British Overseas Trade*, as well as Marshall, *A Digest of All Accounts*, part 2, pp. 6–7 (Customs revenues for the years 1814–29), p. 103 (clover seed prices on the Antwerp market in the years 1814–26); *The Mark Lane Express and Agricultural Journal*, n.s., 1832, 1, 2 January; *The Farmer's Magazine*, n.s., 1839, 25 February; 1857, February, *passim*; 24 August; September, *passim*; 26 October; 23 November. During the nineteenth century import of foreign seeds and botanical specimens was of the greatest importance to improve the flora of Europe: see L. H. Brockway, *Science and Colonial Expansion: the Role of the British Royal Botanical Gardens*, London 1979, and K. Lemmon, *Golden Age of Plant Hunters*, London 1968.

speaking, the trade had maintained that markedly seasonal character already pointed out in the data collected for Carpentras and Paris in the seventeenth century (see Chap. 4, 3.2), which are confirmed by those for London throughout the nineteenth century. The quotations were often only nominal and the commercial correspondent of the *Farmer's Magazine* generally noted with care when real sales picked up again between the end of February, March and April, when large lots of seed were dispatched to the country. The other time of the year when business was brisk was September, when the new seed was harvested, and the prices of the local product were compared with those for French seed, which was the first to arrive on the market, by the end of August in the best years.[88]

Two major factors influenced price formation, the supply of local seed harvested, which depended on rainfall in England, and the fact that English farmers could afford to pay a high price for the foreign product when the price of English wheat was high. The clover cycle was inextricably linked with that of cereals. In capitalist farming, the spread of forage crops and the process of renewing the fertility of the soil depended even then on the commercial value of grain. Despite all the attempts made to diversify English agricultural production in the course of the nineteenth century, English wheat-growing preserved the advantage for, and the enormous power of, the great estates, reinforced by their rearing of livestock, mainly sheep. Therefore, just one model for the whole 1698–1870 period (see Appendix, tables 7 and 8)[89] can be

[88] See for example *The Farmer's Magazine*, ser. 3, 1857, 1858, *passim*.
[89] Besides the sources pointed out in note 85 see G. J. Symons, 'Recent Annual Rainfall compared with that of the Previous 165 Consecutive Years', *British Rainfall*, 1891, pp. 16–18; idem, 'Rainfall from 1725 to 1891', *British Rainfall*, 1896, p. 10; J. Glasspole, 'Two Centuries of Rain', *The Meteorological Magazine*, 63, 1928, pp. 1–6; G. Manley, *Climate and the British Scene*, London–Glasgow 1962, pp. 260 ff., 322–8; idem, *Central England temperatures*. On clover seed prices see: Houghton, *A Collection for Improvement of Husbandry; The London Price Current*, 1779–85, ed. by W. Prince (available at the Guildhall Library in London); A. Young, 'Report respecting Grain and Corn Laws. Lord's Committee', in *BPP*, 1814–15, vol. 5, p. 88, years 1790–1814; *The London New Price Current*, 1814–19; J. E. T. Rogers, *A History of Agriculture and Prices in England*, vol. VI, *1583–1792*, Oxford 1897, pp. 211 ff.; N. J. Silberling, 'British Prices and Business Cycles. 1779–1850', *Review of Economic Statistics*, 5, 1923, suppl. 2; A. D. Gayer, W. W. Rostow and A. J. Schwartz, *The Growth and Fluctuations of the British Economy, 1750–1850*, Oxford 1950, used a series of English red clover as part of the English price index for the years 1750–1850 (I wish to thank Dr A. J. Schwartz, National Bureau of Economics, Washington DC, for kindly supplying these unpublished data); J. M. Price, 'Notes on some London

constructed from data collected on imports of seed, rainfall, the prices of English red clover, the prices of wheat on the London market and then the average wheat prices for the whole of England.

The increase in the volume of seed imports can be explained by taking into account what has been said so far. With the spread of capitalist agriculture, forage-crops acquired a privileged role in the restoration of soil fertility and for the rearing first of cattle and then of sheep. From 1750 on, but above all between 1750 and 1830 the well-known reorganization of vast areas of common fields into enclosures was undoubtedly favoured by the continuous supply of forage seeds from Continental Europe, not so much because they could not have been produced regularly and in sufficient quantity in England but because the population of small farmers was continually diminishing. In a sense, the series of imports of clover seed into England is a measure of the spread of the capitalist system in agriculture, which limited the production of overly expensive goods and services, however useful. Indeed, within the same series lie some quite discordant facts, the sowing of clover in rotation with cereals, the slow spread of forage-crops on permanent pastures and the reduction in wheat cultivation. The results of the multiple regression, calculated on the four series, rainfall, average temperature in August, price of corn and price of English red clover seed, show a stong correlation of the variables (r: 0.746; r²: 0.557). Even higher are the coefficients of the simple regressions between the series recording the average temperature in August (when the new seed was harvested) and rainfall (r: 0.981 and r²: 0.963). That is to say that in central and southern England the low temperature in August, which has a negative influence on the production of clover seed, is linked to the increase in annual rainfall. The same is true for the correlation between the price of wheat and the price of English red clover; when one

Price-Currents, 1667–1715', *EcHR*, ser. 2, 7, 1954, pp. 240–50. On imports see Great Britain, *Trade and Navigation Statistics*, London 1834–70 (annual figures for the United Kingdom); Thompson, 'The Second Agricultural Revolution'. On wheat prices see Mitchell and Deane, *Abstract of English Historical Statistics*, pp. 484 ff.: the prices for the years 1698–1770 are the result of an average of existing prices at Exeter, Eton, Winchester (in *Winchester quarters*), prices for the years 1771–1870 are the national averages published in the *London Gazette* (in *Imperial quarters*: the *Winchester quarter* equals 97 per cent of the *Imperial quarter*); see also Lord W. H. Beveridge, 'A Statistical Crime of the Seventeenth Century', *Journal of Economics and Business History*, 1, 1929, pp. 503–33. On grain growing during times of low prices see Chambers and Mingay, *The Agricultural Revolution*, pp. 181–6.

increased, so did the other (r: 0.839; r²: 0.703).[90] In practice, the imports of clover seed over a period of little less than two hundred years were linked to local production, rainfall and the price of corn. The commercial correspondent of the *Farmer's Magazine* wrote in 1857 that, when the price of corn was low, nobody speculated on importing forage-crop seed.

The cycle of imports behaved in the same way, especially in the years 1750–1870, when three to four years elapsed between the lowest and highest points. In part it was a cycle linked to the four-course rotation (the most famous being the so-called Norfolk course), while the seed used on pastures in mixtures of various kinds was equally distributed over a much longer period. The regional integration which followed the construction of the railway network diminished differences between one area and another and the distinction between mixed farming and sheep- or cattle-rearing, thus making imports more uniform. Perhaps the very distribution of seed among the London firms and the salesmen travelling around the country meant that it took them longer to sell out their stock. The mixture of old and new seed sold by so many dealers might have been the result of a distribution system unable to foresee more accurately the annual consumption of the product or the quantities that would be available for sale. Actually the connection with the grain-market was clearly brought out by the evidence presented before the Committee on the adulteration of seeds.

What happened to the seeds imported to bring about the reorganization and transformation of English agriculture? Did they end up on meadows and pastures or on the best arable land? To this question there is no direct answer, given the ambiguities mentioned above, and for lack of precise data on the state of crops, which only began to be more accurate in the early nineteenth century, with further improvement in the second half of the century. The same is true of the home demand. The aforementioned estimate of 1868, made by the dealer Henry Cutler, that half or two thirds of red clover seed and as much as seven tenths of the white clover seed used in England was imported, is confirmed by the 1866 census on agriculture. As a general rule red clover was sown as a grass crop, in

[90] Regressions have been calculated for the data published in Table 8, see Appendix, using the Systat, Inc. program (I wish to thank Gianni Perona, colleague and friend, for his expert help). The correlation coefficients obtained are much higher than those considered by G. H. Hooker, 'The Weather and the Crops in Southern England, 1885–1921', *Quarterly Journal of the Royal Meteorological Society*, 48, 1922, pp. 115–30 (0.50 for a strict correlation and 0.25 for a probable correlation).

rotation on arable land, while the white variety was preferred for permanent meadows and pastures. Unfortunately, there are no statistics which divide the two products even indicatively.[91] If all the imports of the five-year period 1866–70 had been used on leys (called *temporary grass* in the agricultural census) and, taking the average imports for those years, calculating the usual twelve pounds per acre, we would get 61 per cent of the total area under grass, an average of 2,692,000 acres for that period. But in the years 1866, 1868 and 1869 there were peaks of 74, 81 and 83 per cent.[92] To the leys were added the acres sown with lucerne or trefoil (*M. sativa* or *M. lupolina*), generally not taken into account in the calculation of leys until 1889, giving an average of 10,195 acres for the five-year period (it should be kept in mind that the lucerne field has quite a long life and so the area planted with lucerne is underestimated).[93] The series of imports of forage-crop seed becomes the principal source for an approximate estimate of the acreage under grass between 1750 and 1850.

The crop returns of 1801, collected by clergymen and grouped by diocese, constitute an intermediate reference point. These data have recently been aggregated for the counties, according to their 1801 boundaries, and can thus be compared with the population census begun in the same year.[94] The main difficulty about using these figures lies in the definition of arable. In the census of agricultural land made in 1866 fields kept under grass for less than seven years were also included in this

[91] A few fragmentary observations on the delivery of clover-seed were published in the *Mark Lane Express*.

[92] The above calculation was made on the figures published in Ministry of Agriculture, Fisheries and Food, Department of Agriculture and Fisheries for Scotland (hereafter MAFF), *A Century of Agricultural Statistics: Great Britain 1866–1966*, London 1968, pp. 5–7, 12–13, 34, 45, 97. In the same years the following acreage could have been sown with the imported clover seed: 1866, 1,905,344 acres, 74.6 per cent of 2,553,000 acres; 1867, 1,180,013 acres, 42.4 per cent of 2,779,000 acres; 1868, 1,879,000 acres, 81.6 per cent of 2,699,000 acres; 1869, 1,879,000, 82.9 per cent of 2,266,000 acres; 1870, 1,135,000 acres, 35.8 per cent of 3,165,000 acres.

[93] In the same years 11,016 (1866), 15,640 (1867), 6,344 (1868), 15,360 (1869), 2,616 (1870) acres of lucerne were added to the 11–12 million acres of *tillage* according to the official description. The only figure (18,277 acres for 1890) of lucerne acreage in our possession compares well with the data produced in the previous note. Probably a ten-year moving average of the lucerne seed imports would give a rough estimate of the area used to grow this crop in England and Wales during the eighteenth and nineteenth centuries. See *ibid.*, p. 95.

[94] See M. Turner, 'Arable in England and Wales: estimates from the 1801 Crop Returns', *Journal of Historical Geography*, 7, 1981, pp. 291–301; idem, 'Corn Crises in Britain in the Age of Malthus', in *Malthus past and present*, London 1983.

category, but in the data published from crop returns of 1801 they were not classed as such. In most of the English counties the dominant agrarian feature was a combination of three main cereals, wheat, barley and oats, with beans and peas or turnips in rotation. The difference between the area of cultivated land, namely arable, and permanent pasture, according to the estimates for England and Wales made by B. P. Capper in 1801 and W. T. Comber in 1808, is little over a million acres. The difference lies precisely in the definition of arable, in which Comber includes leys.[95] Although not classified so systematically as for the subsistence crops, legumes also appear in the crop returns for 1801 more frequently than recorded in M. Turner's study, quoted above. The quality of information not explicitly requested is always doubtful in a descriptive source. In Llanycham, Wales, in the diocese of Bangor, 139 acres of pasture were partly clover and rye-grass. In Aller, Somerset, a mainly cattle-rearing county, 292 acres of corn were grown and 73 acres of beans and peas; the rest of the arable land, instead of being left fallow, was sown with vetch and clover. In Combehay and Farley Hungerford 7 acres of vetch were recorded. Elsewhere (e.g. Stowey) owners forbad tenants to plough up natural pastures, as there had been an increase in wheat production at the expense of natural pasture. In more than one village (Creech and Froom Selwood) pasture was considered a good alternative to the hayfield and growing crops.[96] The real alternative to forage-crops in the difficult years of the Napoleonic Wars was peas and beans, which gave a yield equal to or a little lower than wheat (in some cases even higher, as at Otterhampton, Somerset), and had a

[95] See B. P. Capper, *A Statistical Account of the Population and Cultivation, Produce and Consumption of England and Wales*, London 1801, and W. T. Comber, *An Inquiry into the State of National Subsistence*, London 1808. H. C. Prince, 'England circa 1800', in Darby (ed.), *A New Historical Geography of England*, pp. 402 ff., gives the following figures in acres: arable land: 11,350,001 (Capper), 11,575,000 (Comber); pasture and meadow: 16,796,000 (Capper), 17,495,000 (Comber); total cultivated area: 28,146,959 (Capper), 29,070,000 (Comber); (woods and coppices, commons and wastes, buildings, roads, water, etc.) total uncultivated area, 9,118,896 (Capper), 9,430,000 (Comber); grand total, 37,265,855 (Capper), 38,500,000 (Comber). The correct total area of England and Wales is 37,325,000 statute acres. Turner, 'Arable in England and Wales', p. 299, corrects the figures proposed by the above authors to: 8,000,000 acres for Capper, 8,043,000 for Comber, 7,077,000 or 7,860,000 according to the two estimates of the total arable acreage following the 1801 Crop Returns. These figures compare well with the minimum acreage of cultivation reached in 1939 for the whole of Great Britain when by adding Scotland a total of 8,300,000 acres was reached. The maximum figure was for 1869 with 14,200,000 acres: MAFF, *A Century of Agricultural Statistics*, p. 12; see also *AHEW*, 6, pp. 30 ff., 126–34.

[96] See London, PRO, HO 67/1, HO 67/2, ff. 2, 5, 14, 84, 93, 120, 123.

function similar to clover in renewing the fertility of the soil after grain-growing.[97] The production of food was the main concern at the turn of the century. What happened in the west of England, which was pastoral and on the whole backward, was also repeated near London, in Buckinghamshire.[98] In the open-field parishes they had courses of two harvests and a fallow, in the enclosed ones the courses were of five, six, seven or more years, with grain crops alternating with clover, according to local conditions. Wheat was followed by beans and peas, with a deviation from the English tradition, in which barley followed or preceded wheat according to current prices (see Chap. 6, 4.1). Examination of the differentials between income and expenditure for the three categories of land (see footnote 98) shows that only on the best land, which produced twenty-nine bushels of grain, was it worthwhile growing cereals and adopting the three-course rotation (the fallow year meant dividing the income from two years of grain by three). Only under this system did the produce of cereal-growing outweigh that of livestock-rearing, calculated as the product both of fattening and of dairying, while, because of the price of the produce of stock-rearing, it was slightly below this (£1 3s 7d as against £1 10s 6d or £1 4s 10d according to the animals reared). In the second class, the income from grain-growing was much less than from stock-keeping (6s 7d as against £1 7s 5d). Sheep, which were generally reared on fallow, were let out to shepherds and herdsmen, who made a good profit even on small lots of land since they had few expenses. The land in the third category could not have stood the plough regularly and only by removing it from the three-year system and improving it with turnips and legumes could it become advantageous for the owner, the farmer and finally the consumer. However, the habit of using the best land for stock-keeping and the poorer for arable needed to be changed. It had happened because the richest natural pastures had been sufficient to keep cattle and were rented at a price a third higher than arable land. It was a terrible waste. On 120 acres of first quality natural pasture 30 head of cattle, 30 lambing ewes and 10 barren ewes could be kept.[99] Forage-crops would have

---

[97] Yields per acre varied from 16 to 30 bushels for wheat, 20 and 40 for barley, 20–25 (low yields) for beans and peas, 30–35 (high yields) for beans and peas (*ibid.*).

[98] See L. Heslop, *A Comparative Statement of the Food Produced from Arable and Grass Land and the Returns arising from Each; with Observations on the Late Inclosures*, London 1801, *passim*.

[99] Or, in weight, 1108 pounds of wheat from one acre, as against 115 pounds of live weight for dairy cattle and 129 pounds for cattle reared for meat (*ibid.*, pp. 2–3).

turned the poor, light soils into good pastureland, without preventing the naturally fertile soils from being used for grain-growing. This accurate survey for 1801 shows that in central and southern England too, foreign seed was sown preferably not on natural grassland but on poor arable land. The series of seed imports could usefully serve to explain the increase in the productivity of grain-growing in the period from 1750 to 1850, when the area of natural pastures increased, to the detriment of arable land.[100] It should be remembered that cattle consume large quantities of fodder and deposit most of what they eat back on the land; using the best land for cereals increased the productivity per worker, while forage-crops together with cattle on natural pastures enhanced fertility on poor land and increased the yield of cereals when this land was periodically put back under the plough.[101]

How much did the productivity of cereal-growing increase between 1750 and 1830? Was it because of this increase that population growth was maintained in England during this period? Was productivity higher on open fields or on those newly enclosed? Historians reply to these questions in various ways and we have already discussed the results in part. It should be added that the importation of forage-crop seeds enabled farmers to make a clear distinction between arable land and permanent pasture. The best land was ploughed, with an annual rotation based on turnips and clover, to produce good grain crops. It was the droppings of cattle on meadow and pasture, not manure on ploughed fields, that brought about an increase in production. Clover had been given preference over other forage-crops because of its annual cycle, which fitted better with grain-growing. The poorer quality arable land was transformed into meadows or pastures according to need. The yield per acre had increased because the worst arable land had been abandoned (it was failure to do this that kept the yield low in Italy even in the first half of the twentieth century). This could be done both in open-field parishes, with local consent, where social tensions were not too acute (as Lisle pointed out), or, more easily, in the enclosed ones. It has rightly been said

---

[100] See Prince, *England circa 1800*, pp. 417–24.
[101] See M. Turner, 'Agricultural Productivity in England'; idem, 'Agricultural Productivity in Eighteenth century England: further strains of speculations', *Ec. His. Rev.*, 37, 1984, pp. 252–7; M. Overton, 'Agricultural Productivity in Eighteenth Century England: some further speculations', *Ec. His. Rev.*, 37, pp. 244 ff.; R. C. Allen, *Enclosure and the Yeoman*, pp. 210–31. I have pointed out issues other than those stressed by the above authors, who are more concerned with the statistics of crop yields than with the means of obtaining these yields. See also *AHEW*, 6, pp. 134–47.

that enclosure increased the total product of the farm, but not necessarily that of arable land; even the early supporters of enclosure, like Fitzherbert, had said this. First cross-ploughing, and then the fight against Virgilian husbandry, certainly improved cultivation, achieving higher percentages of germination of seed sown. This was important because it is generally accepted that the amount of seed per acre remained constant, and there are no data to prove otherwise.[102]

6. CONCLUSIONS: OLD SOLUTIONS TO NEW PROBLEMS

One of the lasting results of the spread of forage-crops in England was that a greater number of cattle and sheep could be kept, while increasing rather than reducing the area used for growing cereals. This was happening in the decades when the population of the United Kingdom rapidly increased, she was transformed into an industrial economy, and the question of food production was more urgent than ever. Convertible or mixed farming,[103] which spread mainly during the period when the price of wheat was high in the late eighteenth and early nineteenth centuries, increased basic food supplies like cereals and potatoes and allowed a more varied diet to the classes that drew immediate benefit from economic development, through the higher quota of products of animal husbandry and its derivatives. In the following decades this model changed with the general situation. Usually growers of cereals endeavoured to keep yields high and increase productivity without sparing expense. The first Agricultural Revolution, which ended around 1850, was to be followed by a second one based on technical discoveries unknown in the late eighteenth century, such as linseed cake, guano, nitrates extracted from bones, industrial fertilizers, superphosphates and nitrates.[104] But what were the costs for the economic system during the long years of the Victorian Age? The example of guano is the most typical. Although it was a natural fertilizer, with a good proportion of

---

[102] Besides the bibliography already given in notes 95 and 101, it should be remembered that the method for calculating the productivity of English cereal growing in the years 1815–59, used by the firm Cropper Benson & Co and by J. Sandars (described and discussed by M. J. R. Healy and E. L. Jones, 'Wheat Yields in England, 1815–59', *Journal of the Royal Statistical Society*, 1962, part IV, pp. 574–79) is none other than the system proposed by Agostino Gallo as far back as 1564 (see chap. 3, 9).

[103] The terms 'mixed farming' (Jones), 'convertible husbandry' (Chambers and Mingay), 'up and down husbandry' (Kerridge), focus on different elements of farming practice.

[104] See especially Thompson, 'The Second Agricultural Revolution'.

nitrates, phosphates, calcium and potassium, used on light and heavy soils, on meadows and turnips, its market was drastically reduced in the space of a decade, after 1850. The technological problem of the time, the increase in the productivity of cereals on clay and heavy soils in the Midlands, was not solved by the use of guano, for instead of applying it directly on cereals, farmers spread it on the crops which preceded wheat in the rotation. It is true that it would have made the leaves and stems of the wheat develop too much, to the detriment of the ears; in any case it was cheaper to increase the production of manure by increasing fodder. But the fall in the imports of guano from Peru to Great Britain was caused both by the increase in the price of the product to compensate for the lower export figures (between 1854 and 1863) and by the development at home of synthetic alternatives (phosphates, nitrates and super-phosphates) and natural imported ones (nitrates derived from animal bones).[105] The market for guano diminished, but not that for fertilizers in general, in the 1850s and 1860s, when imports of clover seed were still high (an annual average of 200,000 cwt). But this increase in the use of fertilizers was taking place in an agricultural system that was producing progressively less cereals (the level of 3,240,000 tons of wheat produced in 1866 was never reached again until 1943 and the following years), reducing arable land and increasing the area of natural grassland (the 14,266,000 acres of arable in 1866 became 10,998,000 acres in 1914, while permanent pasture rose from 10,256,000 acres in 1866 to 16,116,000 in 1914). The total area cultivated increased a little only because of the increase in natural pastures (from 24,521,000 acres in 1866 to 27,114,000 in 1914).[106] Of the other products of English agriculture, only barley (for fodder) and potatoes increased in the years from 1866 to 1914, and the production of roots and fodder also remained stable. Hop-growing also diminished, while the only improvement in the level of consumption was the considerable increase in horticultural products (from 162 acres for the years 1871–5 to 245,811 acres from 1911–15, one of the highest peaks until 1966) and fresh fruit for the preserved food industry (an average of 60,000–70,000 acres up to

---

[105] See W. M. Matthew, 'Peru and the British Guano Market, 1840–1870', *EcHR*, ser. 2, 23, 1970, pp. 112–28: imports reached £260,000 in 1840 and a maximum 302,207 non-metric tons in 1858; for the years 1855–59 the average was £2,748,034, while the fall in imports began from 1860. In the period from 1859–63 and 1887–91 consumption of fertilizers passed from 347,710 to 996,790 non-metric tons: see Thompson, 'The Second Agricultural Revolution', p. 75.

[106] See MAFF, *A Century of Agricultural Statistics*, pp. 94–5, 98–9.

1915).[107] In the same period, from about 1850 to the First World War, the population engaged in agriculture fell precipitously from 40 per cent in 1851 to 8.7 per cent at the census of 1911. The increase in fertilizers used per ton of product was perhaps made necessary by the fall in agricultural labour expended. The famous expression of Jethro Tull and his school, 'labour as a substitute for manure', proved to be true after a hundred and fifty years of agricultural development. Productivity per acre of wheat had only slightly increased during the First and then the Second World War, reaching 18–20 cwt per acre. Even more illusory were hopes of progress in the production of hay, which fell from an average of 25 cwt per acre in the years 1885–94 to 23.4 in 1910–19 and rose to 25 cwt again only in the decade 1957–66.[108] Present-day critics of the Agricultural Revolution maintain with some foundation that agricultural development did not coincide with the general economic cycle.[109] In practice, the best result of the English agrarian revolution after 1850 was to sustain a growing population with a diminishing number of agricultural workers, while maintaining the yields achieved by good eighteenth-century agronomy.

European governments in general could afford to import half the agricultural produce necessary to fill the gap in their countries' needs during the second half of the nineteenth century.[110] The central role of the United Kingdom in the new colonial order distorted the English farming system favouring the gross saleable produce of every farm rather than the gross national product. Productivity per worker had increased, but so had costs of production because more commodities had been consumed by all industries which contributed to the gross national product, and therefore replaced, according to Sraffa's theory. The answer given to this general problem was to choose the most profitable sectors, leaving the less profitable sectors, such as cattle- and sheep-rearing, to the colonial and ex-colonial countries. The new industrial techniques of food preservation by tinning and refrigerating transformed their products into goods for working-class consumption. The scheme for the constant improvement of the soil to support crop-growing was largely abandoned.

---

[107] See *ibid.*, pp. 100–4, 106.

[108] See *ibid.*, pp. 108–9, 120–1.

[109] See above, note 59.

[110] For an interesting discussion on agricultural stagnation in the late eighteenth and early nineteenth centuries see P. Bairoch, 'Les trois révolutions agricoles du monde développé: rendements et productivité de 1800 a 1985', *Annales (ESC)*, 44, 2, 1989, pp. 317–53.

Such are the cleavages and inversions of tendency within the Agricultural Revolution. The grain crisis of the late nineteenth century and the industrial production of fertilizers and pesticides contributed to the creation of a new technology that reduced agriculture to a chemical equation. But the renewing force of forage-crops, legumes and non-legumes, was kept constantly in mind by practical farmers and land-owners in conflict with official science. The beginnings of what is now called biodynamic agriculture can be found in the period from 1880 to 1930, and its proposals are largely drawn from the experience acquired in the improvement of abandoned land, with the help of forage-crops, vegetal compost and ploughing.[111] Between 1750 and 1880, northern Europe showed how yields could be increased and kept high with the help of white clover and rye-grass on German and Baltic pastures and with legumes, lucerne and sainfoin in northern France. To these forage-crops were added the deposits of nitrates left by crops of beans, peas and lupins. Both heavy and light soils responded well to the increase of potassium provided by grazing animals and legumes which in general restored the quantity lost in the production of wheat.[112] It would have cost less to renew fertility by developing forage-crops than by importing guano and purchasing the fertilizers produced by the chemical industry.

When at the outbreak of the Second World War, the question arose of how to feed a population of forty-five million with the sole resources of the British Isles, the transformation of the thousands of acres of land that had been turned into rough grazing or even left uncultivated from the 1870s presented a series of problems not unlike those that Fitzherbert had described at the beginning of the sixteenth century.[113] Grasses and weeds (bracken, moss, peat, couch-grass, coltsfoot, wild oats and so on), against which generations of English farmers had fought with varying success since the sixteenth century, were attacked once more and overcome, with the help of forage-crops. The good ley of red clover, of lucerne or sainfoin, or the meadow or pasture sown with a mixture of rye-grass, white clover, trefoil and other grasses, were the point of departure for the reclamation of land for cultivation and wheat-growing. The experience

---

[111] See as an example R. H. Elliot, *The Agricultural Changes Required by these Times and Laying Down Land to Grass*, Kelso 1905, pp. 10–15, 28 ff., 58 ff.; E. Pfeiffer, *Soil Fertility, Renewal and Preservation*, London 1947 (Engl. trans.).

[112] See G. P. H. Chorley, 'The Agricultural Revolution in Northern Europe, 1750–1880: Nitrogen, Legumes, and Crop Productivity', *EcHR*, ser. 2, 34, 1981, pp. 71–93, especially pp. 88–9.

[113] See above, chap. 6, notes 59, 63 and 101.

of practical men and farmers, who throughout the first half of the century had continued to regard abandoned arable lands and the invasion of weeds as the tangible signs of agricultural decline and economic unease, was of great moment in regaining rapid control of the situation.[114]

---

[114] See for example Viscount Astor and B. Seebohm Rowntree (eds.), *British Agriculture. The Principles of Future Policy*, Harmondsworth 1939; Sir R. G. Stapledon, *The Plough-up Policy and Ley Farming*, London 1939; Moore, *Grassland Husbandry*; idem, *The Science and Practice of Grassland Farming*, London 1949; T. Bedford Franklin, *Good Pastures. Some Memories of Farming Fifty Years Ago*, Cambridge 1945; Davies, *The Grass Crop*.

Conclusion

When this research was first planned, the political and economic situation was not what it is today and European agricultural history could still be viewed with some degree of optimism. We are living in an age of transition and although the present political changes have little impact on the terms of our analysis, we cannot be indifferent to the destruction and appropriation of Nature that the market economy of our time is wilfully perpetrating. The introduction of forage-crops in early modern Europe, cornerstone in the modernization of agriculture, should be seen as a new way of conducting relations between man and nature. The building of modern society was due to the resumption of ancient crops in a more intensive system of rotation. The greater complexity of the social relations in the late medieval and pre-industrial world needed simplification, to speed up commercial exchange. A market economy tends to create uniformity in productive systems and to break down regional differences, to bring about competition between different areas in such a way that major decisions depend on one economic centre. This is the so-called advanced economic system.[1] Such transformation involved, and still involves, costs. The simplification of existing relations was and is necessary because it is difficult for a capitalist politico-economic system to deal with complex situations; which unfortunately poses a dangerous limit to the possible combinations of productive factors in agriculture.

The international economic system is based on age-old power relations and it is customary for the historian to look to the past, in order to point out the complexity of issues involved in times of transition and crisis. We have seen how, in a given period, activities which gradually

---

[1] I. Wallerstein, *The Modern World-System*, is still the point of reference for a general discussion of these problems.

take on the form of a real innovation, often grow out of experiences that have their roots in distant eras. They have gone through a process of conceptual formulation and trial, not necessarily founded on scientific experiment. Such knowledge is often produced by a social group other than that which appropriates it and treats it as its own. The creative relationship between social groups and their natural environment, which is continually brought out by work on the land, also reveals the links with their culture and their age, on the strength of which a practice can be defined as a technological innovation.[2] This involves tracing the cultural process undergone by technological innovations, before they are taken over by a larger number of people. Then the authors of technical-scientific treatises and their readers, mediators between different cultures, people with practical experience and laymen, become characters in a *Bildungsroman* that has as its setting and its focal point the reorganization of nature according to the economic priorities of a capitalist economy and not according to the natural order of things. Moreover, a process of transformation is always linked to a process of learning, for we do not face a static situation but a continual confrontation between old and new.

Hence the comparison of two possible alternatives is fundamental for the correct reconstruction of the history of change, rather than the description of the path actually followed as if it were the only teleologically possible result. Obviously our knowledge of events depends on the records that survive. The documentary evidence on which this research is based was not selected at the outset, but was built up step by step, following the tangles and inner links left in the historical literature on the subject. It was a matter of reconstructing those links, examining the themes involved, and discovering the real conditions that determined the choice between the old system and the new. In the case of the readers of Pier de' Crescenzi and of those reading in English private libraries, a quantitatively considerable sample was built up, but the model is significant irrespective of the number of copies examined. The

---

[2] We would mention, with no claims to completeness, S. C. Gilfillan, *The Sociology of Invention*, Chicago 1935; N. Rosenberg, *Perspectives on Technology*, Cambridge 1976; P. Stoneman, *The Economic Analysis of Technological Change*, Oxford 1983; see also the bibliography compiled by J. S. Metcalfe and P.C. Stubbs (eds.), *The Economics of Technological Change and Innovation*, Manchester 1973. On agricultural innovations see Z. Griliches, 'Hybrid Corn: an Exploration in the Economics of Technical Change', *Econometrica*, 25, 1957, pp. 501–22, reprinted in idem, *Technology, Education and Productivity. Early papers with notes to subsequent literature*, Oxford 1988, pp. 27–52.

interpretation put forward is true or false according to whether the inner relationships between the facts are true or false. The Middle-English translation of Palladius may testify solely to the interest of Duke Humphrey, and be considered as occasional writing, or it may be introduced into the much longer series of high or low interest in Mediterranean agriculture and agronomy in fifteenth-century England. The facts are true in both cases, but only in the second can the conflict between the old system and the first novelties of fifteenth-century English agriculture be fully understood. The same is true for other situations, such as the return to Classical agronomy, the conflict between northern and southern botanists in France, or the reintroduction of lucerne into Italy. The documents have been presented in a sequence, so that they might serve as unequivocal evidence of the alternatives involved.

Historical research has recently been compared to trial by circumstantial evidence. Personally, I prefer a semantic model, which avoids comparison with the inquisitorial system, for it should not be forgotten that trials based on circumstantial evidence may be founded mainly on the personal prejudices of the inquisitors, and often end by condemning innocent people.[3] Even Bacon recommended torturing Nature (*'torquere naturam'*), proposing the model of the judicial system of his day, to bring Nature up for trial and force her to reveal her secrets, setting this against the traditional school, which preferred to intervene in harmony with natural forces. Natural phenomena, like the historian's documents, are like the tip of an iceberg, and are understandable only if we take into account a qualitative relation between the known and the unknown. If it is true, as Karl Popper believes, that theory predetermines observation and should be distinguished from fact, it should also be remembered that we learn from error, as Lakatos points out.[4] The history of Western agriculture from the end of the Middle Ages to the mid-seventeenth century, and beyond, needs to be seen from the point of view of the resumption of Classical agronomy and its diffusion outside Italy. In this way, a theoretical framework can be laid down, so that a greater number of facts than usual can be taken into account and the scientific development of botany can be connected with the changes in society and

---

[3] Both points are made in C. Ginzburg, *The Cheese and the Worms, the Cosmos of a sixteenth century miller*, Harmondsworth 1982, and his more recent idem, *Clues Myths and the Historical Method*, Baltimore 1989.

[4] See chap. 4, note 2.

agrarian structures. Thus we can consider both the possibility of individual choices in the reorganization of property, and their connection with the general economic trend, keeping in mind a less backward agronomy than that which is generally described.

In the now neglected novel, *Wilhelm Meister*, Goethe, himself deeply interested in the study of nature, outlined a model of learning relevant to what we have just said. When young Wilhelm Meister began his apprenticeship in the theatre, he observed that we copy only the part of a model already known to us; and only exceptionally do we copy directly from nature. To paraphrase what the same poet wrote on the idea of the nation, Nature, too, is a mass of elements which really lack a common purpose. Hence a plan of reorganization is necessary to carry out effective action.[5] To Columella *posse* (to be able) and *velle* (to wish) were inextricably linked, and constituted the foundation of organized agricultural work. Agriculture and botany are similarly related. It was a general plan for the utilization of wild and cultivated plants that made it possible to overcome the impasse of the late Middle Ages, when 'deserted' (i.e. uncultivated) land was impoverished by swarming flocks, threatening the very existence of arable fields. The history of the Italian agrarian landscape provides evidence of the great amount of work done in the early fifteenth century to give shape to the land, to improve the soil and defend it against the all-invading sheep. The Italian pattern was repeated elsewhere, in Provence, and in the open-fields of England, where the early Tudor enclosures constituted a division between arable land and pasture for livestock-keeping.

In Goethe's novel, mentioned above, the nobility constituted the class able to bridge the social gap between high and low, new and old, as one would expect, given Goethe's anti-revolutionary ideas. The two characters in the novel, who exemplify the situation, are the prince, who models his theatrical performances on the ideals of Racine, and Jarno, the official, whose cold, intellectual reasoning leads him to propose Shakespeare's great dramas as a novelty. Novelties and innovations are not necessarily experienced in the same way in upper and lower circles: innovations spring from present and past problems mediated only through that part of nature which is visible.

---

[5] See W. Goethe, *Wilhelm Meisters theatralische Sendung* (1777–92); idem, *Die Schriften zur Naturwissenschaft*, Weimar 1947, and idem, *Gedankausgabe der Werke*, Zürich 1949, 1952, vols. XVI, XVII. See also the English translation by A. Arber (ed.), 'Goethe's Botany: the Metamorphosis of Plants, 1790', *Chronica Botanica*, 10, 1946.

In order to place sixteenth- and seventeenth-century agrarian problems in their context, we have observed how quite a number of English noblemen, not always the richest, acquainted themselves with Continental books on agriculture, revealing deep interest in new technology or their search for a new economic model. But the new crops could be introduced into the English agrarian system only if the main structures of English agriculture were somehow changed. That is to say, that part of Nature which was known and controlled by cultivation had to be extended to include a larger number of cultivated plants. Study of the Classics became one manifestation of the gentleman's nostalgia for Italy and led, as we have seen, to change and innovation, though for the majority of farmers from northern Europe, Italy was a theoretical point of reference rather than an obligatory stage on the agronomic Grand Tour, which few of them could make. Foreigners who went to the peninsula to observe that hot-bed of Classical excellence did not, in fact, find a great many economic institutions to copy.[6] Indeed, comparison between the boasted fertility of Italian soils in Roman times and the agricultural conditions of seventeenth- and eighteenth-century Italy confirmed the superiority of Classical agriculture. Italy was still the most prestigious seat of botanical learning, at least until the national schools prevailed, and began illustrating the flora of the various countries and regions. Then the scientific institutions of Paris and London surpassed the Italian academies. From the first decades of the seventeenth century, slowly but inexorably, the Italian contribution to the development of European agronomy was reduced to more modest dimensions.

Lucerne, the most advanced expression of the agronomic recovery of sixteenth-century Italy, would have given higher yields of grain if grown in the field, or could have become part of the agrarian structures of the time without weakening the predominant position of cereals, had it been cultivated in small plots within the farm. Having been lost sight of because it suffocated or went unnoticed among other meadow grasses, *medica* (lucerne) had even undergone a semantic change to *melica* (sorghum). The effort to reintroduce its cultivation was made by a class of landowners for whom Latin culture was a model of inspiration and behaviour. But the literary model of Cicero and Petrarch tended to exaggerate the landowner's contribution compared with that of the peasant class, who could leave no trace of themselves and their labours

---

[6] See Ambrosoli, *John Symonds.*

in writing.[7] Against this elite can be set a group of more practical men, botanists acquainted with the Classics, who saw the need to bring Classical scientific thought up to date. Among them were Paracelsus, Daléchamps, Anguillara and Turner, who missed no opportunity to take careful note of popular knowledge. In Italy, the academies tended to be more shut off and exclusive than elsewhere, and their disinterest in direct contact with Nature caused a serious delay in the identification of lucerne (1551). Depending as they did, literally, on the Classical sources, they were looking for a plant with red flowers, which was thought to have been described by Dioscorides. In the scientific world of the Renaissance, and hence in agrarian practice, the true and the false were continually weaving their way through the fields of social and technical-scientific knowledge. Different formulations were true, according to varying degrees of truth, in relation to their position in the two areas. What might seem false in one field became true in another.[8]

It has certainly been useful to be able to explain errors and anticipations of practical, pre-scientific agronomy through reference to contemporary agronomy. However, the task of early modern historians is to explain above all else the reorganization of productive choices, while keeping clearly in mind the fundamental economic choices of the dominant social group. It is utterly mistaken to present productive choices as the desire to maximize profits in any and every case. The transformation of pre-industrial agriculture consisted in learning a new system of which every part was representative of that given system. Forage-crops, turnips, flax and hemp grown in rotation with cereals were not easily introduced on Italian, English and French farms until farmers were in full control of their choice of crops and could organize the innovations according to their own needs. The historical evidence gathered about England between 1600 and 1660, or about Sir Richard

---

[7] See G. Misc, *Geschichte der Autobiographie*, Frankfurt 1969; on Italian literary autobiographies see M. Guglielminetti, *Memoria e scrittura. L'autobiografia da Dante a Cellini*, Turin 1977; on one rare example of lower-class autobiography see D. Roche (ed.), *Journal de ma vie: Jacques Louis Ménétra compagnon vitrier du xviiie siècle*, Paris 1982. P. Lejeune, *Le pacte autobiographique*, Paris 1975, D. Vincent, *Bread, knowledge and freedom. A study of nineteenth century working class autobiography*, London 1991.

[8] T. S. Kuhn, *The Copernican Revolution*, Cambridge (MA) Chicago, 1957, and idem, *The Structure of Scientific Revolution*, Princeton 1962, 1970.

Weston, are a fair illustration of the creative contribution of the individual farmer.[9]

The practical knowledge that supported agricultural enterprise was reorganized at the time of the so-called scientific revolution. Until the 1660s the good husbandman had addressed himself to writings on husbandry based on data drawn from experience and sources known both to the owners and to the workers of the land. Ancient and contemporary sources of information were placed on the same footing, interchangeable since they were both part of the owner-occupier's direct experience. Sixteenth-century agriculturalists had brought Classical agronomy up to date and rewritten it according to the regional knowledge and practice of the time. Yet Hartlib's correspondents sent in letters which were clearly already dictated by immediate needs, founded on empirical trials rather than on an economic structure of family farms which had regulated theory until then. High and low culture and/or farming were both to be found, since class divisions meant different needs and different social demands being made on the natural environment. Traditional knowledge was arranged in a series of opposites, hot–cold, dry–wet, wild–sown, which in sixteenth-century natural philosophy were described and updated under the label of *coincidentia oppositorum* and in sayings such as 'agriculture is useful and delightful'. The beginnings of scientific agriculture founded on experiment took place at the same time as the destruction of the peasant family economy and the creation of a labour market. Scientific agriculture started out from the natural history of plants and the Classical study of soils, subjects that, as we have seen, were foremost in the studies of sixteenth- and seventeenth-century English gentlemen. The crisis of the 1620s to 1640s increased the number of unemployed agricultural labourers, for whom provision had to be made, no longer, now, as a family duty only, but also from the point of view of social and Puritan morality. The introduction of new plants into the English agricultural cycle and in general the increase in the number of species cultivated under the watchful eye of a new class of landowner meant going beyond the bounds of the private garden and transforming British flora. This was only possible because agricultural labour was plentiful. The deeply religious landowner, who had to make provision for the poor in his parish, preferred to find them work rather

---

[9] The individual human element is rarely seen as an alternative to the combination of productive factors; see Z. Griliches, 'Education and Production Functions', in idem, *Technology, Education and Productivity*, pp. 147 ff. especially pp. 157 ff.

than let them swell the ranks of the idle poor. The Puritan Common-wealth was based on the principle that the unemployed should not be left without assistance. The landowner became a Schumpeterian entre-preneur, because he organized labour from outside. The new agricultural system passed through various phases. An effort of learning on the part of the landowners was followed by an adaptation of the new Continental techniques to the English situation and, no less important, some time had to elapse for the labourers to understand and apply the new technology. The change from copyhold to tenancy at will, which dates from the seventeenth and early eighteenth centuries, reflected the need for direct control by the landowners of the quality of agricultural work.

Plants grown by the peasantry passed into capitalist agriculture. Unquestionably, the reorganization of western European agriculture was achieved thanks to the botanical heritage already in the possession of the ancient farming world. We owe it to the peasantry that such species survived. Turnips had been grown for human food in peasants' gardens, forage-crops were hidden away in remote valleys of the French Alps. The way forage-crops were spread during the second agricultural revolution takes us back to the more general subject of the domestication of cereals from the first agricultural revolution onwards. The cultivation of cereals spread in semi-arid climates from 7500 BC, and was spontaneously associated with forage-crops. Lucerne, fenugreek, oats and rye grew mixed together with barley and wheat. The domestication of livestock took place side by side with the growing of cereals, which were used to feed the animals, because the farmer was unable to make anything but a rough selection of the crops. It can be maintained that in practice Roman agriculture restricted alternative crops, since, as early as the first century AD, it was founded on the great grain-growing estates and relied on imports from the provinces of Africa and Asia.[10] In Mediterranean Europe and the temperate climates, the starting-point of the second agricultural revolution was the garden, which furnished agriculture with firm support. It was now an integral part of peasant farming, no longer a privilege of oriental monarchs, as it had been in the case of the garden of the Assyrian king, Merodachbaladam. In central and northern Europe, grain cultivation took over space reserved for grazing, the main economic activity on cold, acid soils.[11] The system worked until humans

---

[10] See J. Kolendo, *L'agricoltura nell'Italia romana*, Rome 1980, and L. Capogrossi Colognesi, *L'agricoltura romana. Guida storica e critica*, Bari 1982.

[11] See C. O. Sauer, *Seeds, Spades, Hearths and Herds. The Domestication of Animals and Foodstuffs* (1952), Cambridge (MA) 1975, *passim*.

began to compete with the animal population. Rearing cattle is an extremely wasteful use of vegetal resources. One hectare of natural pasture can support at most three head of cattle, while twenty human beings can live off the same area when it is cultivated with cereals. The northern agricultural system drove livestock onto outfields or even to the most remote parts of the estate, according to von Thünen's geographical arrangement.[12] New forms of soil management, based on private property and continuous cultivation, started out from systems of Mediterranean horticulture. Legumes do not grow spontaneously on northern European pastures because of the acidity and wetness of the soils. Hence their survival is possible not through spontaneous reproduction but through the transformation of the agricultural environment brought about over the centuries by man. Agostino Gallo's explanation of why lucerne disappeared in Italy was ecologically very plausible. He believed that cattle brought into Italy during the invasions of the fifth to sixth centuries had a doubly destructive effect. The large animals, horses and cattle, ate up the most nutritious and tasty plants first, that is lucerne and the other legumes; then the sheep and goats, which crop closer to the ground, destroyed all the rest and finally turned to the foliage of trees. Only the most resistant weeds, of least agronomic value, could then grow on the impoverished pastures.[13] Seventeenth- and eighteenth-century English, and later Scottish, agriculture moved in the opposite direction. Legumes were planted after the land had been prepared by ploughing, draining and liming. Thus the forage-crops adapted well to the fields of northern Europe, since ploughing and harrowing reduced the competition from weeds. French peasant farmers, having kept lucerne and sainfoin alive in small plots, cultivated as gardens, were able to produce seed continuously and in quantities more than sufficient for local needs. The same was true on the small farms of Flanders, where the prevailing legume was clover.[14] Moreover, the costs of producing this botanical plasma-bank, in the critical years of the agricultural revolution,

---

[12] See D. Grigg, *The Agricultural Systems of the World: an Evolutionary Approach*, Cambridge 1974; J. H. Von Thünen, *Der isolierte Staat in Beziehung auf Landwirtschaft und Nationalökonomie*, Berlin 1842; Davies, *The Grass Crop*, p. 176.

[13] A similar phenomenon has been described by Moore, *Grassland Husbandry*, pp. 56 ff., and idem, *The Science and Practice of Grassland Farming*, London 1949.

[14] See M.-J. Tits-Dieuaide, 'L'évolution des techniques agricoles en Flandre et en Brabant'; idem, 'Les campagnes flamandes du xiiie au xviiie siècle, ou le succès d'une agriculture traditionelle', *Annanes (ESC)*, 39, 1984, pp. 590–610; A. Derville, 'Dîmes, rendements du blé et "révolution agricole" dans le nord de la France au Moyen Age', *Annales (ESC)*, 42, 1987, pp. 1411–32.

were extremely low because it was done in the framework of the Continental peasant economy.

Peasant labour was able to produce goods for consumption and productive inputs at lower prices because it transformed labour directly into product and then straightway into capital. Agricultural growth in sixteenth-century Europe depended on the increased productivity of peasant labour, under the strict control of a class of urban landowners.[15] Evictions and dispossession, which happened in many countries throughout Europe, were the result not of the impoverishment of the land, but of the increase in taxes and legal obligations exploited by the urban middle class.

In the fourteenth and fifteenth centuries two writers who represent very well the spirit of the Italian urban middle class, Pier de' Crescenzi and Leon Battista Alberti, recommended buying land that had been little cultivated. In England, in the early eighteenth century, Edward Lisle and Jethro Tull took up the same idea, based on their own experience. The great variability in the value of land is to be attributed to the state of the soil, generally unknown to us, and not merely to the categories assigned in land registers, which only gave an approximate estimate of its average productive capacity. The appropriation of common lands, a phenomenon to be found throughout Europe in the eighteenth and nineteenth centuries, was followed by procedures of improvement, which gradually retrieved the fertility that had accumulated over the centuries in land never regularly cultivated, giving an increase in production in subsequent decades. Yet it became necessary to use phosphates and nitrates as fertilizers to keep up the production of cereals once the area of meadow and pasture increased in nineteenth-century Europe. The ambiguity of agricultural reorganization became even more obvious in the course of the nineteenth century, as permanent meadows took the place of leys. Grain cultivation and stock-keeping also became more dependent on the seed of forage-crops produced by peasant farmers as the century advanced.[16] Thus the agriculture of northern Europe developed with support from the labours of the southern European peasant. The

---

[15] On the Italian situation see Giorgetti, *Contadini e proprietari, passim.*

[16] For example see D. Warriner, *Economics of Peasant Farming* (1939), London 1964, p. 92 on a medium peasant farm of 16 hectares in Western Hungary, producing and exporting lucerne seed. In the countryside between Treviso and Venice, as late as the 1950s, the sedulous *mezzadro* who could spare a small plot of land to grow lucerne for seed obtained a nice income, worth two or three head of cattle, making his neighbours green with envy (Dr. Danilo Gasparini, Treviso, personal communication).

peasant-produced seed of forage-crops made up for the shortcomings of a so-called advanced system. The weak point in northern agriculture, when its cereal-growing was so heavily dependent on hired labour that it was not free to make choices concerning production, lay in its inability to produce sufficient seed for the reproduction of its essential plants. The disappearance of the English yeoman meant that the pattern of urban food consumption determined the productive choices of capitalist agriculture.[17] Regional species and varieties were wiped out as a result of the simplification of diet, which was then regulated according to social class. In Victorian England diet was better in the districts where capitalist reorganization had been less drastic, where yearly tenancies, wages paid in kind, and gardens for the workers were still the norm.

The dependence of northern agriculture on germoplasm from southern countries had already occurred in western history before the mid-sixteenth century. Cereals that were brought from the Middle East had spread through central and northern Europe after adapting to the rainy winter season. Oats and rye, two weeds found among wheat in their countries of origin, had turned into routine crops because they were more suited to harsh winters and poor, acid soils.[18] The same path that crops had followed in the first agricultural revolution of 7500 BC, from the Near East to the Mediterranean basin and on to central and northern Europe, was followed once more after 1550. By then rich in local varieties of cereals, central and northern Europe needed to get supplies of forage-crop seed quickly to improve grasslands where the ecological balance was extremely precarious because so few species grew readily. The thin turf made meadows and pastures inadequate for the intensive animal-raising from which the majority of the population drew sustenance; as Julius Caesar wrote, 'The Britons live on milk and meat' (*Britanni lacte et carne vivunt*). Moreover, the improvement of soil by paring and burning, or burn-baking the clods in small ovens, frequently mentioned between the early sixteenth and the late eighteenth centuries, altered the ecological make-up of natural grasslands and peat-bogs so profoundly that new vegetal germoplasm, that is legumes and rye grass, had to be sown, to create a more botanically balanced combination of grasses capable of growing richly and renewing the fertility of the soil. The endeavours of the innovators, in many English counties, of the

---

[17] In general see J. Burnet, *Plenty and Want. A Social History of Diet in England from 1815 to the Present Day*, Harmondsworth 1968.
[18] See Sauer, *Seeds, passim*.

sixteenth to seventeenth, seventeenth to eighteenth and finally of the late eighteenth and early nineteenth centuries, aimed at reaching a better understanding of the delicate balance between the new species and varieties, so as to replace the old meadows and pastures with permanent meadows or leys. But the undeniable success of many nineteenth-century farmers would never have been achieved without the patient study and experimentation of so many well-known noble landowners and even more unknown farmers. Both what was called the 'nouvelle agriculture' on the Continent and the 'high farming' of England would have come to nothing in the short term, in a time of dire necessity, had they not been preceded by decades of trial and error which had prepared the way to solve the question of wet, acid soils, on the one hand, and botanical innovation on the other.

In England, too, the fact that clover grows spontaneously throughout Europe complicates rather than simplifies the question of when it began to be cultivated.[19] From the time of the earliest experiments it was clear that Dutch red clover was the most suitable on the ley, while English white clover was used for meadows and pastures. The rustic English varieties did not develop so well as those imported from the Continent. What is more, one suspects that in reality even Flemish and Dutch seed came, at least in part, from France. Obviously, rather than relying on continual imports, it was a question of obtaining immissions of southern germoplasm to improve the local varieties. The growth of imports in the eighteenth and nineteenth centuries shows how the work of selection and adaptation by English farmers of the seventeenth and early eighteenth centuries was replaced by commercial dependence on southern germoplasm, which was both better and cheaper.

The whole mechanism for the selection of certain, more productive species, to the detriment of the rustic varieties, from Tarello through to the mid-nineteenth century, is dramatically relevant to the present-day situation. It is only too well known that the loss of vegetal germoplasm is due not only to deforestation in the tropics but above all to the

---

[19] See N. I. Vavilov, *Studies on the origin of cultivated plants*, Leningrad 1926, pp. 147, 203 and *passim*; Vavilov's theories are mentioned by A.-G. Haudricourt and L. Hedin, *L'homme et les plantes cultivées* (1943), Paris 1987, with a bibliography brought up to date by M. Chavet. See now on more recent data Ucko and Dimbleby (eds.), *The Domestication*; J. Renfrew, *Paleoethnobotany. The Prehistoric food plants of the Near East and Europe*, New York 1973; M. N. Cohen, *The Food Crisis in Prehistory. Overpopulation and the origins of Agriculture*, New Haven 1977; C. A. Reed (ed.), *Origins of Agriculture*, La Haye–Paris 1977; J. R. Harlan, *Les plantes cultivées et l'homme*, Paris 1987.

selection of a very few varieties for commercial production, which have been spread throughout the world thanks to capitalist agriculture. In the past ten years the whole of the seed trade and the production of new hybrids has passed into the hands of a dozen multinational companies.[20] This process is destroying the rustic varieties, from which the genes necessary for the production of hybrids are extracted. These come mainly from the southern hemisphere, where the meagre range of remaining seeds is also being grown, in Third World countries such as Chile, Mexico or Tanzania, since the peasant economy and warmer climate ensure higher production rates. When Camillo Tarello asked the Senate of Venice for a patent on the cultivation of clover he was foreshadowing, three hundred years ahead, the colonial appropriation of varieties of great economic importance, such as tulips, cloves, coffee, rubber and so on.

Until the first decades of the nineteenth century, European agriculture developed a great range of cultivated varieties and species, as long as the peasant economy continued to produce highly differentiated seeds with marked regional characteristics. But the need to select the most productive varieties increased the problems of soil tolerance to clover. Even in the seventeenth century there was talk of soils which became 'cloversick' in the course of a few years. The question never arose for sainfoin or lucerne, the seed of which was generally imported.

We have already pointed out that, even in the written documents, fenugreek and melilot always appear at least a generation before lucerne and sainfoin, and that French *sainfoin* gave rise to considerable confusion between the cultivated species and their weeds. For the past three hundred years the development of cultivation has been conditioned by successes and failures in weed-control. Luzzago, one of Agostino Gallo's circle, used to say that the whole art of agriculture consisted in mucking the land well and cleaning it well. This was achieved by ploughing and other mechanical procedures. Passing from the traditional to the so-called Virgilian cultivation with cross-ploughing, and subsequently to Tull's new agricultural methods, brought about a whole succession of interventions on the land which hindered the organic

---

[20] See Brockway, *Science and Colonial Expansion*, and Lemmon, *Golden Age of Plant Hunters*; on the Italian situation see now R. Tolaini, 'Agronomi e vivaisti nella prima metà dell'Ottocento: Mathieu Bonafous e la diffusione del gelso delle Filippine', *Società e storia*, 49, 1990, pp. 567–92; in general see also P. R. Mooney, *Seeds of the Earth. A private or public resource?*, Canadian Council for International Co-operation, 1979, and idem, *The Law and the Seed*, The Dag Hammarskjöld Center, 1983.

reproduction of soil fertility.[21] More frequent tillage tended to cause a loss of humus and a lowering of the fertile surface-soil, which was retrieved by deeper ploughing, bringing the lower layers of soil to the surface. To maintain a constant yield for cereals, instead of seeing it fall rapidly after the first few years of cultivation, fertilizing with phosphates and nitrates became necessary.[22] Published data indicate that towards the mid-nineteenth century the clover seed purchased abroad was used more to improve English meadows and pastures than arable land, on which the products of the chemical industry were lavished. Once more good farming was considered to be that which bowed to the needs of the great capitalist farm, rather than that able to produce at lower costs by using forage-crops to improve the soil.

'The great estates are the ruin of Italy' (*Latifundia perdidere Italiam*). In that famous sentence Pliny the Elder summed up his agronomic and political views.[23] It is well known that the conflict between the two greatest agronomists of the first century AD, Columella and Pliny, needs to be explained not only in terms of the social effects of the great estates but of the technology employed on them as well. Columella held that the environment was transformed by tillage, Pliny that the action of plants transformed the environment. These two alternatives have reappeared at other times in the history of agriculture and continue to constitute possible alternatives in contemporary agronomy. Nothing upsets the agricultural environment more than man's methods of cultivation. Ploughing, burning bushes and land to be cultivated continually alter and worsen soil conditions. The decrease in fertility which occurred in the Middle Ages is generally ascribed to continuous tilling, mostly badly done; for a high standard of tillage would have increased rather than decreased the yield of cereals. Meadows and pastures are, and were considered as, reserves of fertility. It must, however, be borne in mind

---

[21] Two works necessary to re-evaluate the question of soil fertility before 1850 are E. Pfeiffer, *Soil Fertility: Renewal and Preservation*, London 1949, and M. A. Sprague and G. B. Triplett (eds.), *No-tillage and Surface-tillage Agriculture. The Tillage Revolution*, New York 1986.

[22] See M. K. Bennet, 'British Wheat Yield per Acre for Seven Centuries', *EcHR*, 3, 1935; Rothamstead Experimental Station, *Details of the Classical and Long Term Experiments up to 1962*, Rothamstead 1966; G. Porisini, *Produttività e agricoltura: i rendimenti del frumento in Italia dal 1815 al 1922*, Archivio Economico dell' Unificazione Italiana, Turin 1971.

[23] A. Giardina, *Uomini e spazi aperti*, and A. Carandini, *La villa romana e la piantagione schiavistica*, in *Storia di Roma*, 4, *Caratteri e morfologie*, Turin 1989, respectively pp. 71–99, 101–200, have recently questioned this famous sentence by Pliny the Elder.

that this is true of meadows and pastures in good condition, when the turf is well covered with grass for grazing. The wastelands, which were the scene of fifteenth-century transhumance, of herds and flocks passing through, or areas used haphazardly for rough grazing, were often another matter.

Based on Graeco-Roman experience, the new sixteenth-century agronomy reassessed the effect of the plants cultivated on soils. 'Change is the general rule of nature.' In this sentence of the geographer Carl O. Sauer lies hidden a concept generally forgotten by modern historians and late nineteenth-century agronomy that tried to fix production factors in an input–output table. Between the sixteenth and the early eighteenth centuries the greatest effort that European agronomists and farmers had to make was to keep up with the mass of data (and germoplasm) that the botanists unearthed. The historical flora of regions, which could be reconstructed by using the great herbaria of the second half of the sixteenth century, would reveal a much more vital natural environment than the contemporary one. Without doubt the farmers and landowners who decided to follow the path of innovation in subsequent centuries had an advantage in this abundance. The great estates are the ruin of Italy, and not only of Italy. With few exceptions, the agronomic rules which became general principles of cultivation between 1850 and 1950 were informed by the agronomy of the great estate, which was the foundation of the agricultural revolution of 1750 to 1850. Chemical fertilizers and seed selected far away from the centres of production were substituted for the work of selecting and adapting wild plants to the cultivated environment. Experts advertizing new technology and the mechanical means for applying it were substituted for the work of individuals strongly attached to their own environment.[24]

Perhaps that is another story. But only in a manner of speaking, for the history of agriculture is a continual series of recurrences and repetitions. From 7500 BC to the present day, the food crops of the human race have not changed. Indeed, the number of species and varieties has decreased dramatically. Among the conclusions of this research, which discusses the relationship between learning, the new techniques, and the economic growth of the modern age, is a recognition of the fragility of the contemporary agronomic system showing how the choices possible in European agriculture have gradually restricted its capacity to work and grow

---

[24] See P. Bairoch, 'Les trois révolutions agricoles du monde développé: rendements et productivité de 1800 à 1985', *Annales (ESC)*, 44, 1989, pp. 317–53.

through an increase in plant input. It has been limited by the dictates of an agronomy adapted to the needs of the great estates. Quite unintentionally, the peasant farmers contributed to the development of these great estates by preserving rare crops, lucerne and sainfoin in France, clover in Italy, providing seed at times when it was being consumed in large quantities and constituting a valuable reserve. Not only was there no economic compensation for this service. It was passed over by historians, impressed as they were by the achievements of the land-owning classes and large farmers rather than by the work involved in the daily reconstruction of resources rapidly squandered by authoritarian economic decisions.

Appendix

Table 1. *Annotated copies of Pier de' Crescenzi's Liber*[a]

	Owners' signatures, coats of arms	Mss notes, owners' names, underlinings	Clean copies
Italian readers			
Turin	2	1	1
Milan	2	10	0
Venice	5	9	1
Modena	1	3	1
Bologna	3	9	7
Florence	3	12	12
Paris	2	1	1
London	1	1	0
Oxford	0	1	0
Total	19	47	23 = 89
French readers			
Avignon	2	2	0
Carpentras	1	1	1
Paris	11	11	9
Turin	0	2	0
Gorgole de Corne	1	4	6
London	0	1	0
Oxford	0	1	0
Total	15	22	16 = 53
English readers			
Cambridge	1	4	0
London	3	4	8
Oxford	2	2	6
Total	6	10	14=30
Grand total	40	79	53 = 172

[a] The copies in the above table are listed under the owner's town of origin or the language used in the manuscript notes; the very rare copies which had only underlinings to the text are listed under the name of the town where they were found. See text for other remarks on the identification of the owners.

Table 2. *The price of lucerne seed at Carpentras, 1634–1777*[a]

	Month	Price
1634		18
1635	January	18
	February	18
	March	18
1640	November[b]	12
1641	March	8
1644	May	16
1645	January	10
	April	11
	September	10
1646	February	10
	March	9
	April	9
1647	March	9
1648	February	10
	March	9
	April	8.04
	May	9
	November	10
	December	9.04
1649	January	10
	February	10
	March	10
	April	10
1650	January	13
	February	16
	March	16
	October	12.10
1651	March	21
	April	19
	September	11
1652	March	13.12
	April	13
	May	13
	September	14
1653	February	14
	March	14
	April	13.10
	September	13
1654	February	13
	March	13
	April	12.12
	May	11
1655	January	11
	February	12
	March	12.04
	April	12
	September	11.14

	Month	Price
1655	October	12.10
	November	12.08
	December	12
1656	January	11.10
	February	13
	March	13.08
	April	14
	May	14
	June	14
	July	14
	August	13.16
	September	12.14
	October	12.05
	November	12.10
	December	12.10
1657	January	12.12
	February	11.14
	March	10.14
	April	10
	May	10.04
	June	10
	July	10
	August	10.10
	September	10.04
	October	10.10
	November	10.10
	December	10.10
1658	January	10.10
	February	10.10
	March	9.04
	April	7.10
	September	10
	October	10
	November	10
	December	10
1659	January	10
1660	August	12
	September	13
1661	February	11.10
	March	11
1663	March	8
	April	6.10
1664	February	10
	May	10
1665	May	15
1667	February	11
	March	11
1670	February	10

Table 2. (*cont.*)

	Month	Price
1670	April	7
1671	February	8
	March	8
	April	8
1672	September	6
1673	March	8
	April	8
1674	February	12
1675	March	10
1676	March	8.10
1677	March	9.10
	April	8
	May	8
1678	April	11.14
	May	12
1679	February	10
	March	10
	April	10
	May	10
1680	February	11
	March	14.04
	April	15
1681	May	10
	October	11
1682	May	11
	December	12
1683	February	10.06
	March	11
	April	11
	May	10.14
	October	11.10
1684	March	10.06
	April	9.12
1685	February	10
	March	10
	April	10
	May	10
1686	March	13.06
	April	13
1690	March	10
	April	9
1691	May	8
	September	9.18
1692	March	9.10
	April	10
	May	10.10
	October	10
1693	March	10

	Month	Price
1693	April	14.10
1694	March	15.10
	April	13.04
1695	April	18
	May	18
1696	February	12
	March	12.18
	April	12
	May	12.14
1697	March	15
	April	13
	May	12.12
1698	April	20
	October	14
1699	March	20
	April	18.12
	May	20
	December	12
1700	April	14
	May	10
	December	12
1701	April	14
	May	10
1702	January	8
	February	10
	March	8
	April	7.06
	May	8
1703	March	9.06
	April	9.04
	May	10
1704	February	10
	March	9
	April	9.12
1705	February	10
	March	10
	April	9.06
1706	February	12
	March	10
	April	10
	May	10
1707	February	11.10
	March	10
	April	11
1708	February	10
	March	9.14
	April	9.12
	May	10

Table 2. (*cont.*)

	Month	Price
1709	March	13
	April	17
1711	April	10
1714	March	11.04
	April	12.06
1717	April	10
1718	March	7.12
	April	8.06
1720	February	11
	March	11.10
1723	March	10
1725	March	15
1726	April	9
1727	February	9
1728	February	7.10
	March	7.10
1730	March	8
1732	April	11
1733	April	9
1736	April	8
1761	March	9
	April	9.04
1765	March	10.10
	April	9
1766	April	15
	May	16.10
1773	March	14
1777	March	9
	October[c]	12

[a] Prices are given in *florins* up to 1640, thereafter in *livres* and *sous* per *émynée* of Carpentras (equal to approximately 23 litres, see Venard, *L'Eglise d'Avignon*, vol. I, p. 101). The monthly prices are the result of the average of the weekly market quotations for each month. Data missing from the table generally mean that prices of lucerne seed were not quoted on those markets (see text), or else that ledgers have been lost (1634 and 1635 ledgers proved unreadable given their very poor state of conservation).

[b] Please add: December, 3 *écus*.

[c] Please add: 10 October, *esparcet* seed . . . £1 4s; 24 and 31 October, *esparcet* seed . . . £1 18s. 1778: 18 September, *esparcet* seed . . . £1 10s.

Source: see chap. 4, note 66.

Table 3. *Prices of sainfoin seed in Paris: 1683–98 (in* livres *and* sous *rounded to the nearest decimal point per 25 livres of weight)*

	Month	Price
1683	February	9.17
	March	10.13
	April	10.13
1684	March	8.09
	April	7.16
	May	7.15
	August	10
	September	9.01
	October	8
1685	February	9.18
	March	8
	April	7.05
1686	February	10.14
	March	10.09
	April	10
	June	8.10
	July	6.10
	August	6
	September	7
	November	5.10
	December	6
1687	February	10
	March	10.19
	April	10.16
	October	9.13
1688	January	12
	February	11.03
	March	11.16
	April	13.09
	October	9.08
	November	9.10
1689	January	10
	February	10.13
	March	11.13
	April	11.12
	September	8
	October	9.13
	November	7
1690	January	8.05
	February	9.10
	March	8.02
	April	7.09
	May	8
	September	6.14
	October	5.09
1691	January	6.10
	February	6.06

Table 3. (*cont.*)

	Month	Price
1691	March	6
	April	5.07
	May	5.04
	September	4.05
	October	5.15
1692	March	6
	April	6.16
	July	6
	September	5.04
	October	6
	November	5
1693	February	8.15
	April	7.05
	May	8.05
1694	March	11.01
	April	9.15
1695	March	11.02
	April	9.07
	May	9.05
1696	February	10.14
	March	9
1697	February	6.16
	March	8.13
	April	8
	May	9.13
1698	February	11.05
	March	9.14
	April	10.06
	May	9

Source: See chap. 4, note 74.

Table 4. *Classical agricultural writers in English private libraries: 1500–1640*[a]

Pliny	sec. xv*, 1500, 1560, 1572, 1574, 1598, 1634, 1640, 1643[6], 1650
Columella	sec. xv*, 1533, 1566[2], 1569, 1598, 1603, 1604, 1634, 1643, 1644
Cato	1566[2], 1583*, 1583, 1597, 1598, 1603, 1644, 1650
Xenophon	1556, 1583, 1597, 1598[3], 1643[3](?)
Virgil (*Georgics*)	1603, 1615[2], 1635, 1644[3], 1650
Varro	1566[2], 1583, 1598, 1603[2], 1604*
Geoponics	1566, 1603, 1604, 1644
Aristotle	*De natura*, 1598, 1604
	Oeconomicon, 1598

Table 5. *European agricultural books in English private libraries: 1500-1640*[a]

Pier de' Crescenzi	1509*, 1583, 1598, 1603, 1615, 1640*, 1640
Heresbach–Googe	1584, 1643[3], 1644
Countrey Farm	1632, 1643[3], 1649
Gesner	*De animalibus*, 1574, 1598, 1600, 1635
	Historia plantarum, 1644
Praedium rusticum	1600, 1598, 1603, 1640
Maison rustique	1566, 1598, 1640
De Serres	1598, 1600, 1643
Mattioli	1598, 1600[2](?)
Heresbach	1583, 1603
Herrera	1604, 1643
Gallo	1643[2]
Sansovino	1643[2]
Carlo Stefano	1634
Vettori	1649
Falcone	1650

[a] Works are described under author's name in case of works in the original language or translated titles for translations. Years indicate the year in which the titles have been found in the inventories or book lists; * indicates a manuscript book, superscript numbers indicate the number of copies found for that year.

Table 6. *Readers and private libraries according to social classes*

Nobility	35
Liberal professions	13
Scientists, academics	10
Clergy	5
Civil servants	4
No description	4
Total	71

Sources: This sample was based on S. R. Jayne, *Library Catalogues of the English Renaissance*, Berkeley–Los Angeles 1965 brought up to 1980 from other available sources (it has been impossible to take into consideration the second edition of this important work or to bring the sample up to 1990); only the private libraries which included one or more of the books listed above, tables 4 and 5, have been taken into consideration. See the text for discussion of this sample.

The following is the bibliography in chronological order of the private libraries or book lists included in the sample: the number of printed books (pb) or of manuscripts (mss) owned has been indicated whenever known.[a]
1. Fifteenth–sixteenth century: Cambridge, UL, Cambridge Vice Chancellor's Court, Inventories, n.p., n.d.; **2.** c. 1500, Thomas Rotherham, arcbsp of York, 105 mss: A. F. Lead,' Early Yorks. Schools', *Yorks. Arch. Soc. Record Ser.*, 33, 1903, pp. 162–6; **3.** n.d., Martin Collins, canon of York, 150 pb: *Surtees Society*, 53, pp. 279–82; **4.** 1531, Gerald Fitzgerald, Earl Kildare, 92 pb: London, BL, ms Harley 3756, fos. 90, 96v–97; **5.** 1549, John Clement: A. W. Reed, 'John Clement and his books', *The Library*, ser. 4, 6, 1926, pp. 329–39; **6.** 1553, John Bale, 355 mss: H. McCuster, 'Books and mss formerly in possession of J. B.', *The Library*, ser. 4, 16, 1935, pp. 144–65; **7.** 1556, Henry, 1st Baron Stafford, 302 pb: T. F. Dibdin, *Bibliographical Decameron*, London 1817, III, pp. 253–4; **8.** 1558, Richard Brereton: J. C. Piccope,'Lancs. and Chesh. Wills and Inventories', I, *Chetham Soc.*, XXXIII, 1857, pp. 173–5, and *Trans. of Lancs. and Ches. Antiquarian Society*, 11, 1893, pp. 103–12; **9.** 1560, 1565, 1569: Cambridge, UL, Cambridge U. Regist., ms invent., Robert Pember, Thomas Layton, James Kage; **10.** 1565–73, Anonym, physician, 95 pb: London, BL, Add ms 28023, fos. 98–9; **11.** 1566, Sir Thomas Smith: J. Strype, *Life of Sir J. S.*, Oxford 1820, pp. 274–81; **12.** 1574, Sir Nicholas Bacon, Lord Keeper: M. Parker, *De antiquitate Britanniae Ecclesiae*, London 1729, Appendix, pp. xlii–xliii; **13.** 1583, Dr John Dee: J. Orchard Halliwell, 'The private diary of Dr. J. D. and the catalogue of his library', Camden Society, London 1842; **14.** 1583, *idem*: London, BL, ms Harley 1879, fos. 20–108, Catalogue of books; **15.** 1584, Francis Russell, Earl Bedford, 190 mss + 34 pb: M. St Clare Byrne and G. S. Thomson, 'My Lord's books', *Review English Studies*, 7, 1931, p. 396; **16.** 1592, Stephen Vallenger, 100 pb: H. R. Plomer, *The Library*, ser. 2, 2, 1901, pp. 108–12; **17.** 1597, Richard Stonley, 413 pb: L. Holton, 'The library of Elizabeth's embezzling teller', *Studies in Bibliography*, 2, 1949, pp. 49–61; **18.** 1598, William Cecil, Lord Burghley: *Bibliotheca illustris: sive catalogus variorum librorum*, London 1687; **19.** c. 1600 , Sir William Fairfax, 39 pb: E. Peacock, *Inventories made for Sir W. and Sir T. F.*, XLVIII, 1884, p. 153; **20.** 1600, Thomas Sackville, Baron Buckhurst: Oxford, BO, Benefactor's Catalogue; **21.** 1600, George Cary, Baron Hudson: *ibid.*; **22.** 1603, Philip Scudamor: *ibid.*; **23.** c. 1603, William Gent: *ibid.*; **24.** c. 1600, William Allen: *ibid.*; **25.** 1603, George Cary: *ibid.*; **26.** 1603, Walter Ralegh: *ibid.*; **27.** 1603, Thomas Edmund: *ibid.*; **28.** 1603, Thomas Docwra of Puttridge, 17 pb: *ibid.*; **29.** 1603, Michael Dormer, 62 pb: *ibid.*; **30.** 1604, Thomas Kerry, Clerk of the Private Seal, 145 pb: *ibid.*; **31.** 1604, George More, 29 mss: *ibid.*; **32.** 1605, William Hutchinson, archd: *ibid.*; **33.** 1609, Lumley family: S. Jayne and F. R. Johnson, *The Lumley Library. The catalogue*

of 1609, London 1956; **34**. 1610, William Petre, gent: G. E. Dawson, 'A gentleman's purse', *Yale Review*, 39, 1950, pp. 631–46; **35**. 1611, John English, scholar: W. E. Costin, 'The inventory of J. E. B. C. L. Fellow of St John's College', *Oxoniensia*, 11–12, 1946–7, pp. 102–31; **36**. 1615, William Crashaw, 162 mss: CWPO, 'The Southampton mss', *The Eagle*, 39, 1918, pp. 208–13; **37**. 1612, Thomas Twine, M. D.: Oxford, BO, Ben. Cat.; **38**. 1629, William Earl Pembroke: *ibid.*; **39**. 1634, Kenelm Digby, knight, 233 mss: *ibid.*; **40**. 1635, William Laud, archbp Canterbury, 462 pb: *ibid.*; **41**. 1649, Richard Whitaker, bibliophile: *ibid.*; **42**. 1632, Scipio le Squyer, dep chamb Exch, 296 mss + 487 pb: F. Taylor, *Bull. of the John Rylands Library*, 25, 1941, pp. 146–64; **43**. 1632, Henry Percy, Earl Northumberland: *Sotheby Sale Catalogue Library of Petworth Castle*, April 1928, pp. 23–4; **44**. 1634, Sir Edward Coke, lawyer, 1227 pb: W. O. Hassall, *A catalogue of the library of Sir E. C.*, London 1950; **45**. 1634, P. A. Crabe, 5 mss + 51 pb: London, BL, Egerton ms 2983, fo. 28; **46**. 1635, Ben Jonson, poet and dramatist: C. H. Herford and P. Simpson (eds.), *The works of B. J.*, Oxford 1925, Appendix I, pp. 250–71; **47**. 1635–9, Sir Thomas Barrington, 112 pb: M. E. Bohannon, 'A London bookseller's will: 1635–1639', *The Library*, ser. 4, 18, 1938, pp. 432–46; **48**. 1636, Sir Julius Cesar: London, BL, Lansdowne ms 124; **49**. 1637, anonym: Cambridge U. Arch., Donors Book, 44; **50**. c. 1646, John Hatcket, Bsp Litchfield & Coventry: *ibid.*, 81; **52**. 1639, William Sommer, 275 pb: London, BL, ms Burney 368, fos. 59–60; **53**. 1640, John Carter: L. B. Wright, *The first gentleman of Virginia. Intellectual qualities of the early colonial ruling class*, San Marino (CA) 1940, pp. 244–5; **54**. 1640, Sir Henry Spelman, 131 mss + 192 pb: London, BL, Harley ms 7579, fos. 83–6, 87–90; **55**. 1640, Robert Burton, divine, 189 pb: S. Gibson and F. R. D. Needham, 'Two lists of Burton's books', *Oxford Bibl. Soc. Proceedings and Papers*, 1, 1925, pp. 225–46; **56**. 1643, Thomas Bluddow, knight: London, Public Record Office, SP 20/7; **58**. 1643, John Morrison, knight: *ibid.*; **59**. 1643, Sir Francis Windbank: *ibid.*; **60**. 1643, Earl of Northampton: *ibid.*; **61**. 1643, Doctor Watts: *ibid.*; **62**. 1643, Mr Leath, lawyer: *ibid.*; **63**. 1643, Dr Norton: *ibid.*; **64**. 1643, Mr Bronson: *ibid.*; **66**. 1643, Edward Dobson: *ibid.*; **67**. 1643, Dr Lenoyn: *ibid.*; **68**. 1643, Mr Graves: *ibid.*; **69**. 1643, Lord Viscount Conway: *ibid.*; **70**. 1643, Sir Thomas Bludder: J. L. Lievsay and R. B. Davis, 'A cavalier library, 1643', *Studies in bibliography. Papers of the Bibl. Soc. of the Un. of Virginia*, 6, 1953–4, pp. 151–60; **71**. 1644, Bryan Twyne, academic: R. F. Ovenel, 'B. T.'s Library', *Oxford Bibl. Soc.*, n.s., 4, 1950; **72**. 1649, William Drummond: R. Macdonald, *The library of Drummond*, Edinburgh 1971; **73**. c. 1650, John Morris: T. A. Birrell, *The library of John Morris. The reconstruction of a 17th century collection*, London 1976.

[a] Numbers 51, 57 and 65 have been removed from this sample.

Table 7. *Imports, prices, rainfall and temperatures in England and Wales, 1690–1870 (A = clover seed; B = lucerne seed; C = English red clover seed; D = wheat)*

	Imports[a]		Prices[b]		Rainfall[c]	Temperature[d]
	A	B	C	D		
1690	–	–	–	26	–	15.00
1691	–	–	–	37	–	15.50
1692	–	–	26	44	–	15.00
1693	–	–	53	55	–	15.00
1694	–	–	19	31	–	13.00
1695	–	–	–	50	–	13.00
1696	–	–	–	50	–	15.50
1697	–	–	–	55	–	14.50
1698	9	–	–	51	–	15.00
1699	157	–	–	38	–	15.00
1700	346	–	–	32	–	15.00
1701	556	–	–	26	–	16.10
1702	311	–	–	25	–	16.10
1703	16	–	–	36	–	16.10
1704	92	–	–	27	–	16.90
1705	–	–	–	23	–	17.50
1706	156	–	–	24	–	16.70
1707	14	–	–	28	–	16.00
1708	55	–	–	50	–	17.00
1709	3	–	–	68	–	15.50
1710	–	–	–	43	–	15.50
1711	8	–	–	40	–	15.00
1712	–	–	–	34	–	15.00
1713	267	–	–	48	–	15.00
1714	33	–	–	30	–	15.00
1715	–	–	–	39	–	15.00
1716	138	–	–	36	–	15.50
1717	–	–	–	33	–	15.50
1718	–	–	–	27	–	17.00
1719	–	–	–	33	–	17.00
1720	113	–	–	33	–	15.00
1721	–	–	–	28	–	16.00
1722	–	–	–	29	–	15.00
1723	–	–	–	29	–	15.60
1724	221	7	–	34	–	16.20
1725	195	2	–	41	–	13.30
1726	811	23	–	30	109	15.60
1727	–	–	20	102	102	16.90
1728	11	6	22	43	109	16.00
1729	65	5	–	31	97	15.70
1730	995	11	–	28	88	16.30
1731	760	26	–	22	71	16.70
1732	232	2	–	23	83	16.60
1733	1,113	70	–	26	71	16.10

	Imports[a]		Prices[b]		Rainfall[c]	Temperature[d]
	A	B	C	D		
1734	558	42	–	34	114	16.20
1735	284	72	–	34	102	16.20
1736	820	49	–	29	101	17.80
1737	427	16	–	28	110	13.80
1738	1,647	27	–	28	70	16.00
1739	322	47	–	27	89	14.70
1740	916	21	–	50	65	14.70
1741	301	1	–	28	58	16.70
1742	780	2	–	23	65	15.80
1743	131	108	–	20	60	16.90
1744	187	45	37	20	89	15.40
1745	320	18	–	28	80	15.00
1746	519	43	28	30	70	15.90
1747	151	2	–	28	95	18.30
1748	173	22	92	29	65	15.80
1749	80	28	–	28	59	15.60
1750	254	22	26	29	61	15.00
1751	833	22	26	37	108	14.60
1752	575	80	52	36	82	15.70
1753	958	11	–	32	87	15.70
1754	1,220	37	–	27	76	15.70
1755	939	23	32	32	83	14.60
1756	1,247	65	38	50	100	14.70
1757	1,401	69	48	41	93	15.20
1758	1,903	159	16	29	84	16.40
1759	1,647	10	–	29	81	16.30
1760	1,548	28	–	30	70	15.80
1761	893	100	–	28	87	16.40
1762	2,571	52	–	30	71	15.30
1763	3,089	123	–	37	118	15.30
1764	2,088	268	–	40	101	15.20
1765	4,152	527	–	39	82	15.30
1766	2,962	108	–	49	77	16.60
1767	2,178	342	–	50	91	16.10
1768	7,274	12	–	41	128	16.00
1769	8,194	91	–	36	86	15.00
1770	8,243	32	–	44	108	15.80
1771	11,050	50	–	49	70	14.30
1772	3,839	41	–	52	111	16.10
1773	8,280	49	20	53	113	17.20
1774	13,056	54	30	54	129	16.10
1775	16,402	9	–	50	123	15.80
1776	22,919	129	–	39	107	15.20
1777	11,209	151	–	47	89	15.90

Table 7. (*cont.*)

	Imports[a]		Prices[b]		Rainfall[c]	Temperature[d]
	A	B	C	D		
1778	29,154	15	–	43	102	16.80
1779	19,246	26	31	35	83	17.60
1780	8,833	19	33	37	75	17.60
1781	7,402	–	35	46	79	17.40
1782	7.000	–	44	49	131	14.20
1783	12,770	–	69	54	93	15.80
1784	15,709	–	41	54	96	14.00
1785	18,782	–	55	43	77	13.90
1786	11,078	–	–	40	107	15.10
1787	11,386	–	–	42	96	15.60
1788	20,713	–	–	46	65	15.80
1789	33,828	–	–	53	116	16.60
1790	22,915	–	47	53	86	15.60
1791	23,915	–	37	49	105	15.90
1792	52,402	–	38	43	117	16.90
1793	35,476	–	53	49	86	15.00
1794	17,576	–	53	52	104	15.50
1795	8,851	–	69	75	84	16.60
1796	38,548	–	77	79	83	15.90
1797	19,204	–	51	54	106	15.80
1798	28,250	–	57	52	88	16.40
1799	21,342	–	50	69	106	14.40
1800	40,159	–	85	114	90	16.80
1801	23,487	–	89	119	96	17.10
1802	52,786	–	76	70	91	17.20
1803	42,742	–	86	59	77	16.10
1804	47,881	–	78	62	85	15.60
1805	43,395	–	80	90	75	16.40
1806	53,497	–	67	79	96	16.20
1807	55,887	–	68	75	94	16.90
1808	25,419	–	70	81	90	16.70
1809	44,480	576	102	97	88	14.80
1810	70,742	504	102	106	100	14.60
1811	42,886	–	98	95	98	14.40
1812	82,037	336	92	126	97	14.30
1813	–	–	93	110	92	14.50
1814	42,872	631	77	74	92	14.70
1815	54,646	858	69	66	99	15.30
1816	15,076	375	63	78	107	13.90
1817	46,199	268	85	97	100	13.60
1818	121,215	1,750	89	86	102	15.30
1819	72,716	856	76	74	99	17.40
1820	74,030	172	70	68	92	14.70
1821	60,705	277	62	56	106	16.40
1822	37,075	766	45	45	109	15.20
1823	28,874	289	61	53	100	14.40
1824	99,332	713	71	64	117	15.10

	Imports[a]		Prices[b]		Rainfall[c]	Temperature[d]
	A	B	C	D		
1825	128,288	441	67	68	96	16.30
1826	55,391	602	62	59	77	17.60
1827	113,901	1,032	62	58	102	14.80
1828	134,487	1,751	53	60	120	15.30
1829	47,475	761	58	66	102	14.30
1830	87,098	165	79	64	111	13.70
1831	100,925	225	68	66	108	16.90
1832	62,644	461	60	59	98	15.40
1833	62,644	733	65	53	106	14.30
1834	42,256	615	56	46	90	16.20
1835	53,332	656	51	39	99	16.90
1836	64,492	516	60	48	118	14.60
1837	104,816	1,407	59	56	87	15.70
1838	80,491	769	64	64	90	15.10
1839	75,542	829	75	71	107	14.60
1840	120,494	470	70	66	89	15.90
1841	65,346	905	68	64	128	14.60
1842	133,504	568	71	57	91	17.10
1843	53,697	544	52	50	110	15.30
1844	76,278	983	63	51	85	13.50
1845	116,391	1,006	53	57	97	13.50
1846	154,975	805	54	55	108	16.60
1847	136,847	583	46	70	90	15.20
1848	105,262	513	42	50	130	13.60
1849	145,070	722	39	44	98	15.60
1850	97,841	530	42	40	91	14.50
1851	143,413	313	46	38	88	15.50
1852	82,897	435	50	41	138	15.80
1853	236,201	369	55	53	101	14.70
1854	129,231	–	–	73	74	15.20
1855	151,994	1,700	60	75	88	15.70
1856	152,578	1,028	–	69	93	16.90
1857	150,118	348	67	56	97	17.40
1858	90,929	160	58	44	80	15.80
1859	123,389	766	80	44	102	16.20
1860	234,510	218	47	53	122	13.60
1861	179,561	391	72	55	92	15.90
1862	152,974	439	63	55	107	14.60
1863	252,774	455	–	45	89	15.50
1864	201,052	281	–	40	73	14.20
1865	197,320	1.895	–	42	108	15.10
1866	204,144	1.377	–	50	–	14.70
1867	126,440	1.955	–	64	–	16.30
1868	236,150	793	–	64	–	16.80
1869	201,393	1,920	71	48	–	15.50
1870	121,672	327	72	47	–	15.70

Table 7. (*cont.*)

[a] In hundredweights (cwt).

[b] In shillings per cwt for clover seed; in shillings per quarter for wheat. Clover seed prices are the result of the yearly averages of all prices quoted in: *A Collection for Improvement of Husbandry and Trade by John Houghton*, London 1692–3; J. E. Thorold Rogers, *A History of Agriculture and Prices in England*, vol. VI, 1583–1702, Oxford 1887, for the years 1727–85; A. Young, *Statement of the Average Prices of Grass Seeds...*, in *Reports respecting Grain and Corn Laws. Lord's Committee*, in BPP, 1814–15 (1122), vol. V, p. 88, years 1790–1814; A. Schwartz, *National Bureau of Economic Research, seeds: clover, red British* [*i.e. English*], 1790–1850; –*The Farmer's Magazine*, 1838–70, quotations of English red clover seed. When more than one series was available as in the years 1790–1820 and 1838–50, the price given is the average of all available data.

[c] In millimetres.

[d] Average temperature in degrees centigrade for the month of August.

Sources: Public Record Office, Customs Accounts: 1700–80, Cust 3; 1781–90, Cust 17; 1791–1808, Cust 17, 14; 1809–11, Cust 4, 11; 1812–70, Cust 5 (the 1813 ledger is missing). See also *Annual trade and navigation returns, 1837–1870*, and F. M. L. Thompson, 'The second agricultural revolution, 1815–1880', *EcHR*, 21, 1968, pp. 73–4.

Table 8. *Imports of clover seed into England and Wales, 1698–1870 (decennial averages in cwt)*

	Flanders/ Belgium	Holland	France	Germany	Italy	Channel Islands/ Ireland	Other European Countries	America	Total
1698–1709	65	67	–	–	–	–	–	–	132
1710–19	14	19	–	–	–	–	–	–	33
1720–29	62	77	2	–	–	–	–	–	141
1730–39	380	590	2	–	1	–	–	–	973
1740–49	126	219	–	–	–	–	–	–	345
1750–59	72	1,106	–	–	–	–	–	–	1,178
1760–69	248	3,237	–	–	–	–	–	–	3,485
1770–79	467	11,326	18	39	17	–	–	–	11,976
1780–89	2,704	10,526	1,272	279	60	9	9.6	–	14,949.6
1790–99	1,145	18,394	4,115	5,654	20	99	157.1	–	29,577.5
1800–09	6,419	28,776	7,374	2,443	–	92.4	667.6	–	45,827.6
1810–19	7,728	11,875	19,397	6,342	54	148	797.3	1,922.3	51,340.6
1820–29	6,916[a]	19,850[a] 21,996[b]	26,856	14,534	412	3,225	710	1,037	4,184	74,499
1830–39	3,986[c]	23,080[c]	17,482	42,237	561	184	1,562	6,412	95,504
1840–49	2,166	8,650	31,710	54,515	1,776	63	1,896	9,996	110,772
1850–59	9,027	14,364	39,862	57,735	3,555	1.8	2,582	17,454	144,580.8
1860–69	20,113	9,012	68,086	45,908	3,110	40	11,374	43,210	200,853
1870	14,985	5,356	52,926	30,635	2,418	–	5,348	10,004	121,672

[a] 1820–26.
[b] Flanders and Holland, 1826–32.
[c] 1833–39.
Sources: See table 7.

Table 9. *Duty paid on clover seed (in £sd per cwt)*

	Import	Export
1697–1757	ad valorem	ad valorem
1758	0.02.4	0.02.1
1792	0.02.9	duty free export
1798	0.02.3	" " "
1809	0.06.0	" " "
1831	1.00.0	" " "
1842	0.10.0	" " "
1846	0.05.0	" " "
1853	repealed	

Sources: England, *The Act of Tonnage and Poundage and Book of Rates*, London 1689, 1702, 1728, 1737; T. Langham, *The nett Duties and Drawbacks payable on Import and Export of all sorts of Merchandizes*, London 1758, p. 170 (same tariff for lucerne seed); England, *The Consolidated Duties, Drawbacks and Bounties of Customs and Excise . . .* , Liverpool 1792, p. 39; England, *A Table of Additional Duties on Goods and Merchandizes . . .* , Liverpool 1798; England, *The Duties and Drawbacks and Bounties . . .* , Liverpool, p. 48.

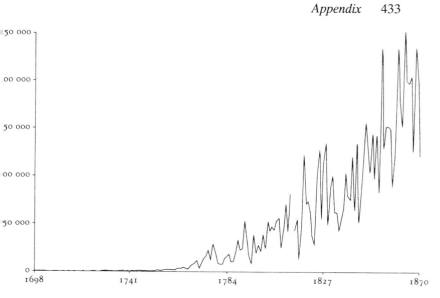

Annual imports of clover seed (figures in cwt)

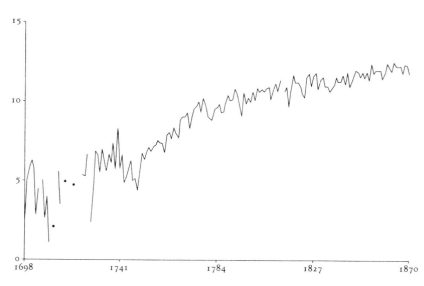

Annual imports of clover seed by year (log e. values)

Index

The index contains the names of people, authors, places and a list of key subjects. People belonging to one family have been grouped together. Names of ancient, medieval and modern authors are given according to the British Museum Catalogue of Printed Books. Regions, counties and départements of small towns and villages are indicated in brackets.

Past and Present Publications

General Editor: JOANNA INNES, *Somerville College, Oxford*

Family and Inheritance: Rural Society in Western Europe 1200–1800, edited by Jack Goody, Joan Thirsk and E. P. Thompson*

French Society and the Revolution, edited by Douglas Johnson

Peasants, Knights and Heretics: Studies in Medieval English Social History, edited by R. H. Hilton*

Town in Societies: Essays in Economic History and Historical Sociology, edited by Philip Abrams and E. A. Wrigley*

Desolation of a City: Coventry and the Urban Crisis of the Late Middle Ages, Charles Phythian-Adams

Puritanism and Theatre: Thomas Middleton and Opposition Drama under the Early Stuarts, Margot Heinemann*

Lords and Peasants in a Changing Society: The Estates of the Bishopric of Worcester 680–1450, Christopher Dyer

Life, Marriage and Death in a Medieval Parish: Economy, Society and Demography in Halesowen 1270–1400, Ziv Razi

Biology, Medicine and Society 1740–1940, edited by Charles Webster

The Invention of Tradition, edited by Eric Hobsbawm and Terence Ranger*

Industrialization before Industrialization: Rural Industry and the Genesis of Capitalism, Peter Kriedte, Hans Medick and Jürgen Schlumbohm*

The Republic in the Village: The People of the Var from the French Revolution to the Second Republic, Maurice Agulhon†

Social Relations and Ideas: Essays in Honour of R. H. Hilton, edited by T. H. Aston, P. R. Coss, Christopher Dyer and Joan Thirsk

A Medieval Society: The West Midlands at the End of the Thirteenth Century, R. H. Hilton

Winstanley: 'The Law of Freedom' and Other Writings, edited by Christopher Hill

Crime in Seventeenth-Century England: A County Study, J. A. Sharpe†

The Crisis of Feudalism: Economy and Society in Eastern Normandy c. 1300–1500, Guy Bois†

The Development of the Family and Marriage in Europe, Jack Goody*

Disputes and Settlements: Law and Human Relations in the West, edited by John Bossy

Rebellion, Popular Protest and the Social Order in Early Modern England, edited by Paul Slack

* Also published in paperback
† Co-published with the Maison des Sciences de l'Homme, Paris